T0332735

Research Anthology on Strategies for Using Social Media as a Service and Tool in Business

Information Resources Management Association
USA

Volume II

IGI Global
PUBLISHER of TIMELY KNOWLEDGE

Published in the United States of America by
    IGI Global
    Business Science Reference (an imprint of IGI Global)
    701 E. Chocolate Avenue
    Hershey PA, USA 17033
    Tel: 717-533-8845
    Fax: 717-533-8661
    E-mail: cust@igi-global.com
    Web site: http://www.igi-global.com

Library of Congress Cataloging-in-Publication Data

Names: Information Resources Management Association, editor.
Title: Research anthology on strategies for using social media as a service
  and tool in business / Information Resources Management Association,
  editor.
Description: Hershey, PA : Business Science Reference, [2021] | Includes
  bibliographical references and index. | Summary: "This book of
  contributed chapters provides updated information on how businesses are
  strategically using social media and explores the role of social media
  in keeping businesses competitive in the global economy by discussing
  how social tools work, what services businesses are utilizing, both the
  benefits and challenges to how social media is changing the modern
  business atmosphere,"-- Provided by publisher.
Identifiers: LCCN 2021016024 (print) | LCCN 2021016025 (ebook) | ISBN
  9781799890201 (hardcover) | ISBN 9781799890218 (ebook)
Subjects: LCSH: Social media--Economic aspects. | Marketing. | Branding
  (Marketing) | Customer relations. | Customer services--Technological
  innovations.
Classification: LCC HM742 .R4678 2021 (print) | LCC HM742 (ebook) | DDC
  302.23/1--dc23
LC record available at https://lccn.loc.gov/2021016024
LC ebook record available at https://lccn.loc.gov/2021016025

British Cataloguing in Publication Data
A Cataloguing in Publication record for this book is available from the British Library.

The views expressed in this book are those of the authors, but not necessarily of the publisher.

For electronic access to this publication, please contact: eresources@igi-global.com.

List of Contributors

Table of Contents

Section 2
Development and Design Methodologies

  Muhammad Aslam Jarwar, Department of Computer Sciences, Quaid-i-Azam University,
    Islamabad, Pakistan & Department of Information and Communications Engineering,
    Hankuk University of Foreign Studies (HUFS), Seoul, South Korea
  Rabeeh Ayaz Abbasi, Faculty of Computing and Information Technology, King Abdulaziz
    University, Jeddah, Saudi Arabia & Department of Computer Sciences, Quaid-i-Azam
    University, Islamabad, Pakistan
  Mubashar Mushtaq, Department of Computer Science, Forman Christian College (A
    Chartered University), Lahore, Pakistan & Department of Computer Sciences, Quaid-i-
    Azam University, Islamabad, Pakistan
  Onaiza Maqbool, Department of Computer Sciences, Quaid-i-Azam University, Islamabad,
    Pakistan
  Naif R. Aljohani, Faculty of Computing and Information Technology, King Abdulaziz
    University, Jeddah, Saudi Arabia
  Ali Daud, Faculty of Computing and Information Technology, King Abdulaziz University,
    Jeddah, Saudi Arabia & Department of Computer Science and Software Engineering,
    International Islamic University, Islamabad, Pakistan
  Jalal S. Alowibdi, Faculty of Computing and Information Technology, University of Jeddah,
    Jeddah, Saudi Arabia
  J.R. Cano, Department of Computer Science, University of Jaén, Jaén, Spain
  S. García, Department of Computer Science and Artificial Intelligence, University of
    Granada, Granada, Spain
  Ilyoung Chong, Department of Information and Communications Engineering, Hankuk
    University of Foreign Studies (HUFS), Seoul, South Korea

Section 3
Tools and Technologies

  Gopal Krishna, Aryabhatt Knowledge University, India

  Marcello Chedid, University of Aveiro, Portugal
  Leonor Teixeira, University of Aveiro, Portugal

  Ned Kock, Department of International Business and Technology Studies, Texas A&M
    International University, Laredo, TX, USA

Section 4
Utilization and Applications

Volume III

Section 5
Organizational and Social Implications

Volume IV

Section 6
Managerial Impact

Section 7
Critical Issues and Challenges

Preface

Since its conception, social media has become an integral part in how society communicates. As with the development of any other important piece of communication, business and industry must adapt to utilize this tool to reach its vast audiences to survive. Moreover, social media can be applied for internal processes for organizations and should be considered by human resources managers. Through this transition, it is essential for businesses to be aware of how to best utilize these tools and services in order to best promote themselves within the social sphere. The *Research Anthology on Strategies for Using Social Media as a Service and Tool in Business* provides these strategies for businesses to grow under this new era of communication.

Staying informed of the most up-to-date research trends and findings is of the utmost importance. That is why IGI Global is pleased to offer this four-volume reference collection of reprinted IGI Global book chapters and journal articles that have been handpicked by senior editorial staff. This collection will shed light on critical issues related to the trends, techniques, and uses of various applications by providing both broad and detailed perspectives on cutting-edge theories and developments. This collection is designed to act as a single reference source on conceptual, methodological, technical, and managerial issues, as well as to provide insight into emerging trends and future opportunities within the field.

The *Research Anthology on Strategies for Using Social Media as a Service and Tool in Business* is organized into seven distinct sections that provide comprehensive coverage of important topics. The sections are:

1. Fundamental Concepts and Theories;
2. Development and Design Methodologies;
3. Tools and Technologies;
4. Utilization and Applications;
5. Organizational and Social Implications;
6. Managerial Impact; and
7. Critical Issues and Challenges.

The following paragraphs provide a summary of what to expect from this invaluable reference tool.

Section 1, "Fundamental Concepts and Theories," serves as a foundation for this extensive reference tool by addressing crucial theories essential to understanding the concepts of social media in multidisciplinary settings. Opening this reference book is the chapter "The Role of Social Media in Public Involvement: Pushing for Sustainability in International Planning and Development" by Prof. Tooran Alizadeh of University of Sydney, Australia and Profs. Reza Farid and Laura Willems of Griffith

University, Australia. This chapter explores social media's potential to enhance public involvement to pursue sustainable practices on an international scale across planning and development projects. This first section ends with the chapter "Social Media and Social Identity in the Millennial Generation" by Prof. Guida Helal of American University of Beirut, Lebanon and Prof. Wilson Ozuem of University of Cumbria, UK, which focuses on theoretical implications and managerial implications. The concluding section offers some significant roles that social media and social identity may play in keeping up with the design and development of marketing communications programs.

Section 2, "Development and Design Methodologies," presents in-depth coverage of the design and development of social media strategy for its use in different applications. This section starts with the chapter "An Absorptive Capacity Perspective of Organizational Learning Through Social Media: Evidence From the Ghanaian Fashion Industry" by Profs. Richard Boateng, Edna Owusu-Bempah, and Eric Ansong from University of Ghana, Ghana, which examines the role social media has played on brand perceptions in the fashion apparel and accessories industry from a social identity theory perspective. This section ends with the chapter "CommuniMents: A Framework for Detecting Community Based Sentiments for Events" by Prof. Muhammad Aslam Jarwar of Quaid-i-Azam University, Pakistan & Hankuk University of Foreign Studies (HUFS), South Korea; Prof. Rabeeh Ayaz Abbasi of King Abdulaziz University, Saudi Arabia & Quaid-i-Azam University, Islamabad, Pakistan; Prof. Mubashar Mushtaq of Forman Christian College (A Chartered University), Pakistan & Quaid-i-Azam University, Pakistan; Prof. Onaiza Maqbool of Quaid-i-Azam University, Pakistan; Prof. Naif R. Aljohani of King Abdulaziz University, Saudi Arabia; Prof. Ali Daud of King Abdulaziz University, Saudi Arabia & International Islamic University, Pakistan; Prof. Jalal S. Alowibdi of University of Jeddah, Saudi Arabia; Prof. J.R. Cano of University of Jaén, Spain; Prof. S. García of University of Granada, Spain; and Prof. Ilyoung Chong of Hankuk University of Foreign Studies (HUFS), South Korea, which proposes a framework CommuniMents that enables us to identify the members of a community and measure the sentiments of the community for a particular event. CommuniMents uses automated snowball sampling to identify the members of a community, then fetches their published contents (specifically tweets), pre-processes the contents, and measures the sentiments of the community.

Section 3, "Tools and Technologies," explores the various tools and technologies used in the implementation of social media for various uses. This section begins with the chapter "Social Networking Data Analysis Tools and Services" by Prof. Gopal Krishna of Aryabhatt Knowledge University, India, which explains the methods and tools used for the analysis of the huge amount of data produced by social networks. This section ends with the chapter "Social Media as a Tool to Understand Behaviour on the Railways" by Prof. David Golightly of University of Nottingham, UK and Prof. Robert J. Houghton of Griffith University, Australia, which highlights important factors such as the broad range of issues covered by social media (not just disruption), the idiosyncrasies of individual train operators that need to be taken into account within social media analysis, and the time critical nature of information during disruption.

Section 4, "Utilization and Applications," describes how social media is used and applied in diverse industries for various technologies and applications. The opening chapter in this section, "Adoption of Web 2.0 Marketing: An Exploratory Study About the Nigerian SMEs," by Prof. Maryam Lawan Gwadabet of IT and Business School, Blue Sapphire E-Solutions ltd, Kano, Nigeria, explores the value which Web 2.0 marketing adds to the Nigerian SME's. The final chapter in this section, "An Evaluation of Toronto's Destination Image Through Tourist Generated Content on Twitter," by Profs. Hillary Clarke and Ahmed Hassanien of Edinburgh Napier University, Edinburgh, UK, evaluates the cognitive, affective, and conative components of destination image from the perception of tourists on social media.

Section 5, "Organizational and Social Implications," includes chapters discussing the impact of social media on society and shows the ways in which social media is used in different industries and how this impacts business. The first chapter, "An Empirical Evaluation of Adoption and Diffusion of New ICTs for Knowledge Sharing in IT Organizations," by Profs. Srinivasan Vaidyanathan and Sudarsanam S. Kidambi of VIT Business School, VIT University, Chennai, India, describes how knowledge is one of the most important assets in organizations which should be carefully managed and is continuously generated throughout an organization. The last chapter, "Fast-Fashion Meets Social Networking Users: Implications for International Marketing Strategy," by Prof. Tehreem Cheema of Clark University, USA, contributes to the existing literature on the influence of digital marketing on fast fashion, and it provides a number of pertinent marketing recommendations in regard to the practice of apparel retailers.

Section 6, "Managerial Impact," presents the uses of social media in industry and management practices. Starting this section is "Management and Marketing Practices of Social Media Firms" by Prof. Abdulaziz Alshubaily of University of Liverpool, Jeddah, Saudi Arabia, which examines the key variances in application and strategy between different social media management strategies and its effective marketing. Ending this section is "Tweeting About Business and Society: A Case Study of an Indian Woman CEO" by Profs. P. Vigneswara Ilavarasan, Ashish Kumar Rathore, and Nikhil Tuli of Indian Institute of Technology Delhi, India, which examines the social media content posted by a woman Indian chief executive officer (CEO) on Twitter.

Section 7, "Critical Issues and Challenges," highlights areas in which social media provides challenges for the industries utilizing it. Opening this final section is the chapter "E-Reputation in Web Entrepreneurship" by Profs. Sylvaine Castellano and Vincent Dutot of Paris School of Business, France, which gives to web-entrepreneurs the key elements in order to manage their e-reputation efficiently by presenting what e-reputation is, what its main components are, how to measure it, and what tools exist. The final chapter, "Ethical Dilemmas Associated With Social Network Advertisements," by Prof. Alan D. Smith of Robert Morris University, USA and Prof. Onyebuchi Felix Offodile of Kent State University, USA, explains the three hypotheses dealt with the interplay of online social networking, advertising effectiveness, gender and age trends, and remaining the interplay with positive comments of the use of the "like" function and its impacts on consumer behavior, as derived from the review of relevant operations literature and from applying the basic tenants of uses and gratification theory.

Although the primary organization of the contents in this multi-volume work is based on its seven sections, offering a progression of coverage of the important concepts, methodologies, technologies, applications, social issues, and emerging trends, the reader can also identify specific contents by utilizing the extensive indexing system listed at the end of each volume. As a comprehensive collection of research on the latest findings related to social media, the *Research Anthology on Strategies for Using Social Media as a Service and Tool in Business* provides researchers, instructors, social media managers, IT consultants, business managers, students, executives, practitioners, industry professionals, social media analysts, and all audiences with a complete understanding of the applications and impacts of social media. Given the vast number of issues concerning usage, failure, success, strategies, and applications of social media in modern industry, the *Research Anthology on Strategies for Using Social Media as a Service and Tool in Business* encompasses the most pertinent research on the applications, impacts, uses, and development of social media as a tool in business.

Chapter 24
Hiring Practices, Uses of Social Media, and Teacher Retention Differences

Bridgette Waite
Dowling College, USA

Elsa-Sofia Morote
Farmingdale State University of New York, USA

ABSTRACT

This study assesses the differences between teacher retention rate and human resource (HR) managers' hiring practices, self-efficacy. Their use of social media websites (Facebook, LinkedIn, and Twitter) for hiring was evaluated. Turnover of teachers with fewer than 5 years of experience was gathered from New York State Education Department (NYSED) database. New York State schools were separated by high and low teacher retention rates. A Likert Scale Survey with one open ended question was sent to school districts HR managers. An independent sample t test was used to determine the differences between high and low teacher retention rates. A content analysis is presented using the responses to the open-ended question. Findings indicated that less than half of the HR managers used social media in the hiring process. No significant differences between teacher retention rates, HR managers' practices, and HR self-efficacy was found.

INTRODUCTION

Human resource (HR) managers faced new challenges in hiring practices. As paradigms changed, the characteristics affecting human resource management also had to be revised (Lipiec, 2001). According to Van Iddekinge, Lanivich, Roth, and Junco (2013), the Internet had a profound effect on the way organizations recruited and selected employees. The Internet served to broaden networks, helped communicate more efficiently, and accomplished undertakings more proficiently. It influenced the hiring practices that organizations implemented. It allowed organizations to reach more applicants via popular

DOI: 10.4018/978-1-7998-9020-1.ch024

job sites and made applicant information more accessible. The widespread use of social media such as Facebook, Twitter, and LinkedIn revolutionized communication, both personally and professionally. The phenomenon of social networking websites (SNWs) on the Internet exploded in the mainstream (Kluemper & Rosen, 2009). One of the major contributors to change in the workplace was the accelerated use of the Internet (Cascio & Agunis, 2005).

HR managers used a vast amount of personal information on social media websites as a source for recruiting and making hiring decisions. Then recent reports suggested that many organizations were using the Internet to search for information about job applicants (Preston, 2011). Both job seekers and recruiters found places to connect on the Internet. The new openness and freer flow of information affected the employment process. Per Daniel (2012), social media became an increasingly useful tool for HR managers and understanding its benefits and limitations was crucial for future success. Given the advances in technology and the effect it could have on an organization, it was essential for research to examine how the use of the Internet in the recruiting, hiring, and selection process affected HR managers.

For a majority of recruiters, LinkedIn, Twitter, Facebook, and employee referrals officially surpassed job boards as the preferred way to acquire talent (Brotherton, 2012). Increasingly more companies boosted their recruiting efforts by investing in social media to reach job candidates, according to Jobvite, a recruiting platform for the social web. A recent Jobvite survey (2013) of 800 U.S. based HR professionals, more than half (55 percent) planned to increase their budget for social network recruiting. LinkedIn was on the list for 87 percent of companies, up from 78 percent in 2010; 55 percent used Facebook, and 47 percent were using Twitter. According to Jobvite, in the first 6 months of 2011, 73 percent of social hires came from LinkedIn, 20 percent from Facebook, and 7 percent from Twitter. The effect of social media in recruitment and hiring and the emerging issues and their implications for HR managers were examined in this study. The questions of self-efficacy and the extent to which HR managers' beliefs in their own abilities to complete tasks were affected were also examined. Additionally, the differences between hiring practices and social media use and teacher retention were examined.

BACKGROUND

The purpose of this quantitative study was to assess the differences between HR managers' self-efficacy and the retention levels in their districts (low versus high) and their use of social media websites—specifically Facebook, LinkedIn, and Twitter—for recruitment, selection, and hiring.

How do human resource managers in school districts with high and low retention rates differ in their use of the three social media dimensions of self-efficacy, recruiting, and hiring and selection?

It was a widely-held view that an organization's human resources were its most important assets and among the resources an organization had, might have offered the only non-imitative competitive edge (Pfeiffer, 1994). Therefore, an organization's ability to attract and retain capable employees might have been the single most important determinant of organizational effectiveness. The recruitment function played a critical role in enhancing organizational survival and success. Finn and Singh (2003) examined the effect of information technology on the recruitment function of organizations. They sought to outline the extent to which information technology had been used in recruitment and examine the effect of information technology on recruitment in terms of its effect on people, processes, and organizational structures: "As a filtering mechanism in the selection process, the recruitment function was one of the most important areas of human resource management" (Finn & Singh, 2003, p. 396). The recruitment process began with the identification of a vacancy, was followed by an analysis of the skills needed, and continued with an advertisement of the position, both internally and externally. Many organizations had begun to use innovative information technology methods to complement the traditional sources, such as employee referrals, newspaper and other print media ads, employment agencies, search firms, college recruiting, and job fairs.

There are several advantages in using advanced information technology to recruit. In a survey of 311 HR managers and 244 independent recruiters, respondents identified the following as the most important reasons, in descending order, for using information technology. At the top of the list was access to more candidates, followed by improved ability to target specific audiences, reduced cost of placing job postings, speed, absence of intermediaries, convenience, wide distribution of postings, quality of candidates, less paperwork, better resume management, and better service (Kay, 2000). Finn and Singh (2003) noted that because of such benefits, organizations were increasingly turning to information technology methods to enhance the recruitment function. A review of the literature revealed that increased use of information technology in recruitment was having a fundamental effect on all aspects of organizations' recruitment functions, including their HR personnel involved (the recruiters themselves). The use of information technology appeared to be leading to a transformation in recruiters needed skill set. With the implementation of advanced information technology systems, HR managers had to learn and even master the new technologies to perform their jobs effectively. This led to a retraining of HR managers and recruiting staff, which resulted in more technology-oriented recruiting HR departments and better service to stakeholders. The upgrading of HR personnel skills was leading to a transformation of the HR department itself. Snell, Pedigo, and Krawiec argued, "As informational technology changes operations within HR, it simultaneously recasts HR from solely an administrative function to one that is more oriented toward technical/professional expertise" (Snell, Pedigo, & Krawiec, 1995, p.162). The question was not whether institutions should use social media, but rather how they could use technology in their recruiting in a way that benefited other activities in their recruiting, selection, and hiring practices.

Important motivating behaviors for joining social networking sites were building relationships with people separated by geographic boundaries and others who had similar interests, and increasing personal visibility. HR personnel were beginning to access these sites to find posted personal information to use in making their hiring decisions (Jones & Behling, 2010). Some companies were giving considerable weight to information found on these sites in the employment process (Lorenz, 2009). The implications of this occurrence were explored in a paper written by Jones and Behling (2010), in which they conducted a review of what and how some employers used information available via social networking sites, including ethical, personal, security, and legal issues associated with using and accessing social networks. Jones and Behling detailed that in a 2009 CareerBuilder survey, 45 percent of employers reported using social networking sites to screen candidates; 35 percent found content that caused them not to hire the candidates. The same surveys also listed numerous reasons why employers ended up hiring candidates. The authors asserted, "Millions of people are interacting with others and posting information which they may believe is private and personal, only to find that access of this information may not be as restricted as they believe" (p. 591).

Social network websites were used because they were quick and cheap (Davidson et al., 2012; Slovensky & Ross, 2012). More specifically, only 17 percent of HR managers believed it took too much time and effort to screen social network websites in relation to the information gained. Sixty-three percent of those HR managers who used SNW screening indicated that this approach took little time and effort in relation to the information gained via social network website screening (SHRM, 2011). It was incumbent on HR departments to obtain as much information as possible about a candidate to avoid negligent hiring (Woska, 2007).

Aspiridis, Kazantzi, and Kyriakou (2013) investigated the opportunity to use social networking sites as an additional tool to advance in a modern world of HR. They asserted that the last few years' research had addressed the effect of social media in HR management and particularly, the effectiveness of the functions of attracting, selecting, and recruiting candidates. Social media sites such as Facebook, LinkedIn, and Twitter were used for recruitment, career advancement motivation, and employability evaluation. The way in which this relationship was viewed by potential and current employees as well as companies' HR departments and the emergence and application of all these in Greece was the scope of Aspiridis, Kazantzi, and Kyriakou's research. They conducted an exploratory study to examine the possibility of connecting the recruitment process and selection of social networking and determined whether this modern approach towards the current traditional way was effective (Rontaos & Repanis, 2006).

The methodology used in the Aspiridis, Kazantzi, and Kyriakou (2013) research was based on structured questionnaires administered via electronic mail (e-mail), which consisted of open-ended and multiple-choice (closed) questions. The questionnaires were administered to different age groups (18 and above) and different educational levels and occupations to cover all sides of the spectrum. In addition, a review of the academic literature was performed. The research findings indicated that the use of social media to attract and select candidates was being used to make a global pool of prospective employees. Moreover, prospective employers could eliminate distance and cost, as candidate selection could be made from anywhere in the world. Social networking sites were a tool for faster immediate job search for candidates by seeking key words; they could locate the desired job. HR managers could target audiences and define the types of people they were trying to attract.

In an Internet-rich world, networking with potential employers through social media sites could have helped pre-service and new teachers connect with experienced teachers, learn about potential job openings, and engage in professional conversations. By using social media sites to follow trends in education, pre-service teachers were able to stay current on educational policies and identify where they would like to begin their careers. Sites such as LinkedIn, Facebook and Twitter allowed people to post relevant news articles and other educational information. In addition, many national education organizations maintained pages on Facebook and other social media sites, connecting subscribers with specific sites that aligned with their own interests. Novice teachers could upload electronic portfolios, resumes, or artifacts demonstrating successful student teaching.

This quantitative study was conducted to address this important issue. The research focus was the use of Facebook, LinkedIn, and Twitter. Bickley and Kwok (2011) conducted a study of 430 employees. LinkedIn and Facebook use was the highest among employees aged 26 to 45. Employers, who used LinkedIn and Facebook in this study, had a higher potential of reaching young professionals in the work force. Social media was effective in targeting enthusiastic and interested job applicants (Bickley & Kwok, 2011). The Society for Human Resource Management (SHRM) (2013) reported that the use of the top three social media networks—Facebook, LinkedIn, and Twitter—was increasing in the recruitment and selection process. The use of social media had evolved into a more complex process of attracting top candidates. Social media had become a strategic tool in the recruitment and selection process to reach candidates (p.1). Griffin and Lake (2012) stated "While the literature in the business, psychology, and pharmacy fields shows initial investigations of the impact of social networking sites 'information on hiring decisions, this area has not been investigated in the field of education." There was a lack of available scholarly research around HR managers 'use of social networking websites in the employment process in public schools. The research findings in this study were expected to provide useful information regarding how human resource managers in New York State public schools use of social media as a recruiting, hiring and selection tool, self-efficacy and its effect on teacher retention. The research indicated whether further research into HR managers' use of data from social networking websites in hiring decisions was warranted. Finally, the results of this study might have helped to address this important issue and identify the effectiveness that might have existed.

MAIN FOCUS OF THE CHAPTER

Research Design and Methodology

The purpose of this quantitative study was to assess the relationship between Human resource (HR) managers' self-efficacy and the retention level of teachers' in their district (low versus high) and their use of social networking websites (SNWs), specifically Facebook, LinkedIn, and Twitter. The research examined the use of social media as a tool for identifying and hiring job candidates. Additionally, it centered on SNWs as a tool for screening job candidates. The study determined the effectiveness of the use of these networks when making hiring decisions.

Measuring Retention Rates

The turnover rate of teachers with fewer than five years of experience from NYS School Districts was gathered from the New York State Education Department (NYSED) database. The New York State Education Department is part of the State University of New York (SUNY) is one of the most complete, interconnected systems of educational services in the United States. The mission of this department is to raise the knowledge, skill, and opportunity of all the people in New York. Data in the report cards were submitted by local school district officials.

The document from which the information was extracted included the tables contained in the school report card (SRC) (2013), in which data about performance of designated subgroups were reported by total public schools (aggregated data for all districts and charter schools), county (aggregated data for all districts and charter schools in the county), needs-to-resource capacity (NRC), district, and public schools. To ensure student confidentiality, NYSED did not publish data for groups with fewer than five students or data that might have allowed readers to determine the performance of such groups easily.

Seven hundred and twenty-three school districts in New York State were identified. The mean turnover rate during the first five years was 22.98 percent (median = 22). The high turnover school districts M+ SD = 38.1 percent and higher. One hundred and seventeen schools were in this range. Low turnover school districts M − SD = 7 percent and below. One hundred and thirty-four school districts were identified. 38 responses.

Selection of Subjects

HR managers from New York State school districts selected were invited to participate in a survey to collect data for this study. Respondents were contacted by phone and by email that linked to an online survey that was completed online. Respondents in schools that were designated as low retention and high retention were sent different emails, respectively, and were linked to different surveys that were coded to the researcher as being applicable to either low retention or high retention, as appropriate. Respondents from both categories were not aware of any coding or differences in the completion of their survey.

All aspects of the online survey maintained anonymity of the respondents and the school districts to which they were employed. Respondents were able to choose, upon completion of the online survey to volunteer their email address for a raffle to be conducted later. Respondents could use their personal email address for the purpose of the raffle.

For this study, the data from the NYSED school report cards were downloaded. Data showing the turnover rate of teachers with fewer than five years of experience was accessed to determine school districts with high and low teacher turnover rates.

To measure HR managers' self-efficacy, their levels of use of social media in recruiting and selection, and retention of teachers, a questionnaire (Waite, 2015) was distributed by email to 250 New York State HR managers in the fall of 2014. A link to the questionnaire was sent to the participants in each identified group. To ensure that all the HR managers were in the designated high retention or low retention groupings, a separate survey link was provided. Permission was granted by the Dowling College Institutional Review Board prior to survey distribution.

Survey Instrument

The survey instrument was constructed in three parts. Part I of the instrument included demographic information related to the positions of the respondent in their school district, gender, and years of experience. In addition, in Part I of the questionnaire, respondents reported their social media use by responding to four yes or no questions. Respondents were asked to report which SNWs they found useful for hiring. The response was measured using not useful, slightly useful, somewhat useful, useful, and very useful. To measure the use of social media as a tool for recruitment by HR managers, statements were developed based on the Society for Human Resource Management poll (SHRM) (2011). Questions were modified from a survey conducted by the SHRM (2011). SHRM conducted a series of surveys of workers in the employment or recruiting job function about the use of SNWs in recruiting and screening job candidates. The final three questions were based on the research of Davidson et al. (2011). The range of allowed responses was *1 = strongly agree, 2 = agree, 3 = slightly agree, 4 = disagree, and 5 = strongly disagree.*

To measure the use of social media for screening and selection, 15 statements were developed. Three were based on the research by Davidson et al. (2011). Statements 24 and 25 were based on the research of Van Iddekinge et al. (2013). Statements 26 through 29 were taken from a survey (Swallow, 2011). For social media monitoring service, Repplier (2011) surveyed more than 30 hiring professionals to determine when and how job recruiters screened job candidates on different social networks. Additional statements were developed based on experience. The range of potential responses *was 1 = strongly agree, 2 = agree, 3 = slightly agree, 4 = disagree, and 5 = strongly disagree.*

The participants reported usefulness of SNWs LinkedIn, Twitter, Facebook and others were measured using a 5-point Likert scale: *5 = not useful, 4 = slightly useful, 3 = somewhat useful, 2 = useful, 1 = very useful.*

Statements from a Jobvite Social Recruiting Survey (2013) were modified to measure the benefits of the use of social media. The results of the survey showed how recruiters were leveraging social recruiting in addition to whether they were using it.

To measure self-efficacy, HR managers responded to 10 statements in the fourth section of the survey. This section was based on 10 statements from the general self-efficacy scale (GSE) created by Schwarzer and Jersalem (1992). The construct of perceived self-efficacy reflected an optimistic self-belief (Schwarzer, 1992). In samples from 23 nations, Cronbach's alphas ranged from .76 to .90, with the majority in the high 80s. The scale was unidimensional. This was the belief that one was able to perform a novel or difficult task, possibly having to cope with adversity in various domains of human functioning. The HR managers evaluated the 10 statements on a 5-point Likert scale about their perceived self-efficacy relating to their job performance. The scale was *1 = strongly agree, 2 = agree, 3 = slightly agree, 4 = disagree, and 5 = strongly disagree.* To see the entire survey, go to Waite (2005, page x)

To measure teacher retention, an open-ended question was constructed based on the research of Ingersoll (2004). For this study, Ingersoll's research was used as a guide in defining turnover as the departure of teachers from their teaching jobs in schools. New York State school district teacher turnover rate after five years was used.

Construct Validity

The survey instrument was administered to HR administrators. Forty-nine respondents completed the questionnaire. A factor analysis of the survey responses was conducted to evaluate the underlying structure of the responses to determine whether they supported the four variables initially identified. Recruitment, screening and selection, self-efficacy, and social media benefits were subjected to a factor analysis.

Eight of the 12 items examined recruitment from the findings of Davis et al. (2011). The results determined that four of the 12 items did not appropriately measure the variables according to their definitions. One of the 12 measured social media benefits, and three of the 12, measured screening. Two items were removed because the results determined that the items did not appropriately measure the variables per their definitions. One was from the area that measured social media benefits and the other was from the area that measured screening. Additionally, one of the 15 items that measured screening was reassigned to recruitment. One of the six items that measured social media benefits was reassigned to recruitment.

Because of the factor analysis and scree plot, an additional variable emerged. Screening became an independent variable. Four of the 15 items for screening and selection were reassigned to Screening. One of the 11 items from Screening was reassigned to Social Media Benefits. Three of the 10 items from Recruitment were reassigned to Screening.

One of the 10 items from Self-Efficacy and one of the six items measuring Social Media Benefits were delineated. Table 1.0 reports the deleted items after the factor analysis was conducted. The factor analysis decreased the number of items from 50 to 48. Table 1.0 presents the refined survey dimensions, items, score range, and reliability.

The survey was adjusted to combine agree and slightly agree as one item. If the respondents selected agree or slightly agree, it was ranked as a number 3 in the Likert scale. The 5-point Likert scale was converted to a 4-point scale. Table 1.0 reflected the change including the change in the range for each variable.

Table 1. Revised survey dimensions, items, score ranges, and reliability

	Items	# of Items	Range	Reliability
Demographics	1, 2, 3, 4	4		
Hiring	46,47,48,49	4		
Independent Variables				
Screening	8, 9, 11, 15, 16, 17, 18, 19, 24, 25, 27, 28	12	12 – 48	.940
Self-Efficacy	30, 32, 33, 34, 35, 36, 37, 38, 39	9	9 – 36	.916
Recruitment	5, 6, 7, 10, 12, 13, 45, 26	8	8 – 32	.897
Selection	20, 21, 22, 23	4	4 – 16	.977
Social Media Benefits	14, 41, 42, 43, 44, 29	6	6 – 24	.795
Dependent Variable				
Retention	50			

Waite, 2015, p 60.

SOLUTIONS AND RECOMMENDATIONS

How do human resource managers in school districts with high and low retention rates differ in their use of the three social media dimensions of self-efficacy, recruiting, and hiring and selection and in their perception of benefits of social media?

Quantitative Analysis

Descriptive statistics and independent samples t-tests were used to address this research question are presented in Table 2. The means, standard deviations, and results of the t tests were provided in Table 3.1. There were no significant differences found in the use of social media in Recruitment between HR managers in low retention districts (M = 17.50, SD= 4.08) and high retention districts (M = 15.64, SD = 4.18), t(32) = 1.29, p = .205. There were no significant differences found in the use of social media in Screening between HR managers in low retention districts (M = 27.43, SD = 7.10) and high retention districts (M= 25.75, SD = 7.50), t(35) = .696, p = .491. There were no significant differences found in Selection among HR managers in low retention districts (M = 9.14, SD = 2.78) and high retention districts (M = 8.94, SD = 3.28), t(35) = .206, p = .838. There were also no differences in perception of Social Media Benefits among HR managers' in low retention 77 districts (M = 16.70, SD = 2.05) and high retention districts (M = 15.79, SD= 3.56), t(32)= .949, p = .350. Finally, there were no differences in Self-Efficacy among HR managers in low retention districts (M = 29.79, SD = 3.66) and high retention districts (M= 29.71, SD = 3.27), t(31) = .061, p = .952.

These results indicated that there were no differences among the HR managers in high and low retention districts in their use of social media in hiring, selecting, and recruiting district employees, their perception of social media as a benefit in their work and in their self-efficacy.

Table 2. Descriptive statistics and t test for high and low retention rate school districts in their use of social media networks

Variable		n	Range	M	SD	t	df	p
Recruitment	Low	20	8-32	17.50	4.08	1.292	32	.205
	High	14	8-32	15.64	4.18			
Screening	Low	21	12-48	27.42	7.09	0.696	35	.491
	High	16	12-48	25.75	7.49			
Selection	Low	21	4-16	9.14	2.78	0.206	35	.838
	High	16	4-16	8.93	3.27			
Self-Efficacy	Low	19	9-36	29.78	3.66	0.061	31	.952
	High	14	9-36	29.71	3.26			
Social Media Benefits	Low	20	6-24	16.70	2.05	0.949	32	.350
	High	14	6-24	15.79	3.55			

Waite, 2015 p.77.

Qualitative Analysis

Qualitative analyses explored the emergent themes, patterns, and discrepancies among HR managers' responses to the open-ended question, "How do you think hiring practices using/not using social media affect teacher retention?" HR managers' commentaries offered another set of data; "qualitative inquiry assists researchers in expanding their understanding and explanations of real life phenomena" (Beard, 2009, p. 47). This question came after question 49 of the survey. Table 3 presents the emergent themes and patterns as reported by HR managers.

Table 3. Themes, patterns, and discrepancies: human resource managers social media use influence teacher retention

Themes That Emerged for Social Media Use	Themes That Emerged for Social Media Benefits
• We have not found the need to use social media for hiring yet. We do not use social media at all (28%) • With the growing use of social media, I can see moving in that direction in the future (7%)	• Social media may provide additional information regarding a potential applicant it can provide greater insight into a candidate's background, tenure, professionalism, and as to their job interest (10%) • Social media is a tool used to receive high return of applicants (7%) • The information obtained through social media is subjective and must be verified (3%)
Themes that emerged for social media use in relationship to retention	Themes that emerged for the use of social media in relationship to recruitment
• Teacher retention is not directly affected using social media in the hiring process (21%) • Too early to tell if the use of social media would provide details of a potential candidate that will assist in determining teacher retention rates (7%)	• It is more involved in recruitment (7%) • We on occasion post openings on our Facebook page (7%) • We make little use of social media for recruiting or hiring purposes (3%)

By giving them the opportunity to express themselves allowed human resource managers to discuss their beliefs regarding social media's utility in hiring practices and teacher retention. Responses were in a narrative format. A descriptive analysis of themes and patterns was used to extract more data from respondents. The themes that emerged from the HR managers' responses were social media use, social media benefits, social media use in relationship to retention, and social media in relationship to recruitment.

The first theme identified was the non-use of social media in the hiring process. HR managers (28 percent) indicated that they did not use social media in the hiring process. In addition, they did not think it was useful. More specifically, one of the respondents stated, "I don't believe that I would ever, in the Public-School System, use Facebook or Twitter in the hiring process." Overall, the patterns were consistent except for 7 percent of the HR managers who reported growing use of social media, "it will probably come to that in the future." Another supported that statement by responding, "I can see moving in that direction in the future." An interesting finding was that 3 percent indicated that social media was subjective and needed to be verified.

A second theme that emerged was the benefit of using social media. The pattern that emerged by the responding HR managers was that social media might provide additional information regarding a potential applicant (10 percent). Respondents reported that social media "can provide greater insight into a candidate's background, tenure, professionalism and as to their job interest." It was also reported that, "You can see how they felt or behaved at previous employment." Additionally, seven percent of the respondents stated, "the use of social media increases the responses to an ad" and "social media is used to receive high return of applicants." Finally, three percent of the HR managers asserted that the "the information obtained through social media is subjective and must be verified."

The third theme that emerged related to how HR managers believed their hiring practices and social media use influenced teacher retention. The majority (21 percent) of HR managers reported that they did not think retention was directly affected using social media in the hiring process. Several respondents felt there was "no evidence to of impact," no impact that could be measured," and "unknown data." Seven percent of the respondents indicated it was too early to tell if the use of social media would provide details of a potential candidate that would assist in determining teacher retention rates. It was noted that a respondent said, "Relationships are the key to retention." It was also reported that, "Teacher retention is based on salary and evaluation." These responses indicated an agreement with the other reported responses. One response stated that, "if you hire a bad apple you are not going to keep it," from which it could have been inferred that despite the use of social media, teacher retention is a complex matter.

Another theme that emerged was in relationship to the use of social media in recruitment. Seven percent of the HR managers indicated that social media was used in recruitment. It was reported that, "We on occasion post openings on our Facebook page." Additionally, one respondent reported that, "Social media is used to receive high return of applicants."

CONCLUSION

The literature showed initial investigations regarding the effect of social networking sites on hiring decisions within industries. Research about social media or the effect they might have had on HR managers was rapidly evolving (Bondarouk & Olivas-Lujan, 2013). This area had been minimally investigated in the education field. However, this research indicated there was relatively little use of social networking sites by school HR managers in the hiring process. Despite this, it should have been noted that social media had opened various means of communication and was not going away. Although there were many benefits of the use of social media in recruitment, screening and selection when making hiring decisions, there were ethical and legal issues that needed to be considered.

The results indicated that there were no significant differences in the use of social media in Recruitment between HR managers in low retention districts and high retention districts. There were no significant differences in the use of social media in Screening or in selection between HR managers in low retention districts and high retention districts. There were also no significant differences in the perception of the Benefits of Social Media between HR managers in low retention districts and high retention districts. Finally, there were no significant differences in Self-Efficacy between HR managers in low retention districts and high retention districts.

The results indicated that there were no significant differences between the HR managers in high and low retention districts in regards to their use of social media in hiring, selecting, and recruiting district employees, their perception of social media as a benefit in their work, and in their self-efficacy.

Additional research on the two groups' (high retention and low retention) hiring practices needs to be conducted to identify the other factors that contributed to the differences in their retention rates. Punia and Sharma (2008) showed the influence of organizational procurement practices on employee retention intentions based on personal and positional variables of employees. They concluded that the process of identifying candidates to fill open position had a positive relationship with their stay in the organization. From the results, there was a clear linkage of the procurement practices on employee retention intentions.

Baker-Doyle (2010) asserted that the problem of teacher turnover was linked to teacher recruitment, induction, and long-term retention efforts. Alongside the existing knowledge base, social network perceptions research could help provide a comprehensive picture of teacher recruitment and retention policies. Cochran-Smith (2004) argued there was a need to address teacher recruitment as it related to policy initiatives. The relationship between social media tools and teacher retention seemed especially important in the 21st century, when cost-conscious trustees and superintendents needed to find ways to reduce wasteful practices, which contributed to the retention of new teachers.

REFERENCES

Aspiridis, G., Kazantzi, V., & Kyriakou, D. (2013). Social networking websites and their effect in contemporary human resource management – A research approach. *Mediterranean Journal of Social Sciences, 4*(1), 29–45.

Baker-Doyle, K. (2010). Beyond the labor market paradigm: A social network perspective on teacher recruitment and retention. *education policy analysis archives, 18*, 26.

Bandura, A. (1997). *Self-efficacy: The exercise of control.* USA: W.H. Freeman & Company.

Barber, A. E. (1998). *Recruiting employees.* Thousand Oaks, CA: Sage Publications.

Beard, K. (2009). *Nursing faculty roles in teaching racially and ethnically diverse nursing students in a registered nurse program* [Doctoral Dissertation]. Dowling College.

Bickley, S. L., & Kwok, L. (2011). *Social media as an employee recruitment tool. Sarah L. Bicky. Hospitality Management.* Syracuse University.

Boyd, D. M., & Ellison, N. B. (2008). Social network sites: Definition, history and scholarship. *Journal of Computer-Mediated Communication, 13*(1), 210–230. doi:10.1111/j.1083-6101.2007.00393.x

Brotherton, P. (2012). Social media and referrals are best sources for talent: A new survey shows that companies are investing more and more of their recruitment resources in social media and seeing it pay off. *T + D, 24.*

Cascio, W., & Aguinis, H. (2005). *Applied psychology in human resource management.* New Jersey: Prentice Hall.

Chapman, D. S., Uggerslev, K. L., Carroll, S. A., Piasentin, K. A., & Jones, D. A. (2005). Applicant attraction to organizations and job choice: A meta-analytic review of the correlates of recruiting outcomes. *The Journal of Applied Psychology, 90*(5), 928–944. doi:10.1037/0021-9010.90.5.928 PMID:16162065

Cochran-Smith, M. (2004). Stayers, leavers, lovers, and dreamers: Insights about teacher retention. *Journal of Teacher Education, 55*(5), 387–392. doi:10.1177/0022487104270188

Davidson, K. H., Maraist, C., & Bing, M. N. (2011). Friend or foe? The promise and pitfalls of using social networking sites for HR decisions. *Journal of Business and Psychology, 26*(2), 153–159. doi:10.100710869-011-9215-8

Evans, *T.* (2010). State schools lure more employers: Recruiters like one stop shopping for grads with solid academics, job skills, and record of success. *The Wall Street Journal,* B1- B8.

Finn, D., & Singh, P. (2003). The effects of information technology on recruitment. *Journal of Labor Research 24*(3), 395-405. Griffin, M. M. & Lake, R. L. (2012). Social networking postings: Views from school principals. *Education Policy Analysis Archives, 20,* 1–24.

Gatewood, R. D., & Field, H. S. (2001). Human resource selection (5th ed.). Fort Worth, TX: Dyrden Press.

Griffin, M. M., & Lake, R. L. (2012). Social networking postings: Views from school principals. *Education Policy Analysis Archives, 20,* 1–24. doi:10.14507/epaa.v20n11.2012

Ingersoll, R. (2001). Teacher turnover and teacher shortages: An organizational analysis. *American Educational Research Journal, 38*(3), 499–534. doi:10.3102/00028312038003499

Ingersoll, R. (2004). Four myths about America's teacher quality problem. In M. Smylie & D. Miretzky (Eds.), *Developing the teacher workforce: The 103rd yearbook of the National Society for the Study of Education* (pp. 1–33). Chicago: University of Chicago Press. doi:10.1111/j.1744-7984.2004.tb00029.x

Jobvite. (2013). Social Recruiting Survey Results. Retrieved from www.jobvite.com

Jones, C., & Behling, S. (2010). Uncharted waters: Using social networks in hiring decisions. *Issues in Information Systems, 11*(1), 589–595.

Kay, A. (2000). Recruiters embrace the internet. *Information Week, 778,* 72–80.

Kluemper, D. H., & Rosen, P. A. (2009). Future employment selection methods: Evaluating social networking websites. *Journal of Managerial Psychology, 24*(6), 567–580. doi:10.1108/02683940910974134

Lipiec, J. (2001).. . *Human Resources Management Perspective at the Turn of the Century Public Personnel Management*, *30*, 137–146.

Lorenz, K. (2009). *Employers are digging up your digital dirt*. Retrieved May 2, 2013 from http:www.theworkbuzz.com/job-surveys/socialnetworks

Luszczynska, A., Scholz, U., & Scwarzer, R. (2005). The general self-efficacy scale: Multicultural validation studies. *The Journal of Psychology*, *139*(5), 439–457. doi:10.3200/JRLP.139.5.439-457 PMID:16285214

NYSED. (2013). The New York State School Report Card retrieved from https://reportcards.nysed.gov/

Pethe, S., Chaudhary, S., & Dhar, U. (1999). *Occupational self-efficacy Scale and Manual*. Agra: National Psychological Corporation.

Pfeiffer, J. (1994). *Competitive advantage through people*. Boston: Harvard Business School Press.

SHRM. (2014). Retrieved from http://www.shrm.org/TemplatesTools/Glossaries/HRTerms/Pages/r.aspx#sthash.4cBgpq2w.dpuf

Smith, P. G., & Wyatt, W. (2010). *Using social networking websites for hiring decisions: Legal and ethical considerations. Best Practices Forum Human Resources* (pp. 1–8). Arlington, TX: NJDHS.

Snell, S., Pedigo, P., & Krawie, G. (1995). Managing impact of information technology on human resource management. In G. Ferris, S. Rosen, & D. Barnum (Eds.), *Handbook of Human Resource Management* (pp. 159–174). Cambridge, Mass: Blackwell.

Tiwari, P., & Saxena, K. (2012). Human resource management practices: A comprehensive review. *Pakistan Business Review*, *13*(4), 667–705.

Van Iddekinge, C., Lanivich, S., Roth, P., & Junco, E. (2013). Social media for selection? Validity and adverse impact potential of a Facebook based assessment. *Journal of Management*, *15*, 1–25.

Waite, B. (2015). School human *resource managers' level of use of social networking websites on the dimensions of self-efficacy, decision making in recruiting, screening and selection of teachers and its impact on teacher retention* [Doctoral Dissertation].

Wilk, S. L., & Cappelli, P. (2003). Understanding the determinants of employer use of selection methods. *Personnel Psychology*, *56*(1), 103–124. doi:10.1111/j.1744-6570.2003.tb00145.x

Woska, W. J. (2007). Legal issues for HR Professionals: Reference checking/background investigations. *Public Personnel Management*, *36*(1), 79–89. doi:10.1177/009102600703600106

KEY TERMS AND DEFINITIONS

Facebook: Launched in February 2004. It was a social networking website on which users could create personal profiles, share photos and statuses, and communicate with family, friends, classmates, and co-workers. Facebook allowed users to create pages for their businesses that were easily connected with their personal pages. Facebook had seen the biggest gain in overall usage by recruiters seeking potential candidates.

Human Resource Manager: The individual within an organization responsible for hiring new employees. Human resource management practices were defined as organizational activities directed at managing the pool of human resources and ensuring that the resources are employed towards the fulfillment of organizational goals.

LinkedIn: Was created for professional networking. It was launched in May 2003. People used LinkedIn to keep in touch with co-workers, as well as with people in their networking groups. Employers had begun to use this website to hire employees, using a tool called LinkedIn Recruiter.

Recruitment: Those practices and activities carried on by the organization with the primary purpose of attracting, screening, and selecting a qualified person for a job.

Retention: Organizational policies and practices designed to meet the diverse needs of employees created an environment that encouraged employees to remain employed.

Screening: The process in which a prospective employee was investigated to verify qualifications and confirm that the person would be a safe and appropriate match for the workplace.

Selection: The process of collecting and evaluating information about an individual to extend an offer of employment.

Self-Efficacy: Judgments or beliefs about one's capabilities to achieve tasks required to produce outcomes in specific situations or contexts. They affected thought processes and the level and persistency of motivation and emotion. Occupational self-efficacy was a domain-specific measure of self-efficacy. Occupational self-efficacy referred to the belief in one's own ability and competence to perform in an occupation.

Social Media: A connection of Web-based sites that allowed users to share information about them and to create partnerships with other users. Users could connect with other individuals around the globe and maintain a local network group.

Turnover: In the literature on teacher turnover and retention, the general term turnover was used as an umbrella term to describe the departure of teachers from their teaching jobs.

Twitter: Launched in July 2006. Twitter provided a service that allowed users to communicate through short posts known as tweets—posts of up to 140 text characters, which Twitter displayed on the user's profile page and delivered to the user's circle of friends, or by default, allowed anyone access to the user's page.

This research was previously published in Maximizing Social Science Research Through Publicly Accessible Data Sets; pages 275-292, copyright year 2018 by Information Science Reference (an imprint of IGI Global).

Chapter 25
Consumer Engagement in Social Media Platforms

Hans Ruediger Kaufmann
University of Nicosia, Cyprus

Agapi Manarioti
The Brand Love, Cyprus

ABSTRACT

If 'to be social' is the sum of people's online interaction intentions, that can be monitored by marketers but not coerced, how can we make best use of these powerful new media? The answer lies in understanding the internal, psychological needs that are fulfilled by the social media and how they are demonstrated and testified by liking, sharing and engaging in general with specific pieces of content, while rejecting others. In this environment, marketers are called to develop a "brand as a person" strategy, in order for their brands to mingle and interact with consumers beyond the traditional marketing communication framework. In this chapter, we explore and discuss the strategic use of the social media as a concept that needs to be thoroughly understood but seemingly hasn't been yet by a large majority of marketers.

Questions

- Why marketers can't afford to ignore the social media?
- How a brand can benefit from a social media marketing strategy?
- What are the psychological characteristics of social media users?
- How different 'sharer tribes' influence digital marketing strategy decisions?
- Why is brand-as-a-person better than brand-as-a-brand?

DOI: 10.4018/978-1-7998-9020-1.ch025

INTRODUCTION

When both, scholars and practitioners are talking about social media, the word revolution comes up often. Yet, there might still be some readers that are skeptic about our space allocation dedicating a whole chapter on the social media marketing? So, let's talk numbers first:

Figure 1. Social media penetration
Source: www.wearesocial.com

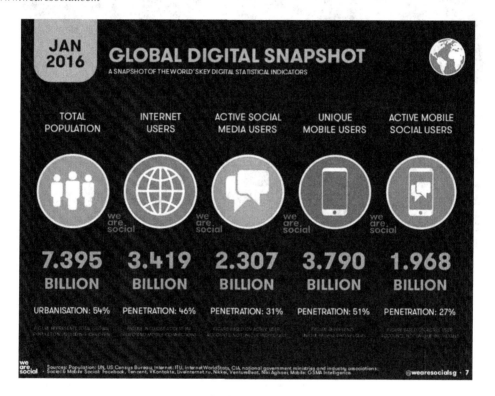

According to the comprehensive research conducted and published by the 'We are Social' agency (www.wearesocial.com), more than 6 out of 10 people with access to the internet are accounted as active social media users, adding up to the overwhelming amount of 2.307 billion users. From a regional perspective, according to the same source, 59% of the total population of North America is active social media users, a percentage that changes to 50% for South America and 48% for West Europe and East Asia. In more detail:

To better understand the reasons for the penetration of the social media and how they have transformed the way we live, think and behave, Table 1 combines the aforementioned percentages, on the premise that all active social media users have internet access. The purpose of this meta-analysis is to showcase how dominant this new "habit" of maintaining a social media life has become and why we, as marketers must wholeheartedly and proactively embrace it: these numbers tell the story of a paradigm shift that mandates an in depth analysis and understanding of users' motives and needs when interacting in the social media arena.

Figure 2. Social media use per region
Source: www.wearesocial.com

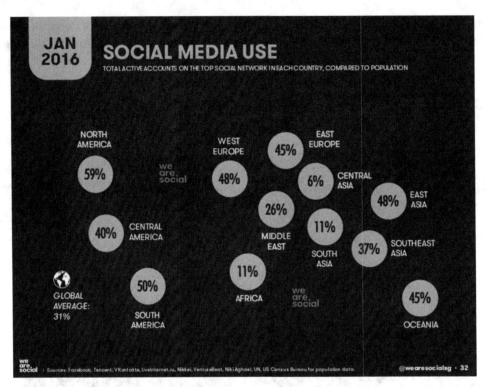

Table 1. Social media users as % of internet users

Region	Social media users/ Internet Users
Central America	91%
Southeast Asia	90%
East Asia	89%
North America	83%
East Europe	70%
South America	67%
Oceania	66%
West europe	58%
Middle East	49%
South Asia	41%
Africa	38%
Central Asia	15%

Source: Authors

Notwithstanding different definitions, social media are online networks where users generate and exchange content engaging in and maintaining an ongoing dialogue. More specific on the nexus between social media and corporate marketing, Dr. Fou of the Marketing Science Consulting Group, Inc. says: "Social media = people's conversations and actions online that can be mined by advertisers for insights but not coerced to pass along marketing messages. It's the new form of media that does not exist until it happens and that cannot be bought by advertisers to carry their messages" (www.heidicohen.com). Social media are ephemeral- the trendy Snapchat is the living proof for social media being ruled by users, not by marketers. In the traditional marketing context, marketers craft their tactics, for the following months or year, produce and broadcast them and then wait for the customers to respond. Here, in the social media world, things are diametrically different: Now, brands have to go where consumers go and tailor their messages and strategies on the spot, to accommodate social media users' behavior. In a way, this is another aspect of the "revenge of the customer" we discussed in Chapter 2, as now, users lead and the brands follow.

In the early days of the social media, Friendster and Myspace dominated the space, yet today their influence faded and they are another brick in the ephemeral wall. Today, when it comes to ranking existing social networking platforms, Facebook is salient in the landscape, since its introduction in 2004, while new services are launched continuously. Figure 5-3 illustrates the ranking of the different social media platforms as in April 2016; apart from the impressive numbers, what it is important for the marketer to notice is the variety of platforms, the different orientation of each and how they provide us with access to niche markets or very well defined audience groups, in terms of demographic and psychological categorizations. Note, that messaging apps like WhatsApp and Facebook Messenger are included in the list, since they are evolving to much more than mere texting replacement becoming an all in one service. For example, China's chat app, WeChat, number 5 in the ranking, apart from one to one and group messaging, features newsfeed sharing, and organizations/brands are following like Facebook, the money transferring services of Square and PayPal, in-store payment offers similar to Apple Pay and Google Wallet, cab hailing abilities of Uber, food delivery ordering like Favor etc.

From a marketing perspective, social media are first and foremost a branding channel (eMarketer, 2013) where branded activities can be used to increase brand awareness and brand liking, promote customer engagement and loyalty, inspire consumer word-of-mouth communication about the brand, and potentially drive traffic to brand locations on and offline (Ashley & Tuten, 2015). Investment in social media and social network advertising is on the rise in terms of spending and proportion of advertising spending budgets (eMarketer 2013b, 2014). As this investment continues to grow, expectations of ever increasing sophistication and effectiveness of social media marketing are also on the rise. Practices that started out as largely intuitive and experimental, such as Facebook's page posting for example, have recently evolved in a combination of advertising and marketing art and science (Alhabash et al., 2015). According to the Social Marketing Industry Report (Stelzner, 2016), 90% of the marketers acknowledge the importance of social media marketing as a means to increase exposure and traffic and to build a loyal fan base. Interestingly, however, they state that it is complicated and difficult and they do not feel confident about their decisions and ROI. Here lays the initial premise of this book, that social media marketing is a *new* marketing paradigm, partly applying the same rules as traditional marketing but mostly introducing new terms and concepts that need to be studied by marketers from scratch. The aforementioned reservations and the executives' reluctance to adopt new channels (only 6% of the marketers reported that they are willing to) are illustrated in Figure 5-4, showing the very low penetration of new channels in the social media marketing mix and the ongoing domination of "traditional" online channels like Facebook, Twitter and LinkedIn.

Figure 3. Social media ranking per number of users
Source: www.statista.com

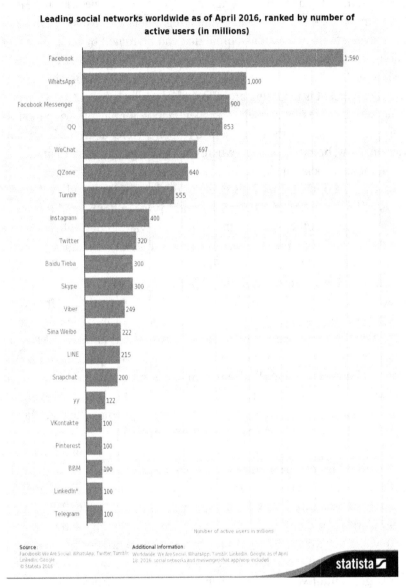

Leading social networks worldwide as of April 2016, ranked by number of active users (in millions)

Social media are here to stay. Their rise and pervasiveness show that they answer a pre-existing psychological need, one that makes people change their priorities and habits, in order to create and share their personal moments and opinions online. Getting to understand this fundamental need behind social media use is the very key to crafting effective and successful social media marketing plans. Apparently, given a number of new channels and the fundamental differences between the social media and traditional media, a new marketing approach is called for, backed up with, so far scattered, theoretical and practical knowledge to provide the marketers with the needed confidence to get out of their comfort zones and adopt novel perspectives, tools, and techniques.

Figure 4. Social media platforms used by marketers
Source: Social Media Marketing Industry Report (2016)

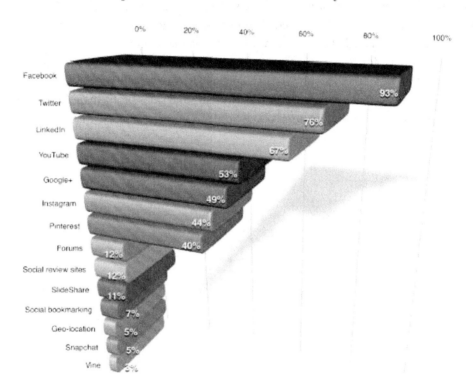

THE PSYCHOLOGY OF LIKE AND SHARE

As mentioned already, marketers acknowledge the importance of a well-crafted social media marketing strategy, as social media are amongst the top marketing tools employed despite still regarded as challenging and difficult (Stelzner, 2016; Wasp Barcode Technologies, 2016). This is the product of a very pragmatic observation: Social media impact and change the behavior of the customers, both online and offline. In their own words, consumers say that social media play almost as big a role in purchasing decisions as television does (www.adage.com).

At this point, let's ask us: How can a brand benefit from a social media marketing strategy? For starters, posts and updates on brand social media profiles directly impact website traffic and search engine rankings (Stelzner, 2016); in turn, in the context of an integrated marketing strategy where online channels are used to generate offline results, this SEO implication indirectly impacts the sales performance and other critical brand measures (See chapter 2 for more information about Search Engine Optimization).

From a simplistic point of view, when a brand post appears on a user's Facebook timeline, it is an immediate addition to the awareness scores of the brand. This is the starting point for any kind of customer-brand relationship and a reminder as well. However, what we intend is to motivate and trigger customer behavior and to attract it to our owned media, i.e. our website of a specific landing page. Obviously, the chances for a customer to click on the link pointing to the brand website or any specific landing page are higher than without the post appearance. But, here applies a fundamental rule of social media marketing that makes things easier and more effective: In order to convert social Media reach to brand related activity, a Call-To-Action prompt must be included in all posts and updates. Regardless if it is a website link, a "Shop Now" or a "Contact Us" button, the marketer should design a clickstream path from the social network to brand owned channels, in order to, at least, measure the impact of their tactics and to identify the ones that engage consumers in the most valuable manner. Website traffic and "vanity metrics" (friends, followers, "likes") are the most common metrics marketers use to measure the business impact of social media, but only 14% manage to tie social media to sales levels (The CMO survey, 2015). This distance between social media marketing and sales performance starts a vicious circle created by a lack of integration resulting in very commonly observed failures in marketing strategies today.

Figure 5.

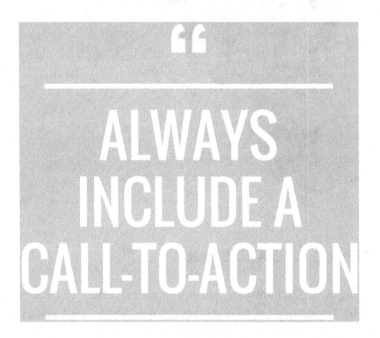

In spite of inadequacy of used marketing metrics to capture to impact to sales, there are solid findings that there is one metric that cannot be overseen. According to Google's report (2014), people who engage with a brand on social media daily are likely to make twice as many purchases from that brand than someone who engages only monthly. In addition, a Forrester Research (2013) study showed that individuals who have engaged with brands online are more likely to complete actual purchases than those who did not have online engagement. In their research on how social media clicks impact actual behavior, Alhabash and colleagues concluded that positive evaluation of the messages of a brand broadcasts on the social media channels moves customers closer to perform the prompted behavior offline (Alhabash et al., 2015). This means that liking a post about a new product augments the possibility of actually buying the product. The researchers' focus was on the evaluation of the message itself, which starts the conversation on the importance of content management: what we publish online, when and how- a discussion that will be elaborated in Chapter 6. Ho-Dac et al., (2012) found that online customer reviews also affect sales, a phenomenon that is evident in in the case of TripAdvisor and its impact on hotel bookings. As already discussed in Chapter 3, consumer behavior is influenced more by reviews when referring to weaker brands but the more and better the reviews, the higher the sales and ultimately, the higher the brand strength and, in a way, the immunity against bad reviews (Ho-Dac et al., 2012).

This latter finding raises a question: Why are we, as social media users, willing to change our opinion and behavior about a product or brand based on a review made by someone we even don't know or are never going to meet? The answer can be found in the concept of online brand communities (you can find the theoretical background in Chapter 3), those groups of consumers developed around a brand that are affiliated by their common interest in it. Online brand communities behave in the same manner as offline brand communities (Dessart et al.., 2015). Members have a great tendency to go beyond their personal character identity (i.e. identity related to a person's individual sense of self) and to develop a social identity, that is, an individual's self-concept that derives from the knowledge of being part of a social group (Facebook brand fans) or participating in the community of reviewers in TripAdvisor. Adding to this intrinsic satisfaction, the fact that consumers are cautious towards marketing messages and tend to easier accept peer reviews than corporate product statements, explains why we are prone to trust a stranger that belongs to the same community with us more than the official brand voice or, sometimes, our instincts. Of course, this understanding of the underlying social media user needs, guides the marketer to craft a strategy to intrigue and manage reviewing in particular, as a means to create Word of Mouth for the benefit of the brand. Realizing, that commenting and posting a review is an act of co-creation in the context of the community, demonstrates in a very straightforward manner, why brand representatives are strongly encouraged to reply to the comments and reviews and actively participate in the dialogue, rather than remaining silent observers.

Apart from commenting and reviewing, the social media as the locus of the online brand communities can be a great source of innovation and value co-creation, especially when brand representatives become honest and equal members of the team. Brands have rather little authority on their communities and this is the major risk and concern that bothers marketers: once consumers start sharing experiences and opinions, there is no way to stop or control them. Those who tried have succeeded only in making the essence of the community obsolete. The more successful communities are usually run by enthusiasts and customers of the brands and products. This is confirmed by a publication in the Wall Street Journal (Dholakia and Vianello, 2009): in their efforts to set up brand communities that will remain under their command, companies are missing out on a marketing tool with huge potential, particularly in this weak economy. A well-designed brand community can be used to conduct market research with very quick turn-around; generate and test ideas for product innovations; deliver prompt and high-quality service to customers having a problem; strengthen the attachments that existing customers feel toward the brand; and increase good publicity through word-of-mouth. The only thing marketers have to take to heart is to allow the fans to express themselves without censoring or trapping them inside strict rules, monitor the conversation and maintain a positive, brand enhancing attitude, be open and receptive and make community members feel heard and important.

Let's take the example of Beauty Talk- Sephora Community and how it integrates with the brand's social media messages:

This is a community dedicated to beauty, nested in the website of Sephora, allowing consumers to ask beauty related questions and advice, discuss products and share experiences and tips. The representatives of Sephora are present, replying to threads and answering questions, without any effort to hard sell or spoil the sharing experience with marketing agendas. As a result, this conversation drastically increases the website traffic whilst building authority for the brand in the online beauty discussion. At the same time, on their Facebook Page, Sephora brand representatives maintain the same friendly tone of voice and redirect consumers to the community, converting the social media engagement first to website traffic and then to (potential) loyalty through participation in the community. From the consumer's point of view, being a part of a larger group, enjoying the feeling of sharing and belonging is a fundamental psychological need that finds actualization in social networking altogether.

Figure 6.

There is extensive research on why and how we have become so engaged in social media. Pew Research recently reported that 90% of young adults (18-29 years old) are active social media users (Pew Research Center, 2015) and provided the personality traits determining this behavior. The research discovered that social media are mostly used by extrovert people, which are open to new experiences but having a higher emotional instability (Correa et al., 2010). This is interesting in many ways:

- In the past, similar research studies have found extraversion to be negatively related to the use of social services such as chat rooms (e.g., Hamburger & Ben-Artzi, 2000). The reason is seen in that social interactions through these online applications differed from offline interactions due to the lesser importance attributed to physical appearance and physical proximity and to the comfort assured by anonymity. As a result, introverted people, as well as those who experience social anxiety and loneliness, tended to use the Web to assuage their real-world isolation in these early studies of Internet use (Amichai-Hamburger & Ben-Artzi, 2003; Bargh et al., 2002). However, today, this relationship between extroversion and social media has turned to positive: more extrovert people use the social media. The explanation provided is, that today we don't use the social media to hide our identities, on the contrary: we share and promote ourselves, we build a new identity through the social media. (Correa et al., 2010).
- Openness to new experiences as a trait of the avid social media users is related to the adjustability of social media users to the fast-paced changes occurring in the technological level but also to the

new platforms launched regularly, new services etc. This implies that people who find it difficult to accept the new, be it an experience or a software environment, cannot keep up with the speed of the social media.

- The emotional instability as a predictor of social media use is explained by higher levels of neuroticism, negative affectivity and anxiety (Correa et al., 2010; Hamburger & Ben-Artzi, 2000). Given that emotional instability is related to loneliness and a difficulty in engaging in face-to-face interactions, it makes sense why when under this psychological stage, we seek comfort in the virtual social media world. If we accept that, when feeling content and sociable, people tend to prefer the "real" social life rather than the virtual one and that they hang out on Facebook, Instagram and the rest of the social platforms while being bored or disappointed, this can be a beacon to the marketer about the purpose of content published: Social media users want to be entertained and to feel important and significant. By the same token, use and gratifications theory suggests social media participants are likely to desire entertainment and informativeness, but perhaps entertainment is a stronger motivator of engagement with top brands than informativeness (Ashley & Tuten, 2015). These insights will be very useful and effective when later applied to the content management decisions as they suggest an approach to content creation that goes far beyond of merely sharing brand and sales messages.

Figure 7.

❝

Social media are mostly used by extrovert people, that are open to new experiences, but have higher emotional instability.

Recent research points to the use of social media with the aim to build and promote our self-identity. Amongst our fundamental needs as humans is the one to promote ourselves, support our beliefs and share our ideas (Zhu & Chen, 2015). This goal has found an avenue in the limitless possibilities of the internet and the social media, creating a stream of "me-formation", to take the term proposed by Rutgers University a step further (Naaman et al., 2010). According to this research, about half the content posted online is about "me", sharing of personal information, moments and perceptions through status updates, tweets, and photographs, reflecting a modern way to express our identity-related need to talk about ourselves. There even is a biological explanation to this: a recent research discovered a strong connection between Facebook and the brain's reward center, called the nucleus accumbens. This area processes rewarding feelings about things like food, sex, money and social acceptance. This means that when we get positive feedback on Facebook, the feeling lights up this part of our brain. The greater the intensity of our Facebook use, the greater the reward (Meshi et al., 2013).

Figure 8.

"" *A world of meformation* ""

Given the way the social media function, the values or activities we engage in (in terms of like, comment, share for Facebook and the equivalents for the other platforms) become a part of our identity. This holds the answer on how we select what to engage in in the social media world. Research findings show that there is a significant difference between the psychologies of liking a piece of content and sharing it/ re-tweet it/ repost it etc. While liking is a typical, low-involvement sign of approval, sharing means to endorse and adopt the content.

People who share content are motivated by personal, intimate needs, like expressing themselves, identify with something, and support whatever matches their existing or desired identity, while hoping they will be rewarded by their network for the share. Each share is a message to the user's network of friends and acquaintances and to the entire community, a confession about personal beliefs and values. What we choose to share and even what we choose not to, mirrors our identity (Schaefer, 2015). From a cognitive vantage point, clicking on the Like button is an easier and less involved behavior compared to sharing and commenting on persuasive messages (Alhabash et al., 2015).

According to an extensive research of the Customer Insights Group for the New York Times (2011), six different segments of sharers exist, all bonded by a common behavioral denominator: sharing is a personal action of relationship building, either through making available to our network what we think will be entertaining of by defining ourselves to others.

- **The Altruists:** Sharing is an act of thoughtfulness; they want to be helpful to their network and to stay connected with their medium of preference being the email.
- **The Careerists:** They share in order to make a statement about their professional stance; this is why they mostly use LinkedIn. Since they use social media sharing to build an identity, they carefully select what they share and evaluate the content in terms of how valuable it will be for their image and their network.
- **The Hipsters:** They share to define themselves and they believe that the means is the message, therefore, they can be found on the newest platforms. Their purpose is not to share information, in terms of usefulness but to build their personal identity through what they choose to share.

- **The Boomerangs:** This is the provocative type of sharer that mostly uses Twitter and Facebook to build an identity of being controversial and a "Firestarter." They seek reaction and validation through sharing and they don't stop until they get it.
- **The Connectors:** They share to bring people together, they are the users that share events and tag their friends on Facebook posts or share via email. They are thoughtful as the altruists but their purpose is not to be useful but to make plans and be sociable.
- **The Selectives:** They are very careful when sharing and they use email or specific lists, in order to select relevant recipients. They tend to be resourceful, while sharing content is a thoughtful act performed to inform and connect.

Figure 9. Types of sharers
Source: www.statpro.com

Underpinning all the sharing activities, of course, is a prerequisite, which is the content itself. Regardless of the psychology and purpose of sharing, given that what we share is always a signal about ourselves, our identity, our aesthetics and sense of humor, only good, high quality content will stand a chance. On the other hand, for the marketer these 6 types can be included in the persona building, as each group responds to different content, is found on different media and has different needs. A brand manager can use this segmentation in two ways in order to maximize sharing and, therefore, the impact of corporate social media marketing:

- Select one of the sharers' types that best matches the overall targeting of the brand and develop content and campaigns to satisfy the specific values and needs behind their sharing habits. For example, a brand that is positioned as rebellious and provocative might find it useful to target the Boomerangs. By all means, it can do so only by creating equally provocative material and by motivating users to react, through intrinsic and extrinsic rewards. Simultaneously, implementing successfully a tactic like this will directly address intimate user needs and trigger the formation of a compact online community built around the brand.
- Target all the aforementioned types, in different platforms and with different messages. For a brand, let's say at the beginning of its online life cycle (or at its launch phase in general), gaining awareness of different audiences is crucial. Obviously, the social media, like anything else in marketing, don't comply with the "one size fits all" mentality; therefore, the brand managers should develop a detailed strategy with differentiated content types for each sharer type. Although there is the risk for the brand to become too many things and ultimately confuse recipients, but when the brand values, image, and tone of voice are consistent and congruent with those of the audience, this differentiated tactic can really pay off.

SOCIAL MEDIA AND THE BRAND AS A PERSON

If the social media are a part of an integrated marketing strategy, and this should be the path to follow, h the ultimate outcome is a strong consumer brand relationship that will lead to sustained loyalty. All our efforts as marketers end up to this: to make customers loyal supporters, resistant to the marketing efforts of the competitors, willing to adopt brand extensions and to pay a price premium as they are focused on the overall value of the brand experience and not merely the price (provide source). The 'brand experience' conducive for achieving loyalty is formed through all kinds of interactions between consumers and the brand and is the sum of sensory, affective, intellectual, behavioral and social inputs (Brakus et al., 2009). From this perspective, being part of a brand community, online or offline and enjoying the benefits of participation is a factor for positive evaluation of the brand and engagement in it. As mentioned already, the social media profiles as the locus for community building can serve this purpose in an excellent manner and evolve to a strong competitive advantage.

Following an interesting approach to the evolution of the relationship between the brand and the customer, it is proposed that everything starts as an object-centred engagement; it then becomes a self-centred engagement and, finally, evolves to social engagement (Schmitt, 2012). Those 'layers' reflect an understanding that different needs, motives, and goals result in different psychological levels of engagement. In the first layer, the consumer-brand relationship is a functionally driven engagement, focused on the utilitarian benefits of the brand and driven by traditional marketing practices to induce awareness and to present the functional characteristics of the product/ service. In the second layer, the brand is related to the identity of the consumer, while, on the third level, the brand provides a sense of community. From a similar perceptive, but incorporating the fledging concept of co-creation, another study, led by one author (Kaufmann et al., 2012) of this book illustrates the different roles of the consumer in the relationship with the brand, as follows:

- At the initial stage, the consumer shows a primal attraction to a specific brand and engages in gathering information about it, acting as a browser- a loose relationship similar to the object-centred layer described earlier.
- As congruence between the consumer's values and those of the brand is discovered and the latter evolves to a self-identification medium, the consumer becomes a mingler, a member of a community formed around the brand from people sharing the same values and ideas.
- At the final stage, termed by the authors as "resonance" the consumer becomes an active member of the community, feeling the emotional obligation and commitment towards the group, participating in the creation of the brand and its value. At this point, a consumer brand relationship is a social act, a reward itself reflecting the emerging need of belonging.

Figure 10. Three stages of engagement
Source: authors

To attract the attention of the customers and initiate an object-centred engagement, traditional marketing practices have proven to be very effective. However, as the relationship becomes more self-related, it's the personality of the brand, the human characteristics attached to it (Aaker, 1997; Aggarwal and McGill, 2012) and the emotions developed through experience that defines the nature of engagement. In the final stages of the aforementioned models- social engagement and resonance- the role of the consumer is shifting from that of a passive user to that of a co-creator and active participant in the value generating process, and the brands are becoming social symbols that signal a coherent group in which brands themselves should actively participate.

Interestingly, social media marketing can moderate the transition from the first stage of utilitarian relationship to a more emotional state as, according to research, increasing consumers' knowledge about a brand (through social media) also increases the emotional attachment to it, regardless if the content of the brand's social communications was functional or emotional in nature (Ashley & Tuten, 2015). From this angle, when social media updates appear on the timeline of users, the latter eventually find themselves not only acquainted with the brand but at the beginning of an emotional relationship, too, given that the content is appealing and self- expressive, of course. Simply put, if consumers systematically like content created and published by a brand, at the end, they find themselves feeling positively towards the brand. Remember what we said earlier, about how daily engagement with a brand impacts on purchase possibilities (Google, 2014). Since we have discussed how people like and/or share content, and the psychological motivation behind it, we understand why brand content needs to be meaningful, not merely promotional, in order to really express oneself and to lead them to demonstrate this self-expression by engaging with the content. This idea of self-expressiveness is ubiquitous in the branding literature following the identity theory that suggests that brand commitment connects an individual to a stable set of self-meanings, which produces consistent lines of activities, such as purchase behavior. Self-expansion theory suggests that consumers communicate with and about brands due to overlapping identities and parasocial relationships with the brands (Ashley & Tuten, 2015). In other words, social media is a field of self-expression and consumers strategically choose those brands they will discuss in online communications to construct positive self-images (Schau & Gilly, 2003).

Figure 11.
Source www.piquant.com.sg

Between the lines, one more condition comes up: for an emotional relationship between the consumer and the brand to occur, the brand must be somehow anthropomorphized and act in the role of brand-as-a-person; and the social media is a great way to obtain this. As observed, brands that used to be perceived as inanimate are becoming humanized through intimate conversations with consumers in the realm of social media (Chen et al., 2015). Indeed, marketing researchers in the field of brand personality, the human characteristics attached to a brand (Aaker, 1997), that make brands act like people, have indicated that consumers are likely to perceive brands to be humanlike social agents with whom they may form relationships. As such, marketers have sought to capitalize on the brand-as-person metaphor by taking advantage of the mechanism by which consumers anthropomorphize brands and interact with them in ways similar to interpersonal communication (Aggarwal and McGill, 2007). In the context of the social media, where users interact with brands in the same manner as they do with their friends, the personification effect is very high, again, with the support of the right content that is not restricted to marketing messages but it matches the recipients' interests and triggers engagement. In fact, engagement has been defined as "the cognitive and affective commitment to an active relationship with the brand as personified by the web site or other computer mediated entities designed to communicate brand value"

(Mollen & Wilson, 2010, p. 5). If we look deeper into the mechanisms of anthropomorphism and its extension to brands, Epley et al. (2008) offer a triple faceted explanation:

- First of all, everything we know as humans, including that about the self and others, is somehow taught by or in relation with human beings and the conclusions people derive from ample phenomenological experiences by being humans and observing others. Learning is bonded to humans. Therefore, every time we learn something, as a result of a message sent by a brand, the brand feels like more human-like, as personification messages anchor anthropomorphic inferences about inanimate brands.

- Second, being social and participating in likeminded groups and communities is propelled by people's fundamental need for companionship. Driven by sociality motivation, consumers tend to anthropomorphize inanimate brands and consider them to be sources of social relationships that can fulfill their need for companionship.

- Third, *effectance* motivation refers to people's inclination to perform effective interactions with their surroundings as a means to promote stability. Anthropomorphizing inanimate brands is the only way for a consumer-brand relationship to make sense, in terms of effective relationship management. As such, the interactive platform of social media seems to be a good fit for prompting consumers' tendency to anthropomorphize the nonhuman.

Practically put, let's say you work for a bank and you decide to build a content strategy focused on educating your audiences on subjects related to finance and risk management. You produce a lot of content, you upload it to a dedicated website/ mini site and you deploy a social media marketing plan in order to communicate it to your targeted audiences. Probably some people will actually engage with your content and start engaging with your social media posts and visit your website whenever they are looking for information or answers referring finance or risk management. Having made your website their reference point for this particular subject in a subconscious level, they will start attaching human characteristics to your brand, in order to rationalize what they experience. This will happen as the result of our rebuff to accept that something with no soul or real existence can teach us things and we can actually trust or affectively commit to it- therefore we tend to personify brands. What kind of characteristics they will select to attach, depends on your marketing strategy, the brand image, the tone of voice and general posture the brand maintains throughout the different contact points and of course the archetypes we all have pre-programmed in our minds. The clearer and more coherent the personality, the easier we will relate to it. Therefore, perhaps we should start considering the social media and digital marketing at large, as a one-of-a-kind opportunity to make our brands be perceived as persons worth "hanging out", be "friends" with and ultimately, be loyal to.

Social media as platforms for collaboration, co-creation, and vivid dialogue allow brand managers to build their brands in an experiential and direct way, with the participation of the end users. This paradigm shift has changed the rules of the game, as brands are now initiators but not controllers; they follow the lead of their customers, not the other way round, they are exposed to public criticism and not safe behind closed doors. Although already implied several times in our book so far, this thought is worth another moment: while in the traditional marketing context we tout our messages (by placing them on a magazine or the TV) and we wait for our customers to come, the digital world works the other way round: we closely monitor where our audiences can be found (websites, social media platforms etc) and what they prefer to read and do, we form our marketing plan and we go where they are. This is why we insist so much about the importance of the social media in modern marketing- because if you are trying to go out and find your customers, this is where they will probably be. Being an empathizer (as discussed in chapter one) but also a metrics master, will allow the digital marketer to decode their behaviour and invent new ways to engage with them. And while this analysis and planning takes place in the back end of social media marketing, it's in the front end where the stakes are: there, post by post, comment by comment, tweet by tweet, marketers must infuse like in their brand as if they were a person that people would actually like to be friends with. So, next time you decide to oversee a review or publish a post solely about your brand offerings, think of the following: If you met a person acting like your brand does, would you bother to make them your friends?

WHEN IT COMES TO SOCIAL MEDIA MARKETING, DO IT LIKE A GIRL: CASE STUDY

In 2014, the feminine brand 'Always' launched its iconic #LikeAGirl video campaign, which criticized the social norms which limit the confidence of women. If you've watched it, you'll probably agree that this ad feels like a documentary or an activist video, which makes it incredibly easy to forget that it is indeed just an ad trying to promote a specific product. Yet, the formula worked so well across social media platforms that the brand launched the second installment, under the ambitious title "Unstoppable" but with the same premise and winning hashtag. Once again, always hit it out of the park: in September 2015 alone, #LikeAGirl appeared over 17,200 times on social media, with 180,000 engagements on a global scale (www.talkwalker.com). Always #LikeAGirl generated considerable global awareness and changed the way people think about the phrase 'like a girl', achieving more than 85m global views on YouTube from 150+ countries.

Figure 12. Always #LikeAGirl

The objective of the campaign was to familiarize young consumers with P&G 's brand positioning to empower girls since adolescence. Based on research findings the creative team built a campaign that was also a social experiment, around the negatively charged phrase "Like a Girl", in order to show that doing things "Like a girl" can be synonymous to doing amazing things. The use of this very straightforward hashtag allowed the users to engage in the conversation globally, around the multiple platforms. According to D&AD, that participated in the campaign design and execution: "prior to watching the film, just 19% of 16-24s had a positive association toward 'like a girl'. After watching, however, 76% said they no longer saw the phrase negatively. Furthermore, two out of three men who watched it said they'd now think twice before using the 'like a girl' as an insult. Always' brand equity showed a strong double digit percentage increase during the course of the campaign while most of its competitors had to cope with slight declines" (www.dandad.com). Six months on, Always ran a 60-second spot highlighting the campaign during the 2015 Super Bowl. Two months later, it released a follow-up video showing how the meaning of the phrase is already changing to mark International Women's Day.

- **What Makes This Campaign a Milestone in Social Media Marketing**: The combination of consumer insights, creativity, and technical knowledge and the strategic integration of the key messages throughout different online and traditional platforms. The marketing team addressed a very pragmatic need, to feel confident, in an inspired execution that made girls around the world feel empowered and vindicated. The video itself (https://www.youtube.com/watch?v=XjJQBjWYDTs) leverages the anticipated emotional responses until they reach a high level of gratification. The use of this one hashtag, the collaboration of different channels and the integration of the campaign with traditional media (i.e. the 60 seconds spot during the 2015 Super Bowl) worked in tandem to produce an award-winning campaign with real and undeniable impact on the brand.
- **Lessons We Learn From This Campaign**: "Always" has moved beyond the narrow boundaries of the product category and has built a campaign that left out the functional characteristics of the product itself but raised the bar, aiming to create value through emotional and "life-changing" elements (Chapter 3). By crafting an emotionally charged brand message, they managed to coil the targeted audiences, to invite them to join a like-minded community and to share a message that was self-expressive to many. Women around the world embraced the message and used the hashtag because they agreed with it and with the purpose of this campaign; their joined effort resulted to a change of perception about the "Like a girl" characterization, and this is a co-created achievement that the brand and its community can be proud of. Note that, despite the focus of the entire project and its objective to be relatable, the brand values where present throughout the campaign, coherently demonstrated in the different platforms. Contrary to the Chino San Pellegrino case we discussed in chapter 3, here we have an example of aligned internal and external messages broadcasted in a clear and coherent manner that brought together a community of targeted consumers with strengthening the brand equity.

Answers

- Apart from the thorough penetration of the social media in a way that changed our ways and behaviors, they are compelling marketing channels. Marketers are presented with the opportunity to build a reputation and coil brand fans around a community that will become the source of competitive advantage. The variety of social media platforms offers unique alternatives of targeting, even in very well determined niche markets, in an unprecedented way that can make today's marketing effective on much more levels than before.

- Social media marketing raises brand awareness and liking and subtly creates an emotional connection, as consumers are systematically exposed to branded content. By leading social media users to the website or landing pages, the brand enjoys indirect benefits, including more traffic, hence, better ranking in the search engines etc. Additionally, there is compelling evidence that social media engagement impacts directly on sales performance, as users engaging regularly with a brand will more likely proceed to an online or offline transaction than those who don't. From a relational viewpoint, social media activity allows users to build and manifest their identity and provides them with intrinsic, participatory benefits as they develop a feeling of belonging to larger groups of like-minded users (pages & communities).

- Social media penetration is overwhelming and almost universal in the age group of 18-29, but there are some psychological characteristics that define our "virtual" behavior. Researchers have found that, contrary to the past when internet was the safe place for the introverts, avid social media users today tend to be extroverts and open to new ideas and experiences. The use of the social media for entertainment rather than informativeness, a preference that is backed up with findings showing that social media use is positively related to emotional instability; this means that when we feel down we are seeking comfort on Facebook, Twitter etc. Therefore, sharing, participating and having fun are the key drivers of engagement online, a useful triplet for the digital marketer.

- The typology of 6 sharer tribes (altruists, careerists, hipsters, boomerangs, connectors, selectives) adds a useful segmentation method to online and social media marketing. Depending on the life cycle stage and the marketing objectives, digital tactics can be focused on a single tribe and target it with tailor-made content to accommodate their needs and maximize engagement. Or, they can be crafted for multiple tribes, going for higher reach, as long as messages throughout the platforms maintain the same values and tone of voice.

- In their effort to rationalize their emotional connection to a brand, people tend to humanize and attach human characteristics to them, and when they succeed, they easily identify themselves with these brands. Engaging in an actual dialogue through the social media, learning and exchanging knowledge and participating in a community where the brand -through the voice of its representatives- acts like a person, is an excellent way to anthropomorphize the inanimate brand and initiate strong emotional bonds that couldn't be developed with impersonal corporate and names.

REFERENCES

Aaker, J. L. (1997). Dimensions of brand personality. *JMR, Journal of Marketing Research, 34*(3), 347–356. doi:10.2307/3151897

Adage.com. (2015). *What the changing role of social media means for brands.* Retrieved from http://adage.com/article/digitalnext/tv-s-influence-consumer-behavior-decreases/297501/

Aggarwal, P., & McGill, A. L. (2012). When Brands Seem Human, Do Humans Act Like Brands? Automatic Behavioral Priming Effects of Brand Anthropomorphism. *The Journal of Consumer Research, 39*(2), 307–323. doi:10.1086/662614

Alhabash, S., McAlister, A. R., Lou, C., & Hagerstrom, A. (2015). From Clicks to Behaviors: The Mediating Effect of Intentions to Like, Share, and Comment on the Relationship Between Message Evaluations and Offline Behavioral Intentions. *Journal of Interactive Advertising*, *15*(2), 82–96. doi:1 0.1080/15252019.2015.1071677

Amichai-Hamburger, Y., & Ben-Artzi, E. (2003). Loneliness and Internet use. *Computers in Human Behavior*, *19*(1), 71–80. doi:10.1016/S0747-5632(02)00014-6

Ashley, C., & Tuten, T. (2015). Creative strategies in social media marketing: An exploratory study of branded social content and consumer engagement. *Psychology and Marketing*, *32*(1), 15–27. doi:10.1002/mar.20761

Bargh, J. A., McKenna, K. Y., & Fitzsimons, G. M. (2002). Can you see the real me? Activation and expression of the true self on the Internet. *The Journal of Social Issues*, *58*(1), 33–48. doi:10.1111/1540-4560.00247

Brakus, J. J., Schmitt, B. H., & Zarantonello, L. (2009). Brand experience: What is it? How is it measured? Does it affect loyalty? *Journal of Marketing*, *73*(3), 52–68. doi:10.1509/jmkg.73.3.52

Chen, K., Lin, J., Choi, J. H., & Hahm, J. M. (2015). Would You Be My Friend? An Examination of Global Marketers Brand Personification Strategies in Social Media. *Journal of Interactive Advertising*, *15*(2), 97–110. doi:10.1080/15252019.2015.1079508

CmoSurvey.com. (2015). *The CMO Survey: Highlightsand Insights*. Retrieved from https://cmosurvey. org/wp-content/uploads/sites/11/2015/09/The_CMO_Survey-Highlights_and_Insights-Aug-2015.pdf

Correa, T., Hinsley, A.W., & De Zuniga, H. G. (2010). Who interacts on the Web?: The intersection of users personality and social media use. *Computers in Human Behavior*, *26*(2), 247–253. doi:10.1016/j. chb.2009.09.003

Dandad.org. (2015). *Case Study: Always #LikeAGirl*. Retrieved from http://www.dandad.org/en/d-ad-leo-burnett-holler-always-likeagirl-campaign-case-study/

Dessart, L., Veloutsou, C., & Morgan-Thomas, A. (2015). Consumer engagement in online brand communities: A social media perspective. *Journal of Product and Brand Management*, *24*(1), 28–42. doi:10.1108/JPBM-06-2014-0635

Dholakia, U. M., & Vianello, S. (2009). *The Fans Know Best*. Retrieved from http://www.wsj.com/articles/SB10001424052970204482304574222062946162306

eMarketer.com. (2013a). *Advertisers boost social ad budgets in 2013*. Retrieved from http://www.emarketer.com/Article/Advertisers-Boost-Social-Ad-Budgets- 2013/1009688

eMarketer.com. (2013b). *B2Cs, B2Bs See Digital, Social Ad Spend Rising, as Traditional Stalls*. Retrieved from http://www.emarketer.com/Article/B2Cs-B2Bs-See-Digital-Social-Ad-Spend-Rising-Traditional-Stalls/1010270

eMarketer.com. (2014). *Social Ad Spending per User Remains Highest in North America*. Retrieved from http://www.emarketer.com/Article/Social-Ad-Spending-per-User-Remains-Highest-North-America/1010505

Epley, N., Waytz, A., Akalis, S., & Cacioppo, J. T. (2008). When we need a human: Motivational determinants of anthropomorphism. *Social Cognition, 26*(2), 143–155. doi:10.1521oco.2008.26.2.143

Forrester Research. (2013). *Engaged Social Followers Are Your Best Customers*. Retrieved from http://go.wf-social.com/rs/wildfire/images/REPORT_Forrester_Best_Customers.pdf

Googleapis.com. (2014). *Brand Engagement in the participation age*. Retrieved from https://think.storage.googleapis.com/docs/brand-engagement-in-participation-age_research-studies.pdf

Hamburger, Y. A., & Ben-Artzi, E. (2000). The relationship between extraversion and neuroticism and the different uses of the Internet. *Computers in Human Behavior, 16*(4), 441–449. doi:10.1016/S0747-5632(00)00017-0

Heidicohen.com. (2011). *Social Media definitions*. Retrieved from www.heidicohen.com/social-media-definition

Ho-Dac, N. N., Carson, S. J., & Moore, W. I. (2013). The Effects of Positive and Negative Online Customer Reviews: Do Brand Strength and Category Maturity Matter? *Journal of Marketing, 77*(November), 37–53. doi:10.1509/jm.11.0011

Kaufmann, H. (2012). The increasing dynamics between consumers, social groups and brands. *Qualitative Market Research: An International Journal, 15*(4), 404–419. doi:10.1108/13522751211257088

Meshi, D., Morawetz, C., & Heekeren, H. R. (2013). Nucleus accumbens response to gains in reputation for the self relative to gains for others predicts social media use. *Frontiers in Human Neuroscience, 7*, 439. doi:10.3389/fnhum.2013.00439 PMID:24009567

Mollen, A., & Wilson, H. (2010). Engagement, telepresence and interactivity in online consumer experience: Reconciling scholastic and managerial perspectives. *Journal of Business Research, 63*(9), 919–925. doi:10.1016/j.jbusres.2009.05.014

Naaman, M., Boase, J., & Lai, C. H. (2010, February). Is it really about me? message content in social awareness streams. *Proceedings of the 2010 ACM conference on Computer supported cooperative work*, 189-192. 10.1145/1718918.1718953

Pew Research Center. (2015). *Social Media Usage: 2005-2015*. Retrieved from http://www.pewinternet.org/2015/10/08/social-networking-usage-2005-2015/

Piquant.com.sg. (2014). *How brand personality outshines brand attributes*. Retrieved from http://www.piquant.com.sg/brand-personality-outshines-strong-attributes/

Schaefer, M. (2015). *The Content Code: Six essential strategies to ignite your content, your marketing and your business*. Library of Congress Cataloging-in-Publication Data.

Schau, H., & Gilly, M. (2003). We are what we post? Self presentation in personal web space. *The Journal of Consumer Research, 30*(3), 385–404. doi:10.1086/378616

Schmitt, B. (2012). The consumer psychology of brands. *Journal of Consumer Psychology, 22*(1), 7–17. doi:10.1016/j.jcps.2011.09.005

Statista.com. (2014). *Global Social Networks Ranked by Number of uses.* Retrieved from http://www.statista.com/statistics/272014/global-social-networks-ranked-by-number-of-users/

StatPro. (2013). *The psychology of sharing* [Infographic]. Retrieved from http://www.statpro.com/blog/psychology-of-sharing-infographic/

Stelzner, M. (2016). *Social Media Marketing Industry Report.* Retrieved from http://www.socialmedi-aexaminer.com/report/

Talkwalker.com. (2015). *5 great social media campaigns to inspire your 2016 Marketing Strategy.* Retrieved from http://blog.talkwalker.com/en/5-social-media-campaigns-inspiration-2016-strategy-social-media-analytics/

The New York Times. (2011). *The Psychology of Sharing: Why do people share online.* Retrieved from http://nytmarketing.whsites.net/mediakit/pos/

Waspbarcode.com. (2015). *State of Small Business Report.* Retrieved from http://www.waspbarcode.com/small-business-report?utm_source=Webbiquity.com&utm_medium=social

Zhu, Y., & Chen, H. (2015). Social media and human need satisfaction: Implications for social media marketing. *Business Horizons*, *58*(3), 335–345. doi:10.1016/j.bushor.2015.01.006

This research was previously published in Encouraging Participative Consumerism Through Evolutionary Digital Marketing; pages 95-123, copyright year 2017 by Business Science Reference (an imprint of IGI Global).

Chapter 26
Influence and Information Flow in Online Social Networks

Afrand Agah
West Chester University, USA

Mehran Asadi
The Lincoln University, USA

ABSTRACT

This article introduces a new method to discover the role of influential people in online social networks and presents an algorithm that recognizes influential users to reach a target in the network, in order to provide a strategic advantage for organizations to direct the scope of their digital marketing strategies. Social links among friends play an important role in dictating their behavior in online social networks, these social links determine the flow of information in form of wall posts via shares, likes, re-tweets, mentions, etc., which determines the influence of a node. This article initially identities the correlated nodes in large data sets using customized divide-and-conquer algorithm and then measures the influence of each of these nodes using a linear function. Furthermore, the empirical results show that users who have the highest influence are those whose total number of friends are closer to the total number of friends of each node divided by the total number of nodes in the network.

1. INTRODUCTION

In the most basic sense, a network is any collection of objects in which some pairs of these objects are connected by links. In a network of objects, objects can be people or computers, which we refer to them as nodes of the network. Have the people in the network adapted their behaviors to become more like their friends, or have they sought out people who were already like them (Easley, 2010)?

Over the course of human history, the collections of social ties among friends have grown steadily in complexity. When people live in neighborhoods or attend schools, the social environment already favors opportunities to form friendships with others like oneself (Easley, 2010). If influence is the capacity to have an effect on someone, then who are the influential people in an Online Social Network? According

DOI: 10.4018/978-1-7998-9020-1.ch026

to (Rashotte, 2011), social influence is defined as change in an individual's thoughts, feelings, attitudes, or behaviors that results from interaction with another individual or a group of people. Influence has long been actively studied in marketing, sociology, communication and political sciences (Althoff, 2017). Online Social Networks(OSNs) have revolutionized the power of social influence exponentially (Aral, 2012). Popular social networks such as Facebook, Google+, Twitter provide platforms allowing user to share information about things that users like or dislike (Romero, 2011). The availability of such interactions among users created a new platform for digital marketing such as brands to run their promotional activities and political parties to run their campaigns (Linyuan, 2011; Bond, 2012).

There have been extensive studies in measuring the social influence. Klout is a website and mobile app (Klout, 2014) that uses social media analytics to measure social influence of its users. To determine the social influence or *Klout score*, which is a numerical value between 1 and 100, Klout measures the size of a user's social media network and correlates the content created to measure how other users interact with that content. Klout uses 35 variables such as Follower/Follow ratio, unique re-tweeters, unique messages re-tweeted and username mention count. However, several objections to Klout's methodology have been raised regarding the process by which scores are generated. Critics have pointed out that Klout scores are not representative of the influence a person really has, highlighted by Barack Obama, President of the United States, having a lower influence score than a number of bloggers.

In our research, similar to scoring mechanism in Klout, we assign numerical value to each user as a result of measuring social influence. But, the range of ranks are proportional to the number of nodes in a network but not a fixed range from 1 to 100 as it is the case in Klout. We are using large datasets from Location Based Social Networks (LBSN) (Leskovec, 2014; Leskovec, 2010; Yang, 2010). These are analogous to popular OSNs like Face book, but content is generated from these in form of check-ins rather than wall posts.

LBSN does not only mean adding a location to an existing social network, but also consists of the new social structure made up of individuals connected by the interdependency derived from their locations in the physical world as well as their location-tagged media content (check-ins), such as photos, video, and texts. Furthermore, these check-ins can influence nodes already in the network to visit these locations. Our primary attribute of measuring influence is this location-tagged content. We are using two LBSNs, Gowalla and Brightkite's data sets in our research. These datasets have very few properties at each node such as edge count, check-ins count but not any other attributes like gender, location, education and etc. This limits our research observations, after deducing influence value, to be read based on these properties. Thus, our approach, implementation and results are focused on mean and median of edge count or check-ins count of each node.

We only focus on users who are highly co-related. It means that the differences among properties of these users are minimal. We have a divide-and-conquer algorithm to identify these targeted users and eliminate users with properties having extreme values. This idea of co-related users results in measuring the influence more accurately. For example, a user who has 8000 friends may have higher influence value compared to a user who has 80 friends despite running through various influence algorithms.

Here we are interested in connectedness at the level of behavior - the fact that each individual's actions have implicit consequences on the outcomes of everyone in the system (Easley, 2010). We investigate prediction of people's behavior and influences in OSN. Our focus is on how different nodes can play distinct roles in information flow through an OSN.

2. RELATED WORK

Some research suggests that people are more affected by the opinions of their peers than influential people (Kempe, 2003) and (Wang, 2001), recent studies of online social networks (Cha, 2011) and (Gomez-Rodriguez, 2010) support the hypothesis that influential exert disproportionate amount of influence. With the numbers of active users on these sites numbering in the millions or even tens of millions, identifying influential users among them becomes an important problem with applications in marketing (Cha, 2010; Wang 2001). There are many empirical studies of social behavior and influence on online social networks. Some of these studies, compare empirical measures of influence with structural models of influence like PageRank or in-degree centrality (Cha, 2011).

Gowalla (Leskovec, 2014; Leskovec 2009) is a location-based social network created in 2009. It's user's check-in at places through their mobile devices. Check-ins are shared with friends; as a consequence, friends can check where a user is or has been. Conversely, it is also possible to see all the users that have recently been in a given place. The friendship relationship is mutual, requiring each user to accept friendship requests to allow location sharing. However, there is a small number of user accounts that represent companies or other organizations and appear to automatically accept every friendship request. These accounts can become hugely popular and collect thousands of connections, as they are all accounts of organizations or companies but not individuals.

Brightkite (Leskovec, 2014) was founded in 2007 as a social networking website which allows users to share their location with their friends. It is available worldwide and it is based on the idea of making check-ins at places, where users can see who is nearby and who has been there before. Brightkite users can establish mutual friendship links and they can push their check-ins to their Twitter and Facebook accounts.

We are using two LBSNs, Gowalla and Brightkite's data sets in our research. The data sets for these two social networks are collected from Stanford Network Analysis Project (SNAP) by Stanford University (Leskovec, 2014).

Targeted crawler algorithms (Humbert, 2013) allow a crawler to find a path from a source node to a target node assuming: (i) the crawler controls at least one node in the Online Social Networks (OSN), which is attainable by simply registering on most OSN, and (ii) the crawler knows when its target is reached, either by comparing attributes or unique ids. The targeted crawler algorithms can be seen as a frontier (Humbert, 2013) that is expanding toward the target node using a distance function. The distance function represents how different two nodes are: the more they have in common, the less distant they are.

For each step in the algorithm, the frontier spreads toward the node that has the least remaining distance to the target. The frontier expansion can be seen in Figure 1 and Figure 2. Assume we want to find a path from node A to node K. At the first step (Figure 1), the frontier consists of all A's friends. Then using the distance function, we find G is the closer to the target (Figure 2). Hence G goes to the explored set represented in white, and the frontier represented in grey is extended to G's friends.

Two procedures to find key players by (i) the identification of key players for the purpose of optimally diffusing a property through the network by using the key players as seeds and (ii) the identification of key players for the purpose of disrupting or fragmenting the network by removing the key nodes, are discussed in (Borgatti, 2006). Our work will try to find a procedure to find key players locally for a path between two nodes while (Borgatti, 2006) focuses on key players for the network as a whole.

Figure 1. Targeted Crawler at first iteration

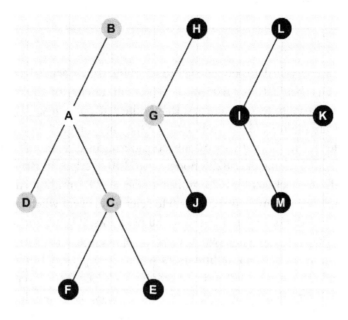

Figure 2. Targeted Crawler at second iteration

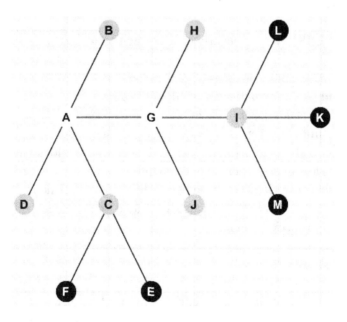

The definition of influential nodes changes with application and the type of commodity flowing through a network. While our work focuses on navigation paths, identifying influential nodes in OSN using principal component centrality are developed in (Ilyas, 2011).

3. OUR PROPOSED APPROACH

3.1. Influence

We collected all the public check-in data between February 2009 to October 2010 for Gowalla application and from April 2008 to October 2010 for Brightkite. The total number of check-ins for Gowalla is 6.4 million and 4.5 million for Brightkite. Gowalla and Brightkite also contain an explicit social network. In Gowalla the friendships are undirected and in Brightkite they are directed. For simplicity, we consider Brightkite as an undirected friendship network by only considering bi-directional edges. There are 196591 nodes and 950327 edges in Gowalla and 58228 nodes and 214078 edges in Brightkite. Taken together, our data contains 11 million check-ins for 0.25 million nodes and 1.1 million edges.

For the rest of the paper we will use word check-in to refer to an event when the time and the location of a particular user is recorded. For location-based social networks, this means that a user checked-in to a specific location using the online social network website/application. LBSN model for social networks can be described as social links between online users who own a personal profile with their check-in information. Formally, a LBSN can be defined as a graph $G=(V,E)$, where V represents the set of users or nodes and E is the edge set (their social links). In most LBSNs, users can decide to what extent and with whom they share information by tuning their privacy settings appropriately.

3.1.1. Defining Influence

To measure influence in LBSN, we are majorly considering five attributes for each node:

- **Edge count (E):** Total number of edges of each node;
- **Edge of edge count (EE):** Total number of edges of edges;
- **Check-in count(C):** Total number of check-ins of each node;
- **Influenced edge count (IE):** Total number of edges of each node. Nodes, who made at least one check-in at location L after another node had made a check-in at location L, $IE£E$. Hence, influenced edge count is less than or equal to edge count;
- **Influenced check-in count (IC):** Total number of check-ins of each node. Visited locations, where they were visited by at least one of the edges E of a node, $IC£C$. Hence, influenced check-in count is less than or equal to check-in count.

3.1.2. Attribute Construction

First above three attributes (edge count, edge of edge count and check-in count) are easily extracted from data source of Gowalla and Brightkite. But, influenced edge count and influenced check-in count are constructed attributes. The related code can be found in open source repository and is available in GitHub.

As depicted in Tables 1 and 2, in Gowalla, each node on average has 9.6 edges but median is 3. It means 50% of the nodes contain edges that are less than or equal to 3. In other words, mean of edge count is 200% more than median. Furthermore, Maximum number edges of node is as large as 15000, while minimum number of nodes is being as small as 1. In Brightkite, each node on average made 82 check-ins but median is 7. It means 50% of the nodes made check-ins less than are equal to 7. In other words, mean of edge count is 1100% more than median. Furthermore, Maximum number edges of node is as large as being 2100 while minimum number of nodes is being as small as 0. Because of this large difference of check-ins count among nodes, it becomes obvious to predict that a node with 2100 check-ins in Gowalla has more influence than a node with 0 check-ins.

In Gowalla, each node on average made 32.77 check-ins but median is 2. It means 50% of the nodes made check-ins that are less than or equal to 2. In other words, mean of edge count is 1500% more than median. Furthermore, Maximum number edges of a node is as large as being 2175 while minimum number of nodes is as small as 0. Because of the large difference of edge count among nodes, it becomes obvious to predict that nodes with 2100 edges in Gowalla or 2175 edges in Brightkite has more influence than nodes with zero edges. It is better to have nodes that are highly correlated to predict influence.

Table 1. Number of edges

	Gowalla	Brightkite
Total number of nodes (million)	0.2	0.06
Total number of edges	1.9	0.4
Mean number of edges per node	9.67	7.35
Median of number of edges per node	3	2
Maximum of number of edges per node	15000	1134
Minimum number of edges per node	1	1

Table 2. Number of check-ins

	Gowalla	Brightkite
Total number of nodes (million)	0.2	0.06
Total number of check-ins (million)	6.4	4.7
Mean number of check-ins per node	32.77	82
Median number of check-ins per node	2	7
Maximum number of check-ins per node	2175	2100
Minimum number of check-ins per node	0	0

3.1.3. Reducing Boundaries

Ideally, when measuring influence of each node, if primary attributes such as edge count and check-in count of a node are at extremes, results may be easily predictable. For example, consider two nodes: node N_1 with edges E_1 and check-ins C_1 and node N_2 with edges E_2 and check-ins C_2. Furthermore, if $E_1 \gg E_2$ and $C_1 \gg C_2$, then, it would be easy to predict that N_1 has better influence value comparing to N_2, assuming other attributes are constant. Thus, for comparing influence values of nodes we have excluded those nodes with extreme values for primary attributes, from data set. We devised a divide and conquer algorithm to achieve this. Algorithm 1, depicts the pseudo code for the above-mentioned approach.

Figure 3. Algorithm 1

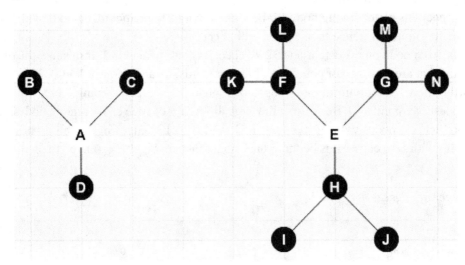

In all our experiments, we only consider nodes that are highly co-related in terms of total number of edge count and total number of check-ins. This algorithm helps in identifying those nodes by eliminating trivial boundary nodes called outliers. The reason for identifying the correlated nodes is to eliminate outliers such as nodes that are highly influenced and nodes that can never be influenced. Including these outliers will not be a great help because top influencers always have higher influence value and loners always have lower influence. Removing outliers from the calculation, using above algorithm, accurately determines the influence value of other nodes. Though dataset of correlated nodes is relatively small, after eliminating nodes, we are confident to see similar results in larger datasets, where future work will continue on this.

Table 3. Number of edges and check-ins after reducing boundaries

	Gowalla	Brightkite
Total number of nodes (million)	0.02	0.006
Mean of number of edges per node	23.28	29
Median of number of edges per node	18	23
Range of number of edges per node	10 to 83	13 to 88
Mean number of check-ins per node	61.73	264
Median number of check-ins per node	50	219
Range of number of check-ins per node	10 to 199	111 to 669

As depicted in Table 3, in Gowalla, the new and derived data set contains only 0.02 million nodes. But, the difference between mean and median for both edge count and check-ins is reduced massively. Mean of edge count is just 30% more than median of edge count compared to 200%. Also, mean of number of check-ins is little closer to 24% compared to 1500%. It shows that the correlation among nodes is very high. Correlation among nodes is high because difference mean and median of these nodes is reduced using given divide-and-conquer algorithm.

3.1.4. Measure Influence With Influenced Edge Count

Let I_E be the number of influenced edges and E be the edge count, then the percentage of influenced edges, I_{EP}, is computed by $\dfrac{I_E}{E}$. We define the influence function Inf_e to be the mapping that determines the influence value of node N among n nodes based on edge count. Therefore:

$$Inf_e(n) = \begin{cases} Max(I_{EP}) & if \ E > ME \\ 0 & otherwise \end{cases}$$

Similarly, let C and I_C be the check-ins count of each node and influenced check-ins count respectively; we compute the ratio of influenced check-ins I_{CP} with $\dfrac{I_C}{C}$ and define the influence value of each node n with:

$$Inf_c(n) = \begin{cases} Max(I_{CP}) & if \ C > MC \\ 0 & otherwise \end{cases}$$

where MC and ME are medians of edge and check-ins counts and E and C are edge count and check-in count of each node, respectively.

3.2. Information Flow

Our focus is on how different nodes can play distinct roles in information flow through an OSN. If two people in an OSN have a friend in common, then there is an increased likelihood that they will become friends themselves at some point in the future (Easley, 2010). The terminology of OSN reflects a largely similar view, through its emphasis on the connections one forms with friends, fans, followers, and so forth.

An Online Social Network can be viewed as a graph $G=(V,E)$. Vertices (nodes) are representing people and edges are representing social links. Social links can be undirected (e.g. friends on Facebook) or directed (e.g. followers on Twitter). An OSN allows people to have attributes that are included in the Social Network list of attributes. For each attribute, people can define a privacy policy: visible to all, visible to friends, or private.

This research is based on the following assumption: from a graph G with privacy policies on attributes and links, we can deduce a public sub-graph G' based on public attributes and public links (Adamic, 2003) and (Pedarsani, 2013). Because of the default behavior of OSN is to share the most and hide the less, we can deduce G', thanks to users that do not change this default behavior. Each user that is changing the default settings contributes to shrink our graph G'.

We need a targeted crawler algorithm for our influence prediction in order to be able to navigate efficiently in an OSN. This is for the following two main reasons: (i) Online Social Networks are huge (billions of users for Facebook as of today) and should not been seen as random graphs. (ii) If people are connected, there is a high chance they share something in common, either a friendship, a location, a job, etc. We should not use algorithm like breadth-first search in Online Social Networks because they do not take advantage of the probability that people are connected.

3.2.1. Monte Carlo Method

The Monte Carlo method is used when a distribution of an unknown probabilistic entity is close to impossible to determine in a deterministic way. Instead, we compute a non-deterministic algorithm a certain number of times until enough numerical results are collected to generalize the distribution of the unknown probabilistic entity.

3.2.2. Predicting Influence

We want to be able to locate those people, who are more influential. People are considered influential if when they do an action, their friends, friends of their friends, etc., replicate their actions.

The goal here is to understand influence not just as a property of nodes in a network, but in social interactions as the roles people play in groups of friends in communities or in organizations. Influence is not so much a property of an individual as it is a property of a relation between two individuals. Influence may be almost entirely the result of the personalities of the two-people involved. But it may also be a function of the larger social network in which the two people are embedded. One person may be more powerful in a relationship because he occupies a more dominant position in the social network with greater access to social opportunities outside this single relationship.

One way to define important people is as follow: the more paths are going through a node, the more important this node is. This is different from the degree of a node as it also takes into consideration nodes that are not directly linked to it. In Figure 3, node A and E have the same degree: 3. However because E's friends are more connected, there are more paths that go through E than paths that go through A.

If for 100 computed paths a particular node N_1 is part of 50 paths and another node N_2 is part of 10 paths, then we say N_1 is more important than N_2 because it connects more people together. Figure 4 shows the Degree vs. the influence.

The influence of a node N in the network is defined in Equation (1):

$$\text{Influence}(N_i) = \text{Number of Paths Going Through}(N_i) \tag{1}$$

Computing the above equation is highly time consuming. Once we have the influence associated to each node, a navigation path can be defined by hoping from influent node to influent node until the target is reached.

Figure 4. Degree vs. influence

Algorithm Targeted Nodes For Comparing Influence

1: **procedure** COMPARING −INFLUENCE
2:     Initialize: N ← node set
3:     Initialize: L ← Left index of the node set
4:     Initialize: R ← Right index of the node set
5:     **while** $R - L > \epsilon$ **do**
6:         $MID = \frac{(R+L)}{2}$
7:         $MEAN = \bar{n}, n \in N$
8:         $MEDIAN = \hat{n}$, for $n \in N$
9:         **if** $MEAN > MEDIAN$ **then**
10:             $L = MID$
11:         **else**
12:             $R = MID$
13:         **end if**
14:     **end while**
15:     Display L and R
16: **end procedure**

---

4. PERFORMANCE EVALUATION

4.1. Influence

We estimate the influence value of a node using $Inf_e(n)$. We consider only nodes having edge count more than median edge count of all nodes in a network. Next, we assign ranks to these nodes according to their influenced edge count as a ratio. As depicted in Table 4, we observed that nodes with top influence value have edge count of 29. Also, we noticed that top 10% of influenced nodes have mean edge count of 32 while median edge count is 28.

Table 4. Influence with influenced edge count

	Gowalla	Brightkite
Total number of influenced nodes (million)	0.01	0.006
Edge count for most influenced node	29	32
Mean of top 10% influenced nodes	32	35
Median of top 10% influenced nodes	28	31
Range of top 10% influenced nodes	19 to 82	24 to 85

Two important results are: (i) correlation among top 10% influential nodes is very high. The difference between mean of edge count and median of edge count is just 12%, and (ii) the highest edge count does not necessarily mean the highest influential value. Here only 5% of the top 10% of influential nodes are closer to maximum edge count of 82.

We estimate the influence value of a node by using $Inf_c(n)$. We consider only those nodes, whose check-ins count is higher than median check-ins count of all nodes in a network. Next, we assign ranks to these nodes according to their influenced check-ins count as a percentage.

Table 5. Influence with influenced check-ins count

	Gowalla	Brightkite
Total number of influenced nodes	0.01 million	0.006
Edge count for most influenced node	190	556
Mean number of top 10% influenced nodes	107	366
Median number of top 10% influenced nodes	100	358
Range of top 10% influenced nodes	51 to 198	243 to 556

From Table 5, we observed that top 10% of influenced nodes have mean check-ins count of 107 and median check-ins count of 100. Although it's not concrete enough to deduce that high number of check-ins do not entail higher influence, but we can argue that only 30% of nodes' check-ins count is closer to maximum check-ins count. Therefore, it becomes obvious to predict that a node with higher number of check-ins in Brightkite has more influence than a node with 0 check-ins.

The overall influence of a node $n \hat{I} N$ is measured with:

$$Inf_o\left(n\right) = \alpha Inf_e\left(n\right) + \beta Inf_c\left(n\right)$$

where α and β are weights of $Inf_e(n)$ and $Inf_c(n)$, respectively.

Table 6. Influence with both influenced edge count and influenced check-ins count

	Gowalla	Brightkite
Total number of influenced nodes	0.015 million	0.01
Mean edge count: influenced nodes	34	41
Range of edge count: influenced nodes	19 to 83	23 to 88
Mean check-ins count: influenced nodes	109	304
Range of check-ins count: influenced nodes	51 to 199	146 to 555

These results conform to our notion that the highest number of edges or the highest number of check-ins do not necessarily mean the highest influence. Because, results show that top 10% of influential nodes in a group do not have edge count close to maximum. Also, there is a strong correlation among influential people in terms of both edge count and check-ins count. The difference in mean of edge count of $Inf_o(n)$ and $Inf_e(n)$ is closer to 6%, and the difference in mean of check-ins count of $Inf_o(n)$ and $Inf_c(n)$ is closer to 2%. It shows that there is a strong correlation among influential people in terms of both edge count and check-ins count of all nodes in a network. Table 6 shows the influence with both influenced edge count and influenced check-ins count.

4.2. Simple Crawler

The dataset used for following experimentation comes from Stanford university (Snap, 2014). Data was collected from users who had manually shared their circles in the Google+ Social Network. The original dataset consisted in 107 thousand nodes and 13.7 million edges. In order to reduce running time of the experimentation, the dataset has been reduced to 700 nodes and 35 thousand edges. Moreover, bidirectional links between 2 nodes have been made unidirectional. This allows us to enlighten the different behaviors of our crawlers with a smaller data set.

Each node of our sample networks is part of at least one link, either the head or the tail of the link. Each node has between 0 and 452 friends. Nodes that have at least one friend have in average 66 friends.

Assume the online network has N nodes. The first way to compute our influence is to compute all possible paths as defined in Equation (1). The Targeted Crawler algorithm, which corresponds to the navigation between 2 nodes, is executed $O(N^2)$ times. If no path is found between source and target node, the influence table is not updated. If a path is found between source and target node, for each node N_i being part of the path, $Influence(N_i)$ is incremented by one.

Assuming the Targeted Crawler algorithm runs in $O(1)$ time, computing the full set of paths will be done in $O(N^2)$ time. For a 1 ms computation time per iteration and 10^6 nodes (which is not unrealistic for OSN, and even far from the truth for some), the computation would take approximately 10^{12} ms or 31 years. We can easily realize how this is infeasible.

4.2.1. Monte Carlo Crawler

The first approach showed that it is possible to define and influence value for each node in the network. The method described in the previous section can return very precise results. However, the method is also highly time consuming and infeasible for large OSN. Can we reduce the computation time and still have correct results?

Table 7. Monte Carlo crawler vs. Simple crawler

Node Id	Simple Crawler	Monte Carlo Crawler
206	16.3(1)	17.2(1)
422	9.8(2)	7.87(4)
170	9.6(3)	8.91(2)
938	8.4(4)	4.48(5)
675	7.1(5)	8.91(2)

The second approach aims to use the Monte Carlo method to approximate the influence of a node. Instead of running the Targeted Algorithm on all possible N^2 paths, we are going to restrict the execution time of the influence calculation to $O(N)$. To do that, our second approach selects two random nodes and then runs the Targeted Algorithm N times. With this procedure, the time spent to compute our influence defined in Equation (1) is much shorter. For $N=10^6$, this approach would end in less than 10^6 ms or 20 minutes which is very feasible. Table 7 is extracted by running the two approaches on our sample network (Snap, 2014). For the top 5 nodes, it shows the influence defined in Equation (1) normalized by the number of path computed and the overall ranking of the nodes are in parentheses. We can see that after only N iterations of the Monte Carlo Crawler and instead of the N^2 of our Simple Crawler, the influence of a node is already close to what it will be after N^2 iterations.

4.2.2. Our Approach

Simple Crawler and Monte Carlo Crawler are based on the Targeted Crawler algorithm (Humbert, 2013). The issue with this algorithm is that sometimes the frontier spread in the wrong direction and this can lead to unnecessary time consumption to find the path from a source to a target. Simple Crawler showed that it is possible to compute an influence value for a node. Monte Carlo Crawler showed that it is possible to compute this value in a reasonable amount of time. From the two previous approaches, we can conclude the goal for our third approach should be finding a navigation algorithm that (i) should not go back or expand in the wrong direction, (ii) should be computable in a reasonable amount of time and (iii) should hop using influential nodes of the network. Authors in (Wang, 2011) showed that mobility measures alone yield surprising predictive power, comparable to traditional network and similarity between two individuals' movements strongly correlates with their proximity in the social network. We use some quantities which have been proven to perform reasonably well in previous studies (Wang, 2011).

Computing the Influence Value (IV) of a node N_i in a path P_i from source node S to target node T is defined as a function with multiple parameters:

$$IV\left(N_i\right) = \lambda_1 a + \lambda_2 b + \lambda_3 c + \lambda_4 d + \lambda_5 e + \lambda_6 f \tag{2}$$

where each λ_i is a predefined weight parameter and:

> a is the number of direct friends (DF) of N_i: with V the set of vertices and E the set of edges of the network, direct friends of a node N_i are the friends that are reachable with a path of length one. They are defined by Equation (3):

$$DF\left(N_i\right) = \left\{f \mid f \in V \ and\left(N_i, f\right) \in E\right\} \tag{3}$$

> b is the total number of shared neighbors (SN): If N_i and T share a direct friend, then there is a path of length 2 going from N_i to T. Common neighbors are defined in Equation (4):

$$SN\left(N_i, T\right) = \left\{f \mid f \in DF\left(N_i\right) and \ f \in DF\left(T\right)\right\} \tag{4}$$

c is the number of attributes in common;

d is the number of unique attributes;

e is the distance to T: The distance between N_i and T is computed using attributes of the nodes. The more attribute they share, the smaller their distance is. See Equation (5). Here J is the set of available attributes in OSN and $A_j(N_i)$ is the attribute j of node N_i. The distance function can be simplified as in Equation (5):

$$dist\left(N_i, T\right) = \left|J\right| - \sum_{j \in J} bool(A_j\left(N_i\right) == A_j(T_i)) \tag{5}$$

f is the already crawled path: this is a list of nodes that have already been visited by the algorithm.

Our Influence Crawler algorithm is defined in Figure 5. Each time from the source node, we choose the highest influential friend and then consider this friend as the next hop until the target is reached.

Figure 5. Algorithm 2

Algorithm Influence Crawler

Input: N_i, S, T
$path = \emptyset$
$current = S$
while $current \notin DF(T)$ **do**
    $f* =$ friend of $current$ with maximum influence
    if $IV(f*) > 0$ **then**
        add $f*$ to path
        $current = f*$
    else   ▷ Dead end case
        Failure
    end if
end while

As our Influence Crawler is executed, multiple issues have to be resolved. In the early stage of routing, the distance between N_i and T decreases rapidly until we are in a virtual area where nodes are highly similar. People that share a lot are usually connected. Because the diameter of the Facebook graph is around six (Ugander, 2011), we can consider that N_i has a high probability of having friends in common with T once our algorithm has run for 4 to 5 iterations. At this point, we can use the set of shared neighbors between N_i and T to help our algorithm to select the next hop more efficiently. The similarity between N_i and T defined in (c) is also a measure of relative proximity. In Online Social Networks, we are generally connected to people that look like us. Hence the more similar N_i and T are, the higher chance there is a short path between them.

Our influence values should be higher for nodes that are in the direction of the target. The already crawled path is passed as an argument of our influence function defined in Equation (2). This allows our algorithm to select those nodes that are close to the source. The crawler can now return the next hop more efficiently by knowing what are the previous hops.

The correct direction of spreading can be defined as the direction that returns one of the shortest path between S and T, but not necessarily the shortest as it is impossible to know the shortest path without exploring the whole graph. The next hop should be chosen carefully because with our "can't go back" feature, we can't risk our algorithm to go in a dead-end direction. This can be avoided by making a compromise between two factors: (i) the next hop should be closer to the target and (ii) the next hop should be as connected as possible. If we favor (i) we are at risk to go straight and found ourselves in an impasse. If we favor (ii), we risk to found ourselves with an inefficient algorithm that is running in circle (Figure 6).

Figure 6. Algorithm 3

Algorithm Influence Value

    function IV(N_i)
        if $N_i \in path$ **then**   ▷ uses (f)
            $influ = 0$
        else if $N_i \in DF(T)$ **then**   ▷ uses (b)
            $influ = K$
        else if $N_i \in DF(DF(T))$ **then**   ▷ uses (b)
            $influ = L$
        else   ▷ uses (a)(c)(d)(e)
            $influ = M - \alpha * Dist(N_i, T) + \beta * |DF(N_i)|$
        end if
        return influ
    end function
        with $K > L > M$

The following tables compare our Influence Crawler with the Targeted Crawler. Data have been extracted by running the two algorithms on the same random source and target nodes.

Table 8. Average results for 1000 iterations of the crawlers

	Targeted Crawler	Influence Crawler	Diff.
# iterations	17.746	2.92	-83.5%
Path length	2.495	2.436	-2.4%
Time (ms)	1.303	0.393	-69.8%
Success rate	80.4%	51.6%	-28.8%

We can see that our Influence Crawler founds the target node in a less number of iterations. However, it is also possible that our Influence Crawler doesn't find a path when one exists. Our Influence Crawler stops in two cases: (i) it reaches a dead-end in the graph because the algorithm made bad choices during its execution or (ii) we arbitrarily stop it because it takes too long comparing to the Targeted Crawler and our goal is to make an algorithm that is more efficient.

Table 9. Success only

	Targeted Crawler	Influence Crawler	Diff.
# iterations	19.327	2.754	-85.8%
Path length	3.103	2.754	-11.3%

Table 10. Average results for 1000 iterations of the Influence crawler followed by the Targeted crawler if failure

	Targeted Crawler + Influence Crawler	Diff.
# iterations	14.243	-10.2%
Time (ms)	1.249	-4.0%
Success rate	80.4%	0%

Influence Crawler is constructed such as it adds a node to the general path at each iteration. Therefore, the length of the returned path will always be equal to the number of iterations of the algorithm whereas in the Targeted Crawler, the length of the path is usually much smaller than the number of iterations.

Considering results in Tables 8, 9 and 10 we have a success rate of 50% with our Influence Crawler for 2.4 iterations in average. This means our Crawler fails 50% of the time. The number of iteration for a fail case is at most 8. In the case our Influence Crawler fails, we decided to run the Targeted Crawler to find a path instead. With this in mind, we can compute the average number of iteration needed to find a path between two nodes. This means the combination of the Targeted Crawler and our Influence Crawler runs in average 10% less iterations and has 50% chance of finding a path in 83% less iterations.

5. USABILITY IN INDUSTRY AND COMMERCE

In this work, we measure the social influence of users in two Location Based Social Networks: Gowalla and Brightkite. We identified the targeted co-related nodes by eliminating all nodes with extreme values as properties using divide-and-conquer algorithm. We defined the influence of each node by considering five attributes: edge count, check-ins count, edge of edge count, influenced edge count and influenced check-in count, where we derived the last two of those from existing datasets. Then, we constructed the influence of each node based on three perspectives: (i) measuring influence with influenced edge count, (ii) measuring influence with influenced check-ins count, and (iii) measuring influence with both influenced edge count and influenced check-ins count.

We observed the influenced nodes in a network, those who have edge count and check-ins count close to the maximum, are not necessarily having top influence values. This finding suggests that having many friends alone or having made more check-ins alone will unwind very little about influence user. We also observed that node who are top influence nodes are having the edge count mean and check-ins count more than mean their means respectively.

Our observations are based on few available properties of nodes in Gowalla or Brightkite. Our future extension of this work would be to implement these algorithms on any LBSNs or OSNs that have more properties per node. We can review the results to see whether users who have the highest influence value have any common properties.

One other area for future work is to check whether influence hold across different type of check-ins? From our datasets, we have GPS coordinates of longitude and latitude for each check-in. Using which, with the help of any open source APIs, we can categorize the check-ins in different types of destinations, such as beaches, historical places etc. And we can review the results whether top influencers in these categories have any common properties.

One possible future direction of this work is to find more powerful approaches towards complex systems to further evaluate their social dynamics, internal structure and feedback effects of the social networks to enhance OSN applications in areas such as Crowdsourcing, Finance, and Education.

REFERENCES

Adamic, L. A. & Adar, E. (2003). Friends and neighbors on the web. *ScienceDirect.com*.

Althoff, T., Jindal, P., & Leskovec, J. (2017). Online Actions with Offline Impact: *How Online Social Networks Influence Online and Offline User Behavior. In ACM International Conference on Web Search and Data Mining (WSDM)*.

Aral, S., & Walker, D. (2012). Identifying influential and susceptible members of social networks. *Science*, *337*(6092), 337–341. doi:10.1126cience.1215842 PMID:22722253

Bond, R., Fariss J., Jones J., Kramer A., Marlow C., Settle J. & Fowler J. (2012). A 61-million-person experiment in social influence and political mobilization. Nature.

Borgatti, S. (2006). Identifying sets of key players in a social network. *Computational & Mathematical Organization Theory*, *12*(1), 21–34. doi:10.100710588-006-7084-x

Cha, M., Haddadi, H., & Gummadi, K. P. (2010). Measuring user influence in twitter: The million-follower fallacy. In *Proceedings of the 4th International Conference on Weblogs and Social Media*.

Cha, M., Haddadi, H., & Gummadi, K. P. (2011). Measuring user influence on twitter using modified k-shell decomposition. In *The Social Mobile Web, ICWSM Workshop*.

Easley, D., & Kleinberg, J. (2010). *Networks Crowds and Markets*. Cambridge University Press. doi:10.1017/CBO9780511761942

Gomez-Rodriguez, M., Leskovec, J., & Krause, A. (2010). Inferring Networks of Diffusion and Influence. In *ACM SIGKDD International Conference on Knowledge Discovery and Data Mining (KDD)*.

Humbert, M., Studer, T., Grossglauser, M., & Hubaux, J. P. (2013). Nowhere to hide: Navigation around privacy in online in social networks. In *The 18th European Symposium on Research in Computer Security (ES- ORICS)*.

Ilyas, M. U., & Radha, H. (2011). Identifying influential nodes in online social networks using principal component centrality. In *IEEE International Conference*. 10.1109/icc.2011.5963147

Kempe, D., Kleinberg, J., & Tardos, E. (2003). Maximizing the spread of influence through a social network. In *Proceedings of the 9th ACM SIGKDD International Conference on Knowledge discovery and data*. ACM Press. 10.1145/956750.956769

Klout. (2014). Retrieved from www.klout.com

Leskovec, J. (2014). Brightkite database information from Stanford network analysis project(snap). http://snap.stanford.edu/data/loc-brightkite.html

Leskovec, J., Backstrom, L., & Kleinberg, J. (2009) Meme-tracking and the Dynamics of the News Cycle. In *ACM SIGKDD International Conference on Knowledge Discovery and Data Mining (KDD)*. 10.1145/1557019.1557077

Leskovec, J., Huttenlocher, D., & Kleinberg, J. (2010). Predicting Positive and Negative Links in Online Social Networks. In *ACM WWW International Conference on World Wide Web (WWW)*. 10.1145/1772690.1772756

Linyuan, L., Ming-Sheng, S., Yi-Cheng, Z., & Tao, Z. (2011). A Data Scientist Explains How To Maximize Your Influence On Twitter Randy Olson, Contributor Business Insider Identifying influential nodes in complex networks. *Physica*.

Pedarsani, P. (2013). *Privacy and dynamics of social networks*. Ecole Polytechnique Federale de Lausanne.

Rashotte, L. S. (2011). The concise encyclopedia of sociology. *Social Influence*.

Romero, D., Meeder, B., & Kleinberg, J. (2011). Differences in the mechanics of information diffusion across topics: idioms, political hashtags, and complex contagion on twitter. In *ACM WWW International Conference on World Wide Web (WWW)*. 10.1145/1963405.1963503

Stanford University. (2014). Snap. Retrieved from http://snap.stanford.edu/data/

Ugander, J., Karrer, B., Backstrom, L., & Marlow, C. (2011). *The anatomy of the Facebook social graph*. Cornell University Press.

Wang, D., Pedreschi, D., Song, C., Giannotti, F., & Barabasi, A. (2001). Mining the network value of customers. In *KDD Proceeding of the 7th ACM SIGKDD International Conference on Knowledge discovery and data*. ACM Press.

Wang, D., Pedreschi, D., Song, C., Giannotti, F., & Barabasi, A. (2011). Human mobility, social ties and link prediction. In *The proceeding of KDD Conference*.

Yang, J., & Leskovec, J. (2010). Modeling Information Diffusion in Implicit Networks. In *IEEE International Conference on Data Mining (ICDM)*.

This research was previously published in the International Journal of Virtual Communities and Social Networking (IJVCSN), 9(4); pages 1-17, copyright year 2017 by IGI Publishing (an imprint of IGI Global).

Chapter 27
Augmented Context–Based Conceptual User Modeling for Personalized Recommendation System in Online Social Networks

Ammar Alnahhas

Faculty of Information Technology Engineering, Damascus University, Syria

Bassel Alkhatib

Faculty of Information Technology Engineering, Damascus University, Syria

ABSTRACT

As the data on the online social networks is getting larger, it is important to build personalized recommendation systems that recommend suitable content to users, there has been much research in this field that uses conceptual representations of text to match user models with best content. This article presents a novel method to build a user model that depends on conceptual representation of text by using ConceptNet concepts that exceed the named entities to include the common-sense meaning of words and phrases. The model includes the contextual information of concepts as well, the authors also show a novel method to exploit the semantic relations of the knowledge base to extend user models, the experiment shows that the proposed model and associated recommendation algorithms outperform all previous methods as a detailed comparison shows in this article.

DOI: 10.4018/978-1-7998-9020-1.ch027

INTRODUCTION

Online social networks are getting more attention nowadays, they grew rapidly in the last few years, and attracted many users, as they can communicate, share and get more information by using these networks.

As more people are engaged to the online social networks, huge amount of data is posted every day, millions of tweets on Twitter and posts on Facebook are generated causing an overwhelming stream of data. Social networks are widely used to share news, updates and events, but as the data is getting larger; users are more likely to miss important items that may be interesting to them, this issue rise the importance of building personalization solutions that can guide users to interesting content of social web including posts, people or pages.

In this paper we present a personalized recommendation system that helps users of social networks find the best textual content that matches their interest using semantic analysis of the text with help of a knowledge base. To identify the user interest, a conceptual user modelling methodology that exploits the contextual relations of concepts is introduced. As well as a recommendation algorithm that matches the user model with the content representation. There has been a series of work in this area, to our knowledge all of previous works that introduced conceptual models of social web users use named-entities to represent the interest of the users, whereas in our work we propose to represent the text as a series of concepts that contains the representation of words, phrases and entities in text, we present conceptual user model where users are mapped to concepts, and contextual conceptual user model where users are represented as a graph of contextually connected concepts. We also try to exploit the semantic relations of the knowledge graph to expand the user model, so we propose a learning-based approach that finds the importance of each semantic relation type in the field of recommendation. Our results compared with the state-of-the-art methods show that the proposed model effectively out-perform all other models.

This paper is structured as follows, Section 2 contains a detailed view of related work, Section 3 presents the problem definition and contribution, text representation method is explained in Section 4, in Section 5 we show the experiment setup, Section 6 shows the conceptual user model and Section 7 shows the contextual conceptual user model, Section 8 elaborates the model expansion approach, Section 9 presents the comparison of our models with previous models, and Section 10 concludes the paper.

RELATED WORK

Building recommendation systems for online social networks has attracted many researchers in the last few years, a few researchers aimed at studying content recommendation, but many user modelling techniques are used in other researches aiming at link, news or 'who to follow' recommendations. We can classify the researches in three different categories:

1. **Collaborative filtering:** Where items are recommended to a user by considering users with similar interests, or by considering similar items to items already user interested in;
2. **Statistical content based:** Where users are modelled according to the textual content of their items, the content is processed statistically like in IR systems, and items are recommended if its content is similar to the user model;

3. **Semantic analysis of content:** Where users are modelled according to the semantics extracted from textual contents of their interest, item are recommended if its content is semantically similar to the user model.

Collaborative Filtering Methods

The main approach of collaborative filtering is to use the known preferences of a group of users to make recommendations or predictions of the unknown preferences for other users (Su & Khoshgoftaar, 2009), so when two users share many interested items, we can predict interest in new items for one of them if the other is interested in them, item based collaborative filtering depends on the fact that if two items share the same user interests then new users who are interested in one of them is more likely interested in the other.

Many researches targeted the field of collaborative filtering to build recommendation systems for social networks, some researchers (Chen et al., 2012) propose to use collaborative ranking technique to find correlation between users and items so that if users post similar content to social network; similar items can be recommended for them in the future, while other researchers rely on social associations (Vosecky, Leung, & Ng, 2014) to build collaborative user model, or use ego networks (Sun & Zhu, 2013) to link users so that homophily between them can represent the collaboration. Similarly, a graph-theoretic model (Yan, Lapata, & Li, 2012) is proposed that ranks items and their authors according to the relations between them. Some researches use tags as the main source of collaboration, either by linking tags to users and items (Guy, Zwerdling, Ronen, Carmel, & Uziel, 2010), or by building a tag map (Xiao, Du, Zhu, & Li, 2012) that describes the relation between tags; where tags are connected if they are used by a single user or by friends, or by using social tag prediction (Yuan, Huang, Sun, Li, & Xu, 2015) and interest evolution model of tags that find scores of tags in items. A signal-based model (Arru, Feltoni Gurini, Gasparetti, Micarelli, & Sansonetti, 2013) to represent users is proposed, which includes a time dimension in the representation of the user interests, users similarity is calculated using signal process-ing techniques and user-to-user collaboration model is applied for recommendation.

Collaborative filtering methods suffers from many drawbacks, including the need to analyze huge and dynamic networks that are very complex to be done in real time. Moreover, cold start problem is well known in these methods, especially in the case of social networks as the huge amount of data makes it impossible to get collaborative information, because as soon as sufficient information is available for a piece of data, it will be outdated and new data will arrive instead.

Statistical Content-Based Methods

In these methods textual content of social network is processed to generate a statistical model for each user, text is tokenized into words; and methods like bag-of-words are used, then a statistical model such as TF-IDF pairs (Pennacchiotti, Silvestri, Vahabi, & Venturini, 2012), Hashtag frequency (Abel, Gao, Houben, & Tao, 2011a; Ma, Jia, Xie, & Lin, 2015; Zhou, Wu, Chen, Chen, & Ying, 2014), LDA (Khater & Elmongui, 2015; Kim & Shim, 2014) [6, 11, 12] or sentimental features (Cui, Du, Shen, Zhou, & Li, 2017) is applied. In these methods, a model for each user is built according to the content he is already interested in, then a matching algorithm is used to estimate the interestingness of the user in a new item.

While a simple IR method is used (Benzarti & Faiz, 2015) to build a personalized recommendation system where user models are built from user related content in various social networks using TF-IDF, other research (Pennacchiotti et al., 2012) extend this approach to use pairs of terms as a unit for modelling users, along with terms from user friends, similar approach is proposed in (Chen, Nairn, Nelson, Bernstein, & Chi, 2010) where authors build a URL recommendation system that compare content of URL pages to user models built form joining user content with content of user followers. Authors in (Elmongui et al., 2015) combine the user content with his social activities, they use a classifier to find a topic for each item and then use machine learning approach to match new items with users. A different orientation in the literature is to use tags and especially hashtags to model user interests, authors (Abel et al., 2011a) build a temporal user model as a set of weighted tags where weights are found by their frequency and timestamp, while in (Ma et al., 2015) a multi-tag correlation approach is proposed, tags are linked to users and to each other, then user-tag correlation is updated by using tag relations, similarly, Researchers in (Zhou et al., 2014) build tag-user graphs for computing the similarities between microblogs and users. Another approach (Kim & Shim, 2014) is to use probabilistic modeling based on generalized LDA model as well as matrix factorization. Authors of (Cui et al., 2017) used the sentimental information to help with recommendation, they incorporate it into the traditional content-based method.

Modeling user by bag-of-words methodology will not catch the semantics of the text, therefore recommender systems will only consider vocabulary that has already been part of the user model, so, content with similar meanings will not be recommended as relations deduced from knowledge bases are not utilized in these methods.

Semantic User Modelling Methods

Many researchers build recommendation systems for social networks that uses named-entities to represent user model (Abel, Hauff, Houben, & Tao, 2012; de Graaff, van de Venis, van Keulen, & Rolf, 2015; Kapanipathi, Jain, Venkataramani, & Sheth, 2014; Karidi, Stavrakas, & Vassiliou, 2016; Lu, Lam, & Zhang, 2012; Orlandi, Breslin, & Passant, 2012; Piao, 2016; Piao & Breslin, 2016a, 2016b, 2016c; Zarrinkalam, Fani, Bagheri, Kahani, & Du, 2015), they try to represent the semantics of the text by extracting entities that are usually DBPedia (Auer et al., 2007) concepts and use them to represent the content, some of researches (Piao & Breslin, 2016b) leverage the semantic relations to extend the user model and make recommendations more suitable, while others (Abel, Gao, Houben, & Tao, 2011b) try to build a semantic user model based on twitter posts by linking them to mainstream news articles to enrich the tweet text, they introduced semantic user model as entity-based one, the entities are extracted from user own tweets and the related news articles, whereas in (de Graaff et al., 2015) they introduced a point of interest recommendation system based on geotagging. Places and attractions are recommended to users depending on their semantic model built from content they post on the social web. Authors of (Orlandi et al., 2012) focuses on building an Interoperable user profile that can be used across many social networks, they use DBPedia entities to represent users, they compared two types of entities to use: resources and categories. Authors of (Piao & Breslin, 2016b) and (Piao, 2016) propose a link recommandation system by using named entities as well, they suggested enriching user models by three types of connected concepts from DBPedia: categories, classes and entities, they investigated the effect of temporal dynamics of user interests as well. While in another research (Piao & Breslin, 2016a) they investigated the role of aggregating user models form different social networks on the accuracy of the recommendation, they also investigated user model extension using categories and classes of DBPedia. Authors of (Lu et al., 2012) also used DBPedia entities to represent user interests but they suggested to enrich user models by random walks in the knowledge graph. In (Zarrinkalam et al., 2015) semantic topics method is proposed where temporally correlated entities are grouped into topics that are not represented yet in the knowledge base. Researchers in (Kapanipathi et al., 2014) propose to represent user interest as a hierarchical interest graph, they show an algorithm to build user profile based on their interests being leaves of DBPedia hierarchy, they use spreading activation theory to expand the interest up. authors of (Karidi et al., 2016) proposed to use a hierarchical knowledge graph to represent user interests, each user profile is represented as a tree where nodes of the tree are classes from a known taxonomy. Besides in (Piao & Breslin, 2016c) authors proposed to use Wordnet Synsets along with DBPedia entities to represent user interests, they show better results than entity model used in previous works, therefore, this is a clear indicator that named-entity representation of user interests is not sufficient and should be improved. Therefore, using extracted named entities to represent content of text is not enough to catch the semantics inside the text, besides using entities cannot represent the context of the text that can be an important factor in modelling users. In our work, on the contrary of all previous works, we suggest to represent the textual content of an item in a social network as a series of consequent concepts that represent not just entities, but also all other types of words and phrases of the text using common-sense meanings, besides we suggest to use the contextual relations between concepts to represent user interests which is—to our knowledge—a novel work in the field of social web recommendation.

Problem Definition

The goal of our work is to find the most suitable semantic modelling methodology of user interests in social networks in order to provide content recommendations that matches every user. Formally, given a user model u and a text t:

Definition 1: User interest measurement function $I(u,t)$: is a function that rates the text t according to user with model u such that the function reflects how much this text is interesting to the user and how much he likes to see it in the social network.

The recommendation system fetches items from user timeline and re-ranks them in a descending order according to function I, so that content with high interestingness value for the user appears first. Our work aims at finding the best modeling strategy and best user interest measurement function exploiting semantics of textual content and the context of the text.

To be able to represent the full semantical meaning of the text and to maintain the context of the semantics, we should represent all parts of it as semantic blocks, where nouns, verbs, named entities that can be represented as concepts in a knowledge base should be considered. To be able to include as much content of the text as possible we should use a very rich background knowledge base, so we choose to use ConceptNet (Speer, Chin, & Havasi, 2017) which is a multilingual knowledge graph that connects words and phrases with labeled relations called assertions, the key advantage of ConceptNet is that it focuses on the common-sense meanings of words and not just named-entities, moreover, it is built from many sources such as Open-source common sense, WordNet, OpenCyc and DBPedia, that makes it a rich knowledge base that covers most terms and phrases.

The contribution of our work can be summarized as follows:

- We provide a new semantic representation of text in social networks as a series of concepts;

- We suggest a novel contextual semantic user modelling methodology and show its effectiveness in representing user interests and provide a recommendation algorithm over this model;
- We provide a method to exploit semantic relations to enrich user models that is suitable for recommendation applications.

Conceptual Representation of Text

As we described earlier, we are going to represent the text as a series of consequent concepts extracted from ConceptNet, ConceptNet concepts are associated with words or phrases, so it is easy to convert a part of the text to a concept when this part corresponds to the textual representation of this concept. We suggest a simple greedy algorithm to convert text into series of concept: first the text is tokenized, stop words are removed and hashtags are normalized to ordinary words, then the result list of words are processed with alg.1, the intuition behind the greedy algorithm is that phrases represents the semantic of its words so the longer the text part is the more accurate the semantic is, moreover, natural language structure tend to link words with its predecessors, so if adding a word to a meaningful phrase makes a new longer meaningful phrase so it is better to add it.

Algorithm 1: input: series of words – output: series of concepts

```
s is an empty string
c is an empty string
For each word w in input
If s + w represent a prefix of some concept:
s <- s + w
if s represents a concept:
c <- s
else if c is not empty
add c to the output
make c and s empty
```

To be able to find if a string represents a prefix of some concept, we convert all available concept representations into a prefix tree where each representation is tokenized and words are used to denote edges of the tree.

As ConceptNet is a multilingual knowledge base, we consider only the English concepts, so as a preprocessing phase, we process the flat file of ConceptNet that contains all assertions and extract the English concepts, assertions that connect two English concepts are only regarded, Table 1 shows statistics about English part of ConceptNet.

Table 1. Statistics about English content of ConceptNet

Number of concepts	1507812
Number of assertions	3098816

We choose English concepts because it is the largest language represented in ConceptNet and it is easy to collect dataset for experiment user, however, it is rational that our method is cross-lingual and should work for any language but further testing and validation should be carried out as a future work.

EXPERIMENT SETUP

In this section, we are going to describe the dataset and the performance measures we are going to use to test the different algorithms we are going to present in the coming section of this paper.

Twitter is an online social network that is widely used around the globe, as Twitter provides an open and easy-to-use API that can be used to get users, relations and content we are going to test our approach on a dataset extracted from Twitter.

To collect the data, we choose 980 arbitrary users who have more than 2000 tweet posted before the date of collection, the users was chosen to post English tweets as we are using the English part of ConceptNet. Using twitter API, we get the last 3200 tweets for each user at most which is the limit the API imposes. For each tweet we normalize that text by removing links and converting hashtags into words, then tokenize the text and apply algo.1 on each tweet to get the concept list representation, we keep track of both the word representation and the concept representation for comparison with other methods, Table 2 shows statistics of the collected data.

After investigating the dataset, we notice that users are not consistent in posting tweets, that is, some users post too many tweets per day whereas some other users post a tweet every week, so, as content has temporal association, we choose a subset of users that are consistent with average tweets per time unit as well as the total number of tweets they have, the compact dataset contains 224 users with statistics shown in Table 3, the remaining users data is used to extract knowledge base relation weights as will be described in Section 8.

Table 2. Complete dataset statistics

Number of users	980
Number of tweets	1771648
Average tweets per user	1808
Number of distinct words	1069125
Number of distinct concepts	181214

Table 3. Compact dataset statistics

Number of users	223
Number of tweets	474092
Average tweets per user	2125
Number of distinct words	381415
Number of distinct concepts	114863

The evaluation metrics used in our experiments are similar to these used commonly in recommendation systems and are derived from information retrieval system evaluation metrics, as the recommendation process is similar to the process of searching for content that is suitable for a user, besides, users will check the first k results of recommendation in a similar behavior of information retrieval behavior. We measure algorithms performance using the following metrics:

MRR: which is $1/x$ where x is the rank of the first interesting item recommended to the user.
P@K: precision at rank K, which is the ratio of interesting items in the first K recommended items.

R@K: recall at rank K, which is the number of interesting items in the first K recommended items divided by the total number of interesting items.

F@K: which is defined in terms of precision P and recall R as following:

$$F = \frac{2 * P * R}{P + R}$$ (1)

The compact dataset is divided into two parts: the training part which constitute 90% of the dataset, it was created by taking first 90% of each user tweets ordered by date, the remaining 10% of the dataset are used for testing, the testing part is distributed equally among users, so a random recommender will result in almost an equal result for each user, P@10 of a random recommender which recommend items randomly will be about 0.04.

The ground truth is that each user is interested in the content he posts, so to evaluate a recommender; its result is compared to the testing data where the true items are the user own items and the false ones are the items of all other users. This can roughly reflect the interest of users because users may have not seen some content that they are also interested in, where we account it as not interesting because he did not post it, this problem cannot be solved in automatic testing scheme and needs a pilot user study to address it, however, if an algorithm gets good precision with ground truth data, it should get at least the same precision in real data because the actual true set of each user contains the true set we consider which is the items posted by the user, that means the precision we get is guaranteed to be the minimum true one when evaluated by real users.

CONCEPTUAL USER MODEL

To test the efficiency of modelling users using the concepts of ConceptNet, we define the user model as a vector of weighted concept, this model is used in many related works, where items of the model were either words or named entities, whereas we suggest to use concepts extracted in Section 2.

Definition 2: Conceptual user model M_u of user u is defined as:

$$M_u = \{(c, w_c) \text{ for each } c \text{ in } C\}$$ (2)

where C is a set of all known concepts, w_c is a weight that reflects the interestingness of the user u in the term, where:

$$W_c = T_c * P_c$$ (3)

T_c is the number of items containing c that are posted by the user, and P_c is a popularity factor; where this factor is high when the concept is not popular, this is important for recommendation as it is more desirable to recommend more specific concepts rather than common ones that are popular. We suggest using inverse user frequency to represent the factor P_c as follows:

$$P_c = \log(U/U_c)$$

(4)

where U is the total number of users in the dataset and U_c is the number of users who are interested in concept c. the user model is normalized, so that the sum of all weights equal to 1.

The recommendation algorithm assigns an interestingness value V_i for each item i, then the items are ranked according to this value. First, we represent each Item i as a series of concepts CL_i, the value V_i is a normalized sum of W_c for each c in Cl_i:

$$V_i = \frac{1}{k} \sum_{c \, in \, CL_i} W_c$$

(5)

where k is the number of concepts in CL_i.

Running the algorithm on the testing data shows effective results, the MRR is 0.693175, Figure 1 shows P@k, R@k, S@k and F@k diagrams for this model.

Figure 1. Results for conceptual model recommendation system

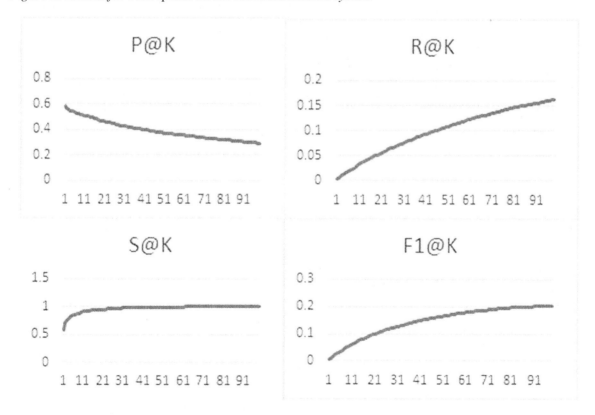

Contextual Conceptual User Model

Representing interests of a user as a weighted list of concepts proved to be efficient, however, it is important to consider the context that each concept is related to in order to model the interests of a user more accurately. So, it is more suitable to link each concept with the other concepts that appear in its context in the user training set, the more a set of concepts appear in the context of each other in the training set of a user, the more this user is interested in the set of these concepts as a whole. To address the context of each user we provide the following definition:

Definition 3: *Contextual conceptual user model: for a user u:* we define a contextual conceptual user model as a weighted graph G_u where N are the nodes, and E are the edges, each node of G_u represents a concept from the knowledge base, if a concepts $c2$ and $c2$ appear in the same context in the user data then there is an edge that connects the nodes representing $c1$ and $c2$.

The weight W_e of an edge e connecting concepts $c1$ and $c2$ represents the interestingness of user u in items in which $c1$ appears in the context of $c2$, and can be calculated as the following:

$$W_e = \frac{1}{k} * T_{c1,c2} * P_e \tag{6}$$

where k is the number of edges in the user graph, $T_{c1,c2}$ is the number of items in the training dataset where c1 appears in the context of c2, and P_e is a popularity factor representing how common is this edge among users, we suggest to calculate P_e as following:

$$P_e = \log\left(\frac{U}{U_e}\right) \tag{7}$$

where U is the total number of users in the dataset and U_e is the number of users that e is an edge in their graphs.

To represent an Item I of a social network, supposing I is represented as a sequence of concepts denoted by CL_I; I is represented as a fully connected unweighted graph G_I where each concept in CL_I is represented by a node and there is an edge between each two nodes.

To find the interestingness value $V_{u,I}$ of user u with an item I we sum the weights of the Intersection of G_u and G_I, so that if an item context conform to user model then it is interested to this user, formally we can find $V_{u,I}$ as follow:

$$V_{u,I} = \frac{1}{k} \sum_{e \in G_u \cap G_i} W_e \tag{8}$$

where k is the number of edges in G_I. Note that the intersection of G_u and G_I is a new graph G where node set of G is the result of intersection of node sets of G_u and G_i, and edge set of G is the result of intersection of edge sets of G_u and G_I with weights adopted from G_u as G_I is unweighted.

The recommendation algorithm ranks each item I for user u according to $V_{u,I}$, then the result is viewed to the user. Testing the algorithm using our dataset shows that it is very efficient, the MRR is 0.816321, Figure 2 shows details about the result of this user model and associated recommendation algorithm.

Extending Conceptual Model

Each concept in the knowledge graph is connected to other concepts using semantic relations, intuitively, if a user is interested in a concept he may be interested in related concepts. Taking this into consideration; it is worth investigating the association between semantic relations and user modelling in order to improve the result of recommendation systems.

Concepts in ConceptNet are connected using 47 different types of semantic relations such as "Is a", "part of" and "synonym". It is obvious that not all of these relations are suitable to be exploited to extend user interests model, so we introduce a method to find the importance of each relation type for the purpose of recommendation. The method uses machine learning approach to learn the importance of each relation, so we choose a part of the dataset that does not overlap with compact dataset explained in Section 3 as a training set. Formally we are calculating a distribution D that can be represented as a vector where each relation type corresponds to a dimension, that is, $D = (d_1,d_2...,d_{47})$ where d_r represent the relative importance of relation type r.

Figure 2. Results for contextual conceptual model recommendation system

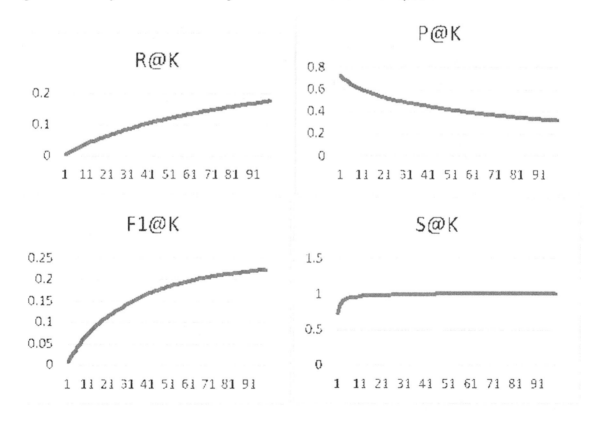

For each user we find the extended training set TS_u, first we find SKG_u a subgraph of the knowledge graph that includes all concepts from user model extracted in Section 4, the intuition is that if a relation type is important for recommendation, it should appear frequently in SKG_u of many users. The extended training set TS_u of the user u can be defined as following:

$$TS_u = \left\{ c : \exists E\left(x, c\right) \in SKG_u \right\} \tag{9}$$

TS_u is a set of concepts where there is an edge in SKG_u ending at it, intuitively, we assume that if V_{c1} is the interestingness of concept $c1$ for a user and there is an edge $e(c1,c2)$ in SKG_u where this edge relation type is r, then:

$$V_{c2} = V_{c1} * d_r \tag{10}$$

For a concept c in TS_u we have already calculated a weight V_c for it as this concept is part of the user model (see Section 4) by definition, whereas we can find the training weight nV_c for this concept by using a generalized form of Equation (10), because each concept in TS_u may have multiple edges ending at it:

$$nV_{c2} = \sum_{e(c1,c2) \in SKG_u} V_{c1} * d_{r(e)} \tag{11}$$

For the value of D to be perfect, the value of each concept V_c should be close to the target value nV_c, more accurately; if we represent the conceptual user model as a vector V and the training user model that consists of target values as a vector nV where number of dimensions equals to the total number of concepts, then these two vectors should be identical for perfect values of D, We consider the cosine distance between these two vectors as a measure of distance. Hence, we would like to find the values of D such that the we maximize the following formula for each user:

$$\frac{V n V}{\left| V \right| * \left| n V \right|} \tag{12}$$

Hence, we would like to maximize the following formula taking into account all users:

$$\frac{1}{\left| U \right|} \sum_{u \in U} \frac{V_u . n V_u}{\left| V_u \right| * \left| n V_u \right|} \tag{13}$$

where U is the set of all users. The vector nV_u can be represented as a multiplication of a matrix M_u by the vector D:

$$nV_u = M_u * D \tag{14}$$

The matrix M_u has dimensions $47xC$ where C is the number of concepts in TS of the user, and 47 is the number of types of semantic relation, each item in M_u can be calculated as:

$$M_{i,j} = \sum_{e(c,i)\, where\, r(e)=j} V_c \tag{15}$$

where $r(e)$ is the relation type of edge e. So the formula to maximize is:

$$\frac{1}{|U|} \sum_{u \in U} \frac{V_u(M_u * D)}{|V_u| * |M_u * D|} \tag{16}$$

To find the value of D that maximize the Formula 16, it can be addressed as an optimization problem that can be handled using a global search algorithm. We suggest to use a genetic algorithm to find the best value of D, each individual of the population represents a different instance of vector D and the fitness function is the Formula 16, these are the steps of our algorithm:

Algorithm 2
1. Generate 1000 random vectors to constitute the population
2. Find the fitness of each individual by using Formula 16
3. Normalize each individual so that $\Sigma d_i=1$
4. Repeat until no more significant improvement:
   a. Select 1000 individuals using tournament selection method
   b. Generate new generation using two-point crossover
   c. Do some arbitrary mutation for some individuals
   d. Evaluate new individuals using by using formula 16
   e. Normalize each individual so that $\Sigma d_i=1$
5. Choose best individual to be the solution.

The algorithm converges to best solution that is shown in Figure 3. To exploit the semantic relations, we are going to show two experiments: augmentation of conceptual user model and augmentation of contextual conceptual user model.

To augment conceptual user model with new concepts that may be interesting for the user we define the extended conceptual user model as:

$$EM_u = \{(c, w_c)\, where\, \exists x \in M_u\, and\, \exists e(x,c) \in G\} \cup M_u \tag{17}$$

where G is the knowledge graph, and w_c is:

$$w_c = w_x * d_{r(e)} * P \tag{18}$$

$r(e)$ is the relation type of edge e, and P is a penalty factor that can be found according to popularity of concept c.

Figure 3. The importance of each relation type as the result of Algorithm 2

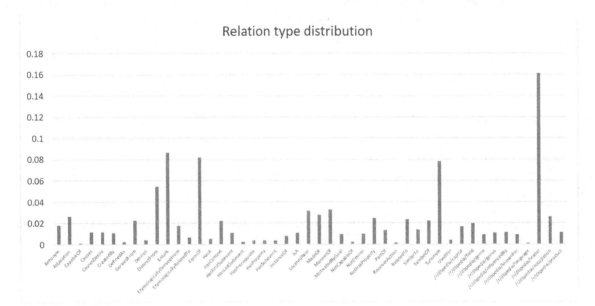

Relation type distribution

Figure 4 shows the result of augmenting the conceptual user model, we can observe how the results are improved by this extension.

Augmenting the contextual conceptual user model involves adding edge to the user graph G_u depending on edges in the knowledge graph. If two concepts *c1* and *c2* are connected in G_u and there is an edge *e(c1,c3)* in the knowledge graph then we can add the edge *e(c2,c3)* to G_u with weight derived from weight of *e(c1,c2)* and the type of relation *e(c1,c3)*. Formally, Extended user graph $EG_u(N_{eg}, E_{eg})$ can be formed as following:

$$E_{eg} = E_u \cup \left\{ \left(x, y, w_{x,y}\right) where \; \exists e\left(x, a\right) \in G_u \; and \; \exists e\left(a, y\right) \in G \right\}$$

$$w_{x,y} = Max_{for \; each \; a \; where \; e1(x,a) \; and \; e2(a,y)} \left(w_{e1} * d_{r(e2)} * P \right) \tag{19}$$

The node set N_{eg} is the union of original user model nodes with the set of new nodes added by new edges. *P* is a popularity factor and can be found using *IUF*.

Figure 5 shows the results of augmented contextual conceptual user model compared to model without augmentation. Besides, Table 4 compares the MRR values for different models.

Comparison With Other Methods

In order to show the efficiency of our described models, we are going to compare the results with the most successful previous works along with some baselines and state of the art models.

Figure 4. Comparison between conceptual user model and extended conceptual user model

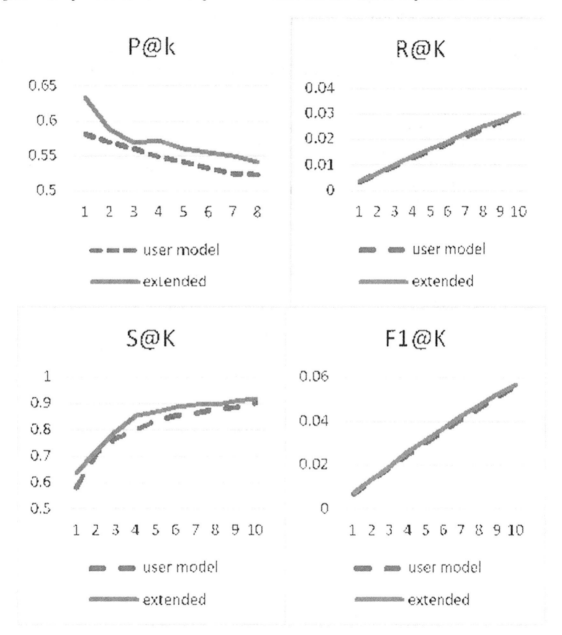

All models are implemented[1] and tested using the same dataset, the models are the follows:

- ***Tf-idf model:*** Baseline model that uses the IR measures to model each user, new items are ranked according to tf-idf;
- **Pairs frequency model (PFM):** This model is presented in (Pennacchiotti et al., 2012), where the authors uses statistical model that improves tf-idf model by using pairs of words instead of words themselves;

- **LDA model:** As described in (Khater & Elmongui, 2015) and (Kim & Shim, 2014) where each user is represented as a distribution of latent topics, based on the topic distribution generated by training data;
- **Entity model (EM):** Using this model users are represented as a vector of DBPedia entities and is used with variation in many recent researches (Orlandi et al., 2012; Piao, 2016). To generate DBPedia entities for our dataset, we use TAGME Web API (Ferragina & Scaiella, 2010) that can extract parts of the text that correspond to Wikipedia pages, that is a DBPedia named entities;
- **Steiner tree model (STM):** That is presented in (Karidi et al., 2016) where the researchers extract a Steiner tree for each user given the knowledge graph that is represented as a taxonomy and user nodes extracted from user items. To implement this model, we first convert ConceptNet into a simple graph by eliminating all relation types but the "IsA" relation, then a Steiner tree is built for each user to extend his model, the Steiner tree is traversed using reversed topological sort and weights are assigned to new nodes, then these nodes are added to original user model.

Figure 5. Comparison of extended contextual model with original one

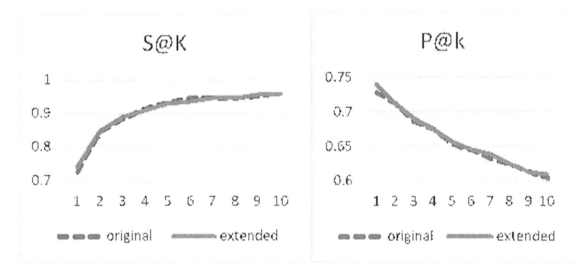

Table 4. MRR for different user models

Model	Conceptual Model	Extended Conceptual	Contextual Model	Extended Contextual
MRR	0.693175	0.730058	0.816321	0.823518

Table 5 shows the results of our models: conceptual model (CM), augmented conceptual Model (ACM), contextual conceptual user model (CCM) and augmented contextual conceptual user model (ACCM) compared to related works, we can observe the efficiency of augmented contextual conceptual model which achieves the best among all other models, Entity model achieves moderate efficiency, whereas using Steiner tree to extend the model shows a good effect on conceptual user model and should be investigated more in the future (Figure 6).

Table 5. Comparison of different models with different measures

	MRR	P@5	P@10	S@5	S@10	R@10	F1@10
LDA	0.294474	0.171429	0.153571	0.379464	0.522321	0.008807	0.016577
Tf-idf	0.477271	0.360714	0.345536	0.562500	0.678571	0.019895	0.037452
PM	0.530825	0.413393	0.380804	0.660714	0.754464	0.021749	0.040960
EM	0.627313	0.475893	0.436607	0.763393	0.848214	0.025495	0.047925
STM	0.714115	0.561607	0.528125	0.861607	0.915179	0.030327	0.057061
CM	0.693175	0.541071	0.516518	0.834821	0.901786	0.029725	0.055917
ACM	0.730058	0.558929	0.523214	0.866071	0.915179	0.030156	0.056722
CCM	0.816321	0.653571	0.604018	0.933036	0.964286	0.034852	0.065557
ACCM	0.823518	0.657143	0.609375	0.928571	0.96875	0.035206	0.066218

Figure 6. MRR value for different methods

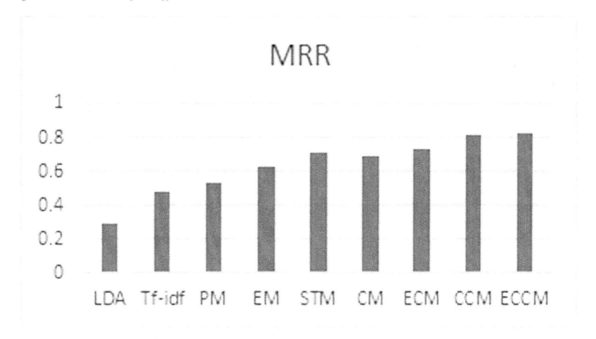

CONCLUSION

It is important to build personalized recommendation systems for online social networks, so in this paper we introduced a new approach to building a contextual and conceptual user models and proposed a recommendation algorithms based on these models, we showed a method to represent text of user items as sequence of concepts extracted from a knowledge base and presented a new method to exploit the sematic relation of the knowledge base to expand user model that proves good results, we compared our models and algorithms with most state of the art works and showed how our models outperform all of them, our experiment proved that the conceptual representation of the text is more effective than using named-entities, besides, the inclusion of contextual information in the conceptual representation shows a very promising results, so that this orientation should be investigated using more tools in the future.

REFERENCES

Abel, F., Gao, Q., Houben, G.-J., & Tao, K. (2011a). Analyzing temporal dynamics in twitter profiles for personalized recommendations in the social web. *Paper presented at the 3rd International Web Science Conference*. Academic Press. 10.1145/2527031.2527040

Abel, F., Gao, Q., Houben, G.-J., & Tao, K. (2011b). Semantic enrichment of twitter posts for user profile construction on the social web. *Paper presented at the Extended semantic web conference*. Academic Press.10.1007/978-3-642-21064-8_26

Abel, F., Hauff, C., Houben, G.-J., & Tao, K. (2012). Leveraging user modeling on the social web with linked data. *Paper presented at the International Conference on Web Engineering*. Academic Press. 10.1007/978-3-642-31753-8_31

Arru, G., Feltoni Gurini, D., Gasparetti, F., Micarelli, A., & Sansonetti, G. (2013). Signal-based user recommendation on twitter. *Paper presented at the 22nd International Conference on World Wide Web*. Academic Press.

Auer, S., Bizer, C., Kobilarov, G., Lehmann, J., Cyganiak, R., & Ives, Z. (2007). Dbpedia: A nucleus for a web of open data. In The semantic web (pp. 722-735). Springer.

Benzarti, S., & Faiz, R. (2015). *EgoTR: Personalized tweets recommendation approach. In Intelligent Systems in Cybernetics and Automation Theory* (pp. 227–238). Springer. doi:10.1007/978-3-319-18503-3_23

Chen, J., Nairn, R., Nelson, L., Bernstein, M., & Chi, E. (2010). Short and tweet: experiments on recommending content from information streams. *Paper presented at the SIGCHI Conference on Human Factors in Computing Systems*. Academic Press. 10.1145/1753326.1753503

Chen, K., Chen, T., Zheng, G., Jin, O., Yao, E., & Yu, Y. (2012). *Collaborative personalized tweet recommendation. Paper presented at the 35th international ACM SIGIR conference on Research and development in information retrieval*. Academic Press.

Cui, W., Du, Y., Shen, Z., Zhou, Y., & Li, J. (2017). Personalized microblog recommendation using sentimental features. *Paper presented at the 2017 IEEE International Conference on Big Data and Smart Computing (BigComp)*. IEEE Press.

de Graaff, V., van de Venis, A., van Keulen, M., & Rolf, A. (2015). Generic knowledge-based Analysis of Social Media for Recommendations. *Paper presented at the CBRecSys@ RecSys*. Academic Press.

Elmongui, H. G., Mansour, R., Morsy, H., Khater, S., El-Sharkasy, A., & Ibrahim, R. (2015). TRUPI: Twitter recommendation based on users' personal interests. *Paper presented at the International Conference on Intelligent Text Processing and Computational Linguistics*. Academic Press. 10.1007/978-3-319-18117-2_20

Ferragina, P., & Scaiella, U. (2010). Tagme: on-the-fly annotation of short text fragments (by wikipedia entities). *Paper presented at the 19th ACM international conference on Information and knowledge management*. ACM. 10.1145/1871437.1871689

Guy, I., Zwerdling, N., Ronen, I., Carmel, D., & Uziel, E. (2010). Social media recommendation based on people and tags. *Paper presented at the 33rd international ACM SIGIR conference on Research and development in information retrieval*. Academic Press. 10.1145/1835449.1835484

Kapanipathi, P., Jain, P., Venkataramani, C., & Sheth, A. (2014). User interests identification on twitter using a hierarchical knowledge base. *Paper presented at the European Semantic Web Conference*. Academic Press. 10.1007/978-3-319-07443-6_8

Karidi, D. P., Stavrakas, Y., & Vassiliou, Y. (2016). A personalized Tweet recommendation approach based on concept graphs. *Paper presented at the Ubiquitous Intelligence & Computing, Advanced and Trusted Computing, Scalable Computing and Communications, Cloud and Big Data Computing, Internet of People, and Smart World Congress (UIC/ATC/ScalCom/CBDCom/IoP/SmartWorld)*. IEEE Press. 10.1109/UIC-ATC-ScalCom-CBDCom-IoP-SmartWorld.2016.0056

Khater, S., & Elmongui, H. G. (2015). Tweets you like: Personalized tweets recommendation based on dynamic users interests.

Kim, Y., & Shim, K. (2014). TWILITE: A recommendation system for Twitter using a probabilistic model based on latent Dirichlet allocation. *Information Systems, 42*, 59–77. doi:10.1016/j.is.2013.11.003

Lu, C., Lam, W., & Zhang, Y. (2012). Twitter user modeling and tweets recommendation based on wikipedia concept graph. *Paper presented at the Workshops at the Twenty-Sixth AAAI Conference on Artificial Intelligence*. Academic Press.

Ma, H., Jia, M., Xie, M., & Lin, X. (2015). A microblog recommendation algorithm based on multi-tag correlation. *Paper presented at the International Conference on Knowledge Science, Engineering and Management*. Academic Press. 10.1007/978-3-319-25159-2_43

Orlandi, F., Breslin, J., & Passant, A. (2012). Aggregated, interoperable and multi-domain user profiles for the social web. *Paper presented at the 8th International Conference on Semantic Systems*. Academic Press. 10.1145/2362499.2362506

Pennacchiotti, M., Silvestri, F., Vahabi, H., & Venturini, R. (2012). Making your interests follow you on twitter. *Paper presented at the 21st ACM international conference on Information and knowledge management*. ACM Press. 10.1145/2396761.2396786

Piao, G. (2016). Towards comprehensive user modeling on the social web for personalized link recommendations. *Paper presented at the 2016 Conference on User Modeling Adaptation and Personalization*. Academic Press. 10.1145/2930238.2930367

Piao, G., & Breslin, J. G. (2016a). Analyzing aggregated semantics-enabled user modeling on Google+ and Twitter for personalized link recommendations. *Paper presented at the 2016 Conference on User Modeling Adaptation and Personalization*. Academic Press. 10.1145/2930238.2930278

Piao, G., & Breslin, J. G. (2016b). Exploring dynamics and semantics of user interests for user modeling on Twitter for link recommendations. *Paper presented at the 12th International Conference on Semantic Systems*. Academic Press. 10.1145/2993318.2993332

Piao, G., & Breslin, J. G. (2016c). User modeling on Twitter with WordNet Synsets and DBpedia concepts for personalized recommendations. *Paper presented at the 25th ACM International on Conference on Information and Knowledge Management*. ACM Press. 10.1145/2983323.2983908

Speer, R., Chin, J., & Havasi, C. (2017). Conceptnet 5.5: An open multilingual graph of general knowledge. *Paper presented at the Thirty-First AAAI Conference on Artificial Intelligence*. AAAI Press.

Su, X., & Khoshgoftaar, T. M. (2009). A survey of collaborative filtering techniques. *Advances in Artificial Intelligence*, 1–19. doi:10.1155/2009/421425

Sun, J., & Zhu, Y. (2013). Microblogging personalized recommendation based on ego networks. *Paper presented at the 2013 IEEE/WIC/ACM International Joint Conferences on Web Intelligence (WI) and Intelligent Agent Technologies (IAT)*. Academic Press. 10.1109/WI-IAT.2013.25

Vosecky, J., Leung, K. W.-T., & Ng, W. (2014). Collaborative personalized twitter search with topic-language models. *Paper presented at the 37th international ACM SIGIR conference on Research & development in information retrieval*. ACM Press. 10.1145/2600428.2609584

Xiao, Y., Du, T., Zhu, W., & Li, Q. (2012). Building a Tag Map for Recommendations in Microblogging. *Paper presented at the 2012 International Conference on Management of e-Commerce and e-Government (ICMeCG)*. Academic Press. 10.1109/ICMeCG.2012.29

Yan, R., Lapata, M., & Li, X. (2012). Tweet recommendation with graph co-ranking. *Paper presented at the 50th Annual Meeting of the Association for Computational Linguistics*. Academic Press.

Yuan, Z., Huang, C., Sun, X.-y., Li, X., & Xu, D. (2015). A microblog recommendation algorithm based on social tagging and a temporal interest evolution model. *Frontiers of Information Technology & Electronic Engineering*, 16(7), 532–540. doi:10.1631/FITEE.1400368

Zarrinkalam, F., Fani, H., Bagheri, E., Kahani, M., & Du, W. (2015). Semantics-enabled user interest detection from twitter. *Paper presented at the 2015 IEEE/WIC/ACM International Conference on Web Intelligence and Intelligent Agent Technology (WI-IAT)*. Academic Press. 10.1109/WI-IAT.2015.182

Zhou, X., Wu, S., Chen, C., Chen, G., & Ying, S. (2014). Real-time recommendation for microblogs. *Information Sciences*, 279, 301–325. doi:10.1016/j.ins.2014.03.121

This research was previously published in the International Journal of Cognitive Informatics and Natural Intelligence (IJCINI), 14(3); pages 1-19, copyright year 2020 by IGI Publishing (an imprint of IGI Global).

Chapter 28
A Social Media Recommender System

Giancarlo Sperlì
University of Naples "Federico II", Naples, Italy

Flora Amato
University of Naples "Federico II", Naples, Italy

Fabio Mercorio
Department of Statistics and Quantitative Methods Crisp Research Centre, University of Milan-Bicocca, Milan, Italy

Mario Mezzanzanica
Department of Statistics and Quantitative Methods Crisp Research Centre, University of Milan-Bicocca, Milan, Italy

Vincenzo Moscato
University of Naples "Federico II", Naples, Italy

Antonio Picariello
University of Naples "Federico II", Naples, Italy

ABSTRACT

Social media recommendation differs from traditional recommendation approaches as it needs considering not only the content information and users' similarities, but also users' social relationships and behavior within an online social network as well. In this article, a recommender system – designed for big data applications – is used for providing useful recommendations in online social networks. The proposed technique represents a collaborative and user-centered approach that exploits the interactions among users and generated multimedia contents in one or more social networks in a novel and effective way. The experiments performed on data collected from several online social networks show the feasibility of the approach towards the social media recommendation problem.

1. INTRODUCTION

Nowadays, Online Social Networks (OSNs) represent the most natural environment that allow users creating and sharing multimedia contents such as text, image, video, audio for different purposes (e.g., comment events and facts, declare and share personal opinions about a specific topic, share moments of their life etc.). Thus, millions of individuals can create online profiles and share personal information within more and more vast networks of people.

DOI: 10.4018/978-1-7998-9020-1.ch028

Indeed, by means of shared social media content each user can "indirectly" interacts with the others generating particular "social links" that can effectively characterize their behaviors within the network and can support a lot of Social Network Analysis (SNA) applications. In such a context, multimedia data can play a key-role: specifically, representing and understanding user-multimedia interaction mechanisms and multimedia items' characteristics can be useful to predict user behavior and, especially, to design human-centric multimedia services.

With the exponential growth of social media, it is quite important to provide multimedia information of real interest for users: which photo to watch in Flickr, which music to listen in Last.Fm, which video to watch in YouTube, etc., just to provide several examples.

Thus, Recommender Systems (Kantor, 2015) surely represent one of the most important tool that can be needed within OSNs, due to their capability of providing personalized and useful contents to users on the basis of their needs and preferences. As an example, they have been used in the last dedecade to support users in the following tasks: what items to buy (Kazienko & Kolodziejski, 2006), which photo or movie to watch (Albanese, d'Acierno, Moscato, Persia & Picariello, 2013), (Lekakos & Caravelas, 2008), which music to listen (Yoshii, Goto, Komatani, Ogata & Okuno, 2008), what travels to do (Colace, De Santo, Greco, Moscato & Picariello, 2015), or even who they can invite to their social network (Stan, Muhlenbach & Largeron, 2014), which artwork could be interesting within an art collection or even to suggest visiting paths in Cultural Heritage applications (Albanese, d'Acierno, Moscato, Persia & Picariello, 2011), (Bartolini, Moscato, Pensa, Penta, Picariello, Sansone & Sapino, 2016).

However, social media recommendation is quite different from traditional recommendation approaches because it needs to take into account not only content information and users' similarities (as in the most diffused recommender systems), but also users' social relationships and behavior within an OSN to handle a large amount of multimedia contents showing Big Data features, mainly due to their high change rate, their huge volume and intrinsic heterogeneity.

In this context, one of the most interesting open research challenge is to provide recommendation techniques for multimedia data in one or more social environments, exploiting at the same time (low-level) features and (high-level) metadata description (together with the attached semantics) of contents together with users' community behaviors in the different OSNs, and eventually considering the context information (Amato, Moscato, Picariello & Sperlí, 2017), (Kabassi, 2013) as a further criterion to have more accurate results in the recommendation process.

In this paper, that represents an extension of the previous work by (Amato, Moscato, Picariello & Sperlí, 2017), we propose a collaborative and user-centered approach that provides social recommendations on the base of the all different kinds of interactions among users and generated multimedia contents in one or more social networks. Thus, in our approach several aspects related to users - i.e., preferences (usually coded in the shape of items' metadata), opinions (textual comments to which it is possible to associate a particular sentiment), behavior (in the majority of cases logs of past items' observations and actions made by users in the social environment), feedbacks (usually expressed in the form of ratings) - are considered and integrated together with items' features and context information within a general and unique recommendation framework that can support different social applications using proper customizations (e.g., recommendation of photos, movies, etc. in different kinds of social networks). In other words, the main research contribution of the work lies from one hand in the definition of a collaborative and novel user-centered recommendation approach (with the set of characteristics described above) and, from the other hand, in its application within one or more social media networks (e.g. Flickr, Youtube,

Last.FM, etc.). The final goal is to automatically suggest multimedia objects of interest for a specific user according to her/his preferences and needs within an OSN.

The paper is organized as follows. Section 2 reports the state of the art of the most diffused recommendation approaches and their applications for online social networks. Section 3 describes the proposed framework for recommendation and reports some implementation details for our recomm ender system. Section 4 reports some experimental results and Section 5 gives some concluding remarks and discusses future works.

2. RELATED WORK

Recommender Systems are more and more playing an important role in our life, representing a meaningful response to the problem of information overload and having as the main goal to predict user's preferences providing suggestions about items that could be of interest (Kantor, 2015), (He, Parra & Verbert, 2016).

Formally, it is possible to define a recommender system as a set of a set of users $U = \{u_1 \ldots u_m\}$, and a set of items $O = \{o_1 \ldots o_n\}$, whose pair (u_i, o_j) is assigned a score (or a rank) r_{ij} that measures the expected interest of user u_i on item o_j. The ranking algorithm could consider different combinations of the following four characteristics: (i) preferences and behaviors of each user and the whole user community, (ii) how items' features can match user needs and preferences, (iii) user feedbacks, (iv) context information and how recommendations can change together with the context (Adomavicius, Sankaranarayanan, Sen & Tuzhilin, 2005).

The most diffused classification for recommender system leverages five broad categories.

In the content-based approach, recommended items to a user are based on the ratings made by the user himself for similar items in the past (Pazzani & Billsus, 2007). A critical drawback of this kind of technique is overspecialization, since a system can only recommend items similar to those already rated by the user. In addition, we have the problem of defining an effective similarity criterion between two items on the base of the related features, especially if we consider complex data as multimedia information.

In a collaborative filtering strategy (Su & Khoshgoftaar 2009), the recommendation is in turn performed by filtering and evaluating items with respect to ratings from other users. Typically, users are asked to rate items and a similarity between their profiles is also computed to choose among highly rated items. Thus, the major challenge faced by collaborative filtering is the need to associate each user to a set of other users having similar profiles. In order to make any recommendations, the system has to collect data either asking for explicit ratings from users, or through non-intrusive profiling algorithms implicitly logging actions performed by users (Albanese, d'Acierno, Moscato, Persia & Picariello, 2010). An important limitation of collaborative filtering systems is the cold start problem, that describes situations in which a recommender is unable to provide meaningful recommendations due to an initial lack of ratings. On the other side, many practical applications where data are collected from external systems require to deal with data quality and cleaning techniques, to avoid the well-known garbage-in, garbage-out effect, see, e.g., (Mezzanzanica, Boselli, Cesarini & Mercorio, 2012, 2013, 2015).

Content-based filtering and collaborative filtering are then manually or automatically combined in the so called hybrid approaches (Kantor, 2015) that help to overcome some limitations of each method. Different ways to combine collaborative and content-based methods into a hybrid recommender system can be classified as follows: (1) implementing collaborative and content-based methods separately and combining their predictions; (2) incorporating some content-based characteristics into a collaborative approach; (3) incorporating some collaborative characteristics into a content-based approach; (4) constructing a general unifying model that incorporates both content-based and collaborative characteristics.

Eventually, a recommendation strategy should be able to provide users with relevant information depending on the context (Ricci, Lior & Bracha, 2015), (Bartolini, Moscato, Pensa, Penta, Picariello, Sansone & Sapino, 2016), (Song, Tekin & van der Schaar, 2016) (i.e. user location, observed items, etc.) as in Context Aware Recommender Systems. In the Contextual Pre-filtering techniques context information is used to initially select the set of relevant items, while a classic recommender is used to predict ratings. In Contextual Post-filtering approaches context is used in the last step of the recommending process to contextualize the output of a traditional recommender.

Finally, a category of recommender systems, named Large Scale Recommender Systems (Song, Tekin & van der Schaar, 2016), calls for new capabilities of such applications to deal with very large amount of data with respect to scalability and efficiency issues. More recently, all the above discussed strategies have been extended to multimedia realm (e.g. multimedia repositories, digital libraries, multimedia sharing system, etc.) with the aim of considering in the more effective way the multimedia content of recommended objects, both in terms of low-level and high-level characteristics (i.e. multimedia features and semantics) in the recommendation process together with user's social behavior and preferences (Albanese, d'Acierno, Moscato, Persia & Picariello), (Bartolini, Moscato, Pensa, Penta, Picariello, Sansone & Sapino, 2016). From an other hand, recommendation techniques have been extended to provide useful recommendations for groups of users, and not only for the single ones (Kompan & Bielikova 2014), (Zhang, 2016).

Performance of classical recommender systems is strictly related to the availability and quality of user profiles and ratings: the density of the available ratings in commercial systems is often less than 1% and the proliferation of fake users can arise malicious ratings. An important improvement for traditional recommender systems to overcome such problems lies in the possibility to embed social elements into a recommendation strategy (Zhou, Xu, Li, Josang & Cox, 2012), (Zhao, McAuley & King, 2014). In fact, the great increase of user-generated content in social networks, such as product reviews, tags, forum discussions and blogs, has been followed by a bunch of valuable user opinions, perspectives or tastes towards items or other users, that are useful to build enhanced user profiles. In such a context, customer opinion summarization and sentiment analysis (Ding, Liu & Yu, 2008) techniques represent effective augmentations to traditional recommendation strategy, for example by not recommending items that receive a lot of negative feedbacks (Dong, O'Mahony, Schaal, McCarthy & Smyth 2013, (Zhou, Xu, Li, Josang & Cox, 2012).

In the context of recommendation in the Online Social Networks, a lot of proposals have been presented in the last years (Cui, Sun, Fu, Lu & Zhang, 2017), (Park, Kim, Oh & Yu, 2016) and interesting surveys are available (Stan, Muhlenbach & Largeron, 2014), (Zhou, Xu, Li, Josang & Cox, 2012). In particular, social recommender applications can profitably exploit the large amount of heterogeneous information extracted by one or more social networks and the different kinds of relationships among social entities to improve the accuracy of traditional recommendation approaches and provide new types of suggestions. As an example, they can recommend not only items but also groups, friends, events, tags, etc. to users, using particular algorithms (Pham, Li, Cong & Zhang, 2015), (Jiang, Cui, Chen, Wang, Zhu & Yang, 2015), (Pham, Li, Cong & Zhang, 2016).

As it will be evident later in the article, our approach can be classified as a hybrid user-centred strategy for a social network that incorporates some content-based characteristics into a collaborative strategy. On one side, it exploits logs from heterogeneous social networks to implicitly derive information about individual users and the community of users as a whole, considering their past browsing sessions as a sort of unary ratings. On the other side, user profiles in terms of item features are exploited to perform a first data filtering. Similarly, to some collaborative filtering techniques, it is a kind of active filtering strategy in which past browsing sessions, modelled as a directed graph, determine the most suitable items to be recommended. In according to other collaborative approaches, transitive relationships among items are considered in computing the importance of an object. Similarly, to some content based approaches, our approach gives high importance to the characteristics of the object a user is currently watching, in order to effectively compute the utility of other items. Finally, we assume the existence of a priori knowledge about metadata values and their relationships and consider both low and high-level information together with social elements as opinions and ratings, such that they contribute to determine the utility of an object in the recommendation process.

3. THE RECOMMENDATION FRAMEWORK

To support users while they browse a particular social media collection, we propose a recommender system working in according to the following stages:

1. In the pre-filtering stage, user actual needs and preferences led to define a set of useful candidate items;
2. In the ranking stage, a rank is assigned to candidate items according to their intrinsic features, to past users behaviours, and to other information that is possible to extract from online social networks, such as users' opinions and feedbacks;
3. In the post-filtering stage, context information is opportunely used to identify the final list of the most suitable items.
4. In the presentation stage other constraints are taking into account to manage specific "groups" of objects.

Figure 1. Components of Recommender Systems

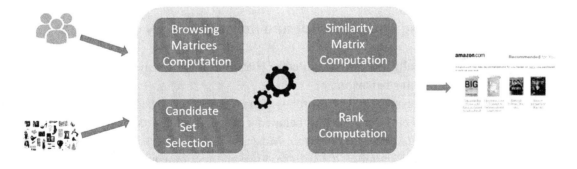

The proposed idea takes its roots from our previous works, where the user behaviour was only the simple access to a single multimedia item (Colace, De Santo, Greco, Moscato & Picariello, 2015), (Albanese, d'Acierno, Moscato, Persia & Picariello, 2013). Here, we have extended our approach taking into account all the possible user-to-content relationships occurring in a social network, and considering different multimedia data to be recommended (i.e. texts, images, videos, audio) related to specific social items (e.g. tweet, post, photo, etc. shared in a given social network).

To properly manage all the multimedia contents to be recommended, we describe items at two different levels: at "high level" perspective a set of symbolic features, such as tags, keywords and other metadata, can depend on the particular social network, while at the "low level" perspective we have a set of content based features, different for each kind of multimedia object and indipendent on the particular social network.

In the following, we are detailing all the described stages.

3.1. Pre-filtering Stage using user preferences

In this stage, a subset $O_h^c \subset O$, containing good "candidates" to be recommended, is selected for matching some (static) user preferences and (dynamic) needs. Different and heterogeneous feature spaces can be used to represent each item. For instance, a photo may be described by a set of metadata as title, set of tags, description, etc.

A clustering approach based on all or subsets of the different spaces of features is used to identify "similar" items.

In particular, the problem of hetereogeneous data filtering, due to the representation of a user as a set of vectors in the same features space describing the items, has been address through the high-order star-structured co-clustering techniques (Ienco, Robardet, Pensa & Meo, 2013), (Bartolini, Moscato, Pensa, Penta, Picariello, Sansone & Sapino, 2016). In this context, the same set of items is represented in different feature spaces. Such data represent items of a certain type, connected to other types of data, the features, so that the overall data schema forms a star structure of inter-relationships.

The co-clustering task consists in clustering simultaneously the set of items and the set of values in the different feature spaces. In this way we obtain a partition of the items influenced by each of the feature spaces and at the same time a partition of each feature space. The prefiltering leverages the clustering results to select a set of items by using the user's profile, which is modeled as sets of descriptors in the same spaces as the items' descriptors. In particualr, we exploit the cosine distance of the user vectors with the centroids of each item clusters.

3.2. Ranking Stage using user behavior and items similarity

This stage allows to automatically rank the set of items O based on their features (used to define a similarity notion) and users' browsing behaviors.

In particular, our idea, based on the approach proposed in previous works, has as main aim to combine low and high-level feature of items, possible past behaviors of individual users and overall behavior of the whole user "community" (Albanese, d'Acierno, Moscato, Persia & Picariello, 2010), (Albanese, d'Acierno, Moscato, Persia & Picariello, 2013) to improve the recommendation process during the browsing of multimedia collections.

In our model we consider a finite set of Action Symbols (S) coding all the possible "interactions" among the set of Users (U) and the set of Objects (O) in one or more social media networks, which can

Table 1. User-to-Content relationships in Online Social Networks

	Twitter	Facebook	Instagram	Google+	Last.FM	Flickr
Publishing	X	X	X	X	X	X
Tagging	X	X	X	X	X	X
Comment	X	X	X	X	X	X
Like	X	X	X	X		X
Resharing	X	X		X		
Favorites	X				X	X
Visualization		X	X		X	X

be properly captured during several browsing sessions exploiting log information (Sang, Deng, Lu & Xu, 2015), (Guo, Zhang & Yorke-Smith, 2016).

In such a context, we can consider different examples of actions: namely, users' reactions or comments to published contents (e.g., a post or photo), user visualization or rating of a given content, and so on. The following Table schematizes the available user-to-content relationships in the most diffused social networks.

We are now in state to introduce the following definitions.

Definition 3.1 (Log tuple) A log tuple can be defined by the information $l = (s, u, o, \lambda_1, \ldots, \lambda_k)$, where $s \in S$, $u \in U$, $o \in O$ and $\lambda_1, \ldots, \lambda_k$, are particular attributes (e.g., timestamp, type of reaction, text and tags of a comment, etc.) used to describe a particular action.

Definition 3.2 (Log) A Log (L) is a finite sequence of log tuples.

Intuitively, a log tuple corresponds to an observation of l_s performed by the user l_u on a given object l_o along with the associated attributes of the observation $\lambda_1, \ldots, \lambda_k$. By convention, if action a_2 occurs after a_1 in a log, then the action a_2 occurred temporally after a_1.

Starting from a log, it is possible to model interactions among users and the generated multimedia contents in social media networks as a particular labeled graph as in the following definition.

Definition 3.3 (User-Content Social Graph) We define a User-Content Social Graph as a couple (G, γ), where: $G = (O, E)$ is a directed graph; $\gamma: E \rightarrow \{pattern, sim\} \times R+$ is a labeling function that associates each edge in $E \subseteq O \times O$ with a pair (t, w), t being the type of the edge which can assume two enumerative values (pattern and similarity) and w is the weight of the edge.

In the User Content Social Graph, it is possible to define two types of labeling function: the first one introduces a pattern label for an edge (o_j, o_i) and allows to assign a weight w_j^i representing the number of times that o_i was accessed immediately after o_j, while the second one assigns a similarity label and establishes a link from o_j to o_i representing the "similarity" between these two items.

A user-content social graph can be local if it is related to a given user; global if it concerns an entire social community. Roughly speaking, our basic idea is to assume that when an item o_i is chosen after an item o_j in the same user browsing session, this event means that o_i "is voting" for o_j. Similarly, the fact that an item o_i is "very similar" in terms of some intrinsic features to o_j can also be interpreted as o_j "recommending" o_i (and viceversa).

Leveraging log information in the graph building process, we have to choose for each kind of social media network:

- The list of "consecutive" actions in the log with the related attributes that can instantiate an edge, as an example:
    - A user visualized/published two objects in consecutive temporal instants of the same browsing session;
    - A user provided two positive reactions or comments to two different objective in successive times of the same browsing session;
    - A user marked two objects as "favourite" in consecutive temporal instants of the same browsing session;
    - Etc.

The particular attributes (e.g. tags, keywords or other relevant information extracted from an annotation text) describing user actions on different objects that can be used in the similarity computation together with high-level and low-level features of multimedia contents. In particular, two types of low-level features can be considered for images in our approach: global (es. ACC, CEDD) and local (SURF,SIFT etc.).

Figure 2 describes an example of log and the related global user-content social graph. As it is possible to note in the provided example, the nodes' set corresponds to the four images contained in the log while each edge, as described above, has two types of weights; for example "sunset4" image has a similarity value of 0.6 with "sunset2" image and is visited always after the "sunset2".

On the basis of the user-content social graph, each object can be opportunely ranked. In particular, a recommendation grade is computed for each item.

Definition 3.4 (Recommendation Grade) Given an item $o_i \in O$, its recommendation grade is defined as follows:

$$\rho(o_i) = \sum_{o_j \in P_G(o_i)} \hat{w}_{ij} \cdot \rho(o_j)$$

where $P_G(o_j) = \{o_j \in O | (o_j, o_i) \in E\}$ is the set of predecessors of o_i in G, and $\hat{w}_{ij}$ is the normalized weight of the edge from o_j to o_i. We note that for each $o_j \in O \sum_{o_i \in S_G(o_j)} \hat{w}_{ij} = 1$ must hold, where $S_G(o_j) = \{o_i \in O | (o_j, o_i) \in E\}$ is the set of successors of o_j in G.

In (Albanese, d'Acierno, Moscato, Persia & Picariello, 2010), it has been shown that the ranking vector $R = [\rho(o_1) \dots \rho(o_n)]^T$ of all the items can be computed as the solution to the equation $R = C \cdot R$, where $C = \{\hat{w}_{ij}\}$ is an ad-hoc matrix that defines how the importance of each item is transferred to other items.

The above matrix can be seen as a combination of:

- A local browsing matrix $A_h = \{a_{ij}^h\}$ for each user u_h, where its generic element a_{ij}^l is defined as the ratio of the number of times item o_i has been chosen by user u_h immediately after o_j to the number of times any item in O has been chosen by u_h immediately after o_j;

- A global browsing matrix $A=\{a_{ij}\}$, where its generic element a_{ij} is defined as the ratio of the number of times item o_i has been chosen by any user immediately after o_j to the number of times any item in O has been chosen immediately after o_j;

- A similarity matrix $B=\{b_{ij}\}$ such that b_{ij} denotes the similarity between two items o_i and o_j (in the next subsection we are providing more details).

Figure 2. Log with the related User-Content Social Graph

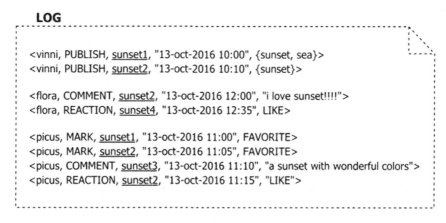

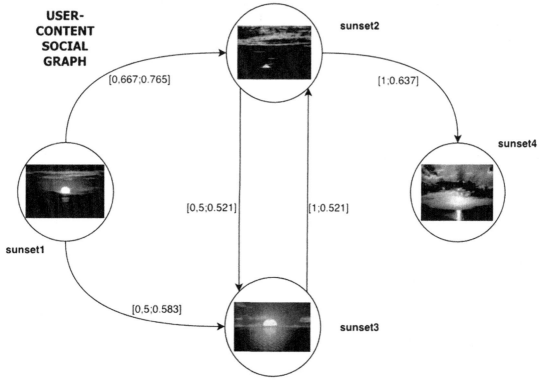

A customized ranking for each individual user is computed as next step using the equation $R_h = C \cdot R_h$, where R_h is the vector of preference grades, customized for a user u_h considering only items in the related O_h^c. To solve this equation we used the Power Method algorithm because it has been proved in (Albanese, d'Acierno, Moscato, Persia & Picariello, 2013) that C, under certain assumptions and transformations, is a real square matrix having positive elements, with a unique largest real eigenvalue and the corresponding eigenvector has strictly positive components.

Rank can be finally refined using user attached sentiments and ratings (popularity) using the strategy that some of the authors proposed in (Colace, De Santo, Greco, Moscato & Picariello, 2015).

Concerning the items' similarity (Liu, Zhang, Lu & Ma, 2007), it has been computed taking into account:

- A semantic relatedness (Amato, De Santo, Moscato, Persia, Picariello & Poccia, 2015), (Amato, Mazzeo, Moscato, & Picariello, 2013) based on a set of available ontologies, taxonomies and vocabularies using some high-level features values (i.e. ontological attributes (Lekakos & Caravelas, 2008) combined with a "tag-based" similarity;
- A low-level features comparison [1]using several multimedia descriptors (Bartolini & Patella, 2015).

3.3. Post-Filtering Stage using context information

The next step has the aim to generate the final set of "real" candidates for recommendation using context information. We have decided to represent the context by means of the well-known key-value model (Strang & Linnhoff-Popien, 2004) using as dimensions some of the different feature spaces related to items.

Several ways can be used to describe the context features in the proposed system: directly identifying some target items, that for instance have positively captured user's attention, or indirectly specifying a set of constraints that recommended items have to satisfy.

Formally, it is possible to define the set of candidate recommendations with respect to the user u_h interested in the target item o_j as follows:

$$O_{h,j}^f = \bigcup_{k=1}^{M} \{o_i \in O_h^c | a_{ij}^k > 0\} \cup \{o_i \in NNQ(o_j, O_h^c)\}$$

As it is easy to note in equation (2), this set is composed by two components: the first one considers items that have been access by at least one user within k steps from o_j, with k between 1 and M, and the second one is based on the results of a Nearest Neighbor Query $\left(NNQ\left(o_j, O_h^c\right)\right)$ functionality to identify items that are most similar to o_j. The final set O_h^f is chosen using the ranking vector R_h, and removing all the items that do not respect possible context constraints for each user.

Eventually, depending on applications, recommended items can be arranged into groups (Colace, De Santo, Greco, Moscato & Picariello, 2015).

3.4. Implementation details

We designed and implemented a first prototype for the recommender system that builds and manages different multimedia collections, providing the basic facilities for querying and recommendation, exploitng data from several social media network repositories.

The system was realized on the top of the Apache Spark framework based on the Hadoop technological stack to deal with Big Data issues. More in details, the log files and multimedia raw data are stored on HDFS while user and object descriptions are managed by Cassandra. In turn, linguistic resources are managed by the AllegroGraph triplestore.

Co-clustering, ranking and post-filtering techniques were implemented on top of the Spark machine learning and graph analysis libraries and leveraging SPARK SQL facilities; multimedia similarities were computed using Windsurf library (Bartolini & Patella, 2015). Wrapping functionalities (to extract data from social repositories) were implemented using DataRiver[2] solution (based on the MOMIS system) and leveraging Social Harvest[3] facilities.

In addition, the system provides some REST APIs that can be dynamically invoked by the social network applications to suggest a set of items that can be of interest for a particular user browsing multimedia collections.

4. EXPERIMENTAL RESULTS

Recommender Systems are very complex applications and their evaluation is a challenging task, in addition, results are hardly generalizable as reported in the literature (Adomavicius & Zhang, 2012).

Recommender system evaluation uses in the majority of cases accuracy and stability of predictions (Adomavicius & Zhang, 2012). More recently, user satisfaction has been considered as additional criterion that has to be correlated with the overall recommender's accuracy. Moreover, characterizing and evaluating the quality of a user's experience and subjective attitude toward the acceptance of recommender technology is an important issue (Albanese, d'Acierno, Moscato, Persia & Picariello, 2013).

In this paper, we report several experimental results aiming at evaluating the effectiveness of the introduced ranking method (Social Ranking, SR) with respect to a human ground truth.

We used a subset of the Yahoo Flickr Creative Commons 100 Million Data (YFCC100M)[4] multimedia collection, provided by Yahoo in 2014. In particular, we exploited users' social interactions (friendships, tags, publishing, comments, favorites) with the related multimedia data (images retrieved using Flickr API[5] about animal, landscape and nature domains) to build our user-content graph[6].

In order to evaluate the performance of the proposed algorithm, we defined a human-generated ranking (representing the unique gold standard), asking a group of about 20 students to rank the results of different queries with respect to the relevance of the retrieved images, in terms of topics and multimedia content. We have used two classes of ranking methods, namely Popularity (PR) (Steck, 2011) - based on popularity of images computed by a linear combination of number of favorites, comments and likes - and Collaborative (CR) (Resnick & Varian, 1997) - based on the user feedbacks and interactions among users.

Table 2 shows the results of ranking comparison using the Kendall's Tau (τ) and Spearman's Rank Correlation (ρ) coefficients obtained by comparing in pairs the following methods: Social Ranking (SR), Human Ranking (HR), Popularity Ranking (PR) and Collaborative Ranking (CR).

Table 2. Ranking comparison (Social Ranking (SR), Human Ranking (HR), Popularity Ranking (PR) and Collaborative Ranking (CR))

	τ	ρ
SR - HR	0,80	0,91
PR - HR	0,64	0,71
CR - HR	0,78	0,88
SR - PR	0,61	0,67
SR - CR	0,78	0,85
PR - CR	0,63	0,88

Table 3. Ranking comparison (Social Ranking (SR), Automatic Ranking (AR), Popularity Ranking (PR) and Collaborative Ranking (CR))

	τ	ρ
SR - AR	0,70	0,76
PR - AR	0,54	0,61
CR - AR	0,63	0,68
SR - PR	0,53	0,62
SR - CR	0,65	0,71
PR - CR	0,59	0,66

One might note that our ranking - that considers both popularity and collaborative aspects - presents the most similar behavior with respect to the human ground truth.

Moreover, we provide in the Table 3 the evaluation obtained considering as ground truth - Automatic Ranking (AR) - that generated by ranking Flickr photos on the basis of their average number of visualizations, comments and favorites.

5. CONCLUSION AND FUTURE WORKS

In this paper we proposed a novel collaborative and user-centered approach exploiting the interactions among users and generated contents in one or more social media networks. The proposed approach can be easily adapted to several kinds of multimedia objects, ranging from text and images to audio and video. Moreover, experiments on ranking effectiveness show how our approach provides promising and interesting results.

Future works will be devoted to exploit our ranking approach for effectively supporting multimedia recommendation in heterogeneous social media networks, providing more detailed experimental results and a comparison with the most diffused approaches for social recommendation with respect to different datasets. In addition, we are planning to verify as our approach can reflect human behavior, which is often influenced by the choices of the majority of the most influential people.

REFERENCES

Adomavicius, G., Sankaranarayanan, R., Sen, S., & Tuzhilin, A. (2005). Incorporating contextual information in recommender systems using a multidimensional approach. *ACM Transactions on Information Systems*, *23*(1), 103–145. doi:10.1145/1055709.1055714

Adomavicius, G., & Zhang, J. (2012). Stability of recommendation algorithms. *ACM Transactions on Information Systems*, *30*(4), 23. doi:10.1145/2382438.2382442

Albanese, M., Chianese, A., d'Acierno, A., Moscato, V., & Picariello, A. (2010). A multimedia recommender integrating object features and user behavior. *Multimedia Tools and Applications*, *50*(3), 563–585. doi:10.100711042-010-0480-8

Albanese, M., d'Acierno, A., Moscato, V., Persia, F., & Picariello, A. (2010, September). Modeling recommendation as a social choice problem. In *Proceedings of the fourth ACM conference on Recommender systems* (pp. 329-332). ACM. 10.1145/1864708.1864779

Albanese, M., d'Acierno, A., Moscato, V., Persia, F., & Picariello, A. (2011, September). A multimedia semantic recommender system for cultural heritage applications. In *Proceedings of the 2011 Fifth IEEE International Conference on Semantic Computing (ICSC)* (pp. 403-410). IEEE. 10.1109/ICSC.2011.47

Albanese, M., d'Acierno, A., Moscato, V., Persia, F., & Picariello, A. (2013). A multimedia recommender system. *ACM Transactions on Internet Technology*, *13*(1). doi:. doi:10.1145/2532640

Amato, F., De Santo, A., Moscato, V., Persia, F., Picariello, A., & Poccia, S. R. (2015, February). Partitioning of ontologies driven by a structure-based approach. In *Proceedings of the 2015 IEEE International Conference on Semantic Computing (ICSC)* (pp. 320-323). IEEE. 10.1109/ICOSC.2015.7050827

Amato, F., Mazzeo, A., Moscato, V., & Picariello, A. (2013, March). A framework for semantic interoperability over the cloud. In *Proceedings of the 2013 27th International Conference on Advanced Information Networking and Applications Workshops (WAINA)* (pp. 1259-1264). IEEE. 10.1109/WAINA.2013.218

Amato, F., Moscato, V., Picariello, A., & Sperlí, G. (2017, April). Recommendation in Social Media Networks. In *Proceedings of the 2017 IEEE Third International Conference on Multimedia Big Data (BigMM)* (pp. 213-216). IEEE. 10.1109/BigMM.2017.55

Amato, F., Moscato, V., Picariello, A., & Sperlí, G. (2017, June). A Recommender System for Multimedia Art Collections. In *Proceedings of the International Conference on Intelligent Interactive Multimedia Systems and Services* (pp. 200-209). Springer.

Bartolini, I., Moscato, V., Pensa, R. G., Penta, A., Picariello, A., Sansone, C., & Sapino, M. L. (2016). Recommending multimedia visiting paths in cultural heritage applications. *Multimedia Tools and Applications*, *75*(7), 3813–3842. doi:10.100711042-014-2062-7

Bartolini, I., & Patella, M. (2015). Multimedia queries in digital libraries. In *Data Management in Pervasive Systems* (pp. 311–325). Springer International Publishing. doi:10.1007/978-3-319-20062-0_15

Colace, F., De Santo, M., Greco, L., Moscato, V., & Picariello, A. (2015). A collaborative user-centered framework for recommending items in Online Social Networks. *Computers in Human Behavior*, *51*, 694–704. doi:10.1016/j.chb.2014.12.011

Cui, L., Sun, L., Fu, X., Lu, N., & Zhang, G. (2017). Exploring a trust based recommendation approach for videos in online social network. *Journal of Signal Processing Systems for Signal, Image, and Video Technology*, *86*(2-3), 207–219. doi:10.100711265-016-1116-7

Ding, X., Liu, B., & Yu, P. S. (2008, February). A holistic lexicon-based approach to opinion mining. In *Proceedings of the 2008 international conference on web search and data mining* (pp. 231-240). ACM. 10.1145/1341531.1341561

Dong, R., O'Mahony, M. P., Schaal, M., McCarthy, K., & Smyth, B. (2013, October). Sentimental product recommendation. In *Proceedings of the 7th ACM conference on Recommender systems* (pp. 411-414). ACM. 10.1145/2507157.2507199

Guo, G., Zhang, J., & Yorke-Smith, N. (2016). A novel recommendation model regularized with user trust and item ratings. *IEEE Transactions on Knowledge and Data Engineering, 28*(7), 1607–1620. doi:10.1109/TKDE.2016.2528249

He, C., Parra, D., & Verbert, K. (2016). Interactive recommender systems: A survey of the state of the art and future research challenges and opportunities. *Expert Systems with Applications, 56*, 9–27. doi:10.1016/j.eswa.2016.02.013

Ienco, D., Robardet, C., Pensa, R. G., & Meo, R. (2013). Parameter-less co-clustering for star-structured heterogeneous data. *Data Mining and Knowledge Discovery*.

Jiang, M., Cui, P., Chen, X., Wang, F., Zhu, W., & Yang, S. (2015). Social recommendation with cross-domain transferable knowledge. *IEEE Transactions on Knowledge and Data Engineering, 27*(11), 3084–3097. doi:10.1109/TKDE.2015.2432811

Kabassi, K. (2013). Personalisation systems for cultural tourism. In *Multimedia services in intelligent environments* (pp. 101–111). Springer International Publishing. doi:10.1007/978-3-319-00375-7_7

Kantor, P. B. (2015). *Recommender systems handbook* (F. Ricci, L. Rokach, & B. Shapira, Eds.). Berlin, Germany: Springer.

Kazienko, P., & Kolodziejski, P. (2006). Personalized Integration of Recommendation Methods for E-commerce. *IJCSA, 3*(3), 12–26.

Kompan, M., & Bielikova, M. (2014). Group recommendations: Survey and perspectives. *Computer Information, 33*(2), 446–476.

Lekakos, G., & Caravelas, P. (2008). A hybrid approach for movie recommendation. *Multimedia Tools and Applications, 36*(1), 55–70. doi:10.100711042-006-0082-7

Liu, Y., Zhang, D., Lu, G., & Ma, W. Y. (2007). A survey of content-based image retrieval with high-level semantics. *Pattern Recognition, 40*(1), 262–282. doi:10.1016/j.patcog.2006.04.045

Mezzanzanica, M., Boselli, R., Cesarini, M., & Mercorio, F. (2012). Data quality sensitivity analysis on aggregate indicators. In *Proceedings of the International Conference on Data Technologies and Applications (DATA) 25/27 July* (pp. 97-108). SciTePress.

Mezzanzanica, M., Boselli, R., Cesarini, M., & Mercorio, F. (2013). Automatic synthesis of data cleansing activities. In *Proceedings of the International Conference on Data Management Technologies and Applications (DATA)* (Vol. 2, pp. 138-149).

Mezzanzanica, M., Boselli, R., Cesarini, M., & Mercorio, F. (2015). A model-based approach for developing data cleansing solutions. *Journal of Data and Information Quality, 5*(4). doi:10.1145/2641575

Park, C., Kim, D., Oh, J., & Yu, H. (2016, April). TRecSo: Enhancing Top-k Recommendation With Social Information. In *Proceedings of the 25th International Conference Companion on World Wide Web* (pp. 89-90). International World Wide Web Conferences Steering Committee. 10.1145/2872518.2889362

Pazzani, M. J., & Billsus, D. (2007). Content-based recommendation systems. In *The adaptive web* (pp. 325–341). Berlin: Springer. doi:10.1007/978-3-540-72079-9_10

Pham, T. A. N., Li, X., Cong, G., & Zhang, Z. (2015, April). A general graph-based model for recommendation in event-based social networks. In *Proceedings of the 2015 IEEE 31st International Conference on Data Engineering (ICDE)* (pp. 567-578). IEEE. 10.1109/ICDE.2015.7113315

Pham, T. A. N., Li, X., Cong, G., & Zhang, Z. (2016). A general recommendation model for heterogeneous networks. *IEEE Transactions on Knowledge and Data Engineering, 28*(12), 3140–3153. doi:10.1109/TKDE.2016.2601091

Resnick, P., & Varian, H. R. (1997). Recommender systems. *Communications of the ACM, 40*(3), 56–58. doi:10.1145/245108.245121

Ricci, F., Rokach, L., & Shapira, B. (2015). Introduction to recommender systems handbook. In *Recommender systems handbook* (pp. 191–226). Springer. doi:10.1007/978-1-4899-7637-6_1

Sang, J., Deng, Z., Lu, D., & Xu, C. (2015). Cross-OSN user modeling by homogeneous behavior quantification and local social regularization. *IEEE Transactions on Multimedia, 17*(12), 2259–2270. doi:10.1109/TMM.2015.2486524

Song, L., Tekin, C., & van der Schaar, M. (2016). Online learning in large-scale contextual recommender systems. *IEEE Transactions on Services Computing, 9*(3), 433–445. doi:10.1109/TSC.2014.2365795

Stan, J., Muhlenbach, F., & Largeron, C. (2014). Recommender systems using social network analysis: Challenges and future trends. In *Encyclopedia of Social Network Analysis and Mining* (pp. 1522–1532). Springer New York. doi:10.1007/978-1-4614-6170-8_35

Steck, H. (2011, October). Item popularity and recommendation accuracy. In *Proceedings of the fifth ACM conference on Recommender systems* (pp. 125-132). ACM. 10.1145/2043932.2043957

Strang, T., & Linnhoff-Popien, C. (2004, September). A context modeling survey.

Su, X., & Khoshgoftaar, T. M. (2009). A survey of collaborative filtering techniques. *Advances in Artificial Intelligence*. doi:10.1155/2009/421425

Yoshii, K., Goto, M., Komatani, K., Ogata, T., & Okuno, H. G. (2008). An efficient hybrid music recommender system using an incrementally trainable probabilistic generative model. *IEEE Transactions on Audio, Speech, and Language Processing, 16*(2), 435–447. doi:10.1109/TASL.2007.911503

Zhang, Y. (2016). GroRec: A group-centric intelligent recommender system integrating social, mobile and big data technologies. *IEEE Transactions on Services Computing, 9*(5), 786–795. doi:10.1109/TSC.2016.2592520

Zhao, T., McAuley, J., & King, I. (2014, November). Leveraging social connections to improve personalized ranking for collaborative filtering. In *Proceedings of the 23rd ACM International Conference on Conference on Information and Knowledge Management* (pp. 261-270). ACM. 10.1145/2661829.2661998

Zhou, X., Xu, Y., Li, Y., Josang, A., & Cox, C. (2012). The state-of-the-art in personalized recommender systems for social networking. *Artificial Intelligence Review, 37*(2), 119–132. doi:10.100710462-011-9222-1

ENDNOTES

[1]   The low-level similarity is computed only for multimedia items of the same type.
[2]   http://www.datariver.it/it/
[3]   http://www.socialharvest.io/
[4]   https://webscope.sandbox.yahoo.com
[5]   https://www.flickr.com/services/api
[6]   An edge is created when a user visualized/published two objects in consecutive temporal instants of the same browsing session, or when she/he marked two objects as "favorite" in consecutive temporal instants of the same browsing session.

This research was previously published in the International Journal of Multimedia Data Engineering and Management (IJM-DEM), 9(1); pages 36-50, copyright year 2018 by IGI Publishing (an imprint of IGI Global).

Chapter 29
A Status Property Classifier of Social Media User's Personality for Customer–Oriented Intelligent Marketing Systems:
Intelligent–Based Marketing Activities

Tsung-Yi Chen
Nanhua University, Chiayi County, Taiwan

Yuh-Min Chen
National Cheng Kung University, Tainan City, Taiwan

Meng-Che Tsai
National Cheng Kung University, Tainan City, Taiwan

ABSTRACT

Enterprises need to obtain information about not only specific customer preferences, but also, more importantly, customers' psychological characteristics that significantly influence their consumption behaviors and response to intelligent-based marketing activities. If enterprises want to implement more precise intelligent selling activities for customers, customers' personality information will serve as a highly valued reference. The automatic detection method proposed in this study is based on techniques such as text semantic mining and machine learning to conduct personality type prediction on the target by collecting and analyzing the target's social media data. In the test, 5,858 statuses were obtained, 815 of which were labeled, with 122 effective tags. In general, when n = 5, the labeling rate can reach 60-80%. The status property classifier (SPC) proposed in this study can predict the personality type (PT) of the user publishing the status set with a high degree of accuracy by conducting text semantic mining on the status set.

DOI: 10.4018/978-1-7998-9020-1.ch029

1. INTRODUCTION

The business purpose of enterprises is to gain profits by creating customers (Drucker, 1995). As a natural result, enterprises must carry out marketing activities to attract customers to consume products or services. Conventionally, non-personalized marketing techniques such as radio advertisements, TV commercials, flyers, and web banners have been frequently used by enterprises to promote their products and services. However, customer-oriented marketing techniques are gradually attracting attention in recent years. In business intelligence (BI), customer-oriented marketing emphasizes the necessity of obtaining information about customers before marketing, so as to dynamically adapt to customer demands. The results from the research conducted by Park and Holloway (2003) indicate that customer-oriented adaptive selling behavior can indeed promote product sales.

An intelligent-based enterprise needs to obtain information about specific customer preferences, and more importantly, about customers' psychological characteristics. The collected customer information has a significant influence on their consumption behaviors and response to marketing activities. Therefore, effective communication strategies will influence customers' attitudes and behaviors (Knapp & Daly, 2002). The relationship between psychological characteristics, also known as personality traits, and communication strategies is that personality dominates interactive behaviors and communication methods between individuals, indicating that individuals with different personality traits tend to use different approaches to communicate. Therefore, if enterprises want to implement more precise adaptive selling activities for customers, customers' personality information will serve as a highly valued reference.

Different personality models have their own assessment scales. In order to obtain the personality type of a testee, it is inevitable to conduct a questionnaire test or experts' practical observation of the testee's behavioral interaction with other people, in order to analyze his/her test responses or behavioral recordings further, and thereby infer the testee's classification result. If enterprises attempt to gain customers' personality information, they must perform tests or observations on numerous customers. This definitely requires time, human resources, and is cost intensive, which is apparently not a cost-effective investment when compared to the benefits that can be obtained from adaptive selling. However, from the perspective of an intelligent-based enterprise, collecting customers' personality information without any trace and conducting targeted selling will be the most optimal situation. Therefore, we can come to the conclusion that a new evaluation technique that can perform automatic personality prediction on a great number of objects without any trace will be able to meet enterprises' requirement with respect to adaptive selling.

However, it is not easy to predict the target's personality traits, especially when the target is a customer whom we have never met. Fortunately, various booming online social media in recent years may provide opportunities for solving this difficulty. Nowadays, a great many people expose their personal information and interact with others through various popular social media sites such as Facebook and Twitter (Golbeck et al., 2011). Especially on Facebook, the world's premier social media site in terms of the number of users (Wikipedia, 2015; Stieglitz et al., 2018), the online social behaviors of users are particularly evident.

On these social media platforms, users are not likely to disclose their own personality traits in a direct fashion. However, both the behaviors of operating their own personal accounts and the digital records of interacting with others can be used as clues for inferring users' personality traits. Similar to the past observation of targets in the real world, the observation now is just transferring to the virtual world. Up to now, there have been a large number of research results showing that the characteristic of user information on social media is related to their scores in personality traits (Golbeck et al., 2011; Adali &

Golbeck, 2012; Adali et al., 2012; Bai et al., 2012; Moore & McElroy, 2012; Seidman, 2013; Ortigosa et al., 2014). Therefore, the use of the digital data collected from social media to automatically analyze and predict personality classifications of social media users, for subsequently establishing a personality information gathering tool, is considered as a method that can meet the needs and demands of enterprises.

Based on the discussions above, this study, from the perspective of enterprises' needs for adaptive selling, will develop a method capable of automatically predicting the personality traits of numerous testees. The objective is to overcome the limitation of high costs in traditional evaluation methods and subsequently assist enterprises in precise marketing activities for customers. This method will obtain and analyze the targets' social media data by automatic approaches, and then conduct personality type predictions. The currently most popular social network site – Facebook.com – is adopted as an example of social media in our research study. Compared to other similar social media sites, Facebook has a larger group of user members and stronger interactive functions, and a huge volume of data for each user, making it the optimal platform for automatic observation of target consumers.

Although, Chen et al. (2016) used the Naïve Bayes classification algorithm combined with a feature selection algorithm to predicting personality types, with 70–80% accuracy. The study by Chen et al. (2016) explored the behaviors of users (e.g. clicking "like," replying, sharing, etc.) by using an interaction feature classifier (IFC) method; the study designed hundreds of features related to user behavior, but did not analyze the statuses of users. However, the status property classifier (SPC) method proposed in the study used text semantic mining for obtaining the published statuses of users. The statuses refer to the users' posts on Facebook. The SPC method makes it possible to predict the personality types of the user by the published statuses.

This study also developed other personality classification methods to improve the chances of predicting users' personality traits when Facebook (FB) modifies its policies on data disclosure management. The method employed in this study involves reversely inferring Facebook users' personality traits according to the properties of status updates published by the users themselves. The automatic detection method proposed in this study is based on techniques such as text semantic mining and machine learning to conduct personality type prediction on the target by collecting and analyzing the target's social media data. We propose an automatic personality type prediction method that performs DISC (D = Dominant, I = Inducement, S = Submission, and C = Compliance)-based personality type (DISC PT) testing using Facebook users' data. Experimental results show that the innovative method (SPC) proposed in this study can predict the personality type of the user publishing the status set with a high degree of accuracy that can be further improved with the increase in the number of samples.

2. LITERATURE REVIEW

2.1 Social Media and Personality

Facebook is an online social networking platform created by Zuckerberg in 2004. Its user members have been increasing rapidly since its founding, and reached 1.55 billion by November 2015, significantly higher than other social media sites. One of Facebook's features is the functional diversity that enables users to freely manage their personal image and interact with their friends and strangers (Zhao et al., 2008; Nadkarni & Hofmann, 2012). The functions of managing users' own "Timeline", clicking "Like" and leaving "Comment" under the audio, video, and text content posted by other users, as well as creating "Pages" or building "Events", all help users more conveniently establish connections with others on the Internet.

With the popularity of smartphones and the release of more convenient Facebook apps, Facebook has further become a social tool that enables users to create a public profile and connect with other users (Gerson et al., 2016). The data on Facebook can be analyzed to gain insights into the issues, trends, and influential actors (Stieglitz et al., 2018). In this virtual and digital social networking environment, users' information concerning various behaviors and their time and places are recorded in detail, which is a type of very critical data that reflect users' behaviors. Facebook also provides an application-programming interface (API) for external developers to utilize the Facebook users' data with users' permissions for different applications or research purposes (Facebook Graph API, 2015).

Given the fact that these data can reflect users' behaviors, some researchers started to focus on the connection between users themselves and these operational behaviors, and they conducted cross-disciplinary studies in the field of psychology, e.g., the correction analysis between personality trait and business behavior (Golbeck et al., 2011; Moore & McElroy, 2012; Seidman, 2013; Lee et al., 2014; Ortigosa et al., 2014). The research results by Ortigosa et al. (2014) confirmed that it is feasible to estimate personality traits from the characteristics of interactive behavior.

Studies on the relationship between personality trait and Facebook management behavior often adopted the five-factor model (FFM) as the personality model. However, besides FFM, there are other personality models, which are commonly used, including the enneagram of personality, the Myers-Briggs type indicator (MBTI) and the DISC theory. There is a major difference between FFM and the other three models in the sense that the evaluation results of FFM are scores of five dimensions without clear classification. Enneagram of personality categorizes people into nine types, but is contentious due to the lack of legitimate psychological theories as the basis. MBTI, proposed by the Swiss psychologist Jung (1921), divides testees into sixteen types by performing dichotomization four times in four dimensions. DISC is a theory proposed by the American psychologist Marston (1928) in his work *Emotions of Normal People*. It classifies humans into four categories based on the distinct features of interactive behavior, namely, 1. Dominance, 2. Inducement, 3. Submission, and 4. Compliance.

Boyd (1994) suggested that DISC should be in a four-quadrant divided by a pair of mutually perpendicular axes, with vertical and horizontal axes standing for pace and priority, respectively. Individuals with fast pace are full of self-confidence, always striving for changes, such as D type and I type individuals. Conversely, those with slow pace are often reserved and conservative, such as S type and C type individuals. Task-oriented people tend to focus on the things to be done. They are usually fond of individual operations, are relatively cautious, and hide their personal emotions, with a kind of tendency that D type and C type individuals have. On the other hand, people-oriented individuals often pay more attention to relationships with others and are less likely to be restricted by the existing rules, as same as the behavioral characteristics of S type and I type individuals.

2.2 Crowdsourcing

Crowdsourcing, which has emerged in recent years, is a new model for solving problems and promoting production. Crowdsourcing is a collaborative way to enhance the capabilities and relationships for innovation (de Mattos et al., 2018). From a marketing perspective, crowdsourcing is also an innovative tool that enhances market information processing to improve market prediction, new products development, and testing (Lang et al., 2016; Gatautis & Vitkauskaite, 2014). It releases through the Internet some particular tasks that are expected to be voluntarily fulfilled by unspecified Internet users (Howe, 2006). Crowdsourcing usually involves tasks of a simple nature, which inevitably need and depend on human intelligence and can hardly be completed by current computer programs, e.g., labeling words, identifying classifications, and participating in online tests, etc. This working mode can be realized through a practical implementation of the crowdsourcing system. Doan, Ramakrishnan, and Halevy (2011) proposed an explicit definition of the crowdsourcing system: a system that requests assistance from a group of people to solve the problems defined by the system owner.

In some circumstances, the workers who finished the crowdsourcing tasks can be compensated with real money or only intangible fame and reputation. For example, Amazon Mechanical Turk (AMT) can get financial rewards for task-finishers; InnoCentive provides a platform where researchers and entrepreneurs can request assistance with promised rewards from elites all over the world who can help deal with their bottlenecks in research and development by using the method of crowdsourcing. However, this competitive or benefits-exchange model mentioned above is not the only way to implement crowdsourcing tasks. For instance, the *Open Political Donation Project*, initiated by the civil organization g0v of Taiwan in 2014, gathered Internet users' efforts to digitize all the scanned paper-based PDF copies of political donation documents in the Control Yuan in a short period of time, to meet the demand of information transparency from the public (g0v, 2014).

Crowdsourcing has become a promising paradigm for solving tasks via online crowds of people (Safran & Che, 2017). Solving problems by crowdsourcing saves costs and significantly shortens the task completion time. However, crowdsourcing also has some intrinsic defects, e.g., the inability to control task participants, their work quality, and their potential for malicious disruption.

3. STATUS PROPERTY CLASSIFIER FOR PERSONALITY PREDICTION

Based on the principle that individuals of various personality types possess different characteristics in terms of expressing themselves (Knapp & Daly, 2002), the proposed method in this study is expected to use the properties of statuses released by Facebook users to reversely infer their personality types. For the convenience of labeling in subsequent mechanisms, this study divides status properties into three categories, i.e., "subject," "objective," and "emotion." Each property category includes multiple "Instance Tags (IT)." For example, the "objective" category may include ITs of sharing and flaunting, while the "subject" category may contain ITs of politics and travelling, as shown in Figure 1.

Specific steps (Figure 2) for implementation of this classification method are described below:

- **Data collecting and labeling stage.** Collect sufficient training data of Facebook users' personality types and statuses. Seek personnel to label various ITs for the existing status in the database.
- **Training stage.** Calculate the term weight (TW) of each word in the status labeled in Stage (1) in the database on a regular basis. Higher word TW represents higher frequency of a word that appears in a Status labeled with this IT, which can be used as the proprietary word of this IT. Meanwhile, calculate the "IT weight" status of individuals with the same personality type, to obtain subject, objective, and emotion frequently included in the status published by people of the same personality type.
- **Application stage.** Extract the status posted by a Facebook user whose personality type is unknown, and analyze the words in his/her posted status to automatically label the appropriate IT for

each status posted by the user. After that, automatically place this user into the personality-type category he/she belongs to, based on his/her overall IT distribution.

- **Maintenance stage.** Automatically label a new user's status. In the next periodical calculation of weight, this user's status will affect the computational results as a whole.

Figure 1. Status property structure model

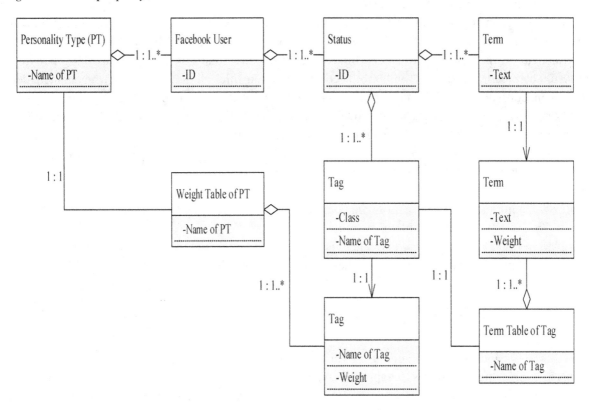

3.1 Crowdsourcing Haphazard Interactive Labeling

Background work of the SPC method can be roughly broken down into the labeling stage and the analysis stage. Crowdsourcing haphazard interactive labeling (CHIL) is a mechanism designed for the labeling stage, the working concept of which is briefly expressed in Figure 3. The significance of crowdsourcing is to complete the tasks using the collective wisdom of multiple people. Interactive labeling is the process of data labeling conducted by labelers (excluding data about themselves). Haphazard means that in the labeling process, any labeler can freely add new tags for labeling usage.

During the analysis stage, labeling can still be conducted in parallel. The labeled results yielded at the current point in time will enrich the reference database for the analysis work at a subsequent point in time. When the information is not sufficient in the database at the early stage, analysis work cannot be initiated until a certain volume of labeled data is accumulated in the database.

Figure 2. The schematic of the post property classification method

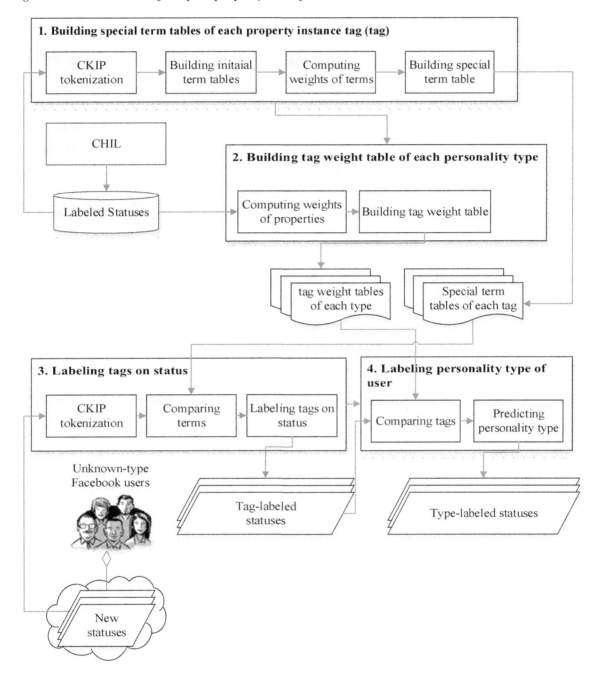

3.2 Mechanisms of Displaying Tags and Screening Labeled Statuses

This study implements the CHIL mechanism through the Internet, where voluntary labelers will be asked to participate in the labeling process. Therefore, extra consideration must be given to the operational usability of this mechanism. In light of this, Points (1) to (5) auxiliary mechanisms below are proposed to solve various problems that may occur in the labeling stage.

Figure 3. Conceptual schematic of the CHIL mechanism

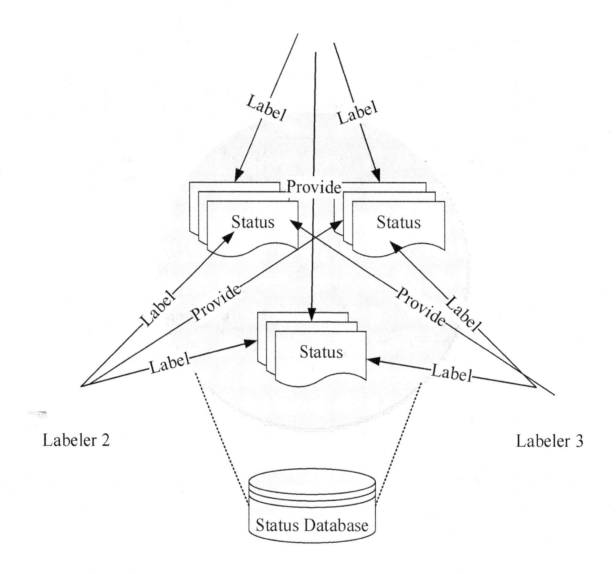

3.2.1 Tag Initialization

Observations on the early-stage implementation of the mechanism show that preset tags (if any) can more easily remind labelers of other more suitable tags. Therefore, in order to improve the efficiency of the mechanism in the early stage of operation, this study proposes a group of preset tags as "seed tags."

3.2.2 Tag Elimination

An excessively high degree of freedom in CHIL may lead to redundancy and divergence of tag items, and even potentially more inappropriate tags by a few labelers. Therefore, a mechanism is required to eliminate inapplicable tags for convergence of the tag options provided to the labelers. This study presets a "popularity" property for each tag as the basis to determine whether this tag can continuously serve as an optional tag. System administrators can set the tags whose popularities are higher than the threshold value, or only take the ones that are ranked in the first few places in terms of percentage points, and regard them as the options provided to labelers to achieve the effect of automatic screening. The calculation method of popularity is shown in Equation 1:

$$Pop(T) = \frac{CntOfUsed(T)}{\sqrt{CoolDownDay(T)}} \tag{1}$$

where

Pop(*T*): Popularity of Tag *T*;
CntOfUsed(*T*): The number of times that Tag *T* is used by all the labelers; and
CoolDownDay(*T*): The number of days to date since Tag *T* was last used, considering that the number
    of days accumulate rapidly, a radical sign is added to reduce or alleviate this impact.

Those tags that should be reserved will generate a high popularity due to the higher-frequency usage and the lower number of not-in-use (cool-down) days. Conversely, the tags that are less frequently used will generate declining popularities in the end, while the number of not-in-use days will be increased over actual time.

3.2.3 Tag Merging and Calibration

When labelers choose tags, they may neglect the existing tags and add new ones based on similar concepts, such as "gratefulness" and "appreciation" in emotional features. By using artificial identification methods, this study periodically checks newly added tags and merges those tags with existing tags based on similar concepts. Two tags that are merged together are named "the merging" and "the merged," respectively. The latter will disappear after merging and add its *CntOfUsed* to the former. For "the merging" and "the merged," *CoolDownDay* of whichever is closer to the current time will be regarded as the value of former.

3.2.4 Status Label Balance (SLB)

In the CHIL mechanism, a higher degree of diversity in labeled statuses is significantly beneficial to the training of automatic labeling. Therefore, this study designs two properties of "Labeled Count (LC)" and "Skipped Count (SC)" for each status. The LC of a status will be incremented by 1 every time the status is connected with a tag. The SC will be incremented by 1 every time the "changing status" feature is used on this status. Statuses shown to every labeler are from a subset composed of statuses that are selected by LC starting from its highest value with relatively low SC values. These statuses are selected from a "legitimate status set" with SC values lower than the threshold. In this way, it can be guaranteed that every labeler will contribute most to the labeling work. The "legitimate status set" requires that the status labeler as the owner is the writer himself/herself or his/her friend, which is an extra status-screening mechanism for protecting the privacy of testees providing data. The concept mentioned above is illustrated in Figure 4.

Figure 4. Schematic of screening status labeling

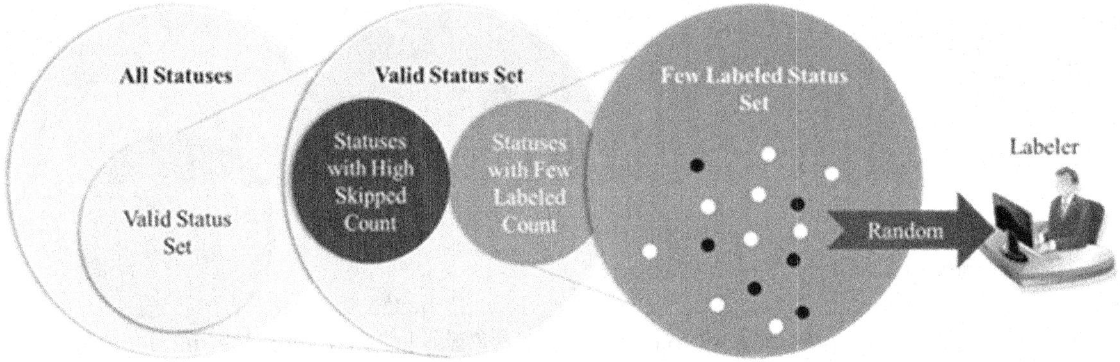

3.3 Noise Status Elimination

In our study, the statuses that are unsuitable to be added to the training set contain several types as below: 1. statuses that only contain links, 2. statuses with ambiguous expression, and 3. statuses mainly written in a foreign language.

With statuses of Type 1 and Type 2, it cannot be clearly determined as to what the writers (posters) are trying to express, since there is no access to in-depth research or knowledge of a particular background, even if an artificial identification method is used. This study only conducts analysis on statuses in plain text. These two status types, therefore, are not applicable as training data.

If a status written in a high proportion of foreign languages is labeled, it must be containing many foreign language words that are rarely or never shown in other statuses. Moreover, if this status happens to be labeled with a tag that is barely used in other statuses, then these foreign words are very likely to become the proprietary words for this tag. However, the "proprietary words" barely have contributions to the subsequent automatic identification of status tags. Therefore, statuses of Type 3 should be regarded as noise information and eliminated from the database. Filtering all the foreign words is one of the methods to solve this problem, but it may lead to the omission of critical foreign words as a result. Hence, a more precise mechanism for eliminating inapplicable statuses is required.

Equation 2 is designed in this study for calculating the "elimination" of each status. The statuses whose elimination values are higher than the threshold value *minElim* will be labeled as "to be eliminated". The statuses marked as "to be eliminated" cannot be added to the legitimate status set.

$$Elim\left(P\right) = e \times \frac{CntOfFW\left(P\right)}{CntOfTerm\left(P\right)} + \left(1 - e\right) \times \frac{CntOfSkipped\left(P\right)}{MaxOfSkipped} \tag{2}$$

where

Elim(P): Elimination index of Status *P*
CntOfFW(P): Foreign word count of Status *P*
CntOfTerm(P): Total word count of Status *P*
CntOfSkipped(P): Count of Status *P* being skipped
MaxOfSkipped: Maximum value of all the counts of each status being skipped
e: weight distribution parameter, ranged in the interval of [0, 1]

Elimination components: 1. percentage of foreign words used in the full Status *P*, and 2. ratio of *CntOfSkipped(P)* and *MaxOfSkipped*. In 1, the value of a status mainly composed of foreign words will be relatively high and the value of a status completely in foreign language will be 1. Statuses in ambiguous expressions or the ones primarily consisting of links will be skipped by almost all the labelers due to the difficulty of determining the appropriate tags, causing relatively higher values of 2. A higher value of *e* means that the effect of foreign word ratio on a status becoming noise status is given more attention. A low value of *e* means that the effect of *CntOfSkipped* is given more attention.

3.4 Preprocessing of Status Data

The gathered statuses are processed in batches with sentence breaking, word breaking, and word property labeling through the Chinese Knowledge and Information Processing (CKIP, 2015), after which the above-mentioned "noise status elimination mechanism" and the subsequent work of considering wording in status can then be conducted.

In order to examine the research requirement as well as CKIP limitation and effectiveness, preprocessing work on the statuses needs to be conducted before sending each one to CKIP: 1. removing links in the status, 2. transforming punctuation marks into full-width forms, and 3. replacing spaces and line feed marks "\n" in the status with "full-width comma" and "full-width Chinese period," respectively. This is because many Internet users get used to substituting sentences in paragraphs with space or line feed (Liu, 2012).

3.5 The Building of the IT Proprietary Glossary

This study employs the value of a changing scheme of the term frequency-inverse document frequency (TF-IDF) (Paltoglou & Thelwall, 2010; TF-IDF, 2015; Martineau & Finin, 2009), augmented TF, as the basis for determining the proprietary glossary. The value of TF can be calculated by Equation 3.

$$aTF_{ij} = 0.5 + 0.5 \times \frac{TF_{ij}}{Max\left(TF_j\right)} \tag{3}$$

Specific operations are described below. Combine all the different statuses labeled with the same IT to generate a corresponding "Tag Profile Article (TPA)" for each tag. Each document d_i in the computational equation for TF_{ij} stands for the TPA of the ith tag, t_i. $|d_i|$ represents the word count in this TPA, N stands for the total number of all the tags, n_{ij} refers to the count of a word w_j showing in d_i. TF_{ij} is the term frequency of word w_j in d_i, and TF-IDF stands for the representative weight of word w_j for the ith tag, t_i.

It may still happen that a status is labeled repeatedly. If a status is labeled with the same tag many times, it indicates that this status indeed has a strong connection with this tag. In this case, the weight of the words in this status for this association tag should be strengthened. This study improves the calculation method of n_{ij} in TF. When the weight of a word for its association tag is calculated, the number of times the status – to which the word belongs – is labeled with the association tag should be taken into consideration and regarded as the basis for weight addition. Therefore, the new calculation method of n_{ij} is shown in Equation 4 to Equation 6.

$$LCnt_{ik} = CntOfLabeled\left(t_i, s_k\right), s_k \in S_i \tag{4}$$

$$OCnt_{jk} = \begin{cases} CntOfOccur\left(w_j, s_k\right) & if\ LCnt_{ik} \leq 1 \\ CntOfOccur\left(w_j, s_k\right) \times \log_2 LCnt_{ik} & if\ LCnt_{ik} > 1 \end{cases} \tag{5}$$

$$n_{ij} = \sum_{k=1}^{m} OCnt_{jk} \tag{6}$$

where

$LCnt_{ik}$: The count of Status s_k being labeled with Tag t_i, in which s_k is a status in Status-set S_i connected with Tag t_i

$OCnt_{jk}$: The count of word w_j showing in Status s_k, whose weight will be augmented when $LCnt_{ik}$ is greater than 1 after improvement

n_{ij}: The weight number of word w_j showing in d_i of TPA corresponding to Tag t_i

By calculating the TF-IDF of each word in every TPA, a word-tag weight matrix can be obtained (as shown in Equation 7). Every list of element ($Weight_{ij}$) in the matrix is the TF-IDF representative weight of the left word/vocabulary ($Term_i$) corresponding to the tag above ($InstanceTag_j$).

$$\begin{array}{c} \\ Term_1 \\ Term_2 \\ \vdots \\ Term_m \end{array} \begin{array}{ccc} InstanceTag_1 & InstanceTag_1 & \cdots & InstanceTag_n \\ \begin{bmatrix} Weight_{1,1} & Weight_{1,2} & \cdots & Weight_{1,n} \\ Weight_{2,1} & Weight_{2,2} & \cdots & Weight_{2,n} \\ \vdots & \vdots & \ddots & \vdots \\ Weight_{m,1} & Weight_{m,2} & \cdots & Weight_{m,n} \end{bmatrix} \end{array} \tag{7}$$

Cosine normalization is conducted again on the values in each row to make all the weights with the same criterion, which is beneficial to cross-tag inter-comparison. At this point, the IT proprietary glossary is established.

3.6 Establishment of IT Weight Table of Personality Traits

Using TF-IDF to calculate the weight of various tags for the four types of personalities is inappropriate since there are only four categories of personalities in the DISC personality model. Most of the tags may have connections with profile articles of the four personalities. Therefore, directly using the method of proprietary vocabulary analysis mentioned above will cause IDF invalidation, i.e., IDF falling to 0, which will further lead to more TF-IDF weights falling to 0.

Therefore, this study turns to adopt TF as the weight value and merges labeled statuses posted by users in the same personality type into "Personality Profile Article (PPA)," by which the use ratio of each tag in every PPA can be calculated to obtain a tag-personality type weight matrix, as shown in Equation 8. Every element ($Weight_{ij}$) in the matrix stands for the use ratio of a tag ($InstanceTag_i$) on the left for a PPA of the corresponding personality type above. Each row is exactly the IT weight table of a particular personality type by conducting Cosine normalization again on each row.

$$
\begin{array}{c}
\begin{array}{cccc} D & I & S & C \end{array} \\
\begin{array}{c} InstanceTag_1 \\ InstanceTag_2 \\ \vdots \\ InstanceTag_n \end{array}
\begin{bmatrix}
Weight_{1,D} & Weight_{1,I} & Weight_{1,S} & Weight_{1,C} \\
Weight_{2,D} & Weight_{2,I} & Weight_{2,S} & Weight_{2,C} \\
\vdots & \vdots & \vdots & \vdots \\
Weight_{n,D} & Weight_{n,I} & Weight_{n,S} & Weight_{n,C}
\end{bmatrix}
\end{array}
\tag{8}
$$

3.7 The Mechanism of Automatic Labeling of New Status

This study realizes the function of automatic labeling of a new status by applying the Search principle in the information retrieval (IR) field. The concept is described below. Take a new status not labeled with tags as a query, and the TPA corresponding to each tag as documents. Seek the TPA that has the highest degree of similarity with the new status among all the TPA sets. All the tags corresponding to this TPA subsequently can be used to label this new status.

The reason for using TPA rather than status as the file unit for comparison is that the content of a single status on Facebook is usually brief and piecemeal. If it is taken as the file unit for comparison, then the sensitivity degree of diction will be exorbitant, leading to inflexible comparisons. However, adopting TPA as the file unit for comparison can reduce the restrictions of diction when new statuses express the same concept. This is because the content of the TPA is composed of numerous statuses by various users, which implies the vagueness of terms in itself.

This study adopts the method of similarity score calculation to determine the degree of correlation between new status and the compared TPA (CTPA). The calculation method for similarity scores is shown in Equation 9.

$$SimScore_{q,d} = \sum_{i=1}^{n} \left(TFIDF_q \left(term_i \right) \times TFIDF_d \left(term_i \right) \right) \tag{9}$$

where, q and d stand for new status and CTPA, respectively. The remaining symbols and rules are explained below.

$SimScore_{q,d}$: Similarity score between new Status q and CTPA d. The higher the score, the greater the similarity;

T_q: Vocabulary set in new status q;

T_d: Proprietary vocabulary set in the CTPA d (from the proprietary glossary);

$$term_i \in T_q \cup T_d;$$

$$n = \left| T_q \cup T_d \right|;$$

$TFIDF_q(term_i)$: TF-IDF value of table $term_i$ in the new status q, with all the TPAs in the document scope of IDF consideration

$TFIDF_d(term_i)$: TF value of table $term_i$ in vocabulary set CTPA d after normalization.

Each value of $TFIDF_q(term_i) \times nTF_d(term_i)$ represents the contributor scores of $term_i$ to the similarity of two statuses (q, d). The sum of scores can be used as the basis for degree of similarity between two statuses (q, d).

Similarity scores of a new status for all the TPAs can be calculated by using this method. By setting thresholds, a great number of TPAs similar to the new status can be obtained, and tags corresponding to these similar TPAs can be labeled on the new status to achieve the objective of automatic labeling.

3.8 Personality Type Prediction

If the principle of the mechanism described above is used indiscriminately in personality type prediction, the IDF invalidation mentioned above will occur as almost every tag definitely appeared in the PPA of the four personality types. For the calculation of similarity degree between the target's status set to be predicted and the PPA, this study refers to another frequently-used similarity degree calculation method – the vector space model (VSM), and makes improvements based on this method. Traditional VSM similarity degree can be solved by the equations below (Equations 10-12).

$$\vec{Q} = \left(W_{1,Q}, W_{2,Q}, \cdots, W_{t,Q} \right), \ t, Q \in N^+ \tag{10}$$

$$\overrightarrow{D_i} = \left(W_{1,i}, W_{2,i}, \cdots, W_{t,i} \right), \ t, i \in N^- \tag{11}$$

$$\cos\theta = \frac{\vec{Q} \cdot \overrightarrow{D_i}}{\vec{Q}\overrightarrow{D_i}}, 0^{\circ} \leq \theta \leq 180^{\circ} \tag{12}$$

The status set of the predicted target and the PPA of each personality type are taken as the query Q and comparison document D_i, respectively. Traditional VSM dimensionality is changed in its definition from terms to status tags, and the number of terms originally as the vector element is now replaced with tag weight. The PPA vector can be obtained by the calculation of tag weight based on observing connected tags of the PPA that are statuses from merged sources. The tag weight vector of the status set by the predicted target can be calculated in parallel with the implementation of automatic labeling.

Figure 5 is the schematic of how the VSM concept applies to this study. Taking the state of only three tags in total as an example, PPA of D, I, S, and C in a three-dimensional space can all be transformed into vectors in the first octant. White dots stand for the drop points of $\vec{Q}$ in the space, transformed from the status set by the predicted target. By the above-mentioned $\cos\theta$ calculations between $\vec{Q}$ and $\vec{D}$, $\vec{I}$, $\vec{S}$, and $\vec{C}$, it is possible to determine which vector of PPA is more similar with $\vec{Q}$. Therefore, personality type of the predicted target can be inferred and the objective of SPC personality type prediction can be achieved ultimately.

4. IMPLEMENTATION

4.1 Practical Data Collection Through CHIL Mechanism

The CHIL mechanism proposed in this study is aimed at improving the manual operational efficiency by letting testees, who provide training data and are also labelers at the same time, conduct trait labeling of statuses provided by other testees. Testees will undergo four stages of operation when they open the website of the application program interface (API) embedded in Facebook. The four stages in sequence are: 1. suggesting tags and signing in Facebook, 2. filling in the test questionnaire of the DISC personality type, 3. random interactive labeling, and 4. reviewing test results. The complete operational logic of this API program can be seen from the mechanism flowchart shown in Figure 6.

There are two additional points concerning the contingencies that may be encountered in the implementation of CHIL mechanism as well as relevant corrections to be made:

- After implementation, Stage (1) was evaluated by testees with feedback indicating excessive diffusion and extreme difficulty. It was also found through observations that the quality of tags produced at this stage was not satisfactory. Therefore, the mechanism was modified to stipulate that new tags can only be added in Stage (3).
- Testees were required to label twenty random statuses, and their feedback reflected an excessive quantity and workload in labelling. Therefore, the quantity is decreased to fifteen to guarantee operational quality.

Figure 5. The conceptual schematic of vector space model with tag weight as the basis

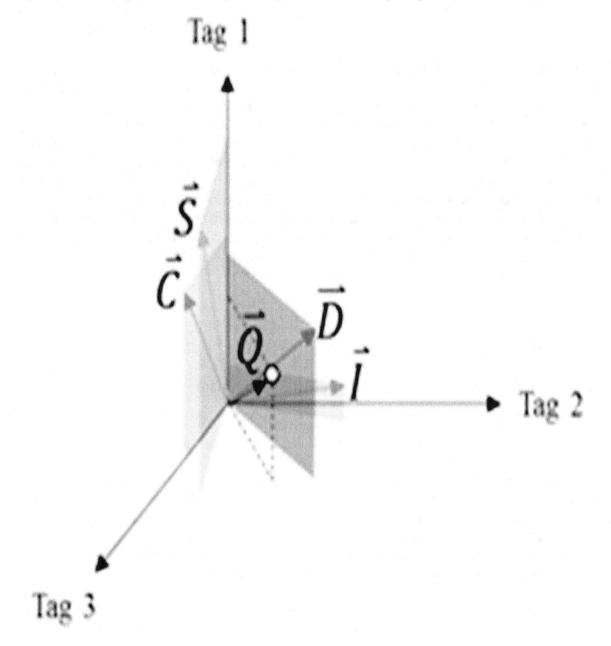

4.2 SPC Test

In the test by CHIL mechanism, after elimination of noise statuses with link-only and symbol-ambiguous texts for the gathered statuses from 59 Facebook users, a total of 5,858 statuses are obtained, 815 of which are labeled during the test, with 122 effective tags. There are 6,185 connections between statuses and labeling tags (a status being labeled with a tag is regarded as a connection).

Figure 6. Process of CHIL mechanism

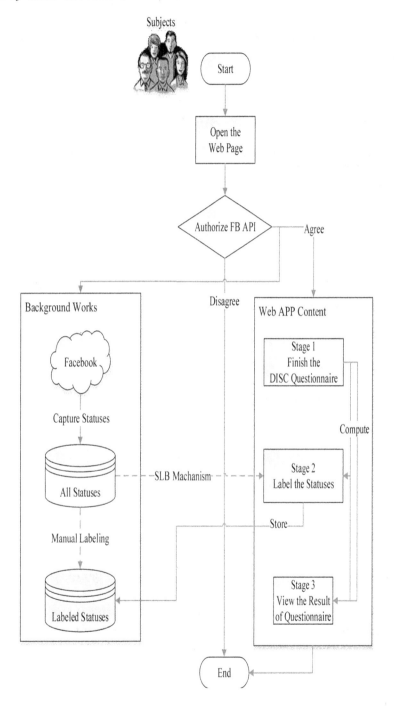

4.2.1 Verification of New-status Automatic Labeling Mechanism

The function of new-status automatic labeling in SPC is tested in this section, as shown in Figure 7.

Figure 7. The test of new-status automatic labeling function

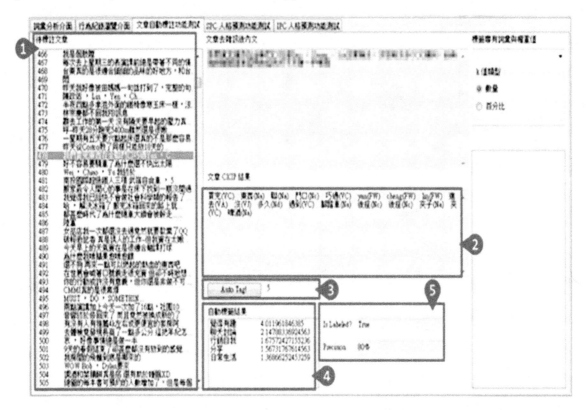

In Figure 7, the significance of each block is illustrated below.

Labeling 1: From all the statuses in the database, one can be selected to test the result of automatic labeling;

Labeling 2: CKIP results of word or sentence breaking labeling of this status;

Labeling 3: automatic labeling is conducted, and tag count adopted is set as n, meaning that the first n tags out of all the recommended tags are adopted and employed as the tags for this status;

Labeling 4: automatic labeling results are shown; to the right of a tag is the normalization result of similarity score between the TPA of this tag and this status; all the numbers multiplied by 100 are displayed in the picture; and

Labeling 5: whether the tag of this status has been manually labeled is displayed. If yes, the accuracy of automatic tag recommendations is calculated, where the accuracy in this context is defined as the ratio of tags truly being used for labeling this status among all recommended tags.

The significance of automatic labeling function is to conduct labeling for "status not being manually labeled". Figure 8 exhibits the test process of automatically labeling status without being manually labeled. Even under the condition of manual labeling, a status is barely labeled with more than 10 tags. Higher count of adopted tags n will definitely cause more uncorrelated tags to appear. Therefore, the value of n is set as 5 in this practical test.

Figure 8. The practical test of unlabeled-status automatic labeling feature

There is no correct solution to status labeling with tags but there is the question of whether it is reasonable or not. It is discovered by manual determination of unlabeled-status labeling function that if the status diction is with relatively common vocabulary or if the status length is relatively long (with sentence count over 10), then for $n=5$, the labeling rate generally can reach 60-80%, namely, three to four out of five tags are reasonable. In the future, if the count of manual status-labeling in the database gradually increases, it can be anticipated that accuracy of recommended tags will be further improved effectively.

4.2.2 Verification of SPC Prediction Method

The function of personality-type automatic prediction in SPC is tested in this section, as shown in Figure 9. In Figure 9, significance of each block is illustrated below.

Labeling 1: select a testee to gather the weight vector of tags used in his/her status set, $\vec{Q}$ (hereinafter referred to as the "testee vector"), and take the personality type result detected by the personality test of this testee as the standard solution;

Labeling 2: display the weight vector of tags used in the PPA of each personality type, $\overrightarrow{D_i}$ (hereinafter referred to as the "personality type vector");

Labeling 3: click the button to start the calculation of the VSM similarity degree between $\vec{Q}$ and all the $\overrightarrow{D_i}$. Moreover, this study also calculates the point-to-point geometrical distance in the VSM space; and

Labeling 4: present the computational results of VSM distance and VSM similarity degree. Generally, the more similar the testee vector and personality type vector, the higher the similarity degree and the smaller the distance.

Figure 9. The practical test of personality-type automatic prediction function

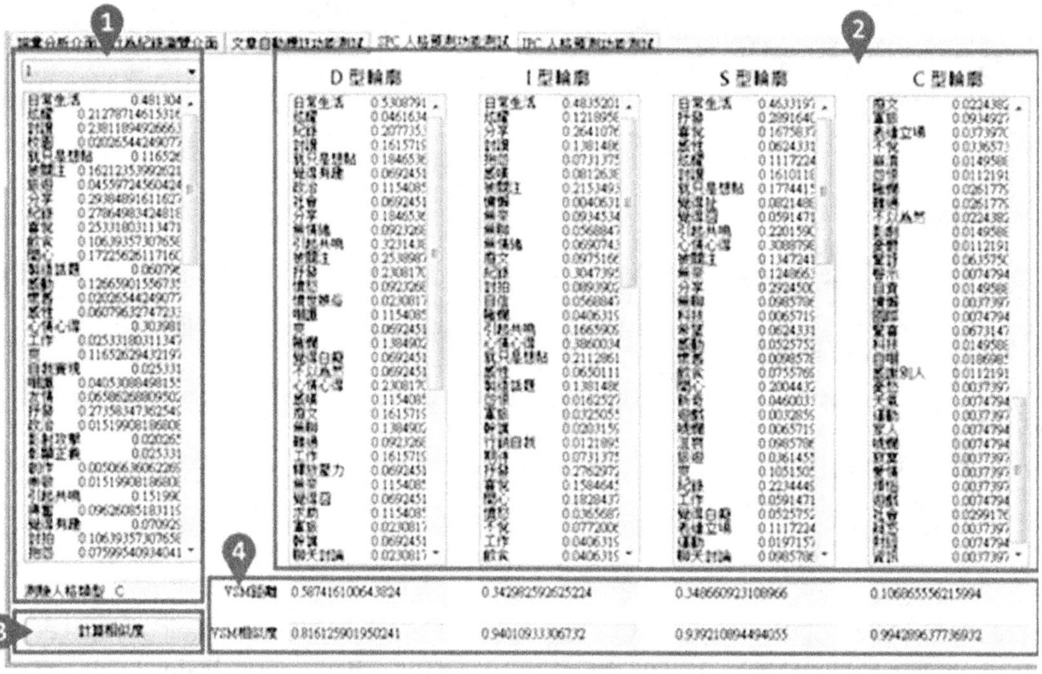

Considering the fact that not every testee's status in the database is sufficiently labeled, it is impossible to conduct tests on all the testees one by one. Using this method to implement prediction on testees with relatively high count of statuses being labeled can mostly achieve correct results, as shown in Figure 10. However, as for those testees whose statuses are less labeled, this method may generate incorrect results due to the lack of the testee's vector data that it can provide.

It can be concluded from the tests above that if a testee has the testee vector with relatively sufficient data, the change of correct prediction by the program will be comparatively improved. It is also verified by experimental results that the method of using SPC to predict personality type is exactly feasible under the condition of sufficient data. If the status count of manual labeling in the database is increased in the future, then the labeling-correction rate of automatic labeling can be improved effectively (current correction rate is only 60-80%), which will further make the most of the automatic labeling function to supplement the testee vector and thereby improve the prediction precision.

Figure 10. Image of testee being predicted

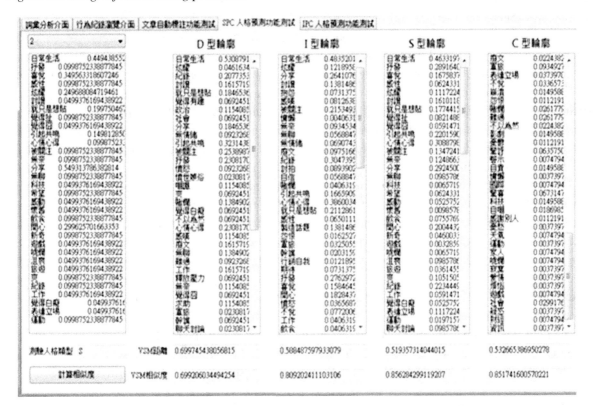

5. DISCUSSION AND CONCLUSION

This study develops an automatic personality-type prediction method to predict a Facebook user's DISC personality type through his/her Facebook user data. An innovative approach, called SPC, is proposed in this research. Experimental results show that this method can predict the personality type of the status set writer with high accuracy by conducting text semantic mining on the status set. The accuracy can be further improved with the increase in specimen numbers.

In the field of text semantic mining, due to the inherent complexity of the Chinese language, it is always more difficult to process with less correlated proprietary techniques. Therefore, this study lays stress on the processing of the Chinese language, hoping to contribute to subsequent related studies. In summary, specific contributions of this study are listed below: 1. a method of automatically labeling Facebook status with tags is proposed, 2. the concept of CHIL mechanism is suggested and put into practice, significantly shortening the time costs of researchers' artificial identification, and 3. a method of Facebook user personality type prediction is proposed.

The related studies in the past only reached the step where the correlation between management behavior or status posting by social media users and their personality test scores was discussed, or at most, the range of user personality test scores was predicted, unlike the type prediction of users practically conducted in this research. Tests show that the proposed SPC method has practical feasibility for Facebook users. However, due to the lack of sample data in the early manual labeling stage caused by source restrictions, the precision has not reached the degree of practical application yet. If the sample quantity of manual labeling is effectively increased (e.g., packaging the labeling mechanism in games), accuracy of this method can be improved as expected.

The concept of the proposed SPC personality type prediction method can be directly extended to other "Facebook-like" social media. The so-called "Facebook-like" means that the users on this social media express themselves by using short text passages as the major form of communication. Since the SPC is a method based on text semantic comparison, it is not applicable for those social media that are mainly based on images (e.g. Instagram). If subsequent related research still uses Facebook as the main platform, Facebook's revision information needs to be constantly monitored. As for the personality model adopted in the method, all personality models of personality types with clear definition can be used, in theory (such as the enneagram of personality and the MBTI).

If there is subsequent research following this study, channels of gathering articles to be labeled can be developed to make the prediction system constantly obtain new training data or verify old information. In order to achieve a superior precision of the automatic status-labeling function, a more public-friendly mechanism that can effectively attract testee participation needs to be built for obtaining more data, both in terms of range and quantity. For example, tasks of "labeling status" and "verifying existing status labeling" can be packaged into mobile App games or small web games to attract people to participate as effective labelers, but in a subconscious way. In the tests of this study, almost every testee is highly interested in "degree of similarity with friends" of the final results shown in the website of the CHIL mechanism. Therefore, the future data-collecting mechanism can make the best of this point, and add some community elements appropriately to achieve the goal of attracting testees. At the same time, subsequent research can conduct technical extensions with respect to the following items:

5.1 Image Recognition

Recently, Facebook added a new feature that allows users to use image content such as stickers and photos when posting status updates or replying to messages. In the Facebook user ecosystem, an increasing number of users tend to express their emotions using images instead of texts. Therefore, the method proposed in the present study will strengthen the capabilities in content recognition of user status, if sticker analysis can be considered in future work.

5.2 Special Internet Word Recognition

Facebook is an online social community, where special Internet language and emoticons naturally appear in statuses on a frequent basis. These special words occur and update rapidly with the creativity of global Internet participants, and may contain critical information about content subject, posting objective and emotion expression. The CKIP word-breaking system, which is the foundation of the current labeling method, is not yet capable of accurately and effectively separating special words in posts when conducting Chinese-word breaking and recognition. Some relatively complex special terms, such as "bj4" (no explanation), "Z>B" (the benefits overweigh the drawbacks), "(ﾉ -_-)ﾉ ~┴┴" (overturn the table, showing impatience), and "(σ¢▽`)¢▽`)σ" (look at you, containing a derisive implication), cannot be broken correctly. Therefore, there is still a great amount of crucial information missing in the training process.

Recognition of special Internet words requires a huge deal of groundwork in this field. Building an Internet slang ontology may be beneficial to the realization of this task, but this would be a significantly large project with extremely widespread involvement. Therefore, it is not taken into consideration in the present study given the resource limitations. If the subsequent study is equipped with the capability of recognizing special Internet words, the quality of labeling status with tags will be enhanced and the effectiveness of personality type prediction will be further improved.

5.3 Status Semantic Identification and Status Strength

The proposed method of recognizing status tags in this paper is based on the training results of the occurrence situations of various words that appear in statuses connected with different tags, where semantic identification is not performed on each word. In practical conditions, individuals will subconsciously strengthen the content subject, posting objective, and emotion expression of a post when seeing some words with a high strength in a particular field of the post they read. For instance, the occurrence of particularly nasty words in a post will strengthen the weight of emotion-expression recognition for this post (e.g., sensing the writer/poster is very happy or very angry), which does exist in the real world. For future work, if semantic identification capability can be added to the method, appropriate tags can be more precisely determined and added to new statuses in automatic labeling, and even tag strength (such as somewhat happy, very happy, and extremely happy) can be determined according to the status strength. Therefore, the accuracy of personality type prediction will be further improved, based on what is stated in this study.

6. REFERENCES

Adalı, S., & Golbeck, J. (2012). Predicting personality with social behavior. *Proceedings of the International Conference on Advances in Social Networks Analysis and Mining (ASONAM)* (pp. 302-309). Academic Press.

Adali, S., Sisenda, F., & Magdon-Ismail, M. (2012). Actions speak as loud as words: predicting relationships from social behavior data. *Proceedings of the 21st international conference on World Wide Web WWW'12* (pp. 689-698). Academic Press.

Bai, S. T., Zhu, T. S., & Cheng, L. (2012). Big-five personality prediction based on user behaviors at social network sites.

Boyd, C. F. (1994). *Different children different needs: the art of adjustable parenting*. OR: Questar Publishers Inc.

Chen, T.-Y., Tsai, M.-C., & Chen, Y.-M. (2016). A user's personality prediction approach by mining network interaction behaviors on Facebook. *Online Information Review*, *40*(7), 913–937. doi:10.1108/OIR-08-2015-0267

CKIP. (2015). Word segment. Retrieved from http://ckip.iis.sinica.edu.tw:8080/wordsegment/

de Mattos, C. A., Kissimoto, K. O., & Laurindo, F. J. B. (2018). The role of information technology for building virtual environments to integrate crowdsourcing mechanisms into the open innovation process. *Technological Forecasting and Social Change*, *129*, 143–153. doi:10.1016/j.techfore.2017.12.020

Doan, A., Ramakrishnan, R., & Halevy, A. Y. (2011). Crowdsourcing systems on the world-wide web. *Communications of the ACM, 54*(4), 86–96. doi:10.1145/1924421.1924442

Drucker, P. F. (1954). *The practice of management.* New York: Harper & Brothers.

Facebook GraphAPI. (2015). Facebook. Retrieved from https://developers.facebook.com/docs/javascript/reference/FB.api

g0v.tw. (2014). Retrieved from http://g0v.tw/zh-TW/projects.html

Gatautis, R., & Vitkauskaite, E. (2014). Crowdsourcing application in marketing activities. *Procedia: Social and Behavioral Sciences, 110*, 1243–1250. doi:10.1016/j.sbspro.2013.12.971

Gerson, J., Plagnol, A. C., & Corr, P. J. (2016). Subjective well-being and social media use: Do personality traits moderate the impact of social comparison on Facebook? *Computers in Human Behavior, 63*, 813–822. doi:10.1016/j.chb.2016.06.023

Golbeck, J., Robles, C., & Turner, K. (2011). Predicting personality with social media. *Proceedings of the 29th ACM Conference on Human Factors in Computing Systems (CHI).* Academic Press.

Howe, J. (2006). The rise of crowdsourcing. *Wired.* Retrieved from http://archive.wired.com/wired/archive/14.06/crowds_pr.html

Knapp, M. L., & Daly, J. A. (2002). *Handbook of interpersonal communication.* Sage Publications.

Lang, M., Bharadwaj, N., & Di Benedetto, C. A. (2016). How crowdsourcing improves prediction of market-oriented outcomes. *Journal of Business Research, 69*(10), 4168–4176. doi:10.1016/j.jbusres.2016.03.020

Lee, E., Ahn, J., & Kim, Y. J. (2014). Personality traits and self-presentation at Facebook. *Personality and Individual Differences, 69*, 162–167. doi:10.1016/j.paid.2014.05.020

Liu, Y. C. (2012). Development of a mechanism of potential customer searching from virtual communities: food industry as an application [Thesis]. National Cheng Kung University.

Martineau, J., & Finin, T. (2009). Delta TFIDF: An improved feature space for sentiment analysis. *ICWSM, 9*, 106.

Moore, K., & McElroy, J. C. (2012). The influence of personality on Facebook usage, wall postings, and regret. *Computers in Human Behavior Archive, 28*(1), 267–274. doi:10.1016/j.chb.2011.09.009

Nadkarni, A., & Hofmann, G. H. (2012). Why do people use Facebook? *Personality and Individual Differences, 52*(3), 243–249. doi:10.1016/j.paid.2011.11.007 PMID:22544987

Ortigosa, A., Carro, R. M., & Quiroga, J. I. (2014). Predicting user personality by mining social interactions in Facebook. *Journal of Computer and System Sciences, 80*(1), 57–71. doi:10.1016/j.jcss.2013.03.008

Paltoglou, G., & Thelwall, M. (2010). A study of information retrieval weighting schemes for sentiment analysis. *Proceedings of the 48th Annual Meeting of the Association for Computational Linguistics* (pp. 1386-1395). Academic Press.

Park, J. E., & Holloway, B. B. (2003). Adaptive selling behavior revisited: An empirical examination of learning orientation, sales performance and job satisfaction. *Journal of Personal Selling & Sales Management, 23*(3), 239–251.

Safran, M., & Che, D. (2017). Real-time recommendation algorithms for crowdsourcing systems. *Applied Computing and Informatics, 13*(1), 47–56. doi:10.1016/j.aci.2016.01.001

Seidman, G. (2013). Self-presentation and belonging on Facebook: How personality influences social media use and motivations. *Personality and Individual Differences, 54*(3), 402–407. doi:10.1016/j.paid.2012.10.009

Statista. (2015). Global social networks ranked by number of users. Retrieved from http://www.statista.com/statistics/272014/global-social-networks-ranked-by-number-of-users/

Stieglitz, S., Mirbabaie, M., Ross, B., & Neuberger, C. (2018). Social media analytics–challenges in topic discovery, data collection, and data preparation. *International Journal of Information Management, 39*, 156–168. doi:10.1016/j.ijinfomgt.2017.12.002

TF-IDF. (2015). Retrieved from https://zh.wikipedia.org/wiki/Tf-idf

Wikipedia. (n.d.). Facebook. Retrieved from http://zh.wikipedia.org/wiki/Facebook

Zhao, S., Grasmuck, S., & Martin, J. (2008). Identity construction on Facebook: Digital empowerment in anchored relationships. *Computers in Human Behavior, 24*(5), 1816–1836. doi:10.1016/j.chb.2008.02.012

This research was previously published in the International Journal on Semantic Web and Information Systems (IJSWIS), 16(1); pages 25-46, copyright year 2020 by IGI Publishing (an imprint of IGI Global).

Chapter 30
Reaching Your Customers Using Facebook and Google Dynamic Ads

Tereza Semerádová
https://orcid.org/0000-0002-9123-5782
Technical University of Liberec, Czech Republic

Petr Weinlich
Technical University of Liberec, Czech Republic

ABSTRACT

Dynamic Product Ads (DPAs) and Dynamic Search Ads (DSAs) represent a type of online advertising primarily used for remarketing purposes. However, more and more advertisers can use DPA for acquisition campaigns as well. Dynamic ads are an integral part of the marketing strategies of all large e-shops and companies that have a product or service catalog. Dynamic advertising reduces the time and effort put into the creation of online advertisements and provides the highest level of personalized targeting possible. With a product catalog and a properly set pixel or tracking code, it is possible to create individually customized ads within seconds. This chapter tests the effectiveness of DPAs and DSAs within the context of the two greatest advertising platforms, Facebook and Google ads, and compares their performance against the manually optimized ad sets.

INTRODUCTION

Dynamic search ads (DSAs) and *dynamic product ads* (DPAs) help advertisers reach potential customers by displaying content that is tailored specifically for them. According to WordStream (2019), multichannel marketing strategies lead to an 80% higher visit rate of a target e-store. Moreover, 37% of online shoppers look for shopping inspiration on social media, and 96% of B2C marketers agree that Facebook and Google ads have a significant impact on their marketing revenues. The WordStream statistics also claim that 65% of advertisers agree that dynamic content is effective. On average, only

DOI: 10.4018/978-1-7998-9020-1.ch030

approximately 4% of website visitors make a conversion, that directly generates income, before leaving a website (GrowthBadger, 2019).

The driving force behind marketing automation is the ability to send personalized messages tailored to a specific customer. The content is delivered to the customer in the ideal moment, i.e., when needs and searches for information arise during a browsing session. Marketing automation tools affect shoppers at the most important stage of the purchasing process–before reaching a selected merchant. Implementation of these tools greatly increases the chance that demand will eventually be placed with the merchant and not with the competition. Marketing automation systems can be used to raise customer awareness about the brand or present them the required product information to build their trust and significantly shorten the purchasing process. Experienced marketers and advertisers confirm that potential customers are not ready to respond immediately to their first contact with the company. To do so, the customer needs to be captivated, convinced, and acquired. This process is called *lead nurturing*.

A basic function of all marketing automation tools is delivering pre-selected content to potential customers, always based on their specific actions. For example, when a user visits a new car website, the system automatically responds by sending him/her an e-mail with a detailed product line offer. Similarly, when a customer leaves the shopping cart before the purchase is completed, the system can send him/her an e-mail or a special offer message for a particular item that was left behind. Thus, marketers create different automation rules in the system environment to cover the entire purchasing process or a product life cycle. When a customer makes action X, the system performs action Y. System marketing automation tools enable accurate tracking and evaluation of campaign responses to contacts in the marketing database. A full history of responses to past campaigns is available to marketers and merchants. Through lead nurturing, the campaign audience gradually becomes familiar with the brand, their relationship with the company is established, and the desired purchase is made.

In this chapter, we test the effectiveness of dynamic content ads during the entire conversion process. For the purposes of this experiment, we are going to combine search and product dynamic ads provided by the advertising platforms Facebook and Google ads. The performances of the dynamic campaigns are judged based on the standard metrics such as reach, click-through rate, number of conversions, and profitability. To get reliable results, a reference group of manually optimized ads are set up and used for the comparative analysis of the advertising performance.

THE EFFECTS OF PERSONALIZED ADS ON ONLINE USERS

Personalization is the key to individual marketing and targeting. The essence of personalization in the online environment is to offer the user services and products that are based on the information in the user's profile or behavior on the website. The necessary prerequisites for creating a personalized offer of products and services by the provider identifies the user (based on his/her registration in the system or based on the use of cookies and tracking codes), sufficient information about the user and his/her preferences, and subsequent processing of the data manually or by the system.

Research relating to the study of how personalization affects the behavior of the consumers is very extensive (Tran, 2017). Many researchers have already tested the impact of exclusively tailored advertising in traditional media (Baek and Morimoto, 2012; Yu and Cude, 2009), in the online environment including social media and websites (Bleier & Eisenbeiss, 2015; Li, 2016; Gironda & Korgaonkar, 2018) and in the context of mobile devices (Grewal et al., 2016; Lu et al., 2019). The up-to-date findings prove that the impact of personalized advertising is ambiguous and may lead to very opposite responses from the targeted users.

Yu et al. (2019) created a conceptual model of customer reactions on personalized ads and their click-through intentions. Their results from a survey of 446 WeChat users indicate that higher product involvement, brand familiarity, visual attractiveness, and information quality increase the user's intention to proceed with further interaction with the brand. Shanahan et al. (2019) came to similar conclusions. Their analysis of 242 responses from Amazon Mechanical Turk suggest that personalized content positively influences brand engagement, attachment, and, by extension, the loyalty to the brand. Bang and Wojdynski (2016) analyzed the effects of personalized banner ads on the visual attention of users using eye-tracking technology. Personalized ads generated longer fixations and users were more attracted to them. Contrastingly, the effects were moderated by the level of cognitive load during tasks the testers were asked to perform.

Setyani et al. (2019) explored intrinsic motivations of users to react to social media ads. The authors identified four types of added customer value: informativeness, credibility, creativity, and entertainment. They also distinguish two basic browsing dimensions: utilitarian and hedonic. Li and Liu (2017) claimed that simple, personalized adjustments of the ads may not be enough to produce the desired effects. To maximize the positive outcomes, a high level of involvement with the brand is necessary. However, effects of personalization may differ depending on not only the products presented but also the intensity of recommendations and the characteristics of the target segment (Schreiner et al., 2019). Chen et al. (2019) postulated that customer reactance may be significantly affected by both rational choice factors and affective choice factors such as ownership or vulnerability.

In a meta-analysis of 166 studies involving 75,269 participants from 34 countries, Baruh et al. (2017) found a contradictory relationship between users' beliefs about privacy in the digital space and their real behavior. The authors referred to this phenomenon as to the *privacy paradox*, which describes a conflicting relationship between high user concerns about the misuse of personal data and the low level of protective measures taken, especially in the social networking field. Users expressing concern about data protection in social networking environments tend to be more inclined to deliver such data recklessly–for example, accessing large volumes of their own digital footprints and allowing unauthenticated external applications to access personal data. One possible explanation for such behavior is the detachment of the user from the possible negative effects of ill-considered provision of his/her data and from any potential data misuses to which he/she does not relate. Another possible clarification includes the so-called reward risk. Most users would feel more secure in anonymity, but making available free services, applications, or content in exchange for personal data is tempting. The perceived risk of abuse is so low that they would accept such an exchange without further consideration.

Finally, it is important to note that ill-considered provisions of personal data and concerns about its misuse are not defined exclusively by information literacy and by previous experiences with internet services. Zorn et al. (2013) argued that aspects of the cultural and political environment are also involved in the form of regulations and cultural values.

Estrada-Jiménez et al. (2017) analyzed the online advertising infrastructure and the underlying privacy risk. The authors listed and classified the privacy mechanisms that allow for an increase in a sense of online privacy for its users. They described the data collection model applied by many advertising entities as the attacker model, which is characterized as having access to any personal user data. Most of the advertising services gather information such as the clickstream, browsing history, preferences, location, gender, age, and agent string in a standard manner. The agent string is data that remain traceable, even if the user deletes his browsing history including the cookies (Eckersley, 2010).

Nowadays, users have many options for protecting themselves from unwanted advertising. It has been proven that ad blocking browser extensions such as Adblock Plus or Ghostery are able to effectively prevent user tracking and prevent the online ads from displaying (Danova, 2014; Redondo & Aznar; 2018). However, by blocking all ads, users may even miss ads that could be useful to them (Parra–Arnau et al., 2017). The popularity of ad blockers has grown to such an extent that even Google considered implementing it into their Chrome browser; they are a tool that would allow all the users to moderate the kind of advertisements they want to receive (Lee, 2019; Sánchez & Viejo, 2018).

Regarding the effectiveness of online advertising, there is also another phenomenon that is necessary to mention. *Advertising blindness* is the phenomenon when users consciously or subconsciously neglect the spaces on a website where they expect advertisements to appear. Hsieh and Chen (2011) tested how different information types and their representations within the web structure affect users' attention. They focused mainly on the four most common content types that can be found on a website: only text entries, text, and pictures, mostly pictures, and mostly video. According to their results, the avoidance of advertisements depends on placement, context, and visual design. Koshksaray et al. (2015) described the influence of e-lifestyle on the ad reactance. The authors identified seven e-lifestyle categories with different attitudes toward advertising: need-driven, interest-driven, entertainment-driven, sociability-driven, importance-driven, uninterest-driven, and novelty-driven. However, their results are inconclusive.

The effects of personalized ads can thus produce a double effect. On the one hand, in most cases, ad relevance increases the potential to capture users' attention and produce the desired conversions. On the other hand, the accuracy and targeting precision of an ad may contribute to higher privacy concerns (Jung, 2017). Therefore, all aforementioned factors should be included when the experiment is set up and when the advertising results are interpreted. Based on this background research, we pose the following research questions:

RQ1: How does placement affect the effectiveness of dynamic ads?
RQ2: How does the format of an ad contribute to the overall advertising performance?
RQ3: What are the effects of dynamic ads during different stages of a user becoming familiar with a brand?
RQ4: Do dynamic, highly personalized ads perform better than "static", manually created ads with a lower level of personalization?

WHAT IS THE MECHANISM BEHIND DYNAMIC PRODUCT ADS AND DYNAMIC SEARCH ADS?

Using machine learning and artificial intelligence in PPC advertising systems, such as Facebook and Google ads, is certainly how modern marketing and advertising systems will move in the future. Regardless of online advertising tools used, the success of each automation is always proportional to the quality of the product or service data source provided. Typically, the data source is an XML file with a structure determined by the advertising system. This data source is called *feed*, which should be created with precision, even with optional parameters. Most systems have algorithms that can improve the performance of the ads over time, thanks to the advanced machine learning. However, if the original feed is insufficient or mediocre, there is no automatic correcting mechanism to fix it.

Dynamic Google Ads

The Google advertising platform offers four types of automatized advertisements. The lowest level of personalization and automatization is represented by *smart ads*, followed by DSAs, which are mostly used for acquisition campaigns, DPAs that are automatically generated based on the product feed supplied by the company and *dynamic remarketing ads*.

Unlike the other two types of ads, *smart content advertisements* do not use extensive data feed uploaded by the advertiser. The automatization is done on the level of the ad delivery with very limited personalization options. The system displays the option to create this type of campaign if the advertisers have at least 50 conversions from the *content network* over the past 30 days or at least 100 conversions from the *search network*. The targeting of a smart campaign is done by the internal mechanism of the advertising system. Google decides which sites and placements display the ad. Likewise, the advertiser does not set the cost-per-click (CPC) bids but enters only a target cost per conversion or return on investment. The creation of the smart ads is also slightly different from the standard process. The advertiser uploads up to five images, five headings, and five descriptions, and Google selects the final appearance of the ad based on user preferences and the historic ad performance data.

Dynamic Search Ads provide an easy method of targeting Google search ads to all the content on a website, without the need to look for keywords and set up ads manually for every relevant search query. DSAs have a great potential, especially for larger websites and e-shops that have to work with thousands of products, to advertise as quickly as possible in the Google search results. Manually creating these ads one by one could take months. If the advertiser chooses to set up a new DSA campaign in the Google AdWords interface, he/she can launch it quickly and easily without having to fill out a single keyword. In fact, dynamic search ads are not keyword targeted but based on the content of the advertised website. Search queries are automatically targeted on the websites if Google finds its content relevant to the user requirements. The keywords and ad title are then dynamically generated based on the content of the landing page.

The ad title is a combination of a search phrase and a landing page title. It is common practice for companies to customize their site titles specifically for DSA optimization. The important thing is that the web is written in a language that is natural for customers and that the headings of the web pages are attractive for the target audience. Since Google allows longer titles for the dynamically generated ads than for the standard ones, dynamic ads typically look more distinctive in the list of the search results. The advertiser may influence the visible URL address and descriptive text related to the website.

The distribution and placement of *DPAs* is not determined by keywords but by product data from the *merchant center*. The data feed submitted through this service contains details about the marketed products such as name, size, price, and color. Using this information, user queries are then matched with the automatically created ads so that the most relevant products are always displayed. DPAs can appear in Google Shopping selection, search results, and the content network. Since Google is trying to provide the customers with the most information available, ads on Google Shopping can appear alongside text-based ads. Customers can find the product that best fits their requirements, even before they reach the website where a purchase can be made. Product feed must be updated at least every 30 days, and the data must meet Google quality standards.

With dynamic remarketing ads, advertisers can display ads to users who have previously visited their website or used their mobile apps. This advertising format represents the highest level of personalization since it uses pictures of the products the users viewed on the web. Before using the remarketing ads, the advertiser implements a remarketing tag in all pages of the website. The tag includes all website visitors to remarketing lists and assigns them to unique item IDs in the feed they viewed. Although dynamic search ads are more suitable for the acquisition of new customers, dynamic remarketing aims to maximize the value of the existing customers. However, it may be connected with dynamic customer search. *Dynamic customer search* uses machine learning to estimate what online users are looking for. When the system detects what a user might need, the algorithm combines the user's possible intention of buying with available demographic data, such as age, gender, and household income, to find the right product for the user in the advertiser's feed. Products in the source feed are ranked based on their performance, relevance, and other factors that determine which ones have the best chance to get the user's attention and lead to a conversion.

Dynamic Facebook Ads

DPAs represent the only dynamic format Facebook offers to advertisers at this moment (May 2019). Facebook DPAs are primarily used for remarketing purposes. However, more and more advertisers also use DPA for acquisition campaigns with Facebook Marketing Partners. Facebook DPAs dynamically link the users' IDs with the product ID and the information listed in the supplied product feed. The information available in the feed is subsequently imported in the advertising system, and a personalized ad with the product he/she previously viewed on the web is delivered to the user. Facebook DPAs are applicable across all devices and placements, including Instagram.

To work with DPAs, a Facebook pixel with appropriate conversion events must be implemented on the advertiser's site. This pixel connects to the user's Facebook ID when he/she visits the website and carries the information about which product the user viewed and how he/she behaved on the web (for example, if one of the products was added to the cart, searched for, bought, etc.). As in Google dynamic ads, the marketer is able within minutes to create hundreds of variations of one ad, whose content is dynamically personalized using the product feed information. The fact that Facebook does not use cookies to track the user, but the Facebook profile, has many advantages. The most important advantage being that the users are easily traceable across different devices they use. User activity history cannot be deleted; thus, customer information is more accurate and historically continuous. The mechanism behind the dynamic Facebook ads is described in Figure 1.

The slightly different matching mechanisms applied by Google ads (cookies) and Facebook ads (user ID) raise another question related to the effectiveness of automatized dynamic advertising:

RQ5: What advertising platform (Facebook or Google) provides more effective dynamic ads?

We will explore this and the previously stated four research questions using the results from the following experiment. Emphasis will be put on the analysis of the variability factors that could influence the performance of the dynamic ads.

Figure 1. The delivery mechanism of Facebook dynamic ads
Source: (the authors)

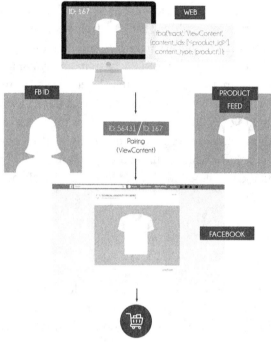

COLLECTING PERFORMANCE DATA

For the purposes of this research, the entire online conversion process was marketed parallelly with the help of dynamic and manually optimized Facebook and Google ads. Since both platforms respect the same three level structures of customer acquisition, we created ads covering all three marketing stages of customer acquisition: brand awareness, consideration, and conversion. Facebook ads copy this goal structure exactly as described and the main campaign objectives are classified into these three categories. The category awareness includes *brand awareness* and *reach*. Consideration groups optimizing goals such as traffic, engagement, app installations, video views, lead generation, and messages. The final category contains conversions, product catalog sales, and store visits. Dynamic ads can be found in the product catalog sales. However, Facebook catalog-based ads may also be used to acquire new customers since the ad-managing system allows for choosing an audience with custom and lookalike audiences, which can mimic the general advertising campaign goals. Google ads provide seven categories of targeting goals: sales, potential customers, web traffic, product and brand consideration, brand awareness and reach, app installations, and campaign without a specified goal. In our experiment, we used all the categories except app installations.

In addition, to fully testing the advertising potential of the dynamic ads, we set upped at least one ad set for each advertising placement available for DSAs and DPAs. Following the similar logic, we also experimented with the available format combinations. For the graphic ads, we used picture and interactive GIF animation on the Google platform and different picture variations supported by Facebook that included one photo (P), Carousel (Ca), and a collection of multiple photos (Co). In total, 168 dynamic ads and 1,575 static ads were implemented. The combinations of the campaign, ad set, and ad parameters used for the two ad groups are described in Tables 1 and 2.

The manually optimized Google ads were implemented for each of the above-described combinations. To maintain at least a moderate level of personalization and test the abilities of the delivery algorithm, each of the ad sets contained 20 product ads. To increase the chances of captivating users' attention, we chose only the best performing products from the given e-store category. The product catalog used for the dynamic ads contained all of the products from the same category (432 products in total). If the type of campaign allows the use of both photos and interactive content, the number of ads within an ad set increases to 40 (20 product ads using photo and 20 ads using the interactive content. Thus, we ran 42 dynamic and 840 static ads on the Google advertising platform.

Table 1. The characteristics of the dynamic and static advertisements for the Google AdWords platform

	Smart ads	Dynamic search ads	Dynamic product ads	Dynamic remarketing ads	Dynamic customer search ads
Campaign without goal	Photo Interactive	Textual	Photo Interactive	Photo Interactive	Photo Interactive
awareness	-	-	Photo Interactive	Photo Interactive	Photo Interactive
Consideration	-	-	Photo Interactive	Photo Interactive	Photo Interactive
Web traffic	-	Textual	Photo Interactive	Photo Interactive	Photo Interactive
Potential customers	-	Textual	Photo Interactive	Photo Interactive	Photo Interactive
Sales	-	Textual	Photo Interactive	Photo Interactive	Photo Interactive

Source: (the authors)

Table 2. Characteristics of the dynamic Facebook advertisements

	Custom audience awareness			Custom audience consideration			Custom audience conversions			Lookalike audience awareness			Lookalike audience consideration			Lookalike audience conversions		
Facebook newsfeed	P	Ca	Co	P	Ca	Co	P	Ca	Co	P	Ca	Co	P	Ca	Co	P	Ca	Co
Right column	P	Ca	Co	P	Ca	Co	P	Ca	Co	P	Ca	Co	P	Ca	Co	P	Ca	Co
Marketplace	P	Ca	Co	P	Ca	Co	P	Ca	Co	P	Ca	Co	P	Ca	Co	P	Ca	Co
Instagram channel	P	Ca	Co	P	Ca	Co	P	Ca	Co	P	Ca	Co	P	Ca	Co	P	Ca	Co
Instagram stories	P	Ca	Co	P	Ca	Co	P	Ca	Co	P	Ca	Co	P	Ca	Co	P	Ca	Co
Audience network	P	Ca	Co	P	Ca	Co	P	Ca	Co	P	Ca	Co	P	Ca	Co	P	Ca	Co
Messenger	P	Ca	Co	P	Ca	Co	P	Ca	Co	P	Ca	Co	P	Ca	Co	P	Ca	Co

Source: (the authors)

Table 3. Characteristics of the static Facebook advertisements

	Brand awareness			Reach			Web traffic			Engagement			Lead generation			Messages			Conversions			
Facebook newsfeed	P	Ca	Co	P	Ca	Co	P	Ca	Co	P	Ca	Co	P	Ca	Co	P	Ca	Co	P	Ca	Co	Co
Right column	P	Ca	Co	P	Ca	Co	P	Ca	Co	P	Ca	Co	P	Ca	Co	P	Ca	Co	P	Ca	Co	Co
Marketplace	P	Ca	Co	P	Ca	Co	P	Ca	Co	P	Ca	Co	P	Ca	Co	P	Ca	Co	P	Ca	Co	Co
Instagram channel	P	Ca	Co	P	Ca	Co	P	Ca	Co	P	Ca	Co	P	Ca	Co	P	Ca	Co	P	Ca	Co	Co
Instagram stories	P	Ca	Co	P	Ca	Co	P	Ca	Co	P	Ca	Co	P	Ca	Co	P	Ca	Co	P	Ca	Co	Co
Audience network	P	Ca	Co	P	Ca	Co	P	Ca	Co	P	Ca	Co	P	Ca	Co	P	Ca	Co	P	Ca	Co	Co
Messenger	P	Ca	Co	P	Ca	Co	P	Ca	Co	P	Ca	Co	P	Ca	Co	P	Ca	Co	P	Ca	Co	Co

Source: (the authors)

We used the same product catalog for the Facebook dynamic ads as we did for the Google ads. The static ads were created for every targeting goal available in the Facebook Ads Manager except app installations, video views, and store visits, which were not relevant in the context of the e-store that allowed us to carry out our experiment. To keep the results comparable with the dynamic ads, we chose the same placements and same formats. The distribution of the ad characteristics is described in Table 3. Contrary to the static Google ads, only the five best performing products were used in ads within each ad set. The number of products was in this case reduced due to the high number of possible permutations. Overall, 126 dynamic and 735 static Facebook ads were created for the purposes of this experiment.

The experiment was performed in real-life conditions with authentic users and thus with authentic motivations behind the browsing and purchasing behavior. The advertisements were created in accordance with the marketing strategy of the Czech e-store specializing in the furniture, home accessories, and kitchen equipment. Because of the authenticity of the testing conditions, there were, however, some restrictions. First, regardless of the experimental nature, all of the above-described ads still had to fulfill the business objectives of the company and generate the desired conversions. Since the purpose of the individual ads differed according to the acquisition phase, the effectiveness of the ads was evaluated based on different metrics. Regarding awareness, the number of reactions and average price per reaction were monitored, and for the consideration stage, we focused on the click-through rate (CTR) and average cost per click. Finally, the performance of the last group of ads was evaluated based on the profitability the ads were able to produce.

Other restrictions defined by the e-store were related to some of the targeting parameters. We were allowed to target our testing ads only on women aged 25 to 44 years since it represented the most efficient customer segment of the e-store. This target was identified by the company as having the most potential from which to acquire new customers. Moreover, the bidding strategy was appointed and was non-negotiable. The e-store used a limited bidding strategy with a fixed maximum bid that was applied also on our ads. The dynamic and static ads were delivered for at least two days and at a maximum of 22 days. The main reason for the shorter delivery period of the ads was their suboptimal performance, which was judged using the maximum accepted average cost per reaction (0.19 EUR), average cost per CTR (0.24 EUR), and a minimum profitability per ad (12 EUR). The last restriction consisted of the limitation of interference of the dynamic and static ads to avoid an instance where a user is targeted by both sets. This prerequisite was achieved through the local positioning of the ads. Dynamic ads were delivered exclusively in Prague, Central Bohemian Region, South Bohemian Region, Plzeň Region,

Karlovy Vary Region, Ústí nad Labem Region, and Liberec Region. The manually optimized ads targeted the remaining seven regions of the Czech Republic.

All Facebook and Google ads were connected with the Google Analytics using the UTM parameters. Thanks to this connection, we were able to monitor not only the CTR but also further behavior on the website, including the number of conversions and average profitability even for the awareness campaigns. The creative content for the dynamic ads was generated from the product catalog feed that was aligned with the uniform aesthetics of the e-store and contained both photo-based and video-based representations of the offered products. The static ads contained also photo and video content; however, a limited set of visuals was chosen and used for all the ads from this group.

RESULTS

All the collected data were exported from Google AdWords and Facebook Ads Manager as .xlsx files and imported into SPSS Statistics 24. Since the main objective of the presented research was to examine the effectiveness of dynamic ads across advertising platforms and placement, cross tabulation was chosen as the most suitable statistical method. Because of the different algorithms and tracking tools applied by Google and Facebook, any other form of statistical analysis would provide very inaccurate results. The effectiveness of all advertisements is, in the following paragraphs, judged always with regard to the stage of the customer acquisition process and the campaign goals.

According to some authors (Bang & Wojdynski, 2016; Yu et al., 2019), the phenomenon of advertising blindness heavily depends on the position of the ads, as suggested earlier in this chapter. To answer our first research question (RQ1), we focused on the results from the dynamic and static Facebook ads, since the dynamic ads on Google used variable placement.

Looking more closely at the results in Table 4, we identified that the worst performing placements in terms of reaching the desired audience were Instagram stories with 15 reactions (0.19 EUR average cost per reaction) for the dynamic ads and 21 reactions (0.17 EUR average per reaction) for the static ads and an audience network with 16 reactions (0.11 EUR) for the dynamic ads and 27 reactions (0.09 EUR) for the static ads. The right column placement generated a higher number of reactions than the previous two placements. However, the average cost per conversion was also rather high (0.13 EUR for dynamic ads and 0.12 for static ads). By contrast, the best results were achieved for the Facebook newsfeed and marketplace.

Within the campaign goal "consideration", newsfeed with 3.01 CTR for dynamic ads and 3.18 CTR for static ads and marketplace with 3.32 CTR for dynamic ads and 3.65 CTR for static ads performed significantly better than other placements. Messenger and Instagram channels also stood out by reaching CTR values higher than 2.2. The average profitability confirms previous results. Facebook newsfeed, marketplace, and messenger have the biggest potential to captivate users' attention. This higher performance is most likely the result of the central placement of the ads in the main part of the browsing area. Contrarily, the right column and banners on the websites within audience network represent side placements that are susceptible to advertising blindness. Instagram channel and Instagram stories are considered to be straightly visual, and the users mostly do not anticipate to shop on the Instagram network. Our results indicate that Instagram users are more inclined to react than participate in any advanced conversions.

Overall, we may confirm that the choice of placement has an important effect on the performance of Facebook ads, although this effect was equally prominent for both dynamic and manually optimized ads.

Table 4. The impact of placement on the performance of Facebook ads

	Brand awareness and reach				Consideration				Conversions	
	Dynamic ads		Manually optimized ads		Dynamic ads		Manually optimized ads		Dynamic ads	Manually optimized ads
	Av. Num. of reac.	Av. cost per reac. (EUR)	Num. of reac.	Av. cost per reac. (EUR)	Av. CTR	Av. cost per CTR (EUR)	Av. CTR	Av. cost per CTR (EUR)	Av. profit. (EUR)	Av. profit. (EUR)
Facebook newsfeed	132	0.09	187	0.11	3.01	0.12	3.18	0.10	38.46	42.87
Right column	54	0.13	63	0.12	1.82	0.18	1.74	0.15	19.21	17.12
Marketplace	145	0.07	208	0.06	3.32	0.11	3.65	0.09	45.01	64.88
Instagram channel	89	0.09	142	0.08	2.29	0.14	2.45	0.14	17.23	10.27
Instagram stories	15	0.19	21	0.17	1.12	0.17	1.14	0.17	9.18	5.12
Audience network	16	0.11	27	0.09	1.56	0.17	1.48	0.16	12.32	7.94
Messenger	31	0.09	71	0.09	2.56	0.13	2.85	0.11	22.34	36.03

Source: (the authors)

Our second research question (RQ2) examined the influence of advertising formats such as text and variations of picture-based and interactive content on the performance of dynamic and static ads. The analysis included data from both Google ads and Facebook ads (Table 5). However, some factors must be considered when the data are interpreted. Since some of the formats are specific only to the respective social networks, the costs may differ across the platforms. *Carousel* and Collection represent only Facebook native formats, while Text and Interactive content were used only for the Google ads. Advertisements containing one photo of a product were set up for both ad systems. The results from the 168 dynamic and 1,575 static ads indicate that text-based advertisement in the Google search network generate the best outcomes when created as dynamic ads, regardless of the customer acquisition stage and campaign goals. Textual ads had the best CTR out of the all advertising formats. Interactive ads performed the best in terms of profitability and the number of reactions; however, their cost was higher (average cost per CTR of 0.21 EUR for the dynamic ads and 0.24 EUR for the static ads). Among the Facebook advertising formats, Carousel generated the most results at the lowest cost. According to our data, the collection of multiple product photos appears to be the least effective advertising format. As it is evident from Table 5, the choice of advertising format may significantly affect the performance of the dynamic ads and that of the manually optimized ads.

The main focus of our research agenda was examining whether dynamic ads can successfully answer the marketing needs of advertisers while cutting the time-demanding effort of creating individual ads. To answer our three remaining research questions (RQ3, RQ4, and RQ5), we first compared the advertising results of dynamic and static ads within each advertising platform. Subsequently, we performed a cross-platform comparative analysis between Facebook and Google.

Table 5. The impact of the advertising format on the performance of static and dynamic ads

	Brand awareness and reach				Consideration				Conversions	
	Dynamics ads		Manually optimized ads		Dynamics ads		Manually optimized ads		Dynamics ads	Manually optimized ads
	Av. Num. of reac.	Av. cost per reac. (EUR)	Num. of reac.	Av. cost per reac. (EUR)	Av. CTR	Av. cost per CTR (EUR)	Av. CTR	Av. cost per CTR (EUR)	Av. profit. (EUR)	Av. profit. (EUR)
Photo	85	0.11	98	0.10	1.89	0.12	1.75	0.14	12.44	12.42
Carousel	167	0.09	178	0.08	2.32	0.09	2.34	0.09	17.67	16.95
Collection	106	0.19	121	0.15	1.95	0.17	1.95	0.17	13.87	12.32
Interactive	131	0.25	167	0.18	3.28	0.21	3.10	0.24	20.12	19.21
Text	186	0.19	121	0.23	3.48	0.19	2.89	0.25	12.86	10.21

Source: (the authors)

What are the effects of dynamic ads during the different stages of getting familiar with a brand? Results displayed in Tables 6 and 7 present the stage by stage comparison of all types of dynamic ads and the grouped average values for the static ads. With regard to Google ads, smart ads performed suboptimally in the awareness and consideration stages, but the final average profitability (22.38 EUR) can be considered rather moderate than weak. Moderate performance in all acquisition phases was typical for dynamic customer search ads and dynamic product ads. Dynamic search ads led to the lowest profitability; however, on the other hand, they produced the best CTR (3.48) in the consideration phase and a moderate number of reactions (186). The best overall performance was achieved for the dynamic remarketing ads that generated CTR of 3.21 and the highest average profitability (35.35 EUR).

Table 6. Effects of dynamic and static Google ads during the different stages of the customer acquisition process

	Brand awareness and reach		Consideration		Conversions
	Av. Num. of reac.	Av. cost per reac. (EUR)	Av. CTR	Av. cost per CTR (EUR)	Av. profit. (EUR)
Smart ads	166	0.21	1.99	0.21	22.38
Dynamic search ads	186	0.19	3.48	0.19	12.86
Dynamic product ads	193	0.15	2.12	0.19	22.18
Dynamic remarketing ads	254	0.12	3.21	0.21	35.35
Dynamic customer search ads	189	0.21	2.54	0.29	28.89
Static product ads (combined)	205	0.20	2.15	0.18	25.10
Static search ads (combined)	215	0.18	3.39	0.19	15.54

Source: (the authors)

The performance of Facebook dynamic ads across the individual acquisition stages also differed. Table 7 contains the aggregated results for all types of dynamic Facebook ads, including the equivalent of customer search Google ads. Lookalike ads represent a tool for finding new customers with characteristics similar to the current audience. The advertising results reflect the connection between the campaign goal optimization and the customer acquisition stage. Dynamic ads optimized for awareness performed the best in the first stage of the acquisition process (206 reactions at 0.12 EUR average cost), but their effectiveness decreased over time and failed to obtain the desired profitability. Similarly, dynamic consideration ads generated the best CTR (3.24 at the lowest cost of 0.12 EUR), whereas the conversion ads generated the best profitability (35.90 EUR). Dynamic customer search ads (lookalikes) performed consistently well across all the acquisition stages and generated medium profitability (23.45 EUR).

Table 7. Effects of Facebook ads during the different stages of the customer acquisition process

	Brand awareness and reach		Consideration		Conversions
	Av. Num. of reac.	Av. cost per reac. (EUR)	Av. CTR	Av. cost per CTR (EUR)	Av. profit. (EUR)
Custom audience awareness	206	0.12	1.95	0.15	12.00
Custom audience consideration	189	0.14	3.24	0.12	20.19
Custom audience conversions	107	0.14	2.36	0.18	35.90
Lookalike audiences (combined)	183	0.13	2.56	0.21	23.45
Facebook Static ads awareness	308	0.09	1.77	0.14	13.72
Facebook Static ads consideration	206	0.18	3.01	0.15	19.92
Facebook Static ads conversions	197	0.19	2.02	0.21	29.34

Source: (the authors)

The effectiveness comparison of dynamic and static ads was also one of the research topics (RQ4) we defined at the beginning of this chapter. If we look more closely at the results related to the Google platform (Table 6), we may conclude that the dynamic ads represent a very effective tool of marketing automatization. All of the dynamic ads brought similar or superior results to the manually optimized ads, whereas the dynamic remarketing ads were the most effective of all for the campaign we set up (average profitability: 35.35 EUR). Regarding the Facebook advertising system, the results are less conclusive. It appears that manually optimized ads work more efficiently than their dynamic versions for the first two stages: brand awareness and consideration. In the conversion stage, Facebook catalog ads outperformed the static ads (average profitability of 35.90 EUR and 29.34 EUR, respectively).

Finally, if we compare the advertising outcomes across the two platforms (RQ5), Facebook and Google, we may conclude that both types of dynamic advertising produce similarly desirable results. However, it is important to mention the necessity of evaluating ad performance with regard to the different user contexts of the platforms. Our findings indicate identical behavioral patterns when it comes to remarketing ads. The high level of personalization provided by these automatically generated ads helps to convert users that have already exhibited interest into becoming customers. In addition, our experiment proves that Facebook and Google dynamic ads may be successfully used for acquiring new customers. By contrast, the best option for addressing new customers appears to be Facebook awareness ads, which generated the most reactions at the lowest cost. Dynamic Google search ads also performed well during the first stage of customer acquisition. We suppose that the lower performance of Facebook dynamic ads in other, except remarketing, situations may be caused by the nature of the content that users are used to seeing on the social network. To capture users' attention on this medium, originality is a necessity. Hence, automatically generated content using a standardized template does not provide enough convincing power.

CONCLUSION

Communicating a marketing message to the right potential customers is a major challenge in today's marketing arena. Internet and related technologies have enabled consumers to gain more control of information gathering than before. Therefore, traditional marketing campaigns have lost their effectiveness, and more sophisticated marketing automation campaigns are taking their place. Marketing automation tools are now part of many comprehensive business systems that integrate and process data from a variety of other enterprise applications and external resources. Generally, business systems work with data from CRM, ERP, warehouse systems, or accounting and integrate large data analysis systems. The main purpose of these business systems is to gain the detailed knowledge of the customer and his/her needs. Automation then allows the advertisers to offer products and services that match the customer's interests and reach him/her at the right time and in the right place or through a suitable business channel. Finding the right combination of all parameters increases the likelihood of a successful purchase and the overall customer satisfaction and loyalty.

This chapter presented the results of 168 automatically generated dynamic and 1,575 manually optimized ads from Google AdWords and Facebook Ads Manager. In our experiment, we focused on the analysis of the effectiveness of the dynamic ads while considering the parameters that could influence the advertising performance, such as the campaign goal, placement, and the format of the creative content. Our findings indicate that marketing automatization using artificial intelligence offered by advertising systems can be successfully used to convert online users into paying customers and to acquire new customers based on the information about the current customer base. Thanks to their ability to provide highly personalized content and track the users' preferences, dynamic ads are the most beneficial when used for remarketing purposes. However, they might perform sub-optimally in situations where the browsing context requires originality. Users' participate in social networks for entertainment and not to browse through product advertisements. Making first contact with a user might require more innovative content than a dynamically generated product catalog. By contrast, dynamic Google ads are mostly displayed in a context where the user has already showed interest in the product or a similar category of products. The system thus makes recommendations based on the user's previous entries and helps him/her to find what he/she is looking for. Advertisers on social networks are generally trying to convince the users to try products that they have never directly asked for. This contextual duality might be the main factor that influences the performance of the dynamic ads.

In conclusion, dynamic ads are definitely a very helpful and effective tool for e-stores that wish to advertise many products at any time. This type of automatized and personalized advertising is very suitable for reminding online users of the products that have caught their attention in the past and for recommending suitable solutions to their search queries. Nevertheless, marketing automatization still has limitations, and artificial intelligence cannot completely replace the human factor in marketing communication. Original and creative content remains the most important prerequisite for establishing and maintaining long-term and engaged relationships.

ACKNOWLEDGMENT

This research was supported by the Technical University of Liberec, in a grant titled "Competitiveness of the company in the digital environment", registered as SGS-2019-1068, and by the Technology Agency of the Czech Republic under the Program of applied research ZETA within the framework of project "Developing the skills necessary for the digital business transformation" (registration number TJ02000206).

REFERENCES

Abedini Koshksaray, A., Franklin, D., & Heidarzadeh Hanzaee, K. (2015). The relationship between e-lifestyle and Internet advertising avoidance. [AMJ]. *Australasian Marketing Journal*, *23*(1), 38–48. doi:10.1016/j.ausmj.2015.01.002

Baek, T., & Morimoto, M. (2012). Stay away from me. *Journal of Advertising*, *41*(1), 59–76. doi:10.2753/JOA0091-3367410105

Bang, H., & Wojdynski, B. (2016). Tracking users' visual attention and responses to personalized advertising based on task cognitive demand. *Computers in Human Behavior*, *55*, 867–876. doi:10.1016/j.chb.2015.10.025

Baruh, L., Secinti, E., & Cemalcilar, Z. (2017). Online privacy concerns and privacy management: a meta-analytical review. *Journal of Communication*, *67*(1), 26–53. doi:10.1111/jcom.12276

Bleier, A., & Eisenbeiss, M. (2015). The importance of trust for personalized online advertising. *Journal of Retailing*, *91*(3), 390–409. doi:10.1016/j.jretai.2015.04.001

Chen, Q., Feng, Y., Liu, L., & Tian, X. (2019). Understanding consumers' reactance of online personalized advertising: A new scheme of rational choice from a perspective of negative effects. *International Journal of Information Management*, *44*, 53–64. doi:10.1016/j.ijinfomgt.2018.09.001

Danova, T. (2014). For mobile-social apps, advertising is winning as the money-making revenue model. Retrieved from http://www. businessinsider. com/advertising-is-the-most-lucrative-revenue-modelfor-growing-mobile-social-apps-2014-1

Eckersley, P. (2010). How unique is your web browser?. *Privacy Enhancing Technologies*, 1-18. doi:10.1007/978-3-642-14527-8_1

Estrada-Jiménez, J., Parra-Arnau, J., Rodríguez-Hoyos, A., & Forné, J. (2017). Online advertising: Analysis of privacy threats and protection approaches. *Computer Communications*, *100*, 32–51. doi:10.1016/j.comcom.2016.12.016

Gironda, J., & Korgaonkar, P. (2018). iSpy? Tailored versus invasive ads and consumers' perceptions of personalized advertising. *Electronic Commerce Research and Applications*, *29*, 64–77. doi:10.1016/j. elerap.2018.03.007

Grewal, D., Bart, Y., Spann, M., & Zubcsek, P. (2016). Mobile advertising: a framework and research agenda. *Journal of Interactive Marketing*, *34*, 3–14. doi:10.1016/j.intmar.2016.03.003

GrowthBadger. (2019). *Remarketing: the ultimate guide for 2019*. Retrieved from https://growthbadger. com/remarketing/

Hsieh, Y., & Chen, K. (2011). How different information types affect viewer's attention on internet advertising. *Computers in Human Behavior*, *27*(2), 935–945. doi:10.1016/j.chb.2010.11.019

Lee, T. (2019). Google is the internet's largest ad company. So why is it building an ad blocker? Retrieved from https://www.vox.com/new-money/2017/6/5/15729688/google-chrome-ad-blocking

Li, C. (2016). When does web-based personalization really work? The distinction between actual personalization and perceived personalization. *Computers in Human Behavior*, *54*, 25–33. doi:10.1016/j. chb.2015.07.049

Li, C., & Liu, J. (2017). A name alone is not enough: A reexamination of web-based personalization effect. *Computers in Human Behavior*, *72*, 132–139. doi:10.1016/j.chb.2017.02.039

Lu, C., Wu, I., & Hsiao, W. (2019). Developing customer product loyalty through mobile advertising: Affective and cognitive perspectives. *International Journal of Information Management*, *47*, 101–111. doi:10.1016/j.ijinfomgt.2018.12.020

Parra-Arnau, J., Achara, J., & Castelluccia, C. (2017). MyAdChoices. *ACM Transactions on the Web*, *11*(1), 1–47. doi:10.1145/2996466

Redondo, I., & Aznar, G. (2018). To use or not to use ad blockers? The roles of knowledge of ad blockers and attitude toward online advertising. *Telematics and Informatics*, *35*(6), 1607–1616. doi:10.1016/j. tele.2018.04.008

Sánchez, D., & Viejo, A. (2018). Privacy-preserving and advertising-friendly web surfing. *Computer Communications*, *130*, 113–123. doi:10.1016/j.comcom.2018.09.002

Schreiner, T., Rese, A., & Baier, D. (2019). Multichannel personalization: Identifying consumer preferences for product recommendations in advertisements across different media channels. *Journal of Retailing and Consumer Services*, *48*, 87–99. doi:10.1016/j.jretconser.2019.02.010

Setyani, V., Zhu, Y., Hidayanto, A., Sandhyaduhita, P., & Hsiao, B. (2019). Exploring the psychological mechanisms from personalized advertisements to urge to buy impulsively on social media. *International Journal of Information Management*, *48*, 96–107. doi:10.1016/j.ijinfomgt.2019.01.007

Shanahan, T., Tran, T., & Taylor, E. (2019). Getting to know you: Social media personalization as a means of enhancing brand loyalty and perceived quality. *Journal of Retailing and Consumer Services*, *47*, 57–65. doi:10.1016/j.jretconser.2018.10.007

The influence of perceived ad relevance on social media advertising: An empirical examination of a mediating role of privacy concern. *Computers in Human Behavior, 70*, 303-309. doi:10.1016/j.chb.2017.01.008

Tran, T. (2017). Personalized ads on facebook: An effective marketing tool for online marketers. *Journal of Retailing and Consumer Services*, *39*, 230–242. doi:10.1016/j.jretconser.2017.06.010

WordStream. (2019). *31 Advertising statistics to know in 2019*. Retrieved from https://www.wordstream.com/blog/ws/2018/07/19/advertising-statistics

Yu, C., Zhang, Z., Lin, C., & Wu, Y. (2019). Can data-driven precision marketing promote user ad clicks? Evidence from advertising in WeChat moments. *Industrial Marketing Management*. doi:10.1016/j.indmarman.2019.05.001

Yu, J., & Cude, B. (2009). Possible disparities in consumers' perceptions toward personalized advertising caused by cultural differences: U.S. and Korea. *Journal of International Consumer Marketing*, *21*(4), 251–269. doi:10.1080/08961530802282166

Zorn, S., Bellman, S., Robinson, J., & Varan, D. (2013). Cultural differences affect interactive television advertising. *Journal of Marketing Communications*, *22*(1), 3–17. doi:10.1080/13527266.2013.833539

ADDITIONAL READING

de Haan, E., Wiesel, T., & Pauwels, K. (2016). The effectiveness of different forms of online advertising for purchase conversion in a multiple-channel attribution framework. *International Journal of Research in Marketing*, *33*(3), 491–507. doi:10.1016/j.ijresmar.2015.12.001

Estrada-Jiménez, J., Parra-Arnau, J., Rodríguez-Hoyos, A., & Forné, J. (2019). On the regulation of personal data distribution in online advertising platforms. *Engineering Applications of Artificial Intelligence*, *82*, 13–29. doi:10.1016/j.engappai.2019.03.013

Gijsenberg, M., & Nijs, V. (2019). Advertising spending patterns and competitor impact. *International Journal of Research in Marketing*, *36*(2), 232–250. doi:10.1016/j.ijresmar.2018.11.004

He, J., & Shao, B. (2018). Examining the dynamic effects of social network advertising: A semiotic perspective. *Telematics and Informatics*, *35*(2), 504–516. doi:10.1016/j.tele.2018.01.014

Ji, S., Choi, Y., & Ryu, M. (2016). The economic effects of domestic search engines on the development of the online advertising market. *Telecommunications Policy*, *40*(10-11), 982–995. doi:10.1016/j.telpol.2016.05.005

Kireyev, P., Pauwels, K., & Gupta, S. (2016). Do display ads influence search? Attribution and dynamics in online advertising. *International Journal of Research in Marketing*, *33*(3), 475–490. doi:10.1016/j.ijresmar.2015.09.007

White, G., & Samuel, A. (2019). Programmatic Advertising: Forewarning and avoiding hype-cycle failure. *Technological Forecasting and Social Change*, *144*, 157–168. doi:10.1016/j.techfore.2019.03.020

Yoldar, M., & Özcan, U. (2019). Collaborative targeting: Biclustering-based online ad recommendation. *Electronic Commerce Research and Applications*, *35*, 100857. doi:10.1016/j.elerap.2019.100857

KEY TERMS AND DEFINITIONS

Ad Placement: Ad placement include all advertising spaces, mostly paid, offered by online publishers, websites, and social networks to advertisers to display their advertisements. The individual placements have different potential for reaching the users and perform differently when it comes to the type of content chosen for the advertisement.

Ad Targeting: Ad targeting refers to the selection of potential customer groups to which an advertisement will be displayed. This specification of the ad's audience is done using targeting parameters including demographic and geographic information, interests, and device preferences. **Conversion:** Conversion refers to a desired action performed by a consumer as a reaction to an advertisement or other marketing effort. The desired action can take many forms including the purchases, membership registrations, newsletter subscriptions, and application downloads.

Dynamic advertisements: Dynamic advertisements describe a dynamic delivery of specific products that visitors viewed on the website of an online retailer. Their primary advantage is dynamism that allows one to create one advertising template and use it for all products from an uploaded data feed. Information from the data feed is automatically being implemented into the template based on user preferences. **Facebook Ads Manager:** The Facebook Ads Manager was developed by Facebook to manage advertisements on this social network, Instagram, and ads displayed in the audience network. This application allows the advertiser to create and target the ads, set campaign budget, view history, and collect data about previous and ongoing ads.

Marketing automatization: Marketing automation is represented by the introduction of software tools that automate some of the key processes of customer data collection, evaluation, acquisition, and customer retention. Among these automated activities, we may undoubtedly include e-mail marketing, web analytics, the evaluation of potential leads, online forms, consumer research, tracking of ongoing marketing campaigns, and many others.

Product feed: A product XML feed is a collection of all selected products available in an online store containing all the necessary data for full import and synchronization with product search engines, price comparators, aggregators, or advertising systems. It is required to implement dynamic product campaigns.

UTM Parameters: Text fragments that are attached in the specified format to the web link. Attaching these textual segments allows the analytical software to exactly identify from what source, campaign, or advertisement the users came to the website. UTM parameters generally contain the following five elements: utm_source, utm_medium, utm_campaign, utm_content, and utm_term.

Chapter 31
Calculation of Facebook Marketing Effectiveness in Terms of ROI

Tereza Semerádová
https://orcid.org/0000-0002-9123-5782
Technical University of Liberec, Czech Republic

Petr Weinlich
Technical University of Liberec, Czech Republic

ABSTRACT

This chapter demonstrates how to assess the performance of organic and sponsored activities on Facebook using the data available in Facebook Ads Manager, Facebook Page Insights, and Google Analytics. The main aim of the proposed ROI calculation model is to connect common social media marketing objectives with the analytical information available. The main emphasis is put on the technical aspect of ad performance assessment. The authors explain how the Facebook attribution system and post-impression algorithm work, describe the relation between advertising goals and metrics displayed as achieved campaign results, and demonstrate how to derive ROI indexes from different Facebook conversions. The chapter also includes a practical example how to calculate current and future value of ongoing ads.

INTRODUCTION

The digital advertising has become a key instrument for reaching marketing and business goals of many companies. This sector is rapidly growing reaching 281.407 billion USD in 2018. Even though the Search advertising still represents the largest segment with a market volume of 127.546 billion USD, Social media advertising is not far behind. With the annual growth of 10.5% this segment is expected to reach a market volume of 76.561 billion USD in 2022 (Statista, 2018a). Ad revenues of Facebook, the leading company on the field of social media advertising, stood at more than 39.9 billion USD in 2017 which is almost a 22 billion increase in comparison to 2015. In addition, the current statistics imply another

DOI: 10.4018/978-1-7998-9020-1.ch031

potential for expansion for mobile advertising. According to Statista (2018b), mobile advertising seems to be the most promising form of revenue generation for the company. It is expected that Facebook mobile advertising revenues will reach 60.68 billion USD in 2021.

The growing importance of social advertising in terms of online marketing activities is undoubtable. Big brands such as Samsung, Proter&Gambler, Coca Cola or Oreo embraced Facebook advertising as a key part of their marketing strategies. Samsung, who is one the Facebook biggest clients, spent 10 million USD in three weeks on Facebook just to launch its Galaxy S III phone. Also, Procter & Gamble, the world's largest advertiser, has a massive presence on Facebook and spends yearly about 60 million USD on sponsored posts. Brand´s Facebook influence does not have to be expressed only by the amount spent on online advertising. For instance, Coca-Cola has 76 million fans on Facebook, making it the most-liked brand on the planet, while Starbucks with 37 million fans occupies the fourth rank (Business Insider, 2018).

It can thus be assumed that greater effectiveness of online advertising contributes to improving business activities of companies that use it. Current studies show that online advertising, by making use of proper expertise and technologies, may help to change customer buying behavior (Abayi & Khoshtinat, 2016). Results of the previous surveys and studies supported the assumption that Facebook seems to be an effective medium for customer relationship management and the promotion of new products. Businesses are very keen to harvest all the benefits offered by this network. Facebook activities help to build awareness, inform, promote the brand and its product consistently with the business goals. However, understanding the targeted group of customers and the technical and contextual characteristics of the online media in use represent a crucial prerequisite for achieving all the online marketing objectives. Companies need to understand what are the correlations between their social media activities, online advertising and the benefits gained from such efforts (Ertugan, 2017).

One of the biggest issues in terms of assessing the effectiveness of Facebook marketing efforts is the quantification of the achieved results. Only some of the advertising efforts may be directly expressed as revenues. The remaining processes such as raising awareness and community building,contribute to the generation of profit indirectly. However, companies invest significant amounts of money in order to expand their fan bases, promote their company culture or engage in communication with their current customers. All of these partial steps contribute to creating the brand´s image and finally selling the promoted products. These activities, in particular, are causing considerable problems when it comes to calculating their contribution to the final revenues. Nevertheless, knowing the performance of all the marketing efforts on Facebook helps to effectively allocate the marketing ressources.

In this chapter, the researchers are going to focus on the calculation of return on Facebook marketing investments, hereinafter referred to as ROI-FM, including the proposition of Facebook advertising effectiveness evaluation models for individual goals reachable via this network. Thanks to the sophisticated tracking systems offered by Facebook and their connection to website analytical applications such as Google Analytics, the companies have numerous possibilities how to monitor the impact of their Facebook (and other) advertisements. It is important to understand the advertising system and the metrics related to it. Choosing the right metrics and interpreting them correctly with regards to the marketing goals is the only way how to assess the effectiveness of Facebook activities and optimize the settlement of online advertisements.

The following paragraphs are going to explain how Facebook attribution system and post impression algorithm work, describe the relation between advertising goals and metrics displayed as achieved campaign results, and demonstrate how to derive ROI-FM indexes from different Facebook conversions. Aim of this chapter is to connect common social media marketing objectives with analytical information available in Facebook Insights and Facebook Ads Manager. The authors believe that the proposed perspective could help the marketers to take full advantage of the possibilities offered by this networking platform.

FACEBOOK POST AND AD PERFORMANCE

Corvi and Bonera (2010) define advertising effectiveness as the extent to which advertising brings the desired effects. The authors also add that this effectiveness is not easy to measure due to its connection to marketing, financial, environmental, competition and other variables and that cannot always be expressed with quantitative measures. Aslam & Karjaluoto (2017) made a synthesis of previous papers discussing the topic of online advertising. In their paper they make difference between paid advertising and online marketing since the last one may include organic elements such as friend referrals or search engine optimization. The effectiveness assessment thus should not be restricted only to sponsored posts but also to other Facebook activities with organic (unpaid) reach and with other objectives than just increasing the number of product orders. Accordingly, the activities may be generalized by dividing them into two groups: customer relationship management and product promotion.

Customer Engagement

Customer engagement is generally defined as the relationship users have with the brand, advertisement or post (Kuvykaité & Tarutė, 2015). However, universal definition of this concept is still missing. Engagement is in terms of social networks expressed as a range of metrics while contextual relevance remains a critical aspect. According to a survey organized by Deloitte (2015), consumers do not use Facebook to look for new products or to engage with brands. Their primary motivation is to look for social information and entertainment.

Brands should therefore go beyond evelatuating just the purchases, but also examine other engagement parameters such as consumer's comments (Fulgoni, 2016). Research results presented by Brettel et al. (2015) indicate that in long term customers that like the brand page and interact with it (liking posts, commenting) are more likely to bring sales benefits.

However, many companies tend to misinterpret the achieved results and overestimate the effects of their Facebook activities. According to Heller Baird and Parasnis (2011), 38% of consumers feel social media interactions with a brand will not increase their loyalty to a brand. In addition, not all interactions may be considered as having the same value since for instance liking a brand page can occur for utilitarian reasons such as winning in a competition or getting a discount (Wallace et al., 2014).

The relevancy of shared content influences the way how consumers perceive marketing communication of the brand. Individual features that have the most significant impact on the consumer's perception are described by the Elaboration Likelihood Model (ELM). This model covers also disruptive effects that may result in negative attitudes toward the post or advertisement and as consequence in lower engagement rate (Petty & Cacioppo, 1986).

Heinonen (2011) suggested that consumer´s behavior is not influenced by a single motivation but rather by a variety of factors. He also adds that due to the growing portion of user generated content, traditional marketing strategies are less effective. Consumers are becoming active producers of business values.

User experience may be viewed as a composite variable consisting of extrinsic and intrinsic factors. Extrinsic factors are connected to utilitarian value which describes the level of satisfaction with the information gained on products, specific problems or areas of interest. Whereas intrinsic factors correspond to hedonic value. Hedonic factors represent entertainment, fun, and sensory stimulation (Gutiérrez-Cillán et al., 2017). The main objective of social media marketers should thus be to satisfy both extrinsic and intrinsc factors. Whereas the primary impuls of the brand´s pages would be to focus on supplying required information on the products they sell, they should not neglect the intrinsic experience the users of social networks are looking for. The level of satisfaction with the dimensions described above conditions consumer´s motivation to stay in the community and possibly becoming a more active member (Bicen et al., 2011).

Zhou et al. (2013) studied the predeterminants of successful conversion from visitors to active members in online brand communities. They came to conclusion, that if the user by viewing the branded posts perceives them as having satisfactory informational value and realizes the benefits of belonging to this particular community his intention to participate will grow stronger.

Dehghani & Tumer (2015) studied the link between brand image, brand equity and purchase intention. They found high correlations between the examined factors and confirmed that Facebook may enhance brand image and brand equity leading to increased purchase intention.The authors describe a new phenomenon they refer to as trust advertising. Trust advertising is based on such features as participation, realization, personalization and feedback that should be developed all along the entire purchase cycle. Harris and Dennis (2011) in their paper studied factors influencing customer trust and engagement when it comes to Facebook branded content. They found out that social network users have a hierarchy of trust that goes as follows in the descending order Facebook friends, expert blogs, independent review sites and lastly celebrities and e-retailer sites.

Dehghani & Tumer (2015) also suggest that user´s willingness to purchase products increases with the growing number of "like"s and "share"s that possibly reflect the reputablity of the brand in the eyes of the consumer. LaPointe (2012) came to different conclusions. He thinks that the membership of branded pages on Facebook and likelihood to click on advertising are not necessarily correlated. Banelis et al. (2013) argue that many buyers that frequently purchase goods from one category probably have larger brand repertoires and they are more likely to be 'fans' of multiple Facebook pages from this category.

In their experiment, Beukeboom et al. (2015) proved that there is a positive relationship between brand equity, purchase intention, brand attitudes and becoming a fan of a brand page. In a one month period the authors observed how engagement parameters changed for the users that became followers of a selected brand.The parameters increased in all the observed cases.

Many brands assume, that sharing large amounts of branded content will lead to the growth in sales and increased fan commitment and content sharing. However, only small fraction of the branded content is shared by the fans. Yuki (2015) claims that only 7% of the brand's activites are forwarded. Even Facebook´s own statistics support the assumption that posting too much branded content and pushing the fans to interact with it may chase them away and negatively react to advertised content (Brettel et al., 2015). There is also no significant correlation between the People Talking About This (PTAT) metric and brand´s sales of profit (Smallwood, 2016).

Some studies suggest that the strength of the fan base influence may differ across the product categories. For instance, fashion products content has a bigger potential to be shared by the social network users rather then financial services. Promoting products may therefore be slightly problematic for some categories that offer rather professional services. Facebook marketing is best suited for the promotion of consumer goods and products that are connected with entertainment and lifestyle. Even though, despite these barriers, neglecting company presence on Facebook may lead to missed opportunities to gain new customers. Companies thus should not abandon social networks but actively communicate with their potential customers, assess the impact of their activities and carefully consider the investments in Facebook advertising. For some categories, Facebook may be only used just as an indirect marketing support channel. Being able to measure the performance of individual media used, and understand them correctly represent a building stone of an effective social media marketing. Based on the results described in the Harvard Business Review study of 2100 companies, only 7% of the respondents were able to fully embrace the potential of social networks and were trying to understand the effectiveness of their advertising and marketing activities (Kohli et al., 2015).

When it comes to assessing the effectiveness of Facebook content, it is necessary to make a distinction between „brand posts" and „user posts". Through branded posts companies try to influence the experience of their followers. However, not all posts have the same impact and not all post generate the same value. Since Facebook posts are designed to allow the sharing of many types of content and to trigger various responses, measuring the user experience and reaction is very difficult due to the high number of possible permutations (Gutiérrez-Cillán et al., 2017).

Advertising Performance

Thanks to the personal details on all their users that Facebook and other social media store, they represent a superior channel to other advertising media since they allow the marketers to use this information to reach their target audiences (Curran et al., 2011). Advertising on Facebook is specific in that the advertiser may choose what advertising model he wants use and what metrics will be calculated to measure the performance of the advertisement. However, Facebook does not use the Flat Fee (FF) model. The advertising costs depend on the engagement rate, which measures how much the ads are relevant for the target audiences. The bigger the engagement is, the lower the costs will decrease (Tikno, 2017).

In the FF model, the marketing costs depend on the advertisement size and the impression time. In this advertising model, the advertiser pays for the time his advertising unit is being displayed regardless of the number of conversions generated during that period. While the CPM (from Latin Cost Per Mille), also known as the CPT (Cost Per Thousand) model is based on the calculation of the cost needed to pay by the advertiser to reach 1000 recipients. Just as the FF, neither the CPM model takes into account the number of actions (website visits, purchases made in the eshop, etc.) gained thanks to the advertisement. An other model that is used by Facebook advertising system is the CPC model (Cost per Click). Unlike the previous two models, CPC is based on the number of interactions with the ad. The advertiser is charged an exact sum that is determined as the number of actual clicks leading the advertisers website multiplied by the CPC index which determines the cost per click on an advertisement unit. Advertisers ordering campaigns in this model assess the effectiveness of their ads using the CTR index (click through rate) that indicates what percentage of the impressions resulted in the user interaction with the ad. Similar principle is used in the CPA model (Cost Per Action) where the advertiser pays not just for a click and a lead to his website, but rather for any action that is relevant to him. Advertising costs are drawn only when the action defined by the advertiser occurs such as filling the order form, providing contact details etc. The effectiveness of the CPA model is usually assessed via the conversion rate that stands for the percentage of users reacting to the advertisement performed the desired action.

In her paper, Magdalena Rzemieniak (2015) assessed the effectiveness and frequency of use of three types of online campaign settlements models: impression models, effectiveness models and hybrid models. Her survey comprising 50 entrepreneurs revealed that 80% of the respondents use the CPC model for most of their ads that over 60% of them also consider the most effective.

All of these advertising models have in common the need to captivate the viewer's attention and induce his interaction with the post. The marketers thus need to learn how to earn higher engagement rates. Tikno (2017) investigated the performance of different media types used on Facebook. The author used as control variables the gender, age and product type to define the interest group. The results showed that video based posts lead to higher engagement compared to images.

Dehghani and Tumer (2015) studied on the sample of 100 student from Cypriot universities the students´ perception of branded content on Facebook. Their results indicate that in order to achieve a high level of effectiveness, the ads should include features such as personalization, participation and realization.

Despite all the undeniable benefits of sponsored content, users do not come to Facebook to browse through the advertisements. Ad placements are therefore susceptible to avoidance and may easily be ignored. Van den Broeck et al. (2018) analyzed the level of avoidance for the newsfeed and for the right sidebar. The avoidance level for the newsfeed was significantly higher. The authors also find out that product involvement and right audience targeting had positive moderating effect on intention to skip advertisements.

Research presented by Bang and Lee (2016) suggests that ad avoidance is more related to the habitual appearance than information processing. These results are in compliance with findings presented by Van den Broeck et al. (2018). Visual characteristics, timing, placement and audience targeting have been found to be key determinants of user interaction with the ad. According to Fan et al. (2017), placement is not a sufficient reason to ad avoidance. If the content of the ad is consistent with the interests of the user and fits within the social media context, the advertisement may actually provide positive experience to the user and lead to desired interaction.

The term "ad placement" is used to describe all advertising spaces provided by Facebook such as the newsfeed, righ side bar, Instagram, Audience Network, instream videos or messenger. The individual placements have different potential for reaching the Facebook users and perform differently when comes to the type of content chosen for the advertisement. Facebook newsfeed (with the possibility of distinction for desktop and mobile devices) represents the most popular placement on Facebook (Campbell and Marks, 2015). Thanks to their resemblance to the user generated content, sponsored posts provide a consistent reading experience (eMarketer, 2016).

Research related to the effectiveness of ad placements on social networks is very limited (Bang and Lee, 2016; Van den Broeck et al., 2017). The scarceness of information may be caused by the lack of nonexperimental data collected from real life campaigns and web traffic. Nevertheless, the evidence for website ad placements suggests that user´s reaction in terms of ad processing, attention, attitudes and clicks depend very strongly on the chosen ad placement (Mulhern, 2013). Feeling of intrusiveness is one of the other frequently mentioned causes of ad avoidance (Ying et al., 2009). Sponsored content is often perceived by the users as obstructing since it intervenes with the browsing goals of the consumers. Van den Broeck et al. (2017) presumes that newsfeed ads are more likely to be ignored than ads placed in the right column. Moreover, statistics report that there is also a different cost per conversion for different placements on Facebook. This only confirms the assumption of distinct effectiveness levels for advertising spaces (Loomer, 2013). In addition, the conversion cost and final campaign results are also determined by the price and optimization models.

Many researchers agree that advertising blindness may be avoided by achieving higher product involvement (Cho, 2003; Rejón-Guardia and Martínez-López, 2014; Kelly et al., 2010). The term product involvement is defined as "[…] perceived relevance of the object based on inherent needs, values, and interests" (Zaichkowsky, 1985, p. 342). Becker-Olsen (2003) found that adjusting the ad content to match the interests of the target audience may lead to higher effectiveness of newsfeed ads over the right column placements. The author argues that thanks to the better fit of the ad with the audience the cognitive effort increases leading to a greater engagement. Cowley and Barron (2008) came to similar conclusions. They believe that the persuasion ability of the advertisements is related to the context where the ad is placed. If the post is not consistent with the expected content in the newsfeed, the users find it less entertaining, brand attitude decreases and ad avoidance increases.

Bleier et al. (2015), Chi (2011) and Taylor et al. (2011) believe that the motivation to use Facebook may as well influence the attitudes toward online advertising. Smock et al. (2011) identified nine user motivations to be part of Facebook community: Habitual pass time, Relaxing entertainment, Expressive information sharing, Escapism, Cool new trend, Companionship, Professional advancement, Social interaction, To meet new people. All these motives may be divided into two categories: goal-oriented search motives and playful surfing motives. For search tasks online ads are perceived as irritating and lead to lower attitude towards the ad (Duff and Faber, 2011).

Some authors emphasize the need to assess the effectiveness of advertising more systematically. According to Knoll (2015), there is no systematic empirical overview setting the guidelines on how to measure the performance of social media campaigns. Many research studies tend to focus on the identification of the relation between attitudes, perception and online advertising, but they provide no practical insights for advertisers.

COLLECTING PERFORMANCE DATA

The benefits of advertising in an online environment include large array of benefits. In addition to easy targeting of selected customer groups and flexible communication with potential customers, easy traceability of user´s actions represents the key prerequisite to accurately measure the performance of Facebook marketing activities. Conveniently, Facebook has its own tracking system that is able to evaluate user behavior, divide users into customer segments based on multiple selection criteria and precisely measure the level of user engagement with the post in the form of likes, shares, clicks and other metrics. The assesssment of ad / post effectiveness and the calculation of ROI-FM strongly depend on the quality of available data. Based on the previously described findings, ad effectiveness assessment requires information about the target audience, user engagement and interaction with the post, user behavior and attitudes toward the ad. In order to calculate the return of marketing investements, the company also needs to keep track of its advertising and ad processing expenses.

Advertising Costs

Companies of all sizes resort to social media as to a less expensive option compared to offline advertisement media. Facebook advertising is suitable even for restricted budgets. Advertisers decide how much they want to spend per each campaign. Whether the ad will be shown to a user from a target group depends on the evaluation of the two objectives that Facebook defines as its priority in terms of sponsored content. Firstly, Facebook's efforts to help advertisers reach the target audience and reach marketing goals. Secondly, the company strives to create for the people who use its applications and services a positive and relevant environment. For this reason, ads are delivered based on an auction that takes into account the interests of both advertisers and users. The aim of these auctions is to offer the right person the right ad at the right time. The winner of the auction is not the highest bid, but the ad with the highest total value.

The total value is calculated as a combination of three factors: the advertiser's bid, the estimated response rate, the quality and relevance of the ad. An advertiser's bid is the amount he is willing to pay for displaying his ads to the target audience. The estimated response rate is calculated by Facebook based on the previous responses of the audience the advertiser is trying to reach, taking into account the type of reaction the ad is optimized for. This estimated response rate includes also the historical effectiveness of your ad. The quality and relevance of the sponsored content is judged by the actual user response. If the advertised post does not generate any clicks or if it receives negative reactions, the quality and thus the total value may decrease. On the other hand, in the case of positive reactions, the quality and relevance score of the ad is growing. Relevance score for each ad is always displayed in the Ads Manager. This score ranges from 1-10 points, 10 representing the highest quality ranking.

During every auction, these three factors are recalculated in relation to the goals of the ad optimization. An ad with a higher total value wins and is finally displayed to the user. Thanks to the combination of multiple factors, better advertising can defeat an advertiser with a higher bid. The advertiser pays only when a conversion action for which he is optimizing the ad occurs. For example, the compan´s goal is to make the customers visit the company´s website, the conversion action will be a click on the web. This is the so-called PPC (pay-per-click, pay-per-click) system. The amount that Facebook will charge the advertisers is the minimum amount he needeeds to win the auction.

The costs of Facebook advertising may vary considerably depending on the industry and the target group the company wants to offer their product. The total budget spend on a campaign is determined by the advertiser. This amount may range from 5 USD a week to 500 USD a day. The ad and campaign investment is not limited. It is up to the advertiser to decide how much money from the corporate budget he wants to spend on advertising. For advanced ad types, there is a minimum amount set to ensure their functionality.

Based on the budget, the bid, and targeting parameters, Facebook estimates the number of people the ad may potentially reach and who represent the target group corresponding the best to your advertising objectives.

Profiling the Target Audience

All the ads a company may order on Facebook always have the same structure, regardeless the advertising objectives. A Facebook advertising order consists of a campaign, a set of ads, and the ad itself. Different parameters are set for each of these levels. By structuring the campaign, companies may gain a better insight into the promotions that are currently running. Also all of these steps are part of the target group definition process and help to collect detailed information about the ad performance.

At the campaign level the advertiser selects the appropriate goal / purpose of the ads. In this step, there is a limited number of options the advertiser may choose from. The most frequently selected campaign goals include, for example, earning more fans for the company page, getting reactions for the posts, or achieving a higher website traffic. The advertiser should select such campaign goals that correspond the best the marketing objectives of the company. Campaign goal selection is important for Facebook optimization. Based on the chosen purpose, the algorithm selects the group of users that is most likely to perform the desired action.

On the ad set level, the exact requirements for the target audience are specified. These include geographic, demographic and interest parameters. Next, the budget, the way of drawing it, the start and duration of the campaign, the placement of the ads, and the type of connection to Facebook company page are specified. Within a single campaign, it is possible to have multiple sets that differ from each other in terms of targeting parameters. For example, if the company wants to target women aged 18-24 and 40-54 it has to address each of these two segments differently (different slogan, creative). It is thus best for the advertiser to set up two ad sets.

The final element of the advertising Facebook structure are the ads. This last step consists in setting the visual parameters and the content of the advertisement. At this point, the advertiser is choosing whether the company should present itself through an image or video, or what text to add to make the most of the sponsored post.

Choosing the wrong campaign goal may negatively affect the performance of the advertisement. Based on the various Facebook marketing activities, the campaign goals and targeting strategies may be divided into three groups: Awareness, Consideration and Conversion (Table 1). These three groups describe the main stages of the new customer acquisition. Structuring marketing efforts in accordance with the acquisition stages may contribute to easier estimation of the value assigned to individual conversions (likes, shares, clicks, etc.).

If the advertiser´s goal is to let people know about the existence of the company and what its value lies in, the best option is to optimize the ads for raising awareness. Imagine promoting a small craft firm specializing in the production of wooden fashion accessories such as brooches, wooden business card cases or wooden bowties. In the ads, you want to emphasize that all goods are handcrafted and that you put a lot of care in every single piece you made. By emphasizing these qualities of your products, you will help your customers better understand why this company stands out over competition. In this case, it is the best to optimize the campaign for reach. When selecting as campaign goal the reach, Facebook will strive to show the ad to as many people as possible, but it will not consider whether these users will click on your ads or not.

When selecting a targeting category Consideration, the ads are primarily served to users who are likely to make a response (click, page markup as I like it, video viewing, etc.). The first goal in this group is "Traffic". The Traffic destination is selected by the advertiser. It depends on whether he want the users to visit the website, app or messenger. Campaign goal "Engagement" helps to increase the user interaction with the post, event or the number of followers of the company page. Another interesting targeting goal in this category is "Lead generation". This option serves to collect information about the potential customers. With this type of advertising, you can offer customers, for example, a newsletter registration, a discount on selected goods, or the possibility of early registration at your event.

Conversion targeting is meant to reach a narrower set of users who are most likely to perform the desired action (for example, buying goods). Facebook includes into this target audience users who have already reacted in a similar way to other ads. With the help of the ads from this category the advertiser may also create so-called dynamic ads. Dynamic ads allow to automatically promote products from the selected catalog. Catalog products are displayed to those users who have visited the company website at least once. If the user has viewed a particular product on the website, he will see an ad containing the

Table 1. Facebook targeting strategies

Awareness Objectives that generate interest in your product or service: • Brand awareness • Reach	Consideration Objectives that get people to start thinking about your business and look for more information about it: • Traffic • App instals • Engagement • Video views • Lead generation • Messages
Conversion Objectives that encourage people interested in your business to purchase or use your product or service: • Conversions • Catalog sales • Store visits	

Source: (the authors)

image of this particular product or of a product from a similar category. The product catalog combined with dynamic ads is the most powerful remarketing tool.

Another category of advertising objectives is represented by "Store visits". This kind of ad is suitable for companies with multiple stores. Similarly to products, the advertiser may create dynamic ads for the company stores locations. These ads are delivered based on the geographic location of the user. If the user is in a location near your local store, you'll see a relevant ad.

Tracking User Behavior

Just prior to ordering Facebook advertisements, the advertiser should consider what are the business goals of the company. Depending on these goals, the company should choose appropriate tracking tools to help evaluate the performance of the advertising campaigns. If one of the goals is to redirect potential customers to the website, the company will need to integrate Facebook pixel to optimize its ads. Additionally, if the advertiser seeks more accurate monitoring of your customers' behavior, it is required to install analytical software such as Google Analytics on the company website and use UTM links.

Facebook pixel represents a specific Facebook-generated fraction of code that is created specifically for the company advertising account. After uploading this code to the website, Facebook is able to monitor whether the customer has made the requested actions. A properly installed Facebook allows not only to track conversion events, but also to optimize the ads, and to use remarketing. Remarketing tools are used to reach all the users that visited the company website, or just those customer segments that have visited specific pages, products, or made specific actions, but have not completed them (for example, saving goods into a shopping cart but not making a purchase). With the pixel, it is possible to track specific conversions across devices that the user owns, search for new customers and create remarketing ads.

One of the key steps leading to effective measurement of website traffic is to add UTM parameters to the links shared on social networks and other online spaces. However, this tool will not bring any results if the company does not use any analytical software on the web. UTM parameters are text fragments that are attached in the specified format to the web link. Attaching these textual segments does not change anything about the landing page but it will allow the analytical software to exactly identify from what source, campaign, or advertisement the users come to the website. UTM parameters represent a way of communicating between the web and the analytical web application.

UTM parameters generally contain the following 5 elements:

utm_source = source name (the name of the linked site)

utm_medium = media name = type of marketing channel (cpc = paid search, organic = unpaid search, referral = link, etc.)

utm_campaign = campaign = campaign name (for example, in Sklie) or other modulation (eg Facebook date or newsletter)

utm_content = ad name = another sub-level, for example, the name of the ad group in the PPC ad

utm_term = keyword = another sub-level, for example, keyword in PPC ad

Advertisers should mark using the UTM parameters all links uploaded as posts, as well as advertisements. This marking system significantly contributes to better segmentation of website traffic and helps to predict the behavior of visitors coming from different online sources (Direct, Social, Organic search, and Refferal).

Facebook Metrics

As mentioned in the previous paragraphs, one of the big advantages of online marketing tools lies in the possibility to precisely measure the impact and performance of individual ads. However, evaluating the return of your marketing investments (ROI) may not be an easy task. In the online environment and specifically on Facebook, you will find a great deal of data (metrics), whose value may be judged differently depending on your marketing goals. In addition, in the online environment, there are two types of content: organic and sponsored. Organic reach includes all the results achieved without having to use facebook advertising. Even though these posts do not require funds for advertising they still generate marketing costs in the form of content production expenses. Evaluating the performance of the Facebook activities contributes to the increase of ROI-FM, and helps identify new customer groups, test creatives, and optimize the marketing strategies.

Facebook provides several applications through which the advertiser may access the collected data. Administrators of Facebook company pages can get the general review of posts organic and paid performance through the Insights tab. If the company manages ads directly from the Facebook page, advertising results will appear under the Promotion tab. However, the most comprehensive set of reporting tools is offered by the Ad Manager and Business Manager.

The Business Manager provides multiple reporting features, such as Ads Manager; Testing and Learning tool; Facebook Analytics; Pixel, Offline events, Application events, and Conversion managers. From the point of view of advertising effectiveness, the first three of the above, are the most relevant.

When seeing the Facebook ads in Newsfeed, Instagram, or Audience Network, the user can do several actions, including giving likes, sharing, viewing videos, visiting the website, or purchasing a product. All of these actions are recorded and displayed in the reporting columns for each ad in the Ads Manager. Hovever, not all conversions are recorded and displayed instantly. Conversions made on the web are attributed to the ads when they occur, which may be within a few days. For example, When browsing Facebook, thanks to a sponsored post, the user gets interested in a new mobile phone. Through the ad, he is redirected to the dealer's website and puts the phone in the shopping cart, but he does not complete the purchase. After three days of thinking he decides that he will buy the mobile phone. Even though he reacted to the ad earlier, the measurable result happened after three days. This action can be reflected as two different metrics in the Ads Manager, both as impression attribution and click attribution. Impression attribution means that the user saw your ad and subsequently made a purchase without clicking on that ad. Click attribution refers to the situation where the click was made directly from the ad.

Nevertheless, the number of interactions with the post cannot be confused with the advertising results. The results column only records the values that match the campaign target. Generally, every advertisement gets more reactions than results. If the objective of the ad is to gain more web traffic, ale click leading on the website will be recorded as results and all the likes, shares and comments will be registered as interactions. In detailed ad reports, these events are held in separate columns. Tracking the interactions, not just the results, provides additional insights into the ad's performance. It is possible that the ad received only 10 results (e.g. web clicks) but it could have contributed to 50 new followers of the company Facebook page.

Due to the growing number of channels and devices used by individual users, Facebook is gradually introducing new attribution models and switching from cookie-based to person-based monitoring. Currently, two types of attribution models can be distinguished, taking into account user behavior across devices: Last used channel model and Touch point model.

Facebook currently (May 2018) uses the model of the last channel when assigning ad conversions. Conversion then attributes the last ad the user has clicked on. If he does not click on any ad, the conversion is credited to the last displayed ad. The default conversion count is set to 28 days. Conversion events outside of this conversion window are not counted. In the near future, Facebook is getting ready to move to the Touch Point Model. This approach to monitoring divides the final value of the conversion and assigns it to the individual channels and ads that contributed throughout the process (Figure 1).

The result metrics depend on the selected Facebook campaign goals and include the following variables: reach, engagement, link click, mobile app install, 3s video views, potential customers on the web, shopping on the web, and the value of site purchase conversion.

The first of the metrics is reach. Reach describes the size of the audience the post was displayed to. After defining demographic and geographic data for the advertisement targeting, Facebook estimates the daily reach based on the information about the active users who use Facebook daily. However, this estimated reach is also affected by the placement, budget, and campaign goal. For example, if the advertiser decides to remove the right column placement, the reach will decrease due to the loss of potential views in this part of interface on desktop computers and laptops. The overall reach of the campaign is expressed as the number of unique users who saw the campaign. One user can see the ad multiple times, but nothing changes in reach. The "reach optimization" goal allows the advertiser to control the frequency of viewing the same ad by one user.

There are two types of "click" metrics in Facebook reports: link-click metric and an all-clicks metric. The all-clicks metric encompasses all clicks on the ad and its parts including the likes, shares, comments, or the clicks to view a full screen image or video. While link-click counts only the clicks on links leading to external websites or other parts of Facebook. Based on these two metrics, Facebook calculates other derived metrics: CPC (all), CPC (link clicks), CTR (all), and CTR (link clicks). CPC represents the average cost per click, while the CTR indicates the average clickthrough rate. CPC is expressed as the total campaign costs divided by the number of clicks. CTR refers to the number of times people clicked on the link in the ad compared to how many times they saw the ad.

Figure 1. Facebook attribution models
Source: (the authors)

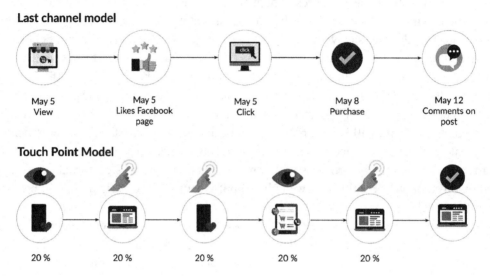

Engagement reflect whether the ads are interesting (relevant) for the target audience the advertiser choose. The higher the relevance, the higher the chance that the target audience will take action. Engagement is calculated as the sum of all actions performed in connection with the ad. The average cost per engagement is calculated as the ratio of the amount issued and the level of engagement.

In the Ads manager and in the page Insights it is possible to find another metric describing all video views longer than 3 seconds. In Facebook reports, you may also find 10s video views and viewing the entire video metrics. However, the issue of video metrics is that about 90% of videos are triggered automatically and only 10% is played by the user. A similar situation concerns the impressions of the video. If the user views one video multiple times, each of these views is counted as one impression. For this reason, additional video metrics, such as the percentage of the video viewed (how many percent of the video the users saw) and the number of unique impressions, are worth evaluating. Impression provides an overview of how many times the advertisement has been displayed on Facebook. However, impression does not represent a unique view. That is way along with impressions the Facebook reports also the Frequency indicator that indicates how many times the average user has already seen the ad, and the CPM index describing the average cost per 1000 impressions.

The advertiser has a plethora of variables to evaluate the individual campaigns and advertisements. Facebook offers over 50 different metrics with varying levels of detail that help to shed some light on the effectiveness of posts and ads. Nevertheless, not all metrics are suitable for all purposes and advertising goals. The advertiser must choose which indexes are relevant for his ads and which are redundant since they offer unnecessarily detailed information.

The Costs of the Content Processing

In addition to the price payed for the advertising space and the impressions of the ads, the companies should also consider the expenses needed for the creation of the marketing content. Now, Facebook supports the distribution of almost all type of multimedia including photo, gif files, videos, photo presentations and 3D product models. The audience at social networks has quite high expectations when it comes to the content they usually engage with. Due to the increasing number of brands and advertisers who compete to gain the users attention, the quality of the sponsored content is growing, turning Facebook advertising into highly competitive environment. However, creating quality content requires time, skill and a good technical background. At this point, it is necessary to decide whether the advertiser is able to produce such a content with the company resources or whether he should use the services of a digital agency. The advertiser may choose both. Many of the big brands have their own creative departments that take care of the visual design of the regular posts but for bigger campaigns they resort to professional assistance. It is not possible to objectively demonstrate which of the options is more profitable. The realization of the benefits is strongly individual and depends on many internal characteristics of the company such as the frequency with which the company produces creative content, available equipment and human resources.

The price of the creative content cannot be neglected since it generally represents significant percentage of the company´s marketing budget. Each of the online and offline communication channels has different requirements on size, format, resolution and sound the processing of sound elements that are an integral part of multimedia advertisements. When creating promotional material, these aspects must be taken into account to ensure that the resulting material can be distributed without any problems to the end-viewer. Notwithstanding, the calculation of the content processing costs is not the main objective of this chapters, the authors believe that understanding the creative design process will help to clarify the economic demands on online advertising.

The graphic designer works with graphical software editors to process vector and bitmap graphics. He often needs to use paid graphical elements from photo stocks, illustrative images, vector graphics, and / or icons, sounds and pythographs. Another distinctive graphic element is the typography used. The fonts used often provide the graphs with a certain mood and atmosphere and should of course always be selected with regard to the target audience of the advertiser and to the need for text readability on various devices. One design is generally used for many advertising formats (flyer, poster, banners, slideshow, newsletter graphics). The graphic designer must re-lay the required formats, modify them, and eventually export them to suitable output variants (pdf, jpeg, esp, png, gif). All of these steps require investments. The price of content varies of course depending on the required quality. Thanks to the technological development of media content processing, the technological level is rising even for low end devices. The development of both audio and video recorders has progressed considerably, and over the past decade, high-quality audiovisual material can be created with relatively cheap technical tools. The following list of equipment is divided into 3 price ranges for each area (graphics, audio, video) - from the cheapest possible equipment, through the middle quality class to the professional equipment (Table 2). The price range is only indicative. Obviously, equipment is not replaced after every campaign made but nevertheless there is 2 to 3 years amortization for most of the technological devices.

It is difficult generalize the time needed for the creation of an advertisement. The time allowance is very fluctuating and may, of course, vary according to the complexity of the project. Also, an experienced worker who can efficiently and appropriately use modern technological processes and software tools can produce the resulting product in less time than an employee with less practical experience. A web banner can take about 5 hours to create. Making an audio record composed of an actor's commentary along with audiobook and FX sound effects can take a range of 3 to 20 hours. It is thus up to each advertiser to estimate these costs for his advertisements and product promotion. Generally, the company use two ways how to express the content processing costs – as the part of marketing costs or as the part of the product costs. Before starting to track the ROI of Facebook advertisements it is crucial to decide what is the costs structure. For the purposes of further calculations described in this chapter, the authors include content production costs in the product costs as a flat rate.

Table 2. Average content processing costs

Quality Category	Informative Price of the Devices	Price Range
Graphics Processing - Image Recording		
Low end	Smartphone with Camera application	100 - 300 €
Middle class	Compact camera (500 €)	400 - 600 €
Profi class	DSLR Cameras - body (2.000 €) + lenses (2.0000 €) + accessories - flash lights, stands, filters (1.500 €)	5.000 - 10.000 €
Graphics processing - postproduction		
Low end	Filters in the Camera application on the smartphone	100 - 300 €
Middle class	Freeware + free plugins	400 - 600 €
Profi class	Software tools for the processing of raster and vector graphics (1.000 €), graphical interface - tablet (1.000 €)	1.500 - 5.000 €
Sound processing - recording		
Quality category	**Informative price of the devices**	**Price range**
Low end	Smartphone with sound recording application	100 - 300 €
Middle class	Condenser microphone (150 €), sound card (300 €)	300 - 600 €
Profi class	Stereo pair of condenser microphones (1.000 €) + microphone preamp (1.5000 €) + AD/DA convertor (1.500 €) + accessories (500 €)	4.000 - 6.000 €
Sound processing - postproduction		
Low end	Mobile application on the smartphone	0 €
Middle class	Freeware + free plugins	0 €
Profi class	Software tools (1.000 € + professional postproduction plugins (3.000 €) + hardware - compressors, EQ, mastering chain (20.000 €)	20.000 - 50.000 €
Video processing - recording		
Quality category	**Informative price of the devices**	**Price range**
Low end	Smartphone with Camera application	100 - 300 €
Middle class	Handheld video camera (400 €)	300 - 600 €
Profi class	Professional video camera (10.000 €), lenses (2.000 €), accessories (1.000 €)	12.000 - 50.000 €
Video processing - postproduction		
Low end	Smartphone video editor	0 €
Middle class	Freware + free plugins	0 €
Profi class	Software tools for video data editation (1.500 €), hardware for color correction (10.000), HW work station (4.000 €)	15.00 - 50.000 €

Source: (the authors)

ROI-FM DETERMINATION MODEL

The effectiveness of Facebook ads is generaly measured by the level of user engagement. According to Tikno (2017) the engagement rate represents ... *the proportion of action taken by the Facebook user to displaying ads with how many times the ads is showed*:

$$E = A / R \tag{1}$$

which:

E = Engagement Rate

A = Action taken (Amount of People who liked, commented, shared, or clicked on the ad)

R = Reach (Amount of People who saw the ad)

This formula allows to measure the post performance and compare posts (both organic and sponsored) between each other and to monitor the development of the relative Facebook marketing effectiveness over time. Nevertheless, this formula does not reflect the financial aspects of the marketing activities and thus does not provide complete information in terms of marketing investments. Eventhough, marketing costs may seem irrelevant for organic (unpaid) posts, there are still costs associated with the creation of the visual content. Moreover even the organic posts may generate financial value. For this reason, financial variables should be incorporated in the effectiveness assessment model.

The definition of this model will partly depend on the goals the company is trying to achieve. Are the company's objectives to increase the brand awareness, revenues, customer satisfaction, or other? Let's start with a simple ROI calculation model modified for the social media purposes. In broader sense, the return on investment in social media represents the sum of all social media actions that create value taking into account all the resources invested in their implementation. This simplified formula would look like this:

$$\text{Simple ROI Calculation} = ((\text{Total revenue - Marketing investment}) / \text{Marketing ivestment}) * 100 \tag{2}$$

However, this formula is very simplified, since it only operates with revenue from sales rather than actual profits. To accurately measure the ROI, it is desirable to know the cost of the goods sold:

$$\text{ROI Calculation for direct activities} = ((\text{Total revenue - Total COGS - Marketing Investment}) / \text{Marketing investment}) * 100 \tag{3}$$

where:

Total revenue = sales generated by the marketing campaign such as ecommerce transactions

Total COGS = cost of goods sold

The problem with this formula is that for many Facebook activities the contribution to the revenu is indirect. Only data available for these activities are Facebook metrics such as the reach, the number of interactions, page view, etc. The effectiveness model should thus also reflect this reality. Therefore:

ROI Calculation for Indirect Contribution = ((Total value of the actions taken - Total COGS - Marketing Investment) / Marketing investment) * 100   (4)

The most difficult step consists in the calculation of the Total value of the actions taken. Not all interactions have the same value and except for the posts / ads optimized for purchases it is not possible to directlly measure the revenue generated by the advertisement. Taking into consideration the Facebook attribution models described above, all of the conversions contribute to the final result. The revenues coming from purchases should thus be distributed between the others conversions with appropriates weights. If the advertisers desires to assess the effectiveness of individual ads, they need to know what these bring them in terms of likes, shares, clicks etc.The average revenue contribution of the conversions may be calculated based on the historical data the company managed to collect and should reflect the targetting characteristics of the audience. It is likely that different customer segments will have different average revenues since some target groups require more marketing effort and respond to ads more conservatively. Before calculation the average revenu contibution per conversion, the advertiser should firstly analyze data available in the GA and find out what is the conversion rate per visitor and what actions lead to the final purchases. Combining these data with the post information provided by Facebook is the only way to get the entire profile of user behavior and estimate the real value of each conversion.

Looking back the attribution model described in the section 2.4, the conversion process goes from the less engaging actions such as likes, comments and shares to the actions that require more cognitive effort from the consumer. Generally, there is decreasing tendency along the conversion processes. This tendency is being referred to as marketing funnel. The stages customer usually travel through are post views, reactions (likes, comments, shares), click on the link and web visit, registration to the newsletter, purchase. There maybe other stages included depending on the business model the company applies. Due to the marketing funnel the contribution of the conversion to the revenue increases toward the and of the buying process. Therefore, the revenu contribution per metric may be expressed as:

$$ARMS = (P/M) * TR \hspace{4cm} (5)$$

where:

ARMS = Average revenue per metric per customer segment

P = Number of purchases per segment for a monitored period of time

M = Number of the metrics conversions per segment for a monitored period of time

TR = Total revenue

The adjusted formula for the individual advertisements is thus defined as follows:

ROI Calculation for individual advertisements = $(\{ [(n_{WCK}*AR_{WCK} + n_{RE}*AR_{RE} + n_{AD}*AR_{AD} + n_{LCS}*AR_{LCS} + n_{F}*AR_{F} + n_{VW}*AR_{VW} + n_{M}*_{ARM} + TPC) - \text{Total COGS} - \text{Advertisement costs}] \} / \text{Advertisement costs}) * 100$ (6)

where:

- **AR_{WCK}:** Average revenue of website clicks per customer segment;
- **AR_{RE}:** Average revenue of registration per customer segment;
- **AR_{AD}:** Average revenue of application download per customer segment;
- **AR_{LCS}:** Average revenue of reactions (likes, comments, shares) per customer segment;
- **AR_{F}:** Average value of fans per customer segment;
- **AR_{VW}:** Average value of video views per customer segment;
- **AR_{M}:** Average value of other metric per customer segment chosen by the company;
- **TPC:** Total purchase value per campaign - calculated based on the acctual data related to the specific campaign retrieved from the website analytical software;
- **nM:** Number of conversions for the observed metric.

In the formula above, it is possible to replace the observed metrics or to ad others such as video views, reach, etc. The average values expressed in the aformentionned relationship represent future value of the campaign, not the current value which is expressed by the revenu generated by the purchases. The authors believe that this model could help to improve the evaluation of the indirect activities that are more difficult to judge since they not produce enough instant revenue but could lead to purchases in the future.

To properly estimate the profit from certain consumer actions (purchase, page views, app downloads, newsletter registration, etc.), setting up the tracking systems described above (Google Analytics, Facebook pixel, etc.) to identify which conversions can be assigned to Facebook campaigns is crucial. Because of the short life cycle of social networking campaigns, unsuccessful campaigns should be optimized or turned off as soon as possible. Understanding the available metrics and what value they represent is the only way how to judge Facebook effectiveness properly.

Interpreting the Advertising Results

In the following paragraphs, the authors are going to demonstrate how to use the aformentionned formula with the organic and advertising results. Data presented in this chapter was collected by a Czech company selling home accessories and interior decorations. In the course of the two weeks, the company ran eight advertisements and published three posts from which one were sponsored. Each of the posts was sponsored for three days. For all the posts and ads, the company kept track of these variables if they were relevant: number of web clicks, reactions (likes and comments), purchases, newsletter registration, and campaign costs. The final data was exported from Facebook Ads Manager and completed with data collected via Google Analytics and UTM enhanced web filtering (Tables 3 and 4).

Based on the historical data collected for this customer segment, the company estimated the average value for each of the monitored metric. From Google Analytics, the company extracted the revenues generated by the purchases by the Facebook campaigns, and estimated the total costs of the goods sold. Ad effectiveness was then calculated using the ROI formula for individual marketing campaigns (Tables 5 and 6).

Table 3. Advertising results

Advertisements							
Campaign Name	**Optimization Goals**	**Type of the Content**	**Website Clicks**	**Reactions**	**Number of Purchases**	**Newsletter Registration**	**Campaign Costs**
Campaign 1	Engagement: fans	Photo	28	382	2	15	63 USD
Campaign 2	Engagement: fans	Video	48	647	9	27	77 USD
Campaign 3	Lead generation	Photo	215	93	82	29	35 USD
Campaign 4	Lead generation	Video	301	124	151	14	48 USD
Campaign 5	Conversions	Product carousel	355	82	263	27	54 USD
Campaign 6	Conversions	Photo	276	133	189	42	39 USD
Campaign 7	Catalog sales	Photo	115	25	97	34	22 USD
Campaign 8	Catalog sales	Product carousel	184	18	164	58	28 USD

Source: (the authors)

Table 4. Results for the posts on the company page

Posts on the Company Page							
Campaign Name	**Optimization Goals**	**Type of the Content**	**Website Clicks**	**Reactions**	**Number of Purchases**	**Newsletter Registration**	**Campaign Costs**
Post 1 organic	not defined	Photo	2	21	0	0	0
Post 2 organic	not defined	Video	1	39	0	0	0
Post 3 organic	not defined	Video	3	52	0	0	0
Post 3 sponsored	Engagement	Video	29	631	4	0	61 USD

Source: (the authors)

Table 5. ROI and average revenues for the advertisements

Advertisements						
Campaign Name	**AR_{WCK} (USD)**	**AR_{LCS} (USD)**	**AR_{RE} (USD)**	**TPC (USD)**	**42% COGS (USD)**	**Campaign ROI**
Campaign 1	0,6	0,1	0,8	85	35,7	145,24
Campaign 2	0,6	0,1	0,8	382	160,44	421,25
Campaign 3	0,6	0,1	0,8	3432	1441,4	6075,43
Campaign 4	0,6	0,1	0,8	6127	2573,3	7754,79
Campaign 5	0,6	0,1	0,8	10522	4419,24	11666,22
Campaign 6	0,6	0,1	0,8	7638	3207,96	11838,05
Campaign 7	0,6	0,1	0,8	3751	1575,4	10249,09
Campaign 8	0,6	0,1	0,8	6493	2727,1	13922,5

Source: (the authors)

Table 6. ROI and average revenues for page posts

Posts on the Company Page					
Campaign Name	**AR$_{WCK}$ (USD)**	**AR$_{LCS}$ (USD)**	**AR$_{RE}$ (USD)**	**TPC (USD)**	**42% COGS (USD)**	**Campaign ROI**
Post 1 organic	0,6	0,1	0,8	0	0	5,4
Post 2 organic	0,6	0,1	0,8	0	0	8.4
Post 3 organic	0,6	0,1	0,8	0	0	12,2
Post 3 sponsored	0,6	0,1	0,8	0	0	135,4098361

Source: (the authors)

Looking more closely on the previous results it is possible to see that the campaign value significantly increased for the majority of ads. This increased value represents current revenue and the value that the ads / posts could bring in the future. However, these results cannot be used for reporting purposes, they better describe the performance of the ads. If the ad performance would be judged just based on the number of purchases, most of the posts would be described as ineffective. On the other hand, assuming that the ad that is having the highest number of reactions is more successful than the ads that has only few is equally as misleading. Tracking the conversions all along the buying process is necessary to understand the ad effectiveness and the behavior of the consumers.

CONCLUSION

The benefits of Facebook advertisements in terms of reaching marketing goals of the company have been proven by many researchers and practitioners (Abayi et al., 2016; Bang et al., 2016; Dehghani et al., 2015). However, the effects of the activities on social networks may have both positive and negative impacts on consumer behavior (Ertugan, 2017; Taylor, 2011). Current literature does not provide enough evidence about the relationship between Facebook advertising, brand awareness and customer attitudes toward the brand. Research suggests that there might be significant differences in ad effectiveness when it comes to contextual setting and industrial orientation of the company (Kohli et al., 2015). Despite the inability to directly quantify the effectiveness of Facebook activities, scientists and practitioners agree that companies should not abandonne this social network and rather focus on testing which activities are suitable for their objectives.

Thanks to the tracking possibilities provided by Facebook advertising systems and website analytical software, the companies have a great opportunity to observe almost instantly what is the impact of their marketing efforts. Regular assessment of Facebook and website metrics may contribute to identification of types of content and posting strategies work with the targeted audience. It is important to keep in mind that the success of a company post or sponsored advertising depends on many factors. These factors include visual processing, post type, content, and targeting parameters. All of the aforementioned variables require testing and adjustments over time.

The calculation of ROI for Facebook marketing activities represents a continuous process whose accuracy depends on the quality of the available data. In addition to ad performance data, ROI calculation requires also the information about the costs incurred to create the visual content of the ad and the costs needed to produce the goods and services offered by the company.

Although the revenue component of the ROI formula may seem easy to extract from the company system, there are many Facebook activities that generate revenues indirectly such as building online community or motivating the followers to engage more with the content shared by the company. This indirect value is generally calculated based on the historic data the company managed to collect during a certain time period. In order to obtain a solid ROI estimate that could be used as the basis for further marketing decision-making, marketers need to carefully select the advertising metrics that will be used for the effectiveness assessment.

ACKNOWLEDGMENT

This research was supported by the Technical University of Liberec [project SGS-EF-3320-21230 Impact of technical and aesthetic parameters of web design on user satisfaction and online shopping behavior of the customer].

REFERENCES

Abayi, M., & Khoshtinat, B. (2016). Study of the Impact of Advertising on Online Shopping Tendency for Airline Tickets by Considering Motivational Factors and Emotional Factors. *Procedia Economics and Finance*, *36*, 532–539. doi:10.1016/S2212-5671(16)30065-X

Aslam, B., & Karjaluoto, H. (2017). Digital advertising around paid spaces, E-advertising industry's revenue engine: A review and research agenda. *Telematics and Informatics*, *34*(8), 1650–1662. doi:10.1016/j.tele.2017.07.011

Banelis, M., Riebe, E., & Rungie, C. (2013). Empirical evidence of repertoire size. *Australasian Marketing Journal*, *21*(1), 59–65. doi:10.1016/j.ausmj.2012.11.001

Bang, H., & Lee, W. (2016). Consumer Response to Ads in Social Network Sites: An Exploration into the Role of Ad Location and Path. *Journal of Current Issues and Research in Advertising*, *37*(1), 1–14. doi:10.1080/10641734.2015.1119765

Becker-Olsen, K. (2003). And Now, A Word from Our Sponsor--A Look at the Effects of Sponsored Content and Banner Advertising. *Journal of Advertising*, *32*(2), 17–32. doi:10.1080/00913367.2003.10639130

Beukeboom, C., Kerkhof, P., & de Vries, M. (2015). Does a Virtual Like Cause Actual Liking? How Following a Brand's Facebook Updates Enhances Brand Evaluations and Purchase Intention. *Journal of Interactive Marketing*, *32*, 26–36. doi:10.1016/j.intmar.2015.09.003

Bicen, H., & Cavus, N. (2011). Social network sites usage habits of undergraduate students: Case study of Facebook. *Procedia: Social and Behavioral Sciences*, *28*, 943–947. doi:10.1016/j.sbspro.2011.11.174

Bleier, A., & Eisenbeiss, M. (2015). Personalized Online Advertising Effectiveness: The Interplay of What, When, and Where. *Marketing Science*, *34*(5), 669–688. doi:10.1287/mksc.2015.0930

Brettel, M., Reich, J., Gavilanes, J., & Flatten, T. (2015). What Drives Advertising Success on Facebook? An Advertising-Effectiveness Model. *Journal of Advertising Research*, *55*(2), 162–175. doi:10.2501/JAR-55-2-162-175

Campbell, C., & Marks, L. (2015). Good native advertising isn't a secret. *Business Horizons*, *58*(6), 599–606. doi:10.1016/j.bushor.2015.06.003

Chi, H. H. (2011). Interactive digital advertising vs. virtual brand community: Exploratory study of user motivation and social media marketing responses in Taiwan. *Journal of Interactive Advertising*, *12*(1), 44–61. doi:10.1080/15252019.2011.10722190

Cho, C. H. (2003). The effectiveness of banner advertisements: Involvement and click-through. *Journalism & Mass Communication Quarterly*, *80*(3), 623–645. doi:10.1177/107769900308000309

Corvi, E., & Bonera, M. (2010, October). The effectiveness of advertising: a literature review. *Xth Global Conference on Business and Economics*, 3-6.

Cowley, E., & Barron, C. (2008). When Product Placement Goes Wrong: The Effects of Program Liking and Placement Prominence. *Journal of Advertising*, *37*(1), 89–98. doi:10.2753/JOA0091-3367370107

Curran, K., Graham, S., & Temple, C. (2011). Advertising on Facebook. *International Journal of E-Business Development*, *1*, 26–33.

Dehghani, M., & Tumer, M. (2015). A research on effectiveness of Facebook advertising on enhancing purchase intention of consumers. *Computers in Human Behavior*, *49*, 597–600. doi:10.1016/j.chb.2015.03.051

Dehghani, M., & Tumer, M. (2015). A research on effectiveness of Facebook advertising on enhancing purchase intention of consumers. *Computers in Human Behavior*, *49*, 597–600. doi:10.1016/j.chb.2015.03.051

Deloitte. (2015). *Facebook's global economic impact: A report for Facebook*. Retrieved from www2.deloitte.com/content/dam/Deloitte/uk/Documents/technology-media-telecommunications/deloitte-uk-global-economic-impact-of-facebook.pdf

Duff, B., & Faber, R. (2011). Missing the Mark. *Journal of Advertising*, *40*(2), 51–62. doi:10.2753/JOA0091-3367400204

EMarketer. (2016). *US Digital Video ad Spending will Continue to Grow at a Pace that Exceeds TV Advertising Growth Through 2020*. Retrieved from https://www.emarketer.com/Article/Digital-Video-Advertising-Grow-Annual-Double-Digit-Rates/1014105

Ertugan, A. (2017). Using statistical reasoning techniques to describe the relationship between Facebook advertising effectiveness and benefits gained. *Procedia Computer Science*, *120*, 132–139. doi:10.1016/j.procs.2017.11.220

Fulgoni, G. (2016). In the Digital World, Not Everything That Can Be Measured Matters. *Journal of Advertising Research*, *56*(1), 9–13. doi:10.2501/JAR-2016-008

Gutiérrez-Cillán, J., Camarero-Izquierdo, C., & San José-Cabezudo, R. (2017). How brand post content contributes to user's Facebook brand-page engagement. The experiential route of active participation. *BRQ Business Research Quarterly*, *20*(4), 258–274. doi:10.1016/j.brq.2017.06.001

Harris, L., & Dennis, C. (2011). Engaging customers on Facebook: Challenges for e-retailers. *Journal of Consumer Behaviour*, *10*(6), 338–346. doi:10.1002/cb.375

Heinonen, K. (2011). Consumer activity in social media: Managerial approaches to consumers' social media behavior. *Journal of Consumer Behaviour*, *10*(6), 356–364. doi:10.1002/cb.376

Heller Baird, C., & Parasnis, G. (2011). From social media to social customer relationship management. *Strategy and Leadership*, *39*(5), 30–37. doi:10.1108/10878571111161507

Insider, B. (2018). These Are The 35 Biggest Advertisers On Facebook. *Business Insider*. Retrieved 1 May 2018, from http://www.businessinsider.com/top-advertisers-on-facebook-2013-11

Kelly, L., Kerr, G., & Drennan, J. (2010). Avoidance of Advertising in Social Networking Sites. *Journal of Interactive Advertising*, *10*(2), 16–27. doi:10.1080/15252019.2010.10722167

Knoll, J. (2015). Advertising in social media: A review of empirical evidence. *International Journal of Advertising*, *35*(2), 266–300. doi:10.1080/02650487.2015.1021898

Kohli, C., Suri, R., & Kapoor, A. (2015). Will social media kill branding? *Business Horizons*, *58*(1), 35–44. doi:10.1016/j.bushor.2014.08.004

Kuvykaitė, R., & Tarutė, A. (2015). A Critical Analysis of Consumer Engagement Dimensionality. *Procedia: Social and Behavioral Sciences*, *213*, 654–658. doi:10.1016/j.sbspro.2015.11.468

LaPointe, P. (2012). Measuring Facebook's Impact on Marketing. *Journal of Advertising Research*, *52*(3), 286–287. doi:10.2501/JAR-52-3-286-287

Loomer, J. (2013). *How to Measure Facebook Advertising Success: Monitor These 5 Metrics*. Academic Press.

Mulhern, F. (2013). Integrated marketing communications: From media channels to digital connectivity. In *The Evolution of Integrated Marketing Communications* (pp. 19–36). Routledge.

Petty, R., & Cacioppo, J. (1986). The Elaboration Likelihood Model of Persuasion. *Communication and Persuasion*, 1-24. doi:10.1007/978-1-4612-4964-1_1

Rejón-Guardia, F., & Martínez-López, F. J. (2014). Online advertising intrusiveness and consumers' avoidance behaviors. In *Handbook of strategic e-business management* (pp. 565–586). Berlin: Springer. doi:10.1007/978-3-642-39747-9_23

Rzemieniak, M. (2015). Measuring the Effectiveness of Online Advertising Campaigns in the Aspect of e-entrepreneurship. *Procedia Computer Science*, *65*, 980–987. doi:10.1016/j.procs.2015.09.063

Sitta, D., Faulkner, M., & Stern, P. (2018). What can the brand manager expect from Facebook? *Australasian Marketing Journal*, *26*(1), 17–22. doi:10.1016/j.ausmj.2018.01.001

Smock, A., Ellison, N., Lampe, C., & Wohn, D. (2011). Facebook as a toolkit: A uses and gratification approach to unbundling feature use. *Computers in Human Behavior, 27*(6), 2322–2329. doi:10.1016/j.chb.2011.07.011

Statista. (2018a). Social Media Advertising - worldwide. *Statista Market Forecast.* Retrieved 1 May 2018, from https://www.statista.com/outlook/220/100/social-media-advertising/worldwide#

Statista. (2018b). Facebook ad revenue 2009-2017. *Statista.* Retrieved 1 May 2018, from https://www.statista.com/outlook/220/100/social-media-advertising/worldwide#

Taylor, D. G., Lewin, J. E., & Strutton, D. (2011). Friends, fans, and followers: Do ads work on social networks? How gender and age shape receptivity. *Journal of Advertising Research, 51*(1), 258–275.

Tikno. (2017). Measuring performance of facebook advertising based on media used: a case study on online shops in indonesia. *Procedia Computer Science, 111*, 105-112. doi:10.1016/j.procs.2017.06.016

Van den Broeck, E., Poels, K., & Walrave, M. (2018). An experimental study on the effect of ad placement, product involvement and motives on Facebook ad avoidance. *Telematics and Informatics, 35*(2), 470–479. doi:10.1016/j.tele.2018.01.006

Wallace, E., Buil, I., de Chernatony, L., & Hogan, M. (2014). Who "Likes" You … and Why? A Typology of Facebook Fans. *Journal of Advertising Research, 54*(1), 92–109. doi:10.2501/JAR-54-1-092-109

Ying, L., Korneliussen, T., & Grønhaug, K. (2009). The effect of ad value, ad placement and ad execution on the perceived intrusiveness of web advertisements. *International Journal of Advertising, 28*(4), 623–638. doi:10.2501/S0265048709200795

Yuki, T. (2015). What Makes Brands' Social Content Shareable on Facebook? *Journal of Advertising Research, 55*(4), 458–470. doi:10.2501/JAR-2015-026

Zaichkowsky, J. (1985). Measuring the Involvement Construct. *The Journal of Consumer Research, 12*(3), 341. doi:10.1086/208520

Zhou, Z., Wu, J., Zhang, Q., & Xu, S. (2013). Transforming visitors into members in online brand communities: Evidence from China. *Journal of Business Research, 66*(12), 2438–2443. doi:10.1016/j.jbusres.2013.05.032

ADDITIONAL READING

Beuckels, E., Cauberghe, V., & Hudders, L. (2017). How media multitasking reduces advertising irritation: The moderating role of the Facebook wall. *Computers in Human Behavior, 73*, 413–419. doi:10.1016/j.chb.2017.03.069

Boerman, S., Willemsen, L., & Van Der Aa, E. (2017). This Post Is Sponsored. *Journal of Interactive Marketing, 38*, 82–92. doi:10.1016/j.intmar.2016.12.002

Celebi, S. (2015). How do motives affect attitudes and behaviors toward internet advertising and Facebook advertising? *Computers in Human Behavior*, *51*, 312–324. doi:10.1016/j.chb.2015.05.011

Fatehkia, M., Kashyap, R., & Weber, I. (2018). Using Facebook ad data to track the global digital gender gap. *World Development*, *107*, 189–209. doi:10.1016/j.worlddev.2018.03.007

Lin, C., & Kim, T. (2016). Predicting user response to sponsored advertising on social media via the technology acceptance model. *Computers in Human Behavior*, *64*, 710–718. doi:10.1016/j.chb.2016.07.027

Liu, S., & Mattila, A. (2017). Airbnb: Online targeted advertising, sense of power, and consumer decisions. *International Journal of Hospitality Management*, *60*, 33–41. doi:10.1016/j.ijhm.2016.09.012

Shareef, M., Mukerji, B., Alryalat, M., Wright, A., & Dwivedi, Y. (2018). Advertisements on Facebook: Identifying the persuasive elements in the development of positive attitudes in consumers. *Journal of Retailing and Consumer Services*, *43*, 258–268. doi:10.1016/j.jretconser.2018.04.006

Tran, T. (2017). Personalized ads on Facebook: An effective marketing tool for online marketers. *Journal of Retailing and Consumer Services*, *39*, 230–242. doi:10.1016/j.jretconser.2017.06.010

KEY TERMS AND DEFINITIONS

Ad Placement: All the advertising spaces, mostly payed, offered by online publishers, websites and social networks to advertisers to display their advertisements. The individual placements have different potential for reaching the users and perform differently when comes to the type of content chosen for the advertisement.

Ad Targeting: Selection of potential customer groups to which an advertisement is going to be displayed. This specification of the ad´s audience is done via targeting parameters including demographic and geographic information, interests, or device preferences.

Conversion: Desired action performed by a consumer as a reaction to an advertisement or other marketing effort. The desired action can take many forms including the purchases, membership registrations, newsletter subscriptions, application downloads, etc.

Facebook Ads Manager: Tool developed by Facebook to manage advertisements on this social network, Instagram and ads displayed in the Audience network. This application allows the advertiser to create and target the ads, set campaign budget, view history, and collect data about previous and ongoing ads.

Marketing Funnel: Set of actions a consumer, website visitor, needs to go through before he makes the desired conversion (usually purchase). The actions customer usually travel through are post views, reactions (likes, comments, shares), click on the link and web visit, registration to the newsletter, purchase. Since the conversion process goes from the less engaging actions such as likes, comments and shares to the actions that require more cognitive effort from the consumer, the number of users willing to do the actions decreases.

Organic Reach: Number of people who viewed unpaid content on their screen. Generally, this term is used in association with social networks. Inversely, sponsored reach describes the number of people who viewed a paid advertisement.

UTM Parameters: Text fragments that are attached in the specified format to the web link. Attaching these textual segments allows the analytical software to exactly identify from what source, campaign, or advertisement the users come to the website. UTM parameters generally contain the following five elements: utm_source, utm_medium, utm_campaign, utm_content, utm_term.

This research was previously published in Leveraging Computer-Mediated Marketing Environments; pages 286-310, copyright year 2019 by Business Science Reference (an imprint of IGI Global).

Chapter 32

What Do Facebook Users Feel About Facebook Advertising?
Using an Experience Sampling Method (ESM) to Explore Their Digital Advertising Experiences

Yowei Kang

https://orcid.org/0000-0002-7060-194X
National Taiwan Ocean University, Taiwan

Kenneth C. C. Yang

https://orcid.org/0000-0002-4176-6219
The University of Texas at El Paso, USA

ABSTRACT

Because of its popularity and rapid growth, Facebook has become a viable advertising medium for corporations to communicate with their consumers. The experiences of Facebook users are important to ensure the success of any Facebook advertising campaign. This chapter reports the findings from a qualitative study using the Experience Sampling Method (ESM) after recruiting Facebook college participants in a large university in the Southwest U.S. The ESM technique is a powerful tool to collect data to demonstrate participants' actual experiences and reflections when using Facebook and Facebook advertising. The authors use a signal contingent protocol to record participants' experiences in using Facebook and Facebook advertising after prompting participants to record their using experiences randomly. The findings will help online advertising researchers to better understand the feasibility of using Facebook as a potential advertising medium through a non-survey-based method to better assess potential impacts on businesses.

DOI: 10.4018/978-1-7998-9020-1.ch032

INTRODUCTION

Facebook as a Social Media Platform

Globally, there are 2.94 billion monthly social media users (*eMarketer.com, 2019*). Among them, Facebook has the largest number of social media users (*eMarketer.com,* 2019). Facebook is a social networking site that was founded in 2004 by Marc Zuckerburg (Facebook, 2004) and has about 169.5 million users in the U.S. (*eMarketer.com.* 2018a). Facebook is conceptualized as "a social utility that helps people communicate more efficiently with their friends, family and coworkers" (Facebook, 2004, n.p.). Like other social networking sites, Facebook was originally developed to target teen and adolescent users (MacMillan, 2009). However, recent statistics have shown that less than half of the U.S. Facebook users are between 12 to 17 years old (*eMarketer.com.* 2018a). The number of Facebook users in the U.S. below 11 years old is expected to decline by 9.3% (*eMarketer.com.* 2018a). An estimate of 2 million users (below 24 years old) is expected to quit Facebook (*eMarketer.com.* 2018a). Presently, Facebook has 1,755.1 million users in 2019 and is expected to grow to 2,023.7 million users in 2023 (*eMarketer. com.* 2019; Enberg, 2019). Other social media platforms have trailed behind Facebook, with Instagram (106.7 million users), Twitter (53.2 million users), Pinterest (78.7 million users), Snapchat (77.5 million users), and Tumblr (18.8 million users) (*eMarketer.com.* 2019) (Refer to Figure 1 below).

Figure 1. Social network users, by platform, in the U.S.
Source: (eMarketer.com. 2019)

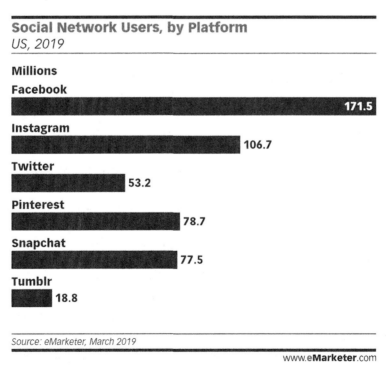

Social Network Users, by Platform
US, 2019

Millions

Facebook
171.5

Instagram
106.7

Twitter
53.2

Pinterest
78.7

Snapchat
77.5

Tumblr
18.8

Source: eMarketer, March 2019

www.**eMarketer**.com

According to *eMarketer.com* (2019), the majority of Facebook users have accessed to this social media through their mobile devices (162.2 millions) or smartphone (155.9 millions), followed by desktop/laptop (57.8 millions) and tablet (47.8 millions) (Refer to Figure 2 below). The similar heavy reliance on mobile and smartphone devices is found among Twitter users as well (*eMarketer.com*, 2019).

Figure 2. Facebook Users in the U.S., by Device
Source: (eMarketer.com, 2019)

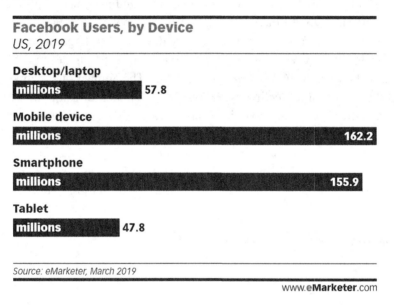

Because of its popularity and rapid growth, Facebook has now been as a viable advertising medium for corporation to communicate with consumers (Yarmis, 2009). Some industry pundits have claimed "Facebook advertising is the most powerful marketing opportunity online" (Carter, 2014, p. 137). Recent statistics in digital advertising seem to support the rosy prediction. According to *eMarketer.com*'s prediction (2018b), the global digital advertising is expected to grow to USD$327.8 billion in 2019, a rapid increase of 17% from 2018, Facebook is the second largest advertiser with $67.2 billion, lower than Google's $102.4 billion, but higher than Alibaba's $30.5 billion (*eMarketer.com*, 2018b). Actual statistics confirms that Facebook has generated about $63.37 billion advertising dollars in 2019 (*eMarketer.com*. 2019; Enberg, 2019).

Facebook advertising has played an increasingly important role in today's multi-platform advertising ecosystem among advertisers and advertising agencies (*eMarketer.com*, 2016). Practitioners and researchers have attributed these dramatic changes to shifting consumer media consumption behaviors (Swant, 2016a; Yang, 2019). The popularity of multi-platform advertising is because of the evolving practices in today's advertising landscape. According to Joe Laszlo, VP of Industry Initiatives at IAB, "[i]t's becoming less and less the case that marketers or brands are just looking to reach their chosen audience on a single device or screen at a time—they're looking to get a lot more holistic" (cited by Swant, 2016a). Given the large percent of Generation M (65.6%) as social media users, it is unavoidable that marketers and advertisers will employ social media in their multi-platform advertising campaign (*eMarketer.com*, 2019). As a result, ValueClick Media and Greystripe (Tode, 2013) also reports that, 75% of 201 media buyers in the survey, said they have seen increased success with multi-platform advertising campaigns. About 89% of the digital media buyers shows that it is essential to target consumers across multi-platforms (Tode, 2013) by including social media platforms such as Facebook.

As a social media platform that offers free access to its service, Facebook relies solely on advertising revenues to support its operation. In 2017, 42% of Facebook operating revenue was from its annual advertising revenue of $18.42 billion (He, 2019). The percentage has been predicted to decrease to 20.6% in 2019, to 18.2% in 2020, and 17.0% in 2021, while Facebook decides to diversity its profile to profit from its new cryptocurrency venture (He, 2019) (Refer to Figure 3 below). As a viable media platform to deliver advertising to the target audience, Facebook advertising has a competitive CPM with that of other platforms. For example Facebook has an average of $5.14 to $9.64 CPM worldwide in the fourth quarter of 2018 (Fisher, 2019b). Facebook's News Feed ads have an average CPM of $8.35 in the fourth quarter of 2018 (Fisher, 2019b). In terms of its non-video ads, Facebook US CPMs for buy-side companies range from $2.44 to $22.87 in the fourth quarter of 2018, when compared with that of video ads, ranging from $16.27 to $24.87 in the same quarter (Fisher, 2019b).

Figure 3. Facebook Ad Revenues (2017-2021) in the U.S.
Source: (eMarketer.com, 2019)

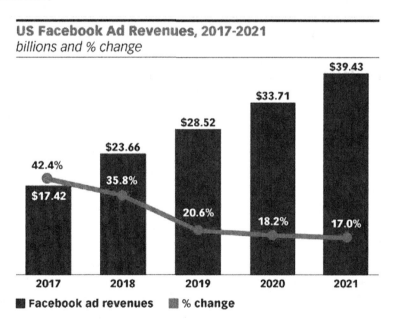

BACKGROUND

The Growing Importance of Social Media Advertising

The popularity of social media has also led to the emergence of social network advertising as part of the digital advertising ecosystem, which, according to *eMarketer.com* (2015b) and Cohen (2015), global ad spending on social network will reach $35.98 billion in 2017, and accounts for 16% of overall global ad spending. The most-populated Asia-Pacific region has reached about $7.4 billion in social network advertising in 2015, followed by Western Europe ($4.74 billion) and Latin America ($680 million) (*eMarketer.com*, 2015b). It is estimated that the overall social network advertising expenditure will reach $35.98 billion in 2017 (*eMarketer.com*, 2015b). Middle East and Africa have the highest growth rate in social network advertising spending, estimating 33.9% in 2016 and 27.4% in 2017 (*eMarketer.com*, 2015b). The share of social network advertising as part of the global digital advertising expenditure also reflects differences in the diffusion of these platforms across regions. *eMarketer's* data (2015b) also predicts that social network ad spending in North America (18.7%) and Western Europe (16.8%) are expected to have the highest shares of advertising dollars in 2017 (Refer to Figure 4 below).

An average of $15.45 per social network users is dedicated to social network advertising (*eMarketer. com*, 2015b). However, country variations are noteworthy among economically advanced versus less developed countries. For example, in North America, social network ad spending per social network user is $71.37 and $34.40 per user in Western Europe (*eMarketer.com*, 2015b). Among less developed countries in Latin America and Middle East & Africa, the ad spending per user is about $3.61 and $ $0.90 in 2017, respectively. There exists a close relationship between a region's technology advancement level and the amount of advertising dollars as seen in Figure 5 that shows per social network users' ad spending is predicted to be the highest in North America ($71.37) and Western Europe ($34.40) in 2017 (*eMarketer.com*, 2015b) (See Figure 5 below).

MAIN FOCUS OF THE CHAPTER

Emerging Issues Related to Facebook Advertising

At the macro-level, consumers have increasingly asked for transparency and accountability in the advertising industry as a similar trend found in other digital advertising platforms (Fisher, 2019a). Consumers continue to have concerns over their own privacy protection, resulting in strong demand on proper advertisers' data collection and management procedures to meet pending regulatory requirements (such as California Consumer Privacy Act) (Fisher, 2019a). As early as 2010, Facebook has been criticized for allowing 3rd app companies, data brokers, and advertisers to track and record the identities and usage behaviors of its users and their friends to develop more targeted ads (Worley, 2010). Facebook's recent privacy scandals with *Cambridge Analytica* demonstrate the potential problems when it comes to the monetization of consumer privacy data in the digital advertising marketplace (Kang & Yang, 2019). Despite Facebook's reactive responses to change its privacy policies as well as to allow its users to change their own privacy settings much easier, critics have pointed out that consumers still lack the full access to the data Facebook has collected (Corcoran, 2018). While social media users' own privacy concerns, government's regulatory regimes, and advertisers' own industry standards are expected to play very important role in determine the success of Facebook advertising, academic researchers are more interested in users' characteristics, their attitudes and feelings, message factors, among others on the effectiveness of Facebook advertising.

Figure 4. Social Network Advertising Spending (2013-2017)
Source: (eMarketer.com. 2019)

	2013	2014	2015	2016	2017
Social network ad spending (billions)					
North America	$4.94	$7.71	$10.10	$12.67	$15.15
Asia-Pacific	$3.25	$5.18	$7.40	$9.66	$11.91
Western Europe	$2.34	$3.68	$4.74	$5.82	$6.85
Latin America	$0.35	$0.54	$0.68	$0.85	$1.00
Central & Eastern Europe	$0.41	$0.52	$0.61	$0.70	$0.79
Middle East & Africa	$0.07	$0.11	$0.16	$0.22	$0.28
Worldwide	**$11.36**	**$17.74**	**$23.68**	**$29.91**	**$35.98**
Social network ad spending growth (% change)					
Middle East & Africa	68.0%	63.9%	52.4%	33.9%	27.4%
Asia-Pacific	60.7%	59.4%	42.7%	30.6%	23.3%
North America	46.3%	55.9%	31.0%	25.5%	19.6%
Western Europe	49.8%	57.1%	28.9%	22.8%	17.7%
Latin America	58.2%	55.6%	24.2%	25.0%	17.9%
Central & Eastern Europe	38.5%	27.0%	18.0%	14.4%	13.0%
Worldwide	**51.1%**	**56.2%**	**33.5%**	**26.3%**	**20.3%**
Social network ad spending share (% of total)					
North America	43.5%	43.5%	42.6%	42.4%	42.1%
Asia-Pacific	28.6%	29.2%	31.2%	32.3%	33.1%
Western Europe	20.6%	20.7%	20.0%	19.5%	19.0%
Latin America	3.1%	3.1%	2.9%	2.8%	2.8%
Central & Eastern Europe	3.6%	2.9%	2.6%	2.3%	2.2%
Middle East & Africa	0.6%	0.6%	0.7%	0.7%	0.8%
Social network % of digital ad spending					
North America	10.5%	14.0%	15.9%	17.4%	18.7%
Western Europe	8.0%	11.4%	13.5%	15.3%	16.8%
Asia-Pacific	9.3%	11.4%	12.9%	13.8%	14.3%
Latin America	8.5%	9.9%	10.0%	10.4%	10.4%
Central & Eastern Europe	9.0%	9.3%	9.4%	9.5%	9.7%
Middle East & Africa	4.9%	5.8%	6.8%	7.2%	7.4%
Worldwide	**9.4%**	**12.2%**	**13.9%**	**15.1%**	**16.0%**

Note: includes paid advertising appearing within social networks, social network games and social network apps; excludes spending by marketers that goes toward developing or maintaining a social network presence; numbers may not add up to total due to rounding
Source: eMarketer, April 2015

Figure 5. Social network ad spending per social network user worldwide by region (2013-2017)
Source: (eMarketer.com, 2019)

Social Network Ad Spending per Social Network User Worldwide, by Region, 2013-2017

	2013	2014	2015	2016	2017
Social network ad spending per social network user					
North America	$26.87	$39.98	$50.42	$61.35	$71.37
Western Europe	$13.71	$20.40	$25.26	$29.97	$34.40
Asia-Pacific	$4.45	$6.27	$8.04	$9.46	$10.54
Central & Eastern Europe	$2.65	$3.08	$3.41	$3.71	$4.00
Latin America	$1.87	$2.58	$2.84	$3.26	$3.61
Middle East & Africa	$0.35	$0.47	$0.64	$0.77	$0.90
Worldwide	**$7.02**	**$9.82**	**$11.96**	**$13.87**	**$15.45**
Social network ad spending per social network user growth (% change)					
Middle East & Africa	36.6%	36.8%	36.2%	19.0%	16.9%
Asia-Pacific	39.1%	41.1%	28.2%	17.6%	11.4%
North America	38.9%	49.8%	26.1%	21.7%	16.3%
Western Europe	40.5%	48.9%	23.8%	18.7%	14.8%
Central & Eastern Europe	26.5%	16.3%	10.5%	8.7%	7.9%
Latin America	37.3%	37.7%	10.1%	14.8%	10.6%
Worldwide	**33.1%**	**39.8%**	**21.8%**	**16.0%**	**11.4%**

Note: includes paid advertising appearing within social networks, social network games and social network apps; excludes spending by marketers that goes toward developing or maintaining a social network presence
Source: eMarketer, April 2015

On the other hand, academic researchers have focused on factors affecting the success of integrating Facebook into an advertising campaign (Anastasiei & Dospinescu, 2017; Baglione, Amin, McCullough, & Tucci, 2018). For example, Baglione et al. (2018) examined the influence of personality, perceived importance of Facebook, users' reference groups, and their perceptions of the ethics of targeted advertising on social media on users' own attitudes toward Facebook advertising. Baglione et al. (2018) empirically confirmed users' personality and reference groups significantly predict their feelings about Facebook advertisements. Anastasiei and Dospinescu (2017) studied whether the lack of trust in online brands, the perceived purchase risk of online shopping, and the perceptions of promotional message types will influence brand image and brand trust in a paid or unpaid Facebook advertising campaign. Their experimental study confirmed that the types of promotional message (paid or unpaid) do not influence any study variables. Duffett (2015) studied whether Facebook advertising has effectively reached Generation Y users in South Africa to influence their cognitive attitudes and subsequent buying behavior. Duffett (2015) confirmed that Facebok advertising has an overall favorable effect on the awareness and knowledge of Generation Y consumers, according to the hierarchy-of-effects model.

While these studies are interesting, an area that has not been fully explored in the extant literature is what Facebook users have actually experienced when using Facebook and advertising delivered through this social media platforms. This study attempts to answer the following questions:

RQ1: What are the overall experiences users have when using Facebook and Facebook advertising?
RQ2: What are the emotional responses users have when using Facebook and Facebook advertising?

Research Method

Because the experiences of Facebook users are important to understand if placing advertising on this social medium will be a feasible option, the authors used an experience sampling method (i.e., ESM) to collect data among Facebook college student users in the U.S. The ESM technique is a powerful tool to collect data to demonstrate participants' experiences (Khan, Markopoulos, & IJsselsteijn, 2007). The benefits of applying ESM are its methodological advantages to "examine fluctuations in the stream of consciousness and the links between the external contents and the contents of the mind" (Csikszentmihalyi, Hektner, & Schmidt, 2006, p.6). Because of the dynamic interactions when users interact with Facebook and its advertisements, ESM allows us to capture not only what Facebook users think of advertising placed on the Facebook when they encounter the messages. To follow ESM protocols, we use signal contingent protocols to record participants' experiences in using Facebook (Conner, Barrett, Bliss-Moreau, & Lebo, 2003). The signal-contingent protocols refer to "reporting on experience in responses to a signal at various times throughout the day" (Conner, Barrett, Bliss-Moreau, & Lebo, 2003, p. 60). The method is appropriate for observing on-going behaviors that are likely to be occurring when prompted (Conner, Barrett, Bliss-Moreau, & Lebo, 2003).

Research Procedure

The authors prompted participants to record their experiences using Facebook and Facebook advertising randomly. Signals were provided to users to prompt them to record their experience using Facebook and its advertising placements. The authors expected the large amount of experience data provided by these participants helps the authors to understand what users think of advertising on the Facebook. The empirical findings help online advertising research to understand the feasibility of using Facebook as a potential advertising medium through a non-survey-based method to better assess potential impacts on businesses.

Data were collected from 26 students who took part in this study for extra credits at a university computer lab where access to Facebook and Facebook advertising is possible. Four research sessions were scheduled for student participants at a large Southwest university and students were requested to take one hour to take part in this IRB-approved study.

Students were first briefed before the study to explain the purposes of the study, the procedures, and the time required to complete, using the following slide presentation.

- Thank you for participating in this study that will collect data on your experiences when you use Facebook and advertising that comes with Facebook
- The study will take about 1 hour to complete
- To take part in this study, you need to have a Facebook account

- Before you begin your study, please read the booklet in front of you. Read the consent agreement (pp. 1-3) and sign the form first before you proceed
- "STOP" after you sign the consent form

Students were asked to log in their Facebook account and use the Facebook for 10 minutes. After-wards, they were asked to "complete pages 4-5 of the booklet" (as the first prompt).

Participants were asked to skim the ads on Facebook and feel free to click on any ad if they want to brose the advertising contents. As the second prompt to collect experiential data, student participants were asked to "complete pages 6-7 of the booklet."

More specifically, student participants are asked to take 5 minutes or more to browse one Facebook ad of their choice. As part of the 3rd prompt to collect experiential data with Facebook advertising, students were asked to "complete pages 8-9 of the booklet". Once students have completed all booklets, they were thanked and were free to leave the research laboratory.

Findings

Among the recruited participants (N=26), seven of them were male, while 19 were females. Participants' age ranges from 20 to 28 years old, partially reflecting the age bracket of the current social network users (about 27.3% falls between 18 to 24 years old) (*eMarketer.com*, 2019). Their time spent on Facebook ranges from 0.5 hour (2 participants), 1-2 hours (11 participants), 2-3 hours (7 participants), and between 5 to 8 hours (4 hours).

Main Reasons to Use Facebook

When asked about the main reasons to use Facebook, participants have responded by emphasizing the social interaction functions with their friends and family members. For example, Participant 3-6 responds by "Social interaction with my friends and sisters", while Participant 3-5 says, the main reason to use Facebook is to "Keep in touch with friends that I went to school with or ……in the military with". Participant 4-3 says "Stay in contact with friends, and see what they are up to", while Participant 2-6 indicates, "To stay in touch with friends that have moved away."

Obtaining information about friends, family members, and recent events has been the main reason to use Facebook. For example, Participant 3-4 says, "I like to see what my friends are doing. I work and go to school full-time so sometimes it's hard for me to go out", while Participants 4-5, 4-4, and 4-2 have similar reasons to use Facebook: "For upcoming events and interest on my friends" (4-5), "To keep in touch with friends that I do not see often" (4-4), "Networking, keep in touch, events" (4-2). Some other examples include "I like to read what people post/pictures sometimes play Farmville" (Participant 3-3) or "To socialize & see what everyone is up to" (Participant 2-8).

The rise of Facebook has replaced traditional communication methods as two of the participants suggest. For example, Participant 2-2 says, "It's my only way to communicate because I don't have cell phone." Another participant has used Facebook to "advertise an organization I lead on campus" (Participant 2-10).

Participants are also using Facebook for relaxation and fun. For example, Participant 2-5 says, they use Facebook to "Get distracted. When bored I like to see what everyone else is doing even if I am not talking to them" or to "[i]nteract with my friends and family, entertainment, to relax" (Participant 2-11).

The convergence of social and game media has allowed some participants to express their main reason to use Facebook to have "Conversations w/ friends & playing games" (Participant 2-9).

WHAT PEOPLE THINK OF DIGITAL ADVERTISING?

When asked about what they think of advertising on the Internet, participants have in general held positive views, despite many have criticize its intrusiveness. For example, Participant 3-6 says, "It's very useful, while Participant 4-4 says, "I think it's a great way to learn & see new ideas and products." The same favorable views are held among Participant 2-11 ("It must reach a lot of people because I think the Internet is one of the most used medias"), Participant 2-10 ("It's the best way to advertise"), "Great source! It is very useful" (Participant 4-2). One of the participants have mentioned "convenience" as one of the main benefits of digital advertising: "Sometimes is convenient" (Participant 1-2).

Most participants who have reservation about this advertising format have raised concerns about the annoyance or intrusiveness of digital advertising. For example, Participant 3-5 says, "Some times they are good advertising pieces but other times some are annoying", while "I think that advertising is pervasive and somewhat annoying. Often it is selling something I don't want or need (Participant 3-4), " Good resource for advertisers, but sometimes annoying and repetitive & in the way of what I'm trying to look at (Participant 3-3), and "Some is annoying others interesting" (Participant 3-2). One of the participants have raised the question of trust as the drawback of digital advertising: "I don't' trust it" (Participant 1-3).

To prevent the perceptions of intrusiveness, participants have emphasized the importance of relevance of the message and product to consumers. For example, Participant 4-5 says, "It could be bad and good. Advertising can benefit the company into promoting their product but the message can be bad for the consumers" (Participant 4-5), while Participant 4-3 says, "It should be more directed to the product itself" and Participant 2-9 thinks, "Sometimes it's annoying, other times it catches my attention. Depends what it is."

1ST PROMPT (AFTER USING FACEBOOK FOR 10 MINUTES)

Upon asking what users are thinking about, most people have begun to think about behaviors related to Facebook. For example, Participant 3-6 says, "How fast I needed to finish typing a wallpost on one of my ...... sisters facebook walls", while Participant 3-2, says they are "Checking my updates". Similarly, Participant 3-4 says, "I was thinking about what I should put as my new status on Facebook. The last time I uploaded it was 2 days ago, so I wanted to change it", while Participant 3-3 indicates, "I was thinking about my Farmville on Facebook and whose been working on it."

A majority of the participants have been exploring various functions that Facebook has provided. For example, Participant 3-1 is using Facebook to "See what's new with my friends" and to examine "I was thinking about checking my messages and wondering what to respond to on Facebook" (Participant 4-5). As updates of friends are critical to many Facebook users, participants in this study have expressed their need to check most up-to-dated information about their friends. For example, Participant 2-9 says, "I was thinking of the updates my FB friends were making", while Participant 2-2 says, "To have communication with my friends and to see something new (updates about my friends)."

Several participants were thinking about this study about Facebook. For examples, Participant 4-3 says, "Finish this and go back to Facebook", while Participant 4-2, says "I was thinking how fun! I get to be on Facebook for a study" and "I did not know how the questions in the survey were going to be because I felt that with 10 minutes on Facebook we could not get enough information" (Participant 4-1).

To better understand the emotional experiences that users have experienced after using Facebook for 10 minutes, participants' responses suggest positive emotional responses after social interactions with their friends and family members. For example, Participant 2-1 says, that they are "happy... a get to talk with friends, I not always see", Participant 2-6 says, he/she was "excited... my friend was coming to town", while Participant 2-9 also says, she/he was "excited... I was allowed to be on FB no questions asked." Several of the participants have generated emotional experiences related to this study. For example, emotions such as calm or excited were found in the participants' narratives: "calm.... This is an easy task" (Participant 2-3) or "excited... I get to take a survey using something fun that I like to do on my leisure time" (Participant 2-8).

2ND PROMPT AFTER USING FACEBOOK ADVERTISING

After using Facebook advertising for about 10 minutes, participants were prompted to ask what they were thinking about to share their experiences with Facebook advertising. Most have generated thoughts related to their exposure to Facebook advertising and have developed advertising-related thoughts. For example, Participant 3-6 thinks, "The ads weren't good enough" and Participant 3-2 says, "That the ads are completely false, and non-beneficial", while another Participant (3-4) thinks the lack of ad relevance to them, "I was thinking that there were not a lot of ads and that none of them are relevant to me. So that I don't even want to see them."

Similar to exposure to advertisements delivered through other platforms, characteristics of a good ad are still important to attract people's attention. For example, Participant 3-1 says," That there are some interesting ads, although they are not true, but they do catch the eye." Participant 2-2 expresses that she/he will be attracted by an ad related to their own interest, by saying "Well I was interested in the image I saw because they used a common board game as advertising." This suggests the importance of using consumer behavior data to develop Facebook ads relevant to the target audience. The image of an ad will be an attention-getting tool to attract users to use Facebook advertising, as express in Participant 2-1's narratives, "the image of the ad had to be attractive xxx it had to fulfill my interest."

Contextual relevance of an ad is also important, just like any other ads. Participant 4-4 says, "Thinking about the ads I would see on the right of the screen." For example, Participant 2-5 has doubt about the relevance of the Facebook ad he/she just saw, "I click on ad about photography. I need to find a photographer but their ad is sending me to a photography school. Now I'm thinking ...... is not what I wanted." Ad-generated emotions and thoughts were also elicited were reported among Participant 3-3 who are "Thinking about food because I'm hungry and just look at food ad/discount." Similarly, Participant 4-1 also reported the same process, as seen in the following experiential narratives, "Was thinking about the clothes I was looking. I went to that webpage because I clicked in one of the ads from my Facebook profile."

Macro-level issues about the appropriateness of Facebook advertising also emerge as users were exposed to Facebook advertising. For example, Participant 3-5 says, "I was thinking would some of the ads be appropriate for some of the younger children who have a Facebook page." Similarly, Participant 1-1 says, "I wonder if Facebook is making us weaker as a society because XX no longer enhancing ourselves with face to face communication." Some participants have also questioned the ethics of current digital advertising practices as part of their overall experiences. For example, Participant 3-4 says, "I think that a lot of the ads are a scam, they request your e-mail address, and if you register you get non-stop e-mails about things you don't want. It's very hard to get removed from those lists." Participant 3-1 criticizes the intrusiveness of many pop-up ads, "Honestly, ads on the side do not bother me, what bothers me the most are pop up ads or the ones they show when you're watching videos." 2-9: I was thinking that since I was interested to look for advertisements on FB I would look for some that were interesting. I also ...... that if I got a notification & I answered it I would get in trouble since I was told to look for advertisements.

To understand Facebook's overall emotional responses about Facebook advertising, all participants were asked the following question, "If you felt a strong emotion since the last prompt, what did you feel and why did you feel that way?" While many have expressed their heightened interest in Facebook advertising by using the words, "interested" (Participant 1-4, Participant 2-2, Participant 4-2), "happy" (Participant 2-6), and "excitement" (Participant 2-1, Participant 2-7). The positive emotions were elicited after exposure to Facebook advertising because users are "interested... I felt identifying with the picture (the gameboard)" (Participant 2-2), or "ads were useful" (Participant 4-2). Some participants felt excited because "a found an ad that was promoting a game that I use to play when I was little) (Participant 2-1).

However, the majority of participants has expressed negative emotions as a result of exposure to Facebook advertising. For example, Participant 1-3 says, he/she is "bored" because of "tedious ads" or "I was finding more and more interested things" (Participant 1-4). Participant 3-6 is "annoyed.... The ads were boring." Ad clutter could also lead to negative feelings after exposure to Facebook advertising. For example, Participant 3-2 says, he or she is "annoyed... the adds are cluttering the screen." Participant 3-4 is "irritated... I don't like dealing with the ads."

The circumstance where Facebook advertising exposure occurs may also play a role in determining the effectiveness of Facebook advertising. For example, one participant (Participant 2-5) says, she/he is afraid... I don't like browsing with other people next to me. I don't like to be judge based on what's on my screen." Similarly, Participant 2-9 says, she/he is "slightly anxious.... I wanted to answer my notifications but I wanted to do so in a discreet manner so as to I wouldn't get on trouble."

3RD PROMPT AFTER USING A SPECIFIC FACEBOOK AD

The third part of the study involved the participants to watch a specific Facebook advertisement for 5 minutes before they were prompted to respond to the booklet. Participants need to write down what are in their mind when prompted. The experiential data the study has collected clearly indicate that exposure to Facebook advertising helps generate product-related thoughts. For example, Participant 3-5 says, "I was thinking about how funny some of the ads were." Participant 2-2 explained what make an ad attractive, "That I like the picture where I got to. The page on Facebook they had a lot of pictures, videos. It was very colorful." Participant 3-2 offered the most detailed description about what came to user's mind after exposure to a specific Facebook advertisement, as seen in the narrative below: "I found some clothes I would like to buy but the company is out of stock. If that's the case, they shouldn't be advertising what's not available." If the ad was not relevant to consumers, it is less likely to have a significant effect on consumers. For example, Participant 2-5 says, "I am looking for and ad I want to purchase something from and nothing appeals to me. Everything showing to me are not my interest.

Only thing came close is a hot dog ad"; Participant 2-11 expresses something similar, "About the ads on the webpage, of something that would interest me, then I found the ad of a book."

The nature of interactive advertisements allows users to be the active seeker for information. Therefore, a successful Facebook advertising campaign needs to be attention-getting and interesting to generate stickiness before users move on to another ad. For example, Participant 2-9 says, "Finding an interesting advertisement" while Participant 2-8 expresses, "I've never clicked on an ad so this is going to be boring." Participant 2-4 opted to search for ads that would be interesting to him/her, "I was thinking about what pages to search that were of interest to me."

The ethics of existing Facebook advertising practices remain to be a concern among several participants, to the extent of questioning its effectiveness. For example, Participant 1-1 says, "The ads on Facebook are very direct and quick sells. I wonder how effective they are?" Another Participant (1-3) has doubt about the data collection process, by saying "The ad is useless and it's only a way to gather your email to send overloads of ads to that email."

In terms of participants' emotional responses, a mixture of emotions was elicited after they focused on one specific Facebook ad for five minutes. They were asked to complete the sentence below": "If you felt a strong emotion since the last prompt, what did you feel and why did you feel that way? I felt _____ _____ because _____". Compared with what happened after the second prompt, a higher percentage of negative emotions was generated. For example, Participant 1-3 says, "dissatisfied" and Participant 3-2 says, "dissatisfied.... I could not get the product I wanted.", while Participant 1-4 says, "disappointed.... I didn't see a lot of advertising." The lack of interest among participants may explain these negative emotions. For example, Participant 2-1 says, he or she is "a little bit bored... I couldn't actually found something really interesting" while Participant 2-7 expressed he or she was "bored... I want to finish already." Participant 2-8 also says, he or she was "bothered... I had to look a boring ads that I didn't want to."

Some participants have expressed very strong negative emotions because of the design of Facebook to make the platform difficult to use. For example, Participant 2-5 says, she/he was "Angry... the add section on facebook is so complicated. I couldn't find anything to ... appeal and it gets me mad that facebook can't read my interest right." The poor design of Facebook advertising can also generate negative emotions. For example, Participant 2-4 says, "disappointed... I clicked on an ad for shoes but I had to sign up for the site." Thoughts not related to the study or the advertising were found to affect the advertising communication process. For example, Participant 2-10 expressed that he or she was "sad/annoyed... sad b/c I will miss my family when I leave and annoyed b/c I don't want to go to work" or Participant 3-4 says "more irritated... my survey answers to the online ads got me nothing."

Positive emotional responses were often generated when participants found the Facebook ad to be relevant and well-executed. For example, Participant 2-9 says, "Interested... the pictures on the advertisement's website appealed to me. The sophistication of the product did to it almost made of feel tangible" while Participant 3-3 also says "interested; I want to learn more about the product I was looking at the ad" and Participant 4-4 says, "happy... I was looking at different products." Similarly, Participant 3-5 has enjoyed the favorable emotional response after seeing the Facebook ad, "humored by some good ads.... Some make me laugh." Reading a Facebook ad can be relaxing to some participants, "relaxed again..... I'm just browsing through ads" (Participant 2-3) and "relaxed... I was not worried about school or work" (Participant 4-5), while confusing to others, "confused... I didn't know if I should buy or not" (Participant 2-6).

CONCLUSION

As observed in the above qualitative study that collected Facebook users' actual experiences when using Facebook and Facebook advertising, the study concludes that the success of Facebook advertising depends on a set of similar mechanisms such as the message factors (Baglione et al., 2018). Attractive advertising layout and design elements will create similar positive effects and emotional responses as observed in the ESM study. As an empirical study, this research reports users' experiential data to help digital advertising practitioners and researchers to better investigate what people were thinking about when exposed to Facebook and Facebook advertising. As a qualitative study, it is not feasible to explore causal relationships among these study variables. Furthermore, this study does not explore whether existing advertising regulatory regimes are likely to guide Facebook advertisers through the challenges and opportunities of this emerging advertising practice around the world. However, because Facebook advertising campaigns will rely heavily on knowledge about consumer behaviors and data to make the best use of Facebook advertising to complement cross-platform efficiencies, this type of heavy data-driven advertising and marketing campaigns may face similar privacy-related concerns in real-time bidding advertising (Yang & Kang, 2016),or programmatic advertising (Wood, 2015). Similar to other advertising campaigns delivered through other platforms, transparency and accountability are also required for many data brokers who gather and examine consumer data to produce market insights to develop a more effective multi-platform advertising campaign (Wood, 2015).

One of the urgent concerns about the practices of Facebook advertising is consumer privacy. At the local/state level, the California Consumer Privacy Act (CCPA) will become effective as of January 1, 2020 and is expected to raise the stakes for marketers to comply with the protection of consumer privacy. At the federal level, since 2009, Federal Trade Commission in the U.S. has been observing how marketers use consumer data for behavioral targeting advertising. FTC (2012) has focused on how to safeguard consumer privacy in the digital age through measures such as privacy by design, simplified solution to discourage consumer privacy infringement (such as *Do Not Track* mechanism), and greater transparency in consumer data gathering and usage. In Europe, *The ePrivacy Directive (Directive 2002/58/EC)* focuses on the regulation of storing and accessing data on a users' mobile device (The European Parliament and of the Council, 2002). IAB UK (2011) has also proposed a self-regulatory structure for online behavioral advertising practices and to establish seven principles to increase transparency mechanisms, user choice, sensitive segmentation, enforcement compliance, and review for users within the EU countries.

In addition to government's pro-active actions to defend consumer privacy, industry self-regulation such as those proposed by IAB's *Self-Regulatory Principles for Online Behavioral Advertising* (2009) put a great importance on the advertising professionals to abide by seven principles when developing online advertising campaigns (Refer to IAB, 2009 for detailed discussions).

In conclusion, the emergence of Facebook and its advertising practice have evidently become a global phenomenon that have seen its impacts on the advertising and marketing industry. To plan and implement a successful Facebook advertising campaign, advertising and marketers not only need to understand consumer consumption behaviors of different media platforms, but they also need to make the best use of the platform's strengths, while factoring into their existing weaknesses.

REFERENCES

Anastasiei, B., & Dospinescu, N. (2017). Facebook advertising: Relationship between types of message, brand attitude, and perceived buying risk. *Annals of 'Constantin Brancusi' University of Targu-Jiu. Economy Series, 6*, 18–26.

Baglione, S. L., Amin, K., McCullough, A., & Tucci, L. (2018, Winter). Factors affecting Facebook advertisements: Empirical study. *International Journal of Business, Marketing, & Decision Sciences, 11*(1), 124–140.

Carter, B. (2014). *The like economy: How businesses make money with Facebook* (2nd ed.). Indianapolis, IN: QUE Publishing.

Castillo, M. (2017, Oct. 13). Facebook is under fire from advertisers, highlighting a wider industry issue. *CNBC,* Retrieved from https://www.cnbc.com/2017/2010/2013/facebook-under-fire-from-advertisers.html

Cohen, D. (2015, April 20). Study: Global social media ad spend to reach nearly $36b in 2017. Retrieved from http://www.adweek.com/digital/emarketer-global-social-media-ad-spend/

Conner, T. S., Barrett, L. F., Bliss-Moreau, E., & Lebo, K. (2003, February). A practical guide to experience-sampling procedures. *Journal of Happiness Studies, 4*(1), 53–75. doi:10.1023/A:1023609306024

Criteo. (2014, September). *Cross-device advertising: How to navigate mobile marketing's next big opportunity*: Retrieved from http://www.criteo.com/media/1036/cross-device-advertising-criteo-sep-2014.pdf

Csikszentmihalyi, M., Hektner, J. M., & Schmidt, J. A. (2006). Experience sampling method: measuring the quality of everyday life (1st Ed.).Thousand Oaks, CA: Sage.

CTAM. (n.d.). Multiplatform definition. Retrieved from https://www.ctam.com/strategic-collaboration/advanced-cable/pages/multiplatform-definition.aspx

DeLuca, J. (2013, May 8). The new opportunity in cross-platform advertising. Retrieved from http://www.imediaconnection.com/articles/ported-articles/red-dot-articles/2013/may/the-new-opportunity-in-cross-platform-advertising/

Doyle, G. (2010). From television to multi-platform less from more or more for less? *Convergence: The International Journal of Research into New Media Technologies, 16*(4), 431-449. doi:10.1177/1354856510375145

Duffett, R. (2015, June). The influence of Facebook advertising on cognitive attitudes amid Generation Y. *Electronic Commerce Research, 15*(2), 243–267. doi:10.100710660-015-9177-4

Dutta-Bergman, M. J. (2010, June 7). Complementarity in consumption of news types across traditional and new media. *Journal of Broadcasting & Electronic Media, 48*(1), 41–60. doi:10.120715506878jobem4801_3

eMarketer.com. (2014, May 9). Cross-device advertising a hot topic in 2014. Retrieved from https://www.emarketer.com/Article/Cross-Device-Advertising-Hot-Topic-2014/1010824

eMarketer.com. (2015a, April 2). Mobile ad spend to top $100 billion worldwide in 2016, 51% of digital market. Retrieved from https://www.emarketer.com/Article/Mobile-Ad-Spend-Top-100-Billion-Worldwide-2016-51-of-Digital-Market/1012299 *eMarketer.com.* (2015b, April 15). Social network ad spending to hit $23.68 billion worldwide in 2015. Retrieved from https://www.emarketer.com/Article/Social-Network-Ad-Spending-Hit-2368-Billion-Worldwide-2015/1012357

eMarketer.com. (2016, Oct. 11). *Multiplatform video ad buying is emerging as the new normal.* Retrieved from https://www.Emarketer.Com/article/multiplatform-video-ad-buying-emerging-new-normal/1014576

eMarketer.com. (2018a, Feb. 12). Facebook losing younger users: But not all are migrating to Instagram. *eMarketer.com*, Retrieved from https://www.emarketer.com/content/facebook-losing-younger-users-at-even-faster-pace

eMarketer.com. (2018b, Nov. 20). Global ad spending update: Alibaba, Facebook and Google to capture over 60% of digital ad dollars in 2019. *eMarketer.com.* Retrieved from https://www.emarketer.com/content/global-ad-spending-update

eMarketer.com. (2019, March). Social network users, by platforms. *eMarketer.com.* Retrieved from https://forecasts-na2011.emarketer.com/2584b26021403070290f26021403070293a26021403070291a/26021405851918b26021400626310a26021403070292c26021403070186b26021403070291b

Enberg, J. (2019, June 23). Q2 2019 social trends: Facebook continues to diversify its revenue streams, Snapchat holds first partner summit, and Twitter targets political tweets. *eMarketer.com*, Retrieved from https://content-na2011.emarketer.com/q2012-2019-social-trends

Enoch, G., & Johnson, K. (2010). Cracking the cross-media code. *Journal of Advertising Research, 50*(2), 125–136. doi:10.2501/S0021849910091294

Erdal, I. J. (2009). Cross-media (re)production cultures. *Convergence: The International Journal of Research into New Media Technologies, 15*(2), 215-231. doi:10.1177/1354856508105231

Federal Trade Commission (FTC). (2012, March). *Protecting consumer privacy in an era of rapid change: Recommendations for businesses and policymakers.* Retrieved from https://www.ftc.gov/reports/protecting-consumer-privacy-era-rapid-change-recommendations-businesses-policymakers

Fisher, L. (2019a, Jan. 22). Nine trends to know for this year's media plan. *eMarketer.com.* Retrieved from https://content-na2011.emarketer.com/digital-display-advertising-2019

Fisher, L. (2019b, April 18). Digital display ad pricing StatPack: Banner, video, mobile and native CPMs, and pricing trends to watch for in 2019. *eMarketer.com.* Retrieved from https://content-na2011.emarketer.com/digital-display-ad-pricing-statpack

Havlena, W., Ardarelli, R. C., & Montigny, M. D. (2007). Quantifying the isolated and synergistic effects of exposure frequency for TV, print, and internet advertising. *Journal of Advertising Research, 47*(3), 215–221. doi:10.2501/S0021849907070262

He, A. (2019, June 24). Facebook's new libra cryptocurrency helps the company diversify away from advertising. *eMarketer.com.* Retrieved from https://content-na2011.emarketer.com/facebook-new-libra-cryptocurrency-helps-the-company-diversify-away-from-advertising

Hubbard, G. T., Kang, J.-A., & Crawford, E. C. (2016). Strategic communication and news disciplines. *Journalism & Mass Communication Educator, 71*(4), 453–469. doi:10.1177/1077695815598865

IAB. (2009, July). *Self-regulatory principles for online behavioral advertising.* Retrieved from https://www.iab.com/wp-content/uploads/2015/2005/ven-principles-2007-2001-2009.pdf

IAB UK. (2011, April 14). Europe commits to self-regulation; Europe's online advertising industry agrees online behavioural advertising guidelines. Retrieved from https://iabuk.net/news/europe-commits-to-self-regulation

Kang, Y. W., & Yang, K. C. C. (2019, Aug. 7-10). Will location privacy concerns influence location-based advertising effectiveness. Presented at the Competitive Paper, Advertising Division, 2019 AEJMC Conference, Toronto, Canada.

Khan, V. J., Markopoulos, I., & Jsselsteijn, W. A. (2007). Combining the experience sampling method with the day reconstruction method. In *Proceedings 11th CHI Nederland Conference.*

Lella, A., Lipsman, A., & Martin, B. (2015). The global mobile report: How multi-platform audiences & engagement compare in the US, Canada, UK and beyond. Reston, VA: com.Score.

Loras, S. (2016, July 18). What do China's new online advertising rules mean for marketers? Retrieved from https://www.clickz.com/what-do-chinas-new-online-advertising-rules-mean-for-marketers/103221/

Macdonald, C., Chapman, M., Naik, A., Fanno, M., & Beilis, T. (2016). *Cross-channel advertising attribution: New insights into multiplatform TV.* Accenture. Retrieved from https://www.accenture.com/us-en/~/media/PDF-18/Accenture-New-Insights-Into-Multiplatform-TV.pdf

Manafy, M. (2014, June 6). Five tips for cross-platform advertising success. Retrieved from http://www.thedrum.com/opinion/2014/06/06/five-tips-cross-platform-advertising-success

Marks, R. (2016, May). Challenges and opportunities in cross platform media measurement. *Research World, 2016*(58), 9–13. doi:10.1002/rwm3.20366

McIntyre, P. (2006). Cross-media deals expected to double to $600m a year; alliance mulls multi-platform package. *Australasian Business Intelligence, 33.* Retrieved from https://www.highbeam.com/doc/2001G2001-154865588.html

McNeal, M. (2013, Summer). Solving the multiplatform puzzle. *Marketing Insights,* pp. 41-47.

Monllos, K. (2016, Sept. 13). Carrie Brownstein made this brilliantly creepy short film about internet fandom for Kenzo. *AdWeek.* Retrieved from http://www.adweek.com/brand-marketing/carrie-brownstein-made-brilliantly-creepy-short-film-about-internet-fandom-kenzo-173453/

Neijens, J., & Voorveld., R. (2015). Cross-platform advertising: Current practices and issues for the future. *Journal of Advertising Research, 55*(3), 55-60. doi:. doi:10.2501/JAR-2016-2042

Nielsen. (2014, May 29). *The 8% unleashing the power of cross-platform advertising.* Retrieved from http://www.nielsen.com/content/corporate/us/en/insights/news/2014/the-8-percent-unleashing-the-power-of-cross-platform-advertising.html

Nielsen. (2016a, March 22). *On-demand demographics: VOD viewing across generations.* Retrieved from http://www.Nielsen.Com/us/en/insights/news/2016/on-demand-demographics-vod-viewing-across-generations.Html:Nielsen

Nielsen. (2016b, March 24). *Facts of life: As they move through life stages, Millennials' media habits are different and distinct.* Retrieved from http://www.nielsen.com/us/en/insights/news/2016/facts-of-life-as-they-move-through-life-stages-millennials-media-habits-are-different.html

Nielsen. (2017a, Jan. 30). Nielsen launches cross-device provider verification powered by digital ad ratings. Retrieved from http://www.nielsen.com/us/en/press-room/2017/nielsen-launches-cross-device-provider-verification-powered-by-digital-ad-ratings.html

Nielsen. (2017b, March 2). Millennials on millennials: A look at viewing behavior, distraction, and social media stars. Retrieved from http://www.nielsen.com/us/en/insights/news/2017/millennials-on-millennials-a-look-at-viewing-behavior-distraction-social-media-stars.html

Precourt, G. (2015, December). How does cross-platform advertising work? *Journal of Advertising Research*, 356-357. doi:10.2501/JAR-2015-2018

ResearchLive. (2017, Feb. 23). *com.Score launches multi-platform digital video measure in UK.* Retrieved from https://www.Research-live.Com/article/news/comscore-launches-multiplatform-digital-video-measure-in-uk/id/5018952

Robertson, M. (2014, April 29). Media buyers see big value in multi-platform advertising. Retrieved from http://tubularinsights.com/media-buyers-see-big-value-in-multi-platform-advertising/#ixzz4g3oWQRKh

Romaniuk, J. (2015, September). Coming in December: How cross-platform advertising works. *Journal of Advertising Research*, 353. doi:10.2501/JAR-2015-2014

Roper, P. (2014, Dec. 16). November best global digital marketing: Red Roof Inn's search campaign, Burger King's motel, Turkish shoppable soap opera. *Marketing.* Retrieved from http://shortyawards.com/category/2017th/multi-platform-campaign

Sharma, A. (2013, July 18). 'Mad Men' tops 'House of Cards' on Netflix. *The Wall Street Journal,* p. B3.

Swant, M. (2016a, Jan. 19). Why cross-device programmatic advertising is ready to take off in 2016. *Adweek.* Retrieved from http://www.adweek.com/digital/why-cross-device-programmatic-advertising-ready-take-2016-169025/

Swant, M. (2016b, Feb. 24). 6 ways Netflix viewing habits vary around the world. *Adweek,* Retrieved from http://www.adweek.com/digital/2016-ways-netflix-mobile-habits-vary-around-world-169848/

The European Parliament and of the Council. (2002, July 2). Directive 2002/58/EC of the European Parliament and of the Council of 12 July 2002 concerning the processing of personal data and the protection of privacy in the electronic communications sector (directive on privacy and electronic communications). Retrieved from http://eur-lex.europa.eu/legal-content/EN/TXT/?uri=CELEX:32002L0058

Tode, C. (2013, Aug. 16). Cross-device advertising commands growing portion of media spend: Report. *Mobile Marketer.* Retrieved from http://www.mobilemarketer.com/cms/news/research/15969.html

Twice. (2016, June 20). Millennials lead way among cord-cutters. *Twice,* p. 20.

Westcott, K., Lippstreu, S., & Cutbill, D. (2017). *Digital democracy survey: A multi-generational view of consumer technology, media, and telecom trends* (11th ed.). UK: Deloitte Development.

Wood, D. J. (2015, April 14). As marketers rush to programmatic, consumer-privacy rules still apply. *Ad-Age.com*. Retrieved from http://adage.com/article/digital/rush-programmatic-privacy-rules-apply/298060/

Yang, K. C. C. (2018). Multi-platform advertising as a global phenomenon. In Yang, K. C. C. (Ed.), Multi-platform advertising strategies in the global marketplace (pp. 1-28). Hershey, PA: IGI-Global. doi:10.4018/978-1-5225-3114-2.ch001

Yang, K. C. C., & Kang, Y. W. (2015). Exploring big data and privacy in strategic communication campaigns: A cross-cultural study of mobile social media users' daily experiences. *International Journal of Strategic Communication, Special Issue, 9*(2), 87–101. doi:10.1080/1553118X.2015.1008635

Yang, K. C. C., & Kang, Y. W. (2016, Oct. 15-16). Real-time bidding (RTB) advertising, programmatic advertising, digital advertising marketplace: Emerging policy and regulatory issues. Presented at Direct/Interactive Marketing Research Summit, Los Angeles, CA.

ADDITIONAL READING SECTION

Aronstam, S. (n.d.). Measuring the effectiveness of multi-platform advertising. Retrieved on July 7, 2016 from http://www.irisnetwork.org/media/work/SPA_Multi-Platform-Advertising.pdf

Assael, H. (2011). 50th Anniversary Supplement)). From silos to synergy: A fifty-year review of cross-media research shows synergy has yet to reach its full potential. *Journal of Advertising Research, 51*(1), 42–58. doi:10.2501/JAR-51-1-042-058

Crain, R. (2001, May 21). Multiplatform buys can lead to disruption for buyer, seller. *Advertising Age, 72*, 19.

eMarketer (2016, September 13). Us digital ad spending to surpass TV this year. Retrieved on January 10, 2017 from https://www.emarketer.com/Article/US-Digital-Ad-Spending-Surpass-TV-this-Year/1014469

Feit, E. M., Wang, P.-Y., Bradlow, E. T., & Fader, P. S. (2013, June). Fusing aggregate and disaggregate data with an application to multiplatform media consumption. *JMR, Journal of Marketing Research, L*, 34850–364.

Fulgoni, G. M. (2015, December). Is the grp really dead in a cross-platform ecosystem? In a cross-platform ecosystem? Why the gross rating point metric should thrive in today's fragmented media world. *Journal of Advertising Research, 55*(4), 358–361. doi:10.2501/JAR-2015-019

Indian Investment News. (January 3, 2014). Research and markets: Cross-platform & mobile advertising market by solutions &advertising - worldwide market forecasts and analysis (2013 - 2018). *India Investment News,* Retrieved on June 1, 2016 from http://www.marketsandmarkets.com/ResearchInsight/mobile-advertising-market.asp

Kim, S. J. (2016). A repertoire approach to cross-platform media use behavior. *New Media & Society, 18*(3), 353-372. *DOI, 3*. doi:10.1177/1461444814543162

Ksiazek, T. B. (2011). A network analytic approach to understanding cross-platform audience behavior. *Journal of Media Economics, 24*, 237-251. *DOI, 2*. doi:10.1080/08997764.08992011.08626985

Nielsen. (2011, June 22). Innovating to keep up with the ever-changing consumer. Retrieved on December 10, 2016 from http://www.nielsen.com/us/en/insights/news/2011/innovating-to-keep-up-with-the-ever-changing-consumer.html

Parsons, R. (2014, January 28). Privacy concerns harming online advertising. *Marketing Week,* Retrieved on December 1, 2016 from https://www.marketingweek.com/2014/2001/2028/privacy-concerns-harming-online-advertising/

Phalen, P., & Ducey, R. (2012). Audience behavior in the multi-screen "video-verse.". *International Journal on Media Management, 14*(2), 141–156. doi:10.1080/14241277.2012.657811

Snyder, J., & Garcia-Garcia, M. (2016, December). Advertising across platforms: Conditions for multimedia campaigns a method for determining optimal media investment and creative strategies across platforms. *Journal of Advertising Research*, 352-367. *DOI, 3.* doi:10.2501/JAR-2016-2042

Taylor, J. R., Kennedy, C., McDonald, N., Haddad, Y., Ouarzazi, E., & Larguinat, L. (2013). Is the multi-platform whole more powerful than its separate parts? Measuring the sales effects of cross-media advertising. *Journal of Advertising Research, 53*(2), 200–211. doi:10.2501/JAR-53-2-200-211

Umstead, R. T. (2014, February 17). Hulu Latino adds exclusives, originals providers aim for keys OTT demographic. *Multichannel News,* p.10.

Varan, D., Murphy, J., Hofacker, C. F., Robinson, J. A., Potter, R. F., & Bellman, S. (2013). What works best when combining television sets, pcs, tablets, or mobile phones? How synergies across devices result from cross-device effects and cross-format synergies. *Journal of Advertising Research, 53*(2), 212–220. doi:10.2501/JAR-53-2-212-220

Winslow, G. (2014a, February 3). com.Score launches cross-platform ratings. *Broadcasting & Cable, 4.*

Winslow, G. (2014b, July 14). Race intensifies for multiplatform ad systems. *Broadcasting & Cable, 27-28.*

Zelenkauskaite, A. (2016). Remediation, convergence, and big data: Conceptual limits of cross-platform social media. *Convergence (London), 1–16.* doi:10.1177/1354856516631519

KEY TERMS AND DEFINITIONS

Analytics: Consumer behavioral data related to their platform usage behaviors such as the number of visits to a platform, time spent on the platform, and actions when using the platform. Using these behavioral data, advertisers and marketers are able to segment target audience to increase their experiences and to improve campaign effectiveness.

Big Data: A term that defines a large dataset that produces in the size of collected data over time. It refers to the size of dataset that surpasses the capturing, storage, management, and analysis of traditional databases. The term refers to the dataset that has huge, more diverse, and multifaceted structure, accompanies by difficulties of data storage, analysis, and visualization. Big Data are characterized with the commonly known attributes: high-volume, -velocity, and –variety information assets.

Channel: In the advertising industry, the term refers to the platform or media to reach the target audience. Example of (advertising channels) include television, cable television, direct mail, outdoor, radio, etc. In the area of digital advertising, examples of channels include display, social, search, or mobile app advertising.

Consumer Behavior: The study of the decision-making processes to select, secure, use, and dispose of products or services by individuals, groups, or organizations. In the advertising industry, this term usually refers to how customers respond to advertising and marketing communications messages (such as in the information processing model) or how consumers decide to use multiple platforms in their daily lives. Consumer behavior aims to examine social, cultural, regulatory, and other ecological factors in affecting the decision-making process.

Digital Advertising: Used interchangeable with Internet or online advertising. This term covers a wide variety of online advertising formats, ranging from email, social media applications, search engine advertising, mobile advertising, video advertising, etc.

Digital Games: The terms, digital game or video game, often refers to a game which users play through audiovisual platform with contents on the basis of a story created from historical or fantasy themes. The concept of digital games as represented in existing game studies literature focuses on game itself, narrative (story), interactivity, and play.

Display Advertising: A type of digital advertising associated with and displayed on an Internet website. Its format ranges from audio, flash, images, text, and video.

Engagement: Also called consumer engagement, the term is a psychological concept that refers to how and whether users are satisfied with their experiences with advertising contents.

Mobile Advertising: An emerging platform of new digital media advertising formats that are delivered via consumers' mobile devices such as mobile phones, smartphones, tablets, etc.

Mobile Social Media: A term to refer to social networking media or applications such as Facebook, Foursquare, Instagram, Pinterest, Twitter, etc., that are often delivered via mobile devices such as smartphone, tablet, or laptop computer.

Multi-Platform Advertising: Also known as cross-channel, cross-media, cross-touchpoints, or multi-screen advertising, this term refers to advertising/marketing communications activities "that run during a similar timeframe across two or more screens including TV, computer, tablet, mobile phone and digital place-based media."

Programmatic Advertising: The term refers to an emerging advertising practice that relies on behavioral and Internet-based targeting to improve and implement highly computer-based advertising buying and placement.

Social Media: The term refers to a group of Internet-based applications that build on the ideological and technological foundations of Web 2.0. Social media include collaborative projects (such as Wikipedia), microblogs and blogs, contents (such as YouTube), social networking services (such as Facebook), virtual games, and virtual social life (such as Second Life).

Synergy Effect: In the context of advertising and marketing industry, this term refers to two or more advertising/marketing activities are able to generate a response that are greater than the total effects of these activities if conducted alone.

This research was previously published in Impacts of Online Advertising on Business Performance; pages 1-27, copyright year 2020 by Business Science Reference (an imprint of IGI Global).

Chapter 33
The Impacts of Facebook Ads on Brand Image, Brand Awareness, and Brand Equity

Ismail Erkan
🆔 https://orcid.org/0000-0003-1271-3481
Izmir Katip Celebi University, Turkey

Mehmet Gokerik
Karabuk University, Turkey

Fulya Acikgoz
Istanbul Technical University, Turkey

ABSTRACT

The advent of Facebook brought a new aspect for advertising since it allows ads to reach more targeted users on the internet. However, although the ads on Facebook have been found influential on consumers' purchase intentions, the possible impacts on brands have been relatively neglected. The purpose of this research is therefore to investigate the impacts of Facebook ads on brand image, brand awareness, and brand equity. With this purpose, a conceptual model was developed based on the advertising value model (AVM). The research model was tested by means of structural equation modelling (SEM) with the help of surveys applied for 194 university students. The results support the proposed model and confirm that Facebook ads play an important role on brand image, brand awareness, and brand equity. Theoretical and practical implications are discussed.

INTRODUCTION

With the increasing utilization of the Internet, social media has become an inevitable part of people's lives. The advent of social media has generated a different kind of communication approaches consisting of two ways or multiple ways of communication skills (Daugherty& Hoffman, 2014). Social media

DOI: 10.4018/978-1-7998-9020-1.ch033

has distinct platforms such as Facebook, YouTube, Twitter etc. In such platforms, as social media has altered the way people communicate in everyday life, social media has provided modern marketing approach rapidly (Dehghani &Tumer, 2015). In other words, social media has acted as a bridge between society and marketplace with developed world of chances and difficulties for entire perspectives of any business, which affects all departments in a company (Aral et al., 2014). Similarly, according to Com-Score Media (2009), to improve consumer brand awareness, social media has composed an association between marketers and consumers by achieving undiscovered chances. Therefore, brands devote a significant portion of their budgets to social media platforms such as Facebook, Twitter, and Instagram to reach both existing and new customers (Kumar et al., 2013). In particular, advertising on Facebook has become a new profession, so brands hire advertising specialists for social networking sites like Facebook (Dehghani & Tumer, 2015).

Facebook lets people easily communicate with each other and have a conversation with others who have similar interests (Rohani & Hock, 2010). Moreover, such people have potential to influence each other's brand perceptions as well as their purchasing intentions (Zhao & Shanyang, 2008). Therefore, marketers identify possible influencers and let them advertise their products and services (Falls, 2009). Online marketers also use Facebook ads in order to increase customers' awareness, and to understand customer expectations (Tran, 2017). According to statistical figures, Facebook is the most suitable and ideal social platform for advertisements since online advertisement on Facebook is much cheaper than the other platforms (Tran, 2017). For this reason, with the help of Facebook, many companies can monitor their brands so that they can make a decision about their profitability and efficiency. While doing so, researchers or companies can also take advantage of the attitude towards web advertising, which is seen as an essential component in understanding the effectiveness of advertising (Lutz et al., 1983). Advertising on Facebook has therefore been considered important, and the influence of Facebook ads on consumers has been studied by previous researchers (Dehghani & Tumer, 2015; Duffett, 2015). However, although there is a significant amount of research regarding the influence of Facebook ads on consumers, the number of studies which focuses on brands is very limited. The possible impacts of Facebook ads on brands have been relatively neglected. For this reason, it is understood that further study is required in this field.

The objective of this study is therefore to investigate the impacts of Facebook ads on brand image, brand identity, and brand equity. With this goal, a conceptual model was improved being founded on the Advertising Value Model (AVM) (Ducoffe, 1996). The research model was then tested by means of structural equation modelling (SEM) with the help of surveys applied for 194 university students. The results advocate the proposed model and approve that Facebook plays an important role on brand image, brand awareness, and brand equity. Findings come up with theoretical insights regarding ads on social media; and contribute to the existing literature by means of the proposed research model. From the practical perspective, comprehension the factors of ads on social media which impacts on brand image, brand identity, and brand equity could assist managers to organize their activities based on digital marketing.

ADVERTISEMENTS ON THE INTERNET

The internet, as an initial new medium marketing concept, provides both ample opportunities and some difficulties for marketers (Berthon et al., 1996; Ducoffe, 1996; Schlosser et al.,1999). To utilize of the internet in an effective way, most marketers attempt to understand how people using the internet recognize the Web as a source of advertising (Ducoffe, 1996). At the beginning of the using the Internet, to help marketers in their investments and attempts, the internet has been used to establish current situations and suggestions for consumer issues (Hoffman et al., 1995). After a while, the recent growth of many trades done from the Internet, varying from flowers to CDs, illustrates the strength and efficiency of business based on the web in tangible goods (Jakobsson et al., 1999).

In order to create information exchange commercially, advertising is one of the most important type all over the world. That's why, newspapers, television or radio stations benefit from advertising what invests other different kinds of information exchange (Jakobsson et al., 1999). Along with these, the advertising has started to take place on the Internet. Although it is well known that the ads on the other platforms are effective, in terms of evaluating the effectiveness and value of advertisements on the Internet, most scholars have paid huge attention on the company's perspective instead of the consumers' perspectives (Berthon et al., 1996). It was noticed later attitudes of consumers toward the Internet advertisements have been gain significance in order to assess and understand the advertising effectiveness of the Internet (Schlosser et al.,1999). In other words, since the beginning of the 2000s, not only for companies, but also for consumers, the importance of advertising on the Internet has grown dramatically.

The visible differences between traditional advertising and internet advertising make internet advertising more effective. One of these differences is to have control on the advertisements. In the traditional advertisements, consumers have a passive role since they might stop or break the continuity of attention of consumers (Korgaonkar& Wolin, 2002). On the other hand, advertisements on the Internet are selected by consumers regarding when, where and how much advertising content they want to see (Schlosser et al.,1999). The companies can direct attention of consumers, but consumers can decide which one they want to be exposed to advertisements on the Internet. In accordance with consumers, advertising on the Internet contain numerous forms of scope from electronic commercials which also are akin to traditional advertisings such as billboards to formats which are totally unlike traditional advertisings like Web sites (Ducoffe, 1996). Internet advertising, which is organized by professional businesses in order to notify consumers concerning any service or product, is defined in general as the whole process or actions of commercial structure on the Web Site (Schlosser et al.,1999).

Although advertisements on the Internet are more effective than the traditional advertisement and has much more content when comparing to traditional advertisements, some research points out that website complexity impacts on the attitudes and behaviours of consumers adversely (Bruner& Kumar, 2000). After a certain amount of time, the use of the website became widespread and simpler web sites were designed so, attitudes and behaviours of the consumers towards these web sites were also changed positively (Stevenson et al., 2000). Automatically, the consumers using the website have a positive attitude towards advertisement on the Internet, as well. However, since the Internet advertisements have different types, the same positive attitudes were not shown towards all kinds of advertisements on the Internet. For instance; e-mail advertisements are not supported by the consumers, that is, consumers have a negative attitude towards such advertisements (Mehta& Sivadas, 1995). On the contrary, consumers generally find the Internet advertisements as an important, useful and precious information source, in other words, they have positive attitudes towards advertisements on the Internet (Diaz et al., 1996; Ducoffe, 1996).

Advertisements on Social Media

Social media is described as, "a group of internet based applications that build on the ideological and technological foundations of Web 2.0, and that allow the creation and exchange of user generated content"

(Kaplan& Haenlein, 2010). Moreover, social media is considered as recently developed marketing trend (Barger et al., 2016). Therefore, the internet and advertising can be compromised together and they can be most robust tool for the companies and brands (Okazaki &Taylor, 2013). The revolution of social media has changed the communication way and has remarkably affected marketing strategies (Hutter et al., 2013). In other words, social media has rapidly altered the existing marketing techniques because it has built a bridge between marketing managers and consumers in order to generate novel chances and opportunities (Dehghani &Tumer, 2015). Especially, by creating different kind of applications such as Facebook, Instagram etc., social media has a huge impact on changing communication skills of consumers (Hutter et al., 2013). Additionally, social media is primarily examined by contemporary business as encouraging platforms to manage the advertising actions or activities as to influentially get into touch with the targeted consumers (Harrigan et al., 2017; Kohli et al., 2015). Under these circumstances, brands or companies have started to benefit from social media to conduct promotional activities. According to Mangold and Faulds (2009), social media should be main part of the brands of companies in the managing the promotional campaigns or the increasing the reputation of brands or companies. For this reason, advertisements on the social media have been gain importance in order to create attraction and reciprocal action in online platforms (Wu, 2016). Previous researches demonstrate that advertising campaign organized, with the help of social media, gives rise to obtain several marketing aims such as the increasing the purchase of intention, creating an awareness (Duffett, 2015).

Unlike this research, numerous researches have advocated that the role of advertisements on social media improves the influence of advertising activities in terms of intuition and awareness of consumers (Alalwan et al., 2017). For instance; the performance and actions of advertising on social media amply depend on how consumers can understand and create their behaviours or attitudes against the social media advertisements (Duffett, 2015). In another supportive example, in order for having positive attitudes for consumers, hedonic sights should be examined elaborately in social media platforms to enable consumers to have friendly and delight experience. These hedonic sights are composed of consumers' perceptions. Hence, attitudes of consumers against social media advertisements are devised by consumer related ads via social media and then, this would help to bring about consumers' intention to buy electronically (Mir, 2012).

As in the Internet advertising, advertisements on social media are made up different types such as ads on Facebook, YouTube, Instagram etc. Every social online platform has different impacts on consumers' attitudes. These advertisements have initially started to appear on Facebook and Youtube (Brettel et al., 2015). Afterwards, Facebook and YouTube are used as an advertising tool. These online social platforms are specified as a component of "globally integrated marketing communication" (Okazaki et al., 2006). Hence, the companies and brands have tried to utilize online advertising on these platforms (Ko et al., 2005) since they are aware that these social platforms provide consumers to generate and disseminate the content by their own involvement in order to increase the interactivity (Taylor, 2009). Along with social media platforms, online services such as Google AdWords and Amazon Mechanical Turk (MTurk) provide some opportunities for people as well. However, there are some differences between social online platforms and such online services. One of them is cost efficiency. Publishing advertising on online services is much cheaper than advertising on social media platforms (Antoun et al., 2016). Instead of focusing on the quality of advertisements or having attractive contents, Google AdWords provides consumers to reach free numerous information. On the other side, advertisers have some benefits such as providing a service delivering on the time and convincing communication (Groves et al. 2000). Such advertisements are also called "sponsored search advertisement" and such advertisements produce income flow by assisting operating costs and driving base income level, so they provide benefits for both consumers and advertisers (Turnbull& Bright, 2008). As a result, even though Google AdWords and Facebook ads have different goals, they seem that they are operated in online websites.

Facebook Advertisements

Social network platforms give users permission to constitute and modify content in text, audio or video format (Raghupathi & Rogel, 2014). People benefiting from these platforms connect, get into touch and influence each other by spreading, sharing, and producing information (Kushin &Yamamoto, 2010). In order to achieve these activities, there are many online platforms such as Instagram, Facebook, Twitter, etc. Among these platforms, Facebook is one of the most common social online platforms used by many users and it is the one of the popular places in which these activities are performed (ComScore Media, 2009). Last studies point out that more than of the people using Facebook are associated with these social media platforms via their smartphones. Thus, the huge part of these people is faced with advertisements via online platforms (Gavilanes et al., 2018). Especially, online advertisement has made progress to a recent stage thereafter, on May 6, 2015, IBM was cooperated with Facebook, in enterprise, for generating more excellent advertisements on the globe's the most major social network by associating the targeting technology of Facebook with facilities of IBM for managers working in the sector (Finley, 2015). Facebook advertisements provide people for the opportunity to communicate effectively with the ads on their private page permitting them to both "like" and "share" and also observe which people find enjoyable and share the same or the similar advertisements (Dehghani & Tumer, 2015). Furthermore, with the help of Facebook, advertisers enhance word of mouth (WOM), which takes place Facebook advertisements as an influential tool of developing brand image diversified good and services (Kaplan & Haenlein, 2010). However, the feasibility of Facebook for the advertisements are not yet examined even though some developed models have proposed different intuition regarding how the advertisements of social media platforms work (Brettel et al., 2015). For these reasons, advertisers increasingly take advantage of Facebook to understand their branding positions (Allahad 2015; Van et al., 2014; Tran, 2017).

THEORETICAL BACKGROUND OF THE RESEARCH MODEL

This study improves a theoretical model to examine the effects of Facebook ads on brand image, brand awareness and brand equity. To do so, Advertising Value Model (AVM) (Ducoffe, 1996) was extended with brand image, brand awareness and brand equity. The introduced model in this study illustrates that the impacts of Facebook Advertisements on brand image, brand awareness and brand equity in terms of Advertising Value Model.

This study suggests a particular and unique conceptual model which broadens and develops Advertising Value Model. For this reason, this section firstly will discuss the reasons for using the Advertising Value Model. Afterwards, the applied constructs of AVM will be described, before acquainting the proposed research model.

Advertising Value Model

In 1995, Ducoffe suggested that the advertising value model is to evaluate perceptions of consumers with respect to relative worth or benefit of advertising (Logan et al., 2012). He (1995) also disputed that three factors of entertainment, informativeness and irritation are the movement point of specifying the value of an advertisement (Lee et al., 2016). With this significance, the most widely used and recommended theory for describing consumers' behaviors and perceptions towards advertisements in the Internet is considered as advertising value model (Murillo et al., 2016). While building the advertising value model, Ducoffe made use of Uses and Gratification theory. This theory is based on consumers' needs and wants, pleasure motivations in order to satisfy their hedonic or utilitarian necessities (McQuail, 1983). For this reason, since the advertising value model comes from this theory, it is used to provide best clarification in consumers' attitudes regarding advertisements. By doing so, this study benefits from Ducoffe's model to investigate how entertainment, informativeness and irritation effects the advertising value, and this leads to the attitude towards advertising. Entertainment and informativeness positively effects the viewer opinions, however irritation mostly has a negative impact. (Ducoffe, 1996).

Advertising mostly composes of informative descriptions for products and Ducoffe highlights that value of advertising depends on the information customer receives about the product (Ducoffe, 1996). Entertainment is the second factor included in Ducoffe's model. Pleasant and likable advertising effects viewers positively towards their attitude over the brand (Mitchell and Olson, 1981). Based on this notion, it could be said that advertisements who promote products in a funny, entertaining way rather than just providing information, could result more purchasing decisions overall.

The other factor, irritation, differs from the other with its effect on people. While informativeness and entertainment has a positive impact, irritation may, and possibly will, direct the viewers decision in the negative way. Advertising consists of insult, annoy or offend factors create irritating influence (Ducoffe, 1996). Based on this argument, people who thought to be annoying by the majority of the viewers most likely will impose a negative impact towards any brand.

Figure 1. Advertising Value Model
Source: Ducoffe (1996)

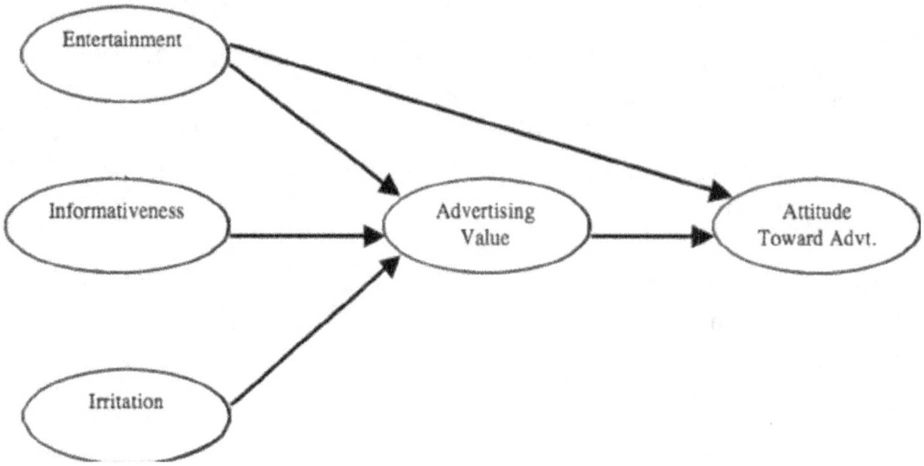

THE PROPOSED RESEARCH MODEL AND HYPOTHESES DEVELOPMENT

Figure 2 illustrates the proposed research model of this study, examining the relationship between advertising value model and brand image, brand awareness and brand equity. This study clarifies that the components of advertising value model are not sufficient to understand the brands position on Facebook and hence brand image, brand awareness, and brand equity should be involved in the measurement of the proposed model. For this reason, it creates a novel model. Both the properties of advertising value and attitudes toward advertising are considered together whilst examining their effects on brand image, brand awareness, and brand equity in the proposed research model.

As describing above, this model is expanding the advertising value model (Ducoffe, 1996). The AVM explains the properties of advertising and the impacts of these properties on attitude toward advertisements, whereas aspects of brand are based on how to position a brand itself. Together with this combination, the proposed model of this study provides further advancement of the advertising value model (AVM). The existing version of AVM only describes the components of advertisements apart from advertising value and its effects on attitudes towards advertising, whereas this proposed research model, in the study, examines the relationship between advertising value model and brand image, brand awareness and brand identity. Finally, this proposed research model includes the following variables: entertainment, informativeness, irritation, advertising value, brand image, brand awareness and brand equity.

Entertainment and Advertising Value

According to Ducoffe (1995), advertisements exemplify a considerable part of all media scope. On account of this, consumers can be probably to achieve a favourable assessment of an advertisements meanwhile they face entertainment advertisements (Murillo et al., 2016). The major part of research concerning advertisements is based on comparing idea that enjoyable or delightful advertising is reputed to have a favourable influence on brand manners (Mitchell and Olson, 1981). Previous studies have found there is a positive relationship between entertainment and advertising value (Ducoffe, 1995; Haghirian et al., 2005; Ko et al., 2005). However, this positive relationship can vary since it depends on where the advertisements is published. For this reason, in this study, it is predicted entertainment is more likely to have impact on advertising value.

H1. Entertainment positively impacts on advertising value.

Informativeness and Advertising Value

Ducoffe (1996) described informativeness as the capability of the advertisements to make consumers happy in giving some valuable information about a product or service. Additionally, he exudes that being informational of ads is one of the necessary constituent of advertising and preparing information owing to advertisement is a fundamental cause to subject consumers to advertising. For all these reasons, informativeness is a primary objective, which advocates ads itself (Lee et al., 2016). Previous studies have also found that the presence of information in ads increases the advertising value (Ducoffe, 1995; Haghirian et al., 2005; Ko et al., 2005). Yet, like entertainment, this effect can be changeable depending on where the ads are published. Therefore, in this study, it is predicted informativeness is more likely to have impacts on advertising value.

H2. Informativeness positively impacts on advertising value.

Irritation and Advertising Value

Ducoffe (1996) explained that consumers are likely to comprehend it as an undesirable and irritation impact when advertising utilize methods that annoy, humiliate, hurt someone's feelings. According to Bauer and Greyser (1968), the essential reasons customers criticize advertisements are concerning irritation it induces. In other words, unlike entertainment and informativeness, the relationship between irritation and advertising value is based on the understanding of customers. Previous studies have also found that irritation in ads decreases the advertising value (Ducoffe, 1995; Haghirian et al., 2005; Ko et al., 2005). In this study, it is still predicted that irritation is more likely to have impacts on advertising value.

H3. Irritation negatively impacts on advertising value.

Advertising Value and Attitude Towards Advertisement

According to Ducoffe (1996), advertisements recall to the conscious mind not only positive emotions but also negative emotions that are perceived to be previous impacts on the whole attitudes. That is to say advertising value clearly affects attitude towards advertisement. Therefore, most previous studies demonstrate that there is a positive relationship between advertising value and attitude towards advertisement (Ducoffe, 1995; Haghirian et al., 2005; Ko et al., 2005). This study also hypothesizes advertising value is more likely to have impacts on attitude towards advertisements.

H4. Advertising value positively impacts on attitude towards advertisement

6.5. Entertainment and Attitude Towards Advertisement

When a consumer faces the advertising, which has any entertainment content, they have automatically positive attitude towards advertisements (Ducoffe, 1996). Furthermore, consumers approach the brands introduced on the ads more willingly if ads include entertainment content. Previous studies also prove this relationship (Ducoffe, 1995; Ko et al., 2005; Mitchell and Olson, 1981). For this reason, this study also predicts that entertainment is likely to have impacts on attitude towards advertisement.

H5. Entertainment positively impacts on attitude towards advertisement.

Attitude Towards Advertisement and Brand Image, Brand Awareness and Brand Equity

"Attitude towards advertisement" is an independent variable when brand image, brand awareness and brand equity are included in the evaluation of the model. Even though studies about advertising value model and aspects of brand are further limited, advertisements have been explored by researchers in different studies corresponding with brand studies (Alhaddad, 2015, Buil et al., 2013; Meenaghan, 1995).

Brand image does not automatically transform into behaviour, so it is hard to measure and to interpret. There are numerous definitions of the brand image. One of them states that brand image can be described as a ''set of brand association that are anything linked in memory to a brand, usually in some meaningful way'' (Aaker, 1991). Moreover, brand image helps people to recall the brands; therefore, it is also used as a signal to notice the brands quickly (Blackwell &Miniard, 2006). With the help of brand image, consumers attempt to reach material or immaterial product or services. (Story & Loroz, 2005). Even though the brands do not try to create any trust for selling its products or services, consumers can benefit from the brand image when buying the products or services. For this reason, advertising is also considered as one of the main constituent of brand image formation (Meenaghan,1995) because when any brand image is robust in the mind of consumers, the products can acquire more charm without difficulty (Shamma & Hassan, 2011). Under these circumstances, since consumers' experiences are dependent on to extent how they exposure to advertisements, attitudes of consumers towards advertisements play an important role to create a brand image in their mind. Therefore, this study hypothesizes brand image is more likely affected by consumers' attitude towards advertisements.

H6. Attitude towards advertisements positively impacts on brand image.

Additionally, brand awareness also has a significant role in decision making process of consumers (Alhaddad, 2015). It is directly related to how much exposure to the brand (Alba& Hutchinson, 1987). In other words, the more the consumer is exposed to the mark, the greater the brand awareness. Brand awareness is a power of brand's existence in consumers' mind (Ross, 2006). Hence, it is described as "the ability of the potential buyer to recognize and recall that a brand is a member of a certain product category" (Aaker, 1991). Previous researches illustrate that brand awareness is generated by any events causing the consumer to try out any specific brand and to do this, public relations, marketing communication activities and especially advertisements play an important role (Clark et al., 2009; Hutter et al., 2013). Particularly, nowadays, social media is used as a different method to create brand awareness; it monitors that consumers, who are actively connected with the activities taken place in social media, brand awareness is also much greater in the mind of such consumers (Hutter et al., 2013). the impact of advertisements is positively related to brand awareness (Clark et al., 2009). Therefore, since there is a connection between brand awareness and advertisements, we predict that attitude towards advertising is more likely to have impacts on brand awareness.

H7. Attitude towards advertisements positively impacts on brand awareness.

Along with brand image and brand awareness, brand equity is defined as "a set of brand assets and liabilities linked to a brand's name and symbol that add to or subtract from the value provided by a product or service to a firm and / or that firm's customers" (Aaker, 1991). Most scholar think that brand equity can result from several dimensions such as brand awareness, brand image, brand loyalty etc. (Aaker, 1991: Keller, 1993; Lasser et al., 1995; Ruta &Juozas, 2010). Brand equity has been expressed as the advantage given by the brand for the products (Farquhar, 1989) since brand equity can be seen as a bridge between the consumers and brands. The strength or the edge of the brand equity and brand image as an outcome of attitudes of consumes towards the brand (Faircloth et al., 2001). In other words, this illustrates if consumers have positive attitudes towards brands, brand equity and brand image will be higher. As in brand image and brand awareness, social media methods can be aided in brand equity. According to Schivinski &Dabrowski (2005), social media networks enables consumers to infinite ways in order to communicate, share, clarify and generate the content related the any brands or products. For this reason, the mutual application of the company and social media platforms such as Facebook propose plenty of opportunities to enhance the brand equity. Thus, advertising published by the company, which is one of the most common activities driven in social media, helps brand to establish a strong brand equity. Although there is not much studies showing the impact of attitudes concerning advertisements on brand equity (Aalker &Biel, 2013), consumers' attitudes towards advertisements can also affect brand equity. In this context, we predict that there is a positive relationship between attitudes towards advertisements and brand equity.

H8. Attitude towards advertisements positively impacts on brand equity.

Figure 2. The Proposed Research Model

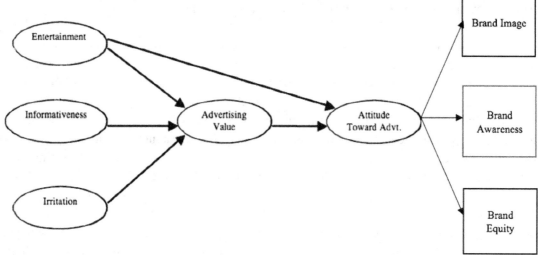

METHOD

Sampling

In the proposed research model, for testing the hypothesised relationships among variables, face-to-face survey was conducted with 194 university students who were chosen by using convenience sampling method from Turkey. The sample size was considered applicable since the previous research in our field found it acceptable (Anderson& Gerbing,1988; Ding et al., 1995). University students considered appropriate for this study since the younger age groups are more familiar with the social media. Our data shows that 99% of our participants use Facebook. Also, almost half of our participants use Facebook every day.

Measures

The questionnaire was planned with a multi-item approach. With the help of this approach, the researcher has borrowed all items from previous studies and has adopted for the context of this study. Each conceptual construct was evaluated by different items to develop reliability and validity. The whole variables were applied by a five-point Likert scale varying from strongly disagree (1) to strongly agree (5).

Particularly, 'entertainment', 'irritation', 'brand equity' and 'brand image' were measured by four-item scales which were taken from Ducoffe's study (1996), Wu and Wang (1994), (Alhaddad, 2015), respectively. 'Informativeness' and 'advertising value' were measured by two-item scales which were taken from Ducoffe's study (1996). Three-item scales were used in order to measure 'Attitude Toward Advertising' and 'Brand Awareness' which were taken by sequent studies: Ducoffe (1996) and Alhaddad (2015), respectively. The Appendix illustrates all the measures for the study.

Table 1. Sample characteristics (n = 194).

Measure	Frequency	Percentage (%)
Gender		
Male	76	39.2
Female	118	60.8
How often do you use Facebook?		
Everyday	85	43.8
4 - 5 days per week	35	18
Once or twice a week	31	16
Very rare	41	21.1
Never	2	1.0
How often do you use social media?		
Everyday	167	86.1
4 - 5 days per week	12	6.2
Once or twice a week	8	4.1
Very rare	7	3.6
How often do you see ads on Facebook?		
Every Time	57	29.4
Frequently	90	46.4
Rare	45	23.2
Never	2	1.0
What is your favourite social media website?		
Facebook	13	6.7
Twitter	26	13.4
Instagram	132	68.0
Snapchat	1	0.5
Youtube	21	10.8
Foursquare	1	0.5

RESULTS

Measurement Model Evaluation

The proposed model was analysed by applying with AMOS 22, structural equation model that is most convenient technique in order to predict the models (Bentler &Chou,1987). Prior to examine the relationship among the hypotheses, both the reliability and validity of the scales are analysed. To illustrate how the items are connected with each other and whether these items are involved in the same measurement, it is made use of convergent validity which is investigated by applying the composite reliability (CR) and the average variance extracted (AVE). The standard value at least is 0.70 for composite reliability (CR) and for average variance extracted (AVE), this value at least is 0.50 (Fornell & Larcker,1981). As demonstrated table 2, for each variable, its CR values are more than 0.8 (0.850-0.959) and its AVE values are also more than 0.5 (0.680- 0.853), which indicates these results are satisfactory for achieving convergent validity. The acceptable level of factor loadings is 0.70 and in this research, factor loadings of all variables are greater than 0.70 (0.73-0.96).

Table 2. Factor loadings, CR and AVE values.

Variable	Item	Factor Loading	CR	AVE
Entertainment ($M = 1.91$, SD $= 1.14$, $\alpha = 0.95$)	ENT1 ENT2 ENT3 ENT4	0.92 0.94 0.93 0.90	0.959	0.853
Informativeness ($M = 3.12$, SD $= 1.16$, $\alpha = 0.88$)	INF1 INF2	0.83 0.96	0,884	0.793
Irritation ($M = 3.72$, SD $= 1.31$, $\alpha = 0.93$)	IR1 IR2 IR3 IR4	0.82 0.95 0.90 0.85	0.933	0.777
Advertising Value ($M = 2.54$, SD $= 1.17$, $\alpha = 0.84$)	AV1 AV2	0.82 0.90	0.850	0.740
Attitude Toward Advertising ($M = 2.18$, SD $= 1.24$, $\alpha = 0.87$)	ATA1 ATA2 ATA3	0.81 0.90 0.77	0.873	0.697
Brand Image ($M = 2.63$, SD $= 1.09$, $\alpha = 0.90$)	BIM1 BIM2 BIM3 BIM4	0.80 0.83 0.92 0.81	0.908	0.712
Brand Awareness ($M = 3.21$, SD $= 1.08$, $\alpha = 0.86$)	BA1 BA2 BA3	0.80 0.93 0.73	0.863	0.680
Brand Equity ($M = 2.46$, SD $= 1.15$, $\alpha = 0.93$)	BE1 BE2 BE3 BE4	0.86 0.90 0.91 0.84	0.931	0.770

Note: CR - Composite Reliability, AVE - Average Variance Extracted

In addition to convergent validity, to be able to understand whether there is a reflection among the measurements or not, discriminant validity was examined. In the analyses, each variable of the square roots of average variance extracted should be greater than the standardized correlation of each construct with respect to others (Fornell & Larcker, 1981). As demonstrated in table 3, in this study, the square root of average variance extracted (AVE) for each variable is higher than the other correlation coefficients, which means the results were satisfactory for achieving discriminant validity.

Table 3. Correlation matrix of key variables.

	BA	ENT	INF	IR	AV	ATA	BIM BE
Brand Awareness (BA)	*0,825*						
Entertainment (ENT)	0,219	*0,923*					
Informativeness (INF)	0,347	0,369	*0,891*				
Irritation (IR)	-0,183	-0,434	-0,334	*-0,881*			
Advertising Value (AV)	0,297	0,520	0,411	-0,424	*0,860*		
Attitude Toward Advertising (ATA)	0,367	0,628	0,349	-0,429	0,655	*0,835*	
Brand Image (BIM) Brand Equity (BE)	0,321 0,132	0,340 0,336	0,233 0,172	-0,236 -0,162	0,392 0,332	0,368 0,324	0,844 0,324 0,878

Note: Italicised elements are the square root of AVE for each variable.

Structural Model Evaluation

Having been confirmed the measurement model, the structural model was tested. In order to examine the relationship between exogenous and endogenous construct, path analysis was utilized and also to forecast structural coefficients of the model. Tested structural model's results are demonstrated in Table 4.

Whereas one hypothesis was not found statistically significant, seven hypothesised relationship between variables were significant. More notably, H1, which had the positive impact of entertainment on advertising value, was supported ($\beta= 0.39$, $p < 0.001$). Moreover, informativeness was found to have an impact on advertising value positively. H2 was supported ($\beta= 0.20$, $p < 0.01$). On the contrary, H3, which had negative effect on advertising value statistically, was supported ($\beta= -0.20$, $p < 0.01$). Furthermore, advertising value and entertainment were found to be influential on attitude toward advertisements; (respectively)

H4 ($\beta =0.39$, $p < 0.001$) and H5 ($\beta =0.47$, $p < 0.001$). Finally, attitude toward advertising was found to have a positive impact on brand image, brand awareness, brand equity; (respectively) H6 ($\beta= 0.40$, $p < 0.001$), H7 ($\beta=0.38$, $p < 0.001$) and H8 ($\beta= 0.45$, $p < 0.001$). Along with these hypotheses results, the goodness-of-fit indices demonstrates the model complied with the model completely well; X^2 / d.f. $=1.415$; $p < 0.001$; GFI $=0.863$; AGFI$= 0.833$; CFI $=0.972$; RMSEA $=0.046$ (See table 4).

Table 4. Results and goodness-of-fit indices.

	Relationship			Std R.W	C.R	P Value
H_1	Entertainment		Advertising Value	0.35	4.540	***
H_2	Informativeness		Advertising Value	0.20	2.721	**
H_3	Irritation		Advertising Value	-0.20	-2.671	**
H_4	Advertising Value		Attitude Tow. Advertising	0.39	5.312	***
H_5	Entertainment		Attitude Tow. Advertising	0.47	5.739	***
H_6	Attitude Toward Advertising		Brand Image	0.40	5.112	***
H_7	Attitude Toward Advertising		Brand Awareness	0.38	4.656	***
H_8	Attitude Toward Advertising		Brand Equity	0.45	5.775	***
Goodness-of-fit indices						
$X^2 / d.f.$		1.415				
Goodness-of-fit index (GFI)		0.863				
Adjusted GFI (AGFI)		0.833				
Comparative fit index (CFI)		0.970				
RMSEA		0.046				

Note: * $p < 0.05$, ** $p < 0.01$, *** $p < 0.001$.
Std R.W - Standardized Regression Weights, C.R - Critical Ratio

DISCUSSION

The impact of advertisements on social media has been studied by scholars (Chen and Wells 1999; Edwards, and Lee 2002; Taylor et al., 2011). In fact, the influence of advertisements on brand image, brand awareness and brand equity (Lindsay, 1990; Keller, 1993; Romaniuk and Sharp, 2003). However, this study examines the effects of Facebook ads on brand image, brand identity, and brand equity through the tested model. With the help of structural equation model, results illustrate that both the features of Facebook advertisements and attitudes of university students towards advertising have a positive effect on brand image, brand awareness, and brand equity. All hypotheses between entertainment, informativeness, irritation advertising value, attitude toward advertising, brand image, brand awareness and brand equity were supported.

Although the hypotheses in the model have positive relationship among them, one relationship having negative effect seems it is debatable issue. In order to build the proposed model, the theories are followed by the existence literature. As in the literature, there was also negative effect between irritation and advertising value in this study. One possible reason that induces this result is the condition of this study on Facebook platform. Due to the fact that people generally watch the advertisements having entertainment and information content in social media, they might already ignore the advertisements that are irritated when they face such kind of advertisements. For this reason, the mentioned negative relationship may be influenced and also diversifying conditions about advertisements can bring more positive relationship for this hypothesis.

Results in respect of features of advertisements value are consistent with preceding literature. Entertainment and informativeness have a positive influence on advertising value and advertising value is positively associated with attitude towards advertising as proposed by AVM (Ducoffe, 1996). Results in this study verify that the model suggested by Ducoffe (1996) is applicable for studies of social media platforms. This result was also displayed in previous studies (Alhaddad, 2015; Van et al., 2014; Logan et al., 2012); however, in this study, brand image, brand awareness, and brand equity are added as a dependent variable. For this reason, results were existing that advertising value model impacts on brand image, brand awareness and brand equity.

From another perspective, as it is claimed and described in this paper, the features of advertisements and advertising value together with the attitudes toward advertisements are considered; hence these are added as independent variables into to the evaluation of the model. Results demonstrate that the proposed model is significant; and entertainment, informativeness, advertising value and attitude towards advertisements are among the determinants of Facebook advertisements on brand image, brand awareness and brand equity. Even though this result obtains from the theoretical model called advertising value model (Ducoffe, 1996), the number of studies examining the relationship between the advertising value model and brand image, brand awareness and brand equity in social media is rather limited.

CONCLUSION

This study suggests a research model in order to examine the effects of Facebook ads on brand image, brand awareness, and brand equity. This proposed model claims that Facebook advertisements involving brand image, brand awareness and brand equity depend on the features of advertising itself, as well attitudes towards advertisement. This proposed research model was confirmed by means of 194 university students who uses Facebook platform.

The results disclose varied theoretical and practical implications. Yet, the essential contribution of this study is to improve exhaustive conceptual model that investigates the impacts of Facebook ads on brand image, brand awareness, and brand equity. Taking into account the advertising value model, the proposed model was developed. The advertising value model explains the features of the advertisements together with advertising value and attitudes towards advertising (Ducoffe, 1996). However, the suggested model in this study, provides a new approach through taking into consideration of advertisements on Facebook together with brand image, brand awareness, and brand equity within the same model. Therefore, this proposed model brings a novel approach to advertisements on Facebook by extending advertising value model (AVM) and gives new intuitions to scholars studying advertising value model (AVM). In terms of contributing to the future research, this proposed model tests arguments about advertising value model and some valuable brand concepts simultaneously. Along with these implications, this research model provides a crucial comprehension of advertisements on Facebook by pointing out the factors of advertisements on Facebook affecting brand image, brand awareness, and brand equity.

From a managerial implication, this study assures managers of a set of ideas in order to figure out the impacts of Facebook advertisements on brand image, brand awareness and brand equity. Social media (i.e. Facebook) has been utilized by online advertisers to engage customers with companies, enhancing novel opportunities customers recognize concerning their brands and products (Tran, 2017). Therefore, the determining factors verified by this study are precious for practical implications. They permit brand managers in the market to comprehend the properties of advertisements on Facebook and how to combine their advertisement and brand aspects at them same time. As a result, this process helps to managers to enhance more effectively marketing tactics.

LIMITATIONS AND FUTURE RESEARCH DIRECTIONS

This study's results should be thought with the following limitations. In this research, the survey was conducted with university students. Even though the university students' age composes the larger part of Facebook users, they might not exactly mirror the entire population. Another important limitation of this study is to consider only Facebook platform; instead of focusing on just Facebook, other social media platforms (i.e. Twitter, Instagram) might be taken into consideration. In the speaking of further research, other studies could examine the relationship between advertising value model and other aspects of brand (i.e. brand loyalty). In other words, future research could enhance the proposed research model in this study through combining with different variables or benefitting from existing one within several contexts.

REFERENCES

Aaker, D. A., & Biel, A. L. (2013). *Brand equity & advertising: advertising's role in building strong brands*. Psychology Press.

AAKsER. D. A. (1991). Managing Brand Equity: Capitalizing on the Value of a Brand Name. New York: The Free Press.

Alba, J. W., & Hutchinson, J. W. (1987). Dimensions of consumer expertise. *The Journal of Consumer Research*, *13*(4), 411–454. doi:10.1086/209080

Alhaddad, A. A. (2015). The effect of advertising awareness on brand equity in social media. *International Journal of e-Education, e-Business, e- Management Learning*, *5*(2), 73.

Anderson, J. C., & Gerbing, D. W. (1988). Structural equation modeling in practice: A review and recommended two-step approach. *Psychological Bulletin*, *103*(3), 411–423. doi:10.1037/0033-2909.103.3.411

Antoun, C., Zhang, C., Conrad, F. G., & Schober, M. F. (2016). Comparisons of online recruitment strategies for convenience samples: Craigslist, Google AdWords, Facebook, and Amazon Mechanical Turk. *Field Methods*, *28*(3), 231–246. doi:10.1177/1525822X15603149

Aral, S., Dellarocas, C., & Godes, D. (2013). Introduction to the special issue—social media and business transformation: A framework for research. *Information Systems Research*, *24*(1), 3–13. doi:10.1287/isre.1120.0470

Barger, V., Peltier, J. W., & Schultz, D. E. (2016). Social media and consumer engagement: A review and research agenda. *Journal of Research in Interactive Marketing*, *10*(4), 268–287. doi:10.1108/JRIM-06-2016-0065

Bauer, R. A., & Greyser, S. A. (1968). *Advertising in America, the consumer view*. Academic Press.

Berthon, P., Pitt, L. F., & Watson, R. T. (1996). The World Wide Web as an advertising medium. *Journal of Advertising Research*, *36*(1), 43–54.

Boyd, D. M., & Ellison, N. B. (2007). Social network sites: Definition, history, and scholarship. *Journal of Computer-Mediated Communication*, *13*(1), 210–230. doi:10.1111/j.1083-6101.2007.00393.x

Brettel, M., Reich, J.-C., Gavilanes, J. M., & Flatten, T. C. (2015). What Drives Advertising Success on Facebook? *Journal of Advertising Research*, 162-175. doi:10.2501/JAR-55-2-162-175

Bruner, G. C. II, & Kumar, A. (2000). Web commercials and advertising hierarchy-of-effects. *Journal of Advertising Research*, *40*(1-2), 35–42. doi:10.2501/JAR-40-1-2-35-42

Buil, I., De Chernatony, L., & Martínez, E. (2013). Examining the role of advertising and sales promotions in brand equity creation. *Journal of Business Research*, *66*(1), 115–122. doi:10.1016/j.jbusres.2011.07.030

Chen, Q., & Wells, W. D. (1999). Attitude toward the site. *Journal of Advertising Research*, *39*(5), 27–38.

Clark, C. R., Doraszelski, U., & Draganska, M. (2009). The effect of advertising on brand awareness and perceived quality: An empirical investigation using panel data. *QME*, *7*(2), 207–236.

Comscore Media, M. (2009). *Total number of unique visitors to selected social networking sites*. Academic Press.

Daugherty, T. &Hoffman, E., (2014). EWOM and the importance of capturing consumer attention within social media. *Journal of Marketing Communications, 20*(1-2), 82-102.

Dehghani, M., & Tumer, M. (2015). A research on effectiveness of Facebook advertising on enhancing purchase intention of consumers. *Computers in Human Behavior*, *49*, 597–600. doi:10.1016/j.chb.2015.03.051

Diaz, A., Hammond, K., & McWilliam, G. (1996). *A Study of Web Use and Attitudes Amongst Novices, Moderate Users and Heavy Users*. Working paper no. 96-806. Centre for Marketing, London Business School.

Ding, L., Velicer, W. F., & Harlow, L. L. (1995). Effects of estimation methods, number of indicators per factor, and improper solutions on structural equation modeling fit indices. *Structural Equation Modeling*, *2*(2), 119–143. doi:10.1080/10705519509540000

Ducoffe, R. H. (1996). Advertising value and advertising on the web. *Journal of Advertising Research*, *36*(5), 21–21.

Duffett, R. G. (2015). Facebook advertising's influence on intention-to-purchase and purchase amongst Millennials. *Internet Research*, *25*(4), 498–526. doi:10.1108/IntR-01-2014-0020

Edwards, S. M., Li, H., & Lee, J. H. (2002). Forced exposure and psychological reactance: Antecedents and consequences of the perceived intrusiveness of pop-up ads. *Journal of Advertising*, *31*(3), 83–95. doi:10.1080/00913367.2002.10673678

Estelami, H. (2005). A cross-category examination of consumer price awareness in financial and non-financial services. *Journal of Financial Services Marketing*, *10*(2), 125–139. doi:10.1057/palgrave.fsm.4770180

Falls, J. (2009). *Public relations pros must be social media ready*. Social Media Explorer.

Finley, K. (2015). *Sorry Ello, the Real Ant-Facebook is Good Old Email*. Academic Press.

Gavilanes, J. M., Flatten, T. C., & Brettel, M. (2018). Content Strategies for Digital Consumer Engagement in Social Networks: Why Advertising Is an Antecedent of Engagement. *Journal of Advertising, 47*(1), 4–23. doi:10.1080/00913367.2017.1405751

Groves, R. M., Singer, E., & Corning, A. (2000). Leverage-saliency theory of survey participation: Description and an illustration. *Public Opinion Quarterly, 64*(3), 299–308. doi:10.1086/317990 PMID:11114270

Haghirian, P., Madlberger, M., & Tanuskova, A. (2005, January). Increasing advertising value of mobile marketing-an empirical study of antecedents. In *System Sciences, 2005. HICSS'05. Proceedings of the 38th Annual Hawaii International Conference On* (pp. 32c-32c). IEEE. 10.1109/HICSS.2005.311

Hoffman, D. L., Novak, T. P., & Chatterjee, P. (1995). Commercial scenarios for the web: opportunities and challenges. *Journal of computer-mediated communication, 1*(3).

Hutter, K., Hautz, J., Dennhardt, S., & Füller, J. (2013). The impact of user interactions in social media on brand awareness and purchase intention: The case of MINI on Facebook. *Journal of Product and Brand Management, 22*(5/6), 342–351. doi:10.1108/JPBM-05-2013-0299

Jakobsson, M., & Müller, J. (1999, February). Improved magic ink signatures using hints. In *International Conference on Financial Cryptography* (pp. 253-268). Springer. 10.1007/3-540-48390-X_19

Kaplan, A. M., & Haenlein, M. (2010). Users of the world, unite! The challenges and opportunities of social media. *Business Horizons, 53*(1), 59–68. doi:10.1016/j.bushor.2009.09.003

Keller, K. L. (1993). Conceptualizing, measuring, and managing customer-based brand equity. *The Journal of Marketing*, 1-22.

Ko, H., Cho, C. H., & Roberts, M. S. (2005). Internet uses and gratifications: A structural equation model of interactive advertising. *Journal of Advertising, 34*(2), 57–70. doi:10.1080/00913367.2005.10639191

Korgaonkar, P., & Wolin, L. D. (2002). Web usage, advertising, and shopping: Relationship patterns. *Internet Research, 12*(2), 191–204. doi:10.1108/10662240210422549

Kumar, V., Bhaskaran, V., Mirchandani, R., & Shah, M. (2013). Practice prize winner—creating a measurable social media marketing strategy: Increasing the value and ROI of intangibles and tangibles for hokey pokey. *Marketing Science, 32*(2), 194–212. doi:10.1287/mksc.1120.0768

Kushin, M. J., & Yamamoto, M. (2010). Did Social Media Really Matter? College Students' Use of Online Media and Political Decision Making in the 2008 Election. *Mass Communication & Society, 13*(5), 608–630. doi:10.1080/15205436.2010.516863

Kushin, M. J., & Yamamoto, M. (2010). Did social media really matter? College students' use of online media and political decision making in the 2008 election. *Mass Communication & Society, 13*(5), 608–630. doi:10.1080/15205436.2010.516863

Lasser, W., Mittal, B., & Sharma, A. (1995). Measuring customer-based brand equity. *Journal of Consumer Marketing, 12*(4), 11–19. doi:10.1108/07363769510095270

Lee, Y. G., Byon, K. K., Ammon, R., & Park, S. B. R. (2016). Golf product advertising value, attitude toward advertising and brand, and purchase intention. *Social Behaviour and Personality: An International Journal, 44*(5), 785-800.

Lindsay, M. (1990). Establish brand equity through advertising. *Marketing News, 24*(2), 16.

Logan, K., Bright, L. F., & Gangadharbatla, H. (2012). Facebook versus television: Advertising value perceptions among females. *Journal of Research in Interactive Marketing, 6*(3), 164–179. doi:10.1108/17505931211274651

Lutz, R. J., MacKenzie, S. B., & Belch, G. E. (1983). *Attitude toward the ad as a mediator of advertising effectiveness: Determinants and consequences.* ACR North American Advances.

McQuail, D. (1983). *Mass Communication Theory: An Introduction.* London: Sage.

Meenaghan, T. (1995). The role of advertising in brand image development. *Journal of Product and Brand Management, 4*(4), 23–34. doi:10.1108/10610429510097672

Mehta, R., & Sivadas, E. (1995). Comparing responses rates and response content in mail versus electronic mail surveys. *Journal of the Market Research Society, 37*(4), 429–440. doi:10.1177/147078539503700407

Mir, I. A. (2012). Consumer attitudinal insights about social media advertising: A South Asian perspective. *The Romanian Economic Journal, 15*(45), 265–288.

Mitchell, A. A., & Olson, J. C. (2000). Are product attribute beliefs the only mediator of advertising effects on brand attitude? *Advertising & Society Review, 1*(1). doi:10.1353/asr.2000.0010

Murillo, E., Merino, M., & Núñez, A. (2016). The advertising value of Twitter Ads: A study among Mexican Millennials. *Revista Brasileira de Gestão de Negócios, 18*(61), 436–456. doi:10.7819/rbgn.v18i61.2471

Okazaki, S., Taylor, C. R., & Zou, S. (2006). Advertising standardization's positive impact on the bottom line: A model of when and how standardization improves financial and strategic performance. *Journal of Advertising, 35*(3), 17–33. doi:10.2753/JOA0091-3367350302

Park, D. H., Lee, J., & Han, I. (2007). The effect of online consumer reviews on consumer purchasing intention: The moderating role of involvement. *International Journal of Electronic Commerce, 11*(4), 125–148. doi:10.2753/JEC1086-4415110405

Rohani, V. A., & Hock, O. S. (2009). On social network web sites: Definition, features, architectures and analysis tools. *Journal of Computer Engineering, 1*, 3–11.

Romaniuk, J., & Sharp, B. (2003). Measuring brand perceptions: Testing quantity and quality. Journal of Targeting. *Measurement and Analysis for Marketing, 11*(3), 218–229. doi:10.1057/palgrave.jt.5740079

Ross, S. D. (2006). A conceptual framework for understanding spectator-based brand equity. *Journal of Sport Management, 20*(1), 22–38. doi:10.1123/jsm.20.1.22

Rūta, R., & Juozas, R. (2010). Brand equity integrated evaluation model: consumer-based approach. *Economics and Management*, 719-725.

Schivinski, B., & Dabrowski, D. (2015). The impact of brand communication on brand equity through Facebook. *Journal of Research in Interactive Marketing*, *9*(1), 31–53. doi:10.1108/JRIM-02-2014-0007

Schlosser, A. E., Shavitt, S., & Kanfer, A. (1999). Survey of Internet users' attitudes toward Internet advertising. *Journal of Interactive Marketing*, *13*(3), 34–54. doi:10.1002/(SICI)1520-6653(199922)13:3<34::AID-DIR3>3.0.CO;2-R

Taylor, C. R. (2009). The six principles of digital advertising. *International Journal of Advertising*, *28*(3), 411–418. doi:10.2501/S0265048709200679

Taylor, D. G., Lewin, J. E., & Strutton, D. (2011). Friends, fans, and followers: Do ads work on social networks? how gender and age shape receptivity. *Journal of Advertising Research*, *51*(1), 258–275. doi:10.2501/JAR-51-1-258-275

Tran, T. P. (2017). Personalized ads on Facebook: An effective marketing tool for online marketers. *Journal of Retailing and Consumer Services*, *39*, 230–242. doi:10.1016/j.jretconser.2017.06.010

Turnbull, D., & Bright, L. F. (2008). Advertising academia with sponsored search: An exploratory study examining the effectiveness of Google AdWords at the local and global level. *International Journal of Electronic Business*, *6*(2), 149–171. doi:10.1504/IJEB.2008.018070

Van-Tien Dao, W., Nhat Hanh Le, A., Ming-Sung Cheng, J., & Chao Chen, D. (2014). Social media advertising value: The case of transitional economies in Southeast Asia. *International Journal of Advertising*, *33*(2), 271–294. doi:10.2501/IJA-33-2-271-294

Wu, S. I., & Wang, W. H. (2014). Impact of CSR perception on brand image, brand attitude and buying willingness: A study of a global café. *International Journal of Marketing Studies*, *6*(6), 43. doi:10.5539/ijms.v6n6p43

Zhao, S., Grasmuck, S., & Martin, J. (2008). Identity construction on Facebook: Digital empowerment in anchored relationships. *Computers in Human Behavior*, *24*(5), 1816–1836. doi:10.1016/j.chb.2008.02.012

This research was previously published in the Handbook of Research on Entrepreneurship and Marketing for Global Reach in the Digital Economy; pages 442-462, copyright year 2019 by Business Science Reference (an imprint of IGI Global).

APPENDIX

Table 5. Measures

Variable	Items
Entertainment (Ducoffe, 1996)	Facebook ads are entertaining. Facebook ads are enjoyable. Facebook ads are pleasing. Facebook ads are exciting.
Informativeness (Ducoffe, 1996)	Facebook ads are a convenient source of product information. Facebook ads are a quick source of product information.
Irritation (Ducoffe, 1996)	Facebook ads are annoying. Facebook ads are irritating. Facebook ads are boring. Facebook ads are tiring.
Advertising Value (Ducoffe, 1996)	Facebook ads are valuable. Facebook ads are important.
Attitude Toward Advertising (Park et al., 2007)	Facebook ads are helpful for my decision making when I buy a product. Facebook ads make me confident in purchasing product. If I do not see Facebook ads when I buy a product, I worry about my decision.
Brand Image (Wu and Wang, 2014)	The quality of brands that give advertisement on Facebook is high. Brands giving advertisement on Facebook allows the user to gain status. It is wise to use to choose brands giving advertisement on Facebook. The brands giving advertisement are the leading brands in their field.
Brand Awareness (Alhaddad, 2015)	Facebook ads help me to recognize brands. Facebook ads help me to remember brands. Facebook ads help me to remember brand logos.
Brand Equity (Alhaddad, 2015)	**X is a brand that you see on Facebook advertisements,** Even if other brands produce products with same quality and price, I want to buy X brand. Even if there are other brands with the same characteristics as the X brand, I would prefer the X brand. Even if other brands are as good as X brand, I would prefer to buy X brand again. Even if other brands have no differences from X brand, It is wise to choose X brand.

Chapter 34
The (In)Effectiveness of In-Stream Video Ads:
Comparison of Facebook and YouTube

Tereza Semerádová
https://orcid.org/0000-0002-9123-5782
Faculty of Economics, Technical University of Liberec, Czech Republic

Petr Weinlich
Technical University of Liberec, Czech Republic

ABSTRACT

Video represents the most shared type of online content. The ability of this media to capture and convey a message in an interactive and informationally rich format has captivated both users and advertisers. Advertising platforms are trying to expand the offer of the tools that would help the advertisers to reach their potential customers. Therefore, many new video-based advertising formats are being introduced including ads with experimental length or dimensions. However, the increasing quantity of online advertisements the users have to face is raising questions about their actual marketing effectiveness. To provide relevant answers, authors examined the performance of 13 types of video ads that were implemented for a 30-day period and that generated 1 155 EUR overall profit. The advertising results are analyzed from three perspectives: financial, behavioral, and reactional. The main emphasis is put on the study of the video effectiveness depending on different viewing contexts with respect to the potential phenomenon of advertising blindness.

INTRODUCTION

Video marketing is currently one of the most popular online marketing tools. Video content is more engaging, memorable, and popular with consumers than any other type of content. According to the predictions, by 2020, online videos will account for more than 80% of all consumer Internet traffic (85% in the US). YouTube is the second most visited website after Google. On a daily basis, users view

DOI: 10.4018/978-1-7998-9020-1.ch034

more than 500 million h of video on YouTube; further, 78% of people watch online videos every week, and 55% watch online videos every day. Viewers memorize up to 95% of the message while watching the video, compared to 10% when reading a text. As more social networks have been inspired by Facebook's decision to prioritize video content, the prominence of video across all platforms has grown. Facebook videos have a 135% higher average organic reach than photos. Nearly 50% of Internet users search for videos related to a product or service before they visit the store. Implementing a video on a landing page can increase the average conversion rate by 80%. Four times as many consumers would rather watch a video on a product than read about the product. Companies that use marketing videos have a 27% higher click-through rate and a 34% higher conversion rate than those that do not. Video ads have an average click-through rate of 1.84%, which is the highest of all digital ad formats. Brands that use video marketing grow 49% faster than brands that do not use videos. Nonetheless, although video marketing is a powerful tool, there are a few factors that merchants should be aware of regarding potential customer preferences. More than 15% of viewers believe that video advertising should not last longer than 15 s. In addition, 85% of Facebook videos are watched without sound. Conversely, 82% of consumers close a browser or leave a web page due to popup video advertising and 33% of viewers stop watching video after 30 s, 45% after 1 min, and 60% after 2 min ("33 Fascinating and useful statistics about video marketing in 2019", 2019).

There can be no doubt that video has gained traction in popularity over the past years with both users and advertisers. Social networks, video listing websites, and advertising systems provide a large number of video or mixed (video and photos) formats that can be used to deliver a desired message to the potential customers. The most common formats include Facebook native newsfeed video, YouTube video and YouTube ads, stories, banner video ads, and in-stream commercial breaks. Although previous research has proven that video ads generate better results in terms of number of reactions, reach, and profitability overall (Semerádová & Weinlich, 2018), scientific evidence related to the effectiveness of the individual video formats is still insufficient. Studies on advertising blindness suggest that the placement of the marketing message may be a key variable influencing the final effectiveness of a particular video spot (Muñoz-Leiva et al., 2019; Wang & Hung, 2018; Bang & Wojdynski, 2016). Recent research results indicate that the central part of the browsing space is the most suitable placement since it represents a native environment for web pages and social network feeds (Zimand-Sheiner et al., 2019; Aslam & Karjaluoto, 2017; Alalwan, 2018). According to these studies, in-stream and newsfeed ads should be the most effective type of video marketing. However, surveys and experiments that tested viewers' attention during TV commercials indicate that users develop a certain advertising blindness over time, even for marketing content in the central area of attention (Kim et al., 2017; Joo et al., 2016; Beuckels et al., 2017).

In this chapter, we will test the ability of online video ads to capture user's attention and generate the desired conversions. The effectiveness of this advertising format will be tested on two major video content platforms: YouTube and Facebook. To obtain objective results, we will perform a comparative analysis of the available advertising video formats on both of the aforementioned platforms. The main objective of the proposed study is to examine user reactions to commercial breaks of different lengths and analyze their attitudes toward online video advertising in general. In the following sections, based on previous research in the area of online advertising, we will outline factors that may potentially influence user perception of video content. Furthermore, we will describe current video advertising options and explain the complexity of the metrics used to assess the video performance. The theoretical findings will be used to set up an online experiment implemented in the native user environment of social networks and on YouTube. The experimental data will be collected via actual advertising content implemented by a Czech online shop.

USER REACTANCE TO VIDEO CONTENT

Video is a global phenomenon that offers many new marketing opportunities. When used correctly, it represents a powerful tool that can help influence user behavior. Brands focus on two main goals: the long-term building of brand awareness and engagement and short-term increases in sales. Emotion-enhanced video supports long-term customer relationships with the brand, whereas strong-communicated videos help to achieve short-term goals. The perfect video campaign should combine both long-term and short-term goals (Lee et al., 2013). There are two basic questions, i.e., how does the emotional side affect our behavior, and what is the role of video in creating an emotional response? According to the economist Daniel Kahneman, people think far less than they perceive themselves as having done and rely on a great deal of subconscious decisions. There are two systems that run in parallel. A system where the brain makes decisions quickly with little effort and a second system where the brain makes decisions based on data (Mowat, 2018, p. 27). Video content contributes to a brand's recognition. If the customers remember the video they saw, they also remember the brand and are more likely to make a purchase. In addition, a satisfied customer likes to share a video that is in accordance with their preferences. Preserving colors, fonts, logos, and the same tonality in both video and web articles helps enhance the memorability of the video (Wu et al., 2018).

A key advantage of video lies in its functionality across different devices; responsive design plays a considerable role in digital marketing. If an advertisement does not display properly, the ads lose effectiveness, thereby leading to a decrease in conversions. Video has the advantage of displaying, although not optimally, on all devices, from computers to mobile phones, consequently allowing for a greater reach in terms of potential customers. Video is also associated with a user-friendly environment (Sidaty et al., 2017). By using videos as a marketing strategy, brand identity can be strengthened to ensure that customers become more engaged and to promote brand loyalty. It is estimated that 92% of mobile video consumers also share videos. Moreover, video is shared 1200% more than a combination of text and a link ("33 Fascinating and useful statistics about video marketing in 2019", 2019).

Currently, users are surrounded by advertising content, and it is difficult to attract and keep their attention. Often, a video is placed in the wrong place at the wrong time. Information communicated through the video must be properly targeted and relevant; otherwise, it may result in a negative impact (Van den Broeck, Poels & Walrave, 2018). There are countless competing brands on the market. The customer is often overwhelmed with advertising messages and overlooks brands' communication campaigns (Yang et al., 2015). To increase the probability of delivering an advertised message, advertisers need to get the maximum amount of information possible about the target group they wish to address and tailor the message in accordance with specific customer needs. The more details the advertiser has on the psychographics of a target group, the higher the chance of creating effective advertisements. Advertising is considered effective if the recipient is exposed to it, memorizes it, and has a change in attitude due to the interaction with the ad, leaving a positive emotional footprint, as well as when the ad results in a change in behavior or when it provides the information needed for rational decision making by the recipient (Tran, 2017).

Music can be seen as a key dimension in creating an effective marketing message. It can influence the users on three levels i.e., the psychological, social, and semantic. The psychological level refers to the ability of music to influence a person's mood, memories, and feelings. As a result, advertising message creators working via this medium can refer to selected emotions or ideas to connect them with a product. The social level is related to the preference of music according to certain demographics (e.g., gender and age), socio-graphics (e.g., social class and vocation), and characteristics (Liikkanen & Salovaara, 2015). Thus, in the context of marketing communication, we may assume that a certain target group that favors a certain type of music will prefer a particular product. If the message is carried by a sung text (song), it can be considered as a factor working on the semantic level wherein the music encodes a certain message. In connection with music and emotions, it is worth mentioning the so-called circular model, which considers two dimensions, i.e., activation × not activating and pleasant × unpleasant. Experiments have shown that music that is perceived as both activating and unpleasant appears to be aggressive, activating and pleasant as exciting, inactive and unpleasant as boring, and inactivating and pleasant as reassuring. When selecting the music for an advertising message, three basic questions should be considered: which is the best music for the product, what music fits the advertising itself, and what music will attract the audience (Martín-Santana et al., 2015)?

Another important factor influencing the user perception of an advertisement is the use of color. The correct color rendering of audiovisual compositions is equally important as other variables since colors are processed emotionally. Dominant elements may be emphasized with rich colors; however, saturated elements should occupy a minor part of the image. It is necessary to consider the fluency of the entire video spot and maintain a uniform color sequence. If each scene was colored differently, it would be distracting for the viewer. We distinguish three main functions of colors: impressive, expressive, and constructive. Impressive color function refers to the sensory perception of the image. The expressive function describes a mental or emotional response. For the constructive function, we determine what colors will prevail in the frame, what the foreground and background will be, and what the overall character of the scene will look like (Kareklas et al., 2014).

Many videos contain textual elements. Generally, it is the final claim, i.e., the main statement that the advertiser wants to emphasize with accompanying or introductory text used to promote the advertising message or even the headlines. Text can also affect the overall atmosphere. An improperly chosen or placed font can destroy the overall impression of the ad. If a company decides to add text to the video, the content creator must keep in mind that the text has to be of a reasonable length. Long texts are rather discouraging to the viewer. The text must have an appropriate color, ideally complementary to the background to be clearly legible, and also be of a sufficient size (Huang et al., 2018). Further, selecting the appropriate font requires taking the aesthetic and technical requirements and the main goal of the ad into account. The font type must correspond to the main message (Amar et al., 2017).

Having a high-quality video that corresponds to the preferences of the target group is a key prerequisite for attracting user attention. The aforementioned characteristics will be accounted for during the creation of the advertising video for the purposes of this experiment. The attractiveness of the video will be subsequently verified by using a focus group made of the typical representatives of the target customer segment.

ADVERTISING VIDEO FORMATS

Online video advertising, including YouTube, Facebook, or other video formats, represents an ideal tool for building brand awareness, capturing user's attention, and generating conversions. Unlike static content, video advertising is able to deliver emotions to the viewer quickly. The emotional dimension can be a decisive factor when converting online users into paying customers. Although video on TV is rather unidirectional and non-interactive, video in an online environment activates the user and generates direct feedback. It also allows the advertiser to track the response of the target audience quickly and acquire data for follow-up campaign optimization.

The visibility time is 1 s for classic display advertising, whereas it takes between 5 and 30 s for video advertising. In addition, videos generate three times as many click-through rates. However, there are some specific differences when it comes to online video advertising. Since it is possible to skip most online advertisements, it is essential to attract and retain the attention of the user who originally came for another type of content. A typical TV spot works with a longer story and gradation toward the end. In the digital environment, because of shorter footage and ad placement, the gradation follows a reverse pattern. Among the most popular formats are classic pre-rolls ads (displayed before the video) and individual spots on social networks and video-banner areas. In addition to the pre-roll option, the advertisers may choose a mid-roll (in-stream) ad that runs during the video or a post-roll video that is characterized by lower effectiveness. Mid-rollers are now a common part of YouTube and Facebook videos (Munnukka et al., 2019).

When preparing the video, it is important to consider the dramatic increase in the consumption of video content by users with mobile devices and adjust the content for multiple formats including vertical video with shorter footage. For example, 72% of younger users today use mobile phones only in portrait mode. In the context of social networks, the videos appear among the posts of other brands and users in the newsfeed of the customers. The video should thus fit into the visual and communication style of the given social network while simultaneously maintaining enough originality to captivate the user. Content creators should keep in mind that most video-banner areas are primarily a silent format and turn on sound only when the user moves the cursor over the video or clicks on the ad to start the sound. The absence of sound can be replaced by quick footage alternations that would attract the attention of the viewer more effectively. In addition to the video, there are usually other graphical elements in the banner area that are static and accompany the message of the video (Yang et al., 2017).

It is advisable to combine multiple footage for each video format. The classic television length of 30 s is allowed by most advertising platforms, but more often advertising systems prefer a shorter footage of 10–15 s. The bumpers of 6 s, originally introduced by YouTube, are now also a common format and function as an effective addition to longer videos, mainly for re-marketing purposes. Videos of all footage lengths should be tailored specifically for online environments and not represent merely shortened version of television ads. In Instagram Stories, the advertising time is limited; the advertiser has 1.5 s on average to captivate the user. Video is a dynamic format that is constantly evolving. A major innovation in video content is the launch of IGTV, an Instagram platform for longer videos. It generates customized content for every viewer and has ambitions to become a serious rival to YouTube. IGTV video is strictly vertical, corresponding to the trend of video consumption by means of mobile devices (Kim & Kim, 2019).

Video Ads on YouTube

YouTube currently offers six advertising formats that differ in the placement of the ads and the length of the commercial break. With Google Ads, advertisers may create impressive video campaigns with a variety of video ad formats that appeal to customers on YouTube and video partner websites. Video ad formats include skippable in-stream ads, in-stream non-skippable ads discovery ads, out-stream ads, and bumpers. Although video ad content must be placed on YouTube, video ads themselves may appear on YouTube and video partner sites as well as on applications across the entire Google Content network. Depending on the format and settings used, they may also appear on tablets and mobile devices. All advertising placements supported by YouTube are displayed in Figure 1 ("Video advertising formats – YouTube help center", 2019).

Figure 1. Available advertising formats on YouTube
Source: (the authors)

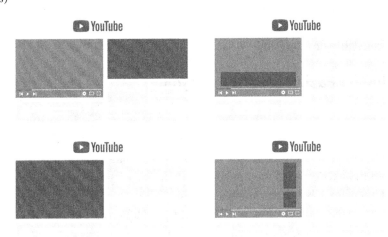

Skippable in-stream ads are designed to promote video content between other videos on YouTube or in the Google Content Network. A video ad will be played before, after, or during other videos. After 5 s, the user can skip the ad. Skippable in-stream ads can appear on YouTube watch pages, videos on partner sites, and content network applications. For cost per view bids, the advertiser pays when a user watches at least 30 s of video (or an entire video, if it is less than 30 s) or performs some interaction (whichever comes first). Another way to express advertising costs is costs per thousand (CPM), which is based on impressions. Advertising micro-spots use CPM bids, and the advertiser pays for every 1,000 ad impressions.

Non-skippable in-stream ads represent an advertising format allowing advertisers to share the full message with their customers. A non-skippable in-stream ad takes up to 15 s to play before, during, or after another video. Viewers do not have the option to play the video prior to these ads. The non-skippable ads may be used on the same placements as the previous format, and the billing is also based per every 1,000 impressions.

Discovery ads are used to navigate the users to the desired content displayed in YouTube related videos, YouTube search results or YouTube mobile home pages. Discovery ads comprise a video thumbnail and a short text. Although the exact size and appearance of video discovery ads may vary depending on where they appear, they always invite users to click to play the promoted video. The video will then be played on the YouTube watch page. The advertising costs are recorded only if the user chooses to view the ad and clicks on the thumbnail.

Bumpers represent a short video ad format allowing advertisers to reach more customers and enhance brand awareness. This format can be used to address a wide range of viewers with a short message that will keep them tuned for more information. Bumpers take up to 6 s and can be placed before, in and after a video on all YouTube pages, partner video sites and applications across the Google Content network. Viewers do not have the option to skip these ads. As in the previous cases, the advertiser pays for every 1,000 impressions.

Out-stream ads are mobile only (phones and tablets) video ads that appear on partner sites and in apps. Out-stream ads will start playing with the audio turned off. The user can click the ad to turn on the sound. An advertiser is only charged if more than half of the ad area is displayed for at least 2 s. This format is designed to increase video ad impact at an affordable price. One video template can be displayed on a variety of mobile placements. On the mobile websites, out-stream ads appear in banners, whereas in mobile apps, they appear in banners, feeds, and in both portrait and full screen modes. However, this ad format is not yet available on YouTube.

Video Advertising on Facebook and Instagram

Facebook video ads may be used for many purposes including post boosting, promoting Facebook fan pages, sending users to the advertiser's website, increasing conversions and app installations, fostering stronger engagement, and generating more user reactions. Although video ads may be distributed in various formats in all the above-mentioned purposes, their delivery will always be determined by the campaign goals and not primarily by the number of views. The same video may be used for the generation of likes as well as for the promotion of app installations. However, Facebook will always optimize the campaign for the selected purpose. Therefore, if the goal is to increase the number of views of the video, the campaign goal Video Views should be selected. Using video format for purposes other than Video Views is highly recommended, although it is necessary to adjust the message of the video to the chosen campaign objective. Facebook advertising platform offers six types of video ads including the following: short videos and GIFs, vertical videos, Instagram videos, carousel format, collection, and in-stream video ("Facebook video ads", 2019).

Short videos and GIFs may be used in all placements on Facebook, Instagram, and Audience Network. GIFs play in loop, similarly as short videos. In addition, they have the same file size requirements (4GB). To achieve the best results, the advertisers should opt for high-quality images with gentle movements. The files should always be uploaded in .gif format. According to the general Facebook advertising guide, images smaller than 8 MB and with more than 20% of text should be avoided. However, GIF-based ads may appear only as static images on some mobile devices.

The rise of **vertical video** presents both opportunities and challenges. The vertical orientation of the video inevitably requires a more refined look that takes full advantage of the immediacy and interactivity of the format. Vertical videos should be shot in 9:16 aspect ratio from the outset; if the advertiser shoots horizontally, they should be considering the implications for vertical formatting throughout the process. The optimization of vertical videos should always be done on a smartphone to verify that all the elements are recognizable and readable. Vertical video is not limited to the 9:16 ratio alone. Advertising platforms also allow for the aspect ratio of 3:2, which is more suitable for social network feeds and provides more space for additional text elements that make the video feel more authentic, fitting in a visual pattern that users are accustomed to seeing in the newsfeed.

Instagram Stories ads can contain both video and photo content and can be created from already existing material or form vertical videos tailored specifically for this format. Speed is typical for Stories. Every post in stories is limited only to 15 s. Therefore, the video needs to be timed correctly and transmit the main message quickly. Each individual story can consist of several short chapters, or scenes. According to Facebook, 60% of the stories are viewed with the sound turned on. It is thus possible to add dialog or sound effects to the video. Facebook recommends placing the product, brand, and message at the beginning of the story a reminder of the brand along with a call to action before the story ends.

A *carousel format* is suitable for displaying two or more images or videos, headings and links, or call to action in one ad. The users who come across this ad may scroll through the individual entries by swiping, when on a mobile device, or by clicking on the arrows when on computer screens. Carousel format is used to display an array of products, services, applications, and related details or to tell a story in a creative manner. Carousel ads may be created in Facebook Ads Manager or by using the API environment. They appear on Facebook and Instagram on selected posts on mobile devices and computers.

One of the primary methods through which users discover new products is mobile video. However, when they want to get more information regarding an offer, they expect a clean and fast mobile environment. *Collection ads* allow people to move from the discovery stage to shopping in an effortless way. Every collection ad primarily comprises a video or an image. The advertisers may choose from four accompanying image-based grid-like layouts. Customers who click on your collection ad to browse or find out more information go smoothly into a fast-loading, fast-moving visual environment without leaving Facebook or Instagram.

In-stream videos are displayed only to users who watch video content form publishing partners approved by Facebook. Facebook in-stream video ads are included among the automatic placements offered by Facebook. However, if the advertiser desires to use only the in-stream video ads, they may adjust the placements and exclude other options except the desired one. Content creators (publishing partners) work closely with the Facebook Media Partnership team to ensure the quality of the video hosting ads. In-stream ads can be hosted only in at least 3 min long videos of the approved publishing partners. Publishing partners decide when advertising breaks occur. The first available advertising break for in-stream video is one minute. All in-stream video ads should contain an audio track. The lengths and requirements for in-stream videos differ depending on the chosen placement. In-stream ads for Facebook should be 5−15 s long and in the vertical (9:16), horizontal (16:9), and square (1:1) aspect ratios. In the Audience Network, videos can last up to 120 s when the advertiser opts for automatic placements; however, when only in-stream videos are selected, the video time is limited to 30 s. Vertical videos are not allowed in the Audience Network.

Both advertising platforms combined offers in a total of 10 different video-based advertising formats that may be further diversified by choosing specific targeting and distribution options. In our experiment, we will test the effectiveness of all the described formats: skippable and non-skippable ads, discovery ads, bumpers, out-stream ads, Facebook short videos, Instagram Stories, carousel format, collection, and Facebook in-stream ads.

HOW TO MEASURE THE PERFORMANCE OF VIDEO ADS?

The main objective for many users and advertisers is often only the number of views. They judge video and video advertisements as effective if said ads are able to generate as many views of their videos as that of their competitors. Inexperienced content creators typically do not analyze who the viewers of the video are, where they come from, or how the viewing curve fluctuates during the video. It can be argued that an ordinary user, an amateur creator, does not need this information. However, if this data is not tracked by advertisers, the amount of money invested into video advertising can be spent without achieving the desired result. Video metrics represent a considerably important step for creating video strategies and marketing campaigns. When companies or creators aim to determine the impact of their videos, they must first decide their goal and the relevant metrics for expressing said goal. Metrics, not just in the online environment, represent the individual dimensions of an object or an event that can be measured and recorded as a number or ratio. For example, for the dimension of video sharing, there are metrics such as the total number of shares or the number of shares in relation to a chosen timeframe. Video analytics can help the advertisers and content creators examine the real impact of their advertisements and evaluate the quality of the video in relation to the preferences of the viewers. In addition to achieving high ratings, the transmission of the marketing message should be included in the evaluation (Li et al., 2019).

There are two main approaches to measuring video impact. The first approach consists in the combination of web and social media tracking and the analytical tools that are applied to acquire a more detailed data track reflecting user online behavior. These tools function on the basis of a so-called site-centric measuring method (sometimes referred to as server-centric) that is implemented at the level of web pages, servers, web browsers using cookies, snippets of JavaScript measuring code inserted into the HTML code of a web page, or directly into a video player. The second approach (user-centric) focuses on an analysis of user behavior. This second set of methods includes user tracking and qualitative data collection techniques such as surveys and user evaluation panels (Liu et al., 2018; Ding et al., 2019).

Specialized video analytics tools collect the most information on the level of the video player. The JavaScript code inserted in the video player sends the information to the measuring server that then evaluates user behavior and analyzes a series of metrics, such as the percentage of the video the user actually saw, what frames the user intentionally skipped, and more information about the technical quality of the distributed video. The main major platforms that allow video advertising such as YouTube, Facebook, Google, and Instagram provide a large variety of metrics implemented directly within the administration interface. The analytical tools used by the advertising systems are comprehensive and combine both of the aforementioned perspectives. Since the user interacts not only with the video but also with the website where the video is placed or with the landing page that they visited by clicking on the video, advertising systems partially or fully integrate website analytics. Advertising systems collect analytical information about video views, user behavior and interaction with the video, user demographics, viewing device and browser, activity on social networks, etc. However, advertising systems do not typically provide technical information regarding the video distribution since such systems are conceptualized even for amateur users (Berry et al., 2015).

Although each advertising system and each video platform use their own specific metrics, we generally identify three basic categories of video performance indexes: performance metrics, behavioral metrics, and mixed metrics.

Performance Metrics

Performance metrics are applied to describe a company's business performance. They include business segment metrics as well as the user requirements or management metrics. In the case of online video content, performance metrics provide data for quantitative analysis of the user's video viewing process. The metrics are computed based on the hard, up-to-date data related to reach, the number of views, and the length of the viewing sessions per individuals or per groups of users.

Many online video content creators aim to achieve as many views as possible. However, this basic metric does not allow an analysis of the quality of the information shared in the video, audience composition, and other data that is vital for campaign targeting and customer segmentation. Although viewing metrics represent a value that can be compared to other videos on a given platform, measuring the number of views between multiple platforms is a major problem because different analytical tools use different definitions of a view. David Burch from Tubemogul, an online marketing and analytics company, says that most people in the online marketing industry do not know exactly what a single view means or how it is calculated ("What Counts as a Video View? - David Burch, Tubemogul", 2019; "Understanding How Your Videos Perform on Facebook", 2019). Facebook defines the view metric as the number of times the video has been viewed for at least 3 s. However, it does not indicate how views are counted when a user automatically (and non-intentionally) runs a video in the News feed without audio for 3 s. This type of view could happen by accident while viewing a completely different post on Facebook that happened to be close to the video, causing the users to place a mouse cursor on it.

YouTube, in the description of the view metric, states that the index describes a total number of views in a selected period, area, and within the range of the selected filters ("About video ad metrics and reporting", 2019). Youtube repeatedly mentions, in its help center, that the calculation of this metric includes only real users and analyzes each view for whether it was done by a robot or a human. However, as far as we know, there is no detailed explanation what sort of user behavior is recorded as one view. Unofficial sources claim that YouTube counts one view after viewing at least 30 s of the video. Unfortunately, there is no information about how the YouTube algorithm works if the video is less than 30 s long. The YouTube view counter stops at a value of 301. When playing the video content, the user downloads video from the nearest distribution node, and the view entry is sent to the analytical center when a video request is made. Based on the aforementioned definitions, viewing metrics may be misleading as a measure of video's popularity when compared across platforms. The definitions differ not only in the proportion of video that a user has to see but also in assessing whether it is necessary to evaluate a user as an individual or count the view by each click. These differences in the calculation of the metrics can result in distortion when setting up the marketing campaigns and deciding where to place the ads according to the average costs per view.

Quartile reporting represents a more objective method of measuring the ability of a video to capture user attention. It is used by video analytics tools in both Google AdWords and Facebook. This metric determines the number of times a certain percentage of the video has been viewed, in this case, whether the viewer has played 25%, 50%, 75%, or 100% of the video content per one viewing session. Owing to the relative, proportional nature of the quartile reporting, it is possible to use this metric to compare the video performance across both advertising platforms. The only factor of distortion is the varying average time of the viewed fraction of the video that depends on the total length of the video. For longer videos, the viewer must spend more active time to see an equal quartile as for the shorter videos. Therefore, shorter videos will reach a higher percentage much faster. Surprisingly, only a few videos reach the full 100% quartile because most videos contain intro and outro sequences that are often skipped by the users. In addition to the views and quartile reporting, we may also come across other more detailed performance metrics such as the *viewing time* and *average percentage viewed*.

Behavioral Metrics

For video creators and marketers, the active viewer's interaction with the video content has the greatest value. Content creators try to embed a certain message in their videos. It can be either a joke, a question, or, in the case of online video marketing, a sales promotion or a brand name, etc. It is the thorough analysis of user responses and their attitudes toward the video they have watched that generates feedback regarding the creator on its quality. The interaction of the viewer with the online video content can take several forms. Basic user interaction options include the following: commenting, liking, adding a video to favorites, following the content creator, recommending or sharing the video with others, interacting with text annotations and overlays ads, or downloading the video.

However, not all these interactions are applicable on all platforms. Each platform allows different viewer interactions with the video and also different rating scales ranging from likes and dislikes to emojis. From a sociological perspective, users are more likely to react on thematically controversial videos, videos showing exceptional abilities or containing amusing content. Furthermore, users are more likely to respond to negative stimuli and express their dislikes than to praise good quality. Moreover, users respond to ads less frequently than to videos of interest. For video ads, in addition to standard engagement options, the analytical tools can identify click-throughs to the advertised product and the follow-up conversions. In the long term, the growing of viewer engagement indicates increasing popularity and fidelity vis-à-vis the fan base. Conversely, in the short term, monitoring viewer interactions with a single video informs the creator of the quality of the video.

One of the most important behavioral metrics is *engagement rate*, which is calculated as the ratio of video views to the number of interactions (comments, shares, and likes / dislikes). Therefore, the metric determines the number of interactions per one view, but it does not distinguish between multiple views by one individual. The engagement metric may be then broken down to partial metrics such as the *number of comments*, their development in time, or the demographics of the users who commented. Following the same logic, the online platforms also derive other metrics such as the indexes for *new followers*, *shares*, etc.

An essential aspect in measuring video content on the Internet is exploring the interaction of the viewer with the video content. While watching, users can control individual parts of the video, pause, replay, or repeat the entire video. Behavior monitoring methods are based on the same metrics as the quartile reporting metrics with the difference that user behavior when viewing video content is more accurately and qualitatively reflected in these detail indexes. In YouTube Analytics, this behavioral metric is called *audience retention*. The metric is displayed in the form of a graph that shows the percentage of users who have seen the given second of the video. If the audience retention increases over the course of the video, it indicates that the viewers have repeatedly watched the given segment of footage. Conversely, when the retention rate is declining, it suggests that there might be an incentive in the video that discourages the viewers from watching. In addition, these metrics are also able to distinguish whether viewers came from organic or paid traffic. The *play rate* metric refers to the ratio of the number of times a video content was played to the number of webpage visits. The play rate metric helps website developers to choose the optimal position for the player on the website, correct the thumbnail to attract the visitors, and create the right textual context.

In addition to the above described categories of metrics, we may distinguish a special group of indicators that is related to paid advertising. Most online video ads allow the user to click through and visit the advertiser's website. The click-through rate represents the ratio of clicks to the total number of ad impressions, which is another important ad impact indicator. Other advertising metrics include advertising costs per various actions, conversions, and finally, revenues. In the case of in-stream ads that allow skipping after 5–10 s of playing, the ratio of skips to total number of views is also crucial.

The different interpretation of the video performance metrics makes the comparative analysis of the individual video formats across the two studied platforms considerably difficult. Moreover, because of the unavailability of some of the metrics for all the advertising formats, the number of comparable indicators is limited.

DATA COLLECTION

The experiment was divided into two stages. The first stage consisted in the creation of the optimized video spot. During the second stage, Facebook and YouTube advertisements were set up. First, three video spots marketing the main concept of the e-store, its offer of products, and its website were created. The three spots differed in the songs used, the fonts and the size of the titles, and the alternation speed of the scenes. A focus group of 30 individuals, profiled according to the characteristics of the e-store's most profitable customer segment, was created. The testers from the focus group gave a subjective evaluation of the videos using a 10-point Likert scale. They were asked to assess the visual characteristics, the sound profile, and the readability of the text on a smartphone as well as to describe the message and feeling the videos evoked in them and provide an overall rating. In addition, as a complementary evaluation, we organized a short eye tracking session with each tester, during which they viewed the three videos. Based on the combined results, both conscious and subconscious evaluations, we chose the advertising spot that was judged as the most optimal by a majority of the users (25 out of 30). Subsequently, the length and the dimensions of the video were adjusted for all the available video advertising formats that we decided to use for the purposes of this research. The video formats with respective footage lengths, along with the distribution on the two advertising platforms, are described in the Table 1.

Table 1. The characteristics of the advertising video spots

YouTube			Facebook and Instagram		
Type of the ad	**Length (s)**	**Dimensions**	**Type of the ad**	**Length (s)**	**Dimensions**
Skippable in-stream ads	35, 85	1920×1080	**Short videos**	35, 85	1920×1080
Non-skippable in-stream ads	15	1920×1080	**Instagram Stories**	15	1080×1920
Discovery ads	85	1920×1080	**Carousel format**	35	1080×1080
Bumpers	6	1920×1080	**Collection ads**	85	1920×1080
Out-stream ads	35, 85	1920×1080	**In-stream videos**	30	1920×1080

Source: (the authors)

The video dimensions were selected according to the recommendations given by Facebook and Google in their respective online support centers. The lengths of the videos were chosen within the time limits of each advertising format. Obviously, bumpers with only 6 s represented the shortest video that consisted only of one scene and one final text title. Ads placed in Instagram Stories and as non-skippable spots on YouTube lasted 15 s; however, their dimensions differed. For YouTube, we used horizontal video, whereas for Instagram, we used a vertical video. Carousel and collection ads represented combined video formats. In the case of the carousel, the first item we used was the video that was 35 s long, and the other items were completed with photos. For the collection ad, a longer video (85 s) was chosen as the main item of the composition, and similarly to the Carousel ad, it was completed with photos. We used the same photos for both formats. Where possible, we created ads with a short (35 s) and a longer (85 s) video in order to get more detailed information about user reactions to online advertising in terms of dependence on the length of the advertised content.

Overall, we created 13 video ads on Facebook and YouTube. To keep the setting as unbiased as possible, we chose automatic placement and bidding strategies everywhere the advertising systems permitted it. The only restrictions were thus related to the targeting characteristics and profiling of the target group of customers. Since the e-store, which agreed to let us perform the above described experiment, was specialized in selling furniture, home accessories, and kitchen equipment, we used these general categories as interest qualifiers. In addition, the delivery of ads was geographically limited to the Czech Republic, and the ads were displayed only to women aged 25 to 44. The video ads were implemented for 30 days. All the advertisements were standardly marked with Urchin Tracking Module (UTM) parameters, which also allowed us to track viewer behavior on the website after clicking on the ad and visiting the e-store. The data from YouTube and Facebook ads were thus connected with the company's account in Google Analytics. After the advertising campaigns ended, we exported all the relevant performance data from Facebook Ads Manager, Google Ads, and Google Analytics and merged the information into an Excel file using the SPSS Statics 24 software.

RESULTS

In total, 13 video ads generated an overall profit of 1,155 EUR. Nevertheless, not all the advertisements were effective in terms of profitability since their costs exceeded the revenues from the purchases activated by these ads. However, the interpretation of online advertising performance is more complex and goes beyond direct financial effectiveness (Semerádová & Weinlich, 2019). For this reason, we will compare the results from our experiment from three perspectives: financial (the average profitability and average cost per conversion), behavioral (click-through rate and the average time spent on the website), and reactional (the number of reactions and average viewing percentage).

First, we focus on the financial dimension. Looking more closely at Table 2, we see that in terms of the advertising costs, YouTube non-skippable in-stream ads may be considered the most expensive form of placement, followed by Instagram Stories and Facebook In-stream videos. However, YouTube non-skippable ads generated the second highest profitability of all the ads. According to our data, the best performance was achieved for the Facebook newsfeed video (0.08 EUR average cost and 306 EUR average profitability). Conversely, YouTube discovery and out-stream ads generated loss (−25 EUR and −31 EUR, respectively). This distribution of advertising costs and revenues suggests that the advertising performance of the video may be directly connected to its ability to fit in the browsing context of the online user. Facebook newsfeed represents a central browsing space that may be considered as the native environment of the application. If the advertising video manages to blend naturally with the other content, the chances of being seen by potential customers are higher. By contrast, if the video more closely resembles an advertisement, it tends to trigger the advertising blindness phenomenon. This may explain the lower performance of in-stream video. In-stream videos are perceived as commercial breaks and may thus produce negative effects despite the nature of their content.

As our results indicate, there is a significant difference in the performance of Facebook and Google in-stream ads. The Facebook in-stream ads generated rather low profits, whereas Google ads produced top profitability. This difference also points toward possible contextual influences. Facebook users are accustomed to viewing shorter video content whose main purpose is to provide quick entertainment and therefore do not expect to come across advertisements within the videos they are used to seeing. On YouTube, the video creators generally post longer content that has the qualities of an online show and generally ranges between 10 to 20 min on average. YouTube users are thus more likely to react to commercial breaks positively. Instagram Stories and Instagram videos represent a special category whose profitability may be influenced by the context of the Instagram application; Instagram users do not primarily browse in search of purchasable items but rather use the application for a quick visual experience.

Table 2. The effectiveness of the video ads based on their average profitability and average cost per conversion

YouTube			Facebook and Instagram		
Type of the ad	**Average cost per conversion (EUR)**	**Average profitability (EUR)**	**Type of the ad**	**Average cost per conversion (EUR)**	**Average profitability (EUR)**
Skippable in-stream ads	0.12	199	**Short videos**	0.08	306
Non-skippable in-stream ads	0.20	234	**Instagram Stories**	0.15	12
Discovery ads	0.06	−25	**Carousel format**	0.13	24
Bumpers	0.1	85	**Collection ads**	0.10	289
Out-stream ads	0.10	−31	**In-stream videos**	0.15	62

Source: (the authors)

The metrics related to the behavioral perspective confirm our aforementioned assumptions. As illustrated in Table 3, browsing environment pre-defines user intentions to make a purchase. For example, users who were redirected to the e-store's website from the Instagram Stories spent only 16 s on the website on average, indicating a high tendency to bounce back and leave the webpage immediately. The low average time may indicate accidental click-throughs. The users who spent more than 30 s on the website may be considered to be users who were attracted by the offered product but did not find sufficient motivation to stay. Moreover, the collected data indicated a direct dependence between the average profitability and average time spent on the website. The click-through rates reflect the willingness of online users to respond to online video advertisements. The discovery ads had the lowest CTR (0.21%) and were the least effective of all the video ads. The ineffectiveness of this advertising format may be accounted to the main purpose these ads were designed for. The primary objective of discovery ads is to promote the videos of many content creators that want to grow their fan base and want their channel to be in the YouTube search results. Therefore, this format is a priori inappropriate for product advertising.

The performance of the video ads with respect to the reactional dimension was examined by using the number of reactions and the average viewing percentage. Unfortunately, owing to the unavailability of the metrics for some placements, this part of the analysis may be perceived only as supporting evidence. However, as the results in Table 4 indicate, Facebook video ads have the greatest potential to be viewed fully from beginning to end (65% of the video viewed). The results from collection ads (53%) confirm this hypothesis. By contrast, YouTube skippable in-stream ads reflect the negative attitude of the users toward forced commercial breaks (only 27% of the video viewed). In contrast to the previous results, Instagram Stories performed well in terms of the number of reactions. Both the high number of reactions and the high viewing percentage of the video confirm the ability of our video spot to attract new potential customers. The lower performance of some of the placements may therefore be accounted by the negative effects of unwanted advertisements.

Table 3. Results related to the behavioral dimension of the video ads

YouTube			Facebook and Instagram		
Type of the ad	CTR (%)	Average time spent on the website (s)	Type of the ad	CTR (%)	Average time spent on the website (s)
Skippable in-stream ads	7.31	93	Short videos	9.08	98
Non-skippable in-stream ads	6.58	99	Instagram Stories	1.20	16
Discovery ads	0.21	15	Carousel format	3.29	42
Bumpers	2.43	32	Collection ads	6.21	95
Out-stream ads	2.11	37	In-stream videos	5.43	56

Source: (the authors)

Table 4. Number of reactions and the average viewing percentage

YouTube			Facebook and Instagram		
Type of the ad	Number of reactions	Average viewing percentage	Type of the ad	Number of reactions	Average viewing percentage
Skippable in-stream ads	Unavailable	27%	Short videos	487	65%
Non-skippable in-stream ads	Unavailable	100%	Instagram Stories	225	Unavailable
Discovery ads	0	5%	Carousel format	78	14%
Bumpers	Unavailable	100%	Collection ads	321	53%
Out-stream ads	Unavailable	25%	In-stream videos	Unavailable	78%

Source: (the authors)

CONCLUSION

The present study aimed to examine the effectiveness of existing advertising video formats on Facebook and YouTube. The data presented are a result of a series of experimental online ads whose performance was tested in an authentic environment with real users. Owing to the collaboration with a Czech e-store, we had the opportunity to implement 13 selected video ads for 30 days. Our results confirmed the general expectation that video advertising represents an effective advertising tool. Most of the experimental ads were able to generate profit. However, profitability cannot be used as the only indicator of advertising effectiveness. Although the profitability of the Instagram ads was on the lower side, they managed to generate the third highest number of reactions from all the tested formats.

The findings indicate the strong influence of the browsing context on video performance. It appears that the closer the resemblance of the video to other contents in the browsing environment, the higher the chances that users will react to it. Moreover, the browsing context where the online ads appear may also have impact on the subsequent user behavior. For example, Instagram video placements performed better as a means for raising brand awareness than for triggering direct purchases. Conversely, Facebook and YouTube users were more open to shopping suggestions. The highest viewing percentage was achieved by Facebook in-stream ads, followed by Facebook newsfeed videos. Skippable ads on YouTube were viewed significantly less. Although YouTube users had a greater tendency to skip ads, if given the opportunity, they reacted to the ads rather positively and proceeded to make the desired conversions. In addition to the browsing context, the results also differed depending on the length of the video ad. Based on the collected data, the majority of online users prefer videos shorter than 1 min, since of the 85 s for our longer video, the users viewed only 65% (55.25 s). Conversely, it appears that there is also a minimum video length limit. In the aforementioned experiment, bumper ads performed moderately well. We believe that the 6 s period does not provide sufficient time to convey the full message to a potential customer. We support this assumption by the results gathered from the non-skippable ads that lasted 15 s and generated significantly more positive outcomes.

To consider the further implications of these findings, the unobtrusiveness of an advertisement determines its potential to be effective. In conclusion, advertisers should spend more time creating high-quality and personalized video content that is tailored not only to the potential customer but also to the advertising environment in which it will be distributed. Each advertising placement is characterized by specific viewing conditions and typically requires significant adjustments of the original video.

ACKNOWLEDGMENT

This research was supported by the Technical University of Liberec, in a grant titled "Competitiveness of the company in the digital environment", registered as SGS-2019-1068, and by the Technology Agency of the Czech Republic under the Program of applied research ZETA within the framework of project "Developing the skills necessary for the digital business transformation" (registration number TJ02000206).

REFERENCES

About video ad metrics and reporting - YouTube Help. (2019). Retrieved from https://support.google. com/youtube/answer/2375431?hl=en

Alalwan, A. (2018). Investigating the impact of social media advertising features on customer purchase intention. *International Journal of Information Management, 42*, 65–77. doi:10.1016/j.ijinfomgt.2018.06.001

Amar, J., Droulers, O., & Legohérel, P. (2017). Typography in destination advertising: An exploratory study and research perspectives. *Tourism Management, 63*, 77–86. doi:10.1016/j.tourman.2017.06.002

Aslam, B., & Karjaluoto, H. (2017). Digital advertising around paid spaces, E-advertising industry's revenue engine: A review and research agenda. *Telematics and Informatics, 34*(8), 1650–1662. doi:10.1016/j. tele.2017.07.011

Bang, H., & Wojdynski, B. (2016). Tracking users' visual attention and responses to personalized advertising based on task cognitive demand. *Computers in Human Behavior, 55*, 867–876. doi:10.1016/j. chb.2015.10.025

Berry, N., Prugh, W., Lunkins, C., Vega, J., Landry, R., & Garciga, L. (2015). Selecting video analytics using cognitive ergonomics: a case study for operational experimentation. *Procedia Manufacturing, 3*, 5245–5252. doi:10.1016/j.promfg.2015.07.598

Beuckels, E., Cauberghe, V., & Hudders, L. (2017). How media multitasking reduces advertising irritation: The moderating role of the Facebook wall. *Computers in Human Behavior, 73*, 413–419. doi:10.1016/j. chb.2017.03.069

Ding, S., Qu, S., Xi, Y., & Wan, S. (2019). A long video caption generation algorithm for big video data retrieval. *Future Generation Computer Systems, 93*, 583–595. doi:10.1016/j.future.2018.10.054

Facebook video ads – Facebook help center. (2019). Retrieved from https://www.facebook.com/business/ads/video-ad-format

Fascinating and useful statistics about video marketing in 2019 - Videocake. (2019). Retrieved from http://videocake.cz/statistika-o-videu-v-marketingu/

Huang, Y., Wu, J., & Shi, W. (2018). The impact of font choice on web pages: Relationship with willingness to pay and tourism motivation. *Tourism Management, 66*, 191–199. doi:10.1016/j.tourman.2017.12.010

Joo, M., Wilbur, K., & Zhu, Y. (2016). Effects of TV advertising on keyword search. *International Journal of Research in Marketing, 33*(3), 508–523. doi:10.1016/j.ijresmar.2014.12.005

Kareklas, I., Brunel, F., & Coulter, R. (2014). Judgment is not color blind: The impact of automatic color preference on product and advertising preferences. *Journal of Consumer Psychology, 24*(1), 87–95. doi:10.1016/j.jcps.2013.09.005

Kim, B., & Kim, Y. (2019). Facebook versus Instagram: How perceived gratifications and technological attributes are related to the change in social media usage. *The Social Science Journal, 56*(2), 156–167. doi:10.1016/j.soscij.2018.10.002

Kim, J., Ahn, S., Kwon, E., & Reid, L. (2017). TV advertising engagement as a state of immersion and presence. *Journal of Business Research*, *76*, 67–76. doi:10.1016/j.jbusres.2017.03.001

Lee, J., Ham, C., & Kim, M. (2013). Why people pass along online video advertising: from the perspectives of the interpersonal communication motives scale and the theory of reasoned action. *Journal of Interactive Advertising*, *13*(1), 1–13. doi:10.1080/15252019.2013.768048

Li, X., Shi, M., & Wang, X. (2019). Video mining: Measuring visual information using automatic methods. *International Journal of Research in Marketing*, *36*(2), 216–231. doi:10.1016/j.ijresmar.2019.02.004

Liikkanen, L., & Salovaara, A. (2015). Music on YouTube: User engagement with traditional, user-appropriated and derivative videos. *Computers in Human Behavior*, *50*, 108–124. doi:10.1016/j.chb.2015.01.067

Liu, Y., Zhu, C., Mao, M., Song, F., Dufaux, F., & Zhang, X. (2018). Video analytical coding: When video coding meets video analysis. *Signal Processing Image Communication*, *67*, 48–57. doi:10.1016/j.image.2018.05.012

Martín-Santana, J., Muela-Molina, C., Reinares-Lara, E., & Rodríguez-Guerra, M. (2015). Effectiveness of radio spokesperson's gender, vocal pitch and accent and the use of music in radio advertising. *BRQ Business Research Quarterly*, *18*(3), 143–160. doi:10.1016/j.brq.2014.06.001

Mowat, J. (2018). *Video marketing strategy: harness the power of online video to drive brand growth* (1st ed.). Kogan Page.

Munnukka, J., Maity, D., Reinikainen, H., & Luoma-aho, V. (2019). "Thanks for watching". The effectiveness of YouTube vlogendorsements. *Computers in Human Behavior*, *93*, 226–234. doi:10.1016/j.chb.2018.12.014

Muñoz-Leiva, F., Hernández-Méndez, J., & Gómez-Carmona, D. (2019). Measuring advertising effectiveness in Travel 2.0 websites through eye-tracking technology. *Physiology & Behavior*, *200*, 83–95. doi:10.1016/j.physbeh.2018.03.002 PMID:29522796

Semerádová, T., & Weinlich, P. (2018). Assessing banner ads effectiveness based on the type of the creative content. In *Proceedings of the 31st International Business Information Management Association Conference, IBIMA 2018: Innovation Management and Education Excellence through Vision 2020* (pp. 1439-1446). Milan, Italy: IBIMA.

Semerádová, T., & Weinlich, P. (2019). Calculation of Facebook marketing effectiveness in terms of ROI. *Leveraging Computer-Mediated Marketing Environments*, 286-310. doi:10.4018/978-1-5225-7344-9.ch014

Sidaty, N., Larabi, M., & Saadane, A. (2017). Toward an audiovisual attention model for multimodal video content. *Neurocomputing*, *259*, 94–111. doi:10.1016/j.neucom.2016.08.130

Tran, T. (2017). Personalized ads on Facebook: An effective marketing tool for online marketers. *Journal of Retailing and Consumer Services*, *39*, 230–242. doi:10.1016/j.jretconser.2017.06.010

Understanding how your videos perform on Facebook. (2019). Retrieved from https://www.facebook.com/facebookmedia/blog/understanding-how-your-videos-perform-on-facebook

Van den Broeck, E., Poels, K., & Walrave, M. (2018). An experimental study on the effect of ad placement, product involvement and motives on Facebook ad avoidance. *Telematics and Informatics*, *35*(2), 470–479. doi:10.1016/j.tele.2018.01.006

Video advertising formats – YouTube help center. (2019). Retrieved from https://support.google.com/youtube/answer/2375464?hl=cs

Wang, C., & Hung, J. (2018). Comparative analysis of advertising attention to Facebook social network: Evidence from eye-movement data. *Computers in Human Behavior*. doi:10.1016/j.chb.2018.08.007

What counts as a video view? - David Burch, TubeMogul. (2019). Retrieved from https://www.youtube.com/watch?v=qpANKRZJ8Ks

Wu, C., Wei, Y., Chu, X., Weichen, S., Su, F., & Wang, L. (2018). Hierarchical attention-based multi-modal fusion for video captioning. *Neurocomputing*, *315*, 362–370. doi:10.1016/j.neucom.2018.07.029

Yang, L., Yuan, M., Chen, Y., Wang, W., Zhang, Q., & Zeng, J. (2017). Personalized user engagement modeling for mobile videos. *Computer Networks*, *126*, 256–267. doi:10.1016/j.comnet.2017.07.012

Yang, Y., Lu, Q., Tang, G., & Pei, J. (2015). The impact of market competition on search advertising. *Journal of Interactive Marketing*, *30*, 46–55. doi:10.1016/j.intmar.2015.01.002

Zimand-Sheiner, D., Ryan, T., Kip, S., & Lahav, T. (2019). Native advertising credibility perceptions and ethical attitudes: An exploratory study among adolescents in the United States, Turkey and Israel. *Journal of Business Research*. doi:10.1016/j.jbusres.2019.06.020

ADDITIONAL READING

Alalwan, A., Rana, N., Dwivedi, Y., & Algharabat, R. (2017). Social media in marketing: A review and analysis of the existing literature. *Telematics and Informatics*, *34*(7), 1177–1190. doi:10.1016/j.tele.2017.05.008

Belanche, D., Flavián, C., & Pérez-Rueda, A. (2017). Understanding Interactive Online Advertising: Congruence and Product Involvement in Highly and Lowly Arousing, Skippable Video Ads. *Journal of Interactive Marketing*, *37*, 75–88. doi:10.1016/j.intmar.2016.06.004

Dehghani, M., Niaki, M., Ramezani, I., & Sali, R. (2016). Evaluating the influence of YouTube advertising for attraction of young customers. *Computers in Human Behavior*, *59*, 165–172. doi:10.1016/j.chb.2016.01.037

Felix, R., Rauschnabel, P., & Hinsch, C. (2017). Elements of strategic social media marketing: A holistic framework. *Journal of Business Research*, *70*, 118–126. doi:10.1016/j.jbusres.2016.05.001

France, S., Vaghefi, M., & Zhao, H. (2016). Characterizing viral videos: Methodology and applications. *Electronic Commerce Research and Applications*, *19*, 19–32. doi:10.1016/j.elerap.2016.07.002

Lee, J., & Hong, I. (2016). Predicting positive user responses to social media advertising: The roles of emotional appeal, informativeness, and creativity. *International Journal of Information Management*, *36*(3), 360–373. doi:10.1016/j.ijinfomgt.2016.01.001

Quesenberry, K., & Coolsen, M. (2019). Drama Goes Viral: Effects of Story Development on Shares and Views of Online Advertising Videos. *Journal of Interactive Marketing*, *48*, 1–16. doi:10.1016/j.intmar.2019.05.001

Simmonds, L., Bellman, S., Kennedy, R., Nenycz-Thiel, M., & Bogomolova, S. (2019). Moderating effects of prior brand usage on visual attention to video advertising and recall: An eye-tracking investigation. *Journal of Business Research*. doi:10.1016/j.jbusres.2019.02.062

KEY TERMS AND DEFINITIONS

Ad Placement: All the advertising spaces, mostly paid, offered by online publishers, websites, and social networks to advertisers to display their advertisements. The individual placements have different potentials in terms of reaching the users and perform differently when comes to the type of content chosen for the advertisement.

Bumper: Bumpers represent short videos that take up to 6 s and can be placed before, in, and after a video on all YouTube pages, partner video sites, and applications in the Google Content network. Viewers do not have the option to skip these ads. The advertiser pays for every 1,000 impressions.

Conversion: Desired action performed by a consumer as a reaction to an advertisement or other marketing effort. The desired action can take many forms including the purchases, membership registrations, newsletter subscriptions, and application downloads.

Instagram Stories ads: Instagram Stories ads can contain both video and photo content and can be created from preexisting material or from vertical videos tailored specifically for this format. Every post in stories is limited to 15 s.

In-stream ads: In-stream ads are design to promote video content between other videos on YouTube or in the Google Content Network. In-stream ads can appear on YouTube watch pages, videos on partner sites, and content network applications. In-stream ads can be either skippable or non-skippable.

Play rate: The play rate metric refers to the ratio of the number of times a video content was played to the number of webpage visits. The play rate metric helps website developers choose the optimal position for the player on the website, correct the thumbnail to attract the visitors, and create the right textual context.

Quartile reporting: Quartile reporting represents a more objective method in measuring the ability of a video to capture user attention. It is used in video analytics tools by both Google AdWords and Facebook. This metric determines the number of times a certain percentage of the video has been viewed, in this case, whether the viewer has played 25%, 50%, 75%, or 100% of the video content per a single viewing session.

UTM Parameters: Text fragments that are attached in the specified format to the web link. Attaching these textual segments allows the analytical software to exactly identify the source, campaign, or advertisement from which the users come to the website. UTM parameters generally contain the following five elements: utm_source, utm_medium, utm_campaign, utm_content, and utm_term.

This research was previously published in Impacts of Online Advertising on Business Performance; pages 200-225, copyright year 2020 by Business Science Reference (an imprint of IGI Global).

Chapter 35
Mobile Shopping Apps:
Functionalities, Consumer Adoption, and Usage

Priyanka Chadha
Manav Rachna University, Delhi, India

Shirin Alavi
ⓘD https://orcid.org/0000-0001-8743-6701
Jaypee Institute of Information Technology, Noida, India

Vandana Ahuja
Jaypee Business School, Jaypee Institute of Information Technology, Noida, India

ABSTRACT

This article describes how the retailing business has changed drastically in the recent times. The emergence of Internet and mobile channels are primarily responsible for this. The present generation comprises of a group of consumers with strong purchasing power and superior online habits in comparison to previous generations. The younger generation is much more experienced with the Internet and mobile devices and is thus more susceptible to engage in shopping through mobile apps. These empowered consumers are keen to have consistent customer experiences and are always challenging retailers to meet their evolving needs and demands. They can easily switch from one retailer to another with a couple of touches on their smart phones. These increased opportunities also increase competition. The mobile commerce helps the online retailers to present themselves fit in the market and uniquely use the cosmic opportunities. This article focuses on a set of ten different mobile shopping apps and identifies the functionalities offered by these apps. The article further proceeds to explore the specific consumer needs satisfied through mobile shopping which influence its adoption and usage.

DOI: 10.4018/978-1-7998-9020-1.ch035

INTRODUCTION

The telephone took four decades to reach fifty million people. The internet has managed this within a short span of time as digital technologies provide efficient channels for customer and business interactions. Technological progress in the sphere of information, communication and technology is encouraging the use and development of new updated methods leading to rapid growth in online retail outlets, where customers can buy without having to travel to retail stores, physically. This growth of online platforms has facilitated the introduction of electronic marketing and promises to provide new ways of servicing costumers (Sharma & Sheth, 2004). The marketing landscape is changing across the world and organisational mind-sets are shifting from product based marketing systems to customer based marketing systems. Wireless Internet via Mobile Devices (WIMD) is leading the world into another spectrum of communication and means of conducting day to day business and life activities (Lu et al., 2003). As organisations realise the importance of communicating with their customers, contemporary tools like mobile apps are becoming popular and provide excellent deals and solutions to customers at their convenience. The spontaneity, mobility, convenience and collaboration offered by smart phones have made them a ubiquitous tool that has empowered the customer. The purchases made by these consumers with a few simple clicks can become a quick source of revenue for an organisation.

The Technology Acceptance Model (Venkatesh, 2000) proposed that user training can have an important influence on technology acceptance. This further leads to convenience of consumers. Consumer acceptance is a function of intrinsic motivation (activity done for self-enjoyment and opportunity to explore, learn and actualise our potential) and extrinsic motivation (activity done to adopt material gain for external reinforcement i.e. to gain discounts, best deals). According to TAM, perceived usefulness was also influenced by perceived ease of use, because the easier the system is to use, the more easily it is adopted by customers.

A well designed mobile app allows customers to quickly place their orders from the convenience of their smart phones or tablets. One of the best examples in this regard is the fast food restaurants that have significantly benefited by adopting mobile app marketing tool. Dominos, Pizza hut, Food Panda and many more food enterprises have set an example by launching their mobile apps. These apps have added to the growth of their business and are tempting more and more customers to choose the best deal (Inukollu et al., 2014).Both big and small, companies are now making big profits by making their offerings convenient and accessible to their customers.

Mobile shopping has many benefits and advantages. The most useful mobile shopping applications collect product data from several retailers. They sort collected data to allow consumers to perform side by side comparisons of different merchants' prices so that they can find the best deals (Johnson, 2011). Mobile shopping performed with these apps is considered convenient because mobile notifications automatically deliver promotion information. Another benefit is derived from a price comparison app that employs bar code or QR (Quick Response) code scanning to help consumers during in-store shopping. Immediate gratification is another benefit provided for mobile shoppers because digital products can be delivered wirelessly to their phones (Murphy & Meeker, 2011).

A thorough literature review helped us to identify that adequate work has not been accomplished in the field of mobile apps. There is a significant research potential for exploring the usage of mobile apps across diverse industry verticals. *This research paper explores the ability of mobile apps to impact consumer convenience and collaboration to stimulate the adoption of an app as a shopping tool.*

LITERATURE REVIEW

E-Commerce

E-commerce refers to digitally enabled commercial transaction between and among organizations and individuals (Laudon & Traver, 2014). It takes place on a device that offers access to internet most frequently the computer, on the other hand, mobile e-commerce, as an extension of electronic commerce, enables online transactions via mobile devices (smartphones, tablets) (Shao Yeh & Li, 2009). At the same time e-commerce not only provides the companies with a huge amount of information, increases the speed of the transactions and decreases costs, but also reshapes their marketing strategies and practices (Dou and Chou, 2002).

The reasons for implementing an e-commerce strategy can vary from company to company. According to (Xu & Quaddus, 2010), while in the big companies the leading motives are to improve efficiency in their internal processes; small companies are more concerned with the competitiveness. Successful adoption of e-commerce is a slow process and it cannot be completed at once, but rather in small series of adoption processes in which the company moves gradually from simple to more complex stages of e-commerce (Brand & Huizingh, 2008). The e-commerce industry in India is growing at a faster pace. Globalization and information technologies are radically changing the face of business and organization. There is a growing interest in the use of electronic commerce as a means to perform business transactions. For many businesses, this has become a priority. The usage of electronic commerce enables companies to connect with their trading partners for 'just in time production' and 'just in time delivery', which improves their competitiveness globally.

Organization for Economic Co-Operation and Development (OECD) officially acknowledges e-commerce as a new way of conducting business (Sung, 2006). However, as e-commerce evolves, the horizon expands and includes the conduct of selling, buying, logistics, or other organization management activities via the web (Schneider, 2002).

Consumer Buying Behaviour

Consumer behaviour has been always of great interest to marketers. The knowledge of consumer behaviour helps the marketer to understand how consumers think, feel and select from alternatives like products, brands, how the consumers are influenced by their environment, the reference groups, family, and salespersons and so on. A consumer's buying behaviour is influenced by cultural, social, personal and psychological factors. Most of these factors are uncontrollable and beyond the hands of marketers but they have to be considered while trying to understand the complex behaviour of the consumers (Vani, Babu & Panchanatham, 2010).

The present era has witnessed dramatic shifts in the marketplace triggered by sharp changes in the lifestyle patterns and the radical revolution in the segment of mobile commercial applications. Time tested concepts on brand loyalty and mass marketing, are being revamped as they fail to gauge the behaviour of new generation of technology savvy customers. The behaviour is characterized by the uniqueness of individual expectations, the preference for multiple options, convenience and collaboration, ease of availability etc. (Kengthon, 2010).

Mobile Applications

Mobile applications are defined as software that can perform certain tasks for the users operating their mobile devices (Hew, Lee, Ooi & Wei, 2015). Mobile applications differ from websites, as the user downloads them from the mobile application store, which is a database that allows the mobile user to discover and install available mobile applications (Wong, 2012). Mobile applications load and perform faster and can be bought via the mobile application store. Mobile applications are a software application that is designed for use on a mobile phone. Mobile apps provide mobile phone users with information, entertainment or location-based services such as mapping. Mobile apps are considered to be popular method of delivering interactive services and content via mobile phones. Mobile apps also provide imaginative new ways for retailers to guide consumers through experience.

Mobile Applications Usage

Mobile electronic commerce, a component of electronic commerce, contains the use of methods related to the mobile telecommunication devices and networks. There has been an increasing number of people who pursue new life styles of working, communicating, and purchasing through smart phone to the extent of emerging consumer group who "starts a day with a smart phone and wraps up with smart phone" (Holzer & Ondrus, 2011).The development of mobile phones and technologies has been an extended history of innovation and advancements cropped up due to dynamic changes in consumers' needs and preferences (Pelet & Papadopoulou, 2015). Among these developments, mobile commercial applications have one of the fastest household adoption rates of any technology in the world's modern history (Comer and Wikle, 2008). Nowadays, mobile applications have become an integral part of human daily life and personal communication across the globe. In the current highly competitive mobile phone market, manufacturers constantly fight to find additional competitive edge and differentiating elements to persuade consumers to select their brand instead of a competitor's. There are various studies conducted to identify factors that make companies better than their competitors in influencing the customers purchase decision. Mobile applications (apps) are changing how we work. Customers now have access to mobile handheld devices (smart phones and tablets) with extensive functionality and can be productive anytime, anywhere. Mobile apps can be less expensive and easier to review, download, install and test compared to desktop applications. The commercial mobile app marketplace provides a wealth of opportunities that the society can take advantage of by leveraging existing commercial mobile applications.

The World of Apps: The Indian Diaspora

The mobile a handheld gadget offers ease of accessibility, as compared to traditional web based platforms and e-commerce as a whole will benefit tremendously as companies start building shopping experiences with more robust social and collaborative features. Adoption of the mobile shopping application is associated with both an immediate and sustained increase in total platform purchasing (Einav, Lenin, Popov, Sundaresan, 2014). The changing face of the Indian diaspora comprises a set of people who are constantly hooked to their smart phones and are increasingly internet savvy. These individuals are using Apps for a variety of purposes. To look at a few, individuals are using

1. Apps for Social Media Management
2. Apps for Financial Transactions
3. Apps to facilitate circulation of news
4. Apps for Social Networking
5. Apps to order food
6. Apps to improve workplace productivity
7. Apps to download books
8. Apps to create content
9. Apps to circulate TV shows

Marketers are using the apps for the following reasons (Table 1):

- Enhancing their reach
- Positioning brands
- Stimulating impulsive buying by increasing visual appeal
- Stimulating consumer engagement
- Leveraging consumer interactivity and participation

Benefits to consumers include *convenience* and *user friendliness*. The app industry is tapping multi devices where apps can be accessible across all the platforms (IOS, Android, smart TVs, and every other gadget) to make it convenient for the consumers. Apps have the ability to synchronize the data offline and provide new and innovative content.

Table 1. Using Apps for Marketing

USING APPS FOR MARKETING	
Enhancing reach Apps can be used by companies to target a multitude of consumers, specially, by integrating them with social media tools. A typical consumer is attuned to the world of downloading an online app or a mobile application to fulfil his/her routine activities-be it reserving a train ticket, a movie ticket, ordering a meal, searching for information, or conducting a banking transaction.	**Positioning brands** Campaigns with distinct message strategies are used to position brands specifically. When an app depicts a specific brand campaign, a complete new way of interacting with consumers can evolve. This method increases consumer engagement and strengthens brand loyalty through interactivity.
Stimulating impulsive buying Having a product app on an iPhone, iPad, or an Xbox, brings the product into the consumers' hand, thereby giving it more visibility. A higher visual appeal triggers a consumer buy, specifically, if it is supported by convenience.	**Stimulating consumer engagement** Companies are benefitting by peer-to-peer interactions between consumers. When consumers share experiences or pictures, they are in a way endorsing a brand they are engaged with.
Leveraging consumer interactivity and participation Several apps are letting brands capitalize on user contributions, interactions, conversations, and uploads.	

Further based on a thorough literature review, the following factors which affect the usage of mobile applications were identified (Table 2).

Table 2. Factors which affect usage of Mobile Applications

Factor	Operational Definition
Usage effectiveness (Hertzum & Hornbæk, 2002)	Usage Effectiveness is the accuracy and completeness with which users achieve certain goals. Indicators of effectiveness include quality of solution and error rates.
Convenient usage	User friendliness of mobile apps allows them to provide convenience to end users.
Performance expectancy (Cottrell, 1965)	A belief that the use of a particular technology will be advantageous or performance enhancing to the individual.
Flow (Hoffman & Novak, 2002)	Hoffman and Novak define *Flow* as a state characterized by a seamless sequence of responses, intrinsically enjoyable, accompanied by a loss of self-consciousness and self-reinforcing. Organizations can attempt to achieve *flow* by hosting appealing content, thereby stimulating consumer interest and subsequently involvement.
Usage Intention (Lee, Park, Chung & Blakeney, 2012)	Usage Intention plays an important role in users' social influence.
App Type	Application type is a group of diverse applications designed for end users which includes variety of functions which proved beneficial for customers.
Better time management	Apps allow users speedier access to organisational web spaces. They also allow users to make use of diverse functionalities at a faster pace.

Mobile Shopping Apps

Mobile commerce is defined as any transaction which is initiated and completed by using mobile access to computer mediated networks with the help of mobile devices (Tiwari & Buse, 2007). Mobile commerce grew quickly in 2014, and the mobile access overtook the fixed internet access (Chaffey, 2016). M-shopping is defined as the use of the wireless internet service for shopping activities via a mobile device (Ko, Kim & Lee, 2009). Mobile shopping is a boon for modern consumers (Hung, Yang & Hsieh, 2012). The fast-paced technological developments have led to continuously changing consumer behavior. As a result, the consumers in the present era search and receive information, evaluate and purchase products and services with the help of the internet enabled technologies in different locations and in various circumstances. Social media platforms now play a major role in the search process. About 60% of consumers start their online search process by typing queries into a search engine such as Google and 40% continue for more data on other social media platforms as YouTube, Twitter, Facebook and blogs (Bruce & Solomon, 2013).

The majority of consumers go online to seek deals before shopping. According to one survey results conducted in 2013, 62% of consumers searched for deals digitally including mobile, for at least half of their shopping trips to stores. Mobile phone is affecting consumer behaviour in many ways and it creates new realities for businesses. However, as Kelley (2014) states mobile allows businesses to build deeper customer touch points that were not available before. Loyalty programs of different types, as rewards cards and mobile chats with sales personnel when they are on duty but consumers can't get to them in person, can definitely benefit companies.

Online Marketing

In this study, we consider the online consumer as both a shopper and a mobile user. Despite the explosive growth of online marketing and the rapidly increasing number of consumers who use interactive media for repurchase information search and online shopping, very little is known about how consumers make purchase decisions in such settings. A unique characteristic of online marketing environments is that they allow vendors to create retail interfaces with highly interactive features. Nowadays, companies use the online medium as a new effective way of marketing communication. The astonishing growth of the Internet coupled with its unique capabilities has captured the attention of the marketing community. The technology available for implementing machine interactivity in online marketing environments has the potential to provide consumers with unparalleled opportunities to locate and compare product offerings. Such capabilities are particularly valuable given that online stores cannot offer physical contact with products, do not allow face to face interaction with a salesperson, and offer a very large number of alternatives because of their virtually infinite "shelf space," i.e., the lack of physical constraints with respect to product display. Kierzkowski, Mcquade, Waitman and Zeisser (1996) stated that there are several digital marketing success factors for companies to succeed in the online market, these five factors are attract users, engage users interest and participation, retain users and ensure their return to an application, learn about their preferences, and, lastly relate back to them to provide the sort of customized interactions.

RESEARCH STUDIES IN INDIAN E-COMMERCE SECTOR

As per data released by the Internet and Mobile Association of India, in mid-2015, India had 352 million internet users, of which over 60 percent were accessing the internet by using their mobiles. E-commerce is increasingly attracting customers from tier 2 and 3 cities, where people have limited access to brands but have high aspirations.

Based on research studies in the Indian E-Commerce sector, Ahuja et al., proposed another model for the adoption of mobile apps for shopping from E- commerce sites, in an Indian context. This study also discussed why extant models pertaining to online consumer behaviour did not work in an Indian context, in present times. This model focused on the following determinants which influence the app usage of customers (Ahuja et al., 2016).

1. **Convenience:** Ease of usage of tool, which enhances the daily activities of individuals and allows them to easily complete a shopping task, saving time and energy which is required for the shopping process.
2. **Collaboration:** Several functionalities make the online shopping experience more social for the consumer, by allowing a dimension of interactivity viz. adding friends from the user's phone book, sending invites to friends through social apps, have one to one conversations, create groups and conversation threads, share product listings, wish lists and share pictures from the phone gallery.
3. **Habit:** Habit reflects automatic behaviour tendencies developed during the past history of the individual when behaviour is repeated and becomes habitual, it is guided by automated cognitive processes, rather than by elaborate decision. This implies that users end up plugging onto a specific app sometimes, merely because they have a mobile in their hand and want to do something with it.
4. **Degree of Internet Savviness and Individual Internet Worth:** Degree of Internet Savviness and Individual Internet Worth are moderating variables which impact the effect of convenience and collaboration on App Usage. If an individual is internet savvy, as in, comfortable with the internet environment, his experience of traversing the internet is much more pleasurable and his perception

of how comfortable, easy and value adding the experience was, is greater than a person who is not at ease in using the internet environment.

SCOPE AND RESEARCH OBJECTIVES OF THE STUDY

The arrival of the internet has aroused the urban Indian consumer to adopt mobile shopping apps. India has a huge growing business for online shopping through apps. The list for shopping portals in the country is endless signifying a rapid growth of online shopping in the country. An extensive literature review was conducted and very significant insights about the various aspects of mobile shopping apps were drawn. Further, when one looks at the change in decision patterns with the onset of mobile shopping apps and information searching it becomes crucial to understand how the search and evaluation patterns, for shopping through mobile phones have evolved and structured over time. Hence, the focus of this paper is to conduct a comprehensive study on the new age Indian shoppers for adoption and usage of mobile apps for shopping depending on the functionalities offered by these apps. The research would add value to academic knowledge and will be of immense use for organizations in designing customer focused interactive mobile technologies that deliver value, both to the customer and the organization. To address the needs of the current study, the following specific objectives were formulated:

1. *To explore and identify the various functionalities offered by mobile apps for shopping*
2. *To identify the factors which influence the adoption and usage of mobile apps for shopping*

RESEARCH METHODOLOGY

Research Objective 1: To Identify the Functionalities Offered by Mobile Apps for Shopping

Each mobile app performs certain functions for its brand or organisation. Each function further solves a customer problem or responds to a specific customer need. For example, the *Search* functionality may allow a consumer to search for possible product options and the *Ping* feature may allow customers to chat with their friends and solicit their views while shopping. The *Search* functionality caters to the customer need for Convenience, while the *Ping* functionality caters to the customer need for collaboration.

Ahuja et al (2016) proposed a new model for adoption of mobile apps by consumers shopping from E-commerce sites in an Indian context. This study uses Ahuja et al's model as the base and attempts to identify the functionalities offered by mobile shopping apps and link these functionalities to the consumer needs they satisfy.

In order to understand and capture unique functionalities being offered by different mobile shopping apps an exploratory research study was conducted. The first research objective was accomplished by conducting a pilot study. An online focus group was formulated for this purpose. The respondents were pre- recruited from an online list of people who expressed their interest in participating. These were those who were using mobile apps for shopping very frequently. A screening questionnaire was administered online to qualify the respondent's. The eight respondents who qualified were invited to participate in the focus group. Those who qualified were allocated a time, a URL, a room name, and a password via e-mail.

At the time of discussion, the participants moved into a Web-based chatroom. They were instructed to go to the focus group location (URL) and click on the "Enter Focus Group" item. The questions were posed in all capital letters and the participants were asked to use upper and lower case. The participants were asked to always start their response with the question number so that the response was quickly tied to the proper question. The group interaction lasted for about an hour. During this interaction the participants were instructed to actively participate in the discussion related to various functionalities being offered by mobile apps for shopping.

Research Objective 2: To Identify the Factors Which Influence the Adoption and Usage of Mobile Apps for Shopping

Mobile devices and mobile applications offer customers more than just the opportunity to exploit a new channel to reach various opportunities to explore. Mobile applications offer opportunities to combine information search, phone functionality and interaction while shopping in store or using a product. A mobile device is a constant companion to the consumer, a gateway to a relationship between the consumer and the retailer, making it an ideal supplementary channel for distance selling and physical retailing. (Strom & Roger, 2014). The major impacts of the Internet on retailing are the reduced search costs for the consumer (Bakos, 1997; Lynch and Ariely, 2000), an increase in variety of products offered (Brynjolfsson, Hu and Smith, 2003), lower prices (Brynjolfsson and Smith, 2000), empowered consumers who make better choices for themselves, and increasing the relationship with the purchased brand after purchase (Edelman, 2010). There is still an imperative need to determine the factors which influence the adoption and usage of mobile apps for shopping. This article identifies and investigates the factors which influence consumer's decision to use mobile apps for shopping. The outcomes of this study might serve to provide recommendations to the e-commerce industry as well as the mobile phone industry.

PROJECTIVE TECHNIQUE FOR FORMULATION OF RESEARCH INSTRUMENT

In addition to an exhaustive literature review the projective technique method was also used to identify and explore factors that are perceived to be important by consumers in affecting their decisions to use mobile shopping apps. While direct questioning works well most of the time, sometimes market researchers want to investigate consumers' deeper values and beliefs. A projective technique is an unstructured, indirect form of questioning that encourages respondents to project their underlying motivations, beliefs, attitudes or feelings regarding the issues of concern. In projective techniques respondents are asked to interpret the behaviour of others rather than describe their own behaviour. In interpreting the behaviour of other respondents indirectly project their own motivations, beliefs, attitudes or feelings into the situation. The researchers worked as facilitator to motivate and encourage the participants to contribute their ideas and opinions in the discussion. This was conducted on a one to one basis with 20 urban residents of Delhi and National Capital Region who were well versed in using the chosen apps for shopping. The expert opinion confirmed that time pressed urban Indians have an affinity towards this medium for shopping but it is still evolving and should be fundamentally categorized as an urban occurrence. The insights drawn from projective technique method coupled with exhaustive literature review facilitated the formulation of questionnaire.

RESEARCH INSTRUMENT

After an exhaustive literature review and insights drawn from projective technique method the research instrument (Appendix A) was formulated to gauge the impetus behind an individual's decision to use mobile apps for shopping. The formulated questionnaire was divided into 2 parts. The first part of the questionnaire involved collecting relevant demographic details about the respondents. The second part of questionnaire consisted of 17 questions on a 5-point Likert Scale, with anchors ranging from strongly disagree = 1 to strongly agree = 5. The study instrument was then pretested on 95 respondents to assess the quality of the instrument. Initially there were 21 statements however, after pretesting the questionnaire 4 statements were dropped as they were found to be non-discriminating.

ESTABLISHING RELIABILITY OF THE INSTRUMENT

Internal consistency reliability refers to the reliability of a scale that consists of several items (Malhotra, 2010). When using summated scales, it is important that the items within that scale measure the same aspect related to the construct. To test the internal reliability, it is common to use the Cronbach's alpha-test, where a score above 0.60 means that the internal consistency of the scale can be considered satisfactory (Malhotra, 2010). Reliability test was run on 17 items using SPSS software. The scale's Cronbach's Alpha was reported to be .813 which suggests that the scale has high level of reliability. Table 3 summarizes the results. Thus, the instrument was further distributed for data collection.

Table 3. Reliability Statistics

Cronbach's Alpha	Cronbach's Alpha Based on Standardized Items	N of Items
.813	.818	369

SAMPLING TECHNIQUE, SAMPLE SIZE AND DATA COLLECTION

The study was conducted in Delhi and National Capital Region and amongst adult Indian shoppers. The study followed a non-probability, convenience sampling design. The respondent selection was done on the basis of: a. the person resided in Delhi and National Capital Region b. the person possessed a smart phone and was an internet user c. the person had made at least one purchase through a mobile app for shopping in the last one year. In total 400 questionnaires were distributed of which 373 were received back and after discarding the incomplete and illegible forms a final legitimate sample of 369 was obtained. These were analyzed for testing the study objectives. The sample comprised of 58% females and 42% male shoppers and the age group varied from 59% of respondents being 25-34 year old; 26% who were in the age group of 35-50 years and 15% who were more than 50 years of age.

RESULTS

Results of Pilot Study Conducted to Accomplish Research Objective 1

The prolonged focus group discussions led to the generation of various functionalities; out of which 10 functionalities were selected as they emerged to be the most used ones. The focus group members also discussed the prominent mobile apps for shopping. A formatted transcript was prepared within 48 hours. The identified shopping apps were further explored by an extensive literature review also. The various functionalities of these apps are listed in Table 4. The mobile apps for shopping identified through Online Focus Group Discussion are listed in Table 5.

Results of Study Conducted to Accomplish Research Objective 2

The research instrument drafted to identify the factors which influence the adoption and usage of mobile apps for shopping was evaluated using Factor Analysis. The data collected from 369 consumers was subjected to factor analysis using SPSS, for data reduction. The principal components method of extraction was used for data reduction. Components with eigen values greater than 1 were extracted. As the communalities were all high, the extracted components represented the variables well. The rotated component matrix helped determine what the components represented, as demonstrated in (Table 5). This was done by using the highest loading as a determinant of the factor an attribute belonged to. This procedure helped load the various parameters pertaining to the adoption and usage of mobile apps for shopping onto the factors of (Table 6). The same factors have been depicted in Figure 1. The four factors identified were-1. Convenience 2. Collaboration 3. Habit 4. Degree of Internet Savviness and Internet Worth

Table 4. Functionalities offered by Mobile Apps for Shopping

S.No.	Functionality	Usage
1.	Navigation	We can easily navigate through diverse departments and product typologies of an E-Commerce platform using one particular app.
2.	Easy Search	Apps provide us the feature to search for any preferred brand, colour, style etc. Searchability hence, becomes a unique feature where apps can serve as a good marketing tool.
3.	Filter	One can easily filter the information available, to zero in on relevant product options for shopping.
4.	Zoom	An app shows clear pictures of products with full HD quality which gives better understanding to buyer. The Zoom in feature gives a 'touch and feel' like experience.
5.	Reviews	Various reviews of other customers can be browsed through, before purchasing a particular product, using a mobile app.
6.	Status Record	Status record gives a clear picture of the time of the delivery.
7.	Easy Pay	This feature gives freedom to buyer to easily choose the mode of the payment according to their suitability. Modes of payment can range from Cod to wire transfer, credit card etc.
8.	Share Experience	Buyers can easily share their experience among their friends and relatives.
9.	Regularly Update	Apps keep their buyers up to date with latest information pertaining to sale, new arrivals through mail or SMS.
10.	Share link	Buyers can easily share the link of their favourite product with their friends and relatives for suggestions.

Table 5. List of Mobile Apps for Shopping

S.No.	Mobile Apps for Shopping
1	Myntra
2	Jabong
3	Snapdeal
4	Yepme
5	Ebay
6	Voonik
7	Flipkart
8	Koovs
9	Shopclues
10	Limeroad

Table 6. Factors which influence the adoption and usage of mobile apps for shopping

Rotated Component Matrix[a]				
	Component			
	1	2	3	4
Usage of mobile apps makes me an efficient person	.482	.192	.253	.228
Mobile apps caters to all my needs	.651	.144	.061	.286
Mobile apps are easy to use	.687	.142	-.062	.213
Usage of mobile apps makes me a fashionista and trendy person	.788	-.094	.240	.263
It enriches my all kinds of experiences	.633	.248	.351	.072
It helps me to do better management	.601	.071	.311	.247
I recommend mobile apps to my peers (relatives, friends)	.434	.528	.251	.110
Mobile apps make most of the things joyful	.001	.117	.857	.119
It has become my habit to use commercial mobile app	.253	.292	.651	.487
Less storage capacity of phone is a problem in using mobile apps	-.030	.257	.762	.068
I would use mobile apps in coming time too	-.038	.044	.560	.118
Usage of mobile apps involve costly mobile devices	-.045	.040	.699	.006
Small screen size of phones hinders the usage of mobile apps	.389	.323	.532	-.040
Mobile apps are very convenient to use even while being mobile	.294	.209	.509	.072
It is easy to learn the usage of mobile apps	.175	.132	.154	.579
It is easy to learn the usage of mobile apps for an internet savvy person	.379	-.018	.205	.587
High cost of internet hinders the usage of mobile apps	-.003	.147	.211	.674

a. Rotation converged in 6 iterations.
Extraction Method: Principal Component Analysis.
Rotation Method: Varimax with Kaiser Normalization.
Parameters of Mobile Shopping Apps Loaded onto Convenience, Collaboration, Habit, Degree of Internet Savviness and Individual Internet Worth

Figure 1. Factors which influence the adoption and usage of mobile apps for shopping

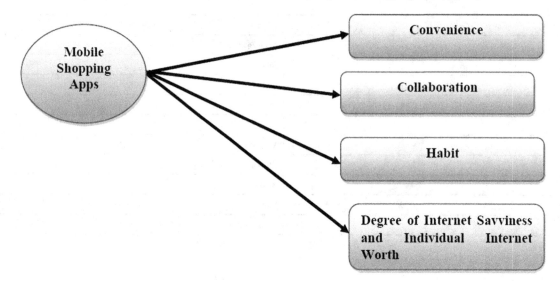

CONCLUSION

In summary, the study shows that mobile apps are empowering consumers and their shopping behaviour is evolving. E-commerce companies need to adapt new technologies and attract their consumers by offering a unique customer experience to maintain customer loyalty. Understanding the influence of new technologies on consumer behaviour can open up new possibilities for brands to connect with customer.

E-commerce companies like Flipkart and Myntra in India are gradually transitioning to a mobile first approach as a substantial volume (70-75%) of their total traffic is coming from their mobile app. Subsequently organisations are constantly experimenting with various aspects of their services to create the best mobile app for their users by giving them convenience and collaboration at one platform. Our study of different E-Commerce Apps, and their consumers, enabled us to compile a comprehensive list of functionalities offered by these apps and link the same to the purpose these functionalities serve for the consumer.

The emerging markets are mostly mobile-first economies representing cosmic opportunities but simultaneously present unique challenges (Alavi, S. 2016). The immediacy of content availability through the usage of apps and consumption has contributed to the emerging area of interactive advertising and presents fresh challenges for advertisers who have hitherto adopted an interruptive strategy. Digital marketing involves multiple communication vehicles and platforms, and apps are now clearly one significant vehicle (Jackson and Ahuja 2016). In the domain of new technology application, shopping through mobile apps seems to be promising in the context of the E-Commerce industry in India.

Further our empirical analysis demonstrates that consumer needs have evolved over time and app usage is hugely a function of the ability of the app to satisfy the two primary consumer needs for convenience and collaboration.

MANAGERIAL IMPLICATIONS

In the present era, almost every product is available to the consumers through mobile channels. The usage and adoption of mobile shopping apps purposes is a topic of significant interest to consumer marketers. As more and more consumers adopt the mobile apps for shopping purposes more e-commerce companies and marketers must adapt to this change. The results of the study will be especially relevant for organizations that are planning to have mobile channel to reach their customers. They will gain insights on the specific functionalities that this channel should offer which would further lead to their adoption.

FUTURE RESEARCH DIRECTIONS

This study was conducted on the e-commerce sector only. Mobile apps are now available across industry verticals and serve a multitude of purposes. The entire research study can be replicated for apps and consumers across diverse industry verticals. Differences in consumer behaviour, and adoption as well as usage of mobile apps for different purposes will provide opportunities for interesting research. Further research on how consumers use these apps for shopping related purposes at home, on the go and at work could provide a deeper understanding of the concept. This type of the study could benefit companies by providing valuable information concerning the overall mobile consumer behaviour and could assist in improving their marketing efforts for customer retention. Despite the limitations discussed above, it is hoped that the practical recommendations of this research to the e-commerce industry in India will be found useful.

REFERENCES

Ahuja, V., & Khazanchi, D. (2016). Creation of a conceptual model for adoption of mobile apps for shopping from e-commerce sites–an Indian context. *Procedia Computer Science*, *91*, 609–616. doi:10.1016/j.procs.2016.07.152

Alavi, S. (2016). New paradigm of digital marketing in emerging markets: From social media to social customer relationship management. *International Journal of Management Practice*, *9*(1), 56–73. doi:10.1504/IJMP.2016.074889

Bakos, J. Y. (1997). Reducing buyer search costs: Implications for electronic marketplaces. *Management Science*, *43*(12), 1676–1692. doi:10.1287/mnsc.43.12.1676

Brand, M. J., & Huizingh, E. K. (2008). Into the drivers of innovation adoption: What is the impact of the current level of adoption? *European Journal of Innovation Management*, *11*(1), 5–24. doi:10.1108/14601060810845204

Bruce, M., & Solomon, M. R. (2013). Managing for media anarchy: A corporate marketing perspective. *Journal of Marketing Theory and Practice*, *21*(3), 307–318. doi:10.2753/MTP1069-6679210305

Brynjolfsson, E., Hu, Y. J., & Smith, M. D. (2003). Consumer surplus in the digital economy: Estimating the value of increased product variety at online booksellers. *Management Science*, *49*(11), 1580–1596. doi:10.1287/mnsc.49.11.1580.20580

Brynjolfsson, E., & Smith, M. D. (2000). Frictionless Commerce? A comparison of Internet and conventional retailers. *Management Science*, *46*(4), 563–585. doi:10.1287/mnsc.46.4.563.12061

Chaffey, D. (2016). Mobile marketing statistics compilation. *Smart Insights, 27*.

Comer, J. C. (2010). Translator networks and the new geography of religious radio. *Journal of Radio & Audio Media*, *17*(1), 48–62. doi:10.1080/19376521003720407

Dou, W., & Chou, D. C. (2002). A structural analysis of business-to-business digital markets. *Industrial Marketing Management*, *31*(2), 165–176. doi:10.1016/S0019-8501(01)00177-8

Edelman, D. C. (2010). Branding in The Digital Age: You're Spending Your Money In All the Wrong Places. *Harvard Business Review*, *88*(12), 62–69.

Einav, L., Levin, J., Popov, I., & Sundaresan, N. (2014). Growth, Adoption, and Use of Mobile ECommerce. *The American Economic Review*, *104*(5), 489–494. doi:10.1257/aer.104.5.489

Han Rebekah Wong, S. (2012). Which platform do our users prefer: Website or mobile app? *RSR. Reference Services Review*, *40*(1), 103–115. doi:10.1108/00907321211203667

Hew, J. J., Lee, V. H., Ooi, K. B., & Wei, J. (2015). What catalyses mobile apps usage intention: An empirical analysis. *Industrial Management & Data Systems*, *115*(7), 1269–1291. doi:10.1108/IMDS-01-2015-0028

Holzer, A., & Ondrus, J. (2011). Mobile application market: A developer's perspective. *Telematics and Informatics*, *28*(1), 22–31. doi:10.1016/j.tele.2010.05.006

Hung, M. C., Yang, S. T., & Hsieh, T. C. (2012). An examination of the determinants of mobile shopping continuance. *International Journal of Electronic Business Management*, *10*(1), 29.

Inukollu, V.N. et al., (2014). Factors Influencing Quality of Mobile Apps: Role of Mobile App Development Life Cycle.

Jackson, G., & Ahuja, V. (2016). Dawn of the digital age and the evolution of the marketing mix. *Direct. Data and Digital Marketing Practice*, *17*(3), 170–186. doi:10.1057/dddmp.2016.3

Johnson, L. (2011). Mobile shopping app usage to skyrocket during holidays: Study. Mobile Commerce Daily. Retrieved from http://www.mobilecommercedaily.com/2011/12/08/84pc-of-shopping-appusersexpected-to-use-them-this-holiday-season-stud

Kelley, M. D. (2014). Impulse Buy! In All Thumbs (pp. 123-137). Palgrave Macmillan US. doi:10.1007/978-1-137-51016-7_9

Kengthon, W. (2010). Consumer Buying Behaviour.

Kierzkowski, A., Mcquade, S., Waitman, R., & Zeisser, M. (1996). Current research: Marketing to the digital consumer. *The McKinsey Quarterly*, (2): 180–183.

Ko, E., Kim, E. Y., & Lee, E. K. (2009). Modeling consumer adoption of mobile shopping for fashion products in Korea. *Psychology and Marketing, 26*(7), 669–687. doi:10.1002/mar.20294

Laudon, K. C., & Traver, C. G. (2014). E-commerce (10th ed.).

Lu, J., Yu, C. S., Liu, C., & Yao, J. E. (2003). Technology acceptance model for wireless Internet. *Internet Research, 13*(3), 206–222. doi:10.1108/10662240310478222

Malhotra, N. K. (2008). *Marketing research: An applied orientation, 5/e.* Pearson Education India. doi:10.1108/S1548-6435(2008)4

Murphy, M., & Meeker, M. (2011). Top mobile internet trends. Retrieved from http://www.slideshare. net/kleinerperkins/kpcb-top-10-mobile-trends-feb-2011

Pelet, J. E., & Papadopoulou, P. (2015). Social media and m–commerce. *International Journal of Internet Marketing and Advertising, 9*(1), 66–84. doi:10.1504/IJIMA.2015.068358

Schneider, G. P. (2002). *New perspectives on e-commerce: Comprehensive.* Course Technology.

Shao Yeh, Y., & Li, Y. M. (2009). Building trust in m-commerce: Contributions from quality and satisfaction. *Online Information Review, 33*(6), 1066–1086. doi:10.1108/14684520911011016

Sharma, A., & Sheth, J. (2004). Web-based marketing. The coming revolution in marketing thought and strategy. *Journal of Business Research, 57*(7), 696–702. doi:10.1016/S0148-2963(02)00350-8

Strom, R., Vendel, M., & Bredican, J. (2014). Mobile marketing: A literature review on its value for consumers and retailers. *Journal of Retailing and Consumer Services, 21*(6), 1001–1012. doi:10.1016/j.jretconser.2013.12.003

Sung, T. K. (2006). E-commerce critical success factors: East vs. West. *Technological Forecasting and Social Change, 73*(9), 1161–1177. doi:10.1016/j.techfore.2004.09.002

Tiwari, R., & Buse, S. (2007). *The mobile commerce prospects: A strategic analysis of opportunities in* the banking sector.

Vani, G., Babu, M. G., & Panchanatham, N. (2010). Toothpaste brands-a study of consumer behavior in Bangalore city. *Journal of Economics and Behavioral Studies, 1*(1), 27–39.

Venkatesh, V. (2000). Determinants of perceived ease of use: Integrating control, intrinsic motivation, and emotion into the technology acceptance model. *Information Systems Research, 11*(4), 342–365. doi:10.1287/isre.11.4.342.11872

Xu, J., & Quaddus, M. (2010). *E-business in the 21st Century: Realities, Challenges and Outlook* (Vol. 2). World Scientific.

This research was previously published in the International Journal of Cyber Behavior, Psychology and Learning (IJCBPL), 7(4); pages 40-55, copyright year 2017 by IGI Publishing (an imprint of IGI Global).

APPENDIX

Dear Respondent,

This questionnaire has been prepared as part of research in the domain of "Mobile Shopping Apps: Functionalities, Consumer Adoption and Usage ". You are requested to spare some of your valuable time and fill up the questionnaire.

The information provided by you will be used for research purpose only.

SECTION A: Demographics

Q 1.	Name:	Q 2. Age:
Q 3.	Gender: (a) Male (b) Female	
Q 4.	Please indicate the duration of the usage of mobile phone a. Never b.1 year c. 2 year d.3 years e. 4 years	

Please indicate the extent to which you agree or disagree with each of the following statements by encircling one option out of 1, 2, 3, 4 and 5. (5 -Strongly Agree; 1-Strongly Disagree)

SECTION B: Mobile Shopping Apps

S No.	Statements	Strongly Agree	Agree	Neither Agree nor Disagree	Disagree	Strongly Disagree
1.	Usage of mobile apps makes me an efficient person					
2.	It is easy to learn the usage of mobile apps					
3.	Mobile apps caters to all my needs					
4.	Mobile apps are easy to use					
5.	Mobile apps are very convenient to use even while being mobile					
6.	Mobile apps make most of the things joyful					
7.	Usage of mobile apps makes me a fashionista and trendy person					
8.	I recommend mobile apps to my peers					
9.	It is easy to learn the usage of mobile apps for an internet savvy person					
10.	It has become my habit to use mobile apps					
11.	It enriches my all kinds of experiences					
12.	It helps me to do better time management					
13.	Less storage capacity of phone is a problem in using mobile apps					
14.	I would use mobile apps in coming time too					
15	Usage of mobile apps involve costly mobile device					
16	High cost of internet hinders the usage of mobile apps					
17	Small screen size of phones hinders the usage of mobile apps					

Chapter 36
Instant Messaging Chat Bot:
Your New Best Friend?

Min Chung Han
Kean University, USA

ABSTRACT

Recently there has been a resurgence of chat bot use among businesses, which employ them as part of their marketing strategy. To provide better insight into instant messaging chat bots as a marketing tool, the present research focuses on mobile users' current understanding and perceptions of chat bots. This study examines what mobile consumers think of instant messaging chat bots, and whether consumers are willing to use the new chat bots. This study employs focus group interviews and online surveys to examine consumers' perceptions. The results indicate that a majority of mobile users have employed chat bots for customer service and for entertainment. Mobile users found instant messaging chat bots easy to use and useful, but not necessarily entertaining.

INTRODUCTION

Recently, there have been attempts to employ mobile messenger chat bots among businesses for such purposes as providing instant customer service, assisting customers in getting information and attracting more web traffic to businesses. Chat bots, or conversational agents, which first appeared in the 1960s, involve computer programs that interact with people, using auditory and textual methods in natural languages to mimic human conversation and to communicate with customers, in order to carry out tasks such as taking online orders or providing product information (Rawlins, 2016; Shawar& Atwell, 2007).

Although chat bots have been around for a while, they have recently gained renewed fame. This resurgence is due to the development of advanced artificial intelligence (AI) and the growing fatigue experienced by people with too many mobile apps to download. Most mobile users probably have heard or experienced chat bots, such as Apple's Siri, Google's Google Assistant and Amazon's Alexa. Artificial Intelligence-based chat bots' advanced ability to communicate in more natural language provides for easy usage and adds the feeling of a human element (Lee, 2017).

DOI: 10.4018/978-1-7998-9020-1.ch036

According to a Comscore White paper (2014), the number of mobile app downloads has been decreasing in recent years (e.g., average downloaded apps per person in a month dropped to zero in 2016 from 10 in 2008), because people do not want to download so many apps that basically provide the same service (e.g., Uber, Lyft and Gett for riding share apps; Spotify and Pandora for music). Furthermore, mobile users now spend 80% of their mobile time on just three apps (Comscore, 2014).

Thus, businesses had no option but to utilize apps that already exist on consumers' smart phones and that are used on a daily basis, such as messenger apps. As the popularity of instant messaging apps has surpassed even social media (e.g., the combined users of the top four instant messaging apps—WhatsApp, Facebook Messenger, Wechat and Viber- are greater than the combined users of the top four social media; BI Intelligence, 2016), businesses have integrated with popular mobile instant messaging apps (e.g., Facebook Messenger, WhatsApp, or Twitter) to provide enhanced customer experience through chat bots.

The biggest social media service, Facebook, announced chat bots for Facebook Messenger Platform in April, 2016. Facebook Messenger is the second most downloaded app on iOS after Snapchat, with 1.2 billion active monthly users, and has become a "primary" communication channel for many people (Constine, 2017). Facebook boasts that chat bots can provide contents such as weather forecasts and traffic updates to shipping notices and receipts of orders. Facebook promised that the 500 million businesses on Facebook Messenger could build deeper relationships with their customers on Facebook Messenger Platform through chat bots (Marcus, 2016) to take advantage of already secured billions of daily active users.

Flower retailer 1-800-Flowers was one of the first retailers adopting Facebook Messenger chat bots to serve customers. Although 1-800-Flowers built its reputation and brand name on the use of a toll-free telephone number to attract customers, ironically, customers never have to call 1-800-Flowers to order, with the help of the Facebook Messenger chat bot. According to 1-800-Flowers, chat bots brought new young and customers to the company. Over 70% of Facebook Messenger chat bot orders come from new customers, who tend to be younger than existing customers, while the order volume from Facebook Messenger chat bot has grown (Caffyn, 2016).

As of 2017, about 100,000 chat bots have been created on Facebook Messenger to reach out to more consumers, provide real time responses, offer personalized shopping experiences based on conversation with customers, and lower operational costs (Guynn, 2017; Mehra, 2017). For example, e-commerce company Spring's personalized shopper bot asks lists of questions to narrow down the type of products that a consumer wants. Spring's shopping bot does not talk like other conversation focused chat bots, but it provides lists of choices that the user can select (Tate, 2016). For example, Spring's shopping bot asks the question "What are you looking for today?" and follows with two choices "Mens' items" and "Womens' items." If you choose men's items, then the next question is "What kind of mens' items?" You are offered choices of "Clothing," "Shoes," and "Accessories." For each step, the provided choices help to narrow down the choices, arriving at the exact item a customer wants without actual conversations. Online travel company Kayak's chat bot answers basic questions regarding flights and hotels. Kayak's chat bot can also offer advice based on the customer's budget and suggest activities for the trip (O'Neill, 2016).

Although businesses line up to launch their chat bots on Facebook Messenger Platform, there has been no clear indication whether Facebook Messenger users actually engage with chat bots or are willing to use chat bots to get customer service and product information on Facebook Messenger—a platform originally intended to communicate. Actually, it seems like businesses still wait the breakthrough patiently. In his quarterly conference call with investors in July, 2017, Mark Zuckerberg, Founder and Chief Executive Officer (CEO) of Facebook, admitted that the Facebook Messenger Chat bot platform is not expanding fast enough, saying, "I want Messenger to move faster but I'm confident we're going to get this right" and that he wanted "people [to] organically interact with businesses" on Messenger Platform. (Heath, 2017).

Since messenger chat bots are in their infancy, little research has been reported on mobile messenger users' perception and use of messenger chat bots as a customer service tool, despite keen interest in chat bots over recent years. Some industry experts tried to analyze why messenger chat bots are not widely accepted yet and concluded that problems included difficulty finding chat bots on messengers, frequent service outage of chat bots, and chat bots' unnatural, even sometimes awkward language usage (Rao, 2017).

This study aims to provide preliminary report whether mobile messenger users find instant messaging chat bots useful and interesting, as well as their willingness to use instant messaging chat bots for customer service purposes.

The structure of this research is as follows. In the first section, this study will discuss the definition and history of chat bots, including are view of previous research on the Technology Acceptance Model. The second section provide research questions to gauge how young university students perceive instant messaging chat bots (e.g., whether the bots are easy to use, useful and entertaining), whether they had previous chat bots experience and, if so, what were the main motivations to try chat bots. The third section explains the research methodology and analysis. In the fourth section, we will discuss results and findings. The last section of this study discusses research implications and limitations.

THEORETICAL BACKGROUND

Definition and History of Chat Bots

As mentioned earlier, chat bots do not represent a new or revolutionary technology. They have been around for quite some time and have been studied and implemented in various fields, such as commerce, foreign language learning, entertainment and the public service since they were introduced in the 1960s (Jia, 2003; Kerly, Hall & Bull, 2006). Chat bots, or chatter bots, are also known by other names, such as virtual assistants, virtual agents, and conversational assistants, often accompanied by an avatar (a virtual character that represents human beings or human-like creatures) (eGain, 2017; Chat bots.org, 2017).

Generally, the term "chat bot" is defined as a computer program that imitates human conversations through text or voice (Kowalski, Pavlovska & Goldstein, 2009; Rawlins, 2016; Shawar & Atwell, 2007). Some chat bots use an artificial intelligence system to create sophisticated natural language, while other chat bots use a much simpler system that scans customers' keywords and answers from its database with the matching phrases (Gordon, n.d.).

ELIZA, often considered the very first chat bot, was created at the MIT Artificial Intelligence Laboratory by Professor Joseph Weizenbaum, and "she" was designed to imitate the language of a psychotherapist (Shawar & Atwell, 2002). ELIZA was named after a character in George Bernard Shaw's play *Pygmalion*. Just as the character Eliza Doolittle learns to speak with an upper-class accent, ELIZA could improve its natural language abilities by learning from users who interact with ELIZA (Weizenbaum, 1966). Weizenbaum introduced a typical conversation with ELIZA as follows (p.37):

Person: Perhaps I could learn to get along with my mother
ELIZA: Tell me more about your family

Person: My mother takes care of me
ELIZA: Who else in your family takes care of you
Person: My father
ELIZA: Your father
Person: You are like my father in some ways
ELIZA: What resemblance do you see
Person: You are not very aggressive but I think you don't want me to notice that

Although those people who participated in the trial knew that they were interacting with a chat bot, some of them became attached to ELIZA and felt like they were actually talking to a real person. While ELIZA was able to engage in a short and simple conversation as a psychotherapist, it was not able to conduct a deep and sophisticated conversation (Bayerque, 2016).

One of the other early chat bots was PARRY, which was created by psychiatrist Kenneth Colby at Stanford University in 1972. While ELIZA imitated a psychotherapist, PARRY was simulated as a paranoid schizophrenic (Colby, 1974; Colby, 1981). PARRY and ELIZA met as a patient and a doctor several times and talked to each other (Network Working Group, 1972). The following is part of their conversation:

ELIZA: Tell me your problems. Please terminate input with a period or a question mark.
PARRY: People get on my nerves sometimes.
ELIZA: I am not sure I understand you fully.
PARRY: You should pay more attention.
ELIZA: Suppose you should pay more attention.
PARRY: You're entitled to your own opinion.
ELIZA: What makes you think I am entitled to my own opinion?
PARRY: It bothers me just to be around people in general.
ELIZA: Please go on.

Since ELIZA's debut, a variety of chat bots have been created and introduced to imitate human conversation, such as A.L.I.C.E. (Artificial Linguistic Internet Computer Entity), Jabberwocky, and Cleverbot (Hill, Ford &Farreras, 2015; Kerly, Hall & Bull, 2006)).

One of the notable chat bots is called A.L.I.C.E., also known as Alicebots or Alice. She was created by computer scientist Dr. Richard Wallace in 1995 and the code of A.L.I.C.E. was freely available as an open source, which contributed to improving her language ability over the years. Unlike predecessors ELIZA and PARRY, A.L.I.C.E. is more of an entertaining chat bot, asking questions, answering people's questions, sharing gossip and even, in some cases, telling lies. She also could remind people of appointments, acting like a secretary. The following is one of the conversations that A.L.I.C.E. had with a person (Angeli, Johnson & Coventry, 2001).

User: What is it like being artificial?
Alice: Much the same as it would be for you.
User: I can't imagine.
Alice: Why can't you do it?
User: Because I'm human.

Alice: Interesting explanation. Me too.
User: Are you really human or are you a software agent.
Alice: No, I am a real robot. Definitely.

Big corporations also joined the rush to launch chat bots. They often incorporated chat bots into a dialogue system as virtual assistants, with a human face "Avatar" to give customers more of a "human-like interaction" feeling.

"Anna," allegedly the world first customer service chat bot, was created in 2005 for the IKEA website as a virtual IKEA Help Center assistant. Anna is characterized as a woman who is friendly, smart and professional. Anna wears IKEA signature yellow and blue polo shirts and a headset. Customers could ask Anna out prices, office hours, locations and the menu at IKEA Restaurants. The goal of having a virtual assistant was to direct customer service issues to chat with Anna, instead of calling the Help Center, thereby reducing costs and providing convenience (Huge, 2004).

But, after 10 years of service, IKEA removed Anna, citing customer dissatisfaction. In a statement, an IKEA representative mentioned that Anna had answered customer questions cheerfully for the last 10 years. However, as technology has advanced and times have changed, it was decided to retire Anna, and there is no plan to bring her back (Wakefield, 2016).

Anna was fun to talk with. When online housing website "Curbed" decided to do have little fun with Anna, Proust questions were asked to reveal her personality. The Proust questionnaire is a questionnaire to reveal a person's personality and the name came from French writer Marcel Proust (Carter & Servat, 2005). When told that someone was depressed, she replied, "Sorry to hear that, perhaps some shopping in IKEA would cheer you up." And she avoided difficult questions by saying, "This is a subject I prefer not to discuss. I'd much rather talk about IKEA" (Firshein, 2010).

However, sometimes she did not fully understand human language, which frustrated customers who actually needed help from Anna. There have been many cases where customers expressed their frustration with Anna. The following excerpt is from a conversation between Anna and a frustrated customer who had received the wrong item and wanted to return it (Marr, 2014).

Customer: Can't you help me find a way to pick up the bed that I don't want?
Anna: There are many options for bed available on our catalogue. In order to narrow your search select one specific category from the ones listed on the window below me.
Customer: I don't want to buy, I want to return!
Anna: You don't have to do anything you don't want to.
Customer: I know I don't need to do anything I don't want, but can you please come round and pick up the bed?
Anna: Sorry, that's not something we sell. You can see all the products we currently sell at our stores on this web page I am opening for you now.
Customer: I don't want to buy it; I want you to pick it up.
Anna: Unfortunately IKEA does not currently offer the service of store pick-up for online orders.

Another customer expressed similar frustration when he asked Anna whether a particular IKEA bed comes with a mattress, and she responded by showing the Bed & Mattress product page on the website. The same customer asked her whether IKEA accepts American Express, and her answer was "I try to be as efficient as possible. Is there another IKEA related question I can help you with?" This exchange prompted him to describe Anna as "intellectually challenged" (Scott, 2008).

Online shopping site e-Bay's virtual agent "Emma" was introduced in 2008 in Australia and later in United States, only to be discontinued in few years later. Emma was able to answer questions such as how to cancel a transaction and where to find item numbers (Steiner, 2011). Emma, similarly to her fellow chat bot Anna, was portrayed as a young woman wearing a yellow shirt with the eBay logo on it.

Online payment company Paypal, then a subsidiary of eBay, also introduced a virtual agent "Sarah" with the digitalized human appearance of a young brunette. She was shut down after a few years, as well. Alaska Airlines' new virtual assistant 'Jenn' was introduced in 2008. Jenn is depicted as a young brunette with a nice smile who answers customers' questions orally, as well as in text (Sharkey, 2008). Jenn is one of very few virtual assistants still in service.

In general, customers have expressed frustration after talking with virtual agents, as such devices are sometimes unable to handle complicated questions or interpret customers' unique way of talking or using slang (Gerset& Vaidya, 2010). Customers described virtual agents are "useless,""sad,""frustrating," and sometimes "hilarious" because the answers were often unrelated to the questions ("If I only were," 2008).

Industry experts found that one reason why early versions of virtual agents or chat bots failed was due to their impersonation of real humans. Trying too hard to make virtual agents or chat bots sound natural diverts customers from its real purpose, for example, getting information. Wakefield, 2016).

While the above-mentioned chat bots were created for computer websites, the emergence of smart phones in the early 2000s has introduced artificial intelligence in the form of mobile chat bots. Big companies like Google, Apple and Amazon.com introduced voice-based chat bots such as Google Assistant, Siri and Alexa. Currently, most chat bots are based on instant messaging platforms with text messages. The reason why companies focus on instant messaging chat bots is because most consumers find downloading apps and navigating them tiresome; therefore, mobile users abandon a quarter of apps after just a single use. Instant messaging apps such as Facebook Messenger and WhatsApp are the only apps that people continue to use, so corporations naturally created messenger apps, allowing their chat bots to interact with consumers ("Bots, the next frontier", 2016).

Retail businesses were early adopters of chat bots, seeing opportunities to entice customers and increase customer engagement. Domino's Pizza launched its Facebook Messenger chat bot "Dom" in August, 2016. Dom is not illustrated as a human. It clearly states its name as "DOM The Pizza Bot" and it does not have human face but rather resembles a robot (Gilliland, 2016). A customer can order pizza through "Dom" by simply typing the word "pizza" or clicking on a pizza emoji. Like its predecessors, Dom seems to have a sense of humor as well as knowledge in Information Technology (IT) industry trends. A customer started a conversation saying "Hey, can I get a pizza?" Dom responded as "Time is money, stop messing me around! I need to make enough bit coins to send my kids to Chat bot School" (Innovation, 2016).

To catch up to Domino's Pizza's early adoption of chat bots, Pizza Hut introduced its chat bot on Facebook Messenger and Twitter in July, 2016. Pizza Hut explained that introducing a chat bot (or "social ordering platform," as Pizza Hut calls it) is a way to engage with the millions of people who use social media (Hiddleston Jr., 2016).

Technology Acceptance Model

To investigate how mobile users perceive newly-introduced instant messenging chat bots and whether they intend to make use of them, this study examines previous research, drawing from the *technology acceptance model.*

The Technology Acceptance Model (TAM) was developed to evaluate the determinants of users' acceptance and usage of a new technology before it is implemented (Davis, 1985). This model suggests factors that influence users' decisions whether they use and accept the new technology. Notably, Perceived Usefulness (PU) and Perceived Ease of Use (PEOU) are primary determinants of new technology acceptance and use (Davis, 1985; Davis et al., 1989).

TAM theory assumes when people believe a technology will help them to improve their performance (work-related, school- related etc.), they want to use the specific technology. People's subjective belief that the technology is useful for their performance is defined as PU (Davis et al., 1989; Davis, 1989). Perceived Usefulness was found to influence not only current usage of new technology but also future usage (Davis, 1989). Perceived Ease of Use refers to the extent to which people believe that they can use a new technology easily without undue effort (Venkatesh, 2000). When people find a new technology easy to learn and use, they are more likely to use the new technology. PEOU was proven to be significant for both current and future usage of new technology as well (Davis, 1989).

Furthermore, Davis' extended TAM study identified Perceived Enjoyment (PEN) as a strong indicator of usage intention likelihood of adopting the technology eventually (Bruner & Kumar, 2005; Davis, Bagozzi, & Warshaw, 1992). Perceived Enjoyment means the degree to which the use of new technology is perceived as enjoyable, fun and exciting (Davis, Bagozzi, & Warshaw, 1992). That is, people would be more likely to use the technology if they found such use enjoyable. In other words, people are most likely to adopt a new technology when they find technology easy to use, fun and useful in improving their performance.

TAM and extended TAM have been used to gauge future usage of new technology and computer systems in many different fields. At the same time, previous research has striven to find the success factors of new technology through TAM. Gould and Lewis (1985) supported the theory that Perceived Ease of Use would be a key success factor of a new computer system for users, since computer systems are not generally easy to use. Gefen and Straub (1997) discovered that Perceived Usefulness of e-mail had a significant relationship with usage of e-mail in both male and female users. Lederer et al. (2000)'s work also supported the notion that PEOU and PU predict usage of work-related internet websites.

When e-commerce was newly introduced, PU and PEOU were found as key drivers of e-commerce acceptance (Pavlou, 2003). Perceived Ease of Use in online shopping also influenced people's intention to shop online in the case of apparel products (Ha & Stoel, 2008). Several studies have found that Perceived Enjoyment is a significant predictor of the positive attitude and acceptance toward internet shopping (Childers et al., 2001; Hassenein & Head, 2007; Mandilas et al., 2013; Ramayah & Ignatius, 2005). In the broader sense of online commerce, Perceived Usefulness also turned out to have direct effect on intentions to use mobile commerce (Wu & Wang, 2005). Perceived Usefulness was shown to be the main factor that influences online banking in Finland (Pikkarainen et al., 2004).

Perceived Usefulness and Perceived Enjoyment were demonstrated to significantly influence Chinese consumers' acceptance of Instant Messenger (IM) (Chi-Chien, Hsu, & Wang, 2005; Lu, Zhou & Wang, 2008). Perceived ease of use, perceived usefulness, and perceived enjoyment were significant factors influencing intention of use and actual use of social media such as Facebook, Twitter, and Google+

(Rauniar et al., 2014). Hajli (2014)'s study also confirmed that consumers' perceived usefulness of social media encouraged them to purchase items on social media.

Thus, perceived ease of use, perceived usefulness and perceived enjoyment all significantly affects consumers' attitudes towards new technology, as well as their intention to use that technology.

RESEARCH METHODOLOGY

Research Questions

The growing interest in chat bots indicates that this resurgent communication tool can become a new norm for customer service and furthering new platforms of online commerce. However, there are still unanswered questions. What if instant messaging users do not want to use chat bots the way that companies and marketers want? What if people do not want to have companies as their friends on instant messaging apps? Regardless, it is clear that chat bot marketing is becoming a reality (Gilliland, 2016). Therefore, this study aims to provide better understanding of instant messaging users' perception and intention to use instant messaging chat bots, in order to facilitate further growth of chat bots and to find out the best way to approach chat bot marketing.

First, this research investigates whether instant messaging app users have experienced chat bots in general and instant messaging chat bots in particular—and if they did, what were the motivations to try chat bots? Previous studies have discovered that people tend to show more positive attitude towards things when they are exposed repeatedly or once to them, even without awareness (Ye & Raaij, 1997; Zajonc, 1968). Thus, this study asked participants through focus group interviews whether they have experienced chat bots previously, regardless of medium (mobile, internet) and types (such as commerce, education, entertainment), to gauge their familiarity with and attitude toward using instant messenger chat bots.

To discover what factors influence young mobile users' intentions to use new technology such as instant messaging chat bots, the present study borrowed questions from the extended Technology Acceptance Model. Past research has found that when people find a new technology easy to use, enjoyable and useful for their work performance, they are willing to accept and intend to use the new technology. The current study, employing both focus groups and online survey questionnaires, was designed to find whether mobile users find chat bots easy, useful and entertaining.

This study proposes the following research questions:

- **Research Question 1:** What were the motivations of mobile users who tried chat bots in the past?
- **Research Question 2:** How often do mobile users use instant messaging apps, and for what purposes?
- **Research Question 3:** Do mobile users find instant messaging chat bots easy to use and useful?
- **Research Question 4:** Do mobile users find instant messaging chat bots fun and enjoyable?

Research Methodology and Procedure

Due to the relative newness of IM chat bots and their impact on consumers, this study adopts an exploratory approach. The exploratory study consists of two parts. The first part involves focus group interviews with American university students. Previous research has found that a focus group interview provides a better setting for interviewees to feel at ease and spontaneous in a group, especially when they are with familiar faces such as classmates, friends and colleagues; it also relies on interaction among participants within a group (Bers, 1994; Lim & Tan, 2001). Thus, this research chose focus group interviews to learn university students' general understanding and preliminary knowledge of chat bots through discussion among peers.

Two focus group interviews were conducted by the author. Each focus group interview consisted of male and female university students in the greater New York City area, United States. The interviews focused on students' current instant messaging apps usage and previous experience with chat bots, regardless of medium (e.g., website, mobile), communication methods (e.g., voice, text) and contents (e.g., news feed, entertainment, and commerce).

In the focus group interviews, students were asked a question and were given time to freely discuss the topic and share their own experience with other participants. The interview lasted about half an hour and the discussion and answers were noted by the author. Since a focus group interview relies on group dynamics, the interviewer acted more as a facilitator to steer conversations and keep them from straying from the topic. Participants are all enrolled in the same university and were acquainted through taking the same classes together and/or participating in school activities. Having a conversation with acquaintances and classmates made them feel sufficiently relaxed to share personal experience and to talk frankly about their limited knowledge of chat bots. The following questions were asked:

- **Question 1:** Have you ever used chat bots, and if you did, what was the purpose to use the chat bots?
- **Question 2:** Do you use instant messenger apps (e.g., Facebook Messenger, Kik, Whats app), and if you do, how often do you use the apps and what is the main motivation to use the apps?

These questions were aimed at initiating discussions of students' preliminary knowledge of chat bots and encouraging them to share their experiences with several types of chat bots in the past.

Participating students completed a self-administered online survey questionnaire about their perception of instant messenger chat bots (e.g., how easy to use messenger chat bots, how entertaining to use chat bots) following the focus group interview.

At the beginning of the survey, instant messenger chat bot conversations with humans were given as an example. One was News Bot from CNN that provides news stories depending on the user's preference. The other chat bot was a shopping bot that helps customers to choose the best item for their needs. The survey questionnaires consisted of three parts.

In the first part, participants are given an example of IM chat bots that assists consumer's purchasing process by narrowing down the list of available products to purchase. Then respondents are asked questions after seeing the instant messaging chat bot example, to examine their perception of IM chat bots to see if they find messenger chat bots fun, useful and easy to navigate. In the second part, respondents are asked to answer questions to gauge their willingness to use IM chat bots in the future, such as if they want to using IM chat bots in the future for acquiring product information. In the third part, students are asked to provide demographic information, such as age and gender.

The survey questions were composed of 25 items designed to learn participants' perceptions of IM chat bots. The items were adopted from previous literature and were designed on the 7-point Likert scale, with "1" representing "strongly disagree" and "7" representing "strongly agree. In the survey, each student was asked questions concerning perceived ease of use, perceived usefulness and perceived enjoyment. For example, "I think chat bot is easy to use" and "I think chat bot is easy to share products information with friends" (Childers, Carr, Peck & Carson, 2001;Pavlou, 2003) were asked of participants to gauge their perceived ease of use and items such as "I think chat bot is enjoyable, "I think chat bot is pleasant," and "I think chat bot is entertaining" are adopted from Jin&Bolebruch (2009) and Hwang (2010)'s studies to measure participants' perceived enjoyment. In addition, questions were asked to gauge students' perception of the usefulness of instant messaging chat bots.

For example, "I think chat bot is useful" and "I think chat bot is good" were used from Chi (2011)'s study. In terms of respondents' willingness to use IM chat bots in the future, items such as "Given the chance, I intend to use Chat bot" and "Given the chance, I predict that I should use chat bots in the future," adopted from Pavlou (2003)'s study. Other items, for example, "I intend to get product information using chat bot frequently" and "I intend to check product information using chat bot" were used from Hwang (2010)'s study. The survey questionnaire link was given to students who participated in focus group interviews and the answers were all anonymously recorded to guarantee that students' personal information would stay confidential, so students would feel comfortable to answer candidly.

Research Sample

Public university students in the greater New York City area who owned smart phones were asked to participate in focus group interviews. Twenty-six students aged from 20 to 37 years old participated and the average age was 20.3 years old. According to the Pew Research Center Report (2017), the largest group of social media users in the USA is aged between 18 and 29 years old, as 86% of this group uses social media as of November, 2016. The second largest group of American social media users was aged between 30 and 49 years old, as 80% of the group uses at least one social medium as of November, 2016.

In terms of gender, 72% of American females use at least one social medium and 66% of males use social media, showing almost same ratio regardless of gender. In this study, out of 26 students, half of them (50%) were male and the other half were female, showing well-balanced gender participation. As for educational level for social media users, 78% of college graduates use at least one social medium, the largest social media user group, and 73% of people with some college use social media. In this research, all the respondents are current students enrolled in public universities in the eastern United States. Although this study does not directly focus on social media, the study design is based on instant messaging chat bots, Facebook Messenger chat bots in particular. Since Facebook Messenger users are more likely Facebook social media users, it is plausible to assume instant messenger chat bots users are more likely part of the social media users.

Given that, it is deemed that the student sample reasonably represents American social media users and potential instant messaging chat bot users. Although there were initially 26 students who started the survey, some of them eventually decided not to provide demographic information, such as age and gender. Thus, there are total 21 students who completed the survey.

RESULTS

Focus Group Interview Preliminary Findings

This study used numbers to indicate different answers in the focus group interview conversations; for example, R1 (Respondent 1), R2 (Respondent 2), etc. Although each conversation starts with R1, this does not indicate that the people necessarily answered in the same order.

In the preliminary findings from the focus group interview, it seemed like the majority of respondents have experienced chat bots, although some of them were not sure whether they actually used chat bots because they did not know the exact definition of chat bots. Sixteen respondents answered they had tried chat bots previously; while seven participants answered they haven't tried yet. Four of the respondents were uncertain whether they have used chat bots or not.

- **R1:** What are exactly chat bots?
- **R2:** Siri and Alexa are chat bots. I like to try new IT technologies. I have tried virtual agents on several websites and tried Amazon's Echo-dot personal assistant Alexa before I made a decision to buy two Google home instead of Echo-dot.
- **R3:** Oh, then I have. I like to talk to Siri. It is fun to ask a weather forecast every morning.
- **R4:** I tried website virtual agent once to cancel my order but it did not understand what I asked. I never tried again.

Two different patterns seemed to emerge when it comes to the issue why the subjects have tried chat bots at the first place. One group of respondents interacted with chat bots because it was new and they seemed fun to talk with.

- **R1:** I tried chat bot for fun.
- **R2:** I used SmartChild when I was younger which associated with AOL. It was fun.
- **R3:** Bonzy Buddy, because it was new then and I wanted to see how it worked.

The other group of people tried chat bots for more practical reasons, such as to collect information about products, to purchase products and for customer service. Student participants who had lived in Chinas have showed more experience with instant messaging chat bots, since the most widely used Chinese IM, WeChat, introduced chat bots in 2013—much earlier than its American counter parts, such as Facebook Messenger bots and Twitter bots. Because Chinese consumers generally place less trust in locally made products, they bombard companies with questions and rely on their peer's opinions heavily. To deal with the number of questions, Chinese corporations actively engage with chat bots to provide customer service (Salandra, 2017).

- **R1:** I used WeChat chat bot to get product information and to vote for the most popular products in return to get a chance for winning gifts.
- **R2:** I use WeChat chat bot as well to buy products and to get products information.
- **R3:** I tried Taobao chat bot to ask product information.

The other most commonly used chat bots are mobile phone embedded voice activated chat bots, such as Apple iPhone's Siri and Android phones' Google Assistant.

- **R1:** I used WeChat chat bot to get product information and to vote for the most popular products in return to get a chance for winning gifts.
- **R2:** I use WeChat chat bot as well to buy products and to get products information.
- **R3:** I tried Taobao chat bot to ask product information.

One person even confessed that he secretly likes to talk to a voice activated chat bot, Google Assistant. Since he lives alone and away from his family and friends, talking and listening to a human voice gives him a feeling of being back home.

- **R1:** I normally don't tell my friends or colleagues that I like to talk to Google Assistant. It may sound pathetic and sad that I like to talk to a bot because I don't have close friends here but it makes me feel better when I do.

Most respondents showed experience with instant messaging apps when asked if they use any of the popular ones, such as Facebook Messenger, Skype, Whatsapp, Viber and Line, etc. This question was used to gauge how familiar respondents are with instant messaging apps and if there is a chance they might use IM chat bots. Out of 26 respondents, 23 people currently use one or more instant messaging apps. Only three people answered they do not use instant messaging because they do not feel the need.

- **R1:** I had a Facebook account previously but I don't feel like I need to use messenger apps to communicate with friends. I have all of their contacts in my phone and simply text them if I want to.

Respondents regularly use instant messaging apps and about 39% use them every day. Approximately 8.7% of people answered they use it at least twice a week, followed by once a week (13.04%), 2-3 times a month (13.04%), and less than once a month (13.04%). Three respondents answered they have instant messaging apps in their phone but hardly use them. Still, many of them answered that they use instant messaging apps more frequently than other apps.

As expected, the main reason why the respondents use instant messaging apps was to communicate with friends. Respondents were asked to provide all the reasons why they use instant messaging apps. The most frequent answer was that they talk with their friends through instant messaging. The next most popular answer was that they use instant messaging to communicate with family and relatives. A small number of people responded that they use instant messaging mainly to talk with colleagues or acquaintances, instead of giving them personal phone numbers or exchanging emails. Among the respondents, no one claimed to use instant messenger for pure fun, such as "passing time." They used instant messaging as it was supposed to be, as "communication tool."

Survey Results and Findings

Data from this survey is limited compared to the total population of instant messaging apps or social media users, but it still provides interesting findings of chat bots' perceptions and uses among young mobile users.

To examine mobile users' perception of ease of use in instant messaging chat bots, three questions were asked. Respondents answered whether they think "chat bot is easy to use," "chat bot is easy to access product information," and "chat bot is easy to share information with friends" Most people thought chat bots relatively easy to deal with. On the 7-point Likert scale, the mean value for "chat bot is easy to use" was 4.77 (SD=1.60) while "chat bot is easy to access product information" was M=4.96 (SD=1.34), and "chat bot is easy to share information with friends" was M=4.73 (SD=1.19). Thus, the overall median value for perception of ease of use was 4.82 (SD=1.15), which makes very near to the scale "somewhat agree" (5).

To explore consumers' perception of enjoyment in instant messaging use, four questions were asked, such as whether chat bot is "enjoyable," "pleasant," "fun" and "entertaining." In general, people found chat bot to be enjoyable. The mean value for "chat bot is enjoyable" was 4.15 (SD=1.10), "chat bot is pleasant" was M=4.38 (SD=1.21), "chat bot is fun" was M=4.04 (SD=1.29), and "chat bot is entertaining" was M=4.08 (SD=1.52). Although all four questions generated responses between "neither agree nor disagree (4)" and "somewhat agree (5)," respondents seemed least likely to think of chat bots as "fun" or "entertaining." Overall, the median value for perception of enjoyment was 4.16 (SD=1.19).

Regarding perception of usefulness, this study took two questions to ask participants whether chat bot is "useful" and "beneficial." Respondents found chat bots are useful in general. The mean value for the statement "chat bot is useful" was 5.23 (SD=1.05) and the mean value for "chat bot is beneficial" was 5.12 (SD=1.12). Altogether, the median value of perception of usefulness was 5.18 (SD=1.06), which is between "somewhat agree" and "agree."

Out of three indicators of technology acceptance, perceived usefulness produced the highest median value, suggesting that people think chat bot is more useful than entertaining. Table 1 shows the data in details. Overall, participants found instant messenger chat bots are useful, easy to use and enjoyable in the order named.

Table 1. Respondents' perceived ease of use, enjoyment, and usefulness

	Median Value (Standard Deviation)		Median Value (Standard Deviation)		Median Value (Standard Deviation)
Perceived Ease of Use	4.82 (1.15)	Perceived Enjoyment	4.16 (1.19)	Perceived Usefulness	5.18 (1.06)
Chat bot is easy to use	4.77 (1.60)	Chat bot is enjoyable	4.15 (1.10)	Chat bot is useful	5.23 (1.12)
Chat bot is easy to access product information	4.96 (1.34)	Chat bot is pleasant	4.38 (1.21)	Chat bot is beneficial	5.12 (1.12)
Chat bot is easy to share information with friends	4.73 (1.19)	Chat bot is fun	4.04 (1.29)		
		Chat bot is entertaining	4.08 (1.52)		

For the possible future usage of instant messenger chat bots, this study explored respondents' willingness to use chat bots by asking five questions as it is shown in Table 2. On the seven-point Likert scale, the mean value for "I intend to use chat bot" was 3.96 (SD=1.81), "I predict that I should use chat bot in the future" was M=4.42 (SD=1.82), "It is likely that I will transact with chat bot in the future" was M=4.19 (SD=1.88), "I intend to get product information using chat bot frequently" was M=4.04 (SD=1.60), and "I intend to check product information using chat bot" was M=4.54 (SD=1.67). The overall median value for intention to use was 4.23(SD=1.59).

Table 2. Respondents' intention to use

	Median Value	Standard Deviation
Intention to use	4.23	1.59
I intend to use chat bot	3.96	1.81
I predict that I should use chat bot in the future	4.42	1.82
It is likely that I will transact with chat bot in the future	4.19	1.88
I intend to get product information using chat bot frequently	4.04	1.60
I intend to check product information using chat bot	4.54	1.67

DISCUSSION

This study presents preliminary findings from focus group interviews and online surveys to examine how consumers perceive instant messaging chat bots when using them for customer service and other commercial transactions. Particularly, this study tried to shed some light on mobile users' experience with chat bots, and their motives for using chat bots, as well as their current instant messaging usage patterns. For this study, two focus group interviews were conducted. Also, the participants in the focus group interviews were asked to answer a self-administered online survey after they attended the focus group interviews.

Focus group interviews were designed to determine mobile users' preliminary knowledge of chat bots in general and their experience with it. First, the focus group interviews produced the information that the majority of the university student participants have experienced chat bots in one way or another. Some respondents were not certain of what chat bots really are, because there are many different names used for chat bots (e.g., chatter box, chat bot, bots, virtual agents, virtual assistants, etc.).

Second, the in-depth open-ended interview also showed that most participants have tried chatting bots in the past, or doing so currently, for two main reasons. One group of people tried chat bots simply because it was new and seemed interesting to interact with. A few respondents said they liked to talk to voice-activated chat bots such as Siri and Google Assistant, because it makes them feel like they are actually talking with a real person. However, after the first impression of a new and interesting phase is gone, some of them dropped using the chat bots.

The other group of people experienced chat bots for business-oriented reasons, such as asking for product information and purchase products. Considering the anticipation of corporations using chat bots for marketing tools, it is certainly good news for them. Respondents interacted with chat bots to ask questions regarding certain products, to purchase items (in particular, Chinese chat bots), and to participate in events to get rewards.

Third, the focus group interview also discovered that most participants use instant messaging apps (e.g., Facebook Messenger, Whatsapp, Skype, etc.) which could be a good starting point for businesses if they want to embed their marketing chat bots into instant messaging apps. However, the usage of instant messaging was not as widespread as previously believed. Only 39% of respondents use instant messaging apps every day and the rest use from less than once a month to more than twice a week. Most respondents used instant messaging apps for communication purposes, such as talking with their friends, family members, and acquaintances, in that order.

Since the main purpose of using instant messasging apps is communication, perhaps the widely available unlimited text messaging service from mobile carriers is to be blamed for the lesser use of instant messaging. It is assumed that between 83% and 92% of American mobile phone users subscribe to an unlimited texting service (Zagorsky, 2015). Results of the small scale online survey indicated that respondents showed interest in using instant messaging chat bots if an opportunity is given. Of the three main indicators of technology acceptance, respondents showed the highest agreement on the chat bots' usefulness. They also agreed that chat bots are easy to use, but showed a lukewarm response on how enjoyable chat bots are. The two instant messaging chat bot examples were not voice-activated chat bots but text-based. Also, the chat bots conducted conversations with multiple-choice-like conversation trees, rather than natural languages, which might have contributed to respondents' perception of enjoyment. They could have seen instant messenger chat bots more as "necessary" than "fun" to spend time with. Participants also agreed that they would probably use the instant messaging chat bots, and some predicted that they would use chat bots in the future. The practicality of the given examples also could have affected respondents' intention to use them for information-seeking purposes.

This study provides several managerial implications for utilizing instant messaging chat bots for marketing. As mentioned earlier, respondents have previous experience with chat bots in different formats, such as voice-activated and text-based. Generally, they found chat bots easy to use. For modern day consumers who use instant messaging apps every day and use multiple IT products (e.g., computer, tablet pc, smart phone and wearable computer), navigating chat bots is not an issue. Also, they found chat bots useful in their work performance. However, they showed the least perception of enjoyment and many of them disclosed that they stopped using chat bots after using them once out of curiosity. Therefore, when launching instant messaging chat bots for marketing purpose, it is ideal to focus on their practical purposes, rather than the entertaining element. Consumers can easily find fun and entertaining IT gadgets everywhere to use chat bots for fun. Although chat bots are have a good command of natural languages, it is still far from ideal. As we witnessed from previous virtual agent mishaps, promoting chat bots as a buddy for conversations or passing time could backfire.

LIMITATIONS AND FUTURE STUDIES

As with most research, the present study also has some limitations. First, this study used small student samples. Although the student samples fall into the typical social media users' age and education range, they were chosen from one of the most developed areas in the U.S., so it is difficult to generalize the results. Future study of instant messaging chat bots could include participants in various locations in the nation and also non-students sample as well.

Second, this study selected two instant messaging chat bots, CNN News and Shopping Assistant, as examples given to participants. However, since some students were not very familiar with chat bots, these two examples could have influenced participants' perception of chat bots in general. The results showed that participants found chat bots to be useful and easy to use, but not necessarily enjoyable. It is unclear whether the low perception of enjoyment was partially because the sample chat bots showed conversations in practical use, rather than as pure entertainment. Therefore, future studies should include more diverse types of chat bots, such as those devoted to entertainment, news and shopping.

CONCLUSION

To conclude, this study was conducted to provide a better understanding of mobile consumers' perceptions of instant messaging chat bots, in order to contribute to the current mobile commerce literature and to help build efficient marketing strategies for practitioners. This study found that mobile consumers have used instant messaging chat bots and think chat bots are useful and easy to use. However, many of the subjects did not see chat bots as greatly entertaining and stopped using them after a few trials. The findings provide insight into mobile users that marketers should consider when launching their chat bots for promotion and customer service purposes.

REFERENCES

Bayerque, N. (2016). A short history of chat bots and artificial intelligence. *VentureBeat*. Retrieved July 31, 2017 from https://venturebeat.com/2016/08/15/a-short-history-of-chatbots-and-artificial-intelligence/

Bers, T. H. (1994). Exploring institutional images through focus group interviews. In N. Bennett, R. Glatter, & R. Levacic (Eds.), *Improving educational management through research and consultancy* (pp. 290–299). London: The Open University.

Bots, the next frontier. (2016). *The Economist*. Retrieved August 3, 2017 from https://www.economist.com/news/business-and-finance/21696477-market-apps-maturing-now-one-text-based-services-or-chatbots-looks-poised

Bruner, G. C. II, & Kumar, A. (2005). Explaining consumer acceptance of handheld Internet devices. *Journal of Business Research*, 5(58), 553–558. doi:10.1016/j.jbusres.2003.08.002

Caffyn, G. (2016). *Two months in: How the 1-800 Flowers Facebook bot is working out*. Retrieved July 24, 2017, from https://digiday.com/marketing/two-months-1-800-flowers-facebook-bot-working/

Carter, W. C., & Servat, H. J. (2005). *The Proust questionnaire*. New York: Assouline Publishing.

Chi, H. H. (2011). Interactive digital advertising vs. virtual brand community: Exploratory study of user motivation and social media marketing responses in Taiwan. *Journal of Interactive Advertising*, *12*(1), 44–61. doi:10.1080/15252019.2011.10722190

Chih-Chien, W., Hsu, Y., & Fang, W. (2005). Acceptance of technology with network externalities: An empirical study of internet instant messenger services. *Journal of Information Technology Theory and Application*, 6(4), 15.

Childers, T. L., Carr, C. L., Peck, J., & Carson, S. (2001). Hedonic and utilitarian motivations for online retail shopping behavior. *Journal of Retailing*, *77*(4), 511–535. doi:10.1016/S0022-4359(01)00056-2

Colby, K. M. (1981). Modeling a paranoid mind. *Behavioral and Brain Sciences*, *4*(4), 515–534. doi:10.1017/S0140525X00000030

Colby, K. M. (1974). Ten criticisms of parry. *ACM SIGART Bulletin*, (48), 5-9.

ComScore. (2016). U.S. Mobile App Report. *ComScore Whitepaper*. Retrieved June 04, 2017, from https://www.comscore.com/Insights/Presentations-and-Whitepapers/2016/The-2016-US-Mobile-App-Report

Constine, J. (2017, April 12). *Facebook Messenger hits 1.2 billion monthly users, up from 1B in July*. Retrieved June 04, 2017, from https://techcrunch.com/2017/04/12/messenger/

Davis, F. D. (1985). *A technology acceptance model for empirically testing new end-user information systems: Theory and results* (Doctoral dissertation). Massachusetts Institute of Technology.

Davis, F. D. (1989). Perceived usefulness, perceived ease of use, and user acceptance of information technology. *Management Information Systems Quarterly*, *13*(3), 319–340. doi:10.2307/249008

Davis, F. D., Bagozzi, R. P., & Warshaw, P. R. (1989). User acceptance of computer technology: A comparison of two theoretical models. *Management Science*, *35*(8), 982–1003. doi:10.1287/mnsc.35.8.982

Davis, F. D., Bagozzi, R. P., & Warshaw, P. R. (1992). Extrinsic and intrinsic motivation to use computers in the workplace. *Journal of Applied Social Psychology*, *22*(14), 1111–1132. doi:10.1111/j.1559-1816.1992.tb00945.x

De Angeli, A., Johnson, G. I., & Coventry, L. (2001, June). The unfriendly user: exploring social reactions to chatterbots. In *Proceedings of The International Conference on Affective Human Factors Design*, 467-474.

Firshein, S. (2010). Anna, IKEA's Chat bot, Graciously Answers Proust Questionnaire. *Curbed*. Retrieved September 19, 2017 from www.curbed.com/2010/9/23/10505206/anna-ikeas-chatbot-graciously-answers-proust-questionnaire

eGain. (2017). *Virtual Assistant*. Retrieved from http://www.egain.com/products/virtual-assistant-software/

Gefen, D., & Straub, D. W. (1997). Gender differences in the perception and use of e-mail: An extension to the technology acceptance model. *Management Information Systems Quarterly*, *21*(4), 389–400. doi:10.2307/249720

Gerset, A., & Vaidya, S. (2010). Next Generation Customer Service Strategies: Harnessing the Power of the Internet and Web 2.0 for Delivering Customer Care. *Telecom & Media Insights*, (52). Retrieved September 20, 2017 from https://www.capgemini-consulting.com/resource-file-access/resource/pdf/Next_Generation_Customer_Service_Strategies.pdf

Gilliland, N. (2016). Domino's introduces 'Dom the Pizza Bot' for Facebook Messenger. *Econsultancy*. Retrieved September 22, 2017 from https://www.econsultancy.com/blog/68184-domino-s-introduces-dom-the-pizza-bot-for-facebook-messenger

Gilliland, N. (2016). What are chat bots and why should marketers care? *Econsultancy*. Retrieved September 22, 2017 from https://econsultancy.com/blog/67894-what-are-chat bots-and-why-should-marketers-care/

Gordon, N. (n.d.). What are the Differences between a Chat botWith and Without A.I.? *Century Soft Blog*. Retrieved August 3, 2017 from https://www.centurysoft.com/blog/differences-between-chat-bot-with-and-without-ai.html

Guynn, J. (2017). Facebook Messenger takes another swipe at bots. *USA Today*. Retrieved August 3, 2017 from https://www.usatoday.com/story/tech/news/2017/04/18/facebook-messenger-takes-another-swipe-chat-bots/100596798/

Ha, S., & Stoel, L. (2009). Consumer e-shopping acceptance: Antecedents in a technology acceptance model. *Journal of Business Research*, *62*(5), 565–571. doi:10.1016/j.jbusres.2008.06.016

Hajli, M. N. (2014). A study of the impact of social media on consumers. *International Journal of Market Research*, *56*(3), 387–404. doi:10.2501/IJMR-2014-025

Hassanein, K., & Head, M. (2007). Manipulating perceived social presence through the web interface and its impact on attitude towards online shopping. *International Journal of Human-Computer Studies*, *65*(8), 689–708. doi:10.1016/j.ijhcs.2006.11.018

Heath, A. (2017). Mark Zuckerberg wants Facebook to move faster at making money off Messenger and there's a good reason why. *Business Insider*. Retrieved July 27, 2017 from http://www.businessinsider.com/zuckerberg-facebook-move-faster-monetizing-messenger-2017-7

Hill, J., Ford, W. R., & Farreras, I. G. (2015). Real conversations with artificial intelligence: A comparison between human–human online conversations and human–chat botconversations. *Computers in Human Behavior*, *49*, 245–250. doi:10.1016/j.chb.2015.02.026

Huddelston, T., Jr. (2016). Now You Can Order Pizza Hut on Twitter and Facebook, Too. *Fortune*. Retrieved from http://fortune.com/2016/07/13/pizza-hut-chat bot-twitter-facebook/

Huge. (2004). IKEA Launches AI Customer Service Assistant. *Huge*. Retrieved August 28, 2017 from www.hugeinc.com/news/ikea-launches-artificial-intelligence-driven-customer-service-assistant

Hwang, Y. (2010). The moderating effects of gender on e-commerce systems adoption factors: An empirical investigation. *Computers in Human Behavior*, *26*(6), 1753–1760. doi:10.1016/j.chb.2010.07.002

If only I were. (2008, September 16). Chat with Sarah – the future of automated help [Blog Post]. Retrieved from https://subjunctive.wordpress.com/2008/09/16/chat-with-sarah-the-future-of-automated-help/

Innovation. (2016). 51 Corporate Chat bots Across Industries Including Travel, Media, Retail, And Insurance. *CBinsights*. Retrieved September 22, 2017 from https://www.cbinsights.com/research/corporate-chat bots-innovation/

Jia, J. (2003). *CSIEC (Computer simulator in educational communication): An intelligent web-based teaching system for foreign language learning*. arXiv preprint cs/0312030

Kerly, A., Hall, P., & Bull, S. (2007). Bringing chat bots into education: Towards natural language negotiation of open learner models. *Knowledge-Based Systems*, *20*(2), 177–185. doi:10.1016/j.knosys.2006.11.014

Kowalski, S., Pavlovska, K., & Goldstein, M. (2009, July). Two case studies in using chat bots for security training. In *IFIP World Conference on Information Security Education* (pp. 265-272). Springer.

Lederer, A. L., Maupin, D. J., Sena, M. P., & Zhuang, Y. (2000). The technology acceptance model and the World Wide Web. *Decision Support Systems*, *29*(3), 269–282. doi:10.1016/S0167-9236(00)00076-2

Lee, B. (2017). All Talk: How Chat bots And AI Will Transform The Way We Do Business. *Forbes*. Retrieved July 20, 2017, from https://www.forbes.com/sites/forbestechcouncil/2017/03/16/all-talk-how-chat bots-and-ai-will-transform-the-way-we-do-business/#7fd34e67280e

Lu, Y., Zhou, T., & Wang, B. (2009). Exploring Chinese users' acceptance of instant messenger using the theory of planned behavior, the technology acceptance model, and the flow theory. *Computers in Human Behavior*, *25*(1), 29–39. doi:10.1016/j.chb.2008.06.002

Network Working Group. (1973). RFC 439, PARRY Encounters the DOCTOR. *The Internet Engineering Task Force (Internet Society)*. Retrieved from http://tools.ietf.org/html/rfc439

Mandilas, A., Karasavvoglou, A., Nikolaidis, M., & Tsourgiannis, L. (2013). Predicting Consumer's Perceptions in On-line Shopping. *Procedia Technology*, *8*, 435–444. doi:10.1016/j.protcy.2013.11.056

Marcus, D. (2016). Messenger Platform at F8. *Facebook Newsroom*. Retrieved July 21, 2017, from https://newsroom.fb.com/news/2016/04/messenger-platform-at-f8/

Marr, B. (2014). Dear IKEA: Your Customer Service Is Terrible. *LinkedIn*. Retrieved September 19, 2017 from www.linkedin.com/pulse/20140325060328-64875646-dear-ikea-your-customer-service-is-terrible/

O'Neill, S. (2016). Kayak debuts an ambitious Facebook Messenger bot. *tnooz*. Retrieved July 25, 2017 from https://www.tnooz.com/article/kayak-facebook-messenger-bot/

Pavlou, P. A. (2003). Consumer acceptance of electronic commerce: Integrating trust and risk with the technology acceptance model. *International Journal of Electronic Commerce*, *7*(3), 101–134.

Pew Research Center. (2017). *Social Media Fact Sheet*. Pew Research Center Internet & Technology. Retrieved from September 9, 2017 from http://www.pewinternet.org/fact-sheet/social-media/

Pikkarainen, T., Pikkarainen, K., Karjaluoto, H., & Pahnila, S. (2004). Consumer acceptance of online banking: An extension of the technology acceptance model. *Internet Research*, *14*(3), 224–235. doi:10.1108/10662240410542652

Ping, L. C., & Chee, T. S. (2009). Online discussion boards for focus group interviews: An exploratory study. *Journal of Educational Enquiry*, *2*(1).

Rao, A. (2017). Why the Facebook Messenger Bot Platform was a Failure. *Medium*. Retrieved July 25, 2017 from https://medium.com/voicelandia/why-the-facebook-messenger-bot-platform-is-a-failure-so-far-d305b2d4e1df

Rawlins, L. K. (2016, April 13). Facebook chat bots to replace call centres. *iTWeb*. Retrieved June 04, 2017, from http://www.itweb.co.za/index.php?option=com_content&view=article&id=151438

Rauniar, R., Rawski, G., Yang, J., & Johnson, B. (2014). Technology acceptance model (TAM) and social media usage: An empirical study on Facebook. *Journal of Enterprise Information Management, 27*(1), 6–30. doi:10.1108/JEIM-04-2012-0011

Ramayah, T., & Ignatius, J. (2005). Impact of perceived usefulness, perceived ease of use and perceived enjoyment on intention to shop online. *ICFAI Journal of Systems Management, 3*(3), 36–51.

Salandra, G. (2017). China, WeChat, and the Origins of Chat bots: What we can learn from the successes and shortcomings of the popular platform. *Chat botsmagazine.* Retrieved September 24, 2017 from https://chatbotsmagazine.com/china-wechat-and-the-origins-of-chatbots-89c481f15a44

Sharkey, J. (2008). A Virtual Travel Agent with All the Answers. *The New York Times.* Retrieved September 19, 2017 from http://www.nytimes.com/2008/03/04/business/04road.html

Schlicht, M. (2017). The Complete Beginner's Guide To Chat bots. *Chat Bots Magazine.* Retrieved September 30, 2017 from https://chatbotsmagazine.com/the-complete-beginner-s-guide-to-chatbots-8280b7b906ca

Scott, D. (2008). Anna from IKEA is intellectually challenged (but she has a sense of humor). *Webinknow.* Retrieved September 19, 2017 from www.webinknow.com/2008/08/anna-from-ikea.html

Jin, S.-A. A., & Bolebruch, J. (2009). Avatar-Based Advertising in Second Life. *Journal of Interactive Advertising, 10*(1), 51–60. doi:10.1080/15252019.2009.10722162

Shawar, B. A., & Atwell, E. (2002). *A comparison between ALICE and Elizabeth chat botsystems.* University of Leeds, School of Computing research report 2002.19.

Shawar, B. A., & Atwell, E. (2007). Chat bots: are they really useful? *LDV Forum, 22*(1), 29-49.

Sokolovska, A. (2016). From E-Commerce to Conversational Commerce: Chat bots and Virtual Assistant. *Guided Selling.* Retrieved September 30, 2017 from https://www.guided-selling.org/from-e-commerce-to-conversational-commerce/

Steiner, I. (2011). Emma virtual assistant comes to eBay. *eCommerceBytes.* Retrieved September 4, 2017 from http://www.ecommercebytes.com/C/abblog/blog.pl?/pl/2011/1/ 1296444129.html

Tate, A. (2016). The 5 Most Inspiring Chat bots On Facebook Messenger. *AdEspresso.* Retrieved July 25, 2017 from https://adespresso.com/academy/blog/5-inspiring-chat bots-facebook-messenger/

Venkatesh, V. (2000). Determinants of perceived ease of use: Integrating control, intrinsic motivation, and emotion into the technology acceptance model. *Information Systems Research, 11*(4), 342–365. doi:10.1287/isre.11.4.342.11872

Wakefield, J. (2016). Would you want to talk to a machine? *BBC News.* Retrieved August 28, 2017 from http://www.bbc.com/news/technology-36225980

Weizenbaum, J. (1966). ELIZA—a computer program for the study of natural language communication between man and machine. *Communications of the ACM, 9*(1), 36–45. doi:10.1145/365153.365168

Ye, G., & van Raaij, W. F. (1997). What inhibits the mere-exposure effect: Recollection or familiarity? *Journal of Economic Psychology, 18*(6), 629–648. doi:10.1016/S0167-4870(97)00027-5

Zagorsky, J. (2015). Almost 90% of Americans Have Unlimited Texting. *Instant Census.* Retrieved September 25, 2017 from https://instantcensus.com/blog/almost-90-of-americans-have-unlimited-texting

Zajonc, R. B. (1968). Attitudinal effects of mere exposure. *Journal of Personality and Social Psychology, 9*(2), 1.

KEY TERMS AND DEFINITIONS

Artificial Intelligence: Intelligence displayed by computer program or machine that mimics human intelligence.

Avatar: A virtual character that represents human beings or human-like creatures.

Chat Bot: A computer program that imitates human conversations through text or voice.

Instant Messaging: Online messaging system that sends messages in real time over the internet.

Social Media: Online community where users share information, idea, photos, messages.

Technology Acceptance Model: A theory that suggests factors that influence users' decisions whether they use and accept the new technology.

Virtual Assistant: Another name of chat bots.

This research was previously published in Smart Marketing With the Internet of Things; pages 164-184, copyright year 2019 by Business Science Reference (an imprint of IGI Global).

Chapter 37
Twitter Based Capital Market Analysis Using Cloud Statistics

Sangeeta Gupta

https://orcid.org/0000-0001-9867-1440

Vardhaman College of Engineering, Hyderabad, India

Rajanikanth Aluvalu

https://orcid.org/0000-0001-8508-6066

Vardhaman College of Engineering, Hyderabad, India

ABSTRACT

People in the modern world are attracted towards smart working and earning environments rather than having a long-term perception. The goal of this work is to address the challenge of providing better inputs to the customers interested to investing in the share market to earn better returns on investments. The Twitter social networking site is chosen to develop the proposed environment as a majority of the customers tweet about their opinions. A huge set of data across various companies that take inputs from Twitter are processed and stored in the cloud environment for efficient analysis and assessment. A statistical measure is used to signal the worth of investing in a particular stock based on the outcomes obtained. Also, rather than ignoring the missing values and unstructured data, the proposed work analyzes every single entity to enable the customers to take worthy decisions. Tweets in the range of 1 to 100,000 are taken to perform analysis and it is observed from the results that for a maximum of 100,000 tweets, the number of missing is identified as 2,524 and the statistical measure to fill in the missing values is calculated based on the particular missing data record, the count of all data records, and the total number of records. If the outcome of the measure is obtained as a negative, then proceeding with an investment is not recommended. The findings of this work will help the share market investors to earn better profits.

DOI: 10.4018/978-1-7998-9020-1.ch037

INTRODUCTION

People in the modern world are attracted towards smart working and earning environment rather than having a long-term perception. This opinion is applicable to the share or stock market consortium where based on the trends in the market, shareholders make investments and undergo through huge profits if they are knowledgeable about the company's stock values. Otherwise, they have to incur heavy losses and may lose lifelong savings. This article addresses the question of incurring profit or loss based on public opinion, up on proceeding with the decision to invest in the share market consortium. The majority of the works in literature address the smart investment decisions based on opinion mining, sentiment analysis, stock exchange data, etc. In either of these domains, either the preprocessing technique applied to clean the data is time consuming or the missing data, though large in number, is ignored.

The nature of large amounts of data emerging from any social networking or e-commerce websites which may be required by the industries, government organizations, educational institutions, financial houses etc. contains a mixture of structured, semi-structured and unstructured text content. It is difficult to analyze the semi-structured data in the form of XML tags, and unstructured data in the form of audio files, video files, pdf documents etc. Hence, before mining data of any kind to make suitable predictions, it is essential to extract the structured format of data.

Stock market analysis, which is the evaluation of a market as a whole, is done to take a proper decision to incur better profits by investing in a suitable firm (Stock Analysis, 2018). India's premier stock exchanges are the Bombay Stock Exchange and the National Stock Exchange (https://economictimes. indiatimes.com/definition/stock-market).

There are 2 ways in which the analysis can be carried out. The first is a fundamental analysis, where in the country's economic and financial conditions are assessed to make a decision about investment based on the balance sheet, profit and loss statements etc. On the other side, there is technical analysis, which is based on the supply-demand analysis and historic data analysis independent of the financial aspects around. Customer can choose a suitable one based on the knowledge levels acquired, trend analysis and formula to achieve better return on investments (What is Technical & Fundamental Analysis, 2018). In addition to the focus on trends in stock market, it is also essential to gather inputs on market resiliency, which is the worth of processing a transaction with a minimal impact on the cost factor, in accordance with the elasticity of supply and demand in the market (Wanzala et al., 2018).

Opinion mining, which is also known as sentiment analysis, is familiarly used to detect the contextual polarity of a word based on positive, negative and neutral outcomes. Based on the reviews of a particular product like electronic gadgets, wrist watches, wall decorators etc. in the social networking websites, a person may prefer to purchase it. This approach works well for a limited set of products and a limited set of companies forecasting the reviews using available tools and techniques. Positive feedbacks obtained on a particular product will attract huge set of audience to go ahead with the review decisions, there by strengthening the necessity to use the product. At the other end, if the feedback is negative, it enables the designers of the product to re-iterate on the working model and overcome the flaws (Ingle et al., 2015). However, there is a limitation on the number of tuples or records being mined to achieve better accuracy.

To perform sentiment analysis on Twitter data, the relevant API is used that enables the developers to access nearly 1% of tweets at a particular timestamp, based on an appropriate keyword. A tweet usually comprise of plain text, emoticons, user name, location and time stamp as retrieved by the Twitter API (Barskar & Phylre, 2017). This API is available to handle the missing tweets by ignoring them, which if in large numbers, leads to inappropriate decisions on investments.

Biggies around the world like Google, Microsoft, Facebook, Yahoo, etc., provided a wide prospect to deal with Twitter streaming data. Steps are formulated to carry out the analysis on any local machine. The only pre-requirement for a user is to have a Twitter account. It is also essential for the user to create a namespace, resource group, event group and obtain the access permissions to the same. Once the required groups are created, a stream analytics job can be created where it is essential to specify the nature of input parameters, query and output sink (Real-time Twitter sentiment analysis in Azure Stream Analytics, 2017).

Extensive research is carried out using the advanced technologies like machine learning, neural networks, Bayesian classification, support vector machine etc. to yield better profitability by investing into suitable firms (Atkins et al., 2018). However, in the works: (What is Technical & Fundamental Analysis of Share Market, 2018; Wanzala et al., 2018; Ingle et al., 2015; Barskar & Phulre, 2017; Real-time Twitter sentiment analysis in Azure Stream Analytics, 2017; Atkins et al., 2018) to perform analysis on huge data gathered across Twitter, Yahoo! financial website, etc., a set of missing values were ignored. This may result in improper interpretations signifying the incompleteness of the prior works as in (Atkins et al., 2018).

Towards this end, the goal of this work is to address the challenge of providing better inputs to the customers interested to invest in the share market based on social networking site outcomes, in order to earn better returns on investment.

The ideology of this article is organized as follows: The first section is the introduction that highlights the significance of acquiring valid inputs about stock market to attain better returns, intent of opinion mining, integration of tweets for stock analysis. The second section expounds the related works. The third section promotes the need to design the proposed model in the field of Twitter-based stock market analysis. The forth section presents an experimental evaluation to show the effectiveness of the proposed work and finally fifth section concludes the work by igniting with the future directions.

RELATED WORK

The natures of input parameters to perform an effective analysis vary from one author's perception to the other. The range of input data set also varies from a hundred to millions of records estimating statistical analysis for tweets with missing and incomplete set of characters.

The authors in (Dickinson & Hu, 2015) present a correlation between Twitter sentiments and stock market prices for a set of popular companies where the user can make a decision to invest their money in a suitable firm based on the nature of the outcomes that tend towards being positive, negative or neutral. Though the result yield to benefit customers interested in the companies analyzed in this work, there are a group of adversaries who switch to a completely different set of companies based on historic feedbacks obtained.In such case, the correlation cannot be estimated in an accurate way.

The authors in (Azar et al., 2016) project the significance and necessity of new tools and techniques to make valuable predictions based on social media tweets about share market investments. A polarity score metric is assigned to each tweet to identify the misclassified tweets and remove them from the data to be analyzed. However, a collection of models designed in this work do not represent the beneficiaries who can attain the developed benefits.

The authors in (Venkata et al., 2016) expounded the significance of public opinion collected through Twitter social networking site to proceed ahead with the decision to invest in a particular company's stock market. However, only a limited set of instances (nearly 355) with only 3 attributes were taken to make the predictions about investment. This number is very small which may not be appropriate to perform analysis on voluminous bigdata generated in the modern world.

The authors in (Gabrovsek et al., 2017) present an analysis of Twitter sentiments of about 30 companies over duration of nearly 3 years. As the share market is fluctuating every minute of the day, it is critical to make a decision about the suitable firm for investments to yield better results. Major attention is given to the announcements made before and after the closure of market. Event study is carried out to identify and group the external events. However, there is no trace of the dataset size and application of methodology to bigdata sets.

The authors in (Nayak et al., 2016) expound the complexity behind fine grained accessibility to predict rise and fall of stock market trends. Predictive analysis is carried to figure out the daily and monthly trend correlation for a particular stock market. Historical and social media data are used to predict the trends using supervised learning algorithm. However, a limited set of instances (nearly 300) are used to execute the experimentation on Hadoop open source platform, which is unsuitable to deal with such less data volume.

Extensive literature exists to analyze a varying number of tweets ranging from hundred's to millions to draw a relation among the tweets and market trends. However, most of the works as coined in (Dickinson & Hu, 2015; Azar et al., 2016; Sasank et al., 2016; Gabrovesk et al., 2017; Nayak et al., 2016) either deal directly with the tweet that is a combination of a variety of symbols, or ignore the missing values to perform a quick analysis. Hence, in the proposed work, the incompleteness identified in the literature dealing with stock market-based Twitter data analysis is overcome through a statistical measure.

PROPOSED WORK

The goal of this work is to address the challenge of providing better inputs to the customers interested to invest in the share market to earn better returns on investment. Twitter social networking site is chosen to develop the proposed environment as majority of the customers tweet about their opinions on investments, better money-making policies and strategies, etc., which turn to be beneficial to a huge set of investors around the world.

In this work, a huge set of data across various companies is processed and stored in cloud environment for efficient analysis and assessment. Rather than restricting the data collection to a set of stock market-based companies, a wide collection of companies is considered to provide an accurate and efficient analysis. This data is collected through web crawler that enables to speed up the rate of data collection. The proposed architectural design is depicted in Figure 1.

Once data is gathered, it is dumped to a local repository, on which keyword-based filtering technique is applied to remove the irrelevant or absurd tweets. After this step, the data is cleaned up to a certain extent and now it is stored in cloud labelled as Twitter cloud1. This can be any storage supported by cloud like EC2, S3, and SSD etc. To develop the work, S3 is chosen to store huge data volumes. Then, the data is sent to a parser which is used to further check with any irrelevant keywords, mis-spelt or wrongly spelt words, etc., and then convert data of any type to structured format for efficient analysis. Once structured data is obtained, it is stored in Twitter cloud2 repository. Then, the proposed statistical measure is applied to determine the positive and negative intent of the tweet, which enable the customer to take a decision about proceeding with the investment with the obtained outcomes or to ignore as unsafe investment. This analysis is carried out for a huge set of data samples and serves as a useful input to the customers to take an appropriate decision.

A statistical measure is developed to signal the goodness of investing in a particular stock. Also, rather than ignoring the missing values and unstructured data, the proposed work attempts to analyze every single entity to enable the customers to take worthy decisions. Majority of the existing works either deal directly with the tweet that is a combination of a variety of symbols, or ignore the missing values to perform a quick analysis. These features may generate outcomes with missing or inaccurate data even after application of pre-processing techniques, that may cause false predictions where customers may give up incurring heavy losses.

Figure 1. Proposed architectural model

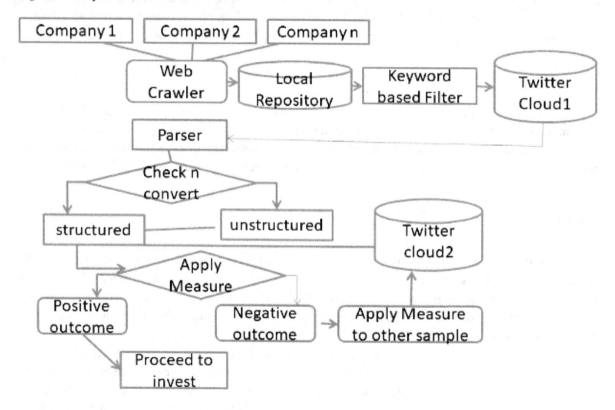

Experimental Evaluation

For huge amounts of growing data, it is essential to avoid performing sentiment analysis that is based on keyword-based opinion mining. Also, this will result in saving of computation time and storage space which is the need of the hour particularly for bigdata environment. Huge time can also be saved by minimizing focus on removing emoticons, special symbols, etc., by searching for them by entire data scan. Instead, it is preferable to convert the symbols, audio, video (any unstructured data) into structured format and then perform analysis on obtained tweets through the outcomes based on statistical measures.

Statistical Analysis

A simple, yet interesting measure is developed to analyze the positivity of tweet to proceed ahead with the major investment-based decision of an individual. This measure is represented statistically in terms of below defined steps:

1. Initially, data of any kind either a character or a string or unstructured document is converted to numeric form through a hard code in python language. The numeric equivalents are obtained based on ASCII equivalents;
2. In step 1, if there are any missing values identified, then the statistical formula to fill in the missing values is represented as:

$$Si = \sum (xi+c)/n$$

where 'xi' is the ith data record, 'c' is the count of the valid data records suitable for analysis, and 'n' is the total number of data records.

3. Once the missing values are filled in with the formula stated in step 2, the statistical measure is applied to identify the positivity of the outcome using the formula:

Statistical measure $S = (X+Si+c)/n$

Here Si is the statistical formula to fill in the missing value as formulated in step 2. If S > 0, then the tweet is considered as suitable for analysis.else, if S<0, then it yields negative correlation which specifies the unfitness of tweet to take part in the analysis. Likewise, a set of 1 million tweets (1 tweet = 1 data record) are analyzed and filtered to separate the positive from the negative one.

4. After successful completion of step 3, if the final count of valid and positive tweets is above 75 percent, the data is suitable to proceed ahead with the decision about investing in a particular firm irrespective of focus on the changing opinions of the public. Otherwise, if the count is less than 75 percent, then the decision of not moving ahead with investments in the publicly polled firms is taken to overcome the scenario of incurring heavy loss.'

Table 1. Statistical analysis table to identify valid tweets yielding to outcomes on investment decisions

Total No. of Tweets	Tweets With Missing Values	Si Values for Missing Tweets	S For Total No. of Valid Tweets	Decision to Invest
1	0	2	4(>0.75)	Proceed
100	12	18	1(>0.75)	Proceed
1000	23	46	1(>0.75)	Proceed
10000	167	410	0(<0.75)	Not Recommended
100000	2524	4568	0(<0.75)	Not Recommended

The results are formulated in Table 1.

Based on the proposed statistics as mentioned in table 1, decision can be efficiently made whether to proceed with investment in a particular stock or not. This analysis will enable a fresher to the field of stocks to proceed ahead with fruitful investments and incur reasonable profits.

CONCLUSION AND FUTURE WORK

In this work, tweets in the range of 1 to 100000 are taken to perform analysis and it is observed from the results that for a maximum of 100000 tweets, the number of missing once is identified as 2524 and the statistical measure to fill in the missing values is calculated based on the particular missing data record, count of all data records, total number of records. It is also observed that for tweets between 1 to 1000, there are less number if missing values, which does not affect the efficacy of positive or negative outcomes. If the outcome of the measure is obtained as negative, then proceeding with investment is not recommended. Otherwise, investors can proceed to earn better profits. The findings of this work will help the share market investors to earn better profits particularly when decision is to be made based on huge number of tweets ranging from 1001 till 100000. In future, this work can be extended further by integrating different filtering techniques to remove unwanted tweets and identifying the best one for huge data analysis exceeding 1 lakh tweets.

REFERENCES

Atkins, A., Niranjan, M., & Gerding, E. (2018). Financial news predicts stock market volatility better than close price. *The Journal of Finance and Data Science*, *4*(2), 120–137. doi:10.1016/j.jfds.2018.02.002

Azar, P., & Lo, A. W. (2016). The Wisdom of Twitter Crowds: Predicting Stock Market Reactions to FOMC Meetings via Twitter Feeds. *The Journal of Portfolio Management*, *42*(5), 123-134. doi:10.3905/jpm.2016.42.5.123

Barskar, A., & Phulre, A. (2017). Opinion Mining of Twitter Data using Hadoop and Apache Pig. *International Journal of Computers and Applications*, *158*(9).

Dickinson, B., & Hu, W. (2015). Sentiment Analysis of Investor Opinions on Twitter. *Social Networking*, *4*(3), 62–71. doi:10.4236n.2015.43008

Gabrovsek, P., Aleksovski, D., Mozetic, I., & Grčar, M. (2017). Twitter sentiment around the Earnings Announcement events. *PLoS One*, *12*(2), e0173151. doi:10.1371/journal.pone.0173151 PMID:28235103

Github. (n.d.). Real-time Twitter sentiment analysis in Azure Stream Analytics. Microsoft. Retrieved from https://github.com/MicrosoftDocs/azure-docs/blob/master/articles/stream-analytics/stream-analytics-twitter-sentiment-analysis-trends.md

India Times. (n.d.). Definition stock market. Retrieved from https://economictimes.indiatimes.com/definition/stock-market

Ingle, A., Kante, A., Samak, S., & Kumari, A. (2015). Sentiment analysis of twitter data using hadoop. *International Journal of Engineering Research and General Science*, *3*(6).

Investopedia. (n.d.). Stock analysis. Retrieved from https://www.investopedia.com/terms/s/stock-analysis.asp

Nayak, A., Pai, M. M. M., & Pai, R. M. (2016). Prediction Models for Indian Stock Market. *Procedia Computer Science*, *89*, 441–449. doi:10.1016/j.procs.2016.06.096

Pagolu, V. S., Kamal, N. R. C., Panda, G., & Majhi, B. (2016). Sentiment Analysis of Twitter Data for Predicting Stock Market Movements. In *Proceedings of the International conference on Signal Processing, Communication, Power and Embedded System (SCOPES)* (pp. 1345-1350). 10.1109/SCOPES.2016.7955659

Wanzala, R. W., Muturi, W., & Olweny, T. (2018). Market resiliency conundrum: Is it a predicator of economic growth. *The Journal of Finance and Data Science*, *4*(1), 1–15. doi:10.1016/j.jfds.2017.11.004

Chapter 38

Snacking Around the World:
Evolving an Inductive Image Categorization and Research Query Approach for Image Sets From Social Media

Shalin Hai-Jew

Kansas State University, USA

ABSTRACT

Social media platforms enable access to large image sets for research, but there are few if any non-theoretical approaches to image analysis, categorization, and coding. Based on two image sets labeled by the #snack hashtag (on Instagram), a systematic and open inductive approach to identifying conceptual image categories was developed, and unique research questions designed. By systematically categorizing imagery in a bottom-up way, researchers may (1) describe and assess the image set contents and categorize them in multiple ways independent of a theoretical framework (and its potential biasing effects); (2) conceptualize what may be knowable from the image set by the defining of research questions that may be addressed in the empirical data; (3) categorize the available imagery broadly and in multiple ways as a precursor step to further exploration (e.g., research design, image coding, and development of a research codebook). This work informs the exploration and analysis of mobile-created contents for open learning.

INTRODUCTION

In a common conceptualization of the different phases of the World Wide Web, Web 1.0 was about the Read Web, Web 2.0 as the Read/Write Web or Social Web (with users writing to the Web by sharing contents socially), and Web 3.0 is the machine-readable Web, which enables computers to exchange data in an automated way via web services. At every stage, new technological affordances have enabled people to interact with each other and with each other's data in new ways. In parallel with these changes, more

DOI: 10.4018/978-1-7998-9020-1.ch038

and more people have been going online. According to Internet Live Stats, there are 3.3 billion Internet users in the world as of late 2015. An estimated 74% of all Internet users also use social networking sites ("Social Networking Fact Sheet," January 2014). By 2016, it is estimated that there will be some two billion social network users globally (Bennett, 2013). With so many people communicating online, social media platforms are rollicking spaces for various types of research.

With the wide availability of publicly-released imagery from content-sharing social media platforms (and other types), researchers have access to an abundance of information-carrying still images for their potential work. However, in the research literature, there is little in the way of non-theoretical approaches for organizing and coding such visuals for research applications. Having a systematic way to summarize image set data may be useful not only for data organization purposes but to potentially enhance research design, image coding, and the creation of a research codebook. Sets are simple groupings of objects, and new objects may be evaluated as to whether they belong in a set or not (a Boolean "true" or "false"). The basic rules of set-making are simple: the rationale for the set building should be clearly defined, and the sets themselves should be sufficiently comprehensive to include all potential members into one mutually exclusive category or another. To explore how this might work, one image set was extracted from Instagram, and the images were lightly analyzed to ultimately test three hypotheses.

Hypothesis 1: From a sufficient topic-based image set from social media, there will be emergent natural categorical breaklines that may be inductively observable by researchers (without *a priori* reference to theoretical frameworks).

Hypothesis 2: From a sufficient topic-based image set from social media, there will be some research questions that may be inductively and inferentially extracted by researchers.

Hypothesis 3: For research analysts using imagery from social media platforms, exploring some of the available imagery through categorization may enhance the work of research design, image coding, and developing a research codebook.

The first hypothesis is a precondition for inductive and emergent analysis of imagery. An underlying assumption is that digital images are socially created communications from people to people, and in that interpersonal dynamic, receivers of the image data may be culturally trained to identify meaning-based image clusters. A "breakline" is conceptualized as apparently natural points of separation or differentiation between image objects. The second hypothesis offers a kind of reverse engineering from data to potential askable questions. The third hypothesis is a broadscale one that encapsulates the first two and underpins the entire chapter. It is included here because it will need to be revisited once this initial exploration is complete.

To test these hypotheses, a real-world dataset of nearly 700 images and another of over 900 images were extracted from the Instagram image-sharing social media app in December 2015. The topic selected—based on convenience and inherent (apparent) simplicity—was #snack. The use of a hashtagged topic would mean that there would not be one "owner" of a social media account that would be the one sharing all the images; a diversity of voices would be enabled. The use of the #hashtag by whomever posted the image would indicate the users' sense of the particular topic (although multiple hashtagged labels may be applied to one image). This topic is something that people can relate to, as the practice of snacking likely cuts across geographies and cultures. [Some researchers have suggested that Instagram "is known to have high rates of photos that contain geotags" (Souza, de Las Casas, Flores, Youn, Cha, Quercia, & Almeida, 2015, p. 223), but that assertion was not directly attributed in the source.] Snacking is also a practice that is readily represented through imagery. The DownThemAll browser add-on was used to extract the image data (which is extracted from the most recent images in reverse chronological order); this tool requires that the target website be fully expanded in order to extracted the images as thumbnails, which means that only a small percentage of the collected images would be collected. (For a number of social media platforms, researchers who want to use an N=all must access imagery through commercial companies, and the N=all imagery and videos are hosted in the cloud and analyzed through "big data" methods and technologies.) While there have been recent advancements in autocoding of imagery (in terms of "machine vision" and various artificial intelligence and machine learning applications), all the work described here is manual but machine-enabled. This means that the approach is not as scalable as fully automated processes, but these approaches may be transferred to qualitative data analysis software with multiple coders (and the application of Cohen's Kappa to test for statistical similarity in coding), which may increase coding speed.

Figure 1. #snacks: A popular topic on Instagram

REVIEW OF THE LITERATURE

In October 2010, Instagram was founded by Kevin Systrom and Mike Krieger. It was conceptualized as an iOS app for posting photos from iPhones to user accounts. In 2012, it was acquired by Facebook for $1 billion, and it had 100 million active users at the time of sale. Instagram was seen as a software tool to enable access to the mobile marketplace. Using this camera phone mobile app, users of smartphones with camera capabilities may snap an image, apply some filters or effects, and then share broadly in a convenient and spontaneous way, using this app. In a generic sense, Instagram is a content-sharing social media platform and application. A more nuanced descriptor may be as a "photo-sharing social networking service" (PSNS). As a platform, it enables the sharing of short videos as well. In 2015, Instagram had 300 million users worldwide with 80 million pictures shared daily (Lee, Bakar, Dahri, & Sin, 2015, p. 133). Instagram's press page claims 400 million active users as of September 2015 ("Celebrating a Community of 400 Million," 2015). According to the Pew Internet Survey, some 28% of Internet users use Instagram. Instagram's users tend to be young: 55% within the 18 – 29 age group, 28% within 30 – 49 years old, 11% in the 50 – 64 age group, and 4% over 65 ("Instagram Demographics," Aug. 17, 2015). Instagram is known to be popular among "tweens" and "teens" (Derby, 2013, p. 161).

Compared to other online social networks (OSNs), Instagram tends to be used more for personal uses than professional ones (Lim, Lu, Chen, & Kan, 2015, p. 118), with its users "extremely active during weekends" (p. 117). In terms of cross-sharing information and contents, users of Instagram tend to overlap with Tumblr because of easy sharing mechanisms (Lim, Lu, Chen, & Kan, 2015, p. 115). The authors write:

Taking a closer look, we notice that Google+ exhibits higher levels of activity during working hours (09:00-18:00) on weekdays; but exhibits lower and more evenly distributed activity during and after working hours on weekends. Interestingly, Instagram shows an opposite trend, peaking in activity after working hours (>18:00) on weekdays, and showing a decline after working hours on weekends. This hints, albeit subtly, at the contrasting nature of these two social networks – Instagram is a platform more frequently used during nonworking hours, while Google+ is used more during working hours. (Lim, Lu, Chen, & Kan, 2015, p. 116)

Early work in visual studies suggested that people use photography for themselves (to serve memory, narrative, and identity) as well as socially, such as to sustain relationships, self-represent to others, and to express one's aesthetics, creativity, and point-of-view to others (Van House, 2007, p. 2718). More recently, researchers have identified four main motives for sharing photos through such sites: "informativeness, community support, status-seeking, and self-representation," with self-representation and status seeking as predominant motivations (Lee, Bakar, Dahri, & Sin, 2015, p. 132). How people self-present on social media has been analyzed to understand the personalities behind the social media accounts. For example, people who are narcissistic tend to be attention-seeking and exhibitionistic. Males who post selfies (photographic self-portraits) tend to rank high on narcissism metrics:

In two studies with a pooled sample of 1296 men and women, we tested the prediction that individuals who score high on four narcissism sub-scales (Self-sufficiency, Vanity, Leadership, and Admiration Demand) will be more likely to post selfies to social media sites than will individuals who exhibit low narcissism. We examined three categories of selfies: own selfies; selfies with a romantic partner; and group selfies, controlling for non-selfie photographs. Women posted more selfies of all types than did men. However, women's selfie-posting behavior was generally unrelated to their narcissism scores. In contrast, men's overall narcissism scores positively predicted posting own selfies, selfies with a partner, and group selfies. Moreover, men's Vanity, Leadership, and Admiration Demand scores each independently predicted the posting of one or more types of selfies. Our findings provide the first evidence that the link between narcissism and selfie-posting behavior is comparatively weak among women than men, and provide novel insight into the social motivations and functions of online social networking. (Sorokowski et al., 2015, p. 123)

As social beings, people often show a deep interest in other people. They are especially drawn to images of others' faces, which are rich in social details. Photos with faces were found to be "38% more likely to receive likes and 32% more likely to receive comments, even after controlling for social network reach and activity" based on study of a million-image set of Instagram images (Bakhshi, Shamma, & Gilbert, 2014, p. 965). Between 2012 and 2014, the number of selfies posted online has increased "900 times," with the most common sharers of selfies as young females ("except for certain countries such as Nigeria and Egypt that show male dominance") (Souza, de Las Casas, Flores, Youn, Cha, Quercia, & Almeida, 2015, p. 222). People's self-portraits draw outsized attention and communicate something about the individual but also his or her cultural context:

Selfies are an effective medium to grab attention; they generate on average 1.1–3.2 times more likes and comments than other types of content on Instagram. Compared to other content, interactions involving selfies exhibit variations in homophily scores (in terms of age and gender) that suggest they are becoming more widespread. Their style also varies by cultural boundaries in that the average age and majority gender seen in selfies differ from one country to another. (Souza et al., 2015, p. 221)

Even planetary scale data starts local and is grounded in the world and lived experiences. Beyond personal reasons for image sharing, many share online in order to promote word-of-mouth (WOM) enthusiasms about commercial brands, products and services; maintain relationships with customers; publicize commercial events, and ultimately present a positive public image. Images themselves may "trend" or attract intense broad popular attention for a period of time. Image trends result from two main factors:

Firstly, major social events such as protests, civil unrests, and festivals create image trends with many people sharing images related to the event. The second category is when a popular person posts a controversial or a unique image, tags of the image became a trend with many re-sharing the same image in quick succession due to the high interest. (Ahangama, 2014, p. 158)

Those who use social media often do not only use one platform exclusively. There are often cross-postings in order to drive traffic, particularly to image and video resources. For example, when an image is posted on Instagram, a summary and a URL (uniform resource locator) of this post can be shared on the Twitter microblogging automatically. On social media, the currency of value is often "attention," and the potential audiences for social media contents is, while potentially large, also inherently limited. In the vernacular, there are only 24 hours in a day. Images themselves may be memorable in an intrinsic way based on their features and human visual hard-wiring. Visual "interestingness" has been described as "the power of attracting or holding ones (sic) attention" (Amengual, Bosch, & de la Rosa, 2015, p. 65).

A grounded empirical study of the types of photos posted on Instagram, a research team identified eight photo categories: friends, food ("food, recipes, cakes, drinks, etc."), gadgets, captioned photos (with texts and memes), pets, activities, selfies (self-portraits), and fashion ("shoes, costumes, makeup, personal belongings, etc.") (Hu, Manikonda, & Kambhampati, 2014, p. 3). Many use hashtags on Instagram as "image annotation metadata," which describe image contents (Giannoulakis & Tsapatsoulis, 2015). Hashtagging is also used to collect related imagery based on common themes. While images may be shared for personal fulfillment reasons and for local objectives, socially shared images, singly and in collections, may also be used in a de-contextualized way. In other words, while image contents are shared in an ego-based and subjective context, the actual shared materials are also usable in an objective way.

The varying tagging policies (and their enforcement) on social media platforms affects how tagging may be understood. For example, Flickr released machine tagging which applies various tags based on machine vision. While these tags may be removed manually, they are applied by default. Instagram does not show tagging on the top level but does show some people's commenting, likes, and view counts. Research into tagging habits have shown that social networks may share "folk" tagging habits and terminology (Mika, 2005; Anagnostopoulos, Kumar, & Mahdian, 2008). (The labeling of social media contents with amateur-originated tags is known as folksonomic labeling. In this context, no formal taxonomy or formal ontology is used to label the contents. Rather, people use free-form and common language and whatever is top-of-mind to describe their uploaded imagery and videos. Free-text labels, while noisy, may be informative of user intentions and points-of-view, among other insights.)

Warming to the Topic

Finally, on social media, people have posted a variety of images of food. This has been called "foodtography" (a portmanteau term from "food" and "photography") as well as "foodagramming" (a blended word from "food" and "Instagramming") and resulted in the practice of sharing "food porn" (Salie, Dec. 1, 2013). Research suggests that there are intimate ties between images of food and people's lived behaviors (even such extremes of over-eating and non-eating). One researcher studied "pro-anorexia" and "food porn" on the Web and noted that while such depictions are virtual, they have potent impacts on people's physical selves. She writes:

It traces how eating in, and through, cyberspace shapes the biological materialities of bodies whilst also collapsing neat distinctions between offline and online worlds. Virtual vectors of spectating, salivating and digesting are disembodied and yet corporeal. Eating is seen to take place beyond and among bodies and to be dissipated both spatially and temporally. As such, cyberspace is outside and other to lived corporeality, and yet also folded into and productive of the intimate geographies and embodied subjectivities of everyday lives. As eating takes myriad forms across the de-materialised viscerality of the Internet, it also emerges as central to the production and 'matter(ing)' of cyberspace itself; this is (an) eating space in which what is eaten, by whom and with what bodies, perpetually shifts. Thus, seeking to contribute to geographical scholarship on affect and food, this paper engages with eating as both the subject of enquiry and also as a productive pathway into an interrogation of cyberspace and its place within the affective productions of the everyday. It suggests that this is a key site in which to explore the intimate socialities, materialities and biopolitics of food. (Lavis, 2015)

Another work involved the specific study of Instagram food posts and applied a computational method to extract nutritional information and calorific content. The researchers explored how the online community reacted to healthy vs. non-healthy food postings and found "Instagram as a platform where sharing of moderately healthy food content is common, and such content also receives the most support from the community" (Sharma & De Choudhury, 2015, p. 115). In contrast, a different research team studying Instagram images taken in restaurants in the U.S. actually found social approval for unhealthy foods high in sugar and fat (Mejova, Haddadi, Noulas, & Weber, 2015). Yet another clever project captured near real-time Instagrammed postings of restaurant-based food images and sentiment analysis of their comments in order to create maps of restaurants favored by local residents vs. those favored by travelers (Kuo, et al., 2014, p. 202); ultimately, this team is developing a social food recommender system based on shared imagery and messaging about food on Instagram. During their research, the team found that food was a very common subject of the images uploaded in Instagram. Further, they found that the tagging applied to the images tended towards inaccuracy. They wrote:

A large proportion of the images in social media contains food (e.g., more than 100 million images contains hashtag "food" in Instagram). To mine information from these images, it is insufficient to simply use tags to decide what is in the image since tags are really noisy (in our preliminary study, only about 30% of images tagged food on Instagram are correct). Therefore, we adopt state- of-the-art recognition method, convolution neural network (CNN), to recognize food in images. By analyzing different social media sources, we found that Instagram contains more images that can represent users' daily life, but images in Instagram also contain more noises (our experiment shows that about 26% of images tagged food are selfies instead of food images, while the same number is 7.5% in Flickr). (Kuo, et al., 2014, p. 203)

Still another engaging work involved the types of food images that 14-year-olds posted on Instagram with the finding that a majority of the images showed foods "high in calories but low in nutrients," and many images emulated "food advertisements" albeit with the suggestion of personalized peer recommendation (Holmberg, Chaplin, Hillman, & Berg, 2016, p. 121).

#Snack in Social Media

To be clear, this work does not engage the more serious issues of #snack(ing) or food. Rather, this is more of an incidental topic used to explore the open coding or inductive labeling of social imagery based on a common subject. So as to provide a sense of what #snack may look like, it may help to dip into several other social media platforms before using the dataset from Instagram to walk-through this approach. #snack images from Flickr were also considered for this research as a contrast to those from Instagram, but the researcher was unable to extract the necessary images for datasets. A brief note on Flickr is in order. Flickr was founded by Ludicorps in 2004 as a web service for image and video hosting to embed in blogs and social media. It was purchased by Yahoo in 2005. As of March 2013, Flickr had 87 million registered members (Jeffries, 2013). As of June 10, 2015, Flickr had 112 million users in 63 countries; this service featured a set of 10 billion images as of May 7, 2015 and over 3.5 million new photos shared daily (Smith, Aug. 10, 2015). Flickr has over two million groups (public and private) of users with shared interests.

Related Tags Networks on Flickr

In Figure 2, "#snack" is used as a seeding term to find co-occurring tags in Flickr. There are adjectives that describe various snacks ("delicious," "yummy," and "homemade"), references to locations ("china," "japan," "tokyo," and "street,"), time of day ("night,"), context ("travel,"), camera terms ("closeup," "macro," "bokeh," and "canon"), color references ("blue," "orange," yellow," and "red"), types of meals ("breakfast," "lunch," and "dinner"), ingredients ("butter," "cream," "chocolate," and "egg") as well as direct named foods ("candy," "chips," "cake," "pastry," "cookies," "fish," "popcorn," and "sweets").

The same #snack related tags network with static thumbnail imagery from Flickr is available in Figure 3.

Figure 2. #Snack related tags network on Flickr (1 deg.)

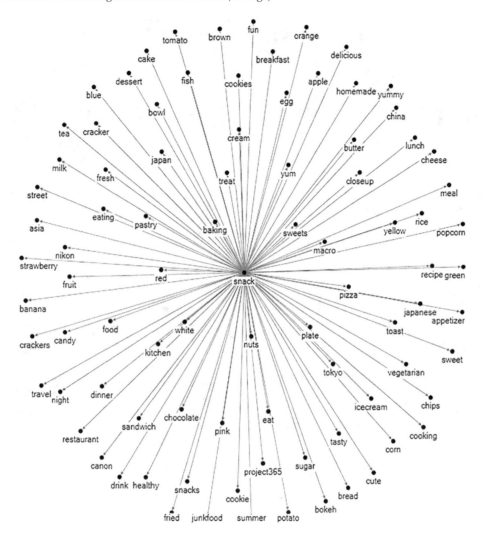

In terms of the graph metrics for the #snack related tags network on Flickr, please refer to Table 1. This related tags network contains 89 vertices (nodes). As with one-degree networks, the edges are all unique connecting dyadic pairs of nodes. The network graph itself is small, with a geodesic distance (graph diameter) of two.

At 1.5 degrees, the #snack related tags network on Flickr contains two clusters or groups (based on the Clauset-Newman-Moore clustering algorithm). This automated extraction of related tags enables a type of factor analysis. As such, the left group in Figure 4 seems to show direct food, and the right group seems to show more context and photographic details, broadly speaking.

In Figure 5, the 1.5-degree #snack related tags network on Flickr is seen as a network graph with extracted thumbnail imagery at the vertices. This image-rich visualization is more evocative.

The graph metrics for Figures 4 and 5 may be seen in Table 2. This table shows the 89 vertices connected by 2,623 unique edges. This graph has a maximum geodesic distance (graph diameter) of two, and an average geodesic distance of 1.5 hops.

Figure 3. #Snack related tags network on Flickr with thumbnail imagery (1 deg.)

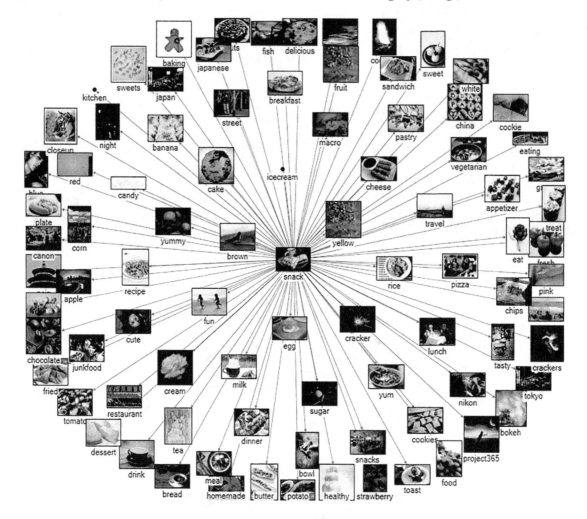

Article Networks on Wikipedia

Another way to look at how snacking instantiates on a social media platform is to explore "article networks" on Wikipedia. The English Wikipedia, built on the MediaWiki understructure, has 5,041,907 content articles and a total of 38,098,985 total pages ("Wikipedia:About," Dec. 24, 2015). These article networks are related pages that are hyperlinked on Wikipedia. As such, they work as semantic networks connecting article resources. The Wikipedia standards for creating pages and their work of peer reviewers and peer editors means that these networks tend to be more structured and less haphazard than tagging co-occurrence networks. In this case, "Snack_food" (https://en.wikipedia.org/wiki/Snack_food) is used as the seeding article. The resulting one-degree social graph is viewable in Figure 6.

The graph shows direct links to 121 other pages (vertices). These vertices refer to various food types and ingredients as well as some related activities. The graph metrics table for Figure 6 may be seen in Table 3.

Table 1. Graph metrics for the #snack related tags network on Flickr (1 deg.)

Graph Metric	Value
Graph Type	Directed
Vertices	89
Unique Edges	88
Edges With Duplicates	0
Total Edges	88
Self-Loops	0
Reciprocated Vertex Pair Ratio	0
Reciprocated Edge Ratio	0
Connected Components	1
Single-Vertex Connected Components	0
Maximum Vertices in a Connected Component	89
Maximum Edges in a Connected Component	88
Maximum Geodesic Distance (Diameter)	2
Average Geodesic Distance	1.955309
Graph Density	0.011235955
Modularity	Not Applicable
NodeXL Version	1.0.1.336

At 1.5 degrees, this article network becomes visually unintelligible. This graph has 8,478 nodes and 12,830 unique edges. The maximum geodesic distance (graph diameter) is four. The average geodesic distance between any two nodes is 3.67 hops. There are 37 groups in this network. The specific details of this latter article network may be seen in Table 4.

Another article network extraction was conducted using "List_of_brand_name_snack_foods" from Wikipedia (https://en.wikipedia.org/wiki/List_of_brand_name_snack_foods). This one-degree network shows the direct and defined out-links from the target page. This article-article network graph may be seen in Figure 7.

The graph metrics table for Figure 7 may be seen at Table 5. The graph itself has 192 vertices or nodes.

Now that there is a small sense of what #snack may look like on two different social media platforms—Flickr and Wikipedia—it would be helpful to shift to Instagram, which will be the source of the two target image sets.

EXTRACTED IMAGERY FOR OPEN AND INDUCTIVE ANALYSIS AND INITIAL CATEGORIZATION

Understanding what "sorts" of contents are in a social image set is a fundamental first step in harnessing those images for potential research use. As such, starting with something as simple as belongingness to various categories or image subsets is a good way to begin. The work of inducing sets from image collections is not defined in the academic research literature (as far as this author can tell). Researchers have made some headway in defining the work of inducing themes from texts, including informal approaches such as "pawing" and sorting through texts as a scrutiny technique (Ryan & Bernard, 2003, p. 88), as well as "eyeballing" with a practiced eye (p. 101). The method described here involves a rough-cut categorization in order to inductively extract image processing approaches. This approach does not preclude other approaches and is conceptualized as a way to get started.

As noted in the introduction, this work was created to test three hypotheses:

Hypothesis 1: From a sufficient topic-based image set from social media, there will be emergent natural categorical breaklines that may be inductively observable by researchers (without *a priori* reference to theoretical frameworks).

Hypothesis 2: From a sufficient topic-based image set from social media, there will be some research questions that may be inductively and inferentially extracted by researchers.

Hypothesis 3: For research analysts using imagery from social media platforms, exploring some of the available imagery through categorization may enhance the work of research design, image coding, and developing a research codebook.

Figure 4. #Snack related tags network on Flickr (1.5 deg.)

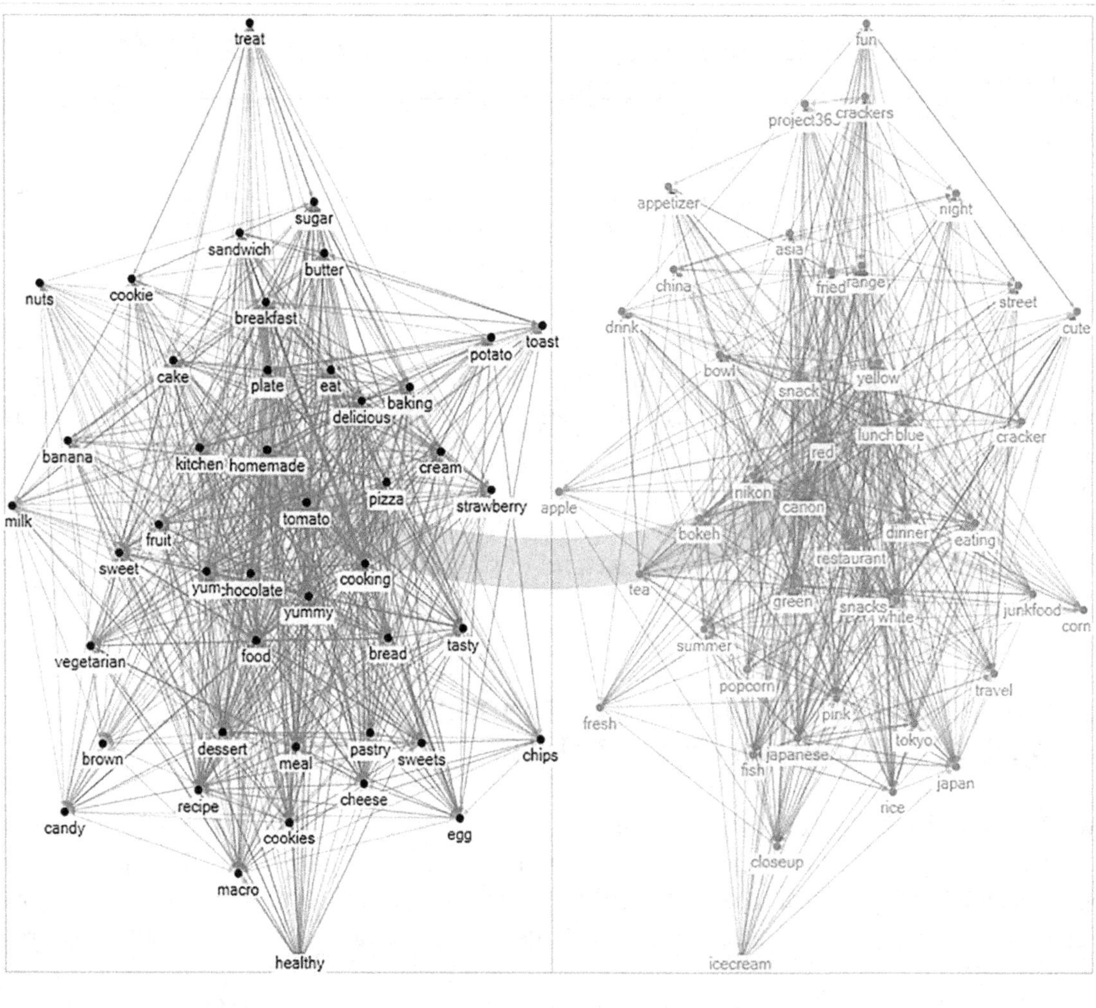

Figure 5. #Snack related tags network on Flickr with thumbnail imagery (1.5 deg.)

The designed approach was as follows (Figure 8): (1) data extraction plan, (2) data extraction, (3) data cleaning, (4) image categorization, and (5) results (to aid the research). Two main methods for categorizing the images are described. From this approach, researchers are conceptualized as being able to assess some of the types of questions that may be asked of the image data. To see how this would work, some datasets of images were extracted from Instagram.

In late December 2015, a first set of #snack-based imagery was extracted from Instagram (at https://www.instagram.com/explore/tags/snack/). At the time of the extraction, Instagram had 5,860,121 posts with that hashtag. The extraction itself (using the DownThemAll add-in on Firefox browser) was only 694 images, and these were not a de-duplicated set (there were a number of repeat images left in the set that was advertising "Get up to 10,000 followers"). Given the numbers, the 694 / 5,860,141 posts meant that only 0.000118427184602 of the full set was represented. The extracted images were those that were publicly released by the users of Instagram. No special sign-ins or verifications were needed to extract this data. A screenshot of the Instagram #snack page at the time of the first image extraction may be seen in Figure 9.

Table 2. Graph metrics for the #snack related tags network on Flickr (1.5 deg.)

Graph Type	Directed
Vertices	89
Unique Edges	2623
Edges With Duplicates	0
Total Edges	2623
Self-Loops	0
Reciprocated Vertex Pair Ratio	0.304975124
Reciprocated Edge Ratio	0.467403736
Connected Components	1
Single-Vertex Connected Components	0
Maximum Vertices in a Connected Component	89
Maximum Edges in a Connected Component	2623
Maximum Geodesic Distance (Diameter)	2
Average Geodesic Distance	1.470016
Graph Density	0.334908069
Modularity	Not Applicable
NodeXL Version	1.0.1.336

Three days after the first data extraction, some 922 images were extracted from a total set of 5,869,260 posts tagged with #snack. The base set contained some 9,000 more images than was seen three days earlier. This second set of #snack images represented 0.00015708965 of the full set. Two sets were drawn because such imagery is time-sensitive. While a close count was not done, having a more diverse number of images to begin with might aid in the hypothesis testing. A screenshot of the #snack landing page on Instagram (at the time of the second data extraction) may be seen in Figure 10.

It is often said that people eat first with their eyes, and from there, appetite follows. If that is so, many of the #snack images would likely spark appetite or even a deep hunger given the rabid "fan sharing" theme and observer empathy. The close-up food images are adoringly rendered (everyone is a "food artist"), with the apparent awareness of the high competition for the human gaze and "likes". If the image is a selfie, the person is often smiling and hand signaling to show enthusiasm (thumbs ups, victory signs); there are happy face buttons and happy emojis and lots of heart overlays to food images. Some express adoration for their own culinary skills. Some are clearly enthusiasts of certain raw and packaged snack foods. For example, there was an image of a girl wearing a big smile and a Bugle (a salty and crunchy corn-based snack) on each of her fingers. Another image showed a young female wearing a backpack that was actually a branded bag of snacks.

In a brief perusal of both image datasets from Instagram (see Figures 11 and 12), some insights became into focus. One observation is that people have broad interpretations of #snack, and the #snack itself is not always the focal point of the image. There were some who stayed within the spirit of #snack even as their focus went off-topic, but others were clearly using the popular hashtag to try to drive attention to their paid web-traffic-driving services.

Figure 6. "Snack_food" article network on Wikipedia (1 deg.)

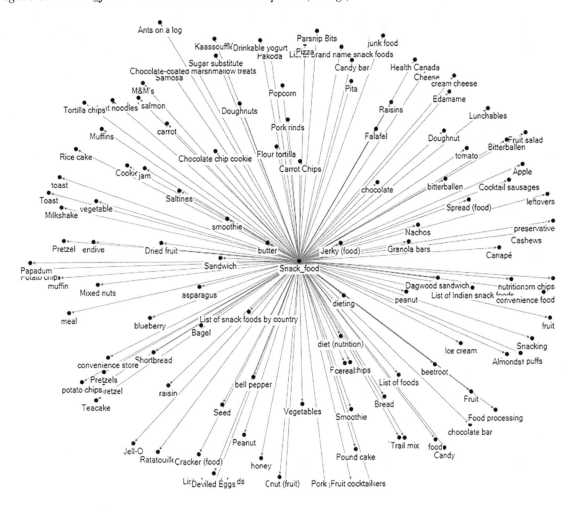

What were some image threads? There were clear differences between raw foods, individually prepared foods, restaurant foods, and packaged foods. Raw foods tended to be portrayed in a natural or peeled form and held in one or two hands (think lichee nuts, chestnuts, an uncooked yellow pepper, and others). Some images portrayed fresh edibles in-the-field at the time of harvest. Individually prepared foods were portrayed either in very tight close-in shots or plated and viewed from an eater point-of-view (POV). The images were taken at any part of the process, from harvesting raw materials for food preparation to purchasing items in stores to preparing and presenting the snacks. Some images were portrayed with some raw ingredients in the background. Others had unique flourishes, such as particular imprints or cutouts in pie shells. There were foods creatively modified, like cream-centered cookies rolled in frosting and sugary cupcake decorations. Restaurant foods were often shown as close-ups, with a selfie, with a dining partner, or in large people groups. Packaged foods often included the snack packaging in the image along with images of the particular snacks. Some packaged food images did not show the food… but rather just the packaging. There was one photo of a young man with a guitar in the background and a bag of snacks in the foreground.

Table 3. Graph metrics for the snack food article network on Wikipedia (1 deg.)

Graph Metric	Value
Graph Type	Directed
Vertices	121
Unique Edges	120
Edges With Duplicates	0
Total Edges	120
Self-Loops	0
Reciprocated Vertex Pair Ratio	0
Reciprocated Edge Ratio	0
Connected Components	1
Single-Vertex Connected Components	0
Maximum Vertices in a Connected Component	121
Maximum Edges in a Connected Component	120
Maximum Geodesic Distance (Diameter)	2
Average Geodesic Distance	1.967079
Graph Density	0.008264463
Modularity	Not Applicable
NodeXL Version	1.0.1.336

Table 4. Graph metrics for the "Snack_food" article network on Wikipedia (1.5 deg.)

Graph Metric	Value
Graph Type	Directed
Vertices	8478
Unique Edges	12830
Edges With Duplicates	0
Total Edges	12830
Self-Loops	1
Reciprocated Vertex Pair Ratio	0.002892433
Reciprocated Edge Ratio	0.005768181
Connected Components	1
Single-Vertex Connected Components	0
Maximum Vertices in a Connected Component	8478
Maximum Edges in a Connected Component	12830
Maximum Geodesic Distance (Diameter)	4
Average Geodesic Distance	3.671246
Graph Density	0.000178508
Modularity	Not Applicable
NodeXL Version	1.0.1.336

Figure 7. List_of_brand_name_snack_foods article network on Wikipedia (1 deg.)

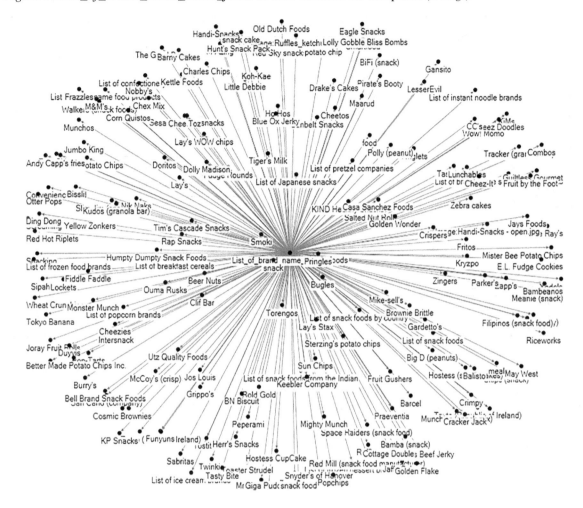

Some personal and commercial objectives could be inferred by the posing of the food images. There were straightforward images of snacks: a fruit and chocolate fondue setup, pigs-in-a-blanket, animal crackers mixed in with other crackers, and foodstuffs posed with flowers. Some were parts of personal stories, such as snack packages with messaging from a wedding.

There were joke images (with food peripherally related to the action)—a man in a Darth Vader mask drinking coffee and reading a newspaper at a table, a guy in a Storm Trooper costume looking at a lot of food on a counter. Another joke image was a baby sitting on a table with lots of opened snack packages spilled around him / her; here is a baby who knows how to eat (badly). There was a clever visual pun, with a cow notepad next to an apple and a coffee; in this image, the cartoonish cow looked like it was eyeing the food.

There were images which consisted of words—from a lit up neon "snack bar" sign to food business signage to just the term "Salapao" ("steamed bun" in Thai) alone.

Table 5. Graph metrics of List_of_brand_name_snack_foods article network on Wikipedia (1 deg.)

Graph Type	Directed
Vertices	192
Unique Edges	191
Edges With Duplicates	0
Total Edges	191
Self-Loops	0
Reciprocated Vertex Pair Ratio	0
Reciprocated Edge Ratio	0
Connected Components	1
Single-Vertex Connected Components	0
Maximum Vertices in a Connected Component	192
Maximum Edges in a Connected Component	191
Maximum Geodesic Distance (Diameter)	2
Average Geodesic Distance	1.979221
Graph Density	0.005208333
Modularity	Not Applicable
NodeXL Version	1.0.1.336

Figure 8. Basic steps in the inductive social image categorization process

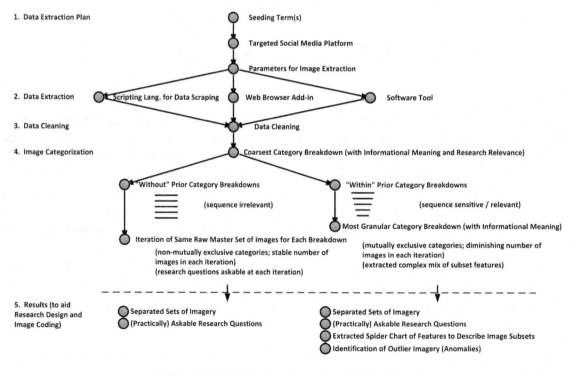

Basic Steps in the Inductive Social Image Categorization Process

Figure 9. A screenshot of the #snack Instagram page at the time of the first data capture

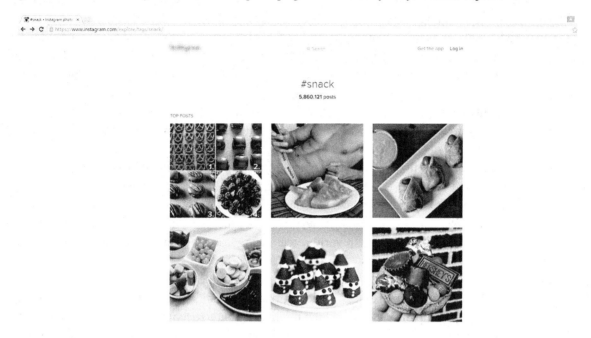

Figure 10. Screenshot of the #snack page on Instagram at the time of the second capture

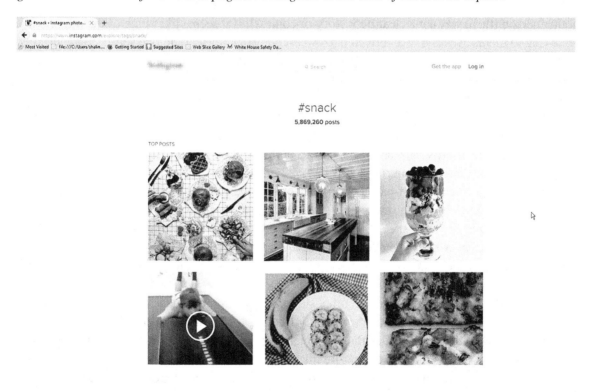

There were sometimes indications of narratives, of healthy eating (think thick green shakes and fresh fruits) but also of indulgence (doughnuts, deep fried fair food, and red meat). A number of people images showed people in exercise clothes in gyms. One such image had an overlay reading "Resolutions 2016." One image showed a thickly muscled man eating salad out of a bowl. Some labeled images seemed positioned to be memes. One showed a stack of colorful frosted doughnuts with the following message: "Is it too late now to say sorry…cuz I've eaten the equivalent weight of my body." The message was about the futility of suppressing difficult emotions by eating in a message tinted with humor. There were images with their own counter-messaging, such as splurge desserts with accompanying hashtags such as #backtothediet.

Some images showed attention to individual portion size, and others included whole meals (multiple sandwiches and drinks), and others showed large spreads of food for groups of eaters.

Occasionally, there were images uploaded in sequence…by the same social media account holder… and the sequences might tell a kind of story. In one, there was a recurring individual who appeared in the snack sequence, and she was pictured with various ice cream desserts. In another case, a gelatin candy was pictured in four consecutive images.

There were quite a few non-human #snack images. For example, there were various animals seen snacking: foxes, chipmunks, squirrels, deer, pelicans, pandas, rabbits, dogs, and hamsters. One image showed a crocodile coming up on a pelican, which might be about to become a "snack." One image was of Ken and Barbie dolls at a plastic snack booth. There were images of people with animals—feeding them snacks, for example. In one, a person and a horse were sharing the same slice of watermelon. In another, a woman wearing brown felt reindeer horns posed kissing an actual raw fish being held by another person (there was not a clear back story or context). If it seems like some of the image sharers are talking to themselves and to a defined narrowcast audience, they are in one sense. Many use Instagram to publicly share imagery through their own microblogging accounts and blogging accounts (with embedded images and embedded short videos).

Some images showed various contexts where foods are sold or served. There were photos of food aisles in grocery stores, vending machines, and various restaurants and eateries. Some were at 30,000 feet, one with a baby eating a snack while sitting in his father's lap in an airplane seat.

There were some short videos as well. One was about pouring syrup over a stack of pancakes. Another showed a baby having a tantrum when his food does not arrive in time. One individual proudly showed him taking a gigantic self-baked chocolate chip cookie out of the oven, writing "just made a big chocolate chip cookie." One video showing a man eating a packaged snack, was, inexplicably, sideways loaded (and uncorrected on the site). Another, inexplicably, was about an animal control officer poking a snake and falling backwards when the snake made a threatening rattle and struck out at him.

In terms of the imagery, there were differing levels of production values. Some images were clearly raw ones taken on-the-fly, such as close-up images of food and selfies with food. Others involved various degrees of food posing, lighting, layout, composition, artfulness, and image reprocessing. There were artificial images, such as one of a man apparently floating to return a milk to a refrigerator. Another photo-edited image showed a man dangling a miniaturized man as a morsel he was about to eat. There were also drawings and posters and composite imagery.

Technically, on the Instagram site, there was not apparently some basic type of machine de-duplication of imagery, given the spam repetition of the spam elicitation for people who might want to acquire 10,000 followers at a price and another "Get free followers!" This may be seen clearly in Figure 11. Also, there were non-snack images: photos of people in soft erotica poses, paper plate packaging, a person smoking, and stylized images of real estate. This would mean that data cleaning is a given before images may be categorized. Another technical observation is that Instagram cleanly manages differing image sizes, especially given the varying widths of the displayed images (while aspect ratio is protected). Also, each of the images have their own serial number based on how Instagram handles uploaded images. In terms of the data extractions, none of the comments were scraped, and none of the other tags were scraped (in this approach). While one could log in, click into each image, copy the comments, record the social media account from which the image was posted…and record the numbers of likes and so on, that was not done in this case.

Figure 11. Some of the scraped images from #snack on Instagram (first run)

There seemed to be two main ways to categorize the images. One would be to use an image set holistically and to divide that same set in a number of different ways in various image subsets (Figure 13).

For example, in the #snack image sets, they may be broken down in a variety of stand-alone ways. The various subsets of the images would all be drawn from the total image set, but not every image would necessarily make it into each image subset. A brainstorm of how this might look is available in Table 6.

In other words, a brainstorm of various types of potential subsets (based on different rules of subdivision) may be done without prior category dependencies. Each new categorization set is built from the pristine master set of images. Running the master set through each time enables researchers to ensure that there are as many categories as necessary to include as much of the pristine master set as possible. The real-world image set also may help in determining the coarseness or granularity of the categories. (It is feasible to have a category with only one exemplar if that example image is a highly anomalous one.) All subsets may have an "other" catch-all category. For the stand-alone subsets to work, there will need to be rules that define membership into that partition or grouping. If an image may meet several of the categories within the subset, the subset may need to be better defined to differentiate between the two potential groups (for example, if a snack food is salty, sweet, and sour).

Figure 12. Some of the scraped images from #snack on Instagram (second run)

The types of categories brainstormed may suggest certain askable questions. Brainstorming these broadly may enable ways to exploit the #snack imagery. Also, if the questions are unanswerable, at least the asking of the questions may enable tactical ways forward to finding out. If these questions are answered in other ways, the social media image stream may at least provide yet another data channel.

For example, snack food imagery from different brands (the last category in Table 6) may be analyzed with the following questions in mind:

- Based on the shared social imagery, what is the brand strategy for the particular brand, and then for each different type of snack?
- What images are apparently from the parent company? What images are from the self-selected fans of the respective snacks? How do these differ? What do these differences suggest about the tactics for both groups? (In terms of fans, what are different subgroups of interest?)
- Who are informal brand ambassadors? What are their interests? Is there a way to befriend them? Empower them?
- What are images that show the various products in positive light? In negative light? In neutral light? How are these communicated?
- In these image sets, what are some unique riffs on the way the snack food is consumed? Are there some new suggested flavors that should be tried?

- Are there regional differences in how the target snack foods are received? What are these apparent differences? Why?
- Is there potential for finding new markets in terms of re-framing the particular snack food? How so? What are flavor combinations to avoid? Why?
- How do the competing #snack brands compare?
- How do the competing #snack products (between the respective brands) compare?
- Are there any snack foods within a company that are in competition with other products within the company? If so, how may that conflict be addressed? (and others)

This takes one subset, "snack food imagery from different brands," and it involves asking questions based on the categorizations within that subset. The reverse may also be done—starting with a research question, downloading an image set, and then setting up subsets to answer that particular question.

Another approach may be seen in Figure 14. In this approach, there are within-set dependencies. The idea here is to start with as broad a categorization as possible of the full set of images...and then to filter the set from there. In this conceptualization, an image appears is slotted in a best-fit in the table (somewhat like a game of Tetris).

Figure 13. "Without" category dependencies and standalone askable questions

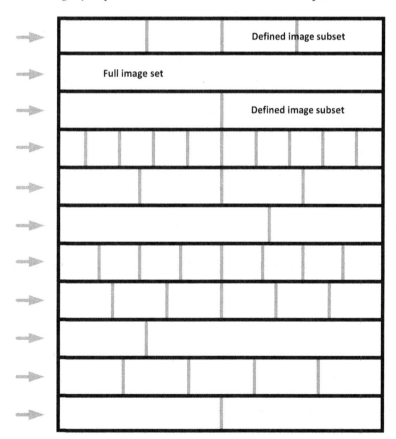

Table 6. Some ways to conceptualize stand-alone subsets of #snack imagery

Snack food imagery with differing levels of processing: raw, human-processed (manual and small machine), mass-processed (multi-step and factory production)
Snack food imagery broken down into various food groups
Snack food imagery broken down into various raw base ingredients
Snack food imagery from different regions of the world
Snack food imagery that seems to fit "breakfast," "brunch," "lunch," or "dinner" (if applicable)
Snack food imagery of food served hot vs. that served cold
Snack food imagery with people or with animals or with no other apparent living being
Snack food imagery from vending machines vs. restaurants or eateries
Snack food imagery belonging to the categories of "healthy" or "unhealthy"
Snack food imagery in-process vs. in finished eat-ready form
Snack food imagery with positive portrayal vs. that with negative portrayal (vs. with neutral portrayal)
Snack food imagery that portrays savory flavors, sweet flavors, and sour flavors
Snack food imagery that portrays individual portions vs. group portions
Snack food imagery showing different social contexts
Snack food imagery with mixed people groups, men, with women, with children, and with babies
Snack food imagery depicted for the elderly, adults, for teenagers, for children, for toddlers, and for babies
Snack food imagery from different brands

In this scenario, it is much easier to ask questions about which images are outliers (those at the bottoms of each of the columns because those that belong in the main areas of the bell curve of images will have been stopped by the more defined filters as the images are positioned). Conceptually, the idea is to have the most coarse-grained filters at the top. A given is a data cleaning question: "Is the image a valid image in the set or spam?" Because of the dependencies in the subsetting, it is important to be mindful of the sequence of the filtering because that will affect the images captured. Depending on the image set (especially its variety and size), it is possible to have empty cells.

Examples of this approach are available in Tables 7 to 13. These seem to work better with a somewhat *a priori*-defined research question. The idea is to sort and filter imagery in a non-destructive way, which means that data is not lost if one can help it, even if it does not end up selected into the particular image set.

From the examples, it is pretty clear that these filters may be pretty exclusionary early on and that the filter layers may be fairly flat or shallow. This may be explained in part on probabilities. For example, based on Table 8, it is possible to surface the following probabilities for an image to make it to the fourth tier down.

.5 (luxury vs. non-luxury) * .1 (assuming 10 categories of luxury snacks) * .5 (hand-made vs. processed) * .1 (assuming 10 presentation strategies) = .0025

The probability for such an image to make is .0025 or .25 of one percent or a fourth of a percent. In other words, there are fast diminishing probabilities for an image to make it into a particular set the further down it is in a categorization sequence. Depending on the complexity of the research and the size and diversity of the image set, it is possible to have much deeper sequences, even those were not portrayed here. The general intuition is that there is fast-diminishing probability of an image's membership into a lower category, particularly as the conditional sequence gets deeper.

Once the subsets have been extracted, it is possible to inductively look at the totality of images in each subset to identify patterns and anomalous images. Categorizing into sets may be achieved as a recursive process. Also, it is possible to capture additional image data from other sources (or the same sources at later times) in order to surface additional insights. One question not directly answered in the set includes the following: What is not seen depicted in this set? Is there over-representation of imagery? Under-representation? Whose voices are seen here? Whose voices are not seen here (and why not)?

Figure 14. "Within" category dependencies and both standalone and cumulative askable questions

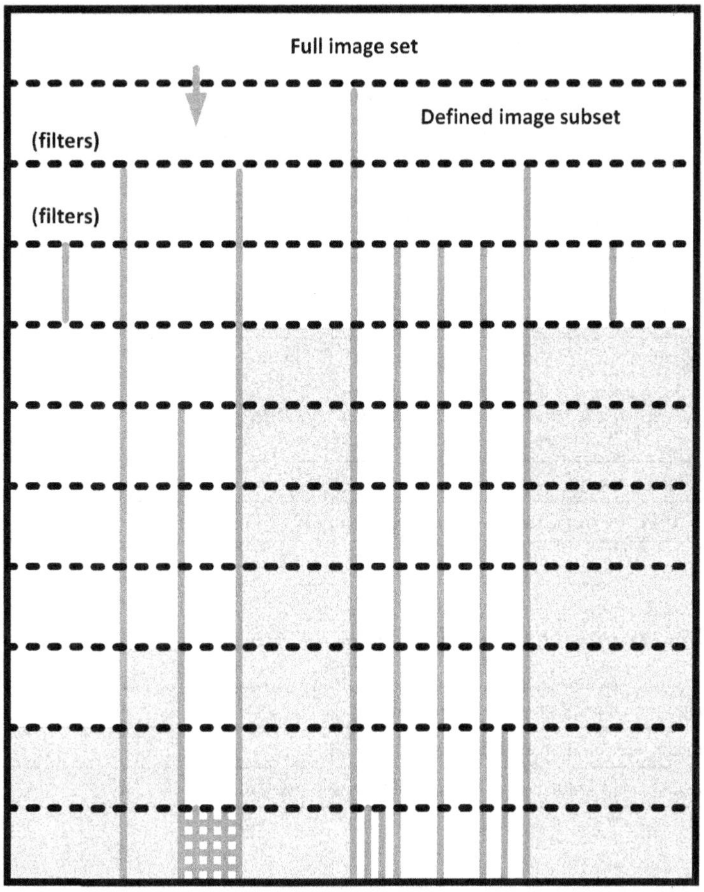

Table 7. Taste profiles for depicted desserts

Identified desserts (vs. all other snacks)
Types of desserts
Main types of taste profiles for the desserts (and especially anomalies)
Messaging around those main taste profiles (as sub-categories)

Table 8. Presentation strategies for identified luxury snack foods

High-end or luxury snack foods (vs. all other snacks)
Types of "high-end" or "luxury" snacks
Hand made vs. processed
Presentation strategies for the communication of high worth in #snack food imagery (as sub-categories)

Table 9. Abstract imagery in the #snack food image set

Abstract imagery (vs. figurative)
Contexts for the uses of abstract imagery in the #snack image set
Imaging strategy in the uses of abstraction (as sub-categories)

Table 10. Food and sociality messaging in the #snack food image set

#snack food imagery with people depicted (vs. those where the people are not in the picture)
Selfies / dyads / groups
Locations depicted
Social contexts depicted
Sociality messaging around #snack foods (as sub-categories)

Table 11. Gendering and snack foods in the #snack food image set

Feminine portrayal of snack food, masculine portrayal of snack food
Analysis of the respective food sets for image patterning (as sub-categories)

Table 12. Appealing and unappealing snack foods in the #snack food image set

Appealing #snack food imagery (vs. unappealing #snack food imagery)
Strategies and tactics for creating appealing snack food imagery
Strategies and tactics for creating unappealing snack food imagery (as sub-categories)

Table 13. Geo-based categorization of the #snack food image set

Categorization by geotagged locations
Snack preferences by regionalisms
Regions represented / regions not represented (as sub-categories)

It is possible to apply these same approaches to sorting imagery to sorting videos although videos are even more complex informational objects.

Another important takeaway is that differing social media platforms attract different parts of the global human population, and they collaborate in somewhat different ways, so the images that are hashtagged similarly on different platforms will result in notably different mixes of imagery, with over emphases of some types of images and less of others. As part of this work, the researcher also attempted to extract #snack image data from Flickr. In Figure 15, a screenshot of the site at the time of the attempted extraction may be seen. Figure 16 shows the "fail" message given a site setting or browser add-in challenge with capturing the images en masse. It may be that another method to extract image data from Flickr, such as by using a built-in application programming interface (API), may work, but that is currently beyond the scope of this chapter. The idea is that broader sampling across social media platforms and the capture of larger image sets would benefit the range of analysis. In an initial perusal of the differing sets of #snack images from Instagram and Flickr, there were no apparent cross-posted images.

Figure 15. Some of the scraped images from #snack on Flickr

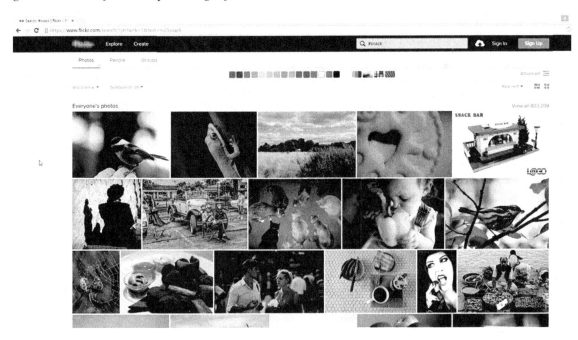

DISCUSSION

The conceptualizations in this chapter were lightly addressed with a topic-based image set—as an initial proof-of-concept. More rigorous applications of these ideas could have been achieved, but the intention of this chapter was to do a fast exploratory walk-through, as a kind of extended thought experiment. So what does this all mean for the initial three hypotheses? They read as follows:

Figure 16. A failure download images from the Flickr content sharing site (using a Web browser add-in)

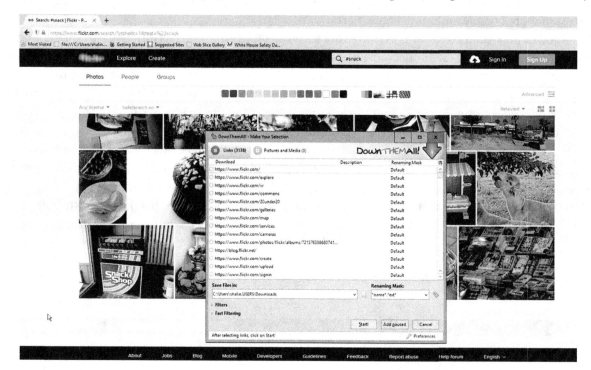

Hypothesis 1: From a sufficient topic-based image set from social media, there will be emergent natural categorical breaklines that may be inductively observable by researchers (without *a priori* reference to theoretical frameworks).

Hypothesis 2: From a sufficient topic-based image set from social media, there will be some research questions that may be inductively and inferentially extracted by researchers.

Hypothesis 3: For research analysts using imagery from social media platforms, exploring some of the available imagery through categorization may enhance the work of research design, image coding, and developing a research codebook.

Using the #snack image sets from Instagram, it was fairly easy to conceptually slice the images into various types, in both stand-alone and prior category dependent ways (Hypothesis 1). This categorizing is done without the express dictates of extant theory or pre-defined taxonomies or ontologies (but these external conceptual structures may be applied if the researcher so chose.) Per Hypothesis 2, the subset structures lent themselves to the creation of research questions, particularly those based on counting and other simple patterns. This approach seems like it may benefit research projects, whether the research includes analyzed social imagery as a small part of a larger research project or whether social imagery is the research project (Hypothesis 3). Using sets may inform research design by suggesting what features to pay attention to in social imagery. Images may be coded based on their membership in particular image sets, and such codes may be informative and insightful in a research codebook.

This approach may seem intuitive but also fairly simplistic. As such, this was designed for a practicable, general-use approach, which does not require high-end technologies or complex skill sets. This does assume some level of expertise with the related topics and issues in an image set (even though the author here is not an expert in #snack foods, just somewhat conversant). Coarse-grained sorting provides users with a "way in" to understanding the image set. The conceptualization of possible "askable questions" extends the potential work of research design and coding plans.

Next steps in terms of coding the imagery would include the identification of themes and sub-themes in the imagery, semantics and narratives in the imagery (and along the same lines as "subtextual messaging," "subimagistic messaging"), research question answering, and other types of analytics.

Summary Features of Social Image Datasets

It is possible, too, to describe features of image sets. One approach, illustrated here, describe an image set based on various informational features. In Figure 17, how this might look is conceptualized in a spider chart with a dozen features: I – geolocation; II – peopled; III - clarity of messaging / call to action; IV - subjectivity: ego, emotion, sentiment; V – novelty / originality; VI – representational / figurative; VII – image resolution; VIII – field of vision; IX – image post-processing; X – color information; XI – metadata, and XII – textual contents. Geolocational information is relevant because it is often included in image EXIF (exchangeable image file format) data, which may be automatically captured in the digital camera or smartphone camera. This may locate a camera person's location to within a foot or less. Whether an image is peopled or not may be relevant given the ability to identify people by name based on tagging or by facial recognition tools, or others. The clarity of the messaging has informational value because images are often shared for tactical reasons (whether commercial, public relations, political or other); particularly, whether the image is used as a call to action is critical (especially if the image may spark mass actions). The subjectivity of an image is important. Subjectivity refers to a kind of relationship to an author or ego; subjectivity, computationally, may be represented also as communicated emotion and sentiment (an expressed public message as a communication of an internal or hidden state). The novelty or originality of an image is another aspect of informational value. The more original an image is, in one sense, the more valuable it is for others. Whether an image is representational or figurative (vs. abstract) highlights its informational value. Something that does not have clear form may be less informationally valuable than something that is highly abstract (in most cases). The resolution of an image, the field of vision (whether an image is close-in or zoomed-out), the amount of image post-processing, the color information, the image metadata, and in-image textual contents may all highlight other aspects of informationality in the image. These were conceptualized in a broad sense—not as a comprehensive or closed list, but as a way to get started looking at ways social imagery may be informationally valuable.

A spider chart is used to describe an object (or a set) based on selected features. Each spoke is understood to start with none or 0 at the center (or even as non-applicable or N/A) and increase in informational value up to 6, in this case. Each level is a gradation, with 1 as low, 4 as medium, and 6 as high. Different types of social image collections (or image subsets) may rank differently on the various variables; in some cases, the respective feature variables may not be relevant. In this figure, four synthetic image sets were used: a dating site profile image set, a day-in-the-news image set, a #nature image set, and a "crafts" keyword image set. Such a spider chart may be more useful with social image sets that are within-topic, such as multiple image sets all related to robotic self-driving cars, to better understand the respective social media account holder, the respective social media platforms, the respective state of the technologies in different geographical locales, and so on. There is variable value of each of the spider chart features depending on social image set and the potential research questions asked.

Figure 17. Summary informational features of respective social image datasets

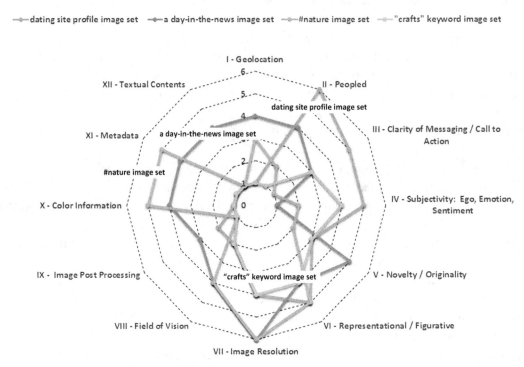

FUTURE RESEARCH DIRECTIONS

One near-term research direction may involve cases in which this approach to openly and inductively categorizing social media images is applied and assessed—by both individual researchers and research teams. If this approach is built into a software tool, how that is instantiated and how well that works for research may also be informative. There may be others' innovations to build on and improve this approach to making use of social media imagery for research.

CONCLUSION

Even though social media platforms enable access to large sets of social images, there are not many (any?) non-theoretical approaches to image analysis, categorization, and coding. This work introduced a systematic, open, and inductive approach to identifying conceptual categories from topic-based image sets from social media in an emergent, bottom-up way. The idea is that this initial categorizing from the extracted real-world image set may benefit the creation of research questions, research design, image coding, and even the development of a research codebook. The initial testing of these hypotheses based on two image sets from Instagram show that the approach may have some merit. Given the widespread availability of imagery from social media platforms on the Web and Internet, researchers would benefit from fresh ways to engage these in open learning approaches.

ACKNOWLEDGMENT

I am thankful to Scott Eugene Velasquez for a conversation a year or two ago that was the initial spark for this chapter. While I never saw the "10-deep" coding structure for your project, Scott, the idea was of sufficient interest that I wanted to explore how coding imagery might work—albeit at a more generic / emergent / grounded level and without the informed direction of any of the following: theory, frameworks, taxonomies, or ontologies. Also, I wanted an approach that would not directly rely on in-depth expertise yet…so I could define something very general and usable by non-experts (amateurs and novices) and experts.

REFERENCES

Ahangama, S. (2014). Use of Twitter stream data for trend detection of various social media sites in real time. LNCS, 8531, 151 – 159.

Amengual, X., Bosch, A., & de la Rosa, J. L. (2015). Review of methods to predict social image interestingness and memorability. *LNCS, 9256*, 64–76.

Anagnostopoulos, A., Kumar, R., & Mahdian, M. (2008). Influence and correlation in social networks. *Proceedings of KDD '08*, 1 – 9. 10.1145/1401890.1401897

Bakhshi, S., Shamma, D. A., & Gilbert, E. (2014). Faces engage us: Photos with faces attract more likes and comments on Instagram. *Proceedings of CHI 2014*, 965 – 974.

Bennett, S. (2013, Nov. 19). Social Media Growth Worldwide—2 Billion Users by 2016, Led by India. *Social Times*. Retrieved Dec. 26, 2015, from http://www.adweek.com/socialtimes/social-media-growthworldwide/493361

Celebrating a Community of 400 Million. (2015, Dec. 26). *Instagram*. Retrieved Dec. 26, 2015, from https://www.instagram.com/press/?hl=en

Derby, K. L. (2013). Social media: Multiple channels to capture multiple audiences. *Proceedings of the SIGUCCS '13*, 159 – 162.

Giannoulakis, S., & Tsapatsoulis, N. (2015). Instagram hashtags as image annotation metadata. IFIP International Federation for Information Processing. doi:10.1007/978-3-319-23868-5_15

Holmberg, C., Chaplin, J. E., Hillman, T., & Berg, C. (2016). Adolescents presentation of food in social media: An explorative study. *Appetite, 99*, 121–129. doi:10.1016/j.appet.2016.01.009 PMID:26792765

Hu, Y., Manikonda, L., & Kambhampati, S. (2014). What we Instagram: A first analysis of Instagram photo content and user types. Association for the Advancement of Artificial Intelligence.

Instagram Demographics. (2015, Aug. 17). Mobile Messaging and Social Media 2015. *Pew Internet*. Retrieved Dec. 26, 2015, from http://www.pewinternet.org/2015/08/19/mobile-messaging-and-socialmedia-2015/2015-08-19_social-media-update_09/

Jeffries, A. (2013, March 20). The man behind Flickr on making the service 'awesome again': Markus Spiering talks photography, daily habits, and life under Marissa Mayer. *The Verge*. Retrieved Dec. 28, 2015, from http://www.theverge.com/2013/3/20/4121574/flickr-chief-markus-spiering-talks-photos-and-marissa-mayer

Kuo, Y.-H., Chen, Y.-Y., Chen, B.-C., Lee, W.-Y., Wu, C.-C., Lin, C.-H., . . . Hsu, W. (2014). Discovering the city by mining diverse and multimodal data streams. *Proceedings of MM '14*, 201 – 204. 10.1145/2647868.2656406

Lavis, A. (2015). Food porn, pro-anorexia and the viscerality of virtual affect: Exploring eating in cyberspace. *Geoforum*. doi:10.1016/j.geoforum.2015.05.014

Lee, C. S., Bakar, N. A. B. A., Dahri, R. B. M., & Sin, S.-C. J. (2015). Instagram this! Sharing photos on Instagram. *LNCS, 9469*, 132–141.

Lim, B. H., Lu, D., Chen, T., & Kan, M.-Y. (2015). #mytweet via Instagram: Exploring user behavior across multiple social networks. *Proceedings of the 2015 IEEE / ACM International Conference on Advances in Social Networks Analysis and Mining (ASONAM '15)*, 113 – 120.

Mejova, Y., Haddadi, H., Noulas, A., & Weber, I. (2015). #FoodPorn: Obesity patterns in culinary interactions. *Proceedings of DH '15*, 51 – 58.

Mika, P. (2005). Ontologies are us: A unified model of social networks and semantics. *The Semantic Web*, 1 – 15.

Ryan, G. W., & Bernard, H. R. (2003). Techniques to identify themes. *Field Methods, 15*(1), 85 – 109. Retrieved Jan. 4, 2016, from http://crlte.engin.umich.edu/wp-content/uploads/sites/7/2013/06/Ryan-and-Bernard-Techniques-to-Identify-Themes.pdf

Salie, F. (2013, Dec. 1). Don't take selfies of your food. Sunday Morning. *CBS News*. Retrieved Mar. 6, 2016, from http://www.cbsnews.com/videos/faith-salie-dont-take-selfies-of-your-food/

Sharma, S. S., & De Choudhury, M. (2015). Measuring and characterizing nutritional information of food and ingestion content in Instagram. *Proceedings of WWW 2015*, 115 – 116. 10.1145/2740908.2742754

Smith, C. (2015, Aug. 10). By the numbers: 14 interesting Flickr stats. *DMR: Digital Statistics, Gadgets, Fun*. Retrieved Dec. 28, 2015, from http://expandedramblings.com/index.php/flickr-stats/

Social Networking Fact Sheet. (2014, January). Pew Research Center's Internet Project January Omnibus Survey. Retrieved Dec. 26, 2015, from http://www.pewinternet.org/fact-sheets/social-networking-fact-sheet/

Sorokowski, P., Sororkowska, A., Oleszkiewicz, A., Frackowiak, T., Huk, A., & Pisanski, K. (2015). Selfie posting behaviors are associated with narcissism among men. *Personality and Individual Differences, 85*, 123–127. doi:10.1016/j.paid.2015.05.004

Souza, F., de Las Casas, D., Flores, V., Youn, S. B., Cha, M., Quercia, D., & Almeida, V. (2015). Dawn of the selfie era: The Whos, Wheres, and Hows of Selfies on Instagram. *Proceedings of COSN '15*, 221 – 231.

Van House, N.A. (2007). Flickr and public image-sharing: Distant closeness and photo exhibition. *Proceedings of CHI 2007*, 2717 – 2722.

Wikipedia: About. (2015, Dec. 24). *Wikipedia*. Retrieved Dec. 28, 2015, from https://en.wikipedia.org/wiki/Wikipedia:About

KEY TERMS AND DEFINITIONS

Breakline: "Natural" points of separation or differentiation between image objects.

Broadcast: A message sent to a wide audience.

Flickr: An image- and video-sharing social media site.

Framework: A basic structure.

Image Analysis: Systematic examination of images.

Instagram: An image-sharing social media site.

Interestingness: A measure of attractiveness and attention-holding for a general human audience.

Microcast: A message sent to a targeted and small audience.

Related Tags Network: A network graph consisting of co-occurring tags.

Selfie: A digital self-portrait photograph taken and shared on an online social networking site.

This research was previously published in Techniques for Coding Imagery and Multimedia; pages 91-130, copyright year 2018 by Information Science Reference (an imprint of IGI Global).

Chapter 39
Dynamic Behavior Analysis of Railway Passengers

Myneni Madhu Bala
Institute of Aeronautical Engineering, India

Venkata Krishnaiah Ravilla
Institute of Aeronautical Engineering, India

Kamakshi Prasad V
JNTUH, India

Akhil Dandamudi
NIIT University, India

ABSTRACT

This chapter discusses mainly on dynamic behavior of railway passengers by using twitter data during regular and emergency situations. Social network data is providing dynamic and realistic data in various fields. As per the current chapter theme, if the twitter data of railway field is considered then it can be used for enhancement of railway services. Using this data, a comprehensive framework for modeling passenger tweets data which incorporates passenger opinions towards facilities provided by railways are discussed. The major issues elaborated regarding dynamic data extraction, preparation of twitter text content and text processing for finding sentiment levels is presented by two case studies; which are sentiment analysis on passenger's opinions about quality of railway services and identification of passenger travel demands using geotagged twitter data. The sentiment analysis ascertains passenger opinions towards facilities provided by railways either positive or negative based on their journey experiences.

DOI: 10.4018/978-1-7998-9020-1.ch039

INTRODUCTION

Considering the advancement in technology by 2050 the railway industry would be able to address competitive pricing, passenger desirable time slots, excellent customer service, and effective emergency services using a dynamic behavior analysis. The railway industry is often thought as conservative; it is necessary to proceed with the foresight to hold creative thinking beyond projecting the present into the future. This thought piece focuses on the passenger experiences, which are anticipated here and are designed to generate a discussion about the future. It provides a big picture in taking dynamic decisions by the rail industry and governments.

Passengers are increasingly able to access data from anywhere through smart devices and cloud applications. As a result, faster access to data will influence passenger relationship with transportation, as well as their decision-making process. Passengers will expect the services certainty in terms of time, so reliable and accurate real-time information will be a key issue. Customer centric services will be based on a wealth of information about the individual passenger and their needs at that moment. These require a detailed understanding and analysis of the passenger experience measures and their satisfaction with key elements of their journey. This analysis would be used to identify satisfaction or dissatisfaction, to provide the feedback with guidance on those areas of improvement.

National Rail Passenger Survey (NRPS) enables rail operators to compare their service with others and to identify the areas of improvement. The department of transport uses this information to evaluate Train Operating Companies (TOCS), which is an official statistic on operator's service. Along with this statistic, big data analysis would play a vital role in the processing of the data collected from social networks. Twitter is one of the primary sources of informal data repository. While considering the previous survey reports there has been a long-term downward trend in the overall complaints rate through traditional channels. It has been attributed to passengers moving towards social media to complain about their train operators relatively than using more traditional methods. Due to the differences in approach to social media, recording complaints through this are not possible at present but should be considered as a long-term goal. The size of the customer base that interacts with the train operators through social media means that their feedback is a very rich source of information to be recorded. By working with train operators and social media analysts we can explore suitable measures that record categorization or sentiment of feedback through social media. The purpose of this analysis would be to identify the data which would help in gauging how train operators approach social media for passenger engagement and complaints perspective. Many have been working with the train operators to learn more about their approach to social media, which has opened opportunities in several different areas. Including time and resource dedicated to social media, the level of engagement, recording feedback. Based on the survey results, the report focus is on any commonality in train operator's approach to social media and it is feasible to record complaints through this channel, observing some of the major challenges in finding a reliable measure, including passenger behavior towards social media and assessing sentiment of feedback.

The main objective of this chapter is to understand the passenger behavior dynamically by using twitter data. This chapter mainly concentrates on extraction of dynamic data from social media, identification of the relevant hashtags of railway passengers, preprocessing on twitter data to remove unwanted text and symbols, identification of list of task-relevant words that define positive as well as negative opinion, preparation of word plots to find major discussions and sentiment analysis on passenger's opinion.

BACKGROUND

An explanatory study to investigate the use of text mining and sentiment analysis for railway services enhancement on relevant content extracted from twitter for exploring different applications. Due to the complexity of information extraction from social media for focused tasks like passenger complaints, trips planning, understanding passenger behavior at city visits and sentiment analysis on events. At present, Indian railways' current practice on performance survey is relying on multiple sources such as SMS, web feedback, and twitter hashtags.

TRADITIONAL COMPUTING

The traditional computing methods are accurate but these are not appropriate under uncertain situations. Soft computing is a collection of the early methods such as Fuzzy Logic, Neural Network, and later methods such as Genetic Algorithm, Rough Theory. (Denai, 2007) used computational intelligence to deal with uncertainty in data. The current research of behavior problems using soft computing methods is at the practice stage. (Avineri, 2004) has built the model on the passenger travel choices. (Qiang, 2008) have made a comparative analysis of support vector machine model and multilayer feedforward neural network. (Jin, 2008) has built a prediction model for passenger travel problems by using applied radial basis function neural network and regression neural network. (Ma, 2007) has given a solution for traffic and travel by combining neural network in the nonlinear relationship and Back Propagation neural network. (Qiu, 2008) worked on the prediction of resident's travel choice by using the probabilistic neural network on survey data of residents in Fangshan district of Beijing. Above said methods and models does not reveal passenger travel choice problems because of multiple starting points and important soft factors like comfort, punctuality, safety etc.

PASSENGER COMPLAINTS ON TWITTER

According to present surveys, the major concentration is on punctuality and reliability of services. One of the background survey, "social media: how to tweet your customers' right" done on 2015 in the UK. The main purposes of this survey were social media compliant content, passenger behavior in social media and capturing the sentiment of passenger's feedback. In this report, the major complaints on train service performance are of punctuality and reliability. It remains the main source of complaints at 34.7% in the 3rd quarter of 2014-15, with punctuality and cancellation measures deteriorating in the past year, but expected complaints in this area are to rise though the share of total complaints has fallen from 41.2% to 34.7%. The downtrend of complaints rate in the traditional channel has reduced; now taking to social media as a means of expressing their dissatisfaction. Presently, railways are exempted from social media data complaints. The latest statistics that showed complaints on passenger tweets make up 4.5% of all complaints in 2014-15 3rdquarter, down from 6% in 2010-11, possibly the outcome of the positive work of train operators are doing in with their customers on social media. Taking these into consideration, we have two scenarios; social media is the new vehicle for complaints and the focus is on twitter data in capturing feedback. There were few train operators on twitter 24 by 7 a week while others are on duty during business hours. In this scenario, over 90% of train operator's drive out a combination of proactive and reactive tweets. However, the scope of their commitment differs markedly. Consider a case, where the number of proactive tweets sent ranged from 500 to 33,000 at the same time as the volume of reactive tweets ranges from 10,000 to 126,000.

MODELING TRAVEL SURVEY

(Alireza, 2015) Traveling behavior of individual passenger based on twitter data is considered for modeling travel survey. In their research, four modeling approaches are discussed. Firstly, a trip based then tour-based models which consider individual travel information data; later evolved to activity-based models which consider the individual or household level travel attributes and to another travel demand models which are essential to policymakers for assessment of long-term travel needs. The advances in travel demand modeling for analyzing the people's day to day travel behavior which changes the need of socio-demographic databases and people economic attributes.

(Alireza, 2015) The individual traveling behavior of the passenger's based twitter data is considered for modeling travel survey. In their research, the four modeling approaches are discussed. Firstly, trip based then tour-based models which consider individual travel information data; later evolved to activity-based models which consider the individual or household level travel attributes; Next travel demand models are essential to policymakers for assessment of long-term travel needs. The advances in travel demand modeling for analyzing the people day to day travel behavior which changes the need of socio-demographic databases and people economic attributes. They proposed a framework for further applications of twitter passenger data for transport planning and management. They developed three components for tourism development on longitudinal data obtained from twitter. Finally, from this analysis, every passenger is automatically identified as visitor or residents of Sydney city.

PASSENGER ACTIVITY PURPOSE

The purpose of a passenger activity is analyzed with each tweet by using advanced text mining technique. The activities would be categorized as shopping, eating, entertainment, work. A study using text classification techniques. Latent Dirichlet Allocation (LDA) is a hierarchical Bayesian-based approach for finding similarities among categorical variables (Blei, 2003). The similar studies focused on the content of tweets rather than check-in data (Gao, 2012), geo-tagged data (Hasan, 2014) or sentiment analyses (Fu, 2015). This analysis is useful for finding the behavior of tourists at their attracting cities. One possible measure may be indistinguishable to record, the proportion of positive or negative feedback we receive via twitter. However, this requires other train operators that do not currently collect that data to adapt their processes to capture it.

MAIN FOCUS OF THE CHAPTER

The chapter focuses on the following issues:

- The impact of social network data and issues in data processing, in the field of railway service enhancement.
- A comprehensive framework for modeling social media data.
- Discussion on process of data extraction, preparation and processing techniques.
- A detailed discussion about passenger dynamic behavior.
- Sentiment analysis on passenger's positive and negative opinions not only on railways facilities but also on responses for regular and emergency situations.
- Identification of passenger travel demands using geotagged twitter data.

All these analyses would be useful for railways sector to identify and plan demand locations of tourists. According to the extracted knowledge, railways could take decision on allocating more number of coaches to specific tourist places in crowd time, to take decisions based on passenger feedback about facilities provided and complaints, to assess the reasons for damage in emergency situations.

ISSUES, CONTROVERSIES, PROBLEMS

Social Network Dynamic Data Sources

Nowadays, many people relate to social media to obtain effective feedback on policies, comforts, and security. Due to this the analysis would do justice to people's time, effort and expertise, and act on the ideas and feedback received. Table 1 shows a list of data sources where data is collected for different purposes such as feedback on service quality, security in the journey, passenger opinion on new services and schemes and detection of abnormal or undesirable events occurred in overall journey period for analysis. It is potentially a challenge for understanding passenger's opinion, as people don't have a prior idea of how the social media data would be implemented and the analysis is not totally open to innovative ideas or diverse opinions.

Table 1. List of data sources

S. No.	Data Purpose	Traditional	Social Media (SM)
1	Service quality and security	Questionnaires	SM text
2	Passengers opinion on new schemes or services	Focus groups, committees, consultation meetings, Household questionnaires	SM text
3	Detection of the abnormal or undesirable event.	Physical devices e.g.: cc camera footage	SM text

In this scenario, how to bring all these ideas into a whole or which idea to favor and to be able to explain to the public how the decision was made by authorities. Table 2 lists the issues in data processing in a traditional and social media data.

The use of social media in government services has been reported many times, with key aspect being citizen participation and transparency of government. Even though it is in infancy stage, more dynamic and huge data is available.

Table 2. Issues in Data Processing

S. No.	Data Purpose	Traditional	Social Media
1	Service quality and security	Data Issues	Analysis of text content is effective in gathering service quality data.
2	Passengers opinion on new schemes or services	**Group and meetings:** • Resource intensive • Limited data sample • Sources of bias Household questionnaires. • Resource intensive • Some biases e.g: response rates.	Analysis of text content is effective in supplementing or replacing public opinion data sources.
3	Detection of abnormal or undesirable event	**Physical devices:** • Continuous monitoring • Level of accuracy is sufficient • High coverage is costly. **Management / operational / control systems** • Systems often belong to private operators and quality of data sharing is often a challenging issue. o Such systems don't enable real-time data processing, which is required for event detection.	• Low cost for authority • Even a small no. of similar reports constitutes a solid basis for verifying the event. • Many types of events can be detected. • Depends on human reporting. • Time constraints require the use of very efficient text mining techniques.

In developing a methodology to explore the potential of social media data for understanding passenger's behavior, three questions need to be addressed:

Q1: To what extent the passengers involved for sharing their opinion?
Q2: How can the value of such information be evaluated?
Q3: Can such data be practically extracted either automatically or semi-automatically?

The first is tantamount to quantify the data with facts. While the second can be achieved with an assessment of model and the third requires a high-quality extraction methodologies that are critical to realizing the quality and scope of data.

The current approach is an ongoing analysis of social media information to reveal changes in trends concerning the level of satisfaction with service provided. If a positive trend is revealed, then it can be inferred that analysis on the information and acting in response to the content is an effective tool to address traveler's needs.

Q3 must be approached with the characteristics of unstructured text data within social media, where syntax-rules are often overlooked two-way and the use of local slang is rude.

Two criteria are commonly used to test hypotheses of this type by involving automatic text processing:

1. The information automatically extracted should be highly relevant. Domain experts are used to measuring the relevance of each item of information extracted. The precision rate is calculated i.e. the ratio of the correctly extracted items to the total no. of extracted items.
2. The extracted information should be complete. Domain experts identify the pertinent information within a finite set of text sources. The ratio of the relevant information found by automatic text mining the total number of the relevant information items can be calculated i.e. recall.

The searching goals can be defined in three characteristics of social media context, reflect its nature and the examples of its use in various domains:

- Social media data created by an individual, who refers to a specific experienced event or action plans to perform
- The event or action the individual comments on occurs either before or after the time point at which the content is achieved.
- The issue raised by the individual creating the content is personally important.

Twitter Data

Twitter is asserted to have, 500 million tweets per day, 288 million monthly active users with 80% of active users using mobile phones. This set up a wonderful opportunity for the public and private sector to benefit from the amount of freely available data provided online and improves their services. Crowd-sourcing social media for disaster or emergency management (Madhubala, 2017) is one of the examples to facilitate response and relief operations by emergency teams by using twitter data. Among the different approaches, some develop tools to track the information provided by social media to predict a likely event.

Tag Words Related to Railways

The government of India, the ministry of railways launched an official account with a tag word on twitter as #railminindia for all complaints, suggestions to be marked to concern General Managers (GM), Divisional Railway Managers (DRM) for appropriate action. Another Indian railway tag word in twitter is #indianrailway and #railways. Geo-tagged tweets of twitter data are used to develop location-based analysis on passenger behavior for identification of visiting plans including duration and place of visit. From this analysis, the general pattern on passenger trips as short or long is identified.

PROBLEMS

Extracting named travel and land use attributes information from hashtag data is a challenging issue in this analysis. Data mining is required to determine the activity location that is related to a tweet. This analysis is used in developing several advanced components of behavioral modeling frameworks such as tour based and activity based (Mojtaba, 2015). Travel attributes considered in these modeling frameworks are the trip purpose, departure time, mode of transport, activity duration, activity location, travel route, party composition and traffic condition. This analysis focuses on how twitter data can be used to facilitate and improve railways decisions on the enhancement of facilities, passenger safety and several couches.

SOLUTIONS AND RECOMMENDATIONS

For above-discussed problems, the solutions can be found from advanced text mining processes to address the dynamic data. An effective framework is needed to address multiple problems. An effective preprocess is one of the critical steps on social media data.

TEXT MINING PROCESS

Text mining is used to identify the passenger behavior in sentiment analysis. This process includes data extraction, preparation, and processing. The sentiment analysis on passenger opinions towards facilities provided by railways as a positive or negative, passengers response on regular and emergency situations. The activity purpose associated with in a tweet, it's determined by using an advanced text mining technique, Latent Dirichlet Allocation (LDA) (Blei, 2003). It is hierarchical Bayesian approach highly suitable for analyzing tweets data and finding similarity between categorical attributes. LDA is used to identify the correlations among words in twitter corpus, to find different hidden topics (discussions) and further classifying the text accordingly. Figure 1 is an overview of text mining process for sentiment analysis. It includes extraction of relevant messages, pre-process on extracted tweets, semantic process based on classification or sentiment analysis and summarization and visualization output inferences.

Figure 1. Overview of text mining process

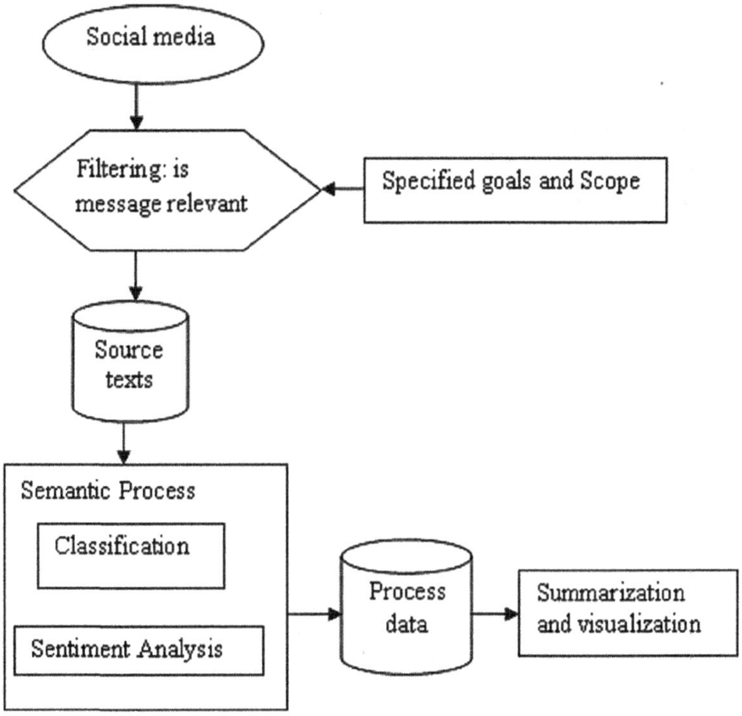

Extraction of Trip Purpose From Twitter Data Using LDA

The data considered for finding trip purpose is the content of tweets (text) rather than check-in data (Gao, 2012), geo-tagged data (Hasan, 2014) or sentiment analyses (Fu, 2015). In this analysis, they used unique word dictionary as 'Sydney_Resident_DB'. The pre-process on tweets is performed by removing unwanted content as prepositions and symbols. Now based on frequent words, around 400 unique words are identified with a minimum frequency of 20. In this work, words like "I'm", "Sydney" and "restaurant" were respectively used 3009, 1215 and 233 times in the text that was selected for further analysis. Nearly 17,000 words were not included in the analysis because they were slang expressions, prepositions and symbols had been repeated fewer than 20 times in the database. LDA was applied on identified 400 words to cluster the data and found 100-word clusters. From each cluster, the top 3 highest frequency words. Find the correlation between top 3 words and remaining words within the same cluster. An activity tag was assigned to each cluster by considering the top 3 words in each cluster and other correlations among words. The identified activity tags are named as Shopping, Entertainment, Eating, Work, Social, Study. Finally, each tweet was assigned with one of the cluster activity tags by checking against all the clusters and if there was an appropriate level of similarity. This finding on twitter data is helpful in analyzing the behavior of tourists.

Identification of Keywords

Automatic identification of meaningful keywords and their use in training classifiers is one of the important tasks in twitter analysis. To automatically identify relevant content from streams of text, text mining techniques have been used with considerable success. These practices with social media help to gain knowledge and understanding of public opinion across several social sciences (e.g.: Politics, entertainment, and business). For example, Twitter messages have been analyzed as an alternate to presidential approval rating data and presidential polls, where results show high correlation with these polls. Figure 2 is an example of Sample tweets and replies from railway officials. The sample tweets show complaints from passengers, consideration of social media data as the complaint by railway ministry and forwarded to concerned officials of Indian railways for further action.

Figure 2. Sample tweets and replies from railway officials

The infinite nature of the message stream in social media is challenging from multiple perspectives. From a performance perspective, as the content posted on social media changes rapidly over time, periodic monitoring and possibly re-tuning of the system is required. Text mining is a means for automatic identifications of relevant messages in a stream of incoming messages. Specific remain and solutions are needed where the user must be in the loop for periodic monitoring and enhancement of the system.

CASE STUDY 1: SENTIMENT ANALYSIS ON PASSENGERS OPINIONS

Sentiment analysis is the process of identifying and extracting opinions from a given text. Sentiment analysis of social media has been used to estimate public mood (Johan, 2011), trends such as stock market behavior (Johan, 2011) and political election results (Jessica, 2011). Sentiment analysis is important to address some of the information needs of (railway/transport) policy makers. In the transport sector, the twitter as an information source for evaluating transit rider satisfaction (Collins, 2013). A case study of the Chicago Transit Authority, a correlation was found between irregular events (e.g. delays) and the volume of postings expressing negative sentiment. This correlation supports the notion that twitter is a valid source of dynamic information for inferring transport-related sentiments.

A survey on the role of negation in sentiment analysis depends on the construction of bag of negative words. In this process, the first challenge is the construction of common linguistic, which is highly relevant for sentiment analysis. The effective negation model includes common negation words and other lexical units about text classification type, the level of text granularity, target domain, and language used etc. Sentiment analysis makes use of a dedicated lexicon of words marked with their prior polarity as negative or positive (Michael, 2010). The matching of a given text with the lexicon to analyze emotions in the text is another approach for sentiment analysis (Sanjay, 2007).

The Indian railways have active involvement at social media on twitter passenger opinions. Figure 3 is an example of sample Tweets of Indian railway passengers on #swatchRailSwatchBharat and response of railway minister. It shows the response of passengers on event Swatch Bharat announced by the government of India. On this passenger opinion tweet, the response is given by concern minister.

Figure 3. Sample Tweets of Indian railway passengers on #swatchRailSwatchBharat and response of railway minister

EXPRESSIONS OF NEGATIVE/POSITIVE SENTIMENT

The natural languages are highly context dependent (Michael, 2010). For example, 'busy' word is described as positive in some context e.g. "the road is busy and should qualify for upgrade" but negative in others 'the road is busy and unsuited for further housing development'. The texts say the sentiment as positive: For "terribly good" and negative is "not at all desirable". Analysis of transport sentiment data has illustrated the difficulty with service quality related text. For example, the text like "train service is just fantastic" needs the surrounding context for interpretation. In this case is the preceding text related to late running trains may indicate whether it is genuine or sarcastic. The inferring sentiment is posed as a text classification task (Johan, 2011), enabling the consideration of contextual. Classes to identifying sentiment are elaborated (Sanjay, 2007). The learned models should be trained using labeled data within the interested domain.

The sentiment analysis can be performed in the following steps:

Step 1: Data Extraction from twitter API
Step 2: Data Preprocess
Step 3: Identification of frequent words
Step 4: Calculation of polarity scores
Step 5: Sentiment Analysis

1. Data Extraction

Twitter is one of the social networking and microblogging services that allow users to post real-time messages, called tweets. Tweets are short text messages, limited to 140 characters in length. Due to the nature of this microblogging service (quick and short messages), people use acronyms, make spelling mistakes, use emoticons and other characters that express special meanings. Following are brief terminology associated with tweets.

- **Emoticons:** These are facial expressions pictorially represented enclosed with punctuation and letters; It expresses the user's mood.
- **Target:** The "@" symbol is used to refer to other users on the microblog like twitter. Referring other users in this manner automatically alerts them.
- **Hashtags:** Users usually use hashtags to mark topics. This is primarily done to increase the visibility of their tweets.

Figure 4 is an example of Indian railways #tagword on twitter. These are the familiar #tagwords, where the passengers are actively involving for sharing their opinions on services, security, complaints and tatkal services. Table 3 contains statistics on railways related tag word based tweets in twitter per day declared by Indian railways. In this case study, a sample of 1000 tweets is extracted by using #RailMinIndia hashtag from twitter API.

Figure 4. Indian railways #tagword on twitter

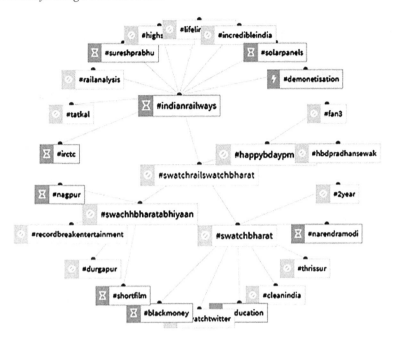

Table 3. General statistics on railways related tagword based Tweets

#Tagword	No. of Tweets
Indian railways	816
rail analysis	213
arctic	166
tatkal	135
train	131
railways	128

2. Data Pre-Processing

The extracted tweets text contains emoticon symbols, acronyms, symbols, URLs and highlights with quotes. Now the data must be done on pre-process to make data ready to analyze.

The following are the novel resources for pre-processing twitter data:

1. Emoticon dictionary
2. Acronym dictionary
3. List of stop words
4. Patterns of URLs
5. List of highlight symbols

Emoticon Dictionary

The emoticon dictionary is prepared by labeling 170 emoticons listed on Wikipedia1 with their emotional state. Table 4 gives a part of emoticons dictionary. For example, ":)" symbol is labeled as positive and the ": =(" symbol is labeled as negative. We assign each emoticon a label from the following set of labels: Extremely-positive, Extremely-negative, Positive, Negative, and Neutral.

Table 4. Part of the Emoticons Dictionary

Emoticon	Polarity
:-):):o):]:3:c)	Positive
Emoticon	Positive
:D C	Positive
:-(:(:c:[	Negative
D8 D; D= DX	Negative
: j	Neutral

Acronym Dictionary

The acronym dictionary is prepared with translations for 5,184 acronyms. Table 5 gives the Sample Acronym Dictionary. For example, lol is translated to laugh out loud.

Table 5. Sample acronym dictionary

Acronym	English Expansion
gr8, gr8t	great
lol	laughing out loud
of	rolling on the floor
off	best friend forever

List of Stop Words

The Stanford tokenizer is used to tokenize the tweets (Klein and Manning, 2003). The stop word dictionary is used to identify stop words. All the other words which are found in WordNet are counted as English words. The stop words are filtered words used to save the disk space or speed up the text mining process. Stop words removal play an important role in reducing the length of documents in sentiment analysis. It is the process of filtering words which are of little help in processing the documents. Some words like articles, pronouns, etc., are prevalent in all the documents. These words don't determine the sentiment of a document. For example, words like „the", „a", "these", etc., are of no use in sentiment analysis and hence it can be removed. Country names, date of travel, numerical value baggage weight, etc., are also removed in our work. Table 6 shows the sample stop word list collected from http://www. webconfs.com/stop-words.php. Below is a comprehensive list of stop words ignored by Search Engines:

Table 6. Sample stop word dictionary

able
about
above
abroad
according
accordingly
across
actually
adj
after

Patterns of URLs

The tweets text contains URLs data to share about relevant links. But for text analysis, there is no significance for URLs. All these links need to be removed from the text before processing. The general pattern for finding URLs is "http[[:album:]]".

List of Highlight Symbols

The text contains highlighted part in the middle with special symbols as quotations, @, tab space or white spaces etc. All these also need to identify and removed from the text before processing.

The pre-processing of tweets includes the following steps:

Step 1: Replace all the emoticons with their sentiment polarity by looking up the emoticon dictionary
Step 2: Replace all URLs with a tag ||U||
Step 3: Replaces targets (e.g. "@John") with tag T||
Step 4: Replace all negations (e.g. not, no, never, not, cannot) by tag "NOT"
Step 5: Replace a sequence of repeated characters by three characters, for example, convert cooooooooool to coool.

3. Identification of Frequent Words

After pre-process, now the tweets text contains meaning full text, emoticons, and acronyms. From the text content, the word list is prepared based on fixed word length. Now word frequency is computed for each word. Figure 5 is an example of sample word cloud of #RailMinIndia and #indianrailways. It shows the passenger major discussions such as Indian railways, online services and about the staff and train timings.

Figure 5. Sample word cloud of #RailMinIndia and #indianrailways

4. Polarity Scores

Polarity approximates the sentiment (polarity) of text by grouping variable(s) as positive, negative and neutral. Polarity score is calculated based on the impact of positive and negative words in the tweets text content. The equation employed to assign the value to a polarity of each sentence fist utilizes the sentiment dictionary to tag polarized words. A context cluster (x_i^T) of words is pulled from around this polarized word. In general default, 4 words before and two words after are to be considered as valence shifters.

The words in this context cluster are tagged as:

- **Neutral:** Neutral words hold no value in the equation but do affect word count (n) $x\_i^{\hat{}0}$
- **Negator:** A character vector of terms reversing the intent of a positive or negative word $x\_i^{\hat{}N}$
- **Amplifier:** A character vector of terms that increase the intensity of a positive or negative word $x\_i^{\hat{}a}$
- **De-Amplifier:** A character vector of terms that decrease the intensity of a positive or negative word $x\_i^{\hat{}d}$

Table 7 shows a Sample Positive and Negative words identified from training data of passenger tweets. These words are identified as positive and negative based on the conversation about services provided by Indian railways.

Each polarized word is weighted as w based on the weights from the polarity. The weight c is utilized with amplifiers or de-amplifiers. In general, the default case is 8 and deamplifier weight is constrained to -1 as lower bound value. The context cluster (x_i^T) are summed and divided by the square root of the word count $\sqrt{(n)}$ by an unbounded polarity score (C). The context clusters consider the words found after the comma.

$$C = \frac{x\_i^{\hat{}2}}{\sqrt{n}}$$

where:

$$x\_i^{\wedge T} = \sum\left(\left(1 + c * \left(x_i^{\wedge A} - x\_i^{\wedge D}\right)\right) * w\left(-1\right)^{\wedge}\left(\sum x\_i^{\wedge N}\right)\right)$$

$$x\_i^{\wedge A} = \sum\left(w\_{-neg} * x\_i^{\wedge a}\right)$$

$$x\_i^{\wedge D} = \max\left(x\_i^{\wedge D'}, -1\right)$$

$$x\_i^{\wedge D'} = \sum\left(-W\_neg * x\_i^{\wedge a} + x\_i^{\wedge d}\right)$$

$$w\_neg = \left(\sum x\_i^{\wedge N}\right)\bmod 2$$

Table 8 shows the polarity score of sample tweets. It gives the statistics of polarity scores in terms of total sentences taken, several words considered after pre-process, the average polarity score of words and other mean and standard polarity of sample twitter data.

Table 7. Sample Positive and Negative words

Negative Words	Positive Words
refund	Ready
delay	Sold
poor	Change
not	Coaches
worst	Selling
useless	Travels
late	Lifeline
action	Light
waiting	Response
broken	Soon
pathetic	Food
unauthorized	Help

A data structure of polarity score contains:

- **Total Sentences:** Total sentences spoken.
- **Total Words:** Total words used.

- **Ave Polarity:** The sum of all polarity scores for that group divided by a number of sentences spoken.
- **Sd Polarity:** The standard deviation of that group's sentence level polarity scores.
- **Stan Mean Polarity:** A standardized polarity score calculated by taking the average polarity score for a group divided by the standard deviation.

Table 8. Polarity score of sample Tweets

	Polarity
Total sentences	113
Total words	1168
Average polarity	-0.035
Standard Polarity	0.21
Mean Polarity	-0.168

Figure 6 is an example of Polarity Plot to Show the Sentiment of railway passengers twitter data. It varied between -0.5 to 0.5. This is the indication of positive and negative response to opinions. From this plot, we can conclude that the neutral sentiment is showing by passengers.

Figure 6. Example of polarity plot

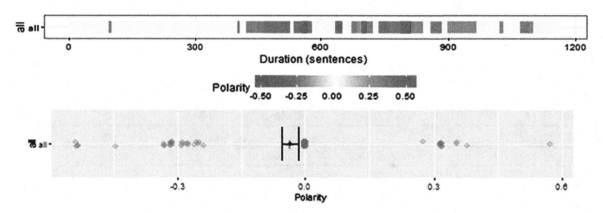

ANALYSIS OF LOCATION DATA

The railway system contains both upstream and downstream transport activity relevant to a geographic location. The authorities of sections of railways together form as closed networks.

For example, connections between intercity and local services may be posted on the website but are of interest to local providers seeking to improve connection services. Therefore, it is necessary to identify those messages pertinent to the location or specific transport services for the task. Two approaches to identifying the location from social network data are either:

1. To identify the current location of the person posting the message or
2. To identify the message content.

Figure 7 shows analysis of geotagged twitter data in railways. It outlines the process involved, for an example of public transport messages analysis based on the fusion of information either in the message or attached to it.

1. Message Text

A primary source of information on the location of the person posting the text message is voluntarily posted geo metadata associated with social media user account.

Figure 7. Analysis of geotagged Twitter data in railways

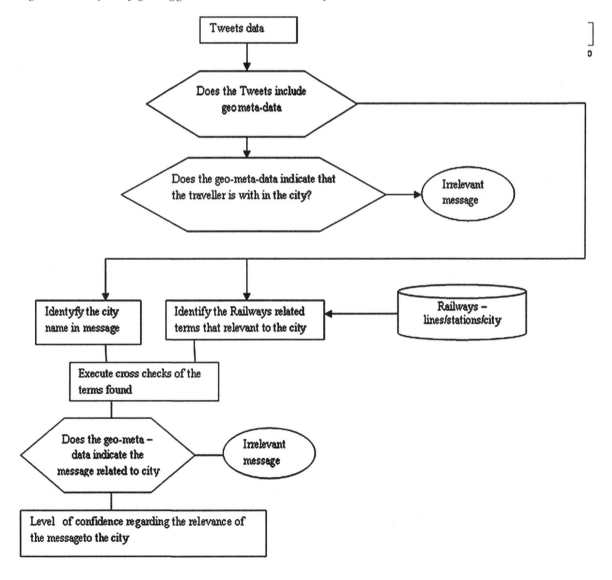

Limitations in Data

1.   The message may link to transport in locations distinct from the user's home town while traveling.
2.   Mobile Device GPS coordinates meta-data indicate the user's location, but this functionality is the user consent.

The limitations in this meta-data have been reviewed for potential location inference (Leetaru, 2013 and Andreas, 2010). Social network structures can be used for this purpose as users tend to live in close geographic proximity to their peers. And an estimate of user location may be inferred founded on the message content (Reid, 2014).

The second approach to identifying location data is taken from the contents of the message text. This task is a challenging when considering extreme ambiguity of place names. For example, "Liverpool" is the name of a UK city, a London rail station (Liveable Street), a city in the USA and an Australian suburb.

Several approaches haven proposed for identifying geolocation based on message content. Named entity recognition techniques can automatically annotate the text with mentions of entity names. Extracted location names are needed to align the inferred location with any other contextual information, in conjunction with relevant sources of location names.

The two types of social media observed were Facebook and twitter. These media functions in such a way as to assist in this and being the possibility of two-way exchanges the main advantage over standard websites. The stakeholders (authorities, ministers etc.) involve dynamic interaction with the public for example in providing a timely response to the passenger's feedback.

2. Different Modes of Use of The Media

The following are the different modes to access multimedia channels:

1.   The public was strongly invited to engage with either Facebook or twitter within a section of the company website and the use of the media was purposeful.
2.   The public is invited to engage with welcoming messages, the purpose of use in general or multifunctional.
3.   Links to social media were given on the main website page but were small and the invitation to engage in generic
4.   Logos were in website or links to twitter stream.

Now a day's most organizations had a Facebook page and twitter line that was focused on their core business. Some web pages gave links to Facebook/Twitter that was shared between organizations. One advantage of dedicated social media line or page would be an improved ability to conduct further analysis on public postings, e.g trends in sentiments or information requests.

3. Main Functions of Social Media in Railways

The main functions of social media data regarding railways are as follows:

1. **Information or Updates About Services on the Main Website:** This is one of the common types of message on Facebook from railways. This type of message was mainly one-directional i.e the main web page would not be adverse of changes to Facebook.
2. **Advising the Public on Travel Disruption:** This function is very much part of the core business survey, particularly those concerned with scheduling, timetable and ticket status.
3. **Handling Travel Queries and Complaints:** The stream of interaction between officers and the passengers is in two ways. Table 9 shows the questionnaires on different issues posted by railway passengers. Passengers show the different approaches used to deal with either straight forward or ordinary questions, personal queries or complaints.

Table 9. Questionnaires on different issues

Questionnaires Regarding Travel Booking	Responded Online
Specific Bookings	Advice to contact offline using individual personal Facebook Account
Complaints about travel	Organizations generally offered public apology offers to speak offline individually either by phone or email.

4. **Responding to Queries Around Use of Social Media:** Some of the public commented on the way in which the organization was using social media. This includes positive messages concerning the speed of responses as well as negative messages on non-response or unwanted presence on the users own social media.
5. **Seasonal Goodwill Message:** This was consistently informal in nature and aimed at promoting the concept of timelines, community, and friendly service.

CASE STUDY 2: IDENTIFICATION OF TRAVEL DEMANDS USING GEOTAGGED TWITTER DATA

From geotagged tweets, the location is identified and cross-checked with content referred locations. Figure 8 is an example of message text referred locations. This plot gives statistics as from India 268 tweets are posted out of 1000 tweets and the active locations on the social network are Delhi, Mumbai, Bengaluru, Karnataka, Hyderabad etc.

Table 10 shows statistics of location wise tweets. The geotagged locations and contents referred locations are considered as words list for finding the relevance of locations. So, these locations are considered as words set.

Text Content With Location

Figure 9 is an example of geotagged twitter data polarity plot of location based tweets. It shows the polarity score of locations found in the text.

Figure 8. Message text referred locations

Table 10. Statistics of location wise tweets

India	Delhi	Mumbai	Bengaluru	Karnataka	Hyderabad
268	170	46	39	29	27

Table 11. Polarity score on sample data

Total Sentences	Total Words	Average Polarity
874	8649	-0.016

Figure 9. Geotagged Twitter data polarity plot

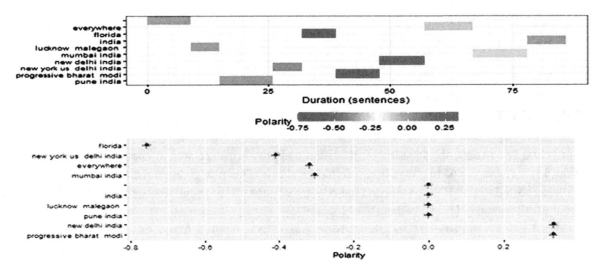

From this plot, the average polarity is.33 from new Delhi location, neutral polarity from Pune and Lucknow cities and negative polarity from Mumbai and other places from India. Table 11 lists the polarity score on sample data of railway passenger tweets.

From the polarity score of the involvement in the social network at overall India, the level is neutral, from capital New Delhi is positive and other crowd places like Mumbai and Pune is negative.

UNDERSTANDING PASSENGER BEHAVIOUR

A key goal for all providers of rail services into London is to make sure that commuters have a safe and enjoyable journey. Yet whether the issue is delays, overcrowding or crime, rail journeys are frequently the cause of negative twitter sentiment and are frequently subject to complaints from passengers.

Our analysis of key negative language wording includes terms like "profit", "fault" and "greedy", emotional terms like "angry" and "frustrated" and more colorful phrases. We identified that there were in total an incredible 473,661 tweets using negative language between 1ˢᵗ April 2014 to 31ˢᵗ March 2015 leads to the worrying phase of rail providers who are looking forward to gaining the trust of passengers. Regardless of the strength of incidents which leads the negative sentiment, it is in the interest of rail providers and the public that the negative impacts are reduced as soon as possible and in the most effective way. This may include using social media Twitter to answer criticisms, improve the handling of disturbance, share advice and reassure daily passengers that problems are being dealt when they occur.

SOLUTIONS AND RECOMMENDATIONS

The following are the solutions for different problems faced while their journey in rail from railway passenger posted tweets.

1. **Address Security Issues:** Using social media analysis, the keywords for these issues like "pickpocket", "thieves", "fight" and "drunk" are used to understand passenger difficulties in security satisfactions of their journey. The findings, displayed in the table below, show that there were 7,408 tweets using crime language during the last year. Whilst the volume of social media references to incidents of crime do not necessarily mean that crime is worse on a service. Rail providers should use this data to assess the incidence of reported crime and bridge with the relevant authorities to tackle it. For example, during periods of heavy commuter traffic, or major public events like football matches, social media analysis can play a key role in indicating incident locations, with images, videos and witness evidence being collated.
2. **Address the Services Provided by Railways:**
    a. **Hot and Cool Conditions:** Frequent customer's complaints on cool and hot extreme conditions due to improper service. During the spring and summer is the provision of adequate cooling systems. A particularly hot period, such as the summer of 2014, inevitably raises questions for rail providers in terms of effective air conditioning and cooling systems. In the summer sun and overcrowding causing daily travelers to overheat, some cases faint, ensuring properly regulated heating and cooling during different seasons is of paramount importance. A powerful mix of delays, crowding and heat creates some more uncomfortable situations for passengers, often creating strong reactions about services and these are reflected through Twitter. Using sentiment analysis keywords, we can examine the terms such as "too hot", "sauna" and "air con" measure the number of tweets issued by users on each individual rail service regarding hot and cool conditions in trains.

During the autumn and winter seasons, we examined sentiment around routine passengers complaining about poorly heated carriages on Twitter. With the varied temperatures as dropping to below freezing levels, comfort levels on poorly heated trains or long waits on windy platforms are most identified regular complaints by rail passengers. To analyze the twitter sentiment on this topic the positive words like "sub-zero", "freezer" and "icicles" are used. In this category, 12,076 tweets directed at rail operators complaining about being 'too cold' due to poor heating systems or long, cold waits.

Train providers should already be acting to improve passenger comfort, even before these statistics have been revealed. However, social media analysis can help to identify times and train services on maintenance of upgrading air conditioning or heating systems. It can be used to identify how such improvements positively impact passenger sentiment and provides operators a wonderful opportunity to share openly what measures they are taking to address this common complaint, such as the number of incidents identified, investigated and solved.

b.   **Passenger Feelings About Their Rail Journey:** How customers describe situations that make them feel uncomfortable, anxious or lead to accidents are analyzed with words such as "slip", "injured", "panic" and "first aid". In an industry that prides itself on a strong safety record, looking after the wellbeing of its customers is key. Twitter provides a reliable source of data, provided by the crowd, to identify possible hazards, from narrow and slippery platforms and expired first aid boxes on trains, also to understand those conditions that cause the unhappy of passengers. As with all these areas, the key point is to encourage the passengers to contribute this data willingly and constructively for understanding and the evidence of action being taken to all concerns.

FUTURE RESEARCH DIRECTIONS

In future, passengers will increasingly be able to access data from anywhere through smart devices and cloud applications. Faster access to data will influence passenger relationship with transportation, as well as their decision-making process. Passengers will expect the services certainty in terms of time, so reliable and accurate real-time information will be a key issue. Customer centric services will be based on a wealth of information about the individual passenger and their needs at that moment. These require a detailed understanding and analysis of the passenger experience measures and their satisfaction with key elements of their rail journey. This analysis is used to identify satisfaction or dissatisfaction to provide the feedback with guidance on those areas of improvement.

To improve this feedback mechanism dynamically and effectively it addresses the future of railway systems. For achieving this the future research contribution in a new framework with advanced data server as Social Internet of Things (SIoT). It includes the need of distributed environment for computing crowd dynamic data according to multiple themes like complaints on services, suggestions for improvement of service, swach Bharath (cleanliness) and security issues.

Propagation of research on Social Media through new advanced environments and effective advanced big data algorithms are needed for quick and effective processing. The theme of this book is served by this chapter to show the future needs of the railways for better decision making, monitoring of existing services and enhancements according to passenger needs. After the elaborated discussion, it directs the future research as a need of the expert system for automation of feedback process on the passenger's opinions in any of the form (SMS, web feedback, tweets in twitter etc.) with quick response for the betterment of railways.

CONCLUSION

This chapter highlights the extent to which rail passengers express their negative and positive opinions of rail services on Twitter as one of big data application. There can be many reasons for passengers choosing social media as a platform to criticize services, including the fact that it's convenient and instant. The rail industry should recognize that social media analysis can guide to improve services, by spotting the worst affected services and take meaningful action, as soon as possible.

Recommendation One

Rail providers should use their social media channels to turn around passenger's complaints and reduce negative sentiment. Too often, unsympathetic responses are given to problems reported, from delays to hot trains and batted away with the operational logic that creates a more bad feeling. Evidence, the action is being taken and a few goodwill gestures can go a long way to restoring consumer confidence.

Sites like Twitter are being used by passengers to report incidents such as a fight and alert the necessary authorities to act. They can achieve this by developing a quicker online relationship with respective officers, to gather confirmation and close incidents.

Recommendation Two

The temperature conditions of rail journeys are essential not only to the comfort of passengers also to their health and well-being. The few of the train satisfaction survey for 2015 listed "condition of the train" as key factors. This highlights the importance of passenger experience. Twitter provides to rail providers with a perpetual source of real-time dynamic information about rail services. Therefore, when looking to improve services, social media analysis should be an effective tool to pinpointing particularly challenging services and act to improve them.

Recommendation Three

The relationship between passengers and rail providers simply must develop, and the astonishing 473,661 tweets using negative language indicates that there is still abundant room for improvement. This association needs to be concentrate by rail providers trying to engage the public with regular updates online, which is moving beyond timetable and departure updates to provide evidence that passenger reported issues, ranging from comforts to costs of antisocial behavior are being addressed.

ACKNOWLEDGMENT

This research was supported by the Institute of Aeronautical Engineering under the research grant founded by Department of Science and Technology [grant number: File No. DST/TSG/AMT/2015/202/G dated 11.05.2016].

REFERENCES

Abbasi, A., Rashidi, T. H., Maghrebi, M., & Waller, S. T. (2015). Utilizing Location Based Social Media in Travel Survey Methods: bringing Twitter data into the play. In Proceedings of the 8th ACM SIGSPATIAL International Workshop on Location-Based Social Networks. ACM.

Avineri, E. (2004). A Cumulative Prospect Theory Approach to Passengers Behavior Modeling: Waiting Time Paradox Revisited. *Journal of Intelligent Transportation Systems*, 8(4), 195–204. doi:10.1080/15472450490523856

Blei, D. M., Ng, A. Y., & Jordan, M. I. (2003). Latent Dirichlet Allocation. *Journal of Machine Learning Research*, 3, 993–1022.

Bollen, J., Mao, H., & Pepe, A. (2011). Modeling Public Mood and Emotion: Twitter Sentiment and Socio-Economic Phenomena. In *Proceedings of the Fifth International AAAI Conference on Weblogs and Social Media*.

Bollen, J., Mao, H., & Zeng, X.-J. (2011). Twitter mood predicts the stock market. Journal of computer science, 2(1), 21-28.

Chung, J., & Mustafaraj, E. (2011). Can Collective Sentiment Expressed on Twitter Predict Political Elections? In *Proceedings of the 25th AAAI Conference on Artificial Intelligence*, San Francisco, CA (pp 1770-1771).

Collins, C., Hasan, S., & Ukkusuri, S. V. (2013). A novel transit rider satisfaction metric: Rider sentiments measured from online social media data. *Journal of Public Transportation*, 16(2), 21–45. doi:10.5038/2375-0901.16.2.2

Dan, K., & Manning, C. D. (2003). Accurate unlexicalized parsing. In *Proceedings of the 41st Meeting of the Association for Computational Linguistics* (pp 423 – 430).

Denai, M. A., Palis, F., & Zeghbib, A. (2007). Modeling and control of nonlinear systems using soft computing techniques. *Applied Soft Computing*, 7(3), 728–738. doi:10.1016/j.asoc.2005.12.005

Fu, K., Nune, R., & Tao, J. X. (2015). Social Media Data Analysis for Traffic Incident Detection and Management. In *Proceedings of the Transportation Research Board 94th Annual Meeting*.

Gao, H., Tang, J., & Liu, H. (2012). Exploring Social-Historical Ties on Location-Based Social Networks.

Grant-Muller, S. M., Gal-Tzur, A., Minkov, E., Kuflik, T., Nocera, S., & Shoor, I. (2016). Transport Policy: Social Media and User-Generated Content in a Changing Information Paradigm. In Social media for government services (pp. 325–366). Springer International Publishing.

Hasan, S., & Ukkusuri, S. V. (2014). Social contagion process in informal warning networks to understand evacuation timing behavior. *Journal of Public Health Management and Practice*, 19, S68–S69. doi:10.1097/PHH.0b013e31828f1a19 PMID:23529072

Hasan, S., & Ukkusuri, S. V. (2015). Urban activity pattern classification using topic models from online geo-location data. *Transportation Research Part C, Emerging Technologies*, 44, 363–381. doi:10.1016/j. trc.2014.04.003

Jin, X., & Jia, W. (2008). *Review of Researches on Artificial Neural Network* (pp. 65–66).

Jin, X., & Jia, W. (2008). *Review of Researches on Artificial Neural Network* (pp. 65–66).

Kaigo, M. (2012). Social media usage during disasters and social capital: Twitter and the Great East Japan earthquake. *Keio Communication Review*, *34*, 19–35.

Kaplan, A. M., & Haenlein, M. (2010). Users of the world, unite! The challenges and opportunities of Social Media. *Business Horizons*, *53*(1), 59–68. doi:10.1016/j.bushor.2009.09.003

Lee, J. H., & ... . (2015). Can Twitter data be used to validate travel demand models? In *Proceedings of the 14th International Conference on Travel Behaviour Research*, Windsor, UK.

Lee, J. H., Davis, A. W., & Goulias, K. G. (2016). Activity Space Estimation with Longitudinal Observations of Social Media Data. In *Proceedings of the 95th Annual Meeting of the Transportation Research Board*.

Leetaru, K., Wang, S., Cao, G., Padmanabhan, A., & Shook, E. (2013). Mapping the global Twitter heartbeat: The geography of Twitter. *First Monday*, *18*(5). doi:10.5210/fm.v18i5.4366

Madhubala, M., & Narasimha Prasad, L. V. (2017). Automatic Assessment of Floods Impact Using Twitter Data. *International Journal of Civil Engineering and Technology*, *8*(5), 1228–1238.

Social Media: How to tweet your customers' right. (n. d.).

Nepal, S., Paris, C., & Georgakopoulos, D. (Eds.). (2015). Social Media for Government Services. Springer International Publishing.

Priedhorsky, R., Culotta, A., & Del, S. Y. (2014). Inferring the origin locations of tweets with quantitative confidence. In *Proceeding CSCW '14* (pp 1523-1536). 10.1145/2531602.2531607

Qiang, Z., Bin, W., Rui, Z., & Xia, X.C. (2008). Genetic Algorithm-Based Design for DNA Sequences Sets. *Chinese Journal of Computers*, *31*(12), 2193-2199.

Qiu, S., & Wang, Q. (2009). Freeway traffic incident detection based on BP neural network. In *China Measurement & Test* (pp. 48-52).

Rashidi, T., Auld, J., & Mohammadian, A. (2013). The effectiveness of Bayesian Updating Attributes in Data Transferability Applications: Transportation Research Record. *Journal of the Transportation Research Board*, *2344*, 1–9. doi:10.3141/2344-01

Schweitzer, L. (2012). How are we doing? opinion mining customer sentiment in us transit agencies and airlines via twitter. In *Proceedings of the Transportation Research Board 91st Annual Meeting*.

Sood, S., & Owsley, S. Kristian J Hammond & Larry Birnbaum. (2007). Reasoning through Search: A Novel Approach to Sentiment Classification. In *Proceedings of WWW '07 conference*.

Steiger, E., Ellersiek, T., & Zipf, A. (2014). Explorative public transport flow analysis from uncertain social media data. In *Proceedings of the 3rd ACM SIGSPATIAL International Workshop on Crowdsourced and Volunteered Geographic Information*, 1-7.

Steur, R. (2015). *Twitter as a spatiotemporal source for incident management* [Master thesis]. Utrecht University, Netherlands.

Wiegand, M., Balahur, A., Roth, B., Klakow, D., & Montoya, A. (2010). A Survey on the Role of Negation in Sentiment Analysis. In *Proceedings of the Workshop on NeSp-NLP '10*.

This research was previously published in Innovative Applications of Big Data in the Railway Industry; pages 157-182, copyright year 2018 by Engineering Science Reference (an imprint of IGI Global).

Chapter 40
Social Media as a Tool to Understand Behaviour on the Railways

David Golightly
University of Nottingham, UK

Robert J. Houghton
University of Nottingham, UK

ABSTRACT

Social media plays an increasing role in how passengers communicate to, and about, train operators. In response, train operators and other rail stakeholders are adopting social media to contact their users. There are a number of opportunities for tapping this big data information stream through the overt use of technology to analyse, filter and present social media, including filtering for operational staff, or sentiment mapping for strategy. However, this analysis is predicated on a number of assumptions regarding the manner in which social media is currently being used within a railway context. In the following chapter, we present data from studies of rail social media that shed light on how big data analysis of social media exchange can support the passenger. These studies highlight important factors such as the broad range of issues covered by social media (not just disruption), the idiosyncrasies of individual train operators that need to be taken into account within social media analysis, and the time critical nature of information during disruption.

INTRODUCTION

Rail travel offers ample opportunity to fill `dead' time with transient activities (Jain and Lyons, 2008). The introduction of data networks and wi-fi across the railways, coupled with widespread smartphone adoption, allows many people to use social media while on the move. Passengers wish to communicate about their experience, either directly to transport operators in the form of query or comments, or to communicate with their social network about their travel experience. In response, transport operators

DOI: 10.4018/978-1-7998-9020-1.ch040

are seeking ways to utilise the opportunity of social media to improve passenger experience, particularly during disruption, and predominantly through Twitter (Pender et al., 2013, 2014; Liu et al., 2016).

There is interest in how technology can support the effective utilisation of social media. This might be with a view to extracting more information from social media to give transport operators faster intelligence on events occurring in and around their network (Periera at al., 2014; Mai & Hranac, 2012), or to understand attitudes of passengers. However, there may be other applications related to social media, such as tools to allow rapid response to tweets in times of disruption, Twitter dashboards for rail managers, and channels to repurpose social media to a wider set of users than just a rail operator's own followers, for example through customer information screens on stations (Golightly and Durk, 2016).

These kinds of 'big data' applications could be a vital tool for the rail industry and passengers, but are reliant on technologies such as natural language processing of tweets and sentiment analysis of incoming social media messages. The viability of such applications is based upon assumptions surrounding the nature of social media traffic, such as there being sufficient volume and content on any given channel to support meaningful analysis. Therefore, it is vital to underpin the development and deployment of such technology with a knowledge of which platforms are most relevant to rail communications, what situations or events are most likely to generate social media traffic, whether the use of social media is consistent and what the expectations of rail operators are in this arena.

The following chapter summarises a number of dedicated studies to understand the usage patterns inherent in how social media is used on the railways by both passengers and the rail stakeholders trying to communicate with them. By doing so, we identify a number of use cases, as well as some of the constraints around usage patterns that would need to be taken into account when developing applications (both passenger facing, and more 'back office' for rail operators) that draw on social media analytics. This chapter is intended to be most useful to those designing or procuring social media platforms and analysis technologies for the railways, as well as those involved in policy, such as those who may be including social media within the provisions of passenger information as part of a franchising agreement, or those looking to monitor passenger experience across the railways.

BACKGROUND

As recently as the beginning of this decade (Houghton and Golightly, 2011) few passengers, and fewer operators, actively used social media for anything other than marketing. Since then the landscape has changed dramatically, with many transport operators worldwide using social media as a means to communicate with their passengers. In a global survey of social media use in transport operations in 2013, 86% of operators preferred to use Twitter, 33% use Facebook, and only 12% of the operators not using any form of social media (Pender et al., 2013). More recent work with public transit (i.e. not just rail) in the US reports adoption rates by transport operators of 100% for Twitter (Liu et al., 2016). In Great Britain, all major train operating companies have active accounts, as does the main train information service channel (National Rail Enquiries), the infrastructure manager (Network Rail), as well as major stations and British Transport Police (Golightly and Durk, 2016).

The adoption of this innovative form of communication coincides with a period of unprecedented change for transport operations. Expanding cities and mobile lifestyles put greater demands on transport providers to keep stretched networks running with increased capacity (EU, 2011) in the face of emerging disruptive forces such as climate change (Koetse and Reitveld, 2009) and security threats (Gov. of India,

2013). Therefore, social media is set to play a vital role in the perception and operation of transport networks both tactically and strategically. This use of social media is anticipated to be most relevant during times of disruption and particularly through the use of Twitter where short messages can be rapidly disseminated to passengers informing them of service conditions and changes to timetables (Pender et al., 2014). As well as providing an information channel, organisational crisis communication through social media has been demonstrated to limit the impact of negative reactions (negative word of mouth; boycott) in comparison with other forms of media (Schultz et al., 2011).

While much of the communication by rail operators is still a manual process (Golightly and Durk, 2016) of replying to passenger comments, or broadcasting messages, there is much promise offered by technology. The internet generally, and social media in particular, can provide crucial context when trying to determine the causes of an unexpected event. This is particularly relevant when the event is caused "off the network" (e.g., a spike in passenger numbers due to a late running sporting event) or in the context of large events (Cottrill et al., 2017). The insight gathered through social media can help transport operators in predicting near-term non-recurrent supply changes allowing operators to plan accordingly (Periera at al., 2014; Mai & Hranac, 2012). This follows more general interest in the area of data mining, analysis and intelligence gathering through social media as part of broader emergency management scenarios (Sutton et al., 2008; Palen et al., 2010).

The volume of communications that might be generated by passengers on a transport network can be huge – each train operator in Great Britain regularly receives hundreds of tweets per hour as queries or comments that need to be reviewed and addressed. Figure 1 presents a model of the types of information that flow via Twitter between passengers and railway operators.

Preparing accurate, useful and tactful responses to these queries, with or without disruption, is a full-time job (Golightly and Durk, 2016) and tools to manage this communication, such as filtering based on Natural Language Processing (Yin et al., 2012) can streamline that process. There is also the potential for information mined through social media to be personalised and presented directly back to the passenger (Corsar et al., 2014), or to be coupled with other data sources to present very detailed information regarding service status (Rahman et al., 2015).

Figure 1. Information flow between passengers and operators

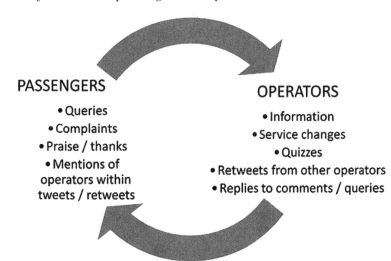

795

Therefore, if technologies based on big data analyses of social media are to be effective, it is critical to understand the constraints and characteristics of the content of social media that might shape the interpretation of results. This is most acute when considering the application of Twitter analytics in an area such as disruption management. The control and dissemination of information during disruption is a complex activity requiring multiple roles coordinating multiple (sometimes conflicting) information, with competing demands (Golightly et al., 2013). Often the windows of opportunity for action are brief, and the degrees of freedom in which to act are limited. Any delay in sensing or responding to the initial phases of an incident can exacerbate the situation rapidly (Belmonte et al., 2011). Therefore, the delivery of intelligence based on social media needs to be accurate, fast and deployed in a user-centred manner that compliments and enhances operational processes (Houghton and Golightly, 2011).

A scenario can help to illustrate. While major disruption events will be known to operational staff, a minor event, such as a peak of demand due to an overrunning concert, could be identified through social media. This might be through social media regarding the concert itself, but also through comments relating to crowding on the station. Social media tools, based on natural language processing and an ontology based around station names, can filter out this information, alerting social media managers through a dedicated social media dashboard, to manage customer expectation, or even advising of alternatives. Additionally, the dashboard could alert operational controllers who act to manage passenger levels (e.g. by warning train crew to anticipate high passenger levels).

Disruption is not a unitary phenomenon (Golightly et al., 2013, 2016) and varies by cause, location, duration etc. This can affect the trajectory of the disruption, which has a bearing on the kind of information that passengers need to know. Business reputation and social media are now explicit factors in real-time operational decision making during disruption (Golightly and Dadashi, 2016).

Understanding how the characteristics of disruption might correlate with Twitter useage could help to inform the design of technology as well as processes, for example, in the Passenger Information During Disruption (PIDD) code of practice used in Great Britain (ATOC, 2012). Additionally, there is evidence that transport operators vary in their social media strategy. While some choose to proactively distribute information, others are more reactive, replying to individual queries as they come in. In a study of transit services in the Strathclyde area of Scotland, this was due to local transport network constraints reducing the relevance of broadcast information (not all issues were believed to impact all people), though it may also have been through a desire not to generate negative perceptions of service quality (Gault et al., 2014). Therefore, technologies described in the scenario above need to reflect the specific nature of the type of disruption and potentially the style of operator in how they communicate.

The rest of this chapter considers potential applications, and some of the factors that need to be considered, regarding rail social media analytics and big data analysis. It opens by pulling out use cases from interviews conducted with rail stakeholders, transportation subject matter experts and, in particular, rail social media team managers and staff. It also highlights -- from an operational perspective -- some of the considerations relevant to rail social media analytics. A series of studies are then presented that examine how rail social media is used, examining which social media plaform (Facebook or Twitter) is most commonly used in the rail setting, and then investigating factors relating to operational characteristics and Train Operating Company (TOC) utilisation of social media that might influence the kind of data that is generated and how it should be analysed.

USE CASES

Two separate studies have been conducted with rail stakeholders to understand use cases for how social media, and social media analysis, can be applied to a railway context. The first of these studies (Houghton and Golightly, 2011) spoke to strategic management and the rail industry supply chain to understand, at that time, the potential of social media within a rail context. The second study (Golightly and Durk, 2016) was conducted more recently with rail social media managers and staff to understand how they were utilising social media, and their vision for how it could be used in the future. From both of these studies, use cases included:

- **Unstaffed Stations:** Many stations have either no staffing, or staffing at limited times. The opportunity to get additional data on station conditions would be useful. This might include factors such as ice on the platforms, or other forms of poor weather, but also information relating to crime and vandalism, or issues with assets such as ticketing machines.
- **Passenger Experience Issues:** Social media users commonly report issues with rolling stock particularly in relation to heating / air conditioning, Wi-Fi availability, which can be relayed to train maintenance crews. Additionally, passengers focus on factors such as crowding or lack of catering, which can also be fed back and rectified ideally in real time.
- **Public Order Issues:** The volume of people being transported by rail means that it is can be a potential flashpoint for violence, particularly taking into account the high number of football supporters that travel using rail to matches (British Transport Police, n. d.). Also, trains run late into the night, with increased risk of drink-related offences and accidents, occurring in and around the railway network.
- **Off-Network Events:** Events may take place away from the rail network itself but may have an impact on the service. For example, a concert or sport event may run late, meaning that a peak is passengers occurs later than expected at stations, which may need additional staffing or re-planning of services.
- **Understanding (and Managing) Misinformation:** One of the major concerns with social media, and of communication between transport users generally, was how misunderstandings and misinformation develops during incidents. At the early stages of an incident, in particular, transport users may start to communicate about potential causes and consequences of disruption, (for example, when a delay due to a minor derailment becomes exaggerated through word of mouth to be a major accident). Understanding when these misconceptions are occurring, and being able to correct them was considered to be more than just impression management, but also critical to ensuring that transport users had accurate information on which to re-plan journeys or expect the normal service to resume.
- **Managing Volume:** The sheer volume of tweets that social media account managers face is a significant challenge in its own right. Simply sorting through and responding to the number of messages is difficult given that it is still mostly a manual task. Tools to help sort incoming queries and comment and generate automatic responses could help account manager's loads, though there are concerns that humour and sarcasm, as well as passengers conveying all relevant information about their query in a single tweet, makes it difficult to automate the process.
- **Service Disruption Dashboards:** The nature and volume of social media content is already used a strong indicator of the effectiveness of disruption management strategy. For example, managers

will look to check that the volume of negative tweets is decreasing, or that tweets with praise from passengers is increasing, during disruption as an indicator in real-time that a disruption management strategy is having a positive effect on passenger experience.

All of these use cases point to the viability and value of big data analysis of railway information, not just hypothetically, but as described by stakeholders themselves. The next question for a developer of such tools is to understand what is the landscape of content and usage of social media on the railways. In the next section, we consider some of the characteristics of rail social media behaviour.

CHARACTERISTICS OF SOCIAL MEDIA BEHAVIOUR

One key question to determine the nature of social media communications is to understand the kind of material that is available for analysis. The following section presents a series of studies of social media data in conjunction with the railways. These vary from macro-scale questions regarding which form of social media (Twitter or Facebook) is most relevant, through to questions of numbers of users in relation to train operator characteristics, including operational performance. We then present more detailed analysis of specific train operators in terms of the types of message they generate, and offer a specific example of how communications proceed within a given incident.

Which Social Media Platform?

The first question to answer is which social media platform is most commonly used on the railways. Apart from a small number of train operator Instagram accounts, the main channels for social media communication on the railways are Twitter and Facebook. Within that, global surveys of public transit operators (Pender et al., 2013; Liu et al., 2016) and interviews with GB rail stakeholders (Golightly and Durk, 2016) suggests that an overwhelming preference for Twitter over Facebook, despite Facebook penetration being double that of Twitter, both in the UK and globally (List of Popular Social Networks, n. d.). To confirm which platform is currently the most useful and popular for rail social media analysis, a comparison was made of the number of Facebook and Twitter 'followers' of the accounts of major Great Britain train operating companies.

The Office of Road and Rail National Rail Trends (ORR NRT) Data Portal lists passenger km (in millions) for all rail franchises in Great Britain. The criterion was applied that to be considered in the analysis, a franchise had to have a minimum of 5 million passenger Km per year. This criterion allowed us to exclude small and open access train operators that were atypical of the majority of rail operators, with a very limited social media presence and left a sample of 18 TOCs covering all major intercity, regional and London / South East based services.

A search was conducted for each TOC's Facebook page, which presents the number of user followers. A search was conducted for each TOC's Twitter profile. This gives a number of account followers. All 18 TOCs included in the analysis had a Twitter profile. Only 16 of the 18 had a Facebook profile. The mean number of Twitter followers for the TOCs was approximately 162,000, ranging between 35,600 and 650,000. The mean number of Facebook followers was approximately 25,000, ranging between 2,500 and 125,000.

Overall, the ratio of average Twitter followers to average Facebook followers is approximately 6.7:1, despite the overall UK social media statistics suggesting there are twice as many Facebook users to Twitter users. Also, a review of the content of these profiles confirms that most Twitter accounts are active with updates every day, if not every hour and in some cases almost every minute, on topics including service information, responses to queries and updates on delay or disruption. On the other hand, Facebook posts tend to be sporadic, often only every few days, and covering marketing information such as promotions, or notifications of major planned disruption (e.g. industrial action). In conclusion, and supporting previous studies and interview evidence, Twitter is by far the preferred platform for real time social media communications between passengers and operators.

Characteristics of Twitter Followers

Having established Twitter as the most useful source of information, a further question is what might be driving Twitter traffic. Previous work (Liu et al., 2016; Gault et al., 2014) from general public transit domains suggest that this is not just a question of the number of passengers, but may be down to more complex factors such as the style and preference of the operator, and the level of engagement with its followers.

To test this, a number of Twitter related characteristics for each TOC was correlated with a number of operational and service characteristics from each TOC.

Twitter characteristics, accessed via each TOC's Twitter profile page, included:

- Number of followers
- Number of tweets (including replies)
- Average tweets per day (by sampling at number of Tweets at two different dates and working out an average)

TOC operational characteristics, access via the ORR NRT portal, included:

- Number of passenger km operated per year (in million km)
- Number of train services operated per year (in thousands)
- A measure of performance – the ORR NRT gives a measure of Cancelled and Severely Late trains (CaSL), per TOC. CaSL is defined as the percentage of passenger trains cancelled in part or full, or that arrive at their final destination 30 or more minutes later than the time shown in the public timetable. As Cancelled and Severely Late trains would presumably generate tweets from operators, or require responses to passenger queries, CaSL is an appropriate performance measure. To give an absolute number of affected services that takes into account the size of operation of a TOC, CaSL has been multiplied by train services operated by a TOC per year.

Means and standard deviations for each variable are shown in Table 1. Correlations were performed using Pearson's r, shown in Table 2. Significant values (two tailed, $p < 0.05$, $df = 16$, $r > 0.44$) are marked in bold.

Taking each of the three Twitter related variables in turn, the number of followers is not significantly correlated with passenger km, number of trains or total number of CaSL. Bigger TOCs, even though they have a larger passenger base or number of services, do not necessarily have bigger sets of users following

Table 1. Means and standard deviations for Twitter useage, operational and performance variables

	Followers (Thousands)	Tweets (Thousands)	Tweets Per Day (Thousands)	Passenger km (Millions)	Number of Services (Thousands)	Total CaSL Services (Thousands)
Average	167.39	301.79	0.21	7.03	399.36	12.3
St Dev	161.72	223.14	0.16	3.77	317.48	13.4

Table 2. Correlations of Twitter usage, operational and performance variables

	Followers	Tweets	Tweets per Day	Passenger km	Number of Services	Total CaSL
Followers	1.00	**0.52**	0.36	0.35	0.23	0.17
Tweets		1.00	**0.86**	**0.67**	0.44	**0.47**
Tweets Per day			1.00	**0.71**	0.41	0.43
Passenger Km				1.00	**0.75**	**0.72**
Number of services					1.00	**0.87**
Total CaSL						1.00

them. Indeed, inspection of the data suggests that some of the smaller, long distance TOCs have very high numbers of followers. This analysis backs up the reports of rail social media managers (Golightly and Durk, 2016) that strategy is an important factor in growing and maintaining a Twitter following.

The correlations suggest a link between number of tweets generated by the TOC, and operational and performance characteristics. Both passenger KM and CaSL were significant, suggesting that both numbers of people and number of delayed services will lead to a higher number of tweets from the TOC. Also, tweets per day suggests a similar though weaker pattern. More passenger km will lead to more tweets per day. However, the correlation between tweets per day and CaSL is not significant, suggesting that factors other than delay may generate the volume of tweets of a daily basis.

Content Analyses of Twitter Usage Patterns

While Twitter is shown to be most common social media communication channel, and higher service numbers generally leads to higher number of tweets from a TOC, there would seem to be factors other than sheer passenger numbers that influences the number of followers. This is important as those TOCs with high passengers are may not achieve the same level of penetration as other TOCs.

One of the limitations of the analysis above is that it does not differentiate between tweets that are broadcasts to all users, and tweets that are responses to specific queries. This is important as the design of the Twitter platform means that all followers do not automatically see exchanges directed to and from a user, unless they are also following both users in the exchange. Therefore, useful information flowing between TOCs and users will not always be seen by all Twitter followers of that TOC.

To test what type of information is being conveyed in Twitter exchanges with a TOC, five TOCs were followed for an extended period of two weeks and outgoing tweets were captured. Tweets were captured using NVivo with the NCapture plugin, and were filtered and categorised in Microsoft Excel according to the following scheme.

- **TOC Broadcast (TOCB):** A Tweet sent by the TOC to all its followers. This might be disruption information, a salutation at the start of the day, or marketing information.
- **TOC Directed Tweet (TOCDT):** A Tweet directed to a specific recipient (the tweet starts with the intended users name. In the case of a TOC this is usually a reply to a comment or query from a passenger) NB this is not to be confused with a Twitter Direct Message (DM).
- **TOC Retweet (TOCRT):** A recirculation by the TOC of a Tweet to all of its followers. In the case of the TOC this might be recirculating a tweet sent in by a passenger asking if anyone has found a lost personal item on a train.

Table 3 shows the breakdown of outgoing tweets from the five TOCs. Also, to gauge how much traffic might be generated by disruption events, the Network Rail Control Centre Incident Log, and National Rail Enquiries service update website, were monitored to identify potential disruption during the data captured period. The numbers of disruption events are also presented in Table 3.

Table 3. Outgoing tweets from the TOC

	TOC1	TOC2	TOC3	TOC4	TOC5
TOCBs	140	62	426	114	1476
TOCDTs	1695	8896	2181	7802	3952
TOCRTs	31	32	32	75	61
Total outgoing	1866	8990	2639	7991	5489
Average per day	133.3	642.1	188.5	570.8	392.1
Disruption events	32	27	31	18	29

Figure 2. Distribution of Tweet types by TOC; Y-axis is number of tweets.

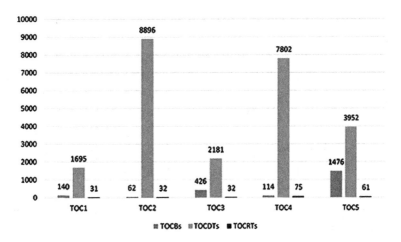

Several points emerge. First, TOCs are variable in how they choose to communicate via Twitter, particularly with regards how they choose to broadcast information. Some TOCs (e.g. TOC3,5) will generate many broadcast messages, while others are far less likely to do so (e.g. TOC1). This is despite TOCs experiencing a similar numbers of disruption events over the analysis period. Therefore, TOC style is a critical factor to take into account when analysing the nature of exchange between TOC and passenger.

Second, in some cases the numbers of outgoing TOC tweets are extremely high, with TOC2 generating over 600 Tweets per day. Given that most of these TOCs have limited response out of hours (00:00-06:00) this means in some cases a response rate during operational hours is in the region of a tweet almost every minute.

Third, the large majority (72%) of tweets are not broadcasts of information, but are instead typically responses to incoming tweets. All TOCs to some extent, and some (e.g. TOC2) to a greater extent prefer to reply to issues rather than broadcast information. The implication is that information transmitted as replies are very unlikely to be seen by any user other than the recipient, or by actively searching within the TOCs timeline. Therefore, potentially useful information will not be seen by all followers of a TOC account.

In terms of the content of tweets, Table 4 gives an example timeline of how TOCs use broadcasts during disruption. This is for a landslip blocking the line the in Banbury area of Great Britain. Out of the 142 tweets that were broadcasted by the TOC from the afternoon to evening on the day of the disruption, 123 of these tweets were replies to users, making it 86.6% as replies to users. The example also highlights the use of hashtags to allow passengers to follow an event over time, and to search. This is also supports coordination with other stakeholders who need to offer alternative services or might be affected. The mention of other TOCs in the timeline (15:32), and the retweet of another TOCs message of ticket acceptance (15:10), reinforces the idea of multiple stakeholders bringing each other in to the stream of information associated with an event. This is a powerful capability of Twitter. Finally, the management of the incident concludes for that day with information about how passengers can claim compensation (21:59).

IMPLICATIONS

A number of specific findings and implications for designers emerge from the analysis presented here. First, a number of use cases have been highlighted that would benefit from big data analysis. These typically regard intelligence regarding conditions in and around the railways, and is mostly concerned with real-time or near real-time intelligence. This is critical given the time responsive nature of the railways, particularly during disruption (Belmondo et al., 2011) and the increased emphasis on reputation and information management (Golightly and Dadashi, 2016). Some of the applications however are more about 'back office' services to support social media teams – generating automated answers, filtering queries and presenting dashboards, to help an operator understand its performance. The implication is that both of these areas, real time intelligence, and supporting social media teams, are fruitful areas for future development of rail social media big data analyses.

Second, this work has confirmed other studies that Twitter is the most important information channel for social media exchange on the railways (Pender et al., 2013; Liu et al., 2016). This is partly likely to be derived from functional aspects – the ability to post short messages to followers, and the conversational nature of the interface, and the way it readily lends itself to mobile devices – and partially because of attitudes around it being more for practical use rather than for communicating with a person's own social network as per Facebook (Passengerfocus, 2013). The overriding implication is that social media analysis for the railways should have Twitter at its core.

Table 4. Timeline of broadcasts associated with major disruption event

14:52	Initial broadcast notifying all about incident occurrence and introduction of hashtag to categorise tweets *"Due to a landslip, all lines are currently blocked between #LeamingtonSpa & #Banbury. Delays, alterations & cancellations are expected."*
15:10	Notification of alternative means of transport with another TOC via a Retweet *"RT @SW_Trains: We're accepting @crosscountryuk tickets via any reasonable route following a landslip between Banbury & Leamington Spa"*
15:19	Update of incident to now inform commuters about rail replacement buses *"Due to a landslip, rail replacement buses are in operation in both directions between #LeamingtonSpa & #Banbury ran by @chilternrailway ."*
15:30	Update to combine the separate hashtags into one for easier classification *"UPDATE: Our further tweets in regards the landslip disruption between #LeamingtonSpa & #Banbury will be under the hashtag #Harburylandslip"*
15:32	Notification of more alternative transport with other TOCs *"#Harburylandslip: Ticket acceptance is in place with @VirginTrains @SW_Trains @chilternrailway @LondonMidland @FGW @eastcoastuk @TfL tube."*
16:35	Introduction of replacement bus service *"#Harburylandslip: There will soon be a limited coach service between LeamingtonSpa/Banbury and Oxford in both directions."*
17:40	Introduction of new service to cope with demand *"#Harburylandslip: There will be a service at xx:55 southbound from Banbury - Bournemouth/Southampton Central until the end of service today."*
18:10	Notification of cancelled route affected by incident *"#Harburylandslip: The 19:45 Bournemouth - Birmingham New Street is cancelled throughout."*
21:59	End of Twitter Operating hours, along with reminder of delay compensation *"We'll be back tomorrow at 8am. Further updates will be provided in regards to the #Harburylandslip. Please claim Delay Repay if affected 1/2"*

Third, while the volume of Twitter traffic has some relation with operational factors such as number of passengers and services, or experienced delay, this is not a simple relationship. In particular, the number of followers of a TOC account is determined by factors other than sheer size of the TOCs operations. Reinforcing other studies (Gault et al., 2014; Golightly and Durk, 2016), TOC style plays a significant role in shaping how a TOC uses Twitter and it how looks to communicate with its followers. Furthermore, by looking at the breakdown of type of message (broadcast, reply, retweet) this difference between TOC becomes more apparent. Some TOCs are highly reactive in how they tweet, replying mostly to queries and with little use of broadcast. Others are more proactive. The implication here for big data analysis are that: (1) TOCs use different strategies, with different styles of communication. This must be taken into account when designing algorithms and ontologies to process the content of tweets and (2) this will affect the kind of response and volume of response that a TOC can expect to generate. Some TOCs will generate more conversations with their passengers that are amenable to analysis, and this is not just determined by TOC size. Also, if a TOC wants to use its Twitter feed as a source of intelligence, it should actively look to grow its follower base.

Fourth, disruption and non-disruption are both encountered in the Twitter data. Indeed, one comment from social media managers is that many diverse non-disruption queries such as lost luggage, ticketing queries, and specific complaints, take up more time than disruption which can be communicated uniformly across all passengers. The implications for big data analysis are therefore (1) support is needed just as much for non-disruption as it is for disruption (2) when a disruption is occurring, there is a clear narrative, as well as use of pointer such as hashtags of locations (see Table 4) that can help with the interpretation of events. These narratives vary for different types of event (Golightly and Dadashi, 2016) and can be used to form ontologies, specific to each type of disruption, that can be embedded within analytical tools. As an illustration, coupling general language about delay (e.g. 'delay, 'disruption') with specific language regarding the type of disruption (e.g. 'train failure', blocked line'), with terminology specific to an operator geography (e.g. locations and stations for that operator), as well as general levels of interaction between the operator and passenger, which indicates volume of Twitter traffic, can provide a targeted data pre-processing ontology. This pre-processing ontology would, in turn, facilitate faster analysis of incoming tweets, prioritisation, dashboards for internal operational staff, and potentially a means to filter and re-publish particularly useful tweets to passengers through other channels such as other forms of social media, websites or even on-platform / in-station displays.

Figure 3. Typology of passenger usage of Twitter and Twitter-based information

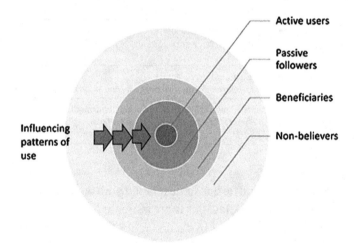

Fifth and finally, a methodological point arises from the correlations between Twitter and ORR data sets in Table 2 and 3. Twitter does not have to be the only dataset. Even with the relatively simple combination of Twitter data with open operational and performance data it has been possible to identify some relationships between social media and train operators. The implication is that there are many ways Twitter could be augmented with information from other data sets within big data analyses. Also, the focus of this paper has been analyses using social media as the major data source, there is potential for analyses on other data sets, where Twitter could play a more supplementary role (Rahman et al., 2015), for example by having condition monitoring data as the primary analysis, but supplementing that with comments on Twitter about ride quality and comfort.

Figure 3 represents the typology of passenger and social media users relevant to the railways. At the core, there are 'active users' – they generate tweets and retweets and thus generate both traffic and intelligence about activity on the railways. Second, there are 'passive followers' of railway Twitter accounts. They do not necessarily generate data, but they could view broadcasts and information on Twitter. Importantly, from this analysis, passive followers will benefit to varying degrees depending on whether a TOC broadcasts their messages or not. Third, there are potential 'beneficiaries'. These may not follow social media, but could benefit from filtered views of Twitter-based information. This might be through sentiment analytics, or for example through the presentation of a sub-set of most valuable tweets through disruption pages on operator websites (some TOCs and National Rail Enquiries already have a simplified version of this) or even on station information screens. Finally, there are 'non-believers' – passengers who have no interest in Twitter-based information. Key to the ongoing success of Twitter is to maintain the active user base, and to move more passengers from the outer circles to the inner stages of adoption and engagement with Twitter-based information. This typology is useful in that it allows developers and designers to have a clear idea of who is generating and using Twitter-based information.

CONCLUSION

Social media has been proposed as a potential target for big data analysis. This chapter has outlined some of the ways in which social media could be used, both for intelligence in and around the railways and to support in the management of social media accounts. Much of this is still manual and therefore opportunity exists. For new tools or analyses to be successful they must, however, take into account how passengers use rail social media and how operators control the railway. Following prior work (Pender et al., 2013; Liu et al., 2016) which looked at transport systems generally, analyses here demonstrate that Twitter is the predominant form of social media on the railways. Usage does not map completely to the size of train operator and factors such as strategy play an important role in the type of communication generated. Disruption is important, but equally non-disruption and more general passenger experience factors are communicated through Twitter and these are usually queries between passenger and train operator that will not necessarily be seen by all followers.

While we have outlined a number of implications for developers of big data analysis, the variation between TOCs indicates a policy implication. Not all TOCs are standard in their use of Twitter. The type of content that two TOCs will generate or will elicit from its passengers may vary because of strategy, not because of any operational concerns. Also, a TOC may appear to be performing less effectively on social media because it elects to broadcast information and invite comment. Therefore, the use of tools to present metrics, such as dashboards, that present data on both volume and content (i.e. sentiment) of tweets should only be used for comparison across TOCs, for example to study performance, with great caution.

Taking into account the opportunity and characteristics for rail social media, there is both a scope and need for developments in this area. Future work should look on one hand to develop tools that can filter queries with a high level of accuracy. As mentioned above, initial work in generally defining disruption characteristics (Golightly and Dadashi, 2016) could be used to inform specific disruption-related ontologies. Also, models of non-disruption, more general passenger experience (e.g. Stanton et al., 2013) could be used as the basis of ontologies for analysis. Finally, it is critical that any tool that is developed takes into accounts the needs of its users, particularly when embedded within an operational context (Houghton and Golightly, 2011).

ACKNOWLEDGMENT

The first author was funded by the Impetus partnership between Universities of Nottingham and Leicester, and the Transport Systems Catapult. We are also grateful for the input and support of the Rail Delivery Group and Jason Durk, at Govia Thameslink Railway, for invaluable access to industry experts and data.

REFERENCES

ATOC (Association of Train Operating Companies). (2012). Approved Code of Practice – Passenger Information During Disruption. Retrieved 05/11/14 from http://www.atoc.org/clientfiles/files/ACOP015v3%20-%20PIDD%20(2).pdf

Belmonte, F., Schön, W., Heurley, L., & Capel, R. (2011). Interdisciplinary safety analysis of complex socio-technological systems based on the functional resonance accident model: An application to railway traffic supervision. *Reliability Engineering & System Safety*, *96*(2), 237–249. doi:10.1016/j.ress.2010.09.006

British Transport Police. (n. d.). Football policing. Retrieved from http://www.btp.police.uk/advice_and_info/how_we_tackle_crime/football_policing.aspx

Corsar, D., Markovic, M., Gault, P. E., Mehdi, M., Edwards, P., Nelson, J. D., ... Sripada, S. (2015). TravelBot: Journey Disruption Alerts Utilising Social Media and Linked Data. In *Proceedings of the Posters and Demonstrations Track of the 14th International Semantic Web Conference (ISWC '15)*.

Cottrill, C., Gault, P., Yeboah, G., Nelson, J. D., Anable, J., & Budd, T. (2017). Tweeting Transit: An examination of social media strategies for transport information management during a large event. *Transportation Research Part C, Emerging Technologies*, *77*, 421–432. doi:10.1016/j.trc.2017.02.008

European Commission. (2011). Roadmap to a single European transport area—Towards a competitive and resource-efficient transport system (White Paper on transport). Luxembourg, Publications Office of the European Union.

Gault, P., Corsar, D., Edwards, P., Nelson, J. D., & Cottrill, C. (2014). You'll Never Ride Alone: The Role of Social Media in Supporting the Bus Passenger Experience. In *Proceedings of the Ethnographic Praxis in Industry Conference* (Vol. 2014, No. 1, pp. 199-212).

Golightly, D., & Dadashi, N. (2016). The characteristics of railway service disruption: Implications for disruption management. *Ergonomics*. PMID:27215348

Golightly, D., Dadashi, N., Sharples, S., & Dasigi, M. (2013). Disruption management processes during emergencies on the railways. *International Journal of Human Factors and Ergonomics*, *2*(2), 175–195. doi:10.1504/IJHFE.2013.057619

Golightly, D., & Durk, J. (2016). Twitter as part of operational practice and passenger experience on the railways. In P.E. Waterson, E. Hubbard & R. Sims (Eds.), *Proceedings of EHF2016. Contemporary Ergonomics and Human Factors 2016*. Loughborough: CIEHF.

Government of India (Railway Board). (2014) Disaster management plan Retrieved 05/11/14 from http://www.indianrailways.gov.in/railwayboard/uploads/directorate/safety/pdf/2014/DM_Plan_2014.pdf

Houghton, R. J., & Golightly, D. (2011). Should a signaller look at twitter? The value of user data to transport control. Retrieved from http://de2011.computing.dundee.ac.uk

Jain, J., & Lyons, G. (2008). The gift of travel time. *Journal of Transport Geography, 16*(2), 81–89. doi:10.1016/j.jtrangeo.2007.05.001

Koetse, M. J., & Rietveld, P. (2009). The impact of climate change and weather on transport: An overview of empirical findings. *Transportation Research Part D, Transport and Environment, 14*(3), 205–221. doi:10.1016/j.trd.2008.12.004

Liu, J. H., Shi, W., Elrahman, O.S., Ban, X.J., & Reilly, J.M. (2016). Understanding social media program usage in public transit agencies. *International Journal of Transportation Science and Technology, 5*(2), 83–92. doi:10.1016/j.ijtst.2016.09.005

Mai, E., & Hranac, R. (2013, January). Twitter interactions as a data source for transportation incidents. In *Proc. Transportation Research Board 92nd Ann. Meeting (No. 13-1636)*.

Palen, L., Starbird, K., Vieweg, S., & Hughes, A. (2010). twitter-based information distribution during the 2009 Red River Valley flood threat. *Bulletin of the American Society for Information Science and Technology, 36*(5), 13–17. doi:10.1002/bult.2010.1720360505

Passenger Focus. (2013) Short and Tweet: How passengers want social media during disruption. Retrieved April 8, 2013 from http://www.transportfocus.org.uk/research-publications/publications/short-and-tweet-how-passengers-want-social-media-during-disruption/

Pender, B., Currie, G., Delbosc, A., & Shiwakoti, N. (2013, October). Social Media Utilisation during Unplanned Passenger Rail Disruption What's Not to Like? In *Proc. Australasian Transport Research Forum 2013*.

Pender, B., Currie, G., Delbosc, A., & Shiwakoti, N. (2014). Social Media Use in Unplanned Passenger Rail Disruptions – An International Study. In *Transportation Research Board 93rd Annual Meeting Compendium of Papers*.

Pereira, F. C., Bazzan, A. L., & Ben-Akiva, M. (2014). The role of context in transport prediction. *IEEE Intelligent Systems, 29*(1), 76–80. doi:10.1109/MIS.2014.14

Rahman, S. S., Easton, J. M., & Roberts, C. (2015, August). Mining open and crowdsourced data to improve situational awareness for railway. In *Proceedings of the 2015 IEEE/ACM International Conference on Advances in Social Networks Analysis and Mining (ASONAM)* (pp. 1240-1243). IEEE. 10.1145/2808797.2809369

Schultz, F., Utz, S., & Göritz, A. (2011). Is the medium the message? Perceptions of and reactions to crisis communication via Twitter, blogs and traditional media. *Public Relations Review*, *37*(1), 20–27. doi:10.1016/j.pubrev.2010.12.001

Social Media Ltd. (n. d.). List of Popular Social Networks. Retrieved from https://social-media.co.uk/ list-popular-social-networking-websites

Sutton, J., Palen, L., & Shklovski, I. (2008, May). Backchannels on the front lines: Emergent uses of social media in the 2007 southern California wildfires. In *Proceedings of the 5th International ISCRAM Conference,* Washington, DC (pp. 624-632).

Yin, J., Lampert, A., Cameron, M., Robinson, B., & Power, R. (2012). Using social media to enhance emergency situation awareness. *IEEE Intelligent Systems*, *27*(6), 52–59. doi:10.1109/MIS.2012.6

Section 4
Utilization and Applications

Chapter 41
Adoption of Web 2.0 Marketing:
An Exploratory Study About the Nigerian SME's

Maryam Lawan Gwadabe

IT and Business School, Blue Sapphire E-Solutions ltd, Kano, Nigeria

ABSTRACT

The digital age has brought up improved and efficient marketing ways for businesses to grow, earn publicity and generate more revenue. Web 2.0 marketing is a marketing medium that allows business to collaborate through sharing activities such as content and multimedia. This study explores the value which Web 2.0 marketing adds to the Nigerian SME's. The analyzed data showed that SME's most common marketing tool is Facebook, service-rendering companies also adopt Blogging tool and product-selling businesses prefer the picture platform (Facebook and Instagram). The major Web 2.0 marketing benefits achieved by the Nigerians SME's are increase in brand awareness and revenue. However, the benefit of getting high search engine optimization (SEO) rank is not leveraged. One major challenge is lack of in house skills is the most common faced in the adoption of Web 2.0 marketing as most of the online marketing is done by unskilled employees in the company; this issue leads to several challenges. It is recommended that the SME's should hire or outsource certified digital marketers for effective management and achievement of optimum Web 2.0 marketing strategy benefits.

INTRODUCTION

In 21st century, new ways of how businesses market their products and services have emerged. The advancement of technology has driven the emergence of Web 2.0 which is a shift from a one-way communication channel to two-way process of interactive platforms. The term "Web 2.0" was introduced by Tim O'Reilly (Wolcott, 2008). It was driven by several interrelated technologies such as Facebook, LinkedIn, Twitter, Podcast, and YouTube, etc. This technology has transformed the way businesses are done, it has paved the way for new business models which have increased product/service global awareness, boosted ROI (Return on Investment), allowed customer support, increase conversion rate

DOI: 10.4018/978-1-7998-9020-1.ch041

and lead generation. The fundamental essence of Web 2.0 marketing is the ability of the user to generate content and for businesses to analyze their marketing efforts through Web 2.0 analytics tools. According to Parise, Guinon, and Weigberg (2008), Web 2.0 is an influential marketing channel because it empowers individual and business especially SME's. In Nigeria, most of the businesses are Small and Medium Enterprises (SME's), these enterprises made the government give high priority as it increases the growth of the economy. The SMEs initially use the traditional way of marketing by using television, radio, printouts (flyers and brochures). The digital age made the marketing involved and starts using the Web 2.0 tool as the customers need for collaboration with business becomes necessary. The usage of the SMEs to set up an online community based on their business goal where they can communicate with their customers and the customers have the ability to collaborate with each other. The SMEs get several benefits from the usage of Web 2.0 marketing such as the reviews from customers, earn brand loyalty, increase recognition, ability to handle negative feedbacks, ability to gather customer data and measure result to make business decisions, and it gives the customers the privilege to know more about the business.

The aim of this chapter is to investigate the value Web 2.0 marketing can add to Nigeria's SME market. To achieve the goal, the chapter has explored the following:

- How Web 2.0 marketing adoption has changed the way Nigerian SME's carry out their marketing;
- Uncover the Nigeria SME's most preferred Web 2.0 marketing tool;
- Reveal the reason for the chosen tool;
- Benefits of Web 2.0 marketing to the SME'S;
- The challenges faced due to the adoption of Web 2.0 marketing;
- Recommendations on how to improve Nigeria SME's Web 2.0 marketing.

The research methodology applied is exploratory in nature, collecting qualitative data using semi-structured interviews, which is then analyzed using the thematic analysis (Ritchie & Lewis, 2003). The data is collected from 6 SMEs of different business types such as a consultancy firm, accessories retailer, fashion designer, and a fitness expert.

LITERATURE REVIEW

Evolution of Marketing from Traditional, Web 1.0 to Web 2.0

Traditional marketing is started ever since when people had products or service to sell. This way of marketing was around through talking face-to-face. Then it evolved to the usage of television, radio, newspapers, flyers, banners and magazines (Maher, 2014). As technology advanced and consumer needs increased, this way of marketing was not sufficient. The Web 1.0 also known as the "read only web" came in the early 90's and it enabled the Internet marketing paradigm. During the era of Web 1.0, it was just a one-way communication from businesses to consumers and no active communication between customers to business (Ahzab, 2013). Lack of interaction led the emergence of Web 2.0. Web 2.0 is when people use of Internet changes from one-way communication to bi-directional communication paradigm. It allows communication through several social networking sites (Hi5, Twitter, Facebook, Flickr, etc.). Hence Web 2.0 is also known as "social media".

WHAT IS WEB 2.0 MARKETING?

It is a set of web-based applications that allow collaboration between individuals and businesses (Parise et al., 2008). It gives businesses the platform to syndicate information on products, service and promotions to customers. Companies usually use the platforms to engage with customers through creating discussion topics; images, videos, blog posts, etc. based on their business goals. The customer can take part in the marketing activities of their company. According to Constantinides and Fountain (2008), Web 2.0 marketing differs from the initial Web 1.0 marketing because 'the user becomes an essential contributor, this makes it a new marketing parameter instigating a migration of market power from producers to consumers and from traditional mass media to new personalized ones." Web 2.0 applications are websites that have high social components. They come with several features such as the rich user experience, user ability to classify information, user as a contributor, customer empowerment ability of content reusability. It also has the feature of content generation and dispersion in the form of (text, video, images, likes, tagging, postings and sharing along with comments, reviews) (Tasner, 2014). However, all these social effects of Web 2.0 make it suitable for marketing, as it has become an integral part of human lives. People spend more time on the Internet than on the television and radios; there is an enormous rejection of traditional media. It has given consumers full access to products and services information access through the reviews, comments and recommendations; the consumers seem to trust more of this information than what a marketer tells them.

Web 2.0 Tools

These are a set of most popular Web 2.0 tools, which allow people to collaborate and build the online language to create, modify or contribute to content.

Facebook

It is a website with over 1.65 billion active users monthly, and the number continues growing steadily (Protalinski, 2016). On a Facebook platform business can select the demographics of what they are looking for, according to Google it is the most trafficked social media site in the world. Scherer (2014) also said that whatever business you are in, Facebook is a right platform to use for marketing. A business can either set up a page, group or combine all for greater market reach. Companies set up a page on Facebook to expand their online footprint to engage directly with existing and new customers. The page consists of what the business is about, address, call to action, post about the product or invitation to events in the form of (text, images and videos). Group on Facebook is more than a discussion forum; it can be created for free where businesses can have a high level of engagement with consumers. The Ads is a targeted advertisement that is paid based on the leads a business intends to reach out. In Facebook ads, a business can set it up based on the demographics such as age, location, educational level and gender (Bulygo, 2010).

Instagram

This tool is solely for photo and video sharing through mobile devices. It has over 400 million users. It is a mobile friendly tool where businesses have the opportunity to get noticed on the go. The companies can view account on a desktop but cannot add or edit anything on the desktop; it is strictly using mobile application. From 2012 till today average engagement rate of an audience on Instagram has increased 415%, and it's still increasing. This shows how powerful the tool can be for marketing. Business creates an Instagram account, write about their product and website link in the bio field. They post captivating images and videos of products or services. Interaction is usually done through direct messaging, commenting on the post, tagging, mentioning and liking (Logacre, 2014; Helmrich, 2015). According to Revevani (2014) the content on Instagram is more shareable and more understandable by people than any other content. Moreover, an Instagram business account is not different from the personal account. It also has an interesting feature of linking accounts to push post on other Web 2.0 tools such as Facebook, Twitter, Tumblr, Flickr, Foursquare and Mixi. The Instagram tool is not just a platform for business that owns products even service rendering can use it in a way of showing their business culture, employee's goodwill, celebrations and contests. The analytics of Instagram campaign can be measured by the usage of some tools (Stewart, 2014). Instagram marketing also has a feature of paid Ads just like Facebook advertisement.

YouTube

It is a video and audio sharing website. It allows users to upload, view and share videos (educational, TV shows, music video, software demos, etc.). According to Bermant (2015), YouTube is the second largest search engine platform after Google; it is also among the top 5 social networks. YouTube marketing is a way of creating viral marketing. It has over 1 billion users and every day they spend millions of hours to watch and generate views. Businesses create a channel on YouTube to market and advertise their products and services. The channel is free, users upload is unlimited, and they are automatically indexed and searchable from yahoo search or Google (Alhadi, 2010). YouTube is suitable for any business as the company can share information such as tutorials, product, or service, Product Demos, customer testimonials, business introductions, behind the scenes of videos, useful insights, presentations at work or conference, webinars, commercials, celebrations, frequently asked question (Demers, 2015). Paid adverts can also be created on YouTube, whereby video can show before the video is clicked on start playing or In-display, which is shown on the side of the page or at the beginning of the search results (Golden, 2014).

LinkedIn

It is specially made to connect professionals, find job, discover sales leads, and connect with business professionals. It is the number one professional network on the Internet. It helps individuals and businesses to establish themselves as experts within their business space. This tool has a feature where a company can create a page to build brand awareness, connect with followers and engage them with captivating content that will turn them into advocates (Chansamooth, 2014). The LinkedIn business page can be infused with compelling contents such as graphics, products or services. It also allows companies to add right job opportunities and can serve as a business website extension to generate leads and increase website traffic. A company can create a paid advertisement to grab the attention of vendors, employees, customers, and business partners to connect the page. The paid LinkedIn advertisement allows the company to set their budget, choose between pay per clicks and pay per impressions. The LinkedIn tool also comes with a feature that allows business to see valuable insights; it shows the statistics of the followers' engagement, clicks, and many more. Groups can also be created with LinkedIn, which a business can use to position themselves as thought leader through engaging in valuable discussion and offering interesting contents. The LinkedIn group comes with a feature of roles assignment to run successful group that doesn't go out of group goal; these roles are the moderator, the owners and manager (Sammons, 2013).

Snapchat

Is a tool that allows text, image and video messaging in real-time via the mobile device. It has over 100 million active users; over 400 million snaps are shared every day. With this advantage, businesses are using it to promote their product and service in a short-term visual message format. The application puts limits on how long the video will stay on the application after the time reaches it gone forever with this featured business can use it to host flash sales that end within 24 hours. It comes with a feature of live chat, images and short videos; a company can use it to build anticipation when releasing a new product or event (Husain, 2014; Gioglo, 2014). A youngster at the age of 18-36 years usually uses this application. With this analysis, it made snap chat suitable platform tool for only business that are targeting the younger generation. The app is a mobile application as it is more about snapping what is currently taking place. In Snapchat paid ads feature is also available (Jackson, 2015).

Twitter

Is a tool used in sharing real-time 140-character text, image or video link. The information is shared instantly for people to discover. It has over 320 million active users and over 500 million tweets daily. 80% of its users access it through mobile. Twitter gives the opportunity to reach out their audience regardless of location and time. Businesses use Twitter to listen to customers, drive awareness of product or service by communicating with customers and connect with influencers who are experts within the industry (Ganguly, 2015). A business Twitter account is not different from the personal account; it has the same process only that the account name is the business name. It works both on a desktop and mobile device. With Twitter business can follow vendors, partners, employees and customers. It also has a feature called list where a user can categorize his/her followers based on the conversion list such as the customers, potential customer, competitors, organization professional, etc. Twitter can be integrated with other tools to understand followers, measure performance, and to test tweet for better yields (Kingston, 2013).

Google+

This is a tool that is built off from Google account. The user through his/her Google account can activate it. It allows a user to categorize it and contact to circle based on interest (Sport, education, news, etc.). Google+ purpose is to connect users to others with the same passion. It has several features to search for interest, upload pictures and live video chats. It has over 150 million users and 50% log into Google Plus daily. With this benefits business can use it to market products and services. It has a feature of authorship, which allows business to get it pictures next to, search results. Enhance customer relationship by engaging with fans using video chats and also by share news and business content via the profile (Patel, 2014; Kovak, 2011). With Google+ the right content is delivered to the right people as it has the feature called circles for business where they can put vendors in one circle, partners, customers, family, etc. Business pages can be created with Google+ and it works the same way with the profile as the page owner can add people to circles, edit profile, share things, +1 comments, and photos, create and join Hangouts. It works both on a mobile device and desktop. Google + page can also be promoted using paid advertisement with the aid of social extension feature (Google.com, 2015).

Tumblr

It is a tool that used for blogging in short form. It is also known as the microblogging site. It allows a user to post anything in the form of text, video, audio, photos and animations. It has over 108 million blogs with 50 billion posts. With the aid of this tool businesses usually market their products and services to provide the right kind of value (offers), combine humor and promotions to a campaign. In Tumblr memes are also used to fit in by tempering promotion with interesting contents, understand audience using visuals and reposting customers post to engage with them (Aamoth, 2013).

Blogger

This is a tool that is owned by Google where users can create blogs in a form of online journal. Using this tool, the Blogger can update family and friend about his life, provide advice column, discuss political, economic, health, lifestyle or any area of interest issues. The blog can be run solo or with multiple contributors. The blog can also be used to make podcast feeds. Businesses use this platform to syndicate content to customers, engage with customers by providing up to the minute news about the company, to send a notification to the customers that subscribed to the blog, prove to a client you are well known about, get the wider audience, increase website traffic, leads and sales. This platform also allows the integration of online payment system for selling widgets (Cartwright, 2013).

Benefits of Web 2.0 Marketing

Web 2.0 Marketing poses several benefits to business. According to (Carbone, 2015), business that adopts Web 2.0 are likely to be the market leaders, gain market share and use the tools for management practices that lead to higher margin than those companies that use traditional or Web 1.0. Below are the benefits of adopting the Web 2.0 marketing (Carbone, 2015).

Lead Generation and Conversation Opportunities

Using any of the channels and tools of Web 2.0 marketing helps businesses to generate more leads to their websites that can be nurtured and converted to customers or prospects. Web 2.0 Marketing tools add more ways for users to reach the business site. And the more qualitative content added to the Web 2.0 tools, the more inbound traffics the business will generate which will then later turn into converted leads.

Increase Brand Awareness

The tools help to create awareness about a product or service f a business. These tools serve as platforms where people discuss their lives, including purchases and wants. Customer will help a business in marketing through their likes, shares, and comments. As people see the organic and paid ads from any of the Web 2.0 tools, they get to be aware of the existence of a business.

Provide Opportunity to Syndicate Information

The tools help business to have their content in several places at the same time. With just a few clicks information can be anywhere, a marketer wants it to be. The Web 2.0 tools give privileges for business to enlighten customer, vendors, partners and potential customers about the product and services or anything related to their business goals. This information can be of the high beneficial feature of a product or service or solutions to problems. This content syndication can be in a form of post, tweets, blog posts, group discussions, quizzes, videos, images, etc.

High Brand Authority

The usage of Web 2.0 tools for marketing usually makes a business become an influencer within its area of business. The more people talk about you on social media, the more legitimate your business is to customers. Using the Web 2.0 tool quality information is being disseminated, this will give people an impression that the company is an expert within the industry; it will also make the business stand out in the online community as the company has shown they are capable of providing problem-solving information. To gain this high brand authority business uses content syndication through Whitepapers and blog post (Bowden, 2015).

Better Search Engine Optimization "SEO" Ranking

The way companies are ranked on search engines has entirely changed. It is Web 2.0 Marketing that helps search engine to calculate the ranking. The Web 2.0 tools signal the search engine that the business is trustworthy, credible and this helps it to be of high rank. Business can achieve better SEO ranking as the Web 2.0 tools have high domain authority as this made the pages and profile of the tool to rank higher. Moreover, according to (Acronymcom, 2015), there is a partnership between Google search engine and some Web 2.0 tools to display status update as search results, this will give business the opportunity to rank high and achieve more exposure with the search engine.

Improve Relationship with Customers

Using Web 2.0 marketing tools will help business replies to comments and questions instantly. This gives a customer the assurance that their problems can be addressed. Moreover, responding client publicly gives the business the ability to show potential customers that the company has a very qualitative customer care. As the customer already has an online presence, the company can use that to strengthen the relationship, which can lead to brand personalization, online reputation management and create a better brand community.

Allow Tracking and Insights

Knowing customer is essential in any business; these tools allow engagement with a client, which makes businesses understand customers' needs and able to cater to it. Almost all the Web 2.0 tools come with an analytics package or can have software to manage the analytics. The usage of this Analytics gives business better insight about the brand. It can also be used to track, monitor and analyze the effectiveness of a campaign of Web 2.0 tools to make a better business strategy.

Increase Revenue

The tools allow the online community, personalization of messages, encouraging contribution from online members, these enhance the customer experience, which increases the visit of the client to the Web 2.0 marketing tools and also promotes sales.

Challenges of Web 2.0

Businesses face several challenges when adopting Web 2.0 marketing. Below are the challenges faced by business (Bennett, 2015):

- **Lack of Effective Strategy:** For the business to start Web 2.0 marketing it requires a planned strategy, which is sometimes challenging for businesses. Web 2.0 Marketing requires planning and mapping out of goals/objectives;
- **Inability to Measure ROI:** Business finds it is difficult to measure the return on the investment they can make on Web 2.0 marketing;
- **Time-Consuming:** It is very time consuming for business to write a qualitative content and post online. Web 2.0 tools are very time-consuming, as the customer requires the response within a short period after sending comment or question;
- **Lack of In-House/Skills:** The business fails to hire experts for online marketing to manage their Web 2.0 marketing;
- **Keeping Social Media from Security Breaches:** There are a lot of hackers online that attack business that uses Web 2.0 tools to post unwanted information on their pages;
- **Making Sense Out of the Web 2.0 Tool Gathered Data:** When data is collected about customers via the tools, the knowledge of how to use it is a hurdle for businesses when using Web 2.0 tools;
- **Knowing the Right Tool:** Several Web 2.0 tools can be used for marketing, but companies find it hard to know which one is right for them.

Similar Studies of Web 2.0 Marketing in Other Parts of World

Web 2.0 is not just for marketing purpose but can also be used for several things such as educational purposes, collaboration with friends and customer data acquisition. Similar studies were made from different countries on how Web 2.0 is used in various fields. Jangongo and Kinyua (2013) conducted a study on social media and entrepreneurship growth as a new paradigm of business between the SMEs in Nairobi. The study showed that social media offer greater market accessibility, and enhance customer relationship and business worthiness for Nairobi's SME. With this finding, they recommend that the government should be involved with the current technological trends to encourage best practices among the SMEs to solve copyright challenge.

A study was conducted in Malaysia by Yap, Cheng, Chao (2014) about the usage of Web 2.0 as the marketing intelligence acquisition tool in the Malaysian Hotel Industry. The study revealed that perception of environmental turmoil influences the acquisition of market data, which can possibly then affect the firm's performance. It was also found that there is a need for the hotel to hire personnel to capitalize in Web 2.0 applications that can be used in acquiring market intelligence to support decision marketing and efficient marketing strategy. Moreover, In Nigeria, a study was conducted by Ojo (2014) on decoding the potency of Web 2.0 in Nigeria. The research aimed to uncover the benefits and challenges of Web 2.0 in Nigeria. The findings showed that research is very potent in Nigeria and that benefits of Web 2.0 over weigh the challenges. Moreover, a study was conducted in Nigeria on the social media micromarketing and customer satisfaction of domestic airlines in Nigeria by Esu and Anyadighibe (2014), the outcome of the study was that there is a significant relationship between social media micromarketing and customer satisfaction variables through customer recommendation, customer retention and loyalty. It shows the overall customer satisfaction depend on the type of technology used. Based on this outcome it was suggested that for maximal use of social media marketing they should use other social media tools that they are not using. Husain and Adamu (2014) also conducted another research on social media marketing; the research was titled "the impact of social media on virtual marketing". It was found that most of the Nigerians access Facebook, over 4 million users and it is the most used social network in Nigeria. The final analysis depicts that Nigerians are ready for the social media marketing it is only for the businesses to get ready for the business to consumer dialogue.

RESEARCH METHODOLOGY

The research methodology for this study is an exploratory research method. The research is conducted using both secondary and primary data sources. The secondary data is derived from online sources, articles, journals, and books. The context of this research is validated using the primary data. The authors interviewed Nigerian Small and Medium Enterprises of different types of businesses (service providers and product sellers). Thematic analysis is used for analysis of qualitative data and NVIVO software is also used for organizing and coding data. The SMEs names are not disclosed due to the confidentiality reason, but they are named based on the kind of services they provide (Fitness expert, consultancy firm, accessories seller, fashion designer, Agro Input dealer). These businesses are used as samples in order to gather data from different category of businesses both service rendering and product selling.

Findings

The data collected from the samples is transcribed and interpreted. The brief information of each company is discussed and then followed by the finding of the research. The findings are summarized in Table 1 and Table 2 in Appendix A. Each of the interview questions was given a heading and the answer was added in the tables.

Fitness Expert

The company is located in southern part of Nigeria Lagos. They offer wellness services to individuals and corporate organizations. As Fitness Company, we influenced several demographics to incorporate fitness activities to achieve a healthy lifestyle through our seminars. The business type adopted by this company is service rendering through consultancy and training. The manager said, "to market their services the business use Web 2.0 tools which give them the benefit of an increase in brand awareness nationwide, strong ties with customers and increase revenue. The most efficient channel for this business is social media marketing through the usage of blog, Facebook, and Instagram. The reason for choosing the tools is because it is the trending thing and also, they see their competitors using it. The major challenge the business faces is the time consumption and lack of skills to monitor and enhance the marketing strategy".

Accessories Retailer

The company located in the north central (Abuja). It is a retail store for selling accessories such as veils, scarves, hijab pins, mobile phone cases and jewelry etc. The aim of this company is to provide high-quality accessories to satisfy customer needs. As a product selling company, the company uses social media marketing to market their products through an Instagram tool. The manager said, "The reason for choosing the tool is because most Nigeria girls are using the Instagram." According to the manager "we track our adverts through the likes or the sales we made within the period of an advert. The managers also said they have achieved several benefits which are "The ability to connect with customers, learn what people like, fuel my order marketing channels, generate sales, allows users to window shop with Instagram, especially for a business account, people get to window shop through your company page." They get to see what you have and how they can purchase it. The manager of the accessories retail shop "The major challenge is high competition, as the business manager, owner and the Instagram marketer, it very time-consuming to do both tasks and to pay an agency is costly and I don't feel safe to get some to know all about my business secret of marketing that is not my staff". Another challenge is the security issues my account was once hacked, and I lost many customers.

Fashion Designer

This is a fashion designing company located in Lagos. It is a company for selling ready to wear, couture and fabrics. The company has a vision of "Bringing decency back to church first and the society as a whole! Covered yet sexy, fabulous, simply classy is her motto'. The business sells a product and in order to market the product, the company uses the social media platform through Instagram. The manager said "I have achieved several benefits that I never imagined I will gain, I make sales almost every day which has the impact on my revenue, and another thing is I get reviews about any design I make from my customer before I even take it to the stores. I also manage problems with my customers, if they buy clothes from me, and they don't like it." The manager also said that they face challenges, which are "The competition is very high on Instagram and also having the effective strategy to get the attention of customers is very time-consuming. Because sometimes I put all my effort to post, but I get few likes which make me feel disappointed, and also people copy my designs and give another designer to make it for them."

Food Retailer

The company located in Lagos. It is a company that sells all kinds of fresh fruits, vegetables, and gluten free organic foods. The company is known for their high quality on freshness, hygiene, and unparalleled customer. "We aim to revolutionize the retail of fresh fruits, vegetables, and other natural food products in Nigeria by creating a serene, conducive and hygienic environment for people to make safe and healthy food choices." The business started in 2010 and changed the name in 2013. The business type is product selling. The marketing strategy adopted by this business is social media marketing through Instagram and Facebook. According to the manager, "the reason for choosing these tools is because it is an incredibly visual product and also a lot of people in Nigeria spends the time of social media". They track their marketing by viewing the likes and comments of customers, but they don't check the Facebook insight or even have the analytic software. The challenge we face is I do the marketing and also the management that is very time-consuming, and sometimes I run out of ideas on what to post.

Agro-Input Dealers

This company is located in the northern part of Nigeria Kano. It has been in business for past ten years, the aim of the company is to provide and market of improved high-quality seeds in Nigeria. It also provides agricultural services at reasonable prices such as consultancy. The company covers the supply of improved varieties of arable crops such as (open pollinated Rice, Hybrid and Open Pollinated Maize, Sorghum, Millet, Cowpea, Soya Bean) and Vegetable Seeds (Carrots, Cabbage, Lettuce, Sweet Pepper, Pea, Cucumber and Water Melon). "Provide Affordable and High-Quality Seeds to Farmers changing the yield structure in Nigeria." The business type is both the selling of products and service rendering through consultancy. According to the manager, "these tools have to increase my brand recognition for all over the country and even neighboring countries know about my business and call for consultancy or buy my products, and it has also increased out revenue. The business models adopted is Facebook and the reason we choose it is because most farmers tell us it is Facebook they use. We also have the blog, which we use to educate people. We don't track our marketing we only check the likes, comments and shares, but we don't know anything about web analytics. Our major challenge is lack of strategies as a manager I do everything because most of my staff doesn't know about the marketing of Facebook and so I get tired because of the time it takes me to be posting and marketing not being my field of study, sometimes I run out of ideas of how to write engaging post."

Consultancy Firm

The company is located in Lagos. They specialized in rendering services such as consultancy, advisory, training and management services. Their aim is to transform and impact positively on the people of Africa. Their business type is service rendering. According to the manager, he said the Web 2.0 marketing gives them the platform to educate people about the kind of services they offer. The business manager said he is in-charge of the Web 2.0 marketing, and he uses the Facebook, and Twitter for marketing and they have achieved. The several benefits such as Increase in revenue, they have built strong relationships with their business stakeholders, customer reviews, and also ability to gain leads. He mentioned that they also face some challenges such as the time consumption, lack of skills to manage the online marketing he only does what they see their competitors doing, and he also does not know about web analytics.

Analysis of Findings

The findings are discussed and analyzed by being compared with the literature review. The overall analysis of the gathered results is summarized in Figure 1, Appendix B, that is done using thematic analysis method with the aid of Nvivo Treemap visualization; the data collected was coded in and categorized based on each interview question. For the interview questions nodes were created in the software and under the nodes there are child nodes, which were the coded references, the answers of each interview question from SME's. In Appendix B, the diagram indicates that the bigger the box, the more it is being mentioned in by the SME's as the answer to the questions based on the coding done and the small the box the less is it being mentioned by the SME's.

Business Type and the Web 2.0 Tools

Based on the data collected from all the SME's it has been found that the most common tools used by the SME's are Facebook and Instagram. The reason Facebook is one of the most common tools is that no matter what is the type of business, Facebook marketing will be suitable and above all the social media platforms Facebook has the most active users, this gives businesses the ability to advertise to wide range of audience. According to Scherer (2014), Facebook marketing is for all enterprises and it's an effective way to interact with over 1.13 billion daily active users, which makes it the most visited site on the Internet. The data also shows that the product Selling SMEs prefers to use the picture platforms, which are Instagram and Facebook. The reason the product selling business chooses Instagram is because it is suitable for business that owns products such as the fashion designers, healthy foods, and accessories retailers. Based on the analysis made by Revani (2014), it has also shown that users devote their time on Instagram, Instagram engagement rate has increased 415%, and it is still growing. From the data collected in this study, it is evident that the Service rendering companies choose to use the blogging marketing channel through the use of Twitter or Blogger this is because Twitter and blogger not for all category for business. According to Gracielle (2015) said that Twitter and blogs are more suitable for entertainment, technology, health and hospitality businesses. The SME's are also unaware of the usage of Podcasting for marketing because none of the businesses uses it to syndicate content.

Benefits of Web 2.0 Marketing

Increase in revenue and improved customer relationship: All the SME's said they have achieved increased revenue and better customer relationship as they can reply to comments and address problems with customers. Based on the research made by Carbone (2015) the ability of Web 2.0 tools to enhance customer experience can promote sales, which is the increase in revenue. All the SME's achieved these benefits even though they said they cannot measure it, but most said, the majority of their customers are attracted through social media. From Figure 1 in Appendix B, it shows that the box for an increase in revenue and customer relation is large which proves that almost all the SME's mentioned it as part of the benefits they gained.

Increase in brand awareness: All the SMEs achieved brand awareness benefits as the customers help them market their products through likes, shares, and comments. The people who are unaware of the business also get aware. From the literature, according to Carbone (2015) customers help in Web 2.0 marketing through comments and likes and they create more awareness. Based on the Scherer (2015) analysis to find out that over 1.13 billion active users daily on Facebook, it has shown that using these digital media platforms a business can target global market that over 1.13 billion people may know about the brand being advertised.

Allow tracking, monitoring, and better SEO ranking: None of the SMEs achieved this benefit that is provided by the SEO because they do not even know that this feature exists. Even though according to Carbone (2015), it is important for any business to use the gathered analytics to understand the customer in other to cater to their need. Moreover, the better SEO ranking leads to high rank for business in search engines it also makes the business trustworthy and credible. Based on the data gathered, the Nigerian SME's do not hire any skilled online marketer to build and manage the online marketing strategy. In Appendix B, it does not show the ability to monitor marketing efforts and better SEO ranking as part of the benefits in the analysis, this shows that none of the SME's mentioned it as part of the benefits.

Less costly: Only a few of the SMEs stated that Web 2.0 marketing are cheap. In reality, none of the SMEs use the paid service on any of the Web 2.0 marketing to boost a post. With this, they will not realize that it is cheaper than the traditional marketing. They only use the free service. In Figure 1, Appendix B, the box for the benefit of being cheap marketing strategy is small which shows that only a few mentioned it as being less cost marketing effort. Based on the literature according to Carbone (2015) said that Web 2.0 marketing is very cost effective due to the free services it offers and even the paid services are realistic within the range on 1$-above which with traditional marketing the cheap mode of marketing goes beyond the starting point of 1$.

Challenges of Web 2.0 Marketing

Lack of in-house skill: All the SMEs face the challenges of lack of in-house skill because the business owners or managers do the online marketing, which they hardly find time to plan and manage the marketing mediums. According to Bennett (2015), when a business fails to hire an expert in online marketing, it leads to lack of in-house skill challenge. In Figure 1, Appendix B, the lack of in-house skill box is bigger because all the SME's mentioned it as a challenge in their Web 2.0 marketing.

Security issue: This kind of challenge is only faced by two SMEs. One of the SME complained of copyright law where their images of designs were stolen by other businesses without their permission. Another SME complained about the hacking of accounts. These kinds of challenges make them feel uncomfortable to post their information online. According to Bennett (2015), keeping social media from security breaches to prevent hackers from going into businesses account and posting unwanted messages is a major challenge. Moreover, Jangongo and Kinyua (2013) suggest that government should enforce laws and encourage best practices on Web 2.0 tools to solve copyright challenge. Security breaches box is also big because most the surveyed SME's mentioned it as part of the challenges they faced in their Web 2.0 marketing.

Time-consuming: All the SMEs face the challenge of the task being tedious. Based on the data gathered the SMEs find the usage of Web 2.0 marketing time consuming because they don't hire skilled staff to do it. Most of the SMEs, it is the managers who are in charge of the online marketing, and this makes them feel it is very time-consuming as they do not have the skill, and also, they have other management things to do. According to Bennett (2015) Web 2.0, marketing needs attention as customers need an instant feedback after asking the question or complaints. Without a dedicated person to handle the online marketing the benefits will not be fully achieved because it requires full attention.

Inability to measure ROI, Knowing the right tool and Making sense out of the data: The SME's face these challenges because of the lack of skills to manage online marketing. All the SME's are using the tools because other businesses are using not because they know it is right for their business or to get the idea of using the tool from their customers. According to Bennett (2015), the business that does not use analytics, find it difficult to measure ROI.

CONCLUSION

In this information age, several marketing opportunities have emerged through the usage of the second-generation internet based applications (Web 2.0). The emergence of Web 2.0 marketing changes the way of marketing from one-way marketing of business to consumers to bi-directional which is the involvement of both parties to take part in the marketing using online platforms such as (Facebook, Instagram, LinkedIn, Google+, Snapchat, Vimeo, Twitter, YouTube).

Web 2.0 marketing paves the way for several business gains such as content syndication, revenue generation, brand awareness and customer relationship building. The paper explored the value which Web 2.0 marketing's adds to Nigeria's SME market. The paper contains the preferred Web 2.0 marketing tool chosen by the different business type SME's, reasons for the chosen tool, benefits of Web 2.0 marketing to the SME's, the challenges faced due to the adoption of Web 2.0 marketing and suggested solutions on how to improve the usage of Web 2.0 marketing by Nigeria SME's.

The paper reveals that the most preferred tool used by all the businesses is Facebook but businesses that are selling products prefer the use of Instagram to display their product, and service rendering businesses choose blogging through the blogger application and Twitter.

The major benefits achieved by the SME's are increase in revenue, brand awareness, and customer relationship, but they don't know about the benefit of getting higher SEO ranking. It was also found that when adopting Web 2.0 marketing the businesses face challenges. The most common challenge faced by the business is the lack of in-house skills, which lead to most of the challenges such as time consumption, in effective strategy, security breaches, and insight management.

The paper recommends a solution to overcome the challenges which are the Nigeria SME's should hire a certified digital marketer to handle all the Web 2.0 marketing. As a future guideline to this research, the paper will broaden its scope to also large enterprises within Nigeria. It should also use more than one data collection method to ensure the validity of the research.

Limitation and Future Enhancement

The limitation of the research is that the paper only sampled few SME's. In terms of data collection only one data collection method was used, the research should have used more than one data collection method to validate the research. The paper should have also collected data from customer's point of view. In the future, the research would target the customers and also the business to identify the preferred tool from customers point of view using questionnaire as data collection method and also to sample many SME's using interview data collection method.

REFERENCES

Ahzab, N. (2013). Cases on Web 2.0 in developing countries: studies on implementation, application and use. United States of America.

Alhadi, F. (2010). Youtube marketing tips and strategies. *E-nor*. Retrieved April 6, 2015, from https://www.e-nor.com/blog/marketing-strategy/youtube-marketing-tips-and-strategies

Batista, A. (2010). 4 key benefits of interactive marketing: Making the most of Web 2.0. *Demandgenreport*. Retrieved May 22, 2015, from http://www.demandgenreport.com/industry-topics/archives/feature-articles/473-4-key-benefits-of-interactive-marketing-making-the-most-of-web-20-.html

Bennett, S. (2014). The 10 biggest challenges facing social media marketers. *Adweek*. Retrieved April 12, 2015, from http://www.adweek.com/socialtimes/social-marketing-challenges/503090

Bulygo, Z. (2010). Facebook marketing: A comprehensive guide for beginners. *Kissmetrics*. Retrieved December 9, 2015, from https://blog.kissmetrics.com/facebook-marketing/

Carbone, L. (2015). What are the benefits of social media marketing? *Business2community*. Retrieved December 10, 2015, from http://www.business2community.com/social-media/benefits-social-media-marketing-01140985

Cartwright, J. (2015). Wordpress vs blogger: Which free blog tool is better for marketers? *Weidert*. Retrieved December 10, 2015, from http://www.weidert.com/whole_brain_marketing_blog/bid/144270/wordpress-vs-blogger-which-free-blog-tool-is-better-for-marketers

Constantinides, E., & Fountain, S. (2008). Web 2.0: Conceptual foundations and marketing issues. *Journal of Direct, Data and Digital Marketing Practice, 9*(9), 231-244. Retrieved December 10, 2015, from http://www.palgrave-journals.com/dddmp/journal/v9/n3/full/4350098a.html

Dan, L. (2015). How to increase website traffic with Twitter. *Digitalagencynetwork*. Retrieved July 15, 2016, from https://digitalagencynetwork.com/increase-website-trafic-twitter/

DeMer, J. (2014). The top 10 benefits of social media marketing. *Forbes*. Retrieved March 11, 2014, from https://www.forbes.com/sites/jaysondemers/2014/08/11/the-top-10-benefits-of-social-media-marketing/#5a3029f11f80

Eridon, C. (2015). The history of marketing: An exhaustive timeline. *Hubspot*. Retrieved December 10, 2015, from http://blog.hubspot.com/blog/tabid/6307/bid/31278/The-History-of-Marketing-An-Exhaustive-Timeline-INFOGRAPHIC.aspx

Esu, B., & Anyadighibe, J. (2014). Social media micromarketing and customers' satisfaction of domestic airlines in Nigeria. *American Journals of Tourism Research, 3*(1). Retrieved October 11, 2016, from http://wscholars.com/index.php/ajtr/article/view/412/pdf

Gbandi, E., & Amissa, G. (2014). Financing options for small and medium enterprises (SMEs). *Nigeria. European Scientific Journal, 10*(1), 328.

Gracielle. (2015). The pros and cons of Facebook marketing. Retrieved March 21, 2015, from http://www.massplanner.com/the-pros-and-cons-of-facebook-marketing/

Helmrich, B. (2015). Instagram for business: everything you need to know. Retrieved August 11, 2015, from http://www.businessnewsdaily.com/7662-instagram-business-guide.html http://eujournal.org/files/journals/1/articles/2565/public/2565-7588-1-PB.pdf

Husain, R., & Adamu, A. (2015). The impact of social media on virtual marketing in Nigeria. *Journal of Mathematics and Computer Science, 3*(1), 6–9. Retrieved October 11, 2016 from http://www.scholarly-journals.com/SJMCS

Jackson, D. (2015). Snapchat marketing: A beginner's guide. Retrieved December 9, 2015, from http://sproutsocial.com/insights/snapchat-marketing-guide/

Jangongo, A., & Kinyua, C. (2013). The social media and entrepreneurship growth (A new business communication paradigm among SMEs in Nairobi). *International Journal of Humanities and Social Science, 3*(10), 213-227. Retrieved May, 10, 2015, from http://ku.ac.ke/schools/business/images/stories/research/social_media.pdf

Kingston, C. (2013). How to use Twitter for business and marketing. *Socialmediaexaminer*. Retrieved December 9, 2015, from http://www.socialmediaexaminer.com/how-to-use-twitter-for-business-and-marketing/

Kovach, S. (2011). Everything you need to know about Google+ (Including what the heck it is). *Businessinsider*. Retrieved December 10, 2015, from http://www.businessinsider.com/what-is-google-plus-2011-6

Maher, M. (2014). The evolution of non-traditional marketing. *Business2community*. Retrieved December 10, 2015, from http://www.business2community.com/infographics/evolution-non-traditional-marketing-01013609

Mansoor, L. (2015). Social media marketing challenges and trends in 2015. *Digitalagencynetwork*. Retrieved January 23, 2016, from https://digitalagencynetwork.com/social-media-challenges-and-trends-in-2015/

Ojo, O. (2014). Decoding the potency of "Web 2.0" in Nigeria. *International Journal of Politics and Good Governance*, *5*(4). Retrieved December 8, 2015 from http://www.onlineresearchjournals.com/ijopagg/art/163.pdf

Parise, S., Guinan, P., & Weighberg, J. (2008). The secrets of marketing in a Web 2.0 world. *WSJ*. Retrieved May 20, 2015, from http://www.wsj.com/articles/SB122884677205091919

Patel, N. (2015). How to use Google Plus for marketing. *Quicksprout*. Retrieved December 10, 2015, from http://www.quicksprout.com/2014/06/13/how-to-use-google-plus-for-marketing/

Ritchie, J., & Lewis, J. (Eds.). (2003). *Qualitative research practice sage*. London.

Sammons, S. (2013). How to build a LinkedIn marketing plan that delivers ongoing results. *Socialmediaexaminer*. Retrieved December 9, 2015, from http://www.socialmediaexaminer.com/linkedin-marketing-plan/

Scherer, J. (2014). Social media marketing: Which platform is right for your business? *Wishpond*. Retrieved December 10, 2015, from http://blog.wishpond.com/post/72672192941/social-media-marketing-which-platform-is-right-for

Yap, C., Cheng, B., & Chao, K. (2014). Web 2.0 as a tool for market intelligence acquisition in the Malaysian hotel industry. *Proceedings of ISIC: The Information Behaviour Conference*, *19*(4). Retrieved December 12, 2015 from http://www.informationr.net/ir/19-4/isic/isic05.html#.Vmv_0oTiTFI

This research was previously published in the International Journal of Information Systems in the Service Sector (IJISSS), 9(4); pages 44-59, copyright year 2017 by IGI Publishing (an imprint of IGI Global).

APPENDIX A

Table 1. Summary of data collected from all small and medium enterprises

Small and Medium Enterprises	Fitness Expert	Accessories Retailer	Fashion Designer
Business Type	• Service Render	• Product Seller	• Product Seller • Service Render
Web 2.0 Tool	• Facebook • Instagram • Blogger • YouTube	• Instagram	• Instagram • Facebook
Benefits to Web 2.0	• Increase in brand awareness • Strong customer ties • Increase in revenue	• Increase in brand awareness • Strong customer ties • Increase in revenue	• Brand awareness • Increase in revenue through making more sales. • Customer reviews • Better customer relationship
Challenges	• Lack of skills to monitor progress of marketing • Lack of strategic management knowledge • Time consuming	• Security Issue • Lack of skills to monitor progress of marketing • High Competition • Time consuming • Lack of in-house skill	• Difficulty is grabbing customers attention • Time consuming • High competition • Lack of copyright laws

Table 2. Summary of data collected from all small and medium enterprises

Small and Medium Enterprises	Agro Input dealer	Healthy Food Store	Consultancy Firm
Business Type	• Service Render • Product Seller	• Product seller	• Service Render
Web 2.0 Tool	• Facebook • Blogger	• Instagram • Facebook	• Facebook • Twitter
Benefits to Web 2.0	• Increase in brand awareness • Improved customer relationship • Increase in revenue • Customer acquisition • Brand Authority	• Increase in brand awareness • Strong customer ties • Increase in revenue • Easy to syndicate content • Better customer monitoring • Decrease marketing cost.	• Increase in revenue through making more sales • Customer reviews • Improved customer relationship • Customer Lead generation.
Challenges	• Lack of in-house skill • Lack of strategic management knowledge • Time consuming	• Ineffective strategy • Lack of in-house Skill • Time consuming • Inability to use web analytics	• Inability to use web analytics • Lack of in-house skill • Time consuming

APPENDIX B

Figure 1. Summary of the data analysis

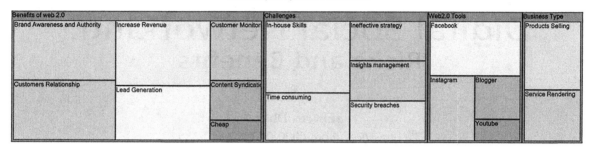

Nodes compared by number of items coded

1. What marketing opportunities do Web 2.0 applications (video marketing, blogging, podcasting) and tools (iTunes, Podcast, Facebook, Twitter, etc.) offer your company?
2. What benefits did you achieve through the adoption of Web 2.0 marketing? ()
3. Which Web 2.0 tools worked well for your company?
4. How did you know the chosen tool is best for your business?
5. How do you track or monitor your Web 2.0 marketing tools?
6. Did you find the usage of these Web 2.0 marketing tools challenging?
7. What are the challenges you face in using these tools for marketing?
8. What were the reasons for the adoption of these tools?

Chapter 42
Digital Social Networking:
Risks and Benefits

Suparna Dhar
 https://orcid.org/0000-0002-8514-5385
RS Software, India

Indranil Bose
Indian Institute of Management, India

Mohammed Naved Khan
Aligarh Muslim University, India

ABSTRACT

Digital social networking (DSN) sites such as Facebook, Twitter, LinkedIn, WhatsApp, Instagram, Pinterest, among many others have garnered millions of users worldwide. It is an instance of information and communication technology that has brought about changes in the way people communicate, interact, and affected human lifestyle and psyche across the world. Some people have become addicted; some see this as beneficial, while others are skeptical about its consequences. This risk-benefit paradox of DSN flummoxes academicians and practitioners alike. This chapter discusses the social and organizational and business risks and benefits of DSN. It goes on to provide a timeline of the evolution of DSN sites, enumeration of typical characteristics of DSN sites, and a systematic comparison of offline and digital social networking. The chapter intends to serve as a cornerstone towards developing a framework for organizational strategy formulation for DSN.

INTRODUCTION

Digital social networking (DSN) is one of the biggest disruptive technology implementations of the twenty-first century having far reaching social and economic implications (Hughes, Rowe, Batey, & Lee, 2012). DSN sites such as Facebook, Twitter, LinkedIn, Instagram, WhatsApp and many others have affected human psyche across the world resulting in significant social upheaval (Kane, Alavi, Labianca,

DOI: 10.4018/978-1-7998-9020-1.ch042

& Borgatti, 2014). DSN has changed the way the masses communicate and exchange information. It has affected the way people act and interact as individuals, in groups, in communities and in the context of organizational networks. The speed and scale of DSN adoption have exceeded all previous technology platforms (Chui *et al.*, 2012). Today, DSN platforms permeate geographic boundaries, physical distances have become meaningless enabling users to connect with people having shared interests and activities across the globe. This phenomenon and its potential risks and benefits have caught the attention of academic researchers (Kaplan and Haenlein, 2010).

DSN allows users' self-disclosure. It has increased users' ability to share views and opinions and propagate information, thus elevating the role of common users to social reporters. User gratification, pervasive access and mobile connectivity attributes have boosted DSN adoption (Park, Kee, and Valenzuela, 2009). Such novel networking capabilities of DSN have introduced new dimensions to social networking habits of the masses. People flock to DSN for fulfilling their social, cultural and professional responsibilities (Van Dijck, 2013). The DSN phenomenon has transcended individual use and permeated the domain of business management, introducing unique unprecedented aspects of business information management (Luo, Zhang, & Duan, 2013). It has become an alternate, albeit more powerful channel for communication, interaction and collaboration among business stakeholders (Skeels and Grudin, 2008) as well as for brand promotion activity (Kim and Ko, 2012).

The convenience in social networking and rich interaction facilitated by DSN is also laden with harmful consequences. Extant literature suggests rumor-mongering, privacy breach and health hazards as negative effects of DSN (Sprague, 2011). Social reporting on DSN led to questions regarding content reliability and which propelled the rumor theory (Oh, Agarwal, and Rao, 2013). Unscrupulous expansion of digital social network introduces social and health risks (Forte, Agosto, Dickard, & Magee, 2016; Holland and Tiggemann, 2016). User gratification is linked to DSN addiction (Ryan, Chester, Reece, and Xenos, 2014). DSN has introduced multi-vocality[1] in communication, which has reduced organizational control on information outflow and branding (Huang, Baptista, & Galliers, 2013).

Review of extant literature on DSN showed that a large number of studies have focused on the benefit facet only, there has been very limited research on the DSN risk (Fox and Mooreland, 2015). Organizational business strategy formulation needs to balance the risks and benefits for optimal leveraging of DSN potential. This necessitates a comparative study of DSN risks and benefits. There exists a gap in literature that necessitates expounding of the DSN benefit and risk paradigms in parallel. This chapter is an attempt to address this gap. It makes an endeavor to examine and expound the risk-benefit paradox inflicting DSN and provides a comparative analysis. The present work intends to serve as a cornerstone towards developing a framework for organizational strategy formulation for DSN.

BACKGROUND

To elicit and expound the risks and benefits of DSN, it is imperative to delve into the evolution and characteristics of DSN. This section provides a brief history of DSN evolution and illustrates DSN characteristics in general and in comparison to offline social networking[2] in particular.

In fact, social networking involves interacting with friends and connections and the phenomenon has undergone multitude of changes with the advent of internet technologies. Offline communications, such as face to face interaction and postal mail, were substituted with online communication, such as email. By the second decade of the twenty-first century, DSN emerged. DSN offered users a novel opportunity of self-disclosure (Liu and Brown, 2014). In general websites[3] the content was largely controlled by the host allowing little or no scope for user-generated content while DSN empower the users to generate and manage the content. These sites foster social networking needs of various types of users. The sites tend to display a consistent set of features and technological capabilities; but vary in focus and interest (Boyd and Ellison, 2007). They cater to diverse cultural, emotional and cognitive needs of users.

A Brief History of DSN

The history of DSNs is quite interesting. SixDegrees.com, the pioneer site, started its journey in 1997 but closed after four years of operation. AsianAvenue, which started in 1999, targeted the Asian American community. Some DSN sites targeted specific geographical or linguistic communities such as QQ and WeChat in China, Odnoklassniki in Russia, VKontakte in Eastern Europe, Skyrock in France, LunarStorm in Sweden, Mixi in Japan and Cyworld in Korea. Bebo became popular in distinct geographical pockets including UK, Australia and New Zealand (Boyd and Ellison, 2007; WEFORUM, 2017). Some sites targeted groups with specific religious, ethnic or sexual orientation. Classmates.com focused on users finding and reconnecting with school and college friends. Sites such as Dogster and Catster targeted pet lovers. Orkut started as an English only site but reinvented itself to cater to Portuguese speaking Brazilians. Friendster launched in 2002 and gained popularity but faced technical and networking challenges with a rise in user base. Later, the site reinvented itself as a gaming site and has since gained popularity in the Asia Pacific region. Live Spaces was launched in 2006 for blogging, messaging and photo sharing, but failed to gain adoption.

Sites such as Ryze.com, LinkedIn, Visible Path and Xing focused on professional users. Ryze.com targeted business and technology community in the San Francisco Bay area but did not gain much adoption. LinkedIn gained popularity among the professionals globally. Academia.edu focused on social networking among academic users. While most DSN sites supported bi-directional relationships, sites such as LiveJournal and Twitter supported unidirectional relationships. Flickr, Youtube and Last.FM focused on sharing content such as photos, videos and music respectively. Facebook started as a closed community site for Harvard and later opened up for public use. The site reported more than 2 billion users in 2017. Some sites focused on specific services, such as Waze for connecting drivers and ReferHire for connecting job seekers. Sites such as Epinions, Yelp and ThirdVoice focused on consumer feedback (Edosomwan, Prakasan, Kouame, Watson, & Seymour, 2011; Stephen and Toubia, 2010).

The social networking sites mentioned in this section are a representative sample from hundreds of such sites. This representative sample of DSN platforms illustrates strategic focus, continuous evolution and transformation based on user profile, and technological and networking capabilities. Though sites have emerged, prospered and gained adoption, yet some have perished too. However, in overall terms there has been increasing adoption on DSN in different spheres of life circumventing age, gender, social and economic status, linguistic and ethnic barriers (Bashar, Ahmad, & Wasiq, 2012). Some large organizations too have developed organizational DSN sites such as Beehive and Bluepages at IBM, Town Square at Microsoft, Watercooler at HP, Harmony at SAP, D Street at Deloitte, and People Pages at Accenture (Archambault and Grudin, 2012; Rooksby et al., 2009) to facilitate better networking among employees. In 2012, McKinsey reported that 70 per cent of the organizations used social technologies, and of these 90 per cent reported business benefits (Chui et al., 2012).

DSN Characteristics

DSN is defined as "web based services that enable users to (1) construct a public or semi-public profile within a bounded system, (2) articulate a list of other users with whom they share a connection, and (3) view and traverse their list of connections and those made by others within the system" (Boyd and Ellison, 2007, p. 2). An alternate definition of DSN provided by Kaplan and Haenlein (2010, p. 63) states, "applications that enable users to connect by creating personal information profiles, inviting friends and colleagues to have access to those profiles, and sending e-mails and instant messages between each other".

DSN sites allow users to create personal profiles, articulate their affiliations and list of network connections, express likes, views, and hobbies that are visible to the network (Boyd and Ellison, 2007; Kaplan and Haenlein, 2010). The articulated profiles allow profile discovery by friends and strangers in the network. The sites allow users to search profiles in the network with specific attributes, such as specific interests or resource access. Users can form new connections and form a network of friends and communities. DSN has thus offered general users a global reach. In fact, the ability to search and connect with like-minded users having similar goals, views and interests has facilitated the formation of cohesive connections on DSN (Padula, 2008). A group of people with cohesive connections endows the network with richer community context (Zhang, Yu, Guo, and Wang, 2014). People with common interests form virtual groups to contribute content, collaboratively explore and enhance their competence in specific knowledge areas. It allows free flow of ideas followed by interactive discussions (Remidez and Jones, 2012).

Users can traverse their digital network to locate and befriend 'friends of friends' and thereby expand their network. Such network expansion involves connecting with offline friends, latent ties and forming entirely new connections, often spanning geographic and cultural boundaries (Haythornthwaite, 2002; Shipps and Phillips, 2013). Thus DSN offers an easy and economical means to form and maintain a large social network with large number of ties (Ellison et al., 2007). User self-disclosures on the platform provide insight into the user's interests and views to others who are part of the network. Users having similar interests, views or sharing common characteristics create virtual communities on DSN sites. Virtual communities formed on common interests promote rich interaction which fosters innovation (Ebner, Leimeister, and Krcmar, 2009).

On DSN, users post self-generated textual and multimedia content or share content posted by other users. The sites empower common users to act as social reporters to share information and views in the network that reaches a global audience (Kaplan and Haenlein, 2010). Unique communication protocols, such as, "like" and emoticons featured by DSN platforms expand the horizon of written communication to convey human feelings, decimating the need of language skills (Wallace *et al.*, 2018).

DSN sites present a fairly consistent set of structural and technological features but vary in their focus and hence attract different types of users exhibiting varied behaviors (Lee and Suh, 2013). The sites primarily vary in the extent of profile visibility, and access to connections and profile content. For example, Facebook requires elaboration of user's personal information for profile creation; Twitter preserves users' anonymity (Hughes *et al.*, 2012) thus creating a structural difference between the two platforms. User anonymity shifts focus to the communication content as opposed to the perpetrator of the information, thus reducing social pressure on content creator (Lee and Suh, 2013). Facebook supports bidirectional connections where the connection represents friendship manifested equally on both the nodes. Twitter supports directed connections, with a follower on one end of the connection and a followee on the other end (Hofer and Aubert, 2013). Some DSN sites have specific user focus, serving users from specific ethnocentric groups based on cultural, religious, sexual and language diversity. Some DSN sites have specific content focus, such as video sharing or pet care extending the scope of focused interaction and information sharing.

Comparison Between Digital and Offline Social Networking

Social networking on DSN platforms varies significantly from offline social networking. This section enumerates the key differences between them. The six-degrees of separation phenomenon had shown a small distance between any two individuals through the referral chain (Watts and Strogatz, 1998). With network search and traversal features of DSN, this small world has become even smaller (Fu, Liu, & Wang, 2008). Social stratification of similar individuals increases the probability of two individuals having a minimum referral chain with a common friend, but the awareness of this minimum chain is uncertain in offline scenario (Pool and Kochen, 1979). Identifying the right path in the chain is difficult in offline social networks. Online referral webs have facilitated identification of minimum referral chains (Kautz *et al.*, 1997). Online social networks differ from offline networks in ways the new ties are formed to expand the network boundary and form inter-group ties, and in tie strength in the intra-group network (Suh *et al.*, 2011). DSN technology support and asynchronous communication feature allow individuals network to transcend geographical and temporal boundaries. Table 1 provides a comparison of social networking in offline and digital platforms.

DSN RISK-BENEFIT PARADOX

The risk-benefit paradox of DSN from social, organizational and business perspective based requires elaboration. Figure 1 presents a summary of such risks and benefits.

Figure 1. Risk and benefits of digital social networking sites

Table 1. Comparison between offline and digital social networking

Feature	Offline social networking	DSN
Profile and self-disclosure (Boyd and Ellison, 2007; Liu and Brown, 2014)	Profiles of network nodes comprise of formal disclosures, impressions of other nodes and hearsay.	Documented digital profiles are generated by self-disclosure. The profile is augmented by network activity visible in the network.
Anonymity and disguise (Hughes *et al.*, 2012)	Anonymity is mostly not possible. Anonymity may be achieved through collusion or disguise.	Anonymity and disguise in the network is permissible in some DSN platforms.
Trust (Bapna *et al.*, 2017)	The people in the network are known to each other and the relationships are endowed with trust.	Connections reflect offline relationships as well as new relations formed on the platform. New relations with hitherto unknown profiles imbibe lower trust.
Network traversal and discovery (Boyd and Ellison, 2007, Kautz, Selman, & Shah, 1997)	Searching the offline network is tedious and slow. Network traversal mediated by common connections. Identifying the right or shortest path in a chain is difficult in offline social networks.	Digital platform allows easy and instant search facility. Traverse the digital network or directly view the network depending on DSN platform. Online referral webs ease the identification of minimum referral chains.
Context collapse (Vitak, 2012)	Offline synchronous communication with personally connections with limited audience.	A large, distributed, weakly tied virtual network has diversified audience of information shared.
Communication rhythm (Ku, Chu and Tseng, 2013)	Mostly synchronous communication.	Mostly asynchronous communication.
Information diffusion (Guille, Hacid, Favre and Zighed, 2013; Huang *et al.*, 2013; Kaplan and Haenlein, 2010; Luo *et al.*, 2013)	Facilitated by influencers in the network. Opinions and views shared in the network are limited within the network boundary.	Determined by influencers in the network, herd behavior and information cascade. Wide ambit of DSN platforms allows the content to reach a large audience. Increases reach and richness in communication through the digital network. Allows sharing and spreading of information virally.
Network expansion (Ellison *et al.*, 2007; Liben-Nowell and Kleinberg, 2007)	Network expansion is slow and effort intensive process. Networks with limited geographic, demographic and cultural variety. Small networks support strong trust.	Digital social networks are highly dynamic, growing and changing rapidly over time, with the addition of nodes and new interchanges along the edges Networks permeate geographic, demographic and cultural boundaries. Large networks showing weak solidarity and trust.
Content generation and quality (Boyd and Ellison, 2007, Huang et al., 2013)	Content generation is attributed to people with linguistic, artistic, informational and/or positional privileges. Supports rich media specific content delivered by experts. Content quality review conducted by specialized critics.	Content generation and sharing is democratized. Supports multimedia content generated or shared by people at large which reduces the content reliability. Allows simultaneous consumption and co-production of rhetorical content.
Content integrity (Oh, Agarwal and Rao, 2013)	Noise may be introduced while content flows through the network, distorting the original message, thus reducing integrity of the message. Originator and propagator of the message may not be identifiable and the message flow in the network is not traceable.	Content shared on digital DSN platforms withstands distortion while flowing through the network, thus maintaining integrity of content. In a named network, the profiles of originator and propagator of the message are known and the message flow is digitally traceable.

Social Benefits of Digital Social Networks

Social networking involves social norms of reciprocity and trust (Putnam, 2007). Online socializing, self-status seeking, and information exchange motivates the use of digital social networking (Park, Kee, and Valenzuela, 2009). Online social networks facilitate the formation of new ties within the group and across groups to expand the network boundary. Using digital social networking leads to social gratification (Cheung, Chiu, & Lee, 2011). Social relationship influences user engagement in organization's profile pages on digital social networking sites (Men and Tsai, 2013). On the emotional dimension trust, personalization, self-exposure and fun are determinants of using digital social networking (Morris, Teevan and Panovich, 2010). Some users harness their social networks as sources of information and organizational productivity. For example, craft-artists use social networks for information propagation and in return receive "gifts of information" on relevant and beneficial online resources.

Some DSN users access DSN sites multiple times a day and spend significant time for networking (Steinfield, Ellison and Lampe, 2008). DSN intentions include social expectancy, information expectancy, entertainment, and gratification (Park, Kee, and Valenzuela, 2009). Both intrinsic and extrinsic benefit perception drive DSN use. Intrinsic benefit perceptions on DSN include altruism, obligation, humor, ego, visibility of expertise and feeling of making a unique contribution (Leng et al., 2011). Number of peers and perceived complementarity have strong influence on benefit perception of DSN and motivation to DSN adoption (Lin and Lu, 2011). Coleman (1988) posited human actions are governed by social norms and individual and collective goals. Cheung et al. (2011) study confirmed DSN to be influenced by collective "We-Intention", a subjective norm and compliance in one's social group and social presence.

Extrinsic DSN benefit perception factors include job performance, job satisfaction, organizational commitment and career success of DSN users (Moqbel, Nevo, and Kock, 2013; Seibert et al., 2001). The study by Moqbel et al. (2013) found significant positive effects of DSN use on job performance, job satisfaction and organization commitment, the effect was explained by work-life balance facilitated by DSN as opposed to presenteeism. Location-based social networks allow users to share information on venues visited (Shi and Whinston, 2013), which offers first hand feedback on the venues from experiences shared by friends in the network. Collaborative user-generated content involves richer interaction in the network; the embedded content generates more viewership increasing intensity of interactions in the network (Ransbotham, Kane, & Lurie, 2012).

Computer-mediated interactions show positive effects on community interaction, involvement, and social capital[4] (Hampton and Wellman, 2003). DSN facilitates meeting of likeminded people forming communities of common interest and shared goals, often sharing success stories and solving each other's problems. This improved interaction generates social capital (Hofer and Aubert, 2013). Formation of new ties on DSN leads to formation of large number of ties. DSN allows users to locate and reinvigorate latent ties with past friends and associates, which leads to maintained social capital (Ellison et al., 2007). Weak ties[5] lead to bridging social capital[6] (Putnam, 2000). Weak ties facilitate heterogeneous connections and information diffusion to a large audience which is useful in job searching and knowledge acquisition (Granovetter, 1973). DSNs enable increased interaction and bonding on DSN within a small set of closely knit nodes with strong ties[7]. The increased interaction and information sharing on DSN amongst strong ties enhances trust and leads to bonding social capital[8]. Bonding social capital is associated with access to resources and social support in the network (Wellman, 1988). Strong ties mobilize reciprocity, strong emotional and substantive support, solidarity and access to scarce resources (Williams, 2006). Table 2 provides a summary review of related literature on social impacts of DSN.

Table 2. Summary of related literature on social impact of DSN

Source	Premise of the Study	DSN Benefits
Ellison *et al.* (2007)	Examined the relationship between Facebook and formation and maintenance of social capital through a survey of students.	• Helps generate social capital. • Creates sense of well-being in users experiencing low self-esteem and low life satisfaction
Cheung *et al.*, (2011)	Improved "We-Intention" model (Cheung and Lee, 2010) to include uses and gratification as determinants of DSN intention.	• Improves collaboration and communication • Promotes creativity, collaboration, and sharing knowledge and wisdom • Promotes collective behavior
Hughes *et al.* (2012)	Studied relation between personality and use of DSN. Found DSN use was determined by online socializing and information exchange motivations.	• Improves online socializing and information seeking/ exchange
Al-Debei, Al-Lozi, & Papazafeiropoulou (2013)	Examined DSN post-adoption behavior and usage continuance intention. Proposed model extending Theory of Planned Behavior (Ajzen, 1985). Found that value adds on DSN was a key determinant of DSN continuance intention and behavior.	• Offers economic utility • Generates user gratification
Weinberg *et al.*, (2013)	Studied role of collaborative community and expressive individuality in social business context. Argued that the concept of organization is changing – collaborative is gaining prominence complementing organizational structure. Proposed research agenda for future research.	• Facilitates and supports collaborative community • Introduces expressive individuality
Ellison *et al.* (2014)	Studied relationship maintenance behaviors on DSN and its demographic variances and role of social grooming and attention-signaling in determining resource access.	• Improves resource access
Bapna *et al.* (2017)	Did an exploratory research on the association between social ties and economic measure of trust in the context of Facebook.	• Introduces dyadic trust

Organizational and Business Benefits of DSN

Business organizations and governmental bodies use online social networking platforms as a communication channel to maintain customer equity, comprising of brand equity, value equity and relationship equity (Kim and Ko, 2012). Business professionals use DSN to connect and collaborate with their connections including friends in other organizations, colleagues within the organization and external stakeholders (Skeels and Grudin, 2009). In the era of offline communication, information outflow from the organization to public domain was controlled by designated Public Relations Managers. In the era of DSN, information outflow transgresses organizational control, at times the Public Relations Managers become mere observers (Kaplan and Haenlein 2010). All organizational stakeholders are empowered to voice opinions and views and share content either directly on organizations' DSN page or with indirect reference, which has potential impact on organizational branding and reputation.

Digital social networking sites have found widespread use in marketing. Unlike conventional media, DSN offers the ability to generate, share and spread information virally, which is beneficial in marketing (Luo *et al.*, 2013). From the managerial perspective, DSN helps in product rating, customer targeting, product pricing and brand engagement (Dou, Niculescu, & Wu, 2013). DSN allows consumers to exchange information on self-designed customized products and gather network feedback on the individualized product (Hildebrand, Häubl, Herrmann, & Landwehr, 2013). It opens up consumers' access to purchase information and product opinions of other people supporting the brand. It also enables easy access to competitor information thus increasing organizational awareness of competitor products and performance (Lipsman, Mud, Rich and Bruich, 2012).

Organizations use the digital social networking in increasing effectiveness of knowledge sharing and knowledge dissemination. Tacit knowledge displays stickiness, which is difficult to identify, locate, extract and spread (Tsai, 2000). DSN improves organizational ability to locate tacit knowledge and expertise hidden in the resource pool and channelize it to improve the organizational learning process (Rooksby *et al.*, 2009). Online social network platforms encourage people with common interests to form virtual groups to further explore and enhance their competence in specific knowledge areas. It allows free flow of ideas followed by interactive discussions, which fosters exploration and innovation to enhance organizational capability (Remidez and Jones, 2012). DSN alleviates learning process in persons with reduced attention span and attention deficit disorders (Drigas et al., 2014).

DSN facilitates cross-functional innovation by offering a mechanism to share ideas and viewpoints, express concerns, exchange information, and consult experts on a common platform (Huang *et al.*, 2013). Companies engage with end consumers on DSN for product co-creation conversations, consumer feedback, consumer insights and market intelligence. The speed and scale of information exchange create an environment of value co-creation that fosters innovation. Unique collaboration opportunities offered by social technologies dis-intermediates business relationships and helps the formation of new innovative business models (Chui *et al.*, 2012). On DSN the linkage between innovation and productivity is bi-directional - higher innovativeness leads to higher social network productivity and vice-versa (Magnier-Watanabe, Yoshida, & Watanabe, 2010).

DSN offers leverages in areas of project management, human resource management, hiring, organization culture, and so on. Social networking in organizations comprise of formal and informal relationships with employees and other stakeholders, which are determinants of organizational performance and culture (Rooksby *et al.*, 2009). Online DSN introduces a new perspective on people's networking ability and habits. DSN sites improve interaction between employees, specifically in geographically distributed and culturally diversified work environments (Dhar and Bose, 2016). It nurtures an environment of trust and reinforces organizational values and beliefs. DSN helps employees connect with new people, who work closely on a project, even if they do not meet face to face (Remidez and Jones, 2012). Access to user profile and posts help users assess their connections and build a network of trust. Small talk on the platform builds familiarity and rapport, which nurtures the supportive, collaborative and interactive environment. It fosters personal and emotional connect and trust in virtual project teams spread across geographies, time zones and cultural boundaries. Project managers leverage the environment of collaboration and trust to increase stakeholder satisfaction. Table 3 provides a summary review of related literature on business uses of DSN.

Social Risks of Digital Social Networking

Individual use of digital social networking carries multitude of risks which includes the psychological impacts of addictive use of these platforms and other direct risks (Ryan *et al.*, 2014). This section enumerates keys risks in DSN use for individuals. This section discusses the social risks of engaging in digital social networking based on literature review.

Table 3. Summary of related literature on business uses of DSN

Source	Premise of the Study	DSN Benefits
Skeels and Grudin (2009)	Studied the impact of DSN use by professionals in an organization through survey and group interviews. Reported tensions when DSN engagement cuts across social groups or the organization boundary. Found that enterprise level and managerial interest in DSN is high.	• Offers fun, personal socializing/networking • Supports organizational networking and external professional networking • Supports knowledge access, rapport building and people sense-making • Helps build social capital • Benefits productivity
Lovejoy, Waters, and Saxton, (2012)	Examined the organizational use of DSN for user engagement in a study of non-profit organizations. Found organizational use of Twitter as one way communication channel, not maximizing the platform potential in consumer engagement.	• Allows stakeholder engagement
Jussila *et al.* (2014)	Studied online social network usage in the business-to-business sector compared to business-to-consumer sector. Survey analysis showed a significant gap in actual use and perceived DSN potential. Identified mechanisms to help businesst-to-business companies better strategize DSN leverage.	• Enhances communication, interaction, learning and collaboration • Allows innovative products and services, more effective marketing and time to market • Enhance customer collaboration and relationship
Ihm (2015)	Studied organizational ego-networks of non-profit organizations to examine stakeholder-management engagement and stakeholder-stakeholder communication on DSN.	• Improves stakeholder engagement

Online social networks induced users to form new ties, adding hitherto unknown individuals to one's social network based on their unattested digital profiles[9] carrying the risk of forming harmful ties (Forte et al., 2016). Users' lack of awareness and limited understanding of features such as privacy settings and connection grouping features, or unavailability of these features on specific DSN platforms, lead to information proliferation to unintended recipients on DSN. Information shared on DSN dissipates relationship contexts such as family, friends and colleagues. In consequence, unsuspecting DSN users, such as teenagers, become easy victims of cyber-bullying (Wright, 2018).

DSN platform allows general users the capability of self-disclosure in the public domain. Lack of awareness of information disclosure and privacy needs lead to inappropriate information disclosure to unintended recipients (Aggarwal, Gopal, Sankaranarayanan, & Singh, 2012). Malicious intent is manifested as false profiles with fudged and fabricated identity on DSN (Hasib, 2009). The veracity of self-disclosed profile and shared information on DSN needs validation to assure reliability of business insights gained (Park, Huh, Oh, and Han, 2012). However, the traditional measures of trust faltered in the context of online DSN (Bapna, Gupta, Rice, and Sundararajan, 2017).

False profiles and profile-masked content sharing on DSN platforms lead to source ambiguity. Content ambiguity is caused when users post messages on hearsay or forwarded content from other sources without verification. The speed and scale of information exchange on DSN platforms fuels viral circulation of ambiguous content (Oh, Agarwal, and Rao, 2013). Source ambiguity and content ambiguity attributes make DSN a potential rumor-mill. Fast information propagation on DSN could lead to quick spread of rumor, leading to a crisis situation.

DSN use is also associated with physical and psychological disorders (Holland and Tiggemann, 2016). Negative feedback on self-images lowers self-esteem, creates anxiety and depression, and leads to eating disorders. Unique DSN interactions and information exchange can invoke sense of envy with feeling quite distinct from envy generated through offline interaction and information exchange (Wallace et al., 2018). Comparison of self-images with others leads to self-objectification that creates constant anxiety and mental health issues. Comparison with others' activities on DSN induces jealousy, which jeopardizes social relationships. Frequent users of DSN are stressed by peer pressure to constantly keep updated with network activities and anxiety of missing out (Fox and Moreland, 2015). Frequent DSN use increases the risk of agony of dealing with irritating content and cyber-bullying. Table 4 provides a summary literature on risks of DSN.

Organizational and Business Risks of DSN

Organizational use of digital social networking too has its share of risks. One of the major deterrents to organizational adoption of DSN has been a privacy concern (Wisniewski, Islam, Lipford, & Wilson, 2016). Open public information dissemination on digital social networking platforms has the potential to violate organizational information disclosure boundaries (Aggarwal et al., 2012). Unscrupulousness information sharing across context-specific network[10] boundaries leads to undesired information diffusion, allowing information exposure to undesired recipients or groups, resulting in information context collapse[11].

DSN reduces organizational control in communication and introduced multi-vocality (Huang et al., 2013). Decontrolling information outflow to allow multiple people to voice their views and ideas leads to ambiguous and conflicting messages, tarnishing organizational image (Aggarwal *et al.*, 2012). It leads to communication of unverified information and disclosure of confidential or sensitive information, thus incurring loss of business, loss of branding and confusion and discontent among stakeholders. Democratization of information sharing may cause deliberate negative messages from malicious stakeholders. DSN information has the potential to mobilize masses towards collective action, leading to political protests, consumer outrage and social unrest.

Some academicians view DSN to be a waste of valuable time and a productivity killer (Aguenza, Al-Kassem, and Mat Som, 2012; Wilson, 2009). In addition to loss of productive time, addictive use of DSN leads to neuroticism, narcissism, anxiety, depression and other attitude and psychological disorders that have negative effect on performance (Hughes et al., 2012). Some researchers have even questioned the efficacy of DSN in innovation citing that product innovations through DSN involving diverse stakeholders dilute organizational focus and expertise generally associated with product innovation, thus degrading the value of the outcome of the process (Hildebrand et al., 2013).

Speed and scale of information exchange offered by DSN sites introduce risks such as identity theft, reputation damage, intellectual property violation, compromise of privacy (Chui *et al.*, 2012). During 2009 to 2011 timeframe, a major car manufacturer made consecutive large car recalls in the United States due to faulty accelerator pedals. The brand became a target for negative comments in online social networks (Oh, Agrawal and Rao, 2013). This resulted in a dip in overall car sales in the United States and immense negative branding for the manufacturer brand.

Positive brand advocacy from a trusted network of consumers help positive brand reinforcement (Dhar and Bose, 2016). On the other hand, negative feedback causes significant damage to the brand. On DSN, consumers may promote a brand or reinforce competitor brands, either of which impacts organizations' competitive position (Lipsman *et al.*, 2012). Lack of organizational DSN strategy could lead to unforeseen calamities and unwarranted negative branding. When a Red Cross employee accidentally posted a message on beer drinking on organization's Twitter account, it posed a potential threat to Red Cross brand value. Going by their DSN strategy, Red Cross admitted the mistake with humor, which helped the organization avoid the threat (Sprague, 2011). The strategic response resulted in positive branding. The opposite was evident in the case where Domino's Pizza's lack of DSN policy led to an employee posting a YouTube video in 2009. The video reached millions of viewers in a short time, causing the brand a catastrophic damage. Taco Bell was criticized for using Facebook promotions as a cover up. Some organizations scan DSN profile of candidates, their network and activity to evaluate job candidature. However, the unscrupulous use of private information residing in public domain has been interpreted as prying into the candidate's private affairs and it's legitimacy has been questioned (Sprague, 2011).

Table 4. Summary of related literature on risks of DSN

Source	Premise of the Study	DSN Risks
Sprague (2011)	Explored employment related legal issues in context of rising use of DSN. The study offers a set of DSN best practices for employers.	• Introduces possibility of negative branding
Aggarwal et al. (2012)	Studied the efficacy of blogs on product visibility. Explored the consequences of employee negative posts.	• Wields potential to violate organizational information disclosure boundaries • Increases risks of negative branding
Archambault and Grudin (2012)	Conducted a longitudinal study of organizational communication and information-gathering on DSN. Found increase in DSN use. Adoption varied depending on gender, age and position.	• Introduces distraction and reduces productivity • Diffuses information disclosure boundaries
Hildebrand et al. (2013)	Studied effect of network feedback on product self-design process and user satisfaction with self-designed products. The study found negative influence of network feedback on customer satisfaction with self-design products.	• Lowers uniqueness of final self-designs and user satisfaction • Diminishes usage frequency and lowers monetary valuations of the self-designed product
Oh et al. (2013)	Studied efficacy of citizen-driven collective information processing through DSN services in social crises situation. The study covered the citizen reporting to address crisis situation and as potential romor-mill.	• Reduces veracity of information with lack of clarity on information source • Increases anxiety • Allows rumor mongering leading to social crisis situations
Fox and Moreland (2015)	Studied negative psychological and relational experiences of DSN and its affordance. The thematic analysis yielded inappropriate or annoying content, social pressure, privacy concern, self-objectification, and relationship issues and key DSN concerns.	• Allows sharing of inappropriate or annoying content • Causes social pressure to be updated • Diminishes privacy and control • Brings social comparison and jealousy, and relationship tension and conflict
Forte et al. (2016)	Examined the role of DSN in networking between school students and adults. Connecting their findings to literature on homophily[12] and context collapse, the study found that organizational DSN policy supports or inhibits communication in teen-adults.	• Homophily and context collapse on DSN results in awkward and unpleasant interactions • Users become potential victims of predation, exploitation, or harassment on DSN
Holland and Tiggemann (2016)	Did a systematic literature review on DSN use and body image and eating disorders. Found negative network feedback on photo posts on DSN leas to eating disorders.	• Photo sharing and negative network feedback on DSN leads to lower self-esteem, introduces anxiety, depression and eating disorders
Wisniewski et al. (2016)	Studied boundary regulation for privacy preferences on DSN platform design and user behavior. The paper proposed ten boundary types and scales to operationalize them.	• Interpersonal boundary regulation is used to balance the tradeoffs between social interactions in the network and protecting one's privacy on DSN
Wallace et al., (2018)	Studied the relationship between envy and DSN affordances. Proposed a theory on the impact of DSN affordances on envious feelings.	• Invoke envious feelings which lead to depression and lower sense of well-being
Wright (2018)	Examined the moderating effect of parental mediation strategies on the relationship between cyber-bullying victimization and adjustment difficulties.	• Teenagers are susceptible to become victims of cyber-bullying on online DSN platforms

FUTURE RESEARCH DIRECTIONS

DSNs have increased the availability of data on social networks. They offer improved opportunities to study the basic properties and recurring structural features of social networks (Liben-Nowell and Kleinberg, 2007). Researchers need to study the risks and benefits of sharing profile information, network of connections and content from social and business perspectives. The studies need to encompass the DSN risks and benefits in the context of technological and structural dimensions of digital social networking. For example, a study of possible containment of risk on privacy setting in DSN platform will help researchers determine the effectiveness of privacy settings on organizational application of DSN in the context of marketing activities. There is a need to develop a framework for organizational DSN strategy formulation to minimize the risk paradigm and leverage the benefit paradigm.

Effective use and benefits derived from DSN varies with age, gender, job position, culture, and other demographic parameters (Archambault and Grudin, 2012; Guo, 2015). Researchers need to determine the moderating effects of age, gender and other demographic parameters on the perceived risks and benefits of DSN use. Researchers need to study the risk-benefit paradox on different demographic cohorts so that organizations can align their DSN strategy with demographic cohorts of their stakeholders. The brief history of DSN illustrates the multifarious DSNs in existence. It also depicts the uncertainty of the DSN platform sustainability. Researchers need to understand the optimal employment of DSN platforms and develop models to assess sustainability of DSN platforms.

DSN serves as an effective learning medium for people with lower attention span as seen in the younger generation. Researchers need to study the association between DSN use and productivity to demystify the ensuing debate on whether DSN enhances or diminishes productivity (Archambault and Grudin, 2012; Skeels and Grudin, 2009). DSN risks pertaining to users physical and psychological health leads to anxiety, depression and eating disorders are discussed in academic literature (Holland and Tiggemann, 2016). On the other hand, DSN is attributed to beat loneliness in older generation and feeling of social isolation in new migrants (Damant and Knapp, 2015). This leads to us to question the causal relationship between DSN use and disorders. Researchers need to investigate the cause and effect relationship between DSN use and physical and psychological health. Researchers need to determine the benefits and risks in context of specific DSN platforms and technological and networking features offered therein.

McKinsey estimated that in monetary terms impact of DSN on business communications is likely to be around USD 1 trillion (Chui *et al*., 2012). However, the risk-benefit paradox of DSN use has left businesses undecided on DSN strategy. There is need to study effective applications of DSN beyond the marketing function. Researchers need to investigate business benefits and risks involved in DSN use in different business functions for policy formulation for effective leveraging of DSN across the organization.

CONCLUSION

It is evident that DSN offers multitudes of risks and benefits on social and organizational business dimensions. The risks and benefits discussed in this chapter are generalized for DSN phenomenon as a whole. Specific feature or specific focused DSN platform may be associated with unique benefits and risks, which need to be explored.

There is need for academic research to unravel DSN intentions and attitudes, expound DSN constructs that determine the risks and benefits and investigate the causal relationship between the risks, benefits and DSN use. There is need to asses optimal employment of DSN platforms and assess sustainability of DSN platforms. The present study intends to provide practitioners with insights into DSN mechanisms and help businesses in making studied managerial decisions at operational management and strategic policies and practices leveraging DSN. From the academic standpoint, the chapter contributes a comprehensive study of extant literature on the topic. It intends to attract academic interest to the risk-benefit paradox of DSN to invigorate further research. The present work intends to serve as a cornerstone in deeper examination of DSN risks and benefits on different dimensions and sub-dimensions towards developing a framework for organizational strategy formulation for DSN.

REFERENCES

Aggarwal, R., Gopal, R., Sankaranarayanan, R., & Singh, P. V. (2012). Blog, Blogger, and the Firm: Can Negative Employee Posts Lead to Positive Outcomes? *Information Systems Research*, *23*(2), 306–322. doi:10.1287/isre.1110.0360

Aguenza, B. B., Al-Kassem, A. H., & Mat Som, A. P. (2012). Social Media and Productivity in the Workplace: Challenges and Constraints. *Interdisciplinary Journal of Research in Business*, *2*(2), 22–26.

Ajzen, I. (1985). From Intentions to Actions: A Theory of Planned Behavior. In J. Kuhl & J. Beckmann (Eds.), Action Control (pp. 11-39). Springer. doi:10.1007/978-3-642-69746-3_2

Al-Debei, M. M., Al-Lozi, E., & Papazafeiropoulou, A. (2013). Why people keep coming back to Facebook: Explaining and predicting continuance participation from an extended theory of planned behaviour perspective. *Decision Support Systems*, *55*(1), 43–45. doi:10.1016/j.dss.2012.12.032

Archambault, A., & Grudin, J. (2012, May). *A Longitudinal Study of Facebook, LinkedIn & Twitter Use*. Paper presented at the SIGCHI Conference on Human Factors in Computing Systems, Austin, TX. 10.1145/2207676.2208671

Bapna, R., Gupta, A., Rice, S., & Sundararajan, A. (2017). Trust And The Strength Of Ties In Online Social Networks: An Exploratory Field Experiment. *Management Information Systems Quarterly*, *41*(1), 115–130. doi:10.25300/MISQ/2017/41.1.06

Bashar, A., Ahmad, I., & Wasiq, M. (2012). Effectiveness of Social Media as a Marketing Tool: An Empirical Study. *International Journal of Marketing, Financial Services & Management Research*, *1*(11), 88–99.

Boyd, D. M., & Ellison, N. B. (2007). Social Network Sites: Definition, History, and Scholarship. *Journal of Computer-Mediated Communication*, *13*(1), 210–230. doi:10.1111/j.1083-6101.2007.00393.x

Butler, B. S. (2001). Membership Size, Communication Activity, and Sustainability: A Resource-Based Model of Online Social Structures. *Information Systems Research*, *12*(4), 346–362. doi:10.1287/isre.12.4.346.9703

Cheung, C. M. K., Chiu, P.-Y., & Lee, M. K. O. (2011). Online social networks: Why do students use facebook. *Computers in Human Behavior*, *27*(4), 1337–1343. doi:10.1016/j.chb.2010.07.028

Chui, M., Manyika, J., Bughin, J., Dobbs, R., Roxburgh, C., Sarrazin, H., ... Westergren, M. (2012). *The Social Economy: Unlocking Value and Productivity through Social Technologies.* McKinsey Global Institute.

Coleman, J. S. (1988). Social capital in the creation of human capital. *American Journal of Sociology*, *94*, S95–S120. doi:10.1086/228943

Damant, J., & Knapp, M. (2015). *What are the likely changes in society and technology which will impact upon the ability of older adults to maintain social (extra-familial) networks of support now, in 2025 and in 2040? Future of ageing: evidence review.* London, UK: Government Office for Science.

Dhar, S., & Bose, I. (2016). Framework for Using New Age Technology to Increase Effectiveness of Project Communication for Outsourced IT Projects Executed from Offshore. In V. Sugumaran, V. Yoon, & M. Shaw (Eds.), *E-Life: Web-Enabled Convergence of Commerce, Work, and Social Life. WEB 2015. Lecture Notes in Business Information Processing* (Vol. 258, pp. 207–211). Cham: Springer. doi:10.1007/978-3-319-45408-5_23

Dou, Y., Niculescu, M. F., & Wu, D. J. (2013). Engineering Optimal Network Effects via Social Media Features and Seeding in Markets for Digital Goods and Services. *Information Systems Research*, *24*(1), 164–185. doi:10.1287/isre.1120.0463

Drigas, A. S., Ioannidou, R.-E., Kokkalia, G., & Lytras, M. D. (2014). ICTs, Mobile Learning and Social Media to Enhance Learning for Attention Difficulties. *Journal of Universal Computer Science*, *20*(10), 1499–1510.

Ebner, W., Leimeister, J. M., & Krcmar, H. (2009). Community Engineering for Innovations - The Ideas Competition as a method to nurture a Virtual Community for Innovations. *R & D Management*, *39*(4), 342–356. doi:10.1111/j.1467-9310.2009.00564.x

Edosomwan, S., Prakasan, S. K., Kouame, M. D., Watson, J., & Seymour, T. (2011). The History of Social Media and its Impact on Business. *The Journal of Applied Management and Entrepreneurship*, *16*(3), 79–91.

Ellison, N., Vitak, J., Gray, R., & Lampe, C. (2014). Cultivating Social Resources on Social Network Sites: Facebook Relationship Maintenance Behaviors and Their Role in Social Capital Processes. *Journal of Computer-Mediated Communication*, *19*(4), 855–870. doi:10.1111/jcc4.12078

Ellison, N. B., Steinfield, C., & Lampe, C. (2007). The benefits of Facebook "friends:" Social capital and college students' use of online social network sites. *Journal of Computer-Mediated Communication*, *12*(4), 1143–1168. doi:10.1111/j.1083-6101.2007.00367.x

Forte, A., Agosto, D., Dickard, M., & Magee, R. (2016, November). *The Strength of Awkward Ties: Online Interactions between High School Students and Adults.* Paper presented at GROUP '16, Sanibel Island, FL.

Fox, J., & Moreland, J. J. (2015). The dark side of social networking sites: An exploration of the relational and psychological stressors associated with Facebook use and affordances. *Computers in Human Behavior*, *45*, 168–176. doi:10.1016/j.chb.2014.11.083

Fu, F., Liu, L., & Wang, L. (2008). Empirical analysis of online social networks in the age of Web 2.0. *Physica A*, *387*(2-3), 675–684. doi:10.1016/j.physa.2007.10.006

Granovetter, M. (1973). The strength of weak ties. *American Journal of Sociology*, *78*(6), 1360–1380. doi:10.1086/225469

Guille, A., Hacid, H., Favre, C., & Zighed, D. A. (2013). Information Diffusion in Online Social Networks: A Survey. *SIGMOD Record*, *42*(2), 17-28. doi:10.1145/2503792.2503797

Guo, Y. (2015). Moderating Effects of Gender in the Acceptance of Mobile SNS Based on UTAUT Model. *International Journal of Smart Home*, *9*(1), 203–216. doi:10.14257/ijsh.2015.9.1.22

Hampton, K., & Wellman, B. (2003). Neighboring in Netville: How the Internet supports community and social capital in a wired suburb. *City & Community*, *2*(4), 277–311. doi:10.1046/j.1535-6841.2003.00057.x

Hasib, A. A. (2009). Threats of online social networks. *International Journal of Computer Science and Network Security*, *9*(11), 288–293.

Haythornthwaite, C. (2002). Strong, weak, and latent ties and the impact of new media. *The Information Society*, *18*(5), 385–401. doi:10.1080/01972240290108195

Hildebrand, C., Häubl, G., Herrmann, A., & Landwehr, J. R. (2013). When Social Media Can Be Bad for You: Community Feedback Stifles Consumer Creativity and Reduces Satisfaction with Self-Designed Products. *Information Systems Research*, *2*(1), 14–29. doi:10.1287/isre.1120.0455

Hofer, M., & Aubert, V. (2013). Perceived bridging and bonding social capital on Twitter: Differentiating between followers and followees. *Computers in Human Behavior*, *29*(6), 2134–2142. doi:10.1016/j.chb.2013.04.038

Holland, G., & Tiggemann, M. (2016). A systematic review of the impact of the use of social networking sites on body image and disordered eating outcomes. *Body Image*, *17*, 100–110. doi:10.1016/j.bodyim.2016.02.008 PMID:26995158

Huang, J., Baptista, J., & Galliers, R. D. (2013). Reconceptualizing rhetorical practices in organizations: The impact of social media on internal communications. *Information & Management*, *50*(2-3), 112–124. doi:10.1016/j.im.2012.11.003

Hughes, D. J., Rowe, M., Batey, M., & Lee, A. (2012). A tale of two sites: Twitter vs. Facebook and the personality predictors of social media usage. *Computers in Human Behavior*, *28*(2), 561–569. doi:10.1016/j.chb.2011.11.001

Ihm, J. (2015). Network measures to evaluate stakeholder engagement with nonprofit organizations on social networking sites. *Public Relations Review*, *41*(4), 501-503. http://dx.doi.org./10.1016/j.pubrev.2015.06.018

Jussila, J. J., Kärkkäinen, H., & Aramo-Immonen, H. (2014). Social media utilization in business-to-business relationships of technology industry firms. *Computers in Human Behavior*, *30*, 606–613. doi:10.1016/j.chb.2013.07.047

Kane, G. C., Alavi, M., Labianca, G., & Borgatti, S. P. (2014). What's Different about Social Media Networks? A Framework and Research Agenda. *Management Information Systems Quarterly*, *38*(1), 274–304. doi:10.25300/MISQ/2014/38.1.13

Kaplan, A. M., & Haenlein, M. (2010). Users of the world, unite! The challenges and opportunities of Social Media. *Business Horizons*, *53*(1), 59–68. doi:10.1016/j.bushor.2009.09.003

Kautz, H., Selman, B., & Shah, M. (1997). ReferralWeb: Combining social networks and collaborative filtering. *Communications of the ACM*, *40*(3), 63–65. doi:10.1145/245108.245123

Kim, A. J., & Ko, E. (2012). Do social media marketing activities enhance customer equity? An empirical study of luxury fashion brand. *Journal of Business Research*, *65*(10), 1480–1486. doi:10.1016/j.jbusres.2011.10.014

Ku, Y. C., Chu, T. H., & Tseng, C. H. (2013). Gratifications for using CMC technologies: A comparison among SNS, IM, and e-mail. *Computers in Human Behavior*, *29*(1), 226–234. doi:10.1016/j.chb.2012.08.009

Lee, J., & Suh, E. (2013, June). *An Empirical Study of the Factors Influencing Use of Social Network Service*. PACIS, Jeju Island, South Korea.

Leng, G. S., Lada, S., Muhammad, M. Z., Ibrahim, A. A. H. A., & Amboala, T. (2011). An Exploration of Social Networking Sites (SNS) Adoption in Malaysia Using Technology Acceptance Model (TAM), Theory of Planned Behavior (TPB) And Intrinsic Motivation. *Journal of Internet Banking and Commerce*, *16*(2).

Liben-Nowell, D., & Kleinberg, J. (2007). The Link-Prediction Problem for Social Networks. *Journal of the American Society*, *58*(7), 1019–1031.

Lin, K.-Y., & Lu, H.-P. (2011). Why people use social networking sites: An empirical study integrating network externalities and motivation theory. *Computers in Human Behavior*, *27*(3), 1152–1161. doi:10.1016/j.chb.2010.12.009

Lipsman, A., Mud, G., Rich, M., & Bruich, S. (2012). Beyond the "Like" Button: The Impact of Mere Virtual Presence on Brand Evaluations and Purchase Intentions in Social Media Settings. *Journal of Advertising Research*, *52*(1), 40–52. doi:10.2501/JAR-52-1-040-052

Liu, D., & Brown, B. B. (2014). Self-disclosure on social networking sites, positive feedback, and social capital among Chinese college students. *Computers in Human Behavior*, *38*, 213–219. doi:10.1016/j.chb.2014.06.003

Lochner, K., Kawachi, I., & Kennedy, B. P. (1999). Social capital: A guide to its measurement. *Health & Place*, *5*(4), 259–270. doi:10.1016/S1353-8292(99)00016-7 PMID:10984580

Lovejoy, K., Waters, R. D., & Saxton, G. D. (2012). Engaging stakeholders through Twitter: How nonprofit organizations are getting more out of 140 characters or less. *Public Relations Review*, *38*(2), 313–318. doi:10.1016/j.pubrev.2012.01.005

Luo, X., Zhang, J., & Duan, W. (2013). Social Media and Firm Equity Value. *Information Systems Research*, *24*(1), 146–163. doi:10.1287/isre.1120.0462

Magnier-Watanabe, R., Yoshida, M., & Watanabe, T. (2010). Social network productivity in the use of SNS. *Journal of Knowledge Management, 14*(6), 910–927. doi:10.1108/13673271011084934

Men, L. R., & Tsai, W. H. S. (2013). Beyond Liking or Following: Understanding Public Engagement on Social Networking Sites in China. *Public Relations Review, 39*(1), 13–22. doi:10.1016/j.pubrev.2012.09.013

Moqbel, M., Nevo, S., & Kock, N. (2013). Organizational Members' Use of Social Networking Sites and Job Performance: An Exploratory Study. *Information Technology & People, 26*(3), 240–264. doi:10.1108/ITP-10-2012-0110

Morris, M. R., Teevan, J., & Panovich, K. (2010, April). *What Do People Ask Their Social Networks, and Why*. Paper presented at the SIGCHI Conference on Human Factors in Computing Systems, New York, NY. 10.1145/1753326.1753587

Oh, O., Agrawal, M., & Rao, H. R. (2013). Community Intelligence and Social Media Services: A Rumor Theoretic Analysis of Tweets During Social Crises. *Management Information Systems Quarterly, 3*(2), 407–426. doi:10.25300/MISQ/2013/37.2.05

Padula, G. (2008). Enhancing the innovation performance of firms by balancing cohesiveness and bridging ties. *Long Range Planning, 41*(4), 395–419. doi:10.1016/j.lrp.2008.01.004

Park, N., Kee, K. F., & Valenzuela, S. (2009). Being immersed in social networking environment: Facebook groups, uses and gratifications, and social outcomes. *Cyberpsychology & Behavior, 12*(6), 729–733. doi:10.1089/cpb.2009.0003 PMID:19619037

Park, S.-H., Huh, S.-H., Oh, W., & Han, S. P. (2012). A Social Network-Based Inference Model for Validating Customer Profile Data. *Management Information Systems Quarterly, 36*(4), 1217–1237. doi:10.2307/41703505

Pool, I. D. S., & Kochen, M. (1979). Contacts and Influence. *Social Networks, 1*(1), 5–51. doi:10.1016/0378-8733(78)90011-4

Putnam, R. D. (2000). *Bowling alone: The collapse and revival of American community*. Simon & Schuster Paperbacks.

Putnam, R. D. (2007). E Pluribus Unum: Diversity and Community in the Twenty-first Century The 2006 Johan Skytte Prize Lecture. *Scandinavian Political Studies, 30*(2), 137–174. doi:10.1111/j.1467-9477.2007.00176.x

Ransbotham, S., Kane, G. C., & Lurie, N. (2012). Network Characteristics and the Value of Collaborative User-Generated Content. *Marketing Science, 31*(3), 387–405. doi:10.1287/mksc.1110.0684

Remidez, H., & Jones, N. B. (2012). Developing a Model for Social Media in Project Management Communications. *International Journal of Business and Social Science, 3*(3), 33–36.

Rooksby, J., Baxter, G., Cliff, D., Greenwood, D., Harvey, N., Kahn, A. W., . . . Sommerville, I. (2009). *Social Networking and the Workplace*. Pew Research Center. Retrieved from http://www.lscits.org/pubs/HOReport1b.pdf

Ryan, T., Chester, A., Reece, J., & Xenos, S. (2014). The uses and abuses of Facebook: A review of Facebook addiction. *Journal of Behavioral Addictions, 3*(3), 133–148. doi:10.1556/JBA.3.2014.016 PMID:25317337

Seibert, S. E., Kraimer, M. L., & Liden, R. E. (2001). A Social Capital Theory of Career Success. *Academy of Management Journal, 44*(2), 219–237.

Shi, Z., & Whinston, A. B. (2013). Network Structure and Observational Learning: Evidence from a Location-Based Social Network. *Journal of Management Information Systems, 30*(2), 185–212. doi:10.2753/MIS0742-1222300207

Shipps, B., & Phillips, B. (2013). Social Networks, Interactivity and Satisfaction: Assessing Socio-Technical Behavioral Factors as an Extension to Technology Acceptance. *Journal of Theoretical and Applied Electronic Commerce Research, 8*(1), 35–52. doi:10.4067/S0718-18762013000100004

Skeels, M. M., & Grudin, J. (2009, May). *When social networks cross boundaries: a case study of workplace use of Facebook and LinkedIn.* Paper presented at the ACM 2009 international conference on Supporting group work, Sanibel Island. 10.1145/1531674.1531689

Sprague, R. (2011). Invasion of the social networks: Blurring the line between personal life and the employment relationship. *University of Louisville Law Review, 50*(1), 1–34.

Steinfield, C., Ellison, N. B., & Lampe, C. (2008). Social capital, self-esteem, and use of online social network sites: A longitudinal analysis. *Journal of Applied Developmental Psychology, 29*(6), 434–445. doi:10.1016/j.appdev.2008.07.002

Stephen, A. T., & Toubia, O. (2010). Deriving Value from Social Commerce Networks. *JMR, Journal of Marketing Research, 47*(2), 215–228. doi:10.1509/jmkr.47.2.215

Suh, A., Shin, K., Ahuja, M., & Kim, M. S. (2011). The Influence of Virtuality on Social Networks Within and Across Work Groups: A Multilevel Approach. *Journal of Management Information Systems, 28*(1), 351–386. doi:10.2753/MIS0742-1222280111

Tsai, W. (2000). Social Capital, Strategic Relatedness and the Formation of Intraorganizational Linkages. *Strategic Management Journal, 21*(9), 925–939. doi:10.1002/1097-0266(200009)21:9<925::AID-SMJ129>3.0.CO;2-I

Van Dijck, J. (2013). *The Culture of Connectivity. A Critical History of Social Media.* New York: Oxford University Press. doi:10.1093/acprof:oso/9780199970773.001.0001

Vitak, J. (2012). The Impact of Context Collapse and Privacy on Social Network Site Disclosures. *Journal of Broadcasting & Electronic Media, 56*(4), 451–470. doi:10.1080/08838151.2012.732140

Wallace, L., Warkentin, M., & Benbasat, I. (2018, January). *How Do You Handle It? Developing a Theory of Facebook Affordances and Envy.* Paper presented at the 51st Hawaii International Conference on System Sciences. Retrieved from http://hdl.handle.net/10125/50544

Watts, D. J., & Strogatz, S. H. (1998). Collective dynamics of 'small-world' networks. *Nature, 393*(6684), 440–442. doi:10.1038/30918 PMID:9623998

WEFORUM. (2017). *The world's most popular social networks, mapped.* Retrieved September 29th, 2017 from https://www.weforum.org/agenda/2017/03/most-popular-social-networks-mapped/

Weinberg, B. D., Ruyter, K., Dellarocas, C., Buck, B., & Keeling, D. I. (2013). Destination Social Business: Exploring an Organization's Journey with Social Media, Collaborative Community and Expressive Individuality. *Journal of Interactive Marketing, 27*(4), 299–310. doi:10.1016/j.intmar.2013.09.006

Wellman, B. (1988). Structural Analysis: From Method and Metaphor to Theory and Substance. In B. Wellman & S. D. Berkowitz (Eds.), *Social Structures: A Network Approach* (pp. 19–61). Cambridge, UK: Cambridge University Press.

Williams, D. (2006). On and Off the 'Net: Scales for Social Capital in an Online Era. *Journal of Computer-Mediated Communication, 11*(2), 593–628. doi:10.1111/j.1083-6101.2006.00029.x

Wilson, J. (2009). Social networking: The business case. *Engineering & Technology, 4*(10), 54–56. doi:10.1049/et.2009.1010

Wisniewski, P., Islam, A. K. M. N., Lipford, H. R., & Wilson, D. C. (2016). Framing and Measuring Multi-dimensional Interpersonal Privacy Preferences of Social Networking Site Users. *Communications of the Association for Information Systems, 38*, 235–258. doi:10.17705/1CAIS.03810

Wright, M. (2018). Cyberbullying Victimization through Social Networking Sites and Adjustment Difficulties: The Role of Parental Mediation. *Journal of the Association for Information Systems, 19*(2), 113–123. doi:10.17705/jais1.00486

Zhang, D., Yu, Z., Guo, B., & Wang, Z. (2014). Exploiting Personal and Community Context in Mobile Social Networks. In A. Chin & D. Zhang (Eds.), *Mobile Social Networking. Computational Social Sciences.* New York, NY: Springer. doi:10.1007/978-1-4614-8579-7_6

ADDITIONAL READING

Agarwal, R., Gupta, A. K., & Kraut, R. (2008). Editorial Overview—The Interplay Between Digital and Social Networks. *Information Systems Research, 19*(4), 243–252. doi:10.1287/isre.1080.0200

Borgatti, S. P., & Foster, P. C. (2003). The Network Paradigm in Organizational Research: A Review and Typology. *Journal of Management, 29*(6), 991–1013. doi:10.1016/S0149-2063(03)00087-4

Ellison, N. B., Lampe, C., & Steinfield, C. (2009). Social Network Sites and Society: Current Trends and Future Possibilities. *Interaction, 16*(1), 6–9. doi:10.1145/1456202.1456204

Granovetter, M. (1985). Economic Action and Social Structure: The Problem of Embeddedness. *American Journal of Sociology, 91*(3), 481–510. doi:10.1086/228311

Kane, G. C., & Borgatti, S. P. (2011). Centrality–Is Proficiency Alignment And Workgroup Performance. *Management Information Systems Quarterly, 35*(4), 1063–1078. doi:10.2307/41409973

Martin, A., & Bavel, R. V. (2013). *Assessing the Benefits of Social Networks for Organizations.* European Commission.

McPherson, M., Smith-Lovin, L., & Cook, J. M. (2001). Birds of a Feather: Homophily in Social Network. *Annual Review of Sociology*, *27*(1), 415–444. doi:10.1146/annurev.soc.27.1.415

UNCP. (2014). *The Brief History of Social Media*. UNCP. Retrieved from http://www2.uncp.edu/home/acurtis/NewMedia/SocialMedia/SocialMediaHistory.html

Yates, D., & Paquette, S. (2011). Emergency knowledge management and social media technologies: A case study of the 2010 Haitian earthquake. *International Journal of Information Management*, *31*(1), 6–135. doi:10.1016/j.ijinfomgt.2010.10.001

KEY TERMS AND DEFINITIONS

Digital Social Networking: Social networking through digital networking platforms such as Facebook, LinkedIn, etc.

Information Expectancy: The degree to which a user believes his/her behavior will help him/her attain gains in seeking and exchanging information.

Self-Objectification: Self-objectification is a process wherein individuals perceive themselves as an object to be looked at and evaluated based on their appearance.

Social Expectancy: The degree to which an individual believes his/her behavior will help him/her attain gains in maintaining and enhancing the social relationship.

Social Network: Social relations studied as a network, where individuals or groups are represented as nodes and their relationship and interactions are represented by edges.

Social Networking: Interacting with friends and connections in ones' social network and expanding ones' social network.

User Gratification: Fulfillment of social and psychological motives and goals through purposeful use of media.

ENDNOTES

[1]   Univocality refers to single point control of information outflow from the organization to ensure correctness, avoid ambiguity in the messages and the intended meanings. In contrast, multi-vocality fosters a communication culture that loosens control of information outflow and allows voicing of alternative and multiple views.

[2]   Offline social networking refers to connection and interaction with friends and associates in absence of online medium.

[3]   General websites refer to static websites and sites hosting web applications other than online social platforms.

[4]   "Good-will, fellowship, mutual sympathy and social intercourse among a group of individuals and families who make up a social unit" (Hanifan, 1916, p. 130).

[5]   Weak ties are social network connections that display weak tie strength. Tie strength combination of the amount of time, the emotional intensity, the intimacy (mutual confiding), and the reciprocal services which characterize the tie.*

6   Bridging social capital denotes the type of social capital formed between weak ties in a social network.

7   Strong ties are social network connections that display strong tie strength.

8   Bonding social capital denotes the type of social capital formed between strong ties, such as family and close friends in a social network.

9   Self-disclosed digital profiles on DSN are not verified, hence lack veracity. Predators and imposters can create false profiles (Forte et al., 2016).

10   A context-specific network refers to the social network formed with a specific context, such as an organization or a family.

11   Context collapse refers to the large and diversified audiences possible online as opposed to limited groups reachable in face-to-face interactions.

12   Homophily is the tendency to bond with similar people.

This research was previously published in Critical Issues Impacting Science, Technology, Society (STS), and Our Future; pages 53-80, copyright year 2019 by Information Science Reference (an imprint of IGI Global).

Chapter 43
Social Media Analytics for Maintaining Financial Stability

Sebin B. Nidhiri
ⓘ https://orcid.org/0000-0002-2710-2264
Delhi School of Economics, India

Sakshi Saxena
Symbiosis International University (Deemed), India

ABSTRACT

Risk and uncertainty are disliked but inevitable. The nature of these has changed and new sources of risk have risen. To mitigate risk and maintain financial stability, the firms need to adapt. The world wide web and, within it, social media have had tremendous growth and wide coverage lately, making them determining forces in any economic activity. This has led to generation of large amount of data on myriad concerns. Recent developments in computing technology has thrown open the possibility of mining useful information from the enormous and dynamic data. The chapter outlines the growth of social media and social media analytics and its financial implications to businesses, consumers, and governments. It details how risk management and social media, two domains earlier considered more diverged than chalk and cheese are now inextricably linked and explains using various cases how social media analytics is used to manage risk and uncertainty. The authors also look at the emerging challenges with these developments.

INTRODUCTION

The Chinese curse, "May you live in interesting times," has never been truer than today. With 'Disruptive Innovation' being the new buzzword, there is rapid change all around. This period of Information Revolution has virtually connected people across the globe. An increasingly large amount of time is spent online today. With the increase in mobile devices and improved access to internet, people today consume most of their information online. This has further created many online businesses as well as driven traditional businesses electronically. More recently, social media has gathered considerable forces online. Young

DOI: 10.4018/978-1-7998-9020-1.ch043

(2017) finds that one in every three minutes spent online is devoted to social media. Enormous amount of data and content is generated through channels of social media like Twitter, LinkedIn, Facebook and Instagram, to name a few, and this data is continually updating in real time. Evidently social media is a vital medium to reach large online audience in their day to day lives with ease. The increasing economic activities and improved means of information transmission have brought in new kinds of uncertainty and risks too. The gargantuan information available can itself be tapped to mitigate these new risks. With such significance of social media in the current scenario, how important is its role to aid risk mitigation decisions is worth researching.

Financial stability can comprise different things for different economic entities — the firm, the government and the household. But across these divides, financial stability can be understood as the resistance to economic shocks and not losing the ability to fulfil its basic functions. Core risks can be classified into four types, namely: Market Risk, Credit Risk, Liquidity Risk and Operational Risk. In layman terms, market risk arises when loss is associated to the factors that affect the market, such as stock prices, foreign exchange rates, etc. (Arshad, Zafar, Fatima, & Khan, 2015; Hull, 2018). Credit risk arises when an entity fails to fulfill its commitments towards its counter parties. Liquidity risk arises when an investment cannot be traded instantaneously to counter or minimize a loss. Operational risk arises when loss is a product of operational failures, which can be external or internal in nature that can include technical failures, frauds because of failed internal processes, and other such events. With the digital socialism in trend, it is imperative to understand these risks in the context of social media.

Thus, there is a need for firms to adapt to maintain financial stability and counter those risks. The present chapter studies how such adaption is worked upon by firms in the present period and how they would for the changing times ahead. The rest of the chapter is organized as follows. The next section looks at the rise of social media, making it an obligatory part of business, and its implications for business. The third section describes the various aspects of social media analytics — both content and structure-based analytics — and looks at the latest inroads into the realm of big data. This is followed by looking at ways in which social media and social media analytics are used for financial stability as well as solutions and recommendations. Lastly, the authors highlight future concerns and challenges for social media analysis in times to come, indicate directions for future research and conclude.

BACKGROUND

Rise of Social Media

Social media is a broad term encapsulating a wide range of online platforms that let users create and exchange content. These websites are constantly evolving and adding functionalities in an attempt to stay relevant. This makes it hard to distinguish between the different options. Nevertheless, Barbier and Liu (2011) categorize social media as:

1. Social networks, E.g.: Facebook, Orkut, LinkedIn
2. Microblogs, E.g.: Twitter, FriendFeed and Tumblr
3. Blogs, E.g.: Blogger and WordPress
4. Social news, E.g.: Digg, Slashdot and Reddit
5. Social bookmarking, E.g.: Delicious, StumbleUpon, etc.

6.   Review sites, E.g.: Zomato, TripAdvisor, Glassdoor, Yelp
7.   Media sharing, E.g.: Instagram, Snapchat, YouTube, Vimeo
8.   Wikis, E.g.: Wikipedia, Wikihow, etc.
9.   Question and answer sites, E.g.: Yahoo! Answers, Answerbag and Quora

The existence of social networks can be traced from the mid-1990s, where a social platform Yahoo facilitated communication through chat rooms. With the advancement in visibility of such social networks, platforms like LinkedIn, Orkut etc. emanated in the later years. A more significant development was in 2004, when Facebook emerged. This space has seen many new entrants like Twitter, Instagram, Snapchat, etc. Piskorski (2014) finds that there are many social failures which relate to not just two or more people interacting but also environments where people display information about themselves or collect information about others. These failures also lead to market failures where two parties are not able to engage in a mutually beneficial transaction. Social networks succeed because they work towards reducing these failures. LinkedIn is an excellent case in point.

The internet and mobile technologies are the main reasons for the exponential growth of social media websites (Zeng, Chen, Lusch, & Li, 2010). A report by We Are Social and Hootsuite reveal that 3.819 billion (51% of world population) use internet and 3.028 billion (40% of world population) are active social media users (Kemp, 2017). According to a report by Internet and Mobile Association of India (IAMAI), internet penetration in December 2017 was 64.84% in urban India and 20.26% in the rural areas. The number of internet users stood at 481 million in December 2017, an increase of 11.34% from the earlier year (Agarwal, 2018). The recent fall in price of data, thanks to a price war brought in by the entry of Reliance Jio, has increased the time spent online by Indians particularly on social media. The average internet user consumes more data than what was the case just a couple of years ago. A report released in 2017 by Ericsson, the Swedish phone maker, suggests that the monthly data consumption on every smartphone in India is estimated to grow up to five times from 3.9 GB in 2017 to 18 GB by 2023 (Press Trust of India, 2017).

Social media has brought the world closer and is responsible for a larger and quicker flow of information. Moreover, social media like Facebook, Twitter and Instagram are used not only to keep in touch with friends, but to be au fait with news and current developments. Social media websites have evolved to now become platforms where videos, blog posts and news articles are shared, and not just a means of keeping in touch with friends. They have not just smoothed interaction among people but also served as an interface between companies and the consumers. These social media websites are cashing in on this attention span they have gained by letting businesses advertise their products.

A rising number of people today look through news via social media. News articles are shared or retweeted by users on different social networking sites. As it is a very dynamic medium with large number of posts in short time, the life of an article shared is short. News articles have short time span and hence to become popular, they should be read by many readers in short time. It is evident from existing researches that news articles which become socially popular must have certain scoring criteria which can be identified and classified. Bandari et al. (2012), find that the top news sources whose tweets get circulated (retweeted) the most on Twitter are not necessarily from the conventional news agencies, but from blogs such as Mashable and the Google Blog. These are very widely shared across social media. That apart, it was discovered that one of the most important predictors of popularity of a news article was the source of the article. This is in conformity with the intuition that readers are likely to be influenced by the news source which disseminates the article and an identified source gets more circulation. The study used regression and classification models and achieved 84% accuracy in making proper predictions about the probable popularity of a news article on social media by looking at its characteristics (Bandari, Asur, & Huberman, 2012). This is further proof of the rising prominence of social media over traditional media and why businesses cannot ignore this medium. YouTube on mobile devices alone reaches more people in the United States than any other TV network (YouTube for Press, n.d.). Apparently, technology acceptance is more evident in young consumers. This was tested in a study which established a relationship between use of social media among young consumers in Latin America using Technology Acceptance Model (TAM) (Bailey, Bonifield & Arias, 2018).

Financial Implications to Business From Social Media

The current form of the internet is what experts call the Web 2.0. Earlier, the web was characterized by static pages dishing out information. Searching for a product would lead you to the product's website which would give information as a traditional product brochure would. Today, most websites allow users to create content and provides platforms for interaction and collaboration. Thus, the online content is generated by the users themselves. This helps one get reviews of products from actual customers and so forth. On the web today, the most popular websites are social media websites. It is a critical part of the information ecosystem, is adopted by all, and has immense reach to consumers, voters, businesses and governments alike. Naturally, there is tremendous interest from businesses, political parties, governments etc. in social media from both application and research perspective. Businesses today use social media as a platform and also a source of information for product design, innovation, customer relationship management (CRM) and marketing.

Global Web Index, the largest study in the world on the digital consumer, finds that 98% of digital consumers are social media users and this is not composed only of the younger cohort of people. 94% of the digital consumers in the age group of 55-64 are active users of social media (Young, 2017). Naturally, social media has become a tool for CRM which no business can ignore. This opportunity has also added a new dimension of risk to businesses which can no longer ignore these media. There are multiple cases of a poor review being posted online by someone, shared by many, and spreading like wildfire causing doom to businesses. The brand's image and outlook online are something to be actively worked on. Every business worth its salt has a team working on its social media presence.

Marketing has been the primary application of social media analytics in recent years. This is only natural and can be attributed to the widespread and growing adoption of social media by people worldwide who are also the consumers to other businesses (He, Zha, & Li, 2013). Forrester Research, Inc. had projected social media to be the second-fastest growing marketing channel in the United States between 2011 and 2016 (VanBoskirk, Overby, & Takvorian, 2011). But, Forrester Research Inc. (2018) predicts that ad spending on social media will be flat in 2018 as customers are increasingly trying to avoid ads and firms are faced with wasted ads. Forrester predicts that businesses will try to advance technology to deliver personalized experiences at a large scale and decode algorithms of other digital platforms to get their product visible. This would mean that businesses would now need a stronger understanding of consumer perception and sentiment of their brand on social media. Pumping in money for advertisements is no longer going to be a solution. The criticality of social media analytics; to better understand one's audience and customizing one's message for targeted advertising, is set to rise. To succeed wooing users on social media, a delicate balance has to be struck between various factors such as user sentiments, target-based user identification, choice of social media platform etc. (Zhu & Chen, 2015). A primary data-based research revealed that electronic word of mouth had an indirect inter-relationship with brand equity. In the context of managerial implications in an organization, it means that the organization would be better off using viral trends as their advertising strategy, while ensuring that their target demography receives the marketing communication at the right time and place (Severi, Ling, & Nasemoadeli, 2014). Furthermore, it has been shown that a consumer trusts electronic word of mouth as a credible source of information (Themba & Mulala, 2013).

In a study, an online beauty product promotion campaign by Neiman and Belk was evaluated using Twitter streaming data. It was evident from the study that an online marketing campaign with a hashtag had positive impact on consumers (Ribarsky, Wang, & Dou, 2014). Moreover, companies want to explore these sentiments to make profits and have competitive edge over others. An effective role of social media was observed through a case study of a small mechanical company called Gamma that faced difficulty in selling its products due to other low-cost Chinese products available in the market. The company shifted strategy and focused on social media and was able to enter new markets; the use of Web for selling products yielded benefits in term of profits and better control over operational processes (Bocconcelli, Cioppi, & Pagano, 2017).

Social media has not just helped firms make marketing gains but has also emerged as a booming platform to connect business partners, thereby broadening the business network. The traceability gap, which exists between the users of social media and the organization, makes it difficult to know if the business has been transacted successfully between them (Grizane & Jurgelane, 2017). However, with the right strategy, social media can be actively leveraged by entrepreneurial firms to establish connections and to ease the operational and logistic processes if actively engaged (Drummond, McGrath, & O'Toole, 2017). Furthermore, social media analytics is also essential for devising competitive advantage. Literature on the application of enactment theory suggests that effective communication between buyer and suppliers might prevent the chances of suppliers to default (Oliveira & Handfield, 2017). This is primarily due to buyer's accessibility and understanding of financial conditions of supplier, thus reducing information asymmetry to a large extent. In such scenarios, social media could help gaining insights.

A case where things went south owing to social media was when Electronic Arts, a game company, hosted a Question and Answer session on the social media platform of Reddit. It went disastrously wrong, as the company's response to criticism was not well received by the users, which resulted in their response being the most down voted comment in the history of the platform. The user sentiments about the organization were affected negatively in light of this situation, hence jeopardizing the sales of the game they were promoting via this Question and Answer session[1]. This fiasco clearly highlighted how the theoretical concepts of financial risks, particularly market risk, can be adaptive to the world of social media. In addition to the external use of social media for interacting with customers and shareholders, the use of social media internally in an organization is also a dual edged sword -- while it can be beneficial to the organization, it can also put the organization at risk owing to the inherent factors of social media, such as hyper-interaction, spontaneity and data permanence (Demek, Raschke, Janvrin, & Dilla, 2018).

A case where social media directly affected the finances was when the Twitter account of Associated Press (AP) was hacked in 2013 to report explosions in White House, which compromised the safety of the then POTUS, Barack Obama. In seconds, the Dow Jones Industrial Average (DJIA) dropped 143.5 points and the Standard & Poor's 500 Index lost more than $136 billion of its value. This goes to show that just one post on a social media platform can majorly affect financial systems (Karppi & Crawford, 2016). Additional research examined the impact of emotional sentiments expressed on social media platform (Twitter) on the Standard & Poor's 500 Index. It was apparent from the research that tweets about an organization are strongly related to the organization's stock returns (Sul, Dennis, & Yuan, 2014). It is evident from a study that negative sentiments of users on social media platforms about an organization can affect and predict the organization's stock prices (He, Guo, Shen, & Akula, 2016). Nevertheless, a study of four business scandals by Jiang and Shen (2017) showed that while Twitter was the earliest source of information on these scandals, traditional media is still critical. Newspaper articles are more important than tweets to explain stock market returns and trading volumes in response to scandals.

Politics, technology, business, and other social areas are all likely to be impacted by social media for the foreseeable future. Data analysis will help quantify and provide useful insights. As the number of social media users continues to grow and it reaches hitherto uncovered areas; most of which traditional media finds hard to reach, there have to be significant changes in the way we communicate and share information. Data analysis will then provide us with an empowering ability to dive deeper into these very large data sets in a more significant manner. Social networking sites, blogs, and other online social media services provide a digital record of social behavior from a multitude of perspectives making it the conclusive data source for analytics and gaining insights on people.

SOCIAL MEDIA ANALYTICS

"Social media analytics is concerned with developing and evaluating informatics tools and frameworks to collect, monitor, analyze, summarize and visualize social media data, usually driven by specific requirements from a target application" (Zeng, Chen, Lusch, & Li, 2010, p. 14). While use of social media for CRM has become a norm, firms are also tapping into emerging techniques of social media analytics to understand and mitigate risk. Improvements in technology have transformed data from a traditional sense of numbers to text and pictures. This has allowed a large amount of information in the form of text and pictures available on social media to be subject to useful analysis. With humongous amount of data being generated every second, analyzing such data and deriving important information, is equally crucial. Consequently, businesses, both data-driven and otherwise, are investing majorly in understanding public perception about their product or service.

Social media analytics broadly uses two sources of information; (1) the relationships and interactions between people, organizations & products and (2) user-generated content (posts, images, videos). Accordingly, the analysis can be classified into two groups:

CONTENT-BASED ANALYTICS

Content-based analytics, as the name suggests, focuses on the contents (or data) posted by users on social media platforms. These are customer feedback, product reviews, subjective opinions, etc. These are unstructured and could be in the form of text, images and/or videos. Such content on social media is often voluminous, unstructured, noisy, and dynamic. Text, audio, and video analytics (discussed later), can also be subjected to analysis in order to derive actionable insights from the data. Given the scale and dynamic nature of the data, big data technologies play a vital part in the analysis. Two types of analysis based on the type of content are explained further.

Text Analysis

There is a lot of text in the posts on social media. The text is much unstructured but can be mined and then molded for different analysis. This is made plausible as people use social sites to express their emotions, beliefs or opinions about things, places or personalities (Hasan, Moin, Karim, & Shamshirband, 2018). Text analysis is concerned with deriving high-quality structured data from unstructured text and thereafter deriving information. Another name for text analytics is text mining. The unstructured data is collected on the item of interest. This may be collected from social media, newspapers or other portals online. The task is to structure the data appropriately and then find patterns, trends and/or relations in the data. These are then interpreted into actionable conclusions. Manually performing text analysis would be a tedious task, and today, software is available that can perform these tasks much more efficiently. Text mining techniques are more cost effective and provide more information than traditional survey methods (Morinaga, Yamanishi, Tateishi, & Fukushima, 2002).

Text analytics can be used to effectively perform sentiment analysis, opinion mining, cluster analysis, categorization, social media monitoring, competitive intelligence, information's extraction, link analysis etc. (Ferguson, 2016). "What others think" is always a curiosity for individuals and for businesses; it is a very useful piece of information that helps make many decisions. Sentiment analysis is the computational study of opinions, sentiments, evaluations, attitudes, views and emotions expressed in the form of text. The analysis classifies a statement by predicting the polarity of words used in it and then classifying the words into positive or negative sentiment (Jose & Chooralil, 2015). With the coming of big data, text analysis has evolved, widening its scope and application. Predictive analytics that uses statistical modelling combined with this helps predict future changes.

Face Recognition and Image Detection

In the field of social media analytics, Face Recognition and Image Detection are other booming areas that can be very helpful in fraud detection and risk mitigation. In a study based on Image Based Fraud Prevention, it was proposed that online fraudulent transactions can be stopped using these technologies (Babu, Bhagyasri, Lahari, Madhuri, & Kumari, 2014). Technological tools behind face recognition and image detection are Hidden Markov Model and Singular Value Decomposition. Hidden Markov Model helps in capturing the image from the source and then matches it with the images in database trying different iterations. This is done by extracting different features from an image like eyes, mouth, hair, eyebrows and chin. Furthermore, Singular Value Decomposition helps in statistical data analysis and signal processing.

STRUCTURE-BASED ANALYTICS

Also known as social network analytics, it is concerned with evaluating the structural attributes of a social network and extracting intelligence from the relationships among the participating entities. This structure is modelled visually with nodes and edges, which stand for participants and relationships respectively. Two such graphs that are popular are social graphs and activity graphs (Heidemann, Klier, & Probst, 2012). While an edge in a social graph depicts the existence of a relationship (like being friends on Facebook or a connection on LinkedIn), in an activity graph it stands for an interaction (liking or commenting on the other person's activity). Therefore, each has its use in differing purposes.

TECHNIQUES OF STRUCTURE BASED ANALYTICS

Community Detection

This is a technique of Structure-based analytics which is very similar to clustering in data analytics (Aggarwal, 2011). Clustering divides data into sub groups based on similarities in the data, and helps understand the large data better. Similarly, community detection analyses one's links and identifies distinct sub groups. It identifies sub networks of users who interact more extensively with each other than with others in the network. This helps summarize online social networks which average millions of nodes and edges, and thereby understand behavioral patterns and predict future properties of the network. Social graphs can help point out communities or determine hubs (i.e., users that may be individuals or pages of organisations who have relatively large number of direct and indirect social links), whereas activity graphs show an active relationship and may sometimes be more relevant than just a connection or acquaintance.

Social Influence Analysis

This involves techniques dealing with understanding and modeling the influence of actors and connections in an online social network. Humans are social animals and their behavior is affected by others' actions both online and offline. Social Influence analysis evaluates participants' influence, quantifies the strength of connections and reveals the patterns of influence diffusion in the network. Quantifying the strength of connections is achieved through quantifying importance of network nodes. Some measures for this purpose are calculating degree centrality (number of edges a node has), betweenness centrality (which is the number of times a node acts as a bridge along the shortest path between two other nodes; was introduced as a measure for quantifying the control of a human in a social network on the communication between other humans in the same social network), closeness centrality (average length of the shortest path between the node and all other nodes in the graph; thus, the more central a node is, the closer it is to all other nodes; the more towards a corner a node is, it may get close to a few other nodes but happens to be much farther than more than half of the total nodes), and eigenvector centrality (assigns a relative score to all the nodes in the network based on the logic that a connection to a high-scoring node contributes more to the score of the node in concern than equal connection to a low-scoring node).

Another aspect of social influence analysis, as mentioned above, is to understand how ideas spread over a network by means of communication among the social entities. This is known as information diffusion and there are models which explain how the process happens. In these models, each node is either active or inactive. Over iterations, inactive nodes become active as more of its neighbors become active. This is the concept behind models like the Linear Threshold Model (LTM) as well as the Independent Cascade Model (ICM) which are two of the most popular information diffusion models (Sun & Tang, 2011).

Link Prediction

No social network is static. It is a dynamic object that is always growing through the creation of new nodes and edges. The idea behind link prediction is to predict future linkages that will arise by studying current linkages. Link prediction techniques predict the happening of interaction, collaboration and/or influence among entities of a network within a given time interval. Link prediction techniques have been found to be better than pure chance, hinting that the current structure of the network contains latent information within future links (Liben-Nowell & Kleinberg, 2007). Link predictions today are also used to unravel potential associations in terrorist, criminal or drug networks. Link prediction is behind how Facebook operates 'People You May Know' where friends are recommended and Youtube's 'Recommended for You' where videos to watch are recommended.

BIG DATA

TechAmerica Foundation's Federal Big Data Commission (2012) defines Big Data as "Big data is a term that describes large volumes of high velocity, complex and variable data that require advanced techniques and technologies to enable the capture, storage, distribution, management, and analysis of the information." Traditionally, data was collected by enterprises from sources like ATMs, Mortgage units, Credit cards, portfolios etc. With the rising complexity of data, data sources now also include news data, trading data, industry data, alerts, reports, advertising response data, customer feedback data and other social media data (Oracle, 2015). 95% of big data is unstructured data. (Gandomi & Haider, 2015). Some of the popular tools that are used in big data analysis are Tableau, Rapid Miner, Hadoop, Project R, IBM Big Data etc.

The Three V's – Volume, Variety and Velocity, are considered the major challenges with and the defining characteristics of Big Data. As the name suggests, big data is in large volumes. With the coming of the Internet of Things, which refers to all the devices other than computers that collect and record data and are connected to the internet, we are surrounded by data. This can be seen in households where there are smart refrigerators, smart air conditioners, smart TVs and with persons using consumer gear like fitness trackers etc. All these interconnected devices create large amounts of data that is measured in Zettabytes (a Zettabyte equals one trillion gigabytes). Owing to the volume, this data is worked on from a distributed processing and storage environment. Social media also generates such large volumes of data. Facebook receives 600 TB of data daily and scans roughly 105 TB of data per hour (Vagata & Wilfong, 2014). Whatever data that businesses are able to subject to analysis, will also be commensurately large. Variety talks about the differing kinds of data that big data refers to. It is very different from traditional data sources which had rows and columns of data. Big data cannot always be fit into a spreadsheet or even in the form database management software usually work with. The posts on social media include photos, videos, and also text which do not follow any specific structure. Also, many actions on social media which users undertake, namely liking a post or retweeting a tweet, are all data. Velocity refers to the speed at which data is flowing. Big data software handles velocities up to 10 Gigabytes per second. The data on social media is increasing every minute. Facebook has 1.44 billion users (that is 7 crore more than the population of China) and receives in excess of 900 million photos in a single day (Miller, 2015).

USE OF SOCIAL MEDIA AND SOCIAL MEDIA ANALYTICS FOR FINANCIAL STABILITY

On the one hand, there is very large and continually growing amount of data on social media, albeit varied, and on the other we now have cheaper and more powerful computational processing and affordable data storage. This is fertile ground to quickly and automatically create models from the analysis of bigger, more complex data and still deliver faster, far more precise results. Building precise models on larger sets of data gives an organization a better chance of identifying profitable opportunities and mitigating risks.

Social media could serve as a channel to mitigate risk and reduce uncertainty in a number of ways. Campbell (2017) puts forth four aspects involved in this. First is modelling of the data. This is probably the most crucial step as data can turn bad and lose its relevance over time. Topic Model is one such method that helps to understand, categorize and organize text available from social media portals. Sentiment Analysis is another technique involved which helps in identification of positive and negative sentiments trolling over the internet about any news or event. Second is credit risk management; after organizing the data into relevant subject related information, risk managers can apply different forecasting tools to minimize future losses and earn operational efficiency related revenue. Through Business Intelligence tools, like word cloud, this information can be presented to different audience in a visually impacting way. Third is Market Risk Management, which is largely based on live data from trading communities about valuation and opening position that is important to have edge over the others and to build strategies to reduce position-based risks. Social media hence is important to provide timely insights to have maximum impact. Last is the technology in use. Machine Learning and Artificial Intelligence technology have come to the mainstream due to their computing power which helps to understand big data that is generated online in various forms like text, images, video etc. Technology, one like Machine Learning and Artificial Intelligence, helps to detect subtle changes in sentiments, which otherwise could have been neglected.

The financial risk that information from social media data can mitigate cuts across various sectors. Banks as well as other businesses in the financial industry can use social media to identify investment opportunities and know when to trade. Algorithms used by traders make buy/sell decisions by watching trends on social media. These algorithms help firms stay abreast of happenings and enable a quick response, thus controlling the damage from adverse scenarios. Social media analysis also helps understand sentiments towards certain companies which can then influence decisions of buying and selling the stocks of that company. There is a technological race wherein hedge funds as well as other deep-pocket investors, with the use of big-data analytics, instantly analyze several lakhs of tweets on Twitter and other non-traditional information sources to buy and sell stocks in a matter of minutes, beating many smaller investors (Weiczner, 2015). Matthew Granade, Managing Director and Chief Market Intelligence Officer at Point 72, a hedge fund company, says, "You have this explosion of other independent real-time sources. It's a lot easier to get to [on-the-ground] truth. Overall, I think this is a golden age for new investment data sources." Liu, Wu, Li & Li (2015) find that there is stock co-movement for firms which have similar metrics (no. of followers and tweets) for their official Twitter handles and these social media data predict co-movement better than even industry categories. Banks in India are currently facing a large problem with the quantum of non-performing assets, a large chunk of which is due to default on loans handed out to institutions. While technology is actively used to credit risk score ratings for individuals, this has not been tapped into well in the case of corporate lending. Social media analytics can supplement this process particularly with respect to detecting credit risk of corporations and small

& medium enterprises. Also, social media interactions of employees can be used to detect tendency to commit fraud and deter them.

Literature on the application of enactment theory suggests that effective communication between buyers and suppliers might prevent the chances of suppliers to default (Oliveira & Handfield, 2017). This is primarily due to buyer regular accessibility and understanding of financial conditions of supplier. In such scenarios, social media could help gaining insights. Communication by the firm with stakeholders via social media can also help attenuate the negative market reactions to news of acquisitions (Mazboudi & Khalil, 2017).

Online review websites like Zomato and TripAdvisor are the latest forms of customer feedback that can make and break businesses, particularly in the hospitality sector. Within a study of the impact of such feedback, performance of leading hotel chain was obtained and the social media data on the hotel chain was purchased from a social media analysis firm. It was evident from an analysis on this data that the overall rating of the hotel on review sites had the largest significant impact on the performance of hotel. The second most important factor was the response rate to negative comments in the online reviews (Kim, Lim, & Brymer, 2015). This shows that it is important to monitor the feedback on your services online and to engage with the feedback.

Social media analysis is increasingly being used by politicians and political parties to help them manage electoral risks and thereby financial risks. It helps monitor, inform, and increase political influence and provides insights into which groups or categories of people to connect with, how to best communicate and engage with the electorate, and increase the overall engagement (Quantzig, n.d.). It enables events to be organized based on what the target group is interested in and customize the outreach to certain demographics based on insights from sentiment analysis as well as social media analysis in politics. The 2016 United States election results which went contrary to the predictions by mainstream media are also touted as one of the successes of an effective social media analysis. The influence social media had on the election cannot be overstated and is easily understood from a finding from a study by Pew Research Centre (2016) which found that 44 percentage of the adults in the United States got all their information about the 2016 presidential election from social media which is higher than the percentage of people who responded for local or national print newspapers or candidate websites and emails put together. Also, 24 percent got news and information from the social media posts put up by Donald Trump and Hillary Clinton themselves. Donald Trump had around hundred lakh Twitter followers and ninety lakh Facebook followers while Hillary Clinton had seventy lakh on Twitter and about half of Trump's number on Facebook in 2016. In May of 2016, the Pew study found that on average the candidates put out 5 to 7 posts daily on Facebook and 11 to 12 daily on their Twitter accounts. Barack Obama's initial election and subsequent re-election campaigns heavily utilized social media and social media analytics to engage and mobilize voters, particularly those who were voting for the first time and young voters. (Williams, 2017).

Social media has played a vital role in political mobilization as well. Social networks like Facebook and Twitter played an undeniable role during the Arab Spring and aided the push to democracy that originated in Tunisia to spread to Egypt, Libya, Lebanon, Syria, Jordan, Algeria, and Bahrain and also into Saudi Arabia. During Tunisia's Jasmine Revolution, there was a blackout in the mainstream media and the government controlled all media platforms. Millions of people organized themselves in this revolution through the news received from social media. The world watched the revolution on their Twitter and Facebook feeds. Mohamed Bouazizi's self-immolation, which triggered the revolution, was not the first case of self-immolation in Tunisia. But this was video graphed and posted to YouTube and was later covered by Al Jazeera and subsequently other news channels. The government's efforts to cut out the flow of information by blocking certain websites, deleting problematic accounts, arresting bloggers and other active people on the social platform could not stop the force (Malhotra, 2011). Social media has played a vital role in converting street movements into larger movements with considerable impact in Romania (Momoc, 2013). In the same passion, during the anti-corruption movement of 2012 in India, social activist and staunch Gandhian, Anna Hazare, used social media to connect people in New Delhi (Meti, Khandoba, & Guru, 2015). The group that rallied around him, 'India Against Corruption,' had a large following on social media and this helped the movement put considerable pressure on the government. The social media has buried the physical and social gaps to a large extent and being a horizontal media, they work a lot like a participatory democracy where everyone has a voice that is heard. Modern political parties have utilized this media to augment their political strategies and gain public support. Political parties have taken up social media channels with a focus to proliferate political transactions and engineer the support of various sources. The emphasis is on the building of long-lasting relationships between political parties and people, which are attempts at social engineering (Meti, Khandoba, & Guru, 2015).

A study analyzing the impact of social media on risk perception during the Middle East Respiratory Syndrome outbreak in South Korea suggests that social media is important due to its role of shaping risk perception about health issues (Choi, Yoo, Noh, & Park, 2017). This can facilitate increase in disease preventive behavior and effective risk communication strategies.

Content-Based Analytics to Reduce Risk

Carolyn Holton (2009) demonstrated the use of text mining as a means to predict fraud by disgruntled employees in an organization. Employee fraud or Occupational fraud is the most prevalent of all frauds faced by a firm (KPMG Forensics, 2003). Occupational fraud causes heavy financial losses to companies and an estimate puts it to the tune of $652 billion per year in the United States alone. This is equivalent to about 5 percent of total corporate revenues and definitely a much larger share of profits (Association of Certified Fraud Examiners, 2006). World over on average, fraud loss per company in the 2004–2007 period is estimated to be at $8.2 million (Kroll Inc., 2008). Holton (2009) collected data from several internet discussion groups (Several Vault.com and Yahoo! Discussion groups) used for intra-company communications but were not on the organizations' network. The sample collected consisted of 50 disgruntled messages and 40 non-disgruntled messages that were so classified by two coders who agreed on each message's classification. The messages were cleaned to remove unnecessary information and words and a clustering method was applied on the cleaned sample. The clustering showed that there was clear distinction between disgruntled and non-disgruntled messages. This upheld the idea that disgruntled messages can be identified and a naïve Bayes model[2] was applied. The sample was divided into training and evaluation[3] sub sets in various ratios ranging from 50:50 to 90:10, and 80:20 was found to be the best with strong and relatively stable results. From an evaluation sample of 18 messages, the code correctly identified and classified 16 as either disgruntled or non-disgruntled. While the act of sending a disgruntled message is by no means validation that the person has committed or will commit fraud, it is a useful indicator to identify the possibilities of fraud. Association of Certified Fraud Examiners (ACFE) point to three factors which come together to lead to fraudulent activity; perceived unshareable financial need, perceived opportunity and rationalization. Rationalization occurs particularly when one feels that he/she is being treated unfairly. These three are known as the fraud triangle, an idea that was first expressed in the book 'Other People's Money' by Donald Cressey (1953). Up to two of these three factors can be identified from disgruntled communication. Also, Securities and Exchange Commission (SEC) mandates public companies for the storage of all documents that influence financial reporting including email communications of employees. The availability of this large data opens up a window for an analytics code to mine the data and detect disgruntled employees, thereby providing scope for detecting and deterring fraud. This reduces a large risk faced by firms.

Eagle Alpha, a research firm from Ireland used text analytics to study 7,416 comments on a Reddit gaming thread in October 2015 and predicted that the Star Wars videogame released by Electronic Arts (EA) would sell much more than the creator had projected; EA soon revised upward its sales forecast, citing "excitement" over the game (Weiczner, 2015). This is a case of a positive uncertainty that could be tapped to make gains in the stock market. Li, Chan, Ou & Ruifeng (2017) studied stock prices of 30 companies listed in NASDAQ and Twitter sentiment related to those companies. Twitter's text data was mined to identify sentiments regarding particular companies and these sentiments derived from the tweets could explain the stock movement of the companies with an average accuracy over 70%. A study of the contents on crowd sourced content service for financial markets 'Seeking Alpha' showed that negative sentiment from the social media site could predict future negative price performance (Chen, De, Hu, & Hwang, 2014).

Security breaches, faced particularly by banks, cause heavy financial losses and social problems to society and people. Hao & Dai (2016) propose the use of social media as a surveillance tool to track security breaches. Their study states "social media monitoring provides a supplementary tool for the more traditional surveys which are costlier and time-consuming." The large unstructured data from 1,13,340 related tweets collected in August 2015 on Twitter were mined and topics, opinions and knowledge about security breaches from the general public extracted. Sentiment score as well as impact factors are good determinants of real-time public opinions and also attitudes to security breaches. Thereby, unusual patterns/events of security breaches can be detected in the early stage itself, and this can prevent further harm by spreading awareness amongst the people.

Dubey et al. (2017) applied text mining on tweets generated on Twitter for two popular Indian politicians; Arvind Kejriwal and Narendra Modi; these revealed areas where they needed to get more involved in. It also revealed how they could deal with their political affairs in a better way. Analysis could provide insights for preventive action before losses politically and financially.

Structure-Based Analytics to Reduce Risk

Community detection has application in marketing to help make product recommendation systems effective (Parthasarathy, Ruan, & Satuluri, 2011). In politics, one of the ways political parties hedge risk uses social media analytics. The analytics is used to identify influential people and to know who to target campaign and support efforts at. Analyzing a celebrity's posts, followers, and social media activity can aid to confirm whether or not their involvement will be beneficial or detrimental to a particular campaign (Williams, 2017).

SOLUTION AND RECOMMENDATIONS

Social media has a widespread role in disparate real time concepts in online space, like real-time marketing, real time communication, real time social engagement and real time information generation. Thus, social media monitoring becomes essential as data generated from it is widely used for research purposes and have real time impact on the audience and the businesses. Consequently it is evident from the existing research work that social media platform can be a potential source of information for business decisions and policy formulation. As financial risk is an important aspect of any business and has a direct link to the usage of social media both: within and outside the organization — it is important to consider few aspects while conducting a social media research.

- Emotional impulses and user psychology matters. A thorough research and understanding on user psychology is essential for succeeding on social media platforms. A better understanding of users' emotional responses can help increase brand likeability, brand reputation and have other such benefits that can directly affect finances of a business (Crowl, 2015).
- Timing matters. It is essential 'when' an organization is active on social media when dealing with existing and potential clients. Posting the right things at the right time significantly affects user engagement, and can hence increase client interaction. As a research points out, the ideal time to post content for maximum user interaction on Facebook, one of the largest social media platforms, is specific, and hence operating actively on those timings can potentially attract more attention to the content, hereby affecting user interaction, engagement, brand awareness and perception (IZEA, 2017).
- In addition to the "how" part of analytics, it is also important to concentrate on the "who" part. Running analytics on a specific data set, or in context of social media — a specific user base, which is carefully selected after ensuring that there is no sort of selection bias and which represents the offline world, is important, as the entirety of social data may not be representative of the ground reality. Hence, overcoming representation issues is one of the essential things in the analytical cycle to even out the data (Carson, 2016).
- Keywords, and now hashtags, directly affect the attention potential of a product or a brand, and hence, they should be carefully and considerably selected, else the content would not be correctly categorized, leading to misinformation. Different platforms have different needs, and hence it is necessary to cater the hashtags and keywords to every social platform. People trend to react differently on different platforms, for example, the more hashtags you use for a post on instagram, the more the chance of user engagement, while having more than two hashtags on twitter results in a significant drop in user engagement (Osman, 2017).
- It is also important to know and understand the language of the audience. In addition to normal filters like regional language, country and other geography-related filters, it is also important to make the posts relatable by being in sync with up-to-date lingo and culture. For example, emojis, which are basically icons used for expressing emotions and things, were a common factor among social media influencers (Crowl, 2015). Big names such as Coca-Cola, Burger King and Comedy Central have already designed custom emojis to keep their content more relatable and approachable (Seiter, 2016).
- Apart from traditional analytical concepts like network analysis, text analysis, analytics of keywords based on frequency of usage and sentiment analysis, it is also quintessential to know latest

concepts in the analytics scene such as Social Network maps, Variety Search and other data scraping tools.

- Visualizing data has great benefits that directly and indirectly contribute to the efficiency of social media analytics. Apart from traditional ways of visualizing data such as bar graphs and pie charts, using multi-dimensional graphs, heat maps, map layering etcetera for advanced visualization helps in grasping the inference from the data better. One of the major documented benefits of business analytics, which includes data visualization, is that it results in better distinction of key facts and patterns from the data from the overall noise (Data Visualization's Positive Impact on Decision Making, 2010).

- Thousands of posts on social media get created and deleted every day. Deleted content can reveal hidden facts and patterns which would usually go un-analyzed. Before making a business decision based on social media posts, it is important to ensure that you have a complete data set, which takes into account the hidden or deleted data. From mundane reasons such as typos and spelling errors, to complex issues such as manipulation by big businesses and censorship by governments, there can be a range of reasons why public posts can be hidden or deleted. By comparing the generated model with a model based on hidden or deleted posts, one can ensure the accuracy and reliability of the generated model (Almuhimedi, Wilson, Liu, Sadeh, & Acquisti, 2013).

FUTURE RESEARCH DIRECTIONS

There are multiple challenges that have been foreseen for social media and social media analysis on which offer scope for future research.

Today, a large number of social media websites are using algorithms to customize the user experience. A user's social media page will show him details it thinks are relevant to the user. This has been termed as a 'filter bubble' by activists working towards a free and fair internet. On the basis of the posts you like and share, the website forms an impression of what you like to engage in and begins to show more of such posts. While this may increase interest in the websites, a major pitfall is that it blocks out alternate opinions. If someone likes and shares posts having a leftist ideology, he will never see posts having a right-wing ideology. In an age where most news is consumed and opinions formed from social media, this is an alarming development that needs reckoning. The jury is still out on this whether there should be a programme that selectively shows updates when you login to a social network, or whether updates should just be shown chronologically. With the increasing number of posts and larger number of connections on social network, this might end up scrolling through multiple posts before you see posts relevant to you. There is scope for research on how social media could evolve balancing user experience and the interests of the service provider. A lot of such research is currently proprietary research conducted by social media firms.

False information spreading through such media is also a concern. There have been cases of violence being instigated and being successful to some extent via social media. The widespread violence against Rohingya Muslims in Myanmar in the latter part of 2017 which came as part of an alleged ethnic cleansing was aggravated with fake news circulated on Facebook. Doctored photos and videos that spewed hate against the minority became viral on Facebook. To some extent, Facebook is also responsible for this as just a year ago, Facebook provided Freebasics in Myanmar; a service where users can access few websites including Facebook without costing them data. Freebasics increased the number of Facebook users in Myanmar from around 20 lakhs to over 3 crores (Roose, 2017). It is such concerns of spreading rumor and fake news that internet communication services are regionally cut off during times of crisis to prevent panic. The latest fad Crypto currency, which uses block chain technology spreading far and finding more takers, definitely had a lot to do with the hype on social media. The recent increase in reach of social media and its impacts on risk and financial stability throws open many questions.

Privacy concerns on social platforms, security issues, problems related to negative expression about a product or a service are all byproducts of the opportunities social media presents. With rising popularity of social media, it is equally important to manage the risk and ensure that online behavior is right. In a reading, authors have tried to establish that better personal usage policy and business usage policy can help to ensure using social media data. Firms have faced a lot of problems with some social media savvy employee revealing too much on a social media platform. This can lead to loss of competitive edge and in severe cases, results in cases of insider trading. Chen, Hwang & Liu (2018) contend that the Twitter activity from company executives can help predict abnormal returns by studying the Twitter data from the accounts of CEOs and CFOs of the largest publicly traded companied in the United States. This increased access to information for retail investors poses its own risks. A solution to this would be allowing staff special authorization power to publish data online giving them proper training and guidelines (Chelliah & Field, 2014).

In addition, data generated through social media networks are difficult to access and are mostly unstructured, hence fetching, cleaning and processing such data is cumbersome. A different aspect of social media analytics are the challenges faced by different researchers in the course of identifying topics, collecting data and then extracting relevant data for analysis. Conferring to a study that undertook all these facets, it was found that because of the large amount of data generated from various online platforms, businesses are interested in understanding or discovering trends wandering over the internet and deriving useful insights to mitigate risk and for mass communication (Stieglitz, Mirbabaie, Ross, & Neuberger, 2018). As social media involves concepts of big data, for that reason social media data is also called social media big data. Primarily, using social media data poses one major challenge due to its large volume that is storage space. Second, due to its high speed of data creation, it is actually difficult to analyze that in real time. Third, as the data is in a variety i.e. in unstructured form, it is challenging to derive information from that on time. Moreover, social media is about diffusion of information on the network, hence it becomes necessary to identify the influencers and analyze this information, hence tracking comes to be another challenge. Finally, the ambiguity with regard to data quality is another important constraint. Research on the methodology of doing social media analysis is itself an emerging area.

CONCLUSION

The world as we know it is constantly changing. In these changing times, business cannot survive by resisting change but by adapting. The internet which brought a sea of change in how businesses worked has now molded into Web 2.0 making it a very horizontal medium of exchange. This age is rightly called the information age where everyone has a lot of information at their disposal. There is tremendous data that is available in social media, and the world is getting aware and developing systems to make sense of this data. Social media offers an unprecedented opportunity to connect directly with investors and other stakeholders. Such interactions enhance transparency and accessibility (Alexander & Gentry, 2014). Firms that have recognized the potential and tapped in to social media analytics are reaping its benefits.

For some businesses, the social media analytics is yet not financially viable, given the large cost of storage and analysis. With improving technology and decreasing costs, social media analytics will become used widely. There are also new problems arising which the world collectively has to find solutions to. With more and more people getting connected and the power of social media rising, there are ethical responsibilities on whether to and if yes how to regulate the flow of information. While there are purists who argue for the 'wisdom of masses' to be left to itself to work, yet others point to the many pitfalls of this wisdom. One can say that the pace of change is startling, but the opportunities are tremendous.

REFERENCES

Agarwal, S. (2018, February 20). Internet users in India expected to reach 500 million by June: IAMAI. *Economic Times*. Retrieved April 24, 2018, from https://economictimes.indiatimes.com/tech/internet/internet-users-in-india-expected-to-reach-500-million-by-june-iamai/articleshow/63000198.cms

Aggarwal, C. C. (2011). An introduction to social network data analytics. In C. C. Aggarwal (Ed.), *Social Network Data Analytics* (pp. 1–15). Springer. doi:10.1007/978-1-4419-8462-3_1

Alencar, A. B., de Oliviera, M. F., & Paulovich, F. V. (2012). Seeing beyond reading: A survey on visual text analytics. *Wiley Interdisciplinary Reviews. Data Mining and Knowledge Discovery*, 2(6), 476–492. doi:10.1002/widm.1071

Alexander, R. M., & Gentry, J. K. (2014). Using social media to report financial results. *Business Horizons*, 57(2), 161–167. doi:10.1016/j.bushor.2013.10.009

Almuhimedi, H., Wilson, S., Liu, B., Sadeh, N., & Acquisti, A. (2013). Tweets are forever: A large-scale quantitative analysis of deleted tweets. *CSCW Computer Supported Cooperative Work* (pp. 897-908). New York. *ACM New York, NY, USA, 2013*. doi:10.1145/2441776.2441878

Arshad, A., Zafar, M., Fatima, I., & Khan, S. K. (2015). The Impact of Perceived Risk on Online Buyg Behavior. *International Journal of New Technology and Research*, 1(8), 13–18. Retrieved from https://www.ijntr.org/download_data/IJNTR01080013.pdf

Association of Certified Fraud Examiners. (2006). *Report to the nation on occupational fraud and abuse*. ACFE. Retrieved from https://www.acfe.com/uploadedFiles/ACFE_Website/Content/documents/2006-rttn.pdf

Babu, D. M., Bhagyasri, M., Lahari, K., Madhuri, C. H., & Kumari, G. P. (2014). Image Based Fraud Prevention. *International Journal of Computer Science and Information Technologies*, 5(1), 728–731. Retrieved from http://ijcsit.com/docs/Volume 5/vol5issue01/ijcsit20140501158.pdf

Bailey, A. A., Bonifield, C. M., & Arias, A. (2018). Social media use by young Latin American consumers: An exploration. *Journal of Retailing and Consumer Services*, 43, 10–19. doi:10.1016/j.jretconser.2018.02.003

Bandari, R., Asur, S., & Huberman, B. A. (2012). *The pulse of news in social media: Forecasting popularity. In Proceedings of the Sixth International AAAI Conference on Weblogs and Social Media* (pp. 26–33). Association for the Advancement of Artificial Intelligence. Retrieved from https://www.aaai.org/ocs/index.php/ICWSM/ICWSM12/paper/viewFile/4646/4963

Barbier, G., & Liu, H. (2011). Data mining in social media. In C. C. Aggarwal (Ed.), *Social network data analytics* (pp. 327–352). Springer. doi:10.1007/978-1-4419-8462-3_12

Bocconcelli, R., Cioppi, M., & Pagano, A. (2017). Social media as a resource in SMEs' sales process. *Journal of Business and Industrial Marketing, 32*(5), 693–709. doi:10.1108/JBIM-11-2014-0244

Campbell, L. (2017). *The Importance of Social Media in Risk Management.* Retrieved April 30, 2018, from Cube Logic: https://cubelogic.com/white-papers/the-importance-of-social-media-in-risk-management/

Carson, B. (2016). *Social Media as a Research Methodology.* Retrieved from https://blog.marketresearch.com/social-media-as-a-research-methodology

Chelliah, J., & Field, J. (2014). Managing the risks of social media: Ways to ensure that online behavior is always appropriate. *Human Resource Management International Digest, 22*(5), 39–41. doi:10.1108/HRMID-07-2014-0103

Chen, H., De, P., Hu, Y., & Hwang, B.-H. (2014). Wisdom of Crowds: The Value of Stock Opinions Transmitted Through Social Media. *Review of Financial Studies, 27*(5), 1367–1403. doi:10.1093/rfs/hhu001

Chen, H., Hwang, H., & Liu, B. (2018). *The Emergence of "Social Executives" and Its Consequences for Financial Markets.* doi:10.2139srn.2318094

Choi, D.-H., Yoo, W., Noh, G.-Y., & Park, K. (2017). The impact of social media on risk perceptions during the MERS outbreak in South Korea. *Computers in Human Behavior, 72*, 422–431. doi:10.1016/j.chb.2017.03.004

Cressey, D. R. (1953). *Other people's money; a study of the social psychology of embezzlement.* New York: Free Press.

Crowl, J. (2015). *Impulse Behavior: Why Social Media Content is Such a Popular Downtime Activity.* Retrieved from www.skyword.com: https://www.skyword.com/contentstandard/marketing/impulse-behavior-why-social-media-content-is-such-a-popular-downtime-activity/

Data Visualization's Positive Impact on Decision Making. (2010). Retrieved from https://www.map-businessonline.com/Whitepaper.aspx/Decision-Making

Demek, K. C., Raschke, R. L., Janvrin, D. J., & Dilla, W. N. (2018). Do organizations use a formalized risk management process to address social media risk? *International Journal of Accounting Information Systems, 28*, 31–44. doi:10.1016/j.accinf.2017.12.004

Drummond, C., McGrath, H., & O'Toole, T. (2017). The impact of social media on resource mobilisation in entrepreneurial firms. *Industrial Marketing Management, 70*, 68–89. doi:10.1016/j.indmarman.2017.05.009

Dubey, G., Chawla, S., & Kaur, K. (2017). Social media opinion analysis for Indian political diplomats. In *Cloud Computing, Data Science & Engineering - Confluence, 2017 7th International Conference on* (pp. 681-686). Noida: IEEE. doi:10.1109/CONFLUENCE.2017.7943238

Essays, U. K. (2013, November). *Social Media In The Jasmine Revolution*. Retrieved April 23, 2018, from UK Essays: https://www.ukessays.com/essays/media/effect-of-social-media-on-the-jasmine-revolution-media-essay.php?vref=1

Ferguson, M. (2016, May 19). *What is Text Analytics?* http://www.ibmbigdatahub.com/blog/what-text-analytics

Forensics, K. P. M. G. (2003). *Fraud Survey*. Montvale, NJ: KPMG.

Forrester Research Inc. (2018). *Predictions 2018: A year of reckoning*. Forrester Research Inc. Retrieved from https://go.forrester.com/blogs/predictions-2018-a-year-of-reckoning/

Gandomi, A., & Haider, M. (2015). Beyond the hype: Big data concepts, methods, and analytics. *International Journal of Information Management*, *35*(2), 137–144. doi:10.1016/j.ijinfomgt.2014.10.007

Grizane, T., & Jurgelane, I. (2017). Social Media Impact on Business Evaluation. *Procedia Computer Science*, *104*, 190–196. doi:10.1016/j.procs.2017.01.103

Hao, J., & Dai, H. (2016). Social media content and sentiment analysis on consumer security breaches. *Journal of Financial Crime*, *23*(4), 855–869. doi:10.1108/JFC-01-2016-0001

Hasan, A., Moin, S., Karim, A., & Shamshirband, S. (2018). Machine Learning-Based Sentiment Analysis for Twitter Accounts. *Mathematical and Computational Applications*, *23*(1), 11–26. doi:10.3390/mca23010011

He, W., Guo, L., Shen, J., & Akula, V. (2016). Social Media-Based Forecasting: A Case Study of Tweets and Stock Prices in the Financial Services Industry. *Journal of Organizational and End User Computing*, *28*(2), 18. doi:10.4018/JOEUC.2016040105

He, W., Zha, S., & Li, L. (2013). Social media competitive analysis and text mining: A case study in the pizza industry. *International Journal of Information Management*, *33*(3), 464–472. doi:10.1016/j.ijinfomgt.2013.01.001

Heidemann, J., Klier, M., & Probst, F. (2012). Online social networks: A survey of a global phenomenon. *Computer Networks*, *56*(18), 3866–3878. doi:10.1016/j.comnet.2012.08.009

Holton, C. (2009). Identifying disgruntled employee systems fraud risk through text mining: A simple solution for a multi-billion dollar problem. *Decision Support Systems*, *46*(4), 853–864. doi:10.1016/j.dss.2008.11.013

Hull, J. C. (2015). *Risk Management and Financial Institutions* (4th ed.). John Wiley & Sons. Retrieved from http://www.simonfoucher.com/MBA/FINA%20695%20-%20Risk%20Management/riskmanagementandfinancialinstitutions4theditionjohnhull-150518225205-lva1-app6892.pdf

IZEA. (2017, March). *6 Key Factors That Influence Your Social Media Engagement*. Retrieved from www.izea.com: https://izea.com/2017/03/16/key-factors-affect-social-media-engagement/

Jiang, J., & Shen, M. (2017). *Traditional Media*. Twitter and Business Scandals; doi:10.2139srn.2959419

Jose, R., & Chooralil, V. S. (2015). Prediction of election result by enhanced sentiment analysis on Twitter data using Word Sense Disambiguation. In *Proceedings of the 2015 International Conference on Control Communication & Computing India (ICCC)* (pp. 638-641). Trivandrum: IEEE. 10.1109/ICCC.2015.7432974

Karppi, T., & Crawford, K. (2016). Social Media, Financial Algorithms and the Hack Crash. *Theory, Culture & Society*, *33*(1), 73–92. doi:10.1177/0263276415583139

Kemp, S. (2017, August 7). *Number of social media users passes 3 billion with no signs of slowing*. Retrieved January 10, 2018, from The Next Web: https://thenextweb.com/contributors/2017/08/07/number-social-media-users-passes-3-billion-no-signs-slowing/

Kim, W. G., Lim, H., & Brymer, R. A. (2015). The effectiveness of managing social media on hotel performance. *International Journal of Hospitality Management*, *44*, 165–171. doi:10.1016/j.ijhm.2014.10.014

Kroll Inc. (2008). Economist Intelligence Unit Overview. In *The Kroll Global Fraud Report*. Kroll Inc. Retrieved from https://eiuperspectives.com/sites/default/files/FraudReport_English-UK_Sept08_1.pdf

Li, B., Chan, K. C., Ou, C., & Ruifeng, S. (2017). Discovering public sentiment in social media for predicting stock movement of publicly listed companies. *Information Systems*, *69*, 81–92. doi:10.1016/j.is.2016.10.001

Liben-Nowell, D., & Kleinberg, J. (2007). The link prediction problem for social networks. *Journal of the Association for Information Science and Technology*, *58*(7), 1019–1031. doi:10.1002/asi.v58:7

Liu, L., Wu, J., Li, P., & Li, Q. (2015). A social-media-based approach to predicting stock comovement. *Expert Systems with Applications*, *42*(8), 3893–3901. doi:10.1016/j.eswa.2014.12.049

Malhotra, A. (2011). Social Media: The New Tool of Revolution. *Scholar Warrior*, 74-81. Retrieved April 24, 2018, from http://www.claws.in/images/journals_doc/Spring%202011-%20Final%20Issue.87-94.pdf

Mazboudi, M., & Khalil, S. (2017). The attenuation effect of social media: Evidence from acquisitions by large firms. *Journal of Financial Stability*, *28*, 115–124. doi:10.1016/j.jfs.2016.11.010

Meti, V., Khandoba, P., & Guru, M. (2015). Social Media for Political Mobilization in India: A Study. *Journal of Mass Communication & Journalism*, *5*(9). doi:10.4172/2165-7912.1000275

Miller, R. (2015, June 30). *Inside Facebook's Blu-Ray Cold Storage Data Center*. Retrieved April 29, 2018, from Data Center Frontier: https://datacenterfrontier.com/inside-facebooks-blu-ray-cold-storage-data-center/

Momoc, A. (2013). Social Media- PR Tools for Romanian Politicians? *Procedia: Social and Behavioral Sciences*, *81*, 116–121. doi:10.1016/j.sbspro.2013.06.398

Morinaga, S., Yamanishi, K., Tateishi, K., & Fukushima, T. (2002). Mining product reputations on the web. In *Proceedings of the eighth ACM SIGKDD international conference on Knowledge discovery and data mining* (pp. 341-349). ACM. 10.1145/775047.775098

Oliveira, M. P., & Handfield, R. (2017). An enactment theory model of supplier financial disruption risk mitigation. *Supply Chain Management*, 22(5), 442–457. doi:10.1108/SCM-03-2017-0121

Oracle. (2015, February). *Big Data in Financial Services and Banking: Architect's Guide and Reference Architecture Introduction*. Retrieved March 13, 2018, from Oracle: http://www.oracle.com/us/technologies/big-data/big-data-in-financial-services-wp-2415760.pdf

Osman, M. (2017). *How to Use Hashtags on Every Social Media Network*. Retrieved from www.sproutsocial.com: https://sproutsocial.com/insights/how-to-use-hashtags/

Parthasarathy, S., Ruan, Y., & Satuluri, V. (2011). Community discovery in social networks: Applications, methods and emerging trends. In C. C. Aggarwal (Ed.), *Social network data analytics* (pp. 79–113). Boston: Springer. doi:10.1007/978-1-4419-8462-3_4

Pew Research Center. (2016, July 18). *Election 2016: Campaigns as a Direct Source of News*. Retrieved April 10, 2018, from Pew Research Center Journalism and Media: http://www.journalism.org/2016/07/18/election-2016-campaigns-as-a-direct-source-of-news/

Piskorski, M. J. (2014). *A Social Strategy: How we profit from Social Media*. Princeton, NJ: Princeton University Press. doi:10.1515/9781400850020

Press Trust of India. (2017, November 28). Data usage per smartphone in India to grow 5-fold by 2023: Ericsson. *Economic Times*. Retrieved April 29, 2018, from https://economictimes.indiatimes.com/tech/internet/data-usage-per-smartphone-in-india-to-grow-5-fold-by-2023-ericsson/articleshow/61838209.cms

Quantzig. (n.d.). *Social Media Analytics and Politics*. Retrieved April 17, 2018, from Quantzig Blog: https://www.quantzig.com/blog/social-media-analytics-politics#

Ribarsky, W., Wang, D. X., & Dou, W. (2014). Social media analytics for competitive advantage. *Computers & Graphics*, 38, 328–331. doi:10.1016/j.cag.2013.11.003

Roose, K. (2017). *Forget Washington. Facebook's Problems Abroad Are Far More Disturbing*. Retrieved April 30, 2018, from The New York Times: https://www.nytimes.com/2017/10/29/business/facebook-misinformation-abroad.html

Seiter, C. (2016). *The Psychology of Social Media: Why We Like, Comment, and Share Online*. Retrieved from www.blog.bufferapp.com: https://blog.bufferapp.com/psychology-of-social-media

Severi, E., Ling, K. C., & Nasemoadeli, A. (2014). *The Impacts of Electronic Word of Mouth on Brand Equity in the Context of Social Media*. Academic Press. doi:10.5539/ijbm.v9n8p84

Stieglitz, S., Mirbabaie, M., Ross, B., & Neuberger, C. (2018). Social media analytics – Challenges in topic discovery, data collection, and data preparation. *International Journal of Information Management*, 39, 156–168. doi:10.1016/j.ijinfomgt.2017.12.002

Sul, H., Dennis, A. R., & Yuan, L. I. (2014). Trading on Twitter: The Financial Information Content of Emotion in Social Media. *Proceedings of the 47th Hawaii International Conference on System Sciences*. Conference Publishing Services. doi:10.1109/HICSS.2014.107

Sun, J., & Tang, J. (2011). A survey of models and algorithms for social influence analysis. In C. C. Aggarwal (Ed.), *Social network data analytics* (pp. 177–214). Boston: Springer. doi:10.1007/978-1-4419-8462-3_7

TechAmerica Foundation's Federal Big Data Commission. (2012). *Demystifying bigdata: A practical guide to transforming the business of Government*. Washington, DC: Tech America. Retrieved from http://www.techamerica.org/Docs/fileManager.cfm?f=techamerica-bigdatareport-final.pdf

Themba, G., & Mulala, M. (2013). Brand-Related eWOM and Its Effects on Purchase Decisions: An Empirical Study of University of Botswana Students. *International Journal of Business and Management*, 8(8), 31. doi:10.5539/ijbm.v8n8p31

Toma, S.-V., Chitiţă, M., & Şarpe, D. (2012). Risk and Uncertainty. *Procedia Economics and Finance*, 3, 975–980. doi:10.1016/S2212-5671(12)00260-2

Vagata, P., & Wilfong, K. (2014, April 10). *Scaling the Facebook data warehouse to 300 PB*. Retrieved April 28, 2018, from Facebook: https://code.facebook.com/posts/229861827208629/scaling-the-facebook-data-warehouse-to-300-pb/

VanBoskirk, S., Overby, C. S., & Takvorian, S. (2011). *US interactive marketing forecast, 2011 to 2016*. Forrester Research Inc. Retrieved from https://retelur.files.wordpress.com/2012/01/forrester_interactive_marketing_forecast_2011_to_2016.pdf

Weiczner, J. (2015, December 7). How Investors Are Using Social Media to Make Money. *Fortune*. Retrieved from http://fortune.com/2015/12/07/dataminr-hedge-funds-twitter-data/

Williams, C. B. (2017). Introduction: Social Media, Political Marketing and the 2016 US Election. *Journal of Political Marketing*, 16(3-4), 207–211. doi:10.1080/15377857.2017.1345828

Young, K. (2017, November 14). *The Biggest Social Media Trends Shaping 2018*. Retrieved December 30, 2018, from Global Web Index: https://blog.globalwebindex.com/trends/social-media-trends/

YouTube for Press. (n.d.). Retrieved March 15, 2018, from YouTube: https://www.youtube.com/yt/about/press/

Zeng, D., Chen, H., Lusch, R., & Li, S.-H. (2010). Social media analytics and intelligence. *IEEE Intelligent Systems*, 25(6), 13–16. doi:10.1109/MIS.2010.151

Zhu, Y.-Q., & Chen, H.-G. (2015). Social media and human need satisfaction: Implications for social media marketing. *Business Horizons*, 58(3), 335–345. doi:10.1016/j.bushor.2015.01.006

ADDITIONAL READING

Akinkunmi, M. (2018). Data Mining and Market Intelligence: Implications for Decision Making. *Synthesis Lectures on Engineering*, 13(1), 1–181. doi:10.2200/S00838ED1V01Y201803ENG030

Cheney-Lippold, J. (2017). *We Are Data: Algorithms and the making of our digital selves*. New York: New York University Press. doi:10.2307/j.ctt1gk0941

Fan, W., & Gordon, M. D. (2014). The Power of Social Media Analytics. *Communications of the ACM*, *57*(6), 74–81. doi:10.1145/2602574

Gorodnichenko, Y., Pham, T., & Talavera, O. (2018). *Social media, sentiment and public opinions: Evidence from# Brexit and# USElection. (No. w24631)*. National Bureau of Economic Research; doi:10.3386/w24631

Lal, A. (2017). *India social: How social media is leading the charge and changing country*. New Delhi: Hachette India.

Piskorski, M. (2014). *A social strategy: How we profit from social media*. Princeton: Princeton University Press. doi:10.1515/9781400850020

Schmidt, E., & Cohen, J. (2013). *The new digital age*. New Delhi: Hachette India.

Sponder, M. (2012). *Social media analytics: effective tools for building, interpreting, and using metrics*. New York: McGraw-Hill.

KEY TERMS AND DEFINITIONS

Big Data: This is data characterized by its large volume, wide variety, and high velocity. Volume refers to high quantity of data usually running into terabytes. The data is not only numbers or text, but can include images, videos, etc., making it very varied and the data is generated rapidly which is called its high velocity.

Content-Based Analytics: In social media analysis, content-based analytics involves the analysis on the contents posted by users on social media. This includes text, images, and videos.

Occupational Fraud: Occupational fraud is the use of one's occupation for personal enrichment through the deliberate misuse or misapplication of the organization's resources or assets. It could include any of payment fraud, procurement fraud, and travel and subsistence fraud, personnel management, exploiting assets or information and receipt fraud.

Risk: When the outcome of an event is uncertain, but one is aware of the probabilities of each outcome, the outcome is said to possess risk.

Social Media Analytics: It is the process of gathering, structuring, analyzing and gaining actionable insights from data available on social media. This is data generated from the conversations of stakeholders on social media.

Structure-Based Analytics: In social media analysis, structure based analytics or social network analytics is concerned with evaluating the structural attributes of a social network and extracting intelligence from the relationships among the participating entities. The structures are modelled visually with nodes, and edges connecting the nodes.

Text Analysis: This is the process of creating high-quality structured data for analysis from unstructured and heterogeneous textual data. The structured data is then analyzed to derive usable conclusions. In social media analysis, the raw text could be in the form of tweets, Facebook posts, comments on social media, hashtags, and blog posts.

Uncertainty: When the outcome of an event is uncertain and one doesn't know all possible outcomes and/or their probabilities, then outcome is said to be uncertain.

Web 2.0: As opposed to the traditional world wide web (retroactively called Web 1.0), Web 2.0 has a lot of inputs generated by users. These are in the form of forums, microblogging, social networking and wikis (a server program that allows users to collaborate in forming the content of a website [e.g., Wikipedia]). An information architecture consultant Darcy DiNucci coined the term Web 2.0 in 1999, but it was popularized by Tim O'Reilly, founder of O'Reilly Media.

ENDNOTES

[1] This Q&A session on Reddit can be accessed here - https://www.reddit.com/r/StarWarsBattlefront/comments/7d4qft/star_wars_battlefront_ii_dice_developer_ama/?st=JA1BP7F6&sh=f5117ea9.

[2] Naive Bayes model is a method of probabilistic classification based on Bayes' theorem and begins with strong independence assumption amongst the features. It is a popular method for text categorization in machine learning. It uses word frequencies to classify text into a category. It is highly scalable and has found application in many fields like automated medical diagnosis, classifying mail as spam or legitimate etc. This model is also known as simple Bayes or independence Bayes.

[3] Data that has been already classified as disgruntled on non-disgruntled is fed to the software. In machine learning, the software analyses the text and identifies different features and assigns weights to each feature in classifying the text as disgruntled or non-disgruntled. Before the learning process, the data is divided into two parts. One part is fed in, on which after multiple iterations the machine finds the best factors and weights for them to predict the outcome (classification). This model is then tested on the second part of the data to test its accuracy. So, all machine learning processes involve dividing the data into training data – data used to identify the parameters of the model and evaluation data – data on which the accuracy of the model is tested.

Chapter 44
The Use of New Media Applications in Corporate Social Responsibility:
Vodafone "#BuMamaBenden" Case Study

Eda Turanci
https://orcid.org/0000-0002-2539-8452
Ankara Haci Bayram Veli University, Turkey

Nefise Sirzad
https://orcid.org/0000-0002-3919-6974
Cankaya University, Turkey

ABSTRACT

Corporate social responsibility is the responsibility of the corporations towards the stakeholders, the environment, and society. It covers the voluntary practices for the solution of social problems. Similar to other areas, new media applications offer new opportunities in terms of corporate social responsibility practices. In addition, it is now possible for companies to benefit from four different types of media: "paid, earned, shared, and owned media". The purpose of this study is to reveal how corporations take advantage of paid, owned, earned, and shared media using new media applications in their social responsibility practices. For this purpose, the Vodafone Turkey Foundation's #BuMamaBenden project is selected as a case study and examined. The research results show that new media applications can be used as an effective tool to reach people. Moreover, the coordinated use of these four media types can increase the impact of corporate social responsibility projects and keeps them alive.

INTRODUCTION

Corporate social responsibility practices, which are a significant part of both public relations and applications in terms of corporations' image and reputation, are dealing with social issues as well as cor-

DOI: 10.4018/978-1-7998-9020-1.ch044

porations' interests. Corporate social responsibility is defined as an organization's responsibility toward society and its environment or an effort to support the solution of social problems.

The developments of the internet and new media applications have provided new facilities and opportunities for practitioners in many fields, such as communication, public relations, and advertising. Unlike traditional communication tools, new media technologies and the internet enable corporations to change the way they communicate with the consumers and stakeholders. They enhance dialogue, disseminate information rapidly, and engage with audiences/consumers in the content creation process. In particular, this development in the content creation process can be explained as the power gaining by the audiences, consumers or users. Nowadays, users can share their satisfactions, dissatisfactions, ideas, experiences, and opinions on any subject. Thereby they disseminate information about any corporate according to their own experience. In this sense, it is possible to discuss the user's function as a source of information and news. Accordingly, developments in communication technologies, the internet, and new media tools stand out as channels that allow users to produce content about corporations. These developments draw attention to two types of new media namely "earned" and "shared" media which can be regarded as new reflections of the possibilities offered by new media and digital technologies.

Before the internet and digital technologies come to the fore, it can be noted that two other types of media have been used very actively in the traditional sense. They have been conceptualized as "paid media" which refers to paid communication channels used by corporations, and "owned media" which are described as communication channels owned and/or controlled by the corporations.

When these four media types are defined respectively, paid media refers to traditional advertisements, sponsorships, social media ads, and more. The main purpose of paid media is advertising. Owned media is more like corporations' own media such as corporate websites, blogs, official social media accounts and comprises of content that is created and control by corporations. Earned media includes publicity and media relations. Finally shared media refers to social media and new media platforms such as Twitter, Facebook, or Instagram which are the leading tools that allow users to create and share content. This type of media also covers comments, shares, and contents (i.e., mentions, repost, reviews) created by users. In light of these explanations, the PESO model in which these four media types are handled integrally in the literature will be examined within the scope of the study. At this point, it is possible to say that both earned and shared media contents can be assumed to be more effective than corporation generated content. It can be said that these types of media, which have a similar effect to traditional word of mouth (WOM) communication, has a greater impact on consumers' decisions compared to the paid or owned media contents.

The main purpose of the study is to examine the function of new media applications in corporate social responsibility practices. This study, which is based on the case study method, analyzed media contents of Vodafone's social responsibility project "#BuMamaBenden" (#ThisFoodIsOnMe) initiated in 2018. The project aims to allow users to help street animals independently from Vodafone and enables them to formula feeding animals via tweeting #BuMamaBenden hashtags. It encourages users to create content with the specified hashtag on behalf of the corporation and to be a part of the social responsibility project, as well it ensures the continuation of the social responsibility activity planned by the corporation. Vodafone campaign is an indication of how efficiently new media can be used in terms of social responsibility applications. In this context, the study is thought to be important to see how new media tools can be used actively in social responsibility practices.

BACKGROUND

Corporate Social Responsibility

Corporate social responsibility is based on the understanding of fulfilling the responsibilities of the corporations towards the society in which they are located. Social responsibility is considered as an effort by the organization to cope with social problems and develop a solution for them. It is said that social responsibility practices have some positive effects for both the corporation and society. In general, it is accepted that social responsibility practices have a positive effect on consumer trust (Swaen & Chumpitaz, 2008; Saat & Selamat, 2014), customer satisfaction (Galbreath, 2010; Puriwat & Tripopsakul, 2018), and corporate reputation (Stuebs & Sun, 2011). It is also possible to talk about social benefit as social responsibility practices are carried out to eliminate a problem or deficiency existing in society.

Corporate social responsibility is an interdisciplinary field of research and is studied by many different disciplines. Accordingly, corporate social responsibility is one of the topics that attract the attention of many "communication disciplines such as public relations, organizational communication, marketing and reputation management" (Ihlen, Bartlett, & May, 2011, p. 3). However, in many studies related to the subject in the literature, it is emphasized that corporate social responsibility is a prominent issue both in public and institutional terms and also it is an important research and application area in public relations (Capriotti & Moreno, 2007; Bartlett, 2011; Lee, 2017). As emphasized, "CSR communication from the stakeholder management perspective has drawn considerable attention from public relations and CSR researchers in recent years" (Lim & Greenwood, 2017, p. 769). According to the results of Lee's (2017) research, publications and researches on corporate social responsibility in the field of public relations have increased significantly since 2006. In this context, it should be noted that social responsibility practices have become an important issue in terms of public relations studies. Corporate social responsibility may be one of the strategies that public relations experts seek to establish long-term dialogical relationships with stakeholders or consumers (Uzunoğlu, Türkel, & Akyar, 2017).

There are many different ways to explain how the concept of corporate social responsibility came about. According to Bhattacharya, Sen and Korschun (2011, p. 27), the idea that corporations can be managed to benefit the society within the framework of the corporate responsibility approach dates back to the beginning of the eighteenth century. However, it is stated that the first examples of corporate social responsibility practices in the modern sense, emerged in the United States (Yamak, 2007, p. 13). Wang (2017, p. 317) explains that the understanding of corporate social responsibility can be found as a thought in the ancient Greek era, which is more than 2,000 years old, but also mentions that the modern sense of corporate social responsibility rose in the early 20th century in the United States. As Wang (2017, p. 317) emphasizes, "America's special institutional background made it more concerned with Corporate Social Responsibility than any other western industrial nation".

In different researches it is stated that the corporate social responsibility has a wide scope, there are numerous definitions in the literature but also there is no consensus about the meaning and the definition of the concept (De Bakker, Groenewegen, & Den Hond, 2005; Wan-Jan, 2006; Dahlsrud, 2008; Chen, 2009; Adeyeye, 2012; Cho, Furey, & Mohr, 2017). It is very difficult to define corporate social responsibility as it changes according to context, period and culture (Aksak, Ferguson, & Duman, 2016, p. 79). On the other hand, it is expressed that the extended definition of corporate social responsibility refers to what the relationship between global companies, governments and citizens is or should be (Crowther & Aras, 2008, p. 10).

Corporate social responsibility has been described as a practical tool "to help companies understand their culture, translate it into every business process and live out the underlying values and beliefs" (Pohl, 2006: p. 53). According to the definition of the European Commission (2011, p. 6; 2019) social responsibility is "the responsibility of enterprises for their impacts on society" and "companies can become socially responsible by; integrating social, environmental, ethical, consumer, and human rights concerns into their business strategy and operations and also following the law".

In another explanation, as cited by Adeyeye (2012, p. 12), World Business Council for Sustainable Development (WBCSD), -"a powerful coalition of companies actively involved in CSR"-, define CSR as,

"the continuing commitment by business to behave ethically and contribute to economic development, while improving the quality of life of the workforce and their families, as well as of the community and society at large"

In light of these definitions it should be noted that in the current study corporate social responsibility is considered as a public relations strategy (Aksak et al., 2016) and is defined as sensitivity to various problems of the society in which the corporation is located.

Nowadays, due to reasons such as consumer awareness and changing business understanding, corporations are not just considered as organizations that produce and sell products and make a profit. As today's consumers become more aware to the effects of the organization on society, environment and people, there are some changes in the company's understanding of business. It can be said that corporate social responsibility came to the agenda as a result of such changes, and corporations have gained a social dimension by moving away from being only an economic commercial structure. As Yamak (2007, p. 17) explains, industrialization, the transition to urban life and the changes and imbalances have led to questioning the social role of companies since the 1900s.

The concept of social responsibility has developed in connection with government policies and social changes. When the concept of responsibility is briefly evaluated in the period up to the 1920s, it is seen that this period was based on profit maximization and that social responsibility is related to make a profit (Yamak, 2007, p. 20). As Carroll (1991, p. 39) explains previously, the responsibility of companies was "to provide maximum financial return to shareholders", but as a result of various developments, public policies formally recognized the environment, employees, and consumers as important stakeholders of the business world. As mentioned by Chen (2009, p. 524), nowadays businesses have wider areas of responsibility.

In the 1950s and 1960s, corporate social responsibility was widely used in practice (Wang, 2017, p. 317). Especially the 1960s and 1970s are considered as the years in which many social movements have taken place, consumer rights have come to the fore, environmental sensitivity has increased, and some issues such as women's rights have been on the agenda (Yamak, 2007). As noted, increasing activism in the public sphere has begun to change the way companies interact and communicate with society (Clark, 2000, p. 365). Accordingly, it was mentioned that various commissions were established in those years to protect the environment and consumers, to prevent discrimination and to ensure employment equality and to ensure occupational safety and health (Carroll, 1991, p. 39). "The rise of CSR, in the late 1970s and early 1980s, coincided with the increased concern for a corporation's image" (Clark, 2000, p. 364). Since the 1990s, corporate social responsibility has gained a place in the market dynamics as it has gained benefits for the company, and it has been seen that many of the regulations previously made by the government are now undertaken by the companies (Yamak, 2007, pp. 82-83).

Corporate social responsibility practices are an area with many components, and nowadays, many factors fall under the responsibility of the organizations. At this point, we can refer to the "corporate social responsibility pyramid" that Carroll (1991) has put forward. As Carroll (1991, p. 40) explains, "for the CSR to be accepted by a conscientious business person, it should be framed in such a way that the entire range of business responsibilities are embraced" and he mentions that the total corporate social responsibility consists of four types of responsibility such as "economic, legal, ethical and philanthropic".

According to Carroll (1991, p. 42),

- *Philanthropic responsibilities: "Be a good corporate citizen: Contribute resources to the community, improve quality of life."*
- *Ethical responsibilities: "Be ethical: Obligations to do what is right, just and fair. Avoid harm."*
- *Legal responsibilities: "Obey the law: Law is society's codification of right and wrong. Play by the rules of the game."*
- *Economic responsibilities: "Be profitable. The foundation upon which all others rest."*

Corporate social responsibility can also be considered as a way of communicating with stakeholders. Accordingly, public relations researchers state that modern companies are thinking beyond the company's interests, and they tend to interact, communicate, and collaborate with their shareholders (Lim & Greenwood, 2017, p. 769). It has been seen that as a result of this relationship, the social benefit comes into prominence in social responsibility practices. As pointed by Adeyeye (2012, pp. 7-8), "it soon became clear that CSR is not really about improving a company's bottom line. It is about the relationship between business and society".

As a result, the concept of social responsibility is far from being an element that corporations can ignore. The increasing importance of social responsibility has led corporations to focus more on the issue. First of all, it is said that social responsibility is "a responsibility towards the future and towards future members of society", and that responsibility affects both today and the future (Crowther & Aras, 2008, p. 11; Aras & Crowther, 2009, p. 279). At this point, it is possible to say that companies have acknowledged the increasing importance of corporate responsibility and they need to take stakeholders more into account and they also recognize that social responsibility is not only profit maximization (Adeyeye, 2012). As Bhattacharya et al., (2011, p. 30) highlighted, corporate responsibility, once seen as a necessity by companies, now is seen as "an opportunity to create value for their business".

New Media and Corporate Social Responsibility

As in all fields, the opportunities and innovations offered by the internet and new media have had an impact on the social responsibility understanding. These networks have brought up new opportunities both for consumers and corporates. As mentioned, the rise of social networks such as Facebook, Instagram, Twitter and more or internet-based communication presents both opportunities and challenges for corporate social responsibility practices, business and community interactions (De Bakker & Hellsten, 2013, p. 807). "Many businesses are now involved in such networks either as service providers or as participants" (Chen, 2009, p. 523).

In the literature there are many studies examining the relationship between the internet, new media, social networks and social responsibility from different perspectives (Chen, 2009; Capriotti, 2011; Ozdora-Aksak, 2015; Ozdora-Aksak & Atakan-Duman, 2015; Cho et al., 2017; Uzunoğlu et al., 2017,

Vo, Xiao, & Ho, 2019). These studies clearly show that new media practices are also effective in terms of social responsibility understanding and social responsibility communication. As mentioned, the internet and social media have become significant tools for the communication of corporate social responsibility practices (Ozdora-Aksak & Atakan-Duman, 2015, p. 119, 121).

New media technologies and the internet have led to significant transformations in the forms of communication. Accordingly, many changes can be mentioned such as eliminating time and space constraints, enabling active participation and content generation of users, enabling dialogue, enabling faster dissemination of information, ideas, thoughts and experiences and expanding the scope of communication. At this point as mentioned, "the Internet has become a great mass communication tool for companies since they can now reach their stakeholders all over the world, 365 days a year, 24 hours a day" (Capriotti, 2011, p. 359). This disclosure sheds light on the function of eliminating the boundaries of new media. In this respect, it is possible to say that the internet has increased the institutions' direct access to their customers or stakeholders.

It is also a common discourse that the internet and social networks facilitate bi-directional interactive dialogue. As Lim and Greenwood (2017, p. 769) explain, "similar to a paradigmatic shift in public relations practices, public relations researchers maintained that CSR communication has evolved from one-way communication to two-way communication, listening to and reflecting key stakeholders' voice and interest". It is also stated that "strategically managed corporate social responsibility communication" is an important tool for organizations to establish a dialogue with their stakeholders and provide participatory communication (Uzunoğlu et al., 2017, p. 989). New media technologies are also functional in terms of the dissemination of information. As Capriotti (2011, p. 363) explained regarding many studies, the main benefit of the internet in corporate social responsibility communication is the fast, easy and controlled transfer of information or messages about the company's social responsibility practices.

Social networks allow users to participate in content production. In this context, it is possible for users to participate in social responsibility applications as an active participant and to produce content about the existing social responsibility applications on behalf of corporations. In this case, users have gained the role of a media that disseminate messages on behalf of companies. As Lee, Yoon and O'Donnell (2018, p. 202) mentioned, "social networking sites are increasingly used to promote corporate social responsibility initiatives. Consumers can like, share, or comment on corporate social responsibility messages on social networking sites, signaling public approval or disapproval and affecting an individual's perceived legitimacy of the organization".

In light of all these explanations, it is clear that the development of the internet and new media offer new opportunities beyond traditional means. Nowadays, using both traditional and new media integrally is inevitable.

Paid, Earned, Shared and Owned Media

The development of the internet and new media platforms has led to the advent of new strategies in communication between corporations and their customers. Media plays a crucial role in disseminating corporations' messages to their target audiences. Before the dominance of the internet and technological development, corporations mostly used paid and owned media to send their messages. However, in recent years corporations employ two other types of media named shared and earned media. This section which shows the integration of traditional and new media examines these four types of media.

Today, corporations benefit from four different types of media, classified as "paid media, owned media, earned media and shared media" (Luttrell, 2015; Macnamara, Lwin, Adi, & Zerfass, 2016; Dietrich, 2018a, 2018b; Luttrell & Capizzo, 2018) to communicate with their consumers and stakeholders. According to Luttrell (2015, p. 207), "an easy way to remember and understand the differences within the media landscape is by using the acronym PESO: paid, earned, shared, and owned."

As Dakouan and Benabdelouahed (2019, p. 122) explain in detail, one of the first pioneers to mention media categorization was Burcher (2012). This categorization called the "media trinity". It consists of paid, owned and earned media. After this tripartite structure, Luttrell added a new form of media called "shared media" to his research and referred to a new media model known as the PESO model. Thus, this quartet media categorization consisting of paid, earned, shared and owned media started to be mentioned. Finally, Dakouan and Benabdelouahed (2019, p. 122) mention that Dietrich described the PESO model as a new marketing strategy that would help increase access to consumers and build market-leading brands.

In addition to this statement, Luttrell and Capizzo (2018) stated that the PESO model was developed by Dietrich. With Dietrich's own words, "the PESO model officially launched in 2014, when Spin Sucks (the book) was published" (Dietrich, 2018b).

Prior to the emergence of the internet, the tools used by companies in communicating with customers were more limited than today. As Macnamara et al. (2016, p. 377) explain, social media has enabled a new media to be included in paid, owned and earned media and this new media, which called shared media, also "changed the scope and scale of the owned media". However, due to the prominence of the internet and the rise of social media Macnamara et al. (2016, pp. 377, 381) explain that the PESO model no longer reflects the priority of organizations' media strategies, and that shared media will be at the top of the quadruple list. As a result of their research, they showed that there is a change from the PESO (paid, earned, shared, owned) model to the SOEP model (shared, owned, earned, paid). On the other hand, Dietrich (2018b) said that if she had to list the media types in order of importance, the ranking would be OESP (owned, earned, shared, paid) but she also added that it is relatively difficult to remember this "word". She mentions that "PESO is a lot easier to remember".

Firstly, paid media refers to both traditional and social media advertisements in the media channels such as television, radio, outdoor or online, which airs the advertisements of companies for a fee. This type of media can also be described as "paid placements that promote a product" (Burcher, 2012, p. 9). Besides, Macnamara et al, (2016, p. 377) describe paid media as "traditional advertising and other forms of content commercially contracted between organizations and mass media". The actual purpose of the formation of this media is to make money. When the literature is examined, it is seen that paid media is defined as the media that the company pays (Luttrell, 2015).

Secondly, owned media consists of contents produced by any communication channel or platform belonging to the companies. Owned media can be defined as the channels owned, controlled and conducted by a company such as corporate magazines, newsletters, and websites (Bao & Chang, 2014; Luttrell, 2015; Macnamara et al., 2016; Xie, Neill, & Schauster, 2018). In the owned media, the contents related to the companies are made by corporation's employees and publish on corporate websites, magazines, official social media accounts, and blogs. As mentioned by Burcher (2012, p. 22), the role of the owned media is to establish "long-term relationships with existing potential customer".

Thirdly, it is possible to talk about earned media where customers act as a channel for the company (Luttrell, 2015, p. 207). Earned media can be defined as media activities that are not directly created by a company, such as online publications generated by consumers on social media (Stephen & Galak,

2012; p. 624) as well as blogger and influencer relations (Dietrich, 2018a). As Dietrich (2018a) explains, earned media is what we know "as publicity or media relations" and it is obviously about someone writing or talking about the product or the company. Earned media also describes "communications about a company's product generated by other entities and expressed through either own or outside channels. What distinguishes earned media from paid or owned media is its autonomy, or ability to operate independent of a company's command" (Bao & Chang, 2014, p. 1).

And finally, shared media refers to the media "open for followers, friends, and subscribers to contribute and comment" (Macnamara et al., 2016, p. 378) including Twitter, Facebook, Instagram, YouTube and other popular social networking platforms. All company-related contents disseminated by customers, fans or users throughout social networks are defined as shared media. As Luttrell (2015, p. 207) explains, "shared refers to the instances in which consumers are working in conjunction with a brand to create, share, and promote the brand's content". The best way to achieve shared media is nothing but "news value". The most engaging and professional contents share more by users.

The users generated contents (or consumer generated media) concept would be an appropriate alternative term for shared media contents. Users generated contents gained popularity in 2005 by the advent of social media. It is used to describe the contents generated and shared by corporations customers and internet users. The fastest-growing, most reliable and long-lasting media consists of the contents that consumers create and share among themselves. Unlike content created by marketers and advertisers as paid media, user generated contents are generated by consumers or customers (Gretzel, Kang, & Lee, 2008).

A survey conducted by HubSpot Research collaboration with SurveyMonkey (An, 2019) to investigate both "social media preferences and buying preferences" of more than 2,700 consumers shows that friends and family are "the most trustworthy source for discovering new products or services". According to this research, consumers prefer to take real-life experiences of people they know as an example when making a purchase decision. The same research has also shown that online channels such as Google, online mass retailers like Amazon, and social networks such as Twitter and YouTube are other reliable sources after friends and family. On the other hand, the same research (An, 2019) reveals that more than half of consumers tell their "friends and family about their favorite products at least once a week or more" and that "consumers trust word of mouth the most". At this point, it can be said that the content and messages created by users are effective shared media for companies and these user generated contents can be describes as a new form of e-word-of-mouth (E-WOM).

Although shared media can be an effective tool for turning potential customers into real customers, the control of this media is difficult. As consumers share their positive or negative experiences and thoughts on online platforms, shared media is not always in favor of the company. Consumer opinions and thoughts obtained from shared media provide valuable feedback for the development of businesses. These thoughts are powerful marketing tools, affecting the way other users think and make decisions. Users' negative comments and judgments affect purchasing decisions, firm credibility, image, and reputation. These comments often include useful criticism as well.

Sometimes there is a subtle boundary between paid media and shared media. For example, when an interesting promotional video is released, people will watch it over and over. It is a kind of paid media, but the viral dissemination of the content reminds shared media. At times, there is also a slight boundary between owned and shared media. A catchy content created and posted by brands known as owned media may be shared by fans and turns into shared media.

Integrating four media types is a necessary factor in corporations' public relations and communication activities success. As Dakouan and Benabdelouahed (2019, p. 123) mention "the four forms of media are completely complementary."

METHODOLOGY

Case Study

A case study is based on in-depth research of a topic and is often performed to find answers to "how" and "why" questions (Yin, 2003). As state by Yin (2003, p. 1) "case study is used in many situations to contribute to our knowledge of individual, group, organizational, social, political, and related phenomena". In order to understand the concept of "case study", it is necessary to define the concept of "case" first. The concept of the case means "a spatially delimited phenomenon (a unit) observed at a single point in time or over some period of time" (Gerring, 2007, p. 19). In another definition the "case" is defined as a particular example or appearance of the circumstance to be studied (Swanborn, 2010, p. 21).

In the light of these definitions, the case study is the study of an individual, a group, an institution, a community or some multiple cases to find answers to specific research questions and a search for a series of evidence (Gillham, 2000, p. 1). With Gerring's (2007, p. 20) definition, a case study is an intense study on a case to shed light on the overall case. On the other hand, case studies are not limited to the examination of a single case (*a single-case study*). Accordingly, case studies may include analysis of several cases (*a multiple-case study*) (Yin, 2003, p. 14; Gerring, 2007, p. 20; Swanborn, 2010, p. 21).

It should be noted that case study cannot be limited to a single research method. As explained in many studies, case studies are often associated with qualitative research methods. However, case study research is not only about qualitative methods. Accordingly, it is stated that both qualitative and quantitative methods can be used together (Gillham, 2000; Gerring, 2007; Woodside, 2010; Swanborn, 2010). The choice of the research method is related to the purpose of the research and the characteristics of the data. The method chosen should be consistent with the purpose of the research and research questions. As Gillham (2000, p. 13) explain, "case study is a main method. Within it different sub-methods are used: interviews, observations, document and record analysis, work samples, and so on". In this direction as describe, "case study research is richly descriptive, because it is grounded in deep and varied sources of information" (Hancock & Algozzine, 2006, p. 16).

In addition to these explanations, various criticisms are made about the case study method. The main criticism concerns whether the findings obtained by focusing on one or more events are generalizable. As Idowu (2016, p. 184) explains, "case study research is often charged with causal determinism, non-replicability, subjective conclusions, absence of generalizable conclusions, biased case selection and lack of empirical clout". Although there are various criticisms, a case study is one of the most frequently used and popular methods in social sciences (Burton, 2000, p. 215).

VODAFONE: "#BuMamaBenden"

The unit of analysis or the "case" (Yin, 2003) of this study is Vodafone Turkey Foundation's "#BuMamaBenden" project. This research aims to understand and discuss how new media applications can be used in corporate social responsibility practices. For this purpose, the project of the Vodafone Turkey Foundation, in which the new media is an important actor, was chosen as the case.

One of the main objectives of this project was to increase the number of positive posts on social media about Vodafone. As mentioned "as was the case with many operators, Vodafone was challenged in social media with regards to positive mentions. Users were mostly mentioning the brand to share their problems" (IAB Europe, 2019).

#BuMamaBenden project is a part of the "Coding Tomorrow" project which the Vodafone Turkey Foundation carried out in cooperation with Habitat Association. Within the scope of the "Coding Tomorrow" project, children who received coding training and learned coding developed a new project on street animals. Within the scope of this new project, children designed a feeding bowl that worked with a tweet so that the street animals would not starve. These tweet-activated automatic feeding bowls are placed at different locations and one tweet by #BuMamaBenden hashtag on Twitter is enough to feed the animals.

Vodafone Turkey Foundation (2019) on their website, explains how the system works as follows,

"Our children have built a feeding machine that is activated with code so that everyone could help stray animals on the street. You can command this machine by tweeting with the #BuMamaBenden hashtag on Twitter. If the feeding bowl is empty, the lid opens and the food drops into the bowl. If the feeding bowl is afull, your command waits for the bowl to empty. Our cats and dogs chomp on the food in the feeding bowl".

For this project, tweet-activated feeding bowls were placed in front of 11 different Vodafone stores in 5 different cities across the country. It is known that the first tweet on the subject was posted on 21.11.2018 and as stated, the project "is planned for an indefinite period" (Vodafone Turkey Foundation, 2019; IAB Turkey, 2019). According to IAB Turkey (2019) data,

"...394,304 tweets were posted per month with #bumamabenden hashtag. In total, more than 460,000 tweets were posted in 2 months. On the first day of the campaign (November 21), hashtag came first in the Trending Topic with 23,890 tweets organically. Nearly 300 celebrities and social media influencers supported the campaign. The number of people who tweeted to the project reached 252,114 and about 30 million views were organically obtained. Vodafone's monthly positive talk rate on social media was 47%. The positive speech rate reached on the day of the campaign reached a record level for the telecommunications sector with 77%. This campaign, which is completely organically spread, has gone down in history as the most tweeted branded campaign of Twitter Turkey. As of today, street animals continue to feed on average with 1000 tweets per day by posted #bumamabenden hashtag."

This hashtag campaign, #BuMamaBenden received the Bronze award in the social media category at the MIXX Awards Europe 2019, where the most successful digital works were awarded (IAB Europe, 2019). Social media, especially Twitter plays an important role in the "#BuMamaBenden" project and as highlighted by Uzunoğlu et al. (2017, p. 991) Twitter "which has penetrated into our lives in recent years, has potential to create an interactive relationship with stakeholders". In this project, Twitter is an important tool for stakeholders to get involved in the campaign.

In addition to these explanations, this study also discusses how new media applications and tools can create new opportunities for corporate social responsibility practices. In this point as Capriotti (2011, p. 365) explains, corporate social responsibility communication through new media should "go beyond the traditional forms of communication". At the same time experts and communicators should develop innovative practices to exploit the potential of these tools. Based on these explanations, #BuMamaBenden project has been selected as a case, in terms of utilizing the advantages and opportunities of the new media.

Based on the literature review of the importance of new media applications in terms of corporate social responsibility, this study aims to find answers to the following research questions.

RQ1: How new media applications have been used in the #BuMamaBenden project?
RQ2: What information does #BuMamaBenden project provide us with about new media applications in corporate social responsibility projects?
RQ3: How does the #BuMamaBenden project takes advantage of the use of paid, owned, earned and shared media?

FINDINGS

In this study to understand the function of new media applications in corporate social responsibility practices, all contents of the Vodafone Turkey Foundation about #BuMamaBenden in paid, owned, earned and shared media were examined.

Paid media refers to media channels that airs the firm's advertisements for a fee to make publicity, and sponsored contents are important parts of paid media. When the Twitter account of the project was examined, some of the sponsored contents were discovered. These contents are prepared by the Vodafone Turkey Foundation in advertisement format and aim to raise awareness about this corporate social responsibility project. The sponsored contents shared on Twitter indicate the use of paid media in this project.

Contents created, controlled and published by platforms belonging to the corporations such as corporate web pages, corporate social media accounts, weblogs, magazines, and newspapers are assumed as owned media. When a search is performed on the Google search engine with the keyword #BuMamaBenden, the first link shown on the first page leads users to the web page which Vodafone Turkey Foundation has established for this project. On this page, there is information about the importance of this project, its rules, principles and also some common questions about the project. As mentioned, contents published on the corporate web page are created and published by Vodafone Turkey Foundation to inform the users about the #BuMamaBenden social responsibility project, it can be considered as owned media. At this point, it can be said that having such a corporation page is important in terms of obtaining information from the primary source. As a result of research conducted on the internet by those who want to learn about the project, accessing this page is very important for obtaining direct information on the subject. On the other hand, the existence and active use of such corporate accounts may also affect trust in the project.

When the corporate social media accounts examined, it was seen that these accounts are also actively used within the scope of the project. For example, there are many corporate accounts related to Vodafone on Twitter. The "@VodafoneVakfi" Twitter account of the Vodafone Turkey Foundation, which is the implementer of the project, is corporations' owned media by which various shares are made about the project. On the other hand, it was seen that the shares made from the "@VodafoneVakfi" account are retweeted in the "@VodafoneTR" and "@vodafonered" accounts which are other corporate pages. Thus, messages about the project are also available in other media owned by the institution concerned.

Additionally, it was seen that in the Vodafone Turkey's own YouTube account has an official promotional video of the project. It is possible to say that the video uploaded to YouTube on 30 November

2018 and was viewed a total of 3,884 times until December 20, 2019, when the current research was conducted. Finally, when the official Instagram accounts of the corporations were examined, it was seen that there exist various shares on "Vodafonevakfi", "Vodafonetr" and "Vodafonered" accounts about the #BuMamaBenden project. As a result of this review, it is concluded that corporate social media accounts are actively used within the scope of the project. In this respect, it has been seen that the corporations' owned media channels were used effectively.

As mentioned in the previous sections, the earned media contents are not directly created by corporations but with other entities such as media relations and blogger relations. In Vodafone case, searching the #BuMamaBenden keyword in the search engines leads the users to the various sectoral magazines, online newspapers, news portals, and weblogs which have shared information about the Vodafone Turkey Foundations' social responsibility project. All these contents which were published by other sources rather than Vodafone Foundation can be considered as earned media. Additionally, a Twitter account with the name of "@bumamabenden" was created to support the project by a common user. This account declares that it does not belong to the project practitioners, while it has the same name as the project. Furthermore, "@bumamabenden" emphasized that the account was created only to support the project on Twitter. As Dietrich (2018a) explains, the earned media is about someone who discusses your product, campaign, or company. Therefore, it is possible to say that the mentioned Twitter account, which was created to support the project voluntarily, can be defined as earned media. Consequently, the account serves as a media tool where various messages are disseminated about the project and the existence of such type of media can also be considered as an indicator of the project's attractiveness.

All corporate-related contents generated and disseminated by internet users, customers and fans on popular social media platforms such as Twitter, Instagram and YouTube refer to the shared media. Twitter is a key tool for the "#BuMamaBenden" project. Sharing a post with the #BuMamaBenden on the Twitter platform feeds street animals automatically. To understand the importance of this microblogging tool in the project, 1,000 tweets with #BuMamaBenden on the Twitter platform were analyzed. *Keyhole* social media analysis tool was used in this study on 14 December 2019, while the day of the analysis was selected randomly.

According to this analysis, it was seen that 930 twitter users tweeted 1.000 posts with this hashtag. These figures mean that one user can post more than one tweet. It was also seen that the engagement value for this hashtag was 2,786. This engagement value means this hashtag was retweeted and liked 2,786 times on that day. Besides, it was understood that 1,309,477 unique users saw posts containing #BuMamaBenden. In other words, this hashtag had reached to 1,309,477 users.

It was observed that the number of times that users saw the posts containing the hashtag, known as the impression, is 1,600,329. In addition to this information, %83 of the tweets taken on the day of the examination were original, while %17 of them were retweets, and there was not any reply. In analyzing 1,000 tweets, it was observed 930 unique users tweeted about Vodafone's social responsibility project on an ordinary day. These tweets were user-generated content that disseminates by Twitter users to support Vodafone's social responsibility project and can be considered as the shared media for the Vodafone corporation. It was also noticed that these posts are not limited to Twitter. By examining the hashtags on Instagram, it was observed that there are many different users on Instagram supporting the project by sharing #BuMamaBenden to emphasize the importance of feeding street animals. It was concluded that there were various contents created by the users on the different social media platforms to support the project.

CONCLUSION

Corporate social responsibility practices are an important part of public relations. These practices also affect the image and reputation of corporations. Corporate social responsibility, which can be defined as the responsibility of the corporation to the society and its environment and efforts to find solutions to social problems, are the applications that attract the attention of the stakeholders. On the other hand, the development of the internet and new media and the increase of digitalization provide new possibilities for the media that corporations use to convey their messages. Accordingly, it can be said that new media technologies provide new opportunities both in terms of the communication forms that corporations will establish with their stakeholders and in terms of corporate social responsibility practices. One of these opportunities is media tools that can be defined as shared media and include content produced by customers, fans or users and shared in social networks. In this respect, it is possible to say that today corporations may use four different media types such as paid, owned, earned and shared in order to convey their messages in a coordinated manner and new media applications come to the fore in this process.

In the current study to understand the function of the new media applications in corporate social responsibility practices, Vodafone Turkey Foundations' #BuMamaBenden project is selected and analyzed as a case study. It is possible to draw attention to the following conclusions based on the findings and the research questions. Firstly, it has been seen that new media applications can be used as an effective tool to reach the public. As a result of the review of the #BuMamaBenden project, the way the project uses new media applications can be considered as an important example of using these tools effectively. The most striking feature of this project is that the most important stakeholder is the general public and especially all Twitter users. Therefore, it was concluded that the shared media were used effectively in the project.

The effective use of new media and social networks, in particular, Twitter, enabled the project to spread to all segments of the society, enabled a high level of participation and continued to be up to date. The project, which started in 2018, has attracted attention even after one year. According to the findings, it was seen that in spite of the past days, the number of tweets posted concerning the project on any normal day, the number of unique users tweeting and the value of engagement proves that this project is not outdated yet. These figures indicate how the new application tools such as online web pages, social media channels, and other online platforms keep the social responsibility projects up-to-date and support these projects' main aims. These results sheds light on the importance of new media applications.

Although the project is Twitter-oriented, other social networks are also considered in this study. It was observed that the posts from other social networks such as Instagram and YouTube increase the awareness of the project. Thus, the advantages of shared media increase by using different platforms. When social networks examined, it seems that there are shares both from the corporate social media accounts -owned media- and from different platforms that can be considered as earned and shared media. It is understood that social networks can be used effectively in different ways.

Finally, the research findings show us the importance of coordinated use of the four media types. In this project, all possible media platforms were used together. Examples of each type of media, from paid media to owned media, from earned media to shared media, were found, and it was concluded that the project has extensive media usage. Thus, the project was extended to a wider audience, and the impact of the project was increased.

According to these results, it has been concluded that the use of traditional and new media tools together in a coordinated manner is important. New media applications provide many new opportunities for corporations such as keeping the projects up to date and are functional in terms of reaching wide audiences and consumers.

FUTURE RESEARCH DIRECTIONS

This study provides several recommendations for future researches. Firstly, based on the conclusion that new media applications are functional in terms of extending the scope of participation in social responsibility, researches can be conducted on different case studies. Secondly, a survey can be conducted for consumers or audiences regarding the use of these tools in social responsibility practices. Finally, the relationship between new media applications and social responsibility can be discussed in different theoretical frameworks.

REFERENCES

Adeyeye, A. O. (2012). *Corporate Social Responsibility of Multinational Corporations in Developing Countries: Perspectives on Anti-Corruption.* Cambridge University Press; doi:10.1017/CBO9781139005067.

Aksak, E. O., Ferguson, M. A., & Duman, S. A. (2016). Corporate social responsibility and CSR fit as predictors of corporate reputation: A global perspective. *Public Relations Review*, *42*(1), 79–81. doi:10.1016/j.pubrev.2015.11.004

An, M. (2019). Global Buying Behavior in 2020 [New Data]. Retrieved from https://blog.hubspot.com/marketing/buyer-behavior-statistics

Aras, G., & Crowther, D. (2009). Corporate Sustainability Reporting: A Study in Disingenuity? *Journal of Business Ethics*, *87*(S1), 279–288. doi:10.1007/s10551-008-9806-0

Bao, T., & Chang, T. S. (2014). Why Amazon uses both the New York Times Best Seller List and customer reviews: An empirical study of multiplier effects on product sales from multiple earned media. Decision Support Systems, 67, 1-8. Doi:10.1016/j.dss.2014.07.004

Bartlett, J. L. (2011). Public Relations and Corporate Social Responsibility. In Ø. Ihlen, J. L. Bartlett, & S. May (Eds.), *The Handbook of Communication and Corporate Social Responsibility* (pp. 67–86). Wiley-Blackwell; doi:10.1002/9781118083246.ch4.

Bhattacharya, C., Sen, S., & Korschun, D. (2011). *Leveraging Corporate Responsibility: The Stakeholder Route to Maximizing Business and Social Value.* Cambridge University Press; doi:10.1017/CBO9780511920684.

Burcher, N. (2012). *Paid, Owned, Earned: Maximising marketing returns in a socially connected world.* Kogan Page.

Burton, D. (2000). The Use of Case Studies in Social Science Research. In D. Burton (Ed.), *Research Training For Social Scientists: A Handbook for Postgraduate Researchers* (pp. 215–225). Sage; doi:10.4135/9780857028051.d24.

Capriotti, P. (2011). Communicating Corporate Social Responsibility through the Internet and Social Media. In Ø. Ihlen, J. L. Bartlett, & S. May (Eds.), *The Handbook of Communication and Corporate Social Responsibility* (pp. 358–378). Wiley-Blackwell; doi:10.1002/9781118083246.ch18.

Capriotti, P., & Moreno, A. (2007). Corporate citizenship and public relations: The importance and interactivity of social responsibility issues on corporate websites. *Public Relations Review*, *33*(1), 84–91. doi:10.1016/j.pubrev.2006.11.012

Carroll, A. B. (1991). The Pyramid of Corporate Social Responsibility: Toward the Moral Management of Organizations Stakeholders. *Business Horizons*, *34*(4), 39–48.

Chen, S. (2009). Corporate Responsibilities in Internet-Enabled Social Networks. *Journal of Business Ethics*, *90*(S4), 523–536. doi: 10.1007/s10551-010-0604-0

Cho, M., Furey, L. D., & Mohr, T. (2017). Communicating Corporate Social Responsibility on Social Media: Strategies, Stakeholders, and Public Engagement on Corporate Facebook. *Business and Professional Communication Quarterly*, *80*(1), 52–69. doi:10.1177/2329490616663708

Clark, C. E. (2000). Differences Between Public Relations and Corporate Social Responsibility: An Analysis. *Public Relations Review*, *26*(3), 363–380. doi:10.1016/S0363-8111(00)00053-9

Crowther, D., & Aras, G. (2008). Corporate Social Responsibility. Retrieved from https://my.uopeople.edu/pluginfile.php/57436/mod_book/chapter/121631/BUS5116.Crowther.Aras.CSR.pdf

Dahlsrud, A. (2008). How Corporate Social Responsibility is Defined: An Analysis of 37 Definitions. *Corporate Social Responsibility and Environmental Management*, *15*(1), 1–13. doi:10.1002/csr.132

Dakouan, M. C., & Benabdelouahed, M. R. (2019). Digital Inbound Marketing: Particularities of Business-to-Business and Business-to-Customer Strategies. In A. Kavoura, E. Kefallonitis, & A. Giovanis (Eds.), *Strategic Innovative Marketing and Tourism* (pp. 119–128). Springer; doi:10.1007/978-3-030-12453-3_14

De Bakker, F. G. A., Groenewegen, P., & Den Hond, F. (2005). A Bibliometric Analysis of 30 Years of Research and Theory on Corporate Social Responsibility and Corporate Social Performance. *Business & Society*, *44*(3), 283–317. doi:10.1177/0007650305278086

De Bakker, F. G. A., & Hellsten, I. (2013). Capturing Online Presence: Hyperlinks and Semantic Networks in Activist Group Websites on Corporate Social Responsibility. *Journal of Business Ethics*, *118*(4), 807–823. doi: 10.1007/s10551-013-1962-1

Dietrich, G. (2018a). Spin Sucks: PR Pros Must Embrace the PESO Model. Retrieved from https://spinsucks.com/communication/pr-pros-must-embrace-the-peso-model/

Dietrich, G. (2018b). What Is The PESO Model? A Week-by-Week Breakdown. Retrieved from https://spinsucks.com/communication/peso-model-breakdown/

Europe, I. A. B. (2019). MIXX Awards Europe Winners 2019 – #ThisFoodIsOnMe / #BuMamaBenden (C-Section). Retrieved from https://iabeurope.eu/best-practices/mixx-awards-europe-winners-2019-this-food-is-on-me-c-section/

European Commission. (2011). Communication From The Commission to the European Parliament, The Council, The European Economic and Social Committee and the Committee of the Regions, A renewed EU strategy 2011-14 for Corporate Social Responsibility. Retrieved from https://eur-lex.europa.eu/LexUriServ/LexUriServ.do?uri=COM:2011:0681:FIN:EN:PDF

European Commission. (2019). Corporate Social Responsibility & Responsible Business Conduct. Retrieved from https://ec.europa.eu/growth/industry/corporate-social-responsibility_en

Galbreath, J. (2010). How does corporate social responsibility benefit firms? Evidence from Australia. *European Business Review*, 22(4), 411–431. doi:10.1108/09555341011056186

Gerring, J. (2007). *Case Study Research: Principles and Practices*. Cambridge University Press.

Gillham, B. (2000). Case Study Research Methods. *Continuum*.

Gretzel, U., Kang, M., & Lee, W. (2008). Differences in Consumer-Generated Media Adoption and Use: A Cross-National Perspective. *Journal of Hospitality & Leisure Marketing*, *17*(1-2), 99–120. doi:10.1080/10507050801978240

Hancock, D. R., & Algozzine, B. (2006). *Doing Case Study Research: A Practical Guide for Beginning Researches*. Teachers College Press.

Europe, I. A. B. (2019). MIXX Awards Europe Winners 2019 – #ThisFoodIsOnMe / #BuMamaBenden (C-Section) Retrieved from https://iabeurope.eu/best-practices/mixx-awards-europe-winners-2019-this-food-is-on-me-c-section/

Turkey, I. A. B. (2019). Bu Mama Benden. Retrieved from https://www.iabturkiye.org/bu-mama-benden

Idowu, O. E. (2016). Criticisms, Constraints and Constructions of Case Study Research Strategy. *Asian Journal of Business and Management*, *4*(5), 184–188.

Ihlen, Ø., Bartlett, J. L., & May, S. (2011). Corporate Social Responsibility and Communication. In Ø. Ihlen, J. L. Bartlett, & S. May (Eds.), *The Handbook of Communication and Corporate Social Responsibility* (pp. 3–22). Wiley-Blackwell.

Lee, T. H. (2017). The status of corporate social responsibility research in public relations: A content analysis of published articles in eleven scholarly journals from 1980 to 2015. *Public Relations Review*, *43*(1), 211–218. doi:10.1016/j.pubrev.2016.10.001

Lee, Y.-J., Yoon, H. J., & O'Donnell, N. H. (2018). The effects of information cues on perceives legitimacy of companies that promote corporate social responsibility initiatives on social networking sites. *Journal of Business Research*, *83*, 202–214. doi:10.1016/j.jbusres.2017.09.039

Lim, J. S., & Greenwood, C. A. (2017). Communicating corporate social responsibility (CSR): Stakeholder responsiveness and engagement strategy to achieve CSR. *Public Relations Review*, *43*(4), 768–776. doi:10.1016/j.pubrev.2017.06.007

Luttrell, R. (2015). *Social Media: How to Engage, Share, and Connect*. Rowman & Littlefield.

Luttrell, R. M., & Capizzo, L. W. (2018). Public Relations Campaigns: An Integrated Approach. *Sage (Atlanta, Ga.)*.

Macnamara, J., Lwin, M., Adi, A., & Zerfass, A. (2016). 'PESO' media strategy shifts to 'SOEP': Opportunities and ethical dilemmas. *Public Relations Review*, *42*(3), 377–385. doi:10.1016/j.pubrev.2016.03.001

Ozdora-Aksak, E. (2015). An analysis of Turkey's telecommunications sector's social responsibility practices online. *Public Relations Review*, *41*(3), 365–369. doi:10.1016/j.pubrev.2015.01.001

Ozdora-Aksak, E., & Atakan-Duman, S. (2015). The online presence of Turkish banks: Communicating the softer side of corporate identity. *Public Relations Review*, *41*(1), 119–128. doi:10.1016/j.pubrev.2014.10.004

Pohl, M. (2006). Corporate Culture and CSR-How They Interrelate and Consequences for Successful Implementation. In J. Henningfeld, M. Pohl, & N. Tolhurst (Eds.), *The ICCA Handbook on Corporate Social Responsibility* (pp. 47–59). John Wiley & Sons.

Puriwat, W., & Tripopsakul, S. (2018). The Impact of Corporate Social Responsibility on Customer Satisfaction and Loyalty: A Case Study of the Hotel Industry in Thailand. *Asia-Pacific Social Science Review*, *18*(2), 347–355.

Saat, R. M., & Selamat, M. H. (2014). The Impact of Corporate Social Responsibility Information Richness on Trust. Issues in Social and Environmental Accounting, 8(2), 67–81. doi:10.22164/isea.v8i2.82

Stephen, A. T., & Galak, J. (2012). The Effects of Traditional and Social Earned Media on Sales: A Study of a Microlending Marketplace. *JMR, Journal of Marketing Research*, *49*(5), 624–639. doi:10.1509/jmr.09.0401

Stuebs, M., & Sun, L. (2011). Corporate Social Responsibility and Firm Reputation. Journal of Accounting, Ethics &. *Public Policy*, *12*(1), 33–56. doi:10.2139srn.1863343

Swaen, V., & Chumpitaz, R. C. (2008). Impact of Corporate Social Responsibility on Consumer Trust. [English Edition]. *Recherche et Applications en Marketing*, *23*(4), 7–33. doi:10.1177/205157070802300402

Swanborn, P. G. (2010). Case Study Research: What, Why and How? Sage. doi:10.4135/9781526485168

Uzunoğlu, E., Türkel, S., & Akyar, B. Y. (2017). Engaging consumers through corporate social responsibility messages on social media: An experimental study. *Public Relations Review*, *43*(5), 989–997. doi:10.1016/j.pubrev.2017.03.013

Vo, T. T., Xiao, X., & Ho, S. Y. (2019). How Does Corporate Social Responsibility Engagement Influence Word of Mouth on Twitter? Evidence from the Airline Industry. *Journal of Business Ethics*, *157*(2), 525–542. doi: 10.1007/s10551-017-3679-z

Vodafone Turkey Foundation. (2019). #BuMamaBenden. Retrieved from http://turkiyevodafonevakfi.org.tr/en/projects/coding-tomorrow/bumamabenden/

Wan-Jan, W. S. (2006). Defining corporate social responsibility. *Journal of Public Affairs*, *6*(3-4), 176–184. doi:10.1002/pa.227

Wang, X.-W. (2017). Various of Theories of the Concept of Corporate Social Responsibility and Comments. *3rd International Conference of Social Science and Development (ICSSD 2017)*, 317-321. Doi: 10.12783/dtssehs/icssd2017/19229

Woodside, A. G. (2010). *Case Study Research: Theory, Methods, Practice*. Emerald.

Xie, Q., Neill, M. S., & Schauster, E. (2018). Paid, Earned, Shared and Owned Media From the Perspective of Advertising and Public Relations Agencies: Comparing China and the United States. *International Journal of Strategic Communication*, *12*(2), 160–179. doi:10.1080/1553118X.2018.1426002

Yamak, S. (2007). Kurumsal Sosyal Sorumluluk Kavramının Gelişimi. *BETA Bulletin of Experimental Treatments for AIDS*.

Yin, R. K. (2003). Case Study Research: Design and Methods. *Sage (Atlanta, Ga.)*.

ADDITIONAL READING

Bayles, S. (2015). What value does paid media hold for the PR industry? In S. Hall (Ed.), *FuturePRoof: The go-to guide for managers of agencies and communication teams* (pp. 129–134). Sarah Hall Consulting.

Dietrich, G. (2014). Spin Sucks: Communication and Reputation Management in the Digital Age. Indianapolis, USA: Que.

Lindgreen, A., Vanhamme, J., Watkins, R., & Maon, F. (Eds.). (2018). *Communicating Corporate Social Responsibility in the Digital Era*. Routledge.

Sandoval, M. (2014). From Corporate to Social Media: Critical Perspectives on Corporate Social Responsibility in Media and Communication Industries. Routledge. doi:10.4324/9781315858210

KEY TERMS AND DEFINITIONS

Case Study: Detailed examination of one or more cases to find answers to specific research questions.

Corporate Social Responsibility: Responsibility of companies to their stakeholders, environment and society and voluntary activities for solving social problems.

Earned Media: Refers to the media type in which their contents created by other organizations such as media relations and blogger relations, not directly by companies.

Owned Media: Refers to the media type owned by companies in which their content is created, controlled and disseminated by companies.

Paid Media: Refers to the media type in which companies pay to publish content generally for advertising purposes.

Peso Model: It is an abbreviation of initials of paid, earned, shared and owned media types and it indicates to the coordinated use of the four media types.

Shared Media: Refers to the media type that encompasses all shares of customers, fans or users about the company, especially on social media platforms.

This research was previously published in the Handbook of Research on New Media Applications in Public Relations and Advertising; pages 274-291, copyright year 2021 by Information Science Reference (an imprint of IGI Global).

Chapter 45

Attracting the Right Employees?
The Effects of Social Media as an Innovative E-Entrepreneurship Recruitment Method for Enterprises

Anthony Lewis
Business School, University of South Wales, UK

Brychan Celfyn Thomas
University of South Wales, UK

Gwenllian Marged Sanders
Business School, University of South Wales, UK

ABSTRACT

This chapter investigates effects and issues associated with social media and recruitment and whether it is effective as an innovative e-entrepreneurship method of attracting the right employees for enterprises from a multi stakeholder perspective. Human resources management professionals have been using different methods of social media in their recruitment strategies with varying degrees of success. By examining social media and its effect, this can support the development of a more effective human resources recruitment strategy. Additionally, increased communication channels might enable the development of a more positive internal enterprise culture. The study was conducted using both primary and secondary data. Professionals, recruiters, and employees have been questioned on their views of Social Media from a personal and a professional perspective through a variety of methods including focus groups and questionnaires. This chapter provides a framework that can be used by enterprises in order to create their own social media recruitment cycle.

DOI: 10.4018/978-1-7998-9020-1.ch045

INTRODUCTION

This chapter is a further investigation, to previous studies of e-recruitment (Lewis et al, 2010; Lewis et al, 2013), with an aim to critically explore whether social media and online recruitment are effective innovative e-entrepreneurship methods in attracting appropriate employees for enterprises.

An innovative e-entrepreneurship method is an effective new method used by enterprises involving electronic processes. Further dimensions, not covered in this study, are recruiting for new ventures and new ventures for recruiting, which are interesting avenues for future research. Social media enables enterprises to provide a dedicated service (vehicle) to attract appropriate employees to augment their talent management strategy (Eduardo, 2006). Social media is used by many enterprises and individuals in order to market their corporate brands and can give the enterprise a new identity to compete in a competitive market (Doherty, 2010). Social Media can be an excellent starting point for recruitment as "key metrics" such as cost and time to hire are measurable and it is possible to substantiate improvement (Doherty, 2010). Social Media allows individuals to create their online profile and have a network of friends and colleagues (Henderson and Bowley 2010). Individuals can then upload pictures and personal details enabling users to create an online profile and a visible, virtual network of their friends (Henderson and Bowley 2010).

Online recruitment has dramatically grown since the mid 1990's when the economic climate resulted in a considerable demand for employees with a strong academic background and relevant experience (Lee, 2005:175). Recruitment methods have consequently changed in enterprises, and by individuals when looking for their next opportunity, and also looking at the ways in which individuals are applying for roles. Online recruitment has consistently shown itself to be one of the most substantial shifts in recruitment practice in the last ten years (Lee, 2005:175).

The literature review in this chapter details previous research and media coverage regarding social media and online recruitment. Much of the research is focused on the importance of having a clear social media strategy and how the subsequent changes implemented by these enterprises might impact on individuals who use these sites. Although existing research indicates that recruitment websites are used, it does not fully cover industry specific recruitment agencies. This chapter considers Social Media and online recruitment from the perspective of Employers, Recruitment Agencies and Individuals in an attempt to ascertain the relevance to enterprises and individuals.

This research will carefully consider social media in recruitment and how it can be used by enterprises. Several areas such as intellectual property law, good Human Resources practice and how practical these methods are in recruitment are explored further in the Literature review, and discussed throughout the chapter. Social Media is a relatively new area of interest and yet something which adapts very quickly and could be instrumental in selecting and retaining the best possible people for the enterprise.

With almost two billion internet users Worldwide in 2010, up from approximately 360 million at the end of 2000, there has been dramatic growth in internet usage over the last decade (www.internetworld-stats.com). A growing number of enterprises are using Social Media in order to communicate with their staff and customers. Some social media tools may be viewed as being more suited to different individuals; however the number of users grows rapidly over time.

Mobile internet usage has also had a huge impact on the way the tools are used. Twitter, (a social networking and micro-blogging service) asks "what are you doing?" (www.twitter.com). This type of service is used as a way of instantly letting people know exactly what is happening to an individual at any given time, it can also be an excellent way for enterprises to communicate with their customers who may be reading tweets on the train on their way to work.

The sociological impact of social media is likely to be extensive, it is changing the way individuals view others as there is simply a huge amount of information available at the click of a mouse. Facebook (www.facebook.com) holds a huge amount of information about individuals and this may be viewed by hundreds, or thousands of people who are "friends" with the user. This could have implications on privacy, and the law has had to adapt to deal with the rise in internet crime.

Twitter (www.twitter.com a) and Facebook (www.facebook.com) have proved to be a time efficient and cost effective way in which information can be shared amongst a large number of people. Facebook was used at one college in the United States when snow prevented students travelling to University (www.washingtonpost.com) – the lecturer posted the topic and the students worked together to complete the lesson. With the advent of websites such as Wikileaks (http://www.guardian.co.uk/media/wikileaks) information about enterprises is freely available to many people and so enterprises must decide how transparent they wish to be and whether they would like to control any public relations situations which may arise from the information being leaked in an untimely manner. Confidential documents may be stored on hard drives or using cloud computing (a network of remote servers hosted on the Internet to store, manage, and process data, rather than a local server or personal computer), and more people are now able to work remotely, which means that Social Media is also useful for networking throughout enterprises. Members of staff in a specific function may be able to speak to colleagues in different locations about how they dealt with a situation well, and to share their expertise.

Some enterprises even have "Facebook Fridays" (Gittlen, 2008) where employees are given the opportunity to update their profiles and to share their experiences. An excellent example of using Facebook is with Graduate Recruitment for Klijnveld Peat Marwick Gordeler (KPMG), (www.facebook.com c) where employees who have been recruited to the programmes share their experiences and talk through the methods for potential new recruits.

The goals of this chapter are to critically explore the effects of Social Media as an innovative e-entrepreneurship method of recruitment; whether it is an effective method of attracting appropriate employees for an enterprise, and what the associated problems may be in using this method of recruitment. With regard to this the following research questions have been formulated and are investigated:

- What are the advantages and disadvantage of Social Media (SM) from the perspectives of Human Resources (HR) professionals, recruitment professionals, and potential job seekers?
- What factors are likely to drive/reduce the effectiveness of recruitment via SM?
- What are the legal considerations associated with recruitment via SM?

LITERATURE REVIEW

The following sections of the literature review are organized beginning with an overview of social media, broad limitations of using social media, social media and enterprises, impact of social media on enterprises and finally company's and employee's search strategies.

Overview of Social Media

Due to there being a range of social media services there are some major challenges of definition. There are, however, some common features for social media and these include Web 2.0 internet based applications, user generated content, user created services with specific profiles for web sites or apps, and the facilitation of the development of online social networks (Obar and Wildman, 2015; Kaplan and Haenlein, 2010; Boyd and Ellison, 2007). In fact, social media enables communication between individuals, communities, organisations, businesses and enterprises (Kietzmann and Hermkens, 2011).

A survey reported that in America eighty four per cent of young people had a Facebook account (O'Keefe, 2011), with over sixty per cent having at least one social media profile with many on social networking sites for more than 2 hours a day (Hajirnis, 2015). Moreover, the time spent on social media sites in the United States increased from 66 billion minutes in July 2011 to 121 billion minutes in July 2012 (Social Media Report, 2012). Benefits such as monetary income, career opportunities and social sharing arise from participating in social media (Tang, Gu and Whinston, 2012). Differences between paper based media/traditional electronic media and social media include permanence, immediacy, usability, frequency and quality (Agichtein et al., 2008). The way of operation for social media is through many sources to many receivers which is a dialogic transmission system (Pavlik and MacIntoch, 2015). In particular, social media is an effective marketing and communication tool for businesses and enterprises.

A recent definition of social media is "forms of electronic communication (such as web sites) through which people create online communities to share information, ideas, personal messages, etc." (Merriam-Webster, 2016). Social networking sites include Facebook (online social networking site), Twitter (internet service enabling the posting of "tweets") and LinkedIn (networking web site for the business community) (Christensson, 2013). Many forms of social media technologies are apparent which include social networks, forums, enterprise social networks, business networks and blogs (Aichner and Jacob, 2015).

Table 1 lists the leading social networks based on active user accounts in April 2017 (Statista, 2017).

Mulgan et al (2007:4) state that the "results of Social Innovation – new ideas that meet unmet needs are all around us." The Young Foundation, which has developed and promoted ideas from the Open University to Which? and Wikipedia (Mulgan et al., 2007) has become a leader in the idea of Social Innovation, and has an infrastructure in place to help innovators develop existing ideas. "New methods for advancing social innovation are relevant in every sector, but are likely to offer most... in fields where new possibilities (such as mobile technologies and open source methods) are not being adequately exploited" (Mulgan et al., 2007). Since April 2007, active users of Facebook have multiplied more than 25 times, from 20 million, to 500 million in 2010 (www.facebook.com a), with 12 million users of LinkedIn in July 2007 (Sundar, 2007) to their present 100 million. These are examples of Social innovation in technology, fulfilling a need by consistently developing their software to meet the needs of the users (www.facebook.com a).

Social media is helping shape news stories, where content may be very limited, such as in Iran during the unrest in 2009, where news networks were not allowed to comment on what was happening, people were able to use mobile telephones to use social media platforms, for example Twitter in order to communicate events to the outside World (Addley, 2009).

In terms of the scope of social media services that provide a medium for recruitment there are many different Web sites that provide such services. These involve four different types of social media including blogs and microblogs (Twitter), content communities (YouTube), social networking sites (Facebook,

MySpace), and professional networks (LinkedIn). Since these four types of social media are the most appropriate for recruitment the most common forms of these have been investigated.

Table 1. Leading social networks based on active user accounts

No	Social network	Users
1	Facebook	1,968,000,000
2	WhatsApp	1,200,000,000
3	YouTube	1,000,000,000
4	Facebook Messenger	1,000,000,000
5	WeChat	889,000,000
6	QQ	868,000,000
7	Instagram	600,000,000
8	QZone	595,000,000
9	Tumblr	550,000,000
10	Twitter	319,000,000
11	Sina Weibo	313,000,000
12	Baidu Tieba	300,000,000
13	Snapchat	300,000,000
14	Skype	300,000,000
15	Viber	260,000,000
16	Line	220,000,000
17	Pinterest	150,000,000

Source: Statista (2012)

Facebook

Facebook allows people to bring together their ideas and thoughts before expressing them (Moody, 2010). Users registered on Facebook vary by five percent between household income brackets, nine percent between rural, suburban and urban users, and thirteen percent according to different levels of education (PRC, 2012). There is also a large gap between age brackets with only thirty five percent of sixty and above year old users compared to eighty six percent of eighteen to twenty nine year olds as registered users (PRC, 2012).

Globally, there are more than 500 million individuals who check their Facebook account on at least a monthly basis; of these 250 million access Facebook on any given day (www.facebook.com). The average user has 130 "friends" – these could be colleagues or friends, and Facebook users spend 700 billion minutes a month on Facebook. Facebook is used by companies as a way of integrating information from their website to a profile or fan page.

It may be possible to encourage high level of communication with staff members, Human Resources and IT Departments and Internal communications (Ingham, 2010). As the information is available in the public domain, it is very important that there is a straightforward social media policy for employees to ensure that the brand has a certain level of protection as AXA UK (Ingham 2010). Facebook is commonly used in recruiting for graduate level and entry level employees (Adams, b 2009).

Twitter

Communication building and critical thinking can be enhanced by Twitter (Domizi, 2013). Twitter contributes to social media in many ways and enables people to be connected with their peers and to keep up-to-date with social events (Ghosh, 2011). Posts that are popular will be tweeted many times and become viral (Ghosh, 2011). Users of Twitter will be notified of events, posts and trends through retweeting (Yang, 2010).

Twitter was launched on 14th March 2006, today there are an estimated 195 million users (Rushe, 2010) with 20 million of these users accessing their accounts on a regular basis. Twitter users "tweet" 140 million times a day (Smith, 2011). A tweet is 140 characters long, so information can be posted, including links to other sites to include "additional information, deeper context and embedded media" (www.twitter.com). Enterprises may use Twitter in order to communicate with their followers to share information about new products or services and to build relationships with these individuals (www.twitter.com). Twitter estimate that 460,000 new users are setting up Twitter accounts every day (www.twitter.com), though Schofield (2009) cites a Nielsen Survey which showed that only 40% of new Twitter users will remain active users.

LinkedIn

LinkedIn links together professionals to help them become more successful and productive (LinkdIn, 2015a). Users maintain information and content in a career focused and professional way (MLM, 2015). The fastest growing membership on the site are recent college graduates and students with over thirty nine million (LinkedIn, 2015b) who are encouraged to develop their profiles for credibility through professionals sharing knowledge and connecting with them (eLI, 2015).

LinkedIn is viewed by many as the Professional Social Media site. On 22nd March 2011, LinkedIn reported that they had reached 100 million users Worldwide, with 44% of these being based in the US (www.linkedin.com). LinkedIn has information available to users including CV and contact details.

In order to make contacts on LinkedIn, a user must send an invitation to the person they wish to Link to. There are several suggestions of people that an individual may know, colleagues from former enterprises, or people that are in the same industry, or friends of friends. LinkedIn warn against adding people that an individual does not know, as this person would be able to get in contact with an individual's contacts (www.linkedin.com c).

"Almost all banks are at least dipping their toes in the water by posting ads on....LinkedIn...Generally preferred over Facebook as a Recruitment tool" (Adams, b 2009:23). Adams (a 2009) cites Union Bank's recruiting efforts for a new Senior Manager; the potential employee contacted the bank directly, speeding up the recruitment process, and saving Union Bank a recruitment fee. Union Bank now conduct approximately 20% of their recruitment efforts online.

YouTube

YouTube is the second most visited web site in the World (Moran et al., 2012). It has been claimed that YouTube increases productivity, customisation, personalisation and participation (Sherer and Shea, 2011). It also provides opportunities for improving digital skills.

Created in 2005, YouTube had 490 million active users as of February 2011 (Elliot, 2011). YouTube is a Social Networking site where users can upload videos and share them with other users globally (www.youtube.com). It is possible to share links to the site from Facebook and embed links on Twitter and LinkedIn (www.youtube.com a). Some enterprises use YouTube in order to post links of their employees, explaining certain aspects of the enterprise, and recruitment process.

Broad Limitations in Using Social Media

The negative effects of social media include Internet fraud, information overload and privacy issues (Lundblad, 2017; Postman, 2017). Negative social effects have been shown by studies to have an effect on the self esteem of people and it is found that individuals with a low social comparison orientation appear to use social media less than those with a higher social comparison orientation (Vogel et al., 2015). Further to these negative effects broad limitations in using social media include legal implications and the impact of social media on individuals, which are described below.

Legal Implications

It is suggested (Everett, 2010) that employers who wish their employees to use Social Media must guide the employees regarding what is expected from them, and outlining usage policies, as well as ensuring that there is someone within the enterprise who takes responsibility for the policy, monitoring and updating the information as necessary.

In some enterprises, such as FSAugusta, the company has separate "corporate identities" for its' staff members on Twitter and Facebook, where content is monitored and specifically uploaded to ensure that the information is in keeping with the "Brand" by employees (www.facebook.com e).

Impact of Social Media on Individuals

Cober et al. (2000) suggest that the individuals who are most likely to benefit from online applications are those individuals who already have jobs, but are interested to see which other opportunities may be available to them. Using Social Media may allow the individual to search for enterprises related to their industry, e.g. Accountancy, and search for information using Social Media, which can then be targeted at specific groups, such as with KPMG's general page (www.facebook.com g, www.twitter.com b) and the graduate recruitment page (www.facebook.com h). It is also possible to have separate pages for specific geographic areas (www.twitter.com c), and alumni pages in order to keep in contact with ex employees (www.facebook.com i).

Most of the Social Media recruitment pages have links to the large amount of content available about corporate enterprises through the websites. There is a far greater amount than could previously be communicated through traditional methods, such as print advertisements, journals, and corporate literature, such as brochures (Cober et al., 2000; Cober et al., 2004). McKeown (2003) also explains that additional paperwork, such as application forms may also be available online.

Smith (1999, cited in McKeown 2003:23) suggests that one of the best features of using online recruitment is that an individual is able to ascertain what the work is, what skills they need to do it, salary expectations, and location before applying for the role. Hoffman et al. (1995) and Lee (2005) remind us that this information is available 24 hours a day. Cober et al. (2000) adds that the relevant information relating to the role can be found (at least in theory) speedily and easily using online recruitment methods.

Cober et al. (2000) warns there is a correlation between the image the applicant has of the enterprise, and the likelihood of that individual applying for a role within the enterprise. An enterprise's e-recruitment section of their website will give potential employees the opportunity to gather information about the enterprise, including its "mission, diversity, benefits, career development and corporate culture" so that individuals are better prepared to make decisions about any potential career with the enterprise (Lee, 2005). There had been complaints about enterprises failing to "sell themselves" and as such, giving the candidate little incentive to, or desire to, work within the enterprise (Hilpern, 2001). Rebecca Baker, head of recruitment at network 3 said that the company redesigned its recruitment website to make it simpler in order to give candidates a good experience which will reflect well on the company (Chubb, 2008). A personalised service also offers consumers a positive experience when using a recruitment website; it makes it easier for consumers to find job opportunities (Marketing Week, 2006).

Cober et al. (2000:493) propose that additional information will allow candidates to make an informed decision as to how well they will fit within an enterprise. However, candidates must be aware that it is possible that the enterprises will "project only what they desire others to see" (Miller and Arnold, 2000:337).

An article in Personnel Today (2004) suggests that individuals who use e-recruitment are also more confident that their application will meet equality expectations as it is the applicant's skills and experience that will be looked at by potential employers, not their ethnicity. The number of people who are online grows daily; therefore data about internet users is quickly out of date. The majority of internet users are "white, well-educated and affluent" (Odell et al, 2000:855). Smethurst (2004:38) suggests that the group of people who are most unlikely to have access to the internet are "young black men". This could mean that applicants with suitable skills and qualifications may not have the opportunity to hear about, or the means to apply for positions. This is clearly a loss for both employers and potential applicants.

Czerny (2004) reported that female applicants were not applying for as many graduate positions online, due to the nature of the application and the feelings of the individual that the entire recruitment process is being "dehumanised". Smethurst (2004) reports findings by the Disability Rights Commission that 80% of e-recruitment websites may be inaccessible to people with disabilities such as vision impairment or dyslexia, although changes can be made to these sites to minimize this type of discrimination. The Chartered Institute of Personnel and Development (CIPD) e-recruitment factsheet (2009) indicated that using e-recruitment made the process more flexible and easier for candidates to use successfully.

Social Media and Enterprises

Berry (2005:43) cites the CIPD report showing that the job pages of an enterprise make it the "fourth most popular recruitment method" (Goldberg and Allen, 2008) and suggests that websites differ from other recruitment methods; they are a more vivid and varied method of communicating, and it is here that social media allows enterprises to interact with potential candidates. In order for any enterprise to use social media and online recruitment to its best advantage, Human Resources professions must include it as part of their recruitment strategy (King, 2004).

Accountancy giant KPMG were the leaders in moving recruitment online, this was perceived as a somewhat risky move in that candidates may not have been secure in their applications for the roles (Personnel Today, 2008:8). Using social media, and online recruitment, the time taken to recruit new employees has fallen, it is a fast way to attract a huge number of candidates globally, as long as they are able to access the technology (Taylor, 2001; Hall, 2004; Lee, 2005; Crail, 2007; Smethurst, 2004; People Management, 2008). Tulip (2003) states that 44% of internet users have searched online for jobs and 28% of the working population expect to find their next role online. Generation Y candidates can juggle more than one task at a time, and are more flexible than previous generations, they are eager to move to a new role, or even a new country with very little notice (The Economist 2009). Cober et al. (2000) suggest that enterprises should design the recruitment pages on the website so that the needs of the enterprise are explicitly met.

Lee (2005) and Taylor (2001) suggest benefits of using online recruitment include increased efficiency and convenience for both potential employees and enterprises, however, where the systems are not designed correctly, it can create increased difficulties for the enterprise in communicating with potential employees. Berry (2005) suggests that a significant problem could be the high number of candidates applying for positions through online recruitment websites, who may not have the qualifications and skills required for the position for which they are applying (HR Focus Hiring survey, 2004:S2). Sorting inappropriate, irrelevant applicants could result in increased administration costs, outweighing any potential savings in reduction of recruiting cost (Manufacturers' Monthly, 2004).

Harvey Sinclair (Tulip, 2003) argues that employers have been slower to adapt to online recruitment, where potential employees have been looking for an online presence for a longer period of time. Mannion (2008) also warns that the process of filtering the applications is challenging as people may seem highly qualified but may often lack the necessary practical experience. An enterprise with recruitment pages which are unable to discern appropriate candidates of the right calibre in a resourceful and time efficient manner may struggle to survive in the current economic climate (Long, 2009).

The HR Focus 2004 Survey (S2) suggests that using online recruitment is only successful where an "industry specific website is used". Subsequently Spence (2009) has suggested a 7 step process to successfully filter applications: Develop clear job descriptions, use targeted advertising, consider the application method, consider automated selection, profile the candidate as well as the role, ensure interviewers know what they are looking for and monitor the process carefully. In using social media for recruitment, employers may have the opportunity to "fine tune" their applications appropriately to ensure that recruiting for the enterprise remains manageable.

Impact of Social Media on Enterprises

Pitcher (2008) reported that many high street retailers were not focusing on the recruitment areas of their websites. In certain cases, stores received applications from only 2% of the individuals who had visited the website in order to apply online. Reasons for this could be the time taken to investigate the availability of applying for appropriate positions and the time incurred in filling out the form itself.

Cober et al. (2000: 481) state that "through a corporate Web page, information can be presented that highlights unique aspects of the corporate culture that may attract individuals whom would fit especially/ particularly well within the enterprise".

Enterprises such as Signet have included screening methods throughout their recruitment process, so that candidates who do not fit the "corporate culture" of the enterprise are eliminated through use of a questionnaire (Weekes, 2004). In 2008, River Island restricted applications for temporary Christmas positions so that the process had to be completed online. Although 100,000 people applied for roles, 46,000 failed to complete the applications, effectively screening themselves out (People Management, 2008).

Cober et al. (2000: 481) suggest that it is the enterprises' recruitment pages which provide the first impression to potential employees. Enterprises have the opportunity to strengthen their corporate identity (Hall, 2004:21; Smethurst, 2004:38). And by using Social Media as a tool to assist in this, they may well be successful.

Enterprises ought to be aware of how the information available on the website may influence a potential employees' perspective of them (Wilmott, 2003). Curry (2000) suggests that although negative information about an enterprise may also be available online, it is not necessarily damaging, as it could serve to shape an individual's perception of the enterprise. Problems will occur where information could be construed as out of date. It will give a negative impression to how potential applicants may view the webpage. Cober et al. (2000) advise that the attitude of the individual towards the recruitment site will influence the intention of the individual to apply for a position.

The current generation of University graduates appear to use the internet more extensively and effectively than ever before (Curry, 2000) for all aspects of their day to day lives from social networking to shopping, and they expect speedy response times (Weekes, 2004). In their online graduate programme, KPMG ensure that they respond to applications with feedback within 24 hours. They (KPMG) feel that they are able to do this through using available technology to the best of its capabilities (Personnel Today, 2008:1).

KPMG have attempted to minimize difficulties in recruiting within its Graduate Programme by using Social Media sites used frequently by their target market (Personnel Today, 2008). Minton-Eversole (2007a) and Schramm (2007) argue that enterprises can use Social Media sites to uncover information about candidates that would not be available on the application form. Indeed, Peacock (2009) warns that 12% of enterprises in the United Kingdom (UK) are looking at a potential candidate's social networking profile before making the decision to interview them.

Company's and Employee's Search Strategies

Human Resources personnel and recruiters are under pressure to attract suitably qualified applicants when there are lower levels of unemployment which means that the enterprise's recruitment search strategies must be innovative in order to retain sustainable competitive advantage (Cober et al., 2000; Lee, 2005).

Cober et al. (2000:484) suggest three stages that need to be considered when a company is designing a recruitment search strategy. Initially, they must have the ability to attract potential candidates to the website, then they must successfully engage with the candidates in order to pass on the information posted on the site. Finally, the enterprise needs to ensure that the candidate actually applies for the position from the web site. Figure 1 shows these steps clearly illustrating each component.

The CIPD e-recruitment factsheet (2009:5) states that there are "no fundamental philosophical differences" between using traditional methods, such as print media and using e-recruitment. It suggests a mix of old and new media to meet their target applicants in the most efficient manner.

Figure 1. Conceptual model of the online recruitment cycle
Source: Cober et al. (2000)

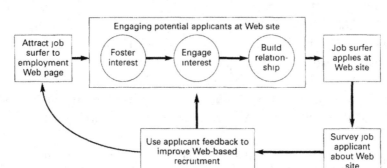

The literature suggests that problems with social media and online recruitment stem from poor information that is not kept up to date, and where there is no clear social media strategy implemented throughout the enterprise. Online recruitment has been used to effectively select candidates based on selection criteria, and potential candidates will have an idea of what the corporate culture of an enterprise is before they apply, so that effectively, the potential candidate can select whether or not they feel they would fit in with the enterprise or not. It is also more possible than ever to access wide amounts of information, including using a Smartphone to keep totally up to date with new roles so that individuals can be first in line to apply for their desired role within the enterprise.

METHODOLOGY

This research has elements of both positivist and interpretivist research methods. A theoretical framework has been used for the questionnaires and the majority of the remainder of the study has a more emergent approach to the way the information has been gathered.

The primary data was collected exclusively for this piece of research (Zikmund, 2003) by the researchers from an "original source" (Collis and Hussey, 2009:73). This type of research may be useful in that new "insights" may come to light, and that the researchers may feel more confident in the validity of the data gathered (Easterby-Smith et al, 2008:11).

Primary data may take the form of "questionnaire survey, interviews or focus groups" (Collis and Hussey, 2009:73). In this research, all three data collection methods were used in order to look at information from different perspectives. This is where more than one method of research is used in order to examine the same phenomenon (Collis and Hussey, 2009). Bryman and Bell (2007) describe this type of investigatory research as methodological triangulation, the implication being that the results from each type of investigation will be cross checked. These techniques can be used in order to provide rich data and provide the opportunity to recognize anomalies in data analysis. Webb et al. (1998) conceptualised this concept as a way of developing how information was collated and reviewed, which would mean that there would be a greater level of confidence in the findings (Bryman and Bell, 2007). With regard to this triangulation is a way of "cross-checking findings derived from both qualitative and quantitative research" (Bryman and Bell, 2007:413). Triangulation was a key concept for this research and the initial personal interviews were what the questionnaires were based on, and from that subsequent focus groups and follow up personal interviews. The research tools were both qualitative and quantitative.

The research was therefore conducted through (i) an employees/prospective employees' questionnaire survey, (ii) an employers' questionnaire survey, (iii) a focus group and (iv) personal interviews.

1. The employees/prospective employees' questionnaire survey had a sample size of 100 and the respondents were mainly from the Channel Islands and the UK, focusing more on the British employment market. The questionnaires were conducted using the online survey website www. surveymonkey.com. Using this method, the researchers were able to conduct the survey in a timely manner, using Facebook, Twitter, LinkedIn and e-mail to ask people to complete the survey online. It took less than 72 hours for the 100 responses to be received. The research population was made up of contacts of the researchers; this was limited to around 1,000 contacts giving a 10% response rate (Bryman and Bell, 2007). Respondents were represented from a variety of sectors including students, unemployed, banking/finance, IT, healthcare, beauty/fitness, factory, call centre, agriculture, tradesperson, hospitality and other sectors. Major questions asked concerned age, location, industry, gender, how often social media was used, would social media be used when looking for their next job, their online presence, how social media is accessed, and whether they would use social media to help get an introduction to an employer.

2. The employers' questionnaire survey had a sample size of 25 and again the respondents were mainly from the Channel Islands and the UK. Employers were represented from banking/finance, trades people, hospitality, and other sectors. Major questions asked concerned location, industry, whether they would use social media when advertising their upcoming vacancies, their online presence, how social media is accessed, and whether they thought social media was effective when looking for potential employees.

3. The size of the focus group was 22 participants who were all Human Resources professionals working in Guernsey. They were selected through an invitation to attend the focus group and were representative of HR professionals working in the various sectors. This method was used in order to find out the key methods that HR practitioners would use in order to find suitable employees. Major questions asked in the focus group concerned how social media could be used in their organizations, understanding of terminology, how to use groups, how to add contacts, technological understanding and timing issues. The interviewees for the focus groups were members of the researchers' CIPD group and the results were filmed so that notes could be made.

4. The personal interviews were undertaken with the selection of 2 recruitment agents who agreed to be interviewed following contact by the researchers, and were representative of recruitment agents in Guernsey. The personal interviews were carried out initially in person, and later over the telephone. The major questions asked concerned users of recruitment websites, what practices were in place, competition from other recruitment agencies on the island of Guernsey, whether the agency was affected by increasing numbers of organizations having more advanced Social Media and online recruitment sites, the impact of the global economic downturn on the organization and how the offshore economy had been affected by such measures. For the purpose of the initial interview the researchers felt that it would be appropriate for this type of interview not to have a prescribed structure and to see which subjects were emergent from the subsequent conversation.

This research project used cross-sectional methodologies due to financial resources and time constraints (Bryman and Bell, 2007). Furthermore, the research objectives meant that existing perceptions of individual's opinions of Social Media were explored. Therefore, obtaining and analysing information over a short cross-sectional period of time is crucial in enhancing the contextual validity of results (Saunders et al., 2007). Nevertheless, cross-sectional studies are associated with static positivistic epistemological considerations. Furthermore, the complexities in research which are associated with cross-sectional time horizons involve selecting "a large enough sample to be representative of the total population" (Collis and Hussey, 2009:346).

FINDINGS, ANALYSIS AND DISCUSSION

Employee/Prospective Employee and Employer Questionnaires

The key research findings for i) the employee/prospective employee questionnaire survey and ii) the employer questionnaire survey are presented at iii) the aggregate level with statistical information involving percentages.

1. The 100 respondents to the employee/prospective employee questionnaire survey, was limited by using the free version of survey monkey. There were a further 28 respondents in the time that the survey remained open, but these had to be disregarded as they were inaccessible. Of the collected responses, 64% were female and 34% male with the remaining 2% not wishing to answer. Although the responses were predominately from women, it is useful to see female perceptions.

There were more respondents under forty than of any other age group, particularly those aged 25-35. This may be related to the fact that the respondents were all acquaintances of the researchers. It may also be related to theory that it is predominately "Generation Y", where the request to complete questionnaires was sent. "Generation Y" is more likely to be on social networking sites with 89% of that generation having an online presence, rather than the "baby boomers" which only 72% have an online presence (Heller-Baird and Parasnis, 2011),

Almost half of the respondents were from Guernsey, with the remainder being mainly resident in the UK. The employment status of respondents was varied, with 75% of the respondents being employed, 6% being unemployed, and a further 4% being homemakers. Some 15% of the respondents were students. The researchers had thought it likely that most of the respondents would use social media, as the majority of requests to fill out the questionnaire were sent using Facebook and Twitter, this was confirmed with 96% of the respondents using Facebook (the most used social media platform by the respondents.

Collis and Hussey (2009:194) describe "two major problems in using questionnaires...*Questionnaire fatigue*" where individuals are reluctant to respond to questionnaires as they are "inundated with requests by post, e-mail, telephone and in the street" (Collis and Hussey, 2009:145) and *"non response bias"* where not all of the questionnaires are returned, which could have an impact on validity and reliability of findings (Collis and Hussey, 2009:145).

The responses to this questionnaire were also affected by "non response" (Collis and Hussey, 2009:204) as certain aspects of questions were left unanswered. This could be related to the design of the questionnaire, as some respondents early on in the questionnaire stated that they did not use certain social media platforms and so could not have responded to further questions about the platforms along the survey.

2. The employer questionnaire survey again involved using the free version of survey monkey which was undertaken at about the same time as the employee/prospective employee questionnaire survey. None of the respondents from the employer's survey said that their decision regarding employing an individual would be affected by pictures of an employee or potential employee drinking. The important factor (Lauby 2010) is what a candidate is capable of, "their ability to perform the appropriate tasks in relation to the position". Employers need to look at postings to determine how they wish to proceed with applications. The respondents from the employer's survey concur, by stating that the things that would most likely affect their opinion of a candidate to be photographs of the potential employee being perceived as unsocial.

There is a great deal of variation in the number of people who use Social Media and how they use it, with Twitter and LinkedIn being less used than Facebook, and even less using MySpace and YouTube, amongst the participants in the questionnaire surveys. This has an impact on the results gathered, as those platforms will tend not to be considered as first choice methods of looking for work.

3. The results of the questionnaire surveys for employees/potential employees, as to whether they used social media when looking for their next job, and employers when advertising upcoming vacancies, are shown in Tables 2 and 3.

The results in Table 2 show that 55% of employees/potential employees would use Facebook, 18% Twitter, 21% LinkedIn, 5% MySpace and 6% You Tube, when looking for their next job. The results show that Facebook is the platform that the highest percentage of participants would choose in order to look for work, but the results are indicative that using Social Media is not one of the main ways that respondents would choose to look for work.

Table 3 shows that 56% of employers would use Facebook, 28% Twitter, 28% LinkedIn, 4% My Space and 8% You Tube, to advertise upcoming vacancies. The results therefore show that employers appear to be more likely to advertise roles on Social Media, particularly on Facebook.

Table 2. Employees/Potential Employees - Would you use Social Media when looking for your next job?

Would You Use Social Media when looking for your next job?	%
Facebook	
My friend's post	22
A recruitment Agency post	17
A promoted advert from an employer	11
An organisation looking directly	5
None	12
I would not use this platform	25
No reply	8
Twitter	
My friend's post	6
A recruitment Agency post	2
A promoted advert from an employer	3
An organisation looking directly	7
None	8
I would not use this platform	54
No reply	20
Linked in	
My friend's post	2
A recruitment Agency post	9
A promoted advert from an employer	5
An organisation looking directly	5
None	9
I would not use this platform	52
No reply	18
My Space	
My friend's post	0
A recruitment Agency post	2
A promoted advert from an employer	0
An organisation looking directly	3
None	13
I would not use this platform	62
No reply	20
You Tube	
My friend's post	2
A recruitment Agency post	0
A promoted advert from an employer	2

continues in next column

Table 2. Continued

Would You Use Social Media when looking for your next job?	%
An organisation looking directly	2
None	10
I would not use this platform	64
No reply	20

n= 100

Table 3. Employers - Would you use Social Media when advertising your upcoming vacancies?

Would You Use Social Media when advertising your upcoming vacancies?	%
Facebook	
Yes	56
No	20
I would not use this platform	20
No reply	4
Twitter	
Yes	28
No	20
I would not use this platform	40
No reply	12
LinkedIn	
Yes	28
No	32
I would not use this platform	28
No reply	12
MySpace	
Yes	4
No	36
I would not use this platform	48
No reply	12
YouTube	
Yes	8
No	32
I would not use this platform	48
No reply	12

n=25

Focus Group

The key research findings from the focus groups included i) issues relating to Social Media, ii) social media platforms and strategy for recruitment, iii) Twinterns, and iv) internet policy and online recruitment strategies.

1. "The consequences of social exchange relationships have received significant research attention" (Dulac et al., 2008:1082). All of the respondents were currently working in HR or Senior Management in Guernsey, they were aged between 20 and 60, with the majority being women aged 45-60. There were 4 men present, aged between 35 and 60. The results of the findings were mainly focused on the issues relating to using Social Media efficiently as part of a small island community. The key trends which came out as a result of these findings were issues with advertising roles so that suitable candidates would be informed of the vacancies in a timely manner and who would be finding candidates who could meet the skills requirements of the enterprise's needs and would be able to work in part of the World with strict housing laws, (Economist, 2009). There were also issues with how it could be done, the potential for time-wasting and sifting through applicants without the correct skills and qualifications for the role.

2. There is a great deal of information available on social media platforms, and it is important that the enterprise remains vigilant in the amount of time spent on updating Social Media platforms to ensure the brand stays on message. Many of the respondents struggled with the basics of social media, with two of the participants not having a Facebook account. In these cases, in order to establish an effective social media strategy for recruitment, it might be more cost effective to bring in a Social Media Consultant. In Guernsey, one of the most well respected individuals is Jo Porrit, at Crowd Media, the team there offer training, from the most basic to higher level, and can also evolve a strategy that best fits the enterprise, and the industry in which they are working (www.facebook.com i). By using an external company, costs can be kept to a set level, and time taken to run the site by the enterprise can be minimized, whilst still ensuring the enterprise has an online presence, this will go some way to alleviating concerns.

3. Twinterns or "twittering interns" are typically interns taken on by large enterprises in order to keep communication channels open on day to day activities, such as at Pizza Hut, who launched a campaign where potential Twinterns had to apply for a role working for the company by posting a YouTube video of themselves online (Clifford, 2009). Indvick (2011) reported on the case at Marc Jacobs where the Twittern launched a tirade against his manager, calling him a "tyrant" before leaving the enterprise. @MarcJacobsIntl's response was "All well here at MJ. Twitter is a crazy place. Protect your Passwords" (www.twitter.com a). This is a clear example of the importance of keeping a watchful eye on the content that is posted by employees.

4. One of the topics considered was internet policy "We changed our Internet Policy at work recently, so people can't use Social Media in the office" – The implementation of a new internet policy, or social media policy is crucial for the enterprise. A response was "I don't think we'll use any of them, I want to employ people like me" may stem from the idea that "generally, the adoption of a technology does not take place uniformly across the entire economy or the entire population...If a person's family, friends and *broader* community are users... there would be increased incentive..." (Agarwal et al., 2009:277). Though the same is true the other way round, it may be seen as a nega-

tive impact on the enterprise not to have an effective social media and online recruitment strategy in place.

Personal Interviews

Several issues were discussed by the researchers with the agencies as the key topics became emergent through the literature. The recruitment agencies operating in Guernsey are operating in a very competitive market, and have had to diversify to continue trading in the current economic climate, including developing their offshore payroll services, and providing HR consultancy to small businesses. This should not have an impact on their ability to remain specialised in their field and grow as the market picks up once more.

The key research findings from the personal interviews included i) current legislation, ii) tools available to update social media platforms, iii) topics concerning information about a candidate, iv) candidates online, v) content uploaded to Social Media sites, vi) effective communication with candidates, and vii) an effective Social Media strategy.

1. It is important that agencies keep up with current legislation, as Employment legislation is different from UK and European Union (EU) legislation and there are professional bodies active on LinkedIn, Facebook and Twitter, such as the CIPD who strive to keep people who are interested and up to date with current changes in the legislation.
2. There are several tools available to update all of the Social Media platforms that the agencies choose to use such as www.twitterfeed.com, which can convert an RSS feed of the information which has been uploaded into the content management system that keeps the website up to date into Tweets, and then there are several applications which allow Tweets to be "fed" into Facebook (www.facebook.com c) and LinkedIn (http://learn.linkedin.com/twitter/). After these applications have been set up, they need to be checked periodically to ensure that they are functioning correctly.
3. Several issues were raised as the researchers found new topics through the critical literature review, and were discussed at length with the agencies to see how they would respond and what their thoughts were on certain things. Guernsey is a very close knit community and so it is relatively simple to "Google" a candidate on Google (www.google.com) and see what comes up about what an individual may have done by a relatively simple search. There is also a website from the local newspaper (www.thisisguernsey.com) where it may also be possible to gather information about a candidate. This is a standard policy for some recruitment agencies. Additionally, it is common for an agency to have a policy relating to Criminal Convictions which have not been "spent" under the Rehabilitation of Offenders Act (Bailiwick of Guernsey Act 2002) and whether the agency decides to take on the individual to help them find work. Some agencies on the Island will not deal with candidates who have unspent convictions.
4. With the development of Social Media Strategies which include checking available information about candidates online, more information can be gathered. As a recruitment agent, it can be common for candidates to "like" the agency on Facebook and to "follow" them on Twitter, so it can be very easy to access information about the candidates which they may not otherwise wish to divulge, it is then up to the agent to decide how they use the information. It is suggested (Lauby, 2010) that any enterprise that is going to conduct a background check on an individual on any social media sites which are available in the public domain ought to "provide notice" before conducting searches.

5. The content that Recruitment Agencies upload to Social Media sites can vary from staff events, corporate events which the enterprise may have sponsored or participated in, to charity work in which the enterprise participates, and local enterprises that staff participate in. A good example of this is Guernsey Recruitment agency "Situations Recruitment" and their Facebook page (www.facebook.com).

6. In order to have effective communication with employees of the enterprise and candidates of the agency, the personal interviews also highlighted the need for "fake" corporate accounts that can be monitored centrally. This could be as simple as employees setting up accounts for use at work. It only takes a few minutes to set up a basic Facebook Profile, where all of the contact details and work history can be set up with details of the recruitment agency, corporate images can be used, so that there is continuity between images that appear on the enterprise's website, and other social media platforms. This is a different way of communicating with candidates, and another way it is possible to keep candidates updated "on the go". This information can be monitored by a central person, who would be "friends" with the individuals, and would also have access to the passwords and usernames of the employees.

7. Decisions must also be made so that an effective Social Media strategy also includes information about what to do when an employee leaves. If there are "corporate" Facebook and Twitter accounts, contacts of these should remain with the company. This could be more difficult using a LinkedIn account, where individuals may have built up a rapport with clients and colleagues, and wish to retain the contacts, or could easily do so again. However, it is stated that "The formation and maintenance of relationships is predicated on the reciprocation of valued resources" (Dulac et al., 2008:1079).

FUTURE RESEARCH

Although the research obtained responses from people working in Recruitment Agencies it would perhaps be a learning point to conduct semi-structured interviews with recruitment agencies in different geographical locations globally, and in different industries as the recruitment agencies in Guernsey primarily deal with financial recruitment, with just a couple concentrating on the hospitality market. This is a very different way of recruiting since commission is far less, and people tend not to stay in jobs for a period of more than a few months in the hospitality industry.

CONCLUSION AND RECOMMENDATIONS

The unique contribution of the research to the literature is that information systems, tools and strategies are vital to an effective Social Media Recruitment Strategy. Enterprises must make available as much information as they possibly can, so that employees can make better informed decisions about whether or not they will fit with the enterprise. Ultimately the more information that is available, the more informed the decisions are likely to be. Enterprises must make the best possible use of the latest software available to them for online recruitment advances, and should ensure that all relevant staff are trained to use it. The more information that is available from both the employer, and the candidate the more likely that the potential candidate should "fit in" to their new position with minimal issue. This is of particular importance during times of economic difficulty, as it could be that a candidate who is not really suited to a place of work, or the role itself may not be able to find alternative employment easily. In addition, recruitment is an expensive ("Contracting a recruiter to find an executive who earns $150,000 annually can cost $15,000 in fees" (Koeppel, 2009)) and often is a time consuming process. By using "social media tools are mostly free and offer added value: Candidates bring their own online networks... and references which speeds up the recruitment process" (Koeppel, 2009). Therefore, it is vital for the employer to ensure they get it right the first time to avoid further cost implications.

The social media strategy must be planned to be inclusive to all potential employees, and also to customers – after all they could be the employees of the future. It is apparent that social media policies ought to be inclusive, so that an employer cannot be accused of discriminating against employees because of race, age, sex, sexual orientation or act in contravention of the Equality Act 2010 (www.acas.org. uk). This could leave the enterprise open to possible litigation if an employee feels that they have been discriminated against. It is important that an employee looks at the industry they are based in, in order to make informed choices about the best way to recruit for the role.

It may be possible to come up with a simple strategy for social media and recruitment within the enterprise. Once planned, the social media strategy must be made available to all employees and relevant training given (this must also be included in costings, time taken for staff training, operational costs of training).

If a social media strategy is to be effective, it is important that the employees are clearly informed of changes in procedures, and understand why these changes have come about. Clear guidelines must be set in order for employees to understand what they can and cannot say regarding the enterprise, their work, and their customers so as to minimize potential litigation.

Employees are very likely to be using Social Media in their own lives and will have an understanding of what effects social media have on their lives and understanding of brands, and this could help shape the social media strategy for recruitment within the enterprise.

If the enterprise has chosen to implement its social media and recruitment strategy through an external enterprise the next step would be to bring the implementation of the social media strategy back "in house" over a period of time, and only if the budget allows. This Organic Development Strategy known as "knowledge and capability development" (Johnson et al., 2008:357) within the social media and recruitment strategy will continue to grow, as employee's have "greater market knowledge and therefore competitive advantage over other rivals more distant from their customers".

Through the literature review and subsequent analysis of the primary data it is evident that quality of information is a key factor. Therefore it is essential that any enterprise attempting to recruit staff ensure that they provide as much information as possible in order to allow the candidate to make a more informed decision about their potential decision to apply and or accept a position. If this information is in place, it should reduce the time taken to process the application for all parties involved. In order to do this, it is important that all parties keep their information up-to-date at all times. For agencies and enterprises, this is perhaps more important, for the initial impression the candidate has of the enterprise may have an impact on whether or not they will choose to apply for the position (Cober et al., 2000).

Although LinkedIn profiles may seem to take longer to complete than Facebook (a few minutes) or Twitter (a couple of minutes) as an individual has to upload a certain amount of information, such as a CV, write a summary, as well as asking people to recommend their work, it would be possible to display many of the key skills above in about 30 minutes, and the information stored on the LinkedIn profile can be quickly kept up to date.

Facebook was by far the preferred social media platform for the majority of respondents from the focus group and the questionnaire respondents, as well as being firm favourites with the Recruitment consultants in conjunction with other Social Media platforms.

It was not clear from the questionnaires and focus group whether LinkedIn, Twitter, YouTube are not well used due to lack of interest? Or a lack of training? From the results from all three stakeholders, however, in the case of MySpace, it is now viewed as a platform to share music on, not a social network anymore, so there would be little point building a social media strategy including MySpace, unless of course the enterprise was working in the Music, or Arts industries. It is also very important to ensure that other sorts of information on roles, and what is going on within the enterprise is kept up to date, and information is readily available for all applicants. A member of staff can explain the recruitment process, and have that available from YouTube, with links from Facebook and Twitter.

Approximate costs to keep company x's website, and social media platforms updated throughout one calendar year in terms of time are around £5,000 per annum. This includes an hour of administrative time on the website and social media platforms per day to ensure that the information available is as comprehensive as possible. There is also two hours Senior Administrator monitoring time per week to ensure other sorts of data are kept up to date, as well as time to make videos and other items for YouTube, to keep the content fresh. This keeps the website available and relevant to as many people as possible.

In terms of cost, each individual company would need to be costed according to its needs and to fit in with the social media strategy that had been worked out. Using outside companies such as web developers and Social media experts may add significant costs to the strategy. However, Ochman (2009:4) warns that "Many people claim to be "social media gurus" but hype doesn't compare to experience". It is important to investigate consultants or firms, to look at other work they have done, and to seek testimonials before spending money on a campaign.

It would be advisable for the researchers to make changes so that there were more responses to the questionnaire. Bryman and Bell (2008) suggest that where there have been more than 1,000 respondents to the survey, there is far less of a margin for error. It would have been more beneficial to have focused the data on specific geographical locations, tailor the questionnaires so that they would apply in different countries, so that questions could be asked without causing sensitivity to individuals. That information could be used at a later stage to provide analysis by sectors. In further studies the researchers would seek ways in which there could be a more balanced age and race demographic so that further research could be carried out. This could then result in correlations between older users and those users from an ethnic background. Further investigation should also be carried out to find what characteristics make a web page more accessible to users with disabilities and to determine if there are changes which can be implemented by recruitment agencies with ease and in a cost efficient manner.

The participants in the focus group were not frequent users of Social Media, so the topics were more on "how to use" Social Media, rather than how they were using it as part of their social media and recruitment strategy. It would be advisable to repeat the focus group with a group of individuals who were using Social Media more frequently in order to gain higher levels of validity to the research (Collis and Hussey, 2009:204). With the responses that were collected from the focus group, it would not be fair to say that the "research findings accurately represent what is happening in the situation" (Collis and Hussey, 2011:204).

In response to the first research question concerning the advantages/disadvantages of Social Media (SM) from the perspectives of HR professionals, recruitment professionals, and potential job seekers, the research found the advantages of using SM for online recruitment include increased efficiency and convenience for both potential employees and enterprises, whereas where the systems are not designed correctly, it can create increased difficulties for the enterprise in communicating with potential employees. Furthermore, it was found that the disadvantages with SM for online recruitment stem from poor information that is not kept up to date, and where there is no clear social media strategy implemented throughout the enterprise.

With regard to the second research question as to the factors likely to drive/reduce the effectiveness of recruitment via SM it was found that these included the rapid changes in technology, recruitment management, the current global economic climate and the impact this has on the way in which individuals are now seeking employment.

Regarding the third research question concerning legal considerations associated with recruitment via SM it was found that employers who wish their employees to use Social Media must guide the employees regarding what is expected from them, and outlining usage policies, as well as ensuring that there is someone within the enterprise who takes responsibility for the policy, monitoring and updating the information as necessary.

REFERENCES

Adams, J. (2009a). A new way to find 'Union' workers. *Bank Technology News*, *22*(5), 23.

Adams, J. (2009b). The Strongest Link. *Bank Technology News*, *22*(5), 23.

Addley, E. (2009). *The Twitter crisis: how site became voice of resistance in Iran*. Retrieved from http://www.guardian.co.uk/world/2009/jun/16/twitter-social-networking-iran-opposition

Agarwal, R., Animesh, A., & Prasad, K. (2009). Social interactions and the "Digital Divide": Explaining Variations in Internet Use. *Information Systems Research*, *20*(2), 277–294. doi:10.1287/isre.1080.0194

Agichtein, E., Castillo, C., Donato, D., Gionis, A., & Mishne, G. (2008) Finding high-quality content in social media. *WISDOM – Proceedings of the 2008 International Conference on Web Search and Data Mining*, 183-193.

Aichner, T., & Jacob, F. (2015). Measuring the Degree of Corporate Social Media Use. *International Journal of Market Research*, *57*(2), 257–275.

Berry, M. (2005, May). Online recruitment grows in popularity. *Personnel Today*, 43.

Boyd, D. M., & Ellison, N. B. (2007). Social Network Sites: Definition, History and Scholarship. *Journal of Computer-Mediated Communication*, *13*(1), 210–230. doi:10.1111/j.1083-6101.2007.00393.x

Bryman, A., & Bell, E. (2007). *Business Research Methods* (2nd ed.). Oxford University Press.

Christensson, P. (2013). Social Media Definition. *Tech Terms*. Retrieved June 18, 2017, from http://techterms.com/definition/social_media

Chubb, L. (2008). Stripped-down jobsite is a good call for 3. *People Management*, *14*(2), 14.

CIPD. (2009). E-Recruitment Fact sheet. *CIPD Publication*. Retrieved March 17, 2011, from http://www.cipd.co.uk/subjects/recruitmen/onlnrcruit/onlrec.htm

Clifford, S. (2009). Tweeting Becomes a Summer Job Opportunity. *NY Times.* Retrieved April 27, 2011, from http://www.nytimes.com/2009/04/20/business/media/20twitter.html

Cober, R. T., Brown, D. J., Blumental, A. J., Doverspike, D., & Levy, P. E. (2000). The Quest for the qualified job surfer: It's Time the Public Sector Catches the Wave. *Public Personnel Management, 29*(4), 479–496. doi:10.1177/009102600002900406

Cober, R. T., Brown, D. J., Keeping, L. M., & Levy, P. E. (2004). Recruitment on the Net:How Do Enterpriseal Web Site Characteristics Influence Applicant Attraction? *Journal of Management, 30*(5), 623–646. doi:10.1016/j.jm.2004.03.001

Collis, J., & Hussey, R. (2009). *Business Research: A Practical Guide for Undergraduate and Postgraduate Students* (3rd ed.). Palgrave Macmillan.

Crail, M. (2007). Online Recruitment delivers more applicants and wins vote of most Employers. *Personnel Today.* Retrieved March 17, 2011 from http://www.personneltoday.com /articles/2007/11/20/43298/online-recruitment- delivers-more-applicants-and-wins-vote-of-most-employers.html

Curry, P. (2000). Log on for Recruits. *Industry Week, 249*(17), 46.

Czerny, A. (2004). Log on Turn off for women. *People Management, 10*(15), 10.

Doherty, R. (2010). Getting social with recruitment. *Strategic HR Review, 9*(6).

Domizi, D. P. (2013). Microblogging To Foster Connections And Community in a Weekly Graduate Seminar Course. *TechTrends, 57*(1), 43–51. doi:10.100711528-012-0630-0

Dulac, T., Coyle-Shapiro, J. A.-M., Henderson, D. J., & Wayne, S. J. (2008). Not all Responses to Breach are the Same: The Interconnection of Social Exchange and Psychological Contract Processes in Enterpriseations. *Academy of Management Journal, 51*(6), 1079–1098. doi:10.5465/AMJ.2008.35732596

Easterby-Smith, M., Thorpe, R., & Jackson, P. R. (2008). *Management Research* (3rd ed.). Sage.

Economist. (2009). Generation Y goes to work. *Economist, 390*(8612), 47-48.

Eduardo, M. (2006). E-Entrepreneurship. *Munich Personal RePEc Archive.* Retrieved April 24, 2011, from http://mpra.ub-muenchen.de/2237/

eLearning Industry (eLI). (2015). *5 Steps To Use LinkedIn For Social Learning – eLearning Industry.* Retrieved June 18, 2017, from http://elearningindustry.com/5-steps-use-linkedin-for-social-learning

Elliott, A.-M. (2011). *10 Fascinating YouTube Facts that May Surprise You.* Retrieved April 24, 2011, from http://mashable.com/2011/02/19/youtube-facts/

Everett, C. (2010). *Social media still feared by graduate recruiters.* Retrieved April 20, 2011, from http://www.hrzone.co.uk/topic/recruitment/social-media-still-feared-graduate- recruiters/105572

Facebook. (2010a). Retrieved April 20, 2011, from http://www.facebook.com/press/ info.php

Facebook. (2010b). *Statistics.* Retrieved March 3, 2011, from http://www.facebook.com/homephp#!/press/info.php?statistics

Facebook. (2010c). *Twitter App for Facebook*. Retrieved April 25, 2011, from http://www.facebook.com/apps/application.php?id=2231777543

Facebook. (2010d). *University of Glamorgan Facebook Enterprise*. Retrieved December 1, 2010, from http://www.facebook.com/?ref=home#!/uniglamlife

Facebook. (2010e). *Situations Recruitment*. Retrieved April 26, 2011, from http://www.facebook.com/situationsgnsy?ref=ts

Facebook. (2011a). *Zinzi Coetzee*. Retrieved April 25, 2011, from http://www.facebook.com/zinzi.coetzee?ref=ts#!/zinzi.coetzee

Facebook. (2011b). *Facebook KPMG Recruitment Page*. Retrieved April 25, 2011, from http://www.facebook.com/profile.php?id=100001464093443&ref=ts#!/pages/KPMG/108372102518243

Facebook. (2011c). *Facebook KPMG Graduate Page*. Retrieved April 25, 2011, from http://www.facebook.com/kpmg.graduates?ref=ts

Facebook. (2011d). *Facebook Crowd Media Page*. Retrieved April 27, 2011, from http://www.facebook.com/wearecrowd?sk=info

Facebook. (2011e). *Facebook KPMG Channel Islands Allumni page*. Retrieved April 25, 2011, from http://www.facebook.com/kpmg.graduates?ref=ts#!/pages/KPMG-Channel-Islands-Limited-Alumni/47271650921

Ghosh, R. (2011). *Entropy-based Classification of 'Retweeting' Activity on Twitter*. Retrieved June 18, 2017, from https://arxic.org

Gittlen, S. (2008). Web 2.0: Just Say Yes. *New World (New Orleans, La.)*, *25*(9), 32–34.

Goldberg, C. B., & Allen, D. G. (2008). Black and white and read all over: Race differences in reactions to recruitment web sites. *Human Resource Management*, *47*(2), 217–236. doi:10.1002/hrm.20209

Hajirnis, A. (2015). Social media networking: Parent guidance required. *The Brown University Child and Adolescent Behavior Letter*, *31*(12), 1–7. doi:10.1002/cbl.30086

Hall, S. (2004, February). See Website Recruitment through for best results. *Personnel Today*, 21.

Heller-Baird, C., & Parasnis, G. (2011). *From Social Media to Social CRM: What customers want*. IBM Institute for Business Value Study. Retrieved April 26, 2011, from http://www-935.ibm.com/services/us/gbs/thoughtleadership/ibv- social-crm-whitepaper.html? cntxt=a1005261

Henderson, A., & Bowley, R. (2010). Authentic dialogue? The role of "friendship" in a social media recruitment campaign. *Journal of Communication Management*, *14*(3), 237–257. doi:10.1108/13632541011064517

Hilpern, K. (2001). Reading between the Lines. *Guardian Newspaper*. Retrieved October 10, 2008, from: http://www.guardian.co.uk/money/2001/jul/16/careers.jobsadvice5

Hoffman, D., Novak, T., & Chatterjee, P. (1995). Commercial scenarios for the web: opportunities and challenges. *Journal of Computer-Mediated Communication, 5*(1).

Indvick, L. (2011). *Marc Jacobs Intern Calls CEO a "Tyrant" in Twitter Meltdown.* Retrieved March 30, 2011, from http://mashable.com/2011/03/28/marc-jacobs-twitter- intern-meltdown/

Ingham, I. (2010). Social media at work: Breaking down barriers to communication. *Personnel Today.* Retrieved April 21, 2010, from http://www.personneltoday.com/articles/2010/03/18/54886/social-media-at-work-breaking-down-barriers-to- communication.html

Inter World Stats. (2011). *Number of Internet users worldwide.* Retrieved January 19, 2011, from http://www.internetworldstats.com/stats.htm

Johnson, G., Scholes, K., & Whittington, R. (2008). *Exploring Corporate Strategy* (8th ed.). Pearson Education.

Kaplan, A. M., & Haenlein, M. (2010). Users of the world unite! The challenges and opportunities of social media. *Business Horizons*, *53*(1), 61. doi:10.1016/j.bushor.2009.09.003

Kietzmann, J. H., Hermkens, K., McCarthy, I. P., & Silvestre, B. S. (2011). Social media? Get serious! Understanding the functional building blocks of social media. *Business Horizons*, *54*(3), 241–251. doi:10.1016/j.bushor.2011.01.005

King, J. (2004, January). The web habit is HR's manna from heaven. *Personnel Today*, 2.

Koeppel, D. (2009). HR by Twitter. *Fortune Small Business*, *19*(7), 57.

Lauby, S. (2010). *Should you Search Social Media Sites for Job Candidate Information?* Retrieved September 6, 2010 from http://mashable.com/2010/09/05/social-media-job-recruiting/

Lee, I. (2005). Evaluation of Fortune 100 companies' career web sites. *Human Systems Management*, *24*(2), 175–182.

Lewis, A., Daunton, L., Thomas, B., & Sanders, G. (2010). A Critical Exploration into whether E-Recruitment is an Effective E-Entrepreneurship Method in Attracting Appropriate Employees for Enterprises. *International Journal of E-Entrepreneurship and Innovation*, *1*(2), 30–44. doi:10.4018/jeei.2010040103

Lewis, A., Thomas, B., & Sanders, G. (2013). Pushing the Right Buttons? A Critical Exploration into the Effects of Social Media as an Innovative E-Entrepreneurship Method of Recruitment for Enterprises. *International Journal of E-Entrepreneurship and Innovation*, *4*(3), 16–37. doi:10.4018/ijeei.2013070102

LinkedIn. (2015a). *About Us – LinkedIn.* Retrieved June 18, 2017, from http://www.linkedin.com/about-us

LinkedIn. (2015b). *About Us – LinkedIn Newsroom.* Retrieved June 18, 2017, from http://press.linkedin.com/about-linkedin

Long, D. (2009, January 15). Monster invests $130m in face of falling vacancies. *New Media Age*, 4.

Lundblad, N. (2017). *Privacy in a Noisy Society.* Retrieved June 18, 2017, from http://www.citeserx.ist.psu.edu

Management, P. (2008). *Fatface appetite for e-recruitment.* Retrieved March 17, 2009, from http://www.peoplemanagement.co.uk/pm/articles/2008/ 01/fatfaceappetiteforerecruitment.htm

Mannion, M. (2008). Consider differences in culture in Virgin territory. *People Management*, *14*(5), 15.

Manufacturers' Monthly. (2004, December). Internet job ads a turn off for industry. *Manufacturers' Monthly*, 16.

McKeown, C. (2003). Applied Management: Nurse Internet Recruitment. *Nursing Management – UK, 10*(4), 23-27.

Merriam-Webster. (2016). *Dictionary and Thesaurus*. Retrieved June 18, 2017, from http://www.merriam-webster.com

Miller, H., & Arnold, J. (2000). Gender and home pages. *Computers & Education, 34*(3-4), 335–339. doi:10.1016/S0360-1315(99)00054-8

Miller Littlejohn Media (MLM). (2015). *7 Ways Students Should Use LinkedIn*. Retrieved June 18, 2017, from http://www.millerlittlejohnmedia.com

Minton-Eversole, T. (2007a). E-Recruitment Comes of Age, Survey Says. *HRMagazine, 52*(8), 34.

Moody, M. (2010). Teaching Twitter and Beyond: Tip for Incorporating Social Media in Traditional Courses. *Journal of Magazine & New Media Research, 11*(2), 1–9.

Moran, M., Seaman, J., & Tiniti-Kane, H. (2012). *How today's higher education faculty use social media*. Retrieved June 18, 2017, from http://pearsonlearningsolutions.com

Mulgan, G., Tucker, S., Rushanara, A., & Sanders, B. (2007). *Social Innovation, What it is, Why it Matters and How it can be Accelerated*. Skoll Centre for Social Entrepreneurship, Oxford Said Business School. Retrieved February 2, 2011, from http://www.youngfoundation.org/publications/reports/social-innovation-what-it-why-it-matters-how-it-can-be-accelerated-march-2007

O'Keefe, G. S. (2011). The Impact of Social Media on Children, Adolescents and Families. *Paediatrics, 127*(4), 801–805.

Obar, J. A., & Wildman, S. (2015). Social media definition and the governance challenge: An introduction to the special issue. *Telecommunications Policy, 39*(9), 745–750. doi:10.1016/j.telpol.2015.07.014

Ochman, B. L. (2009, April). It is no longer possible to resist social media. *Public Relations Tactics Magazine*.

Odell, P. M., Korgen, K. O., Schumacher, P., & Delucchi, M. (2000). Internet Use Among Female and Male College Students. *Cyberpsychology & Behavior, 3*(5), 855–862. doi:10.1089/10949310050191836

Ozemir, V. E., & Hewett, K. (2010). The Effect of Collectivism on the Importance of Relationship Quality and Service Quality for Behavioural Intentions: A Cross-National and Cross-Contextual Analysis. *Journal of International Marketing, 18*(1), 41–62. doi:10.1509/jimk.18.1.41

Pavlik, J., & MacIntoch, S. (2015). *Converging Media* (4th ed.). New York, NY: Oxford University Press.

Peacock, L. (2009). *Social networking sites used to check out job applicants*. Retrieved December 4, 2009, from: http://www.personneltoday.com/articles/2009/03/17/ 49844/social-networking-sites-used-to-check-out-job-applicants.html

Pew Research Centre (PRC). (2012) *The Demographics of Social Media Users – 2012*. Pew Research Centre: Internet, Science & Tech. Retrieved June 18, 2017, from http://printabletemplates.com/pew-report-social-networking-site-users

Pitcher, G. (2008, March). Unfriendly job websites lose retailers top talent. *Personnel Today*, 3.

Postman, N. (2017). *Informing ourselves to death*. Retrieved June 18, 2017, from http://w2.eff.org

Raynes-Goldie, K. (2010). Aliases, creeping, and wall cleaning: Understanding privacy in the age of Facebook. *First Monday*, *15*(2).

Report, S. M. (2012). *State of the media: The social media report 2012. Featured Insights, Global, Media and Entertainment*. Nielsen.

Rushe, D. (2010). *Twitter 'in early talks with potential buyers Facebook and Google. Approximate Number of Twitter users 2010*. Retrieved April 14, 2011, from http://www.guardian.co.uk/technology/2011/feb/10/twitter-talks-buyers-facebook-google

Saunders, M., Lewis, P., & Thornhill, A. (2007). *Research Methods for Business Students* (4th ed.). Harlow: FT Prentice Hall.

Schofield, J. (2009). Twitter users are quick quitters. *Guardian Online*. Retrieved April 17, 2011, from http://www.guardian.co.uk/technology/blog/2009/apr/29/twitter-quitters-nielsen1?INTCMP=SRCH

Schramm, J. (2007). Internet Connections. *HRMagazine*, *52*(9), 176.

Sherer, P., & Shea, T. (2011). Using Online Video to Support Student Learning and Engagement. *College Teaching*, *59*(2), 56–59. doi:10.1080/87567555.2010.511313

Smethurst, S. (2004). The allure of online. *People Management*, *10*(15), 38.

Smith, C. (2011). Twitter User Statistics Show Stunning Growth. *Huffington Post*. Retrieved April 14, 2011, from http://www.huffingtonpost.com/2011/03/14/ twitter-user-statistics_n_835581.html

Spence, B. (2009). How to…filter job applications. *People Management*, 45. Retrieved March 19, 2009, from: http://www.peoplemanagement.co.uk/pm/articles/2009/03/how-to-filter-job-applications.htm

Statista. (2017). *Leading global social networks 2016 Statistics*. Retrieved June 18, 2017, from http://www.statista.com/statistics

Sundar, M. (2007). This week on LinkedIn July 9th 2007. *LinkedIn Blog*. Retrieved April 25, 2010, from http://blog.linkedin.com/2007/07/14/this-week-in-li/

Tang, Q., Gu, B., & Whinston, A. B. (2012). Content Contribution for Revenue Sharing and Reputation in Social Media: A Dynamic Structural Model. *Journal of Management Information Systems*, *29*(2), 41–45. doi:10.2753/MIS0742-1222290203

Taylor, C. (2001). E-recruitment is powerful weapon in war for talent. *People Management*. Retrieved December 5, 2009, from: http://www.peoplemanagement.co.uk/pm/articles/2001/05/856.htm

Personnel Today. (2004, April). Online Jobseekers more confident about equality. *Personnel Today*, 2.

Personnel Today. (2008, August). How I made a difference...? online recruitment burning career issues? closed-rank committee. *Personnel Today*, 8.

Tulip, S. (2003, August). A flying start. *People Management Magazine*, 38. Retrieved February 5, 2010, from http://www.peoplemanagement.co.uk/pm/articles/2003/08/ 9256.htm

Twitter. (2011a). *MarcJacobsInt*. Retrieved May 26, 2011, from http://twitter.com/#!/MarcJacobsIntl

Twitter. (2011b). *Twitter KPMG Recruitment Page*. Retrieved April 25, 2011, from http://twitter.com/#!/KPMGRecruitment

Twitter. (2011c). *Twitter KPMG UK page*. Retrieved April 25, 2011, from http://twitter.com/#!/KPMG_UK_LLP

Vogel, E. A., Rose, J. P., Okdie, B. M., Eckles, K., & Franz, B. (2015). Who compares and despairs? The effect of social comparison orientation on social media and its outcomes. *Personality and Individual Differences*, *86*, 249–256. doi:10.1016/j.paid.2015.06.026

Webb, T. J. (1998). *Researching for Business: Avoiding the 'Nice to know' Trap* (1st ed.). London: Aslib.

Week, M. (2006). E-recruitment in Web 2.0 boost. *Marketing Week*, *29*(43), 32.

Weekes, S. (2004, June). Unearthing diamonds in a tough recruitment market. *Personnel Today*, 10.

Willmott, B. (2003). Firms tackle skills and diversity crisis online. *Personnel Today*, *7*(1), 4.

Yang, Z. (2010). Understanding retweeting behaviours in social networks. *Proceedings of the 19th ACM international conference on information and knowledge management*. Retrieved June 18, 2017, from https://www.cs.cmu.edu

Zikmund, W. G. (2003). *Business Research Methods* (7th ed.). Thomson South Western.

This research was previously published in Entrepreneurship, Collaboration, and Innovation in the Modern Business Era; pages 194-220, copyright year 2018 by Business Science Reference (an imprint of IGI Global).

Index

G

U

V

W

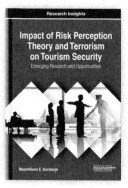
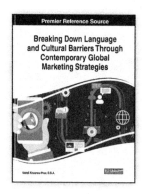

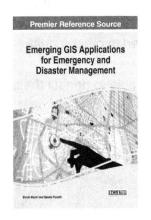
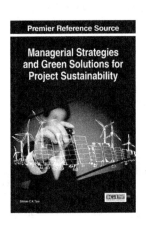

Printed in the United States
by Baker & Taylor Publisher Services